To Janet, Stacey and Emma:
I cannot get better than the best.

Martin C. Calder

To Helen for her unwavering support

Simon Hackett

Contents

The Editors

Martin C. Calder MA, CQSW is a Child Protection Co-ordinator with City of Salford Community and Social Services Directorate. The generic nature of the assessment framework has identified the need for more specific and individualised frameworks and Martin is keen to furnish overstretched front line workers with accessible evidence-based assessment tools to assist them in their job. Martin has written extensively on many child protection matters and is keen to bridge theory, research and practice to enhance outcomes for children.

Simon Hackett is a Lecturer in the Centre for Applied Social Studies at the University of Durham, UK. He has a wide range of interests relating to childcare practice and research. A qualified social worker, Simon was previously employed by NSPCC and was involved in the investigation of allegations of institutional abuse in North Wales children's homes, arising from the Waterhouse Inquiry. A co-founder and a former Programme Director of G-MAP, a leading community-based organisation working with young people who sexually abuse others, he has substantial practice and training experience in sexual aggression work. He is an active researcher in the field and, with Helen Masson, is currently leading a two-year project examining policy and practice in the adolescent sexual aggression field across the UK and Republic of Ireland. He has published variously in relation to child maltreatment, social work practice and sexual aggression. Since moving into academia Simon has taught extensively on child protection matters on the post qualifying award, developing unique frameworks for practitioners.

The Contributors

Patrick Ayre is a qualified social worker and university lecturer. Working in the Department of Applied Social Studies at the University of Luton, he teaches and researches in the field of child protection and child welfare.

Alan Cooper qualified in 1982 from the London School of Economics with a CQSW and MSc in social work, psychology and social policy. He has worked for several local authorities and an NSPCC special unit. With his colleague Judith Tuck he now runs Osiris Training and Consultancy.

Dr Lenard Dalgleish is a Senior Lecturer in Psychology at the University of Queensland, Australia. From 1981 to 1988 he was a Lecturer in Social Work where his interest in child protection decision making developed. He has given many keynote talks, conference presentations and workshops on risk assessment and decision making. He is a member of the editorial board of *Child Abuse Review*.

Dr Celia Doyle is a Senior Lecturer in Behavioural Studies at University College Northampton. Having worked in the field of child protection for thirty years, she also remains in independent practice. Her main research interest is the emotional abuse of children, particularly the nature of supports which can ameliorate their circumstances. However, she has also written extensively on working with abused children and on child sexual abuse.

Richard Fountain is a qualified social worker with over 25 years experience of child and family work both as a practitioner and manager. He is currently the manager of Family Support and Child Protection services for Luton Housing and Social Services Department.

Dr Neil Frude is a clinical psychologist. He is Clinical Research Tutor on the South Wales Doctoral Course in Clinical Psychology and a Consultant Clinical Psychologist with the Cardiff and Vale NHS Trust. He has written and edited a number of books and papers, mainly on issues within the fields of child abuse, family psychology and abnormal psychology.

Fiona Harbin has worked as a senior social worker specialising in substance misuse and child protection, for Bolton social services department, since 1996. Prior to this she worked for eight years in Wigan then Bolton as a childcare social worker. In her current role she has a particular interest in developing new services for working with drug using parents and their children. Within this she has developed group and individual interventions for working specifically with children who have experienced parental substance misuse.

Dr Anne Hollows is Principal Lecturer in Social Work at Sheffield Hallam University. She qualified as a social worker in 1974 and has worked in both probation and social work. Before working in higher education she headed the Child Abuse Training Unit at the National Children's Bureau. She is a member of the international faculty of ISPCAN. Her doctoral thesis was entitled 'Good Enough Judgements: a study of judgement making in social work with children and families.'

David Howe is Professor of Social Work at the University of East Anglia. He has research and writing interests in adoption, attachment theory, and child abuse and neglect. He is the author of a number of books and Editor of the journal *Child and Family Social Work*.

Dorota Iwaniec is Professor of Social Work and Director of the Institute of Child Care Research at Queen's University Belfast. Before coming to Queen's in 1992 she worked in Leicester as a practitioner, researcher and trainer. She has been involved in failure-to-thrive research for the last 25 years and has finished a 20-year follow-up study on children who failed-to-thrive. She has published extensively in the area of child care.

Lynne Jones has worked in Social Services since 1973, qualifying in 1979 and specialising in children and families work in 1982. She has a broad expertise having worked in six Northwest authorities during her career. She completed her Masters in Child Care Law and Practice in 1991 and joined Bolton as Principal Officer Child Protection and Quality Assurance in 1995. She has recently been promoted to Assistant Director in the same authority.

Margaret Kennedy has pioneered work in issues of disability and child protection. She has written extensively on the subject and is co-editor and co-author of the ABCD – *ABuse and Children who are Disabled* – training and resource pack. She chaired the BASPCAN Disability and Abuse working party and is on the Editorial Board of the *Journal of Adult Protection*. Margaret is disabled and is a qualified nurse and social worker. She is a certified counsellor and has an advanced certificate in Child Abuse Studies. She has also studied the issues of Christianity and Child Abuse. Margaret has lectured and taught extensively throughout the British Isles: her audiences have included police, social workers, health workers, clergy, pastoral workers, probation officers and medical staff.

Michael Murphy has been involved in childcare work for over twenty years. He is currently the resource co-ordinator for Bolton ACPC and a member of PIAT (Promotion of Interagency Training) although he is soon to move to the University of Salford as Senior Lecturer. He is the author of *Working Together in Child Protection* (Ashgate, 1995) and *The Child Protection Unit* (Avebury,1996). He is the co-author of *Dealing with Stress* (Macmillan, 1994) and *Meeting the Stress Challenge* (Russell House Publishing, 1996).

Tom O'Loughlin has worked in Social Services since 1975. He worked initially for Trafford Social Services and since 1980 has been with Bolton Metro. He has specialised in work with children and families. In Bolton he was formerly Principal Officer Child Protection and for the last six years has managed the Advice and Assessment service. He is the manager responsible for the Implementation of the Assessment Framework.

Anne Peake is an Educational Psychologist with Oxfordshire Social Services. She has worked as a psychologist since 1976, for Education and Social Services, in Liverpool, the London Borough of Haringey, and now in Oxfordshire. Her main area of professional interest is in Child Protection work.

Gretchen Precey is an independent social worker, trainer and consultant. Her background is in child protection work. In addition to having a clinical interest in MSBP from her experience as a practitioner, Gretchen has trained widely on the *Framework for the Assessment of Children in Need and their Families*.

Barry Raynes is the executive director of Reconstruct. He has twenty five years of experience of working in all aspects of social care. He has worked as a trainer or consultant in most of the country's social services departments.

Caroline Rowsell is a feminist activist and researcher who has worked within a Social Services Training Section for the past 10 years. She specialises in issues related to violence against women and children, and is particularly concerned with the development of policy and strategy in relation to this field. She has worked extensively with local authorities, domestic violence fora, and domestic violence providers to extend knowledge and awareness of domestic violence issues. She is employed by the Department of Transport, Local Government and the Regions as one of two National Domestic Violence Co-ordinators, and is currently working to ensure that both local authorities and domestic violence providers are fully engaging with the Government's Supporting People programme.

Dr Prakash Srivastava is a Consultant Community Paediatrician whose main interest has been the effect of life experiences on child development. Though he currently works in Luton, Bedfordshire, the Graded Care Profile sprang principally from twelve years experience of working in a multi-agency setting in a socially and economically deprived part of South Yorkshire.

Janice Stewart is a qualified nurse and health visitor with many years experience as a practitioner and manager. She is now the Designated Nurse Child Protection for Bedfordshire Health, covering both Luton and Bedfordshire and also the Senior Nurse Child Protection for the Luton and Bedfordshire Community NHS Trust.

Bill Stone qualified as a social worker in 1981 after taking a degree in Social Policy at Nottingham University. Since then he has had a varied career in social work, primarily with children and families. He developed a particular interest in issues around parenting and child neglect and has trained extensively on this subject. He now works on a freelance basis with a mixed portfolio of practice, research, training and consultancy.

Amy Weir MA (Oxon.), MBA (OBS), CQSW. Amy was until recently the national lead inspector at the Department of Health for the Quality Protects Programme. She is currently seconded from the Department of Health to be Head of Children and Family Services in the London Borough of Harrow. She is particularly interested in the questions of how to ensure that the needs of children are assessed and met safely and effectively across agency and specialism boundaries. Amy co-edited *Conflict of Interest: Child Protection and Adult Mental Health* (Routledge, 1999) with Anthony Douglas. She evaluated and contributed to the Department of Health Training Pack – *Crossing Bridges: Training Resources for Working With Mentally Ill Parents and Their Children* (Pavilion, 1998).

Jane Wonnacott is a freelance trainer and consultant who has many years experiences of child protection training and practice. She runs training courses for local authorities and voluntary organisations and is particularly interested in supervision and the role of line managers in developing practice. She has recently carried out extensive training for local authorities on the New Assessment Framework. She has undertaken Part 8 enquiries for Area Child Protection Committees as well as providing consultancy on ACPC development. She is a consultant to Social Services departments on all aspects of child protection training. Jane has a long-standing interest in the integration of child protection and disability training, particularly in the area of assessment of risk.

Part One: The DoH Framework for the Assessment of Children in Need and their Families: Overview and Critique

Chapter One

Introduction

Martin C Calder and Simon Hackett

The Assessment of Children in Need and their Families (DoH, 2000) signalled a significant desire on the part of central government to improve assessment practice in childcare social work. It is a central part both of the Quality Protects agenda (DoH, 1998) and of the modernisation of social care services (DoH, 1998b). Although the consultation period was lengthy, the time allowed for agency and worker preparation pre-implementation was relatively short. Evidence from a wide range of agency contacts suggests that many people in the field remain at different points in their understanding of what is expected. This has direct implications for the capacity of agencies and individuals to implement the Assessment Framework across different practice settings and in response to wide-ranging practice issues. This book is designed to help with these challenges.

The Assessment Framework is a bold attempt to articulate, and indeed standardise, some of the current themes and issues in practice and to learn the lessons from past failures and weaknesses in assessment practice. The principles underpinning the Framework, with the emphasis on developmentally sensitive approaches, strengths perspectives, ecological concepts and the importance of underpinning assessments with research evidence are laudable. The Framework and accompanying guidance and scales represent a considerable conceptual step forward. However, we believe that there are gaps in several key respects and areas for development at a number of different levels. In particular, many important questions remain unanswered:

- Why, at least on an overt level, has the concept of 'risk' been deleted from the Framework? What are the implications of this for practice? How does this fit with other frameworks e.g. ASSET (YJB, 2000) where risk remains a key issue? Practitioners have repeatedly stated

that this is a matter of confusion to them. Should they jettison all their skills in the area of risk evaluation? Is risk no longer a useful concept for practice? Does the emphasis on strengths invalidate a perspective on risk?

- If the Framework is needs-led, but if the core business of social services remains child protection, does the Framework run the risk of skewing professional thinking in such cases in an overtly positive light? How should practitioners balance the relative weight of strengths and risks, or conflicting information across the different dimensions or domains in the Framework?

- Is the Framework equally applicable to all practice issues, or are there areas where it is less relevant? Child sexual abuse appears to be an area which is not discussed in any shape or form (see Calder, 2000; 2001; 2002 for further details).

- Are 'context issues' likely to undermine the scope of the Framework and its effectiveness? Are the staffing and wider resource implications of the Framework being given enough emphasis? How do other developments and issues impact upon implementation, for example, new legislation governing the exchange of information between busy and over-stretched professionals?

- Is there a reliable evidence-base upon which assessment practice can be built and do practitioners (and agencies) have the skills, resources and time to access this?

- Are the enormously tight timescales set realistic? Is it possible to engage parents, develop their trust and retain the child in focus or does the completion of the Assessment Forms come to dominate within such short timescales?

- Does the Framework fit with other key documents, for example, 'Safeguarding Children' (DoH, 1999)?

- Are the materials which underpin the Framework and significantly add to its usefulness available to all those who need them on the frontline?
- Does the Framework help or exacerbate difficulties associated with working together across professions and professionals (see Calder, 1999 for a review)?
- Does the proposed universality of the Framework allow sufficient specificity to children from minority groups, whose needs have traditionally often been overlooked?

These are the kind of questions which have motivated us to work together to produce this volume. We hope that the contributors who have provided their expertise in assessing complex and wide-ranging issues will be able to assist in the task of adding flesh to the bare bones provided by the Framework.

The book is designed to address the questions about the Framework both *operationally* and *conceptually* and to begin to provide some ideas as to how deficits may be overcome. Additionally, it seeks to help practitioners to identify and contextualise the relevant domains to explore in response to a range of presenting situations which are common features of childcare practice. The book does not include an explicit chapter on sexual abuse as this complex area has already been addressed elsewhere (Calder, 2000; 2002; Hackett, 2001).

Evidence and practice evolves quickly and thus there is some responsibility for workers to update themselves. This clearly needs to take place within a flourishing and nurturing organisational context. Good practice can emerge but cannot be sustained in a non-supportive organisation.

If the Framework is to be successful in improving the quality of assessments for children and their families, then there needs to be a continual process of development and enhancement. This book, we hope, will represent a contribution to this process.

All the opinions expressed are those of the authors of the particular chapters.

Happy reading!

Martin C Calder
Simon Hackett
December 2002

References

Calder, M. C. (1999) A Conceptual Framework for Managing Young People Who Sexually Abuse: Towards a Consortium Approach. In Calder, M. C (Ed.) *Working With Young People Who Sexually Abuse: New Pieces of the Jigsaw Puzzle*. Dorset: Russell House Publishing, 109-50.

Calder, M. C. et al. (2000) *A Complete Guide to Sexual Abuse Assessments*. Dorset: Russell House Publishing.

Calder, M. C. et al. (2001) *Juveniles and Children Who Sexually Abuse: Frameworks for Assessment*. (2nd edn) Dorset: Russell House Publishing.

Calder, M. C. (Ed.) (2002) *Young People Who Sexually Abuse: Building the Evidence Base for Your Practice*. Dorset: Russell House Publishing.

DoH (1998) *Quality Protects: Transforming Children's Services*. LAC (98) 28. 11 Nov.

DoH (1998b) *Modernising Social Services*. London: The Stationery Office.

DoH et al. (1999) *Working Together to Safeguard Children: A Guide to Inter-agency Working Arrangements to Safeguard and Promote the Welfare of Children*. London: The Stationery Office.

DoH et al. (2000) *Framework for the Assessment of Children in Need and Their Families*. London: HMSO.

Hackett, S. (2001) *Facing the Future: A Guide for Parents of Young People Who Have Sexually Abused*. Dorset: Russell House Publishing.

Youth Justice Board (2000) *Asset Assessment Profile*. London: Youth Justice Board.

Chapter Two

The Assessment Framework: A Critique and Reformulation

Martin C Calder

Introduction

The government is changing the way social workers do business. They are attempting to provide a framework for holistic, proactive and inclusive assessments within prescribed timescales. They have built their multi-component framework from research findings, modelling for practitioners what they expect in terms of 'evidence-based' practice. There are some positive points to the framework they propose, although there are many limitations, omissions and conflicts. The aim of this chapter is to chart the territory which surrounds these latter points: not in an attempt to discredit or sideline the materials produced, but to provide ideas and stimulus to the debate surrounding implementation strategies. The Framework is here to stay and we need to utilise the strengths and tackle the limitations if we are to practice effectively in the arena of childcare.

Origins of the assessment framework

The UK government has recently introduced (1st April, 2001) a new assessment framework for compulsory adoption by those agencies under the umbrella of the Department of Health, the Department for Education and Employment, and the Home Office (DoH et al., 2000), reinforced by the Children's Fund (DfEE, 2001). This has been driven by several different forces and the training pack accompanying the Assessment Framework (The NSPCC and The University of Sheffield, 2000) identifies the following:

- A central policy context that sees the government committed to ending child poverty, tackling social exclusion, and promoting the welfare of all children – so that children can thrive and fulfil their potential as citizens throughout their lives. There is also a drive to improving the quality and management of services responsible for supporting children and families through modernising social services, promoting co-operation between all statutory agencies, and building partnerships with the voluntary and private sector.

- Government objectives for children's social services that include ensuring that children are protected from emotional, physical and sexual abuse and neglect (significant harm); ensuring that children in need gain maximum life chance benefits from educational opportunities, health care and social care; and to ensure that referral and assessment processes discriminate effectively between different types and levels of need and produce a timely response (Quality Protects agenda – see DoH, 1998).

- The current legal framework as set out in the Children Act (1989) which states that every Local Authority has a general duty to:
  - safeguard and promote the welfare of children within their area who are in need; and
  - so far as is consistent with that duty, to promote the upbringing of such children by their families. [Section 17(1)].

There is also a clear definition of children in need as follows:
- he is unlikely to achieve or maintain, or to have the opportunity of achieving or maintaining a reasonable standard of health or development without the provision for him of services by local authority
- his health or development is likely to be significantly impaired, or further impaired, without the provision for him of such services or
- he is disabled [Section 17(10)].

Under Section 47 of the Children Act the local authority has a statutory duty to investigate wherever it has reasonable cause to suspect that a child who lives, or found, in their area is suffering, or is likely to suffer, significant harm or where a child is the subject of an emergency protection order or is in police protection. The authority is required to make such enquiries as it considers necessary to enable it to decide whether it should take any action to safeguard or promote the child's welfare, either by applying for a court order or by providing services or other help for the child and his family. If access to the child is denied or information withheld the authority must take reasonable steps to obtain access or information unless it is satisfied it already has sufficient information. The investigating authority may call upon other local authorities', health authorities', education authorities' and other specified agencies for assistance and these authorities have a duty to assist unless it would be unreasonable in the circumstances (Section 23).

- The findings from 'Messages from Research' (DoH, 1995) that pointed to a need to refocus all the energies and time away from the child protection system at the expense of other children found to be 'in need', but not in need of protection. This had created a system whereby professionals framed cases in such a way as to try and access resources through the child protection system, but these failed when allegations were unsubstantiated and the case was closed without assessing or attending to other needs or problems, or when cases were deferred as a gate keeping mechanism (Calder, 1993). Working Together to Safeguard Children (DoH et al., 1999) sets out the following selective findings from this research to embellish this point:
  - Some professionals were using Section 47 enquiries inappropriately, as a means of obtaining services for children in need;
  - Over half of the children and families who were the subject of Section 47 enquiries received no services as the result of professionals' interest in their lives. Too often, enquiries were too narrowly conducted as investigations into whether abuse or neglect had occurred, without considering the wider needs and circumstances of the child and family;
  - Enquiries into suspicions of child abuse can have traumatic effects on families. Good professional practice can ease parents' anxiety and lead to co-operation that helps to safeguard the child. As nearly all children remain at, or return home, involving the family in child protection processes is likely to be effective. Professionals could still do more to work in partnership with parents and the child;
  - Discussions at child protection conferences tended to focus too heavily on decisions about registration and removal, rather than focusing on future plans to safeguard the child and support the family in the months after the conference (although this misses

the central role of the core group – see Calder, 2001);
  - While inter-agency work was often relatively good at the early stages of enquiries, its effectiveness tended to decline once child protection plans had been made, with social services left with sole responsibility for implementing the plans;
  - There was inconsistent use made of the child protection register, which was not consulted for 60% of children for whom there were child protection concerns.

- The previous central assessment guidance 'Protecting Children' (DoH, 1988) predated the Children Act (1989) and the accompanying child protection guidance 'Working Together' (DoH, 1991) was restricted to comprehensive assessments that followed child protection registration and was structured in such a way that it was used mechanistically by practitioners. We also know that the central guidance was fundamentally flawed in a number of other respects that include:
  - The fact that it does not address in any shape or form the complexities of child sexual abuse (see Calder, 2000 for a detailed critique).
  - The fact that the guidance was issued at a time when the emphasis was on controlling dangerous families and we have moved away from this towards a partnership-based approach (see Calder, 1995; DoH, 1995b).
  - A failure to provide sufficient guidance in the arena of post-registration practice (see Calder and Horwath, 1999).
  - The lack of detailed guidance on how to harness the information collected to move into either a short or long-term plan. The emphasis of the 167 questions was on structured information collection (a process often done well by workers) rather than their repeatedly defined area of weakness (using it to guide their intervention).
  - No reference to the assessment of risk to children who have been placed on the child protection register so that a clear child protection plan can be formulated (Katz, 1997).
  - It contained hidden assumptions about what 'normal' families should look like, i.e. they should resemble middle-class white families as closely as possible. Families who deviate from this norm are seen to be unable to provide adequate care for their children.

Furthermore, the whole process of assessment is seen as setting a middle-class agenda by which clients are 'tricked' into co-operation (McBeath and Webb, 1990).
- The text reflected ideas and practices which predate current thinking about children's rights (Schofield and Thoburn, 1996).
- The lack of focus on anti-racist and anti-discriminatory practice: as the tenor of all the questions is Eurocentric – very few focus on the child's identity and identity development, nor on links with his/her own community. The role of oppression in the construction of child abuse is not addressed at all.
- The question and answer format has been criticised for being overtly restrictive and that other observations and methods should be used. The questions themselves are often inappropriate in particular situations and therefore the overall headings are more often used than the individual questions.
- The assessments were static and not dynamic: not because the text advised this, simply that the format encouraged it.
- Inspections of social work practice had identified variable performance in assessments that were often of poor quality; the assessment process was often unclear and unco-ordinated; families were given inadequate early responses when asking for help; there was a lack of systematic approaches to information gathering; a failure to obtain children's views and wishes; a variability of time scales for assessment; and an absence of inter-agency protocols or frameworks for assessing children in need.
- There was also a great deal of concern being expressed by children and young people about their experiences of being assessed with some recommendations on how that might be improved (see The NSPCC and The University of Sheffield, 2000).

Taking these concerns collectively there is a very clear and a powerful argument for change in terms of updating the kind of central guidance needed to guide frontline workers in their approach. This was reinforced by parallel findings that uncovered the secondary disadvantages of children in the public care system (DfEE/DoH, 2000) and the quality of the assessments post core assessment. This led to a view that we could attempt to integrate the looked after children system with the assessment process from the point of first contact to enhance the quality of provision and add some continuity and consistency. The assessment framework thus started with the developmental dimensions for the child, deemed helpful in the looked after system, and was then added to. What is of concern is the assessment framework that was finally issued, particularly since it only purports to be a framework and not in itself a tool for assessment practice. My concern is that if you have a fundamentally flawed framework then it is setting practitioners up to fail when they endeavour to add flesh to the bones (Calder, 2000). Before I move into a detailed critique of the framework, it is important to provide a summary overview of the content.

Content of the assessment framework: A summary

The following section details briefly the main components of the assessment framework:

- Assessment is one of six key areas in the **Quality Protects** programme.
- The new framework will provide a **systematic** way of assessing children and families.
- The assessment will address **three domains**: the child's developmental needs; parental capacity; family and environmental factors.
- The assessment framework will be **integrated** into the revised 'Working Together to Safeguard Children'.
- The guidance will be accompanied by **tools** to assist assessment and by **schedules** designed to systematically collect and collate material from individual child and family assessments. The schedules will be the subject of **further development** over a two-year period.

Key principles

- It is **child centred**:
- It is rooted in **child development** (which includes recognition of the significance of timing in a child's life):
- It takes an **ecological approach** of locating the child within the family and the wider community;
- It is based on ensuring **equality of opportunity** for all children and their families;
- It is based on **working in partnership** with families and young people;
- It **builds on the strengths** in each of the three domains;

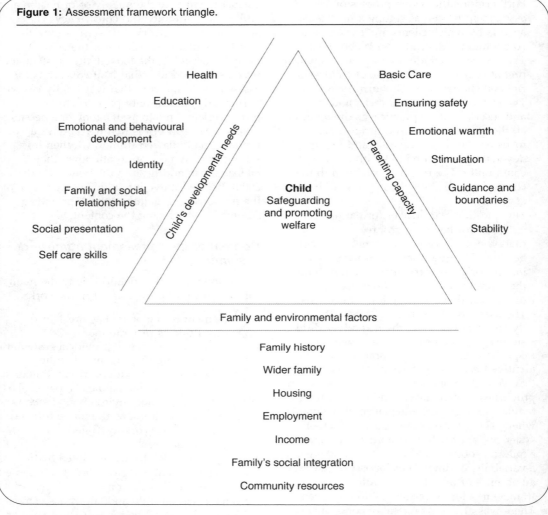

Figure 1: Assessment framework triangle.

- It is a **multi-agency approach** model in which it is not just social services departments who are the assessors and providers of service;
- Assessment is seen as a **process** not just a single event;
- **Action and services** should be provided in parallel with assessment, according to the needs of the child and family – not to await 'completion of assessment';
- It is **grounded in knowledge** derived from theory, research, policy and practice.

The assessment framework is presented visually above (see Figure 1) and is followed by a description of the key components of each strand. There are several key issues arising from this that will be addressed under the critique later in this chapter.

Dimensions of child's developmental needs

1. **Health**
   Includes growth and development as well as physical, and mental, well being. Involves receiving appropriate health care when ill, an adequate and nutritious diet, exercise, immunisations and developmental checks, dental and optical care and for older children appropriate advice and information on issues that have an impact on health.

2. **Education**
   Covers all areas of a child's cognitive development which begins from birth. Includes opportunities for play and interaction with other children and adults, access to books, an adult interest in school

work, progress and achievements and acquiring a range of skills and interests. Appropriate developmental progress involves taking account of a child's starting point and any special educational needs.

3. **Emotional and behavioural development**
Concerns the appropriateness of response in feelings and actions by a child, initially to parents and caregivers and increasingly to others beyond the family. Includes nature and quality of early attachments, characteristics of temperament, adaptation to change, response to stress and degree of appropriate self-control.

4. **Identity**
Concerns the child's growing sense of self as a separate and valued being. Includes how a child views himself and his abilities, feelings of belonging and acceptance by the family and wider society and strength of a positive sense of individuality.

5. **Family and social relationships**
Development of empathy and the capacity to place self in someone else's shoes. Includes quality of relationships with parents or caregivers, increasing importance of age appropriate friendships within peers and other significant persons in the child's life and response of family to these relationships.

6. **Social presentation**
Concerns child's growing understanding of the way in which appearance and behaviour are perceived by the outside world and the impression of being created. Includes appropriateness of dress for age, gender, culture and religion, cleanliness and personal hygiene and availability of advice from parents or caregivers about presentation in different settings.

7. **Self care skills**
Concerns the acquisition by a child of competencies required for increasing independence, from early skills of dressing and feeding, to opportunities to learn safe care beyond the family and independent living skills as older children. Includes encouragement to acquire skills and impact of disability and other special needs on how skills are gained.

Dimension of parenting capacity

1. **Basic care**
This dimension involves providing for the child's physical needs, and appropriate medical and dental care.
Includes provision of food, water, shelter, clean clothing and adequate personal hygiene.

2. **Ensuring safety**
Ensuring the child is adequately protected from harm or danger.
Includes protection from harm or danger, and from contact with unsafe adult/other children and from self-harm.

3. **Emotional warmth**
Ensuring the child's emotional needs are met.
Includes ensuring the child's requirements for secure attachment with significant adults and appropriate sensitivity; and responsiveness to the child's needs. Demonstration of affection and positive regard for the child and appropriate physical contact, comfort and cuddling sufficient to demonstrate warm regard.

4. **Stimulation**
Promotion of child's learning and intellectual development through encouragement and cognitive stimulation.
Includes facilitating the child's cognitive development and potential through interaction, communication, talking and responding to the child's language and questions, encourage and joining the child's play, and promotion of educational opportunities. Ensuring school attendance or equivalent opportunity.

5. **Guidance and boundaries**
This comprises enabling the child to regulate their own emotional state, and develop an internal model of conscience and appropriate behaviour, while also promoting pro-social inter-personal behaviour and social relationships.

    The key parental tasks are *demonstrating and modelling* of appropriate behaviour, emotional regulation and interactions with others, and *guidance*. Limit setting boundaries, so that the child is able to develop an internal model of moral values and conscience, and social behaviour appropriate for the society within which they will grow up. The aim is to enable the child to grow into an autonomous adult, holding their own values, and able to demonstrate pro-social behaviours with others, rather than having to be dependent on rules outside themselves.
Includes social problem-solving, anger management, consideration for others, and effective discipline and shaping behaviour.

6. **Stability**
Providing a *sufficiently* stable family environment to enable the above dimensions of parenting to operate reasonably consistently.
Includes responding in a similar manner to the same behaviours, providing consistency of emotional warmth over time.

Family and environmental factors

1. **Family history**
Who is living in the household and how are they related to the child?
Chronology of significant life events and their meaning to family members. Nature of family functioning and its impact on the child. Parental strengths and difficulties, including those of an absent parent.

2. **Wider family**
Who are considered to be members of the wider family by the child and the parents? This includes related and non-related persons and absent wider family. What is their role and importance to the child and parents and in precisely what way?

3. **Housing**
Does the accommodation have basic amenities and facilities appropriate to the age and development of the child and other resident members? Includes the interior and exterior of the accommodation and immediate surroundings. Basic amenities include water, heating, sanitation, cooking facilities, sleeping arrangements and cleanliness, hygiene and safety and their impact on the child's upbringing.

4. **Employment**
Who is working in the household and their pattern of work? How does this impact on the child? How is work or absence of work viewed by family members? How does it affect their relationship with the child?

5. **Income**
Sufficiency of income to meet the family's needs. Are there extreme financial difficulties which affect the child?

6. **Family's social integration**
Exploration of the wider context of the local neighbourhood and community and its impact on the child and parents. Includes the degree of the family's integration or isolation, their peer groups, friendship and social networks and the importance attached to them.

7. **Community resources**
Describes all facilities and services in a neighbourhood, including universal services of primary health care, day care and schools. Includes availability, accessibility and standard of resources and impact on the family.

The critique and reformulation

(a) Context issues

Since the early 1990s child protection agencies have been under siege as evidenced by a dramatic upsurge in referrals, increasingly high caseloads, inadequate supervision, severe financial cuts and ever-shrinking resources, continuous change, and negative media portrayal. These have all impacted acutely on workers with low morale as the norm. It is against this background that an agenda for practice must be set (Calder, Peake and Rose, 2001).

The refocusing of children's services aims to promote child protection within the context of wider services for children in need and children should not be routed inappropriately into the child protection system as a means of gaining access to services. It is argued that many families who find themselves enmeshed in the child protection system suffer from multiple disadvantages and that they need help at an earlier stage to tackle their problems before parenting difficulties escalate into abuse. A more holistic view of the needs of vulnerable children and their families is required. The development of what has come to be called 'family support' has taken on a strategic significance for bringing about these changes.

The aim of the central government guidance on the assessment framework is to achieve a rebalancing of child protection (Section 47, Children Act, 1989) towards children in need (Section 17, Children Act 1989) thus extending the assessment catchment for agencies coupled with an improvement in the quality of assessments. What is problematic is that this has not been accompanied by an increase in resources especially as we know that our child protection services are under-resourced to start with and this is probably a major contributor to tragedies such as the death of Victoria Climbie in Haringey. 'We need to recognise our child protection system for what it is: an under-resourced and understaffed system battered by years of reactive policy change, and a hostile, uncomprehending media onslaught; a system in which individuals are too often overburdened and unsupported' (Comment, *Community Care*, 26th April–2nd May 2001, p2). It thus becomes important for the public inquiry to 'examine the reality gap between policies such as the refocusing of resources onto family support and what actually takes place on the ground'. Let us hope that the inquiry brief extends beyond establishing the circumstances surrounding her death to embrace staffing issues, resource levels, workloads, professional confidence, and the increasing gaps between central expectation and local practice, particularly conceptual acceptance and the capacity to deliver.

The shift towards family support (DoH, 1995) and a slower recourse towards child protection intervention provides an opportunity for social services departments to offer services to these families who have in the past been filtered out or whose situations have sometimes worsened when they have been brought into the child protection system. Support is often correlated with improved outcomes for their children, although exactly what the interface is between family support and child protection remains unclear and hugely variable. This has led to concerns that in some cases children do not remain safeguarded, particularly where some cases of child protection are defined as children in need of family support (*Community Care*, 30th August–5th September, 2001, p5).

Valios (2001b) has noted that many local authorities have been unable to carry out the spirit of 'Messages from Research' (DoH 1995) because the document did not tell them how to. This has resulted in family support services being layered on top of child protection, with many agencies running their entire child welfare service as child protection. This is fuelled by myths that child protection referrals are self-evident and they rarely are, with workers trying to fit the enormous variety of child rearing practices into vague and unstable definitions of neglect, sexual and physical abuse. At the same time as the government is encouraging us to move towards a more supportive approach, they have commissioned an inquiry into the Victoria Climbie affair and this is likely to result in tighter procedures, more accountability and therefore a more cautious professional approach. The government have indicated they will introduce any major changes recommended, out of the

context that they are already introducing major changes through the revised working together, the assessment framework, Quality Protects, etc.

I have chosen to address the following issues to support my belief that the assessment framework is misguided in the above climate and actually aggravates some of the known and established difficulties and problems:

- The increasing obstacles to inter-agency working.
- The development of thresholds for the provision of a social work service.
- The barriers to information exchange between professionals.
- The lack of fit between the assessment framework and 'Working Together'
- The lack of inter-governmental department liaison resulting in parallel ASSET guidance being issued. (Youth Justice Board, 2000).

The increasing obstacles to inter-agency working

It is hoped that the development of a standardised assessment framework will provide a language which is common to children and their families, as well as to professionals and other staff. This should make multi-disciplinary working easier and provide a more effective service response, which in turn should lead to better outcomes for children.

(Adcock, 2000, p478).

This appears idealised in the face of the following discussion.

Child protection is not the exclusive province of any one agency. Unfortunately, different constituent agencies of the child protection system are guided by different legislation and government guidance, and these, at times, seem to pull in different directions (Margetts, 1998, p28). Working together among different professionals and between different agencies is also not a uniform activity. It can range from the face-to-face contact between a doctor and a health visitor concerned about a shared patient, to a network of professionals employed by different agencies to meet the needs of a particular client group (Loxley, 1997, p42).

There is ample evidence in the child protection arena that individuals and agencies have found it most difficult to co-operate. This goes beyond individual personality conflict and professional incompetence. They are rooted in a variety of differences in values, practices, perspectives, and professional ethos, arising out of a range of social, cultural and historical processes. I have previously extended and adapted (see Calder, 1999) the work of Olive Stevenson and Marion Charles (see Charles and Stevenson, 1990; and Stevenson, 1989) to explore some of the explanations why working together often runs into difficulties. This is important given the potential direct and indirect effect of the new assessment framework to aggravate these further.

1. Differences in background and training: Professionals bring a range of personal and professional experiences combined with extensive differences in temperament and views of life and society. They will differ greatly in their educational experiences, particularly their professional training which has a profound socialising effect upon them. Their expectations of training will also differ. For social workers, they will have experienced training, which encourages the development of self-awareness and is based on abstract values like self-determination. This mirrors the complex and uncertain situations which they will face in practice. Other professionals will have experienced more decisive and directive training and may be frustrated by the lack of definitive answers to child protection problems.

2. Varied attitudes to family life: Individual attitudes to family life are shaped by personal experiences, ethnic origin, culture and social class combining with the effects of professional socialisation. It follows, therefore, that attitudes will vary over issues such as what constitutes good/bad family life, 'normal' behaviour, etc.

3. Stereotypes and prejudices: Are a pervasive feature held by us in relation to disciplines we rarely encounter, and have the potential to damage trust and create stress and confusion about what skills and responsibilities they actually have to offer. The different approaches necessarily adopted by professional groups may give rise to stereotypical 'cardboard' images of each other. Such stereotyping can be dangerous when it allows us to distance ourselves from others, and to fail to see the individual through the distorting lens of our own prejudices. It can be used defensively to convince ourselves we do not need to take their ideas, understandings and values seriously, and to reinforce our own superior knowledge.

4. Role identification and socialisation: Each professional will have been socialised into their particular role, and will have a value system and language unique to their particular profession. These value systems are constant sources of potential conflict, which affect how professionals view each other's work and the level of risk acceptable to the respective professions. This has a profound effect on how they see each other, on the nature of their interaction and on their perceptions of specific family situations and the action taken. Stevenson (1989) has reminded us that we should not overlook the effect of role definition upon the attitudes and feelings of the worker's involved. Roles have emotional as well as intellectual dimensions. There can be consequences for staff within their own agencies of subscribing to their role in the child protection system, e.g. they are pilloried and may have their career prospects affected.

5. Differences within and between professionals: No individual is the same, whether they are from the same agency or from a different one. Subsystems exist – each with different aims and values, relating to personal and social characteristics (such as class and gender). Not all individuals hold the same interests, beliefs or expertise.

   Status and power: Differences in contracts of employment, the different types and standards of professional training, occupational status and prestige, gender, race, class, language, and public image all contribute to the real and felt power differentials within the interagency network. Working together means contact between different emotional realities, different systems of meaning and different types of bias. At its most acute, the statutory responsibility of social services for the protection of abused children is at odds with its low status, salary and less certain identity. Professionals working together requires significant personal investments, inducing a sense of vulnerability, such as exposing practice to peer scrutiny and with it the prospect of being assessed as being incompetent. Such anxieties can become infectious and compound the presenting problems. One profession may regard another as hostile or inferior to their own and shape their attitudes accordingly. Status affects performance: those who perceive themselves of low status may offer no contributions or feel unable to question information or comments made by those of seeming high status or power.

6. Professional and organisational priorities: The nature of the work undertaken by the various agencies varies greatly. Those with statutory and lead procedural responsibilities will spend much of their time doing child protection work, compared to other agencies where it plays one part of a much more generic caseload. For example, Hallett (1995) found that teachers only spent half a day a month on child protection and thus remain detached from the system. The importance of staff training will be given different emphasis by the various agencies (varying from essential to being seen as a 'luxury').

7. Structures, systems and administration: The variety of structures, and the systems within them, of the different agencies create difficulties and make co-ordination difficult. Agencies hold different powers and duties, and some do not have coterminous geographical boundaries. Accountability and authority is fragmented, with individuals having differing degrees of authority with which to speak for their agencies. All these differences affect co-operation and inhibit the transfer of information between agencies. Each agency has a different job to do, a different area of activity, and different interests and concerns. Some have a focused role at a particular stage whilst others have a more diffuse role that spans all the stages. Similarly, within any stage, different agencies may need to focus on different aspects (Stainton-Rogers, 1989, p88-9). Charles and Stevenson (1990) have argued that we must all have some appreciation of the diversity of employing agencies, with their differing structures, nature and functions. They noted that many of the professionals involved in child protection work belong to agencies featuring strict hierarchical structures, e.g. the police, whilst local authority departments are ultimately accountable to committees of elected representatives, who delegate powers and duties through senior officers to teachers and social workers. GPs and consultants, although immediately accountable to their

relevant professional bodies, are less directly influenced or constrained in their day-to-day actions by a professional hierarchy. Other doctors, such as hospital and community paediatricians, have clear lines of accountability from basic staff through more senior staff to lead workers. As such, the agency structure inevitably poses limits to the degree of professional autonomy exercised by the various disciplines. For those whose freedom of action is constrained by agency structures, a certain tension exists between the exercise of individual professional judgement and what is agency permissible. This tension is easily compounded by the attitudes of other professionals, who may express frustrations about delays in decision making, being unaware of the processes needing to be gone through. Organisational structures affect the availability of staff, e.g. surgery hours, shift systems, daily patterns of working and duty rotas all influence the nature of inter-professional co-operation (p86–88).

8. Different roles and responsibilities: The issue of role clarity is important, particularly when their blurring can relieve staff of knowing who is doing what and why and who should be held accountable in the event of failure. Hallett (1995) found some confusion about the roles of various professionals in the system, partially supported by the research of Calder and Barratt (1997) in the core group. Here, the authors found a discrepancy between what health visitors, teachers and social workers conceptualised as their own roles and those of others with what was found in practice. They concluded that roles had to be grounded in what was realistic rather than being overtly idealistic. There appears to be a shift towards acceptance that whilst there is an expectation of collective responsibility, the reality is that social services have the lead responsibility and any offers of support will be gratefully received. Yet unless this is agreed and understood formally and locally, there will be confusion and a culture of blame will prevail. There is also a need to acknowledge that child protection is dirty work and it can lead to social worker's defining their own role and that of others in such a way to enable them to ditch the dirty work on to others (Blyth and Milner, 1990, p197). Social services have a broad role in

the management of child abuse, ranging from partnership and rehabilitation to investigation and removal. The police have a duty to prosecute (punitive), whilst probation has a crime prevention role, plus working with those convicted of sexual offences. Morrison (1998b) pointed out that, for the police and probation, the concept of risk is overwhelmingly a negative association, e.g. the risk of danger. This is in stark contrast to debates in the child protection field in which the risk of potential danger is continually weighed against risk of potential benefit (p4).

9. Lines of authority and decision-making: Social services are the lead agency in child protection, joined by the police and others. Only recently has the law required key agencies to co-operate with social services in the investigation of child abuse. The problem with such mandated working together is that people and agencies will not necessarily collaborate just because someone tells them to do so. This is most acute when seen in the context that few professionals would choose to work together given a choice. Different agencies and individuals may have varying degrees of acceptance of, or commitment to, co-operate and differing capacities to resist. The recommendations of a child protection conference are not binding and agencies can, and do, act independently of them (especially when they did not sign up to them originally). Within agencies, the aims and approaches of people at different levels are often at odds, e.g. 'managerial safety' versus practitioner option for risk.

10. Different perspectives: Professionals define and explain child abuse in different and sometimes conflicting ways and adopt quite different stances about the way work should be undertaken. Different theories often emerge from particular disciplines and are maintained without reference to, or acknowledgement of, parallel theories. This blinkered approach to problem definition affects our ability to provide a problem resolution.

11. Complexity and co-ordination: Rai (1994) defined complexity as the degree of structural differentiation or internal segmentation, as reflected by the number of divisions, number of hierarchical levels, and the number of geographical locations of the organisation (p90). He found a very clear negative relationship between complexity and co-ordination in child welfare agencies, particularly relating to communication.

12. Communication: Information is power and sharing it symbolises some ceding of autonomy. Disagreements exist both as to the content of what is to be shared and about the actual value of talking together at all. What seems essential to communicate for one may seem a breach of confidentiality or peripheral to another. Professionals from different fields are used to working within their own particular culture and organisational structure with their established rules on issues such as confidentiality. The very differences in language and traditions can lead to a breakdown in communication, especially when dominated by technical terms and/or jargon. The differences in status, position and hierarchy inhibit communications among members of an organisation, particularly inter-level. These concerns have been aggravated further by the recent introduction of the Data Protection Act (1998) and the impact on information exchange outside of the child protection banner (discussed later in this chapter).

13. 'Underlapping service provision': is a tactic employed by agencies where they choose the narrowest possible view of their duties and then they discharge them in as perfunctory a way as possible. Once one agency has taken this view, others may do so to avoid 'dumping', thus depriving the client of any service rather than a complementary interagency response (Margetts, 1998). The threshold for receiving a social work service is discussed later in this chapter.

14. Changes in philosophy: is a pervasive feature of current child protection work. Following the Children Act (1989) and the introduction of parental responsibility and partnership (see Calder, 1995); and the report 'Messages from Research' (DoH, 1995), which recommended that we review the balance between family support and child protection approaches, there has been conflict between agencies on how to respond to these concepts. This is important, as we cannot separate partnership with families from partnership practice between and within agencies (Morrison, 1996). If there are deficits in collaboration between

agencies, then it undermines the experience of partnership for the families: 'If partnership is to become a reality, it must be ingrained and modelled within organisational structures, cultures, and working relationships which seek to reward collaboration rather than competition' (Morrison, 1996, p135).

15. Organisational restructuring: Reorganisations in key agencies have taken place in the context of tight financial constraints on local government. There has been a major shift in the balance of power from local to central government as local authority expenditure and taxation has been brought firmly under central control. As Morrison (1998) has noted:

> *The past seven years have seen an escalation in both the extent and rate of organisational change across the public sector. No agency or discipline has been left unaffected . . . Reforming legislation has occurred in social services, health, education, and criminal justice sectors, in pursuit of greater efficiency and effectiveness with the introduction of market principles against a backcloth of fiscal retrenchment . . .*
> (p122–3).

This has led to agencies redefining their core business and basing collaboration on fiscal as opposed to inter-professional arrangements. The result is that 'collaboration is currently dangerously over-dependent on the commitment and skills of individuals, rather than organisations, and thus too easily disrupted by their departure. Unfortunately, this means that whilst the quality of response may be very good if it involves individuals committed to collaboration, it cannot guarantee it maintains that response across populations or over time.' Morrison also notes that the organisational context has therefore become less predictable, less stable and more conflictual in the short-term, as the competition for resources becomes even more acute. Whilst the emphasis on contractual, accountable and targeted services may in the longer-term result in strategic inter-agency partnerships for the planning, commissioning and evaluating of child protection services, in the short-term at least, 'partnerships' across agencies are under severe strain (p125). Morrison (1997) concluded that these cumulative forces have 'placed an almost intolerable strain on

inter-agency work and the ethos of collaboration which has been the heart of modern child protection work. Given that, even under reasonable conditions, multi-agency work is not easy, current conditions mean that its undergoing its sternest test since its importance was first recognised in the early 1970s' (p196). These changes may spell the end of specialist knowledge and the need to train and support more, but smaller, teams of staff. Morrison (1996) also pointed out that the fragmentation of central structures means that it is no longer possible for senior managers to guarantee a response to child protection throughout their agency. The result is that a culture of 'survivalism' has developed, in which individual energies are directed towards self-protection, with little spare energy left to engage with the external world of other agencies. For an excellent article reviewing the impact of a market forces approach on the organisation of child protection services, the reader is referred to Barker (1996); and for a review of the implications of the purchaser-provider separation for service delivery, the reader is referred to Hood (1997). To conclude, Corby (1995) has argued that 'the assumption that co-ordination is inevitably the best way to achieve goals is questionable. Indeed, there is a distinct possibility that co-ordinated action can be misused as a substitute for shortage of resources' (p212).

16. Anxiety and child protection: Morrison (1995) has argued that anxiety runs like a vein throughout the child protection process. This can relate both to the work as well as the struggle to survive in the current external climate of change. If it is not contained, learning cannot take place. Failures at an organisational level to appropriately contain anxiety can permeate all aspects of the agency's work, as well as affecting its relations with the outside world and other agencies. This is demonstrated in the dysfunctional learning cycle described by Vince and Martin (1993)-see Figure 2. In this environment, anxiety is seen as unprofessional, a sign of weakness and not coping. As a result, uncertainty is suppressed through fight and flight mechanisms. The absence of forums where feelings and doubts can be safely expressed leads to defensiveness, and a resistance to

Figure 2: Dysfunctional learning cycle. Vince and Martin (1993).

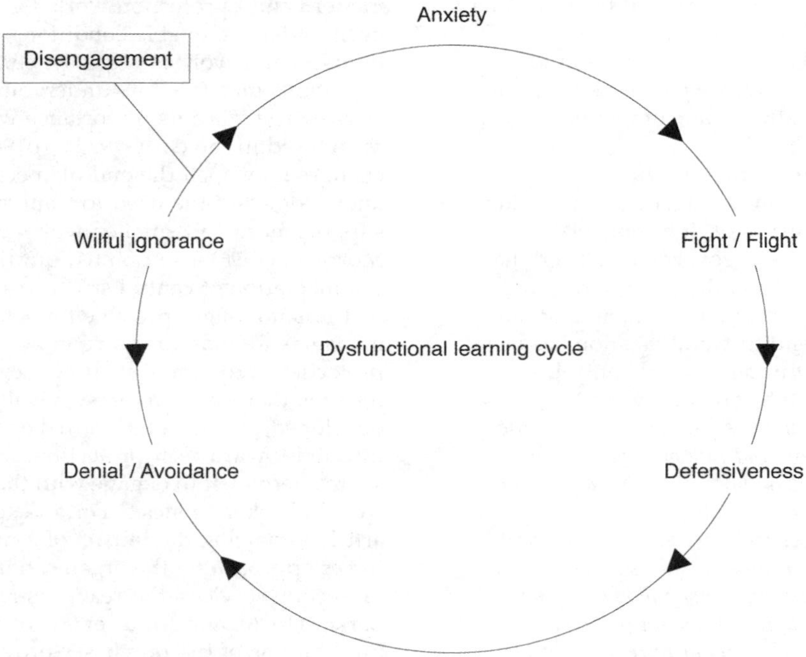

share and reflect on practice. It also undermines confidence to experiment with new practice. Emotional defensiveness then deepens into cognitive distortion whereby the principal reality is warded off via denial of dissonant information and attitudes, offering a temporary but false sense of security. If this process worsens with more wilful and sustained ignorance, it may lead eventually to total disengagement.

Could the situation get worse and in what circumstances is clearly an important question to be asked, and then answered. I believe that the assessment framework contributes to this in a number of ways. Firstly, the process of consultation on the framework was a protracted one with several draft documents being issued for comment (see DoH, 1999) – primarily to local authority social services departments. The reason for this narrow approach is linked to the Quality Protects agenda that is targeted exclusively on social services, and also on the need to improve the quality of assessments that social workers invariably retain lead casework responsibility for. One of the consistent messages fed back to the Department of Health throughout the

process of consultation was that any new assessment framework had to be issued to the inter-agency network, since there is a central mandate to work together to achieve better outcomes for children. This was repeatedly ignored until the last minute when the logos of the Department for Education and Employment and the Home Office joined with that of the Department of Health. Whilst this was a good outcome, the process of arriving at this is problematic. For example, all the other agencies appear to have been excluded from the process of consultation. When the final document appeared with cross-governmental department support, this was not accompanied by internal departmental guidance from the DfEE, the Home Office or the Department of Health (to some of the affected branches, such as health visitors, doctors, etc.) so it has been a lottery as to who has been told of, or learned about, this development. There are also two different models of training delivery to frontline staff to prepare them for implementation: to social services staff alone under the banner of Quality Protects (aggravating the other agencies perception of being isolated) or through the Area Child Protection Committee (ACPC) – although the latter is not truly multi-disciplinary in its delivery since other agency staff were not deemed eligible for the training on the trainers programme mobilised (rather late and without the finished training pack) by the Department of Health. To add to the problems is the dichotomy between a multi-agency understanding that they will be able to refer more cases at an earlier stage to social services (to bring alive the Section 17 criteria) and a need for social services to actively restrict the work it will take on in line with the available resources rather than the identified needs. This is aggravating tensions between agencies further as health and education staff grapple with the concern that they will have a restricted capacity to access a social work service when in fact they think they should access it much more freely. This is dealt with in the next section.

The development of thresholds for the provision of a social work service

Need is not an absolute concept. People have to agree on who is in need and who is not. Certain aspects of children's services are socially constructed. This means that society may decide, for example, which children are in need, when it is right to intervene, what type and quality of services to offer and what outcomes are sought. In most Western developed nations, when need is defined by fiscal criteria, it appears to outstrip resources available to meet it by a ratio of three to one. As a consequence, society must prioritise the support it is prepared to offer to different groups of children in need (Dartington Social Research Unit, 1998).

Guidance on a response to the task of identifying 'children in need' has to balance the clear spirit and intention of the Children Act with the constraints on resources in which Local Authority departments and agencies involved with children and families operate. As a result, there is a need to set priorities and identify target groups. Valios (2001) reported on the drastic financial problems facing ALL social services child care departments. She found that of the projected social services overspend of £200 million for 2000-1, 64% was attributable to children's services. According to the Department of Health, gross expenditure by local authorities in England on personal social

services was just over £12 billion in 1999-2000, with services to children and older people accounting for nearly three quarters of the total spend (DOH, 2000d). There are several integrated factors accounting for the increase in expenditure on children's services: the national rise in the number of children entering the care system; the rising number of staff vacancies and the need to recruit agency staff or place children in outside placements at great cost; the impact of private foster care agencies on driving the cost of the same service up; and the need to offer financial incentives to attract staff. What is clear is that the government agenda cannot be translated into practice at a local level without more resources. The government have been told that the formula for the standard spending assessment is wrong and out of date and ignores the special features of social services generally and children's services in particular. Authorities continue to massively exceed the allotted monies but this is in order to deal with children in need of protection or who need to be taken into care rather than financial mismanagement. The government needs to get out its credit card and fund the services it so clearly wants in place. At present, it is only the government ministers who seriously believe that social services have enough money to do the job asked of it.

Local authorities cannot limit the legal definition of 'children in need' (Section 17) to certain groups or categories of children, but they can give guidance as to how the definition of 'in need' should be interpreted. Many local authorities have thus responded by formulating local guidance to help staff in the allocation of staff and services according to locally agreed priorities. Quite apart from the need to narrow the Section 17 criteria down to manage scarce resources, Social Services are now required under the modernising agenda (DoH, 1998b) to set down and publicise widely its services so as to achieve total transparency. The following discussion derives from the work the author did in Salford to develop a threshold for the provision of a social work service (Calder, 2000b).

The definition of 'in need' provided by the Children Act has the potential to embrace large numbers of children who might benefit from the provision of a service. The definition does not indicate how we should set about the task of determining which children should have priority. The fact that a child is considered to be 'in need' does not automatically lead to a duty to provide services. The Guidance to the Children Act 1989 (Vol. 2) states:

Local Authorities are not expected to meet every individual need, but they are asked to identify the extent of need and then make decisions on the priorities for service provision in their area in the context of that information and their statutory duties.

The Act does specify that services should be directed towards safeguarding and promoting the welfare of children. For the Local Authority, the adoption of an approach which sees its core business as safeguarding activity ensures that there is not a net-widening effect of pulling more children into services, whilst also reducing the vulnerability of the Authority to legal challenge from parents who felt that they should receive a wide range of services which, in their opinion, would promote the welfare of their children. Conversely, this narrow approach has the effect of other agencies pushing cases 'up-tariff' to attract a service because it is perceived that family support services receive little priority. If the choice is a child protection service or nothing, more cases will continue to be sucked into the child protection system, either because those making or receiving referrals will continue to believe that that is the only way to receive a service, or because staff feel uncomfortable in screening out people when the alternative is no service at all.

The duty to provide services to children in need falls on the Local Authority and is a shared corporate responsibility. Clearly the philosophy underpinning the act extends that shared responsibility to all of those providing services to children and families. The Children Act 1989 made it clear that, although the Social Services Department has the lead responsibility with regard to children in need, there is a clear expectation that other Departments within the local authority, the Health Authority and Voluntary agencies will provide assistance. No single agency has the responsibility, the resources, the skills or the expertise to meet all the needs of the children in greatest need. The Social Services clearly has a responsibility to co-ordinate the services for those children identified as being in need and to promote a network of services to meet their needs.

Thresholds are of two types. A pure threshold describes in a language accessible to all professionals working with children in need the seriousness of a child's situation. A process threshold describes the point beyond which an agency will decide to support a child in need and the activity (e.g. case conference or checking a register) required to permit an intervention. Presently, the disjunction between pure and process thresholds is great, meaning that agencies intervening with many of the less serious cases may overlook the circumstances of children at great risk of harm (Dartington Social Research Unit, 1998, p23).

The adoption of a threshold for a social work service should enable several objectives to be achieved:

- Consistency and equity in response to need across the areas.
- Equitable provision of limited resources across the local authority area according to levels of need (i.e. targeting) – on the assumption that we cannot respond to all the identified need, it is important that service users and other professionals see the provision of services as fair.
- Improved management information about the type of need, which is not receiving a response – which should allow us to develop and commission services in relation to changing need (see the discussion below on the Children in need database return).
- The recording of assessed needs and of decisions that need cannot be met because of lack of financial and/or other resources.
- Analysis of service response to enhance discussions with other Departments and agencies as to their input.

The following framework sets out a categorisation of need along a continuum and within which we can easily locate a threshold for the provision of a social work service.

In the government paper addressing eligibility criteria for adult services (DoH, 2001) they encourage services to move away from focusing on those in the greatest immediate need, believing that prevention now is better than emergency intervention later. This surely does not mean that services to those in greatest need are overlooked for the sake of those in less need, but that we should create services to meet a broader range of needs. What the guidance does not say is where the money is to come from.

In Salford, as in many local authorities known to the author, the threshold for the provision of a social work service is just below the critical category (simply to embrace Section 7 and

Figure 3: Service eligibility levels (Calder, 2000b).

Level	Category	Definition
Level 5	Collapsed	Children looked after or living away from home as a result of actual or likely significant harm or family breakdown.
Level 4	Critical	Families in which there is clear evidence that children are suffering or likely to suffer significant harm. Social work intervention is urgently required in order to prevent family breakdown and avoid the children's removal from home.
Level 3	Compromised	Families who are experiencing substantial difficulties in meeting their children's needs and where some form of intervention is required in order to prevent or delay further deterioration.
Level 2	Vulnerable	Families in which children have acquired or encountered some difficulty, which requires additional help if their life chances are to be optimised or the risk of social exclusion is to be averted.
Level 1	Prevention	Selective services targeted at families or sections of the community where research evidence indicates an above average vulnerability to social exclusion.
Level 0	Promotional	Universal services aimed at promoting the welfare of all children in the community.

Section 37 reports in the compromised category) and this reflects the numbers on the Child Protection Register and/or in the Looked After System where there are increasingly onerous tasks set for the social worker and no ability to delegate their responsibilities elsewhere. It also reflects the drive from government to offer significant resources to new initiatives such as Sure Start, Health and Education Zones, and Youth Offending Teams to address preventative work. The problem with this is that they remain unco-ordinated and this makes any coherent planning difficult, especially in the absence of any local audit. More recently, the guidance on the Children's Fund (DfEE, 2001a and b) is geared towards 5–13-year-olds at risk of social exclusion and expects services to be provided at an early stage, pre-crisis. 'Preventive services provide support for the child, young person or family before they reach crisis, with the aim of reducing the future probability of poor outcomes and maximising their life chances. Birth to adulthood can be likened to a game of snakes and ladders. Ladders represent positive supports and enablers, and snakes the mishaps, miseries and mistreatment. The role of preventive services is to provide more ladders and reduce the number of snakes ... We know enough about risk and protective factors to be able to identify at an early stage children and young people and families who are at risk of adverse outcomes, and to intervene early ... (DfEE, 2001a, p2). This requires a change in culture and a change in the way services are co-ordinated and delivered in the community. They identify four levels of prevention:

1. **Level One: Diversionary**: where the focus is before problems can be seen – thus prevention strategies are likely to focus on whole populations.
2. **Level Two: Early prevention**: implies that problems are already beginning to manifest themselves and action is needed to prevent them becoming serious or worse.
3. **Level Three: Heavy-ended prevention:** would focus on where there are multiple, complex and long-standing difficulties that will require a customisation of services to meet the needs of the individual concerned.
4. **Level Four: Restorative prevention:** focuses on reducing the impact of an intrusive intervention. This is the level of prevention that would apply to such as children and young people in public care, those permanently excluded from school or in youth offender institutions/supervision and/or those receiving assistance within the

---

Figure 4: Levels of need and prevention: an integrated framework.

Levels of need	Levels of prevention
Collapsed	Critical/compromised
Vulnerable prevention	Promotional
Restorative prevention	Heavy-end prevention
Early prevention	Diversionary

---

child protection framework (DfEE, 2001a, p14).

One of the worries about this initiative for local authorities is that many will have located preventive work below their threshold for the provision of a social work service, and they are now faced with a new initiative with a lot of attached monies to bid from. However, it is clearly possible to creatively integrate the framework for determining eligibility and the levels of prevention (see Figure 4 above).

A more complex and contentious consideration is, then, whether the threshold is a universal one for all social work services, or whether there are different thresholds for different social work services. For example, should there be a different threshold for a social work service for disabled children? Or for children in hospital where they may be suffering from a terminal illness? Or for family support services provided by the social services department? The latter is a crucial consideration. If other agencies see the development of a threshold as similar to pulling up the drawbridge and leaving other agency colleagues behind, then they would want access to family centre places for families in the compromised category to prevent the situation becoming more acute. However, since there is a detailed assessment needed on all open cases to social workers, there is a need to prioritise such cases for a family centre place over a more 'preventative' approach. This has the potential of leaving other agencies with more work and fewer resources. They have no greater resources, either financially or in worker numbers, to absorb 'the ineligible cases'. This then aggravates other agency perceptions about social workers and contributes to the mounting obstacles to inter-agency practice. Amadi (2001) has commented that 'from a health visitor's point of view, the threshold where a child is deemed to be at risk has increased. This has

meant that there are fewer children on the at-risk register, but if they are not taken on by social services it increases the onus on the health visitor or school nurse to support these families. Unfortunately, this often comes at the expense of other equally vulnerable families.'

There is a need for social service departments to identify at which point in the process they are to apply their threshold and this is likely to be after 24 hours to filter out quickly the need for initial or core assessments. There is also an issue about which cases and in what circumstances a referral can be accepted (see Data Protection section for details) in the first instance.

What has become confusing for social services is that the government have provided two further pieces of guidance on defining 'children in need' that differ from Section 17 of the Children Act 1989. The Department of Health's statisticians have produced a new and detailed definition for children in need to inform them about which cases of children in need social workers are currently working with as well as where the allocated monies are currently spent (see DoH, 1999b). These are reproduced as Figure 5 overleaf. What is interesting is that the operational branch of the Department of Health have taken issue with them and a revised definition is awaited.

The second issue relating to the definition of 'children in need' derives from the consultation paper (DoH, 2000) on the future of Children's Service Planning (the sister body to the ACPC locally that addresses all matters across agencies relating to children in need). This introduced the concept of a vulnerable child (defined in Figure 3) but states that the child in need is to be seen as a subcategory of this, thus implying a narrower definition of a 'child in need' than set out in the Children Act. The final document (DoH, 2001) offered the following definitions:

- By 'vulnerable' we mean children whose life chances will be jeopardised unless action is

Figure 5: Children in Need Definitions (DoH, 1999).

1   Abuse or Neglect

Definition

Children in need as a result of, or risk of, abuse or neglect.

Guide to inclusions and exclusion from this category

All children whose names are on the child protection registers or who are subject to Section 47 inquiries should be included.

Children who have just been referred with evidence of possible neglect or abuse should be included here.

Children who are living within a situation of domestic violence which triggers Section 47 inquiries during the census week should be included here.

Children whose needs arise out of their involvement (actual and suspected) in prostitution which has triggered Section 47 inquiries should be included here.

Children whose needs arise primarily out of their abusing other children which has triggered Section 47 inquiries should be included here.

Children whose needs arise from being abandoned by their families in circumstances which trigger Section 47 inquiries during the census week should be included here.

Possible sub-categories

As per Working Together

2   Disability

Definition

Children and their families whose main need for services arises out of the children's disabilities or intrinsic condition.

Guide to inclusions and exclusion from this category

This category embraces children who are suffering impairment to their health and development as a result of their own intrinsic condition. The resulting needs require more support than is available through the capacity of their parents or carers and hence there is a need for social services. These are likely to be provided in conjunction with other services, particularly health and education.

The use of the term 'disability' here embraces any illness which causes the disability.

Although the majority of the children included in this category will be permanently disabled, this does not have to be the case for inclusion in this category. A child requiring social services during the course of recovery from a disabling illness, or whose prognosis is uncertain, should be included here.

Most children whose needs fall within this category will have a medically diagnosed condition such as cerebral palsy, autism, or Downs syndrome.

There are some conditions where there is uncertainty or controversy about whether it is appropriate to regard them as intrinsic to the child. This used to be the case with autism, but it is now acknowledged to be overwhelmingly genetic in origin. Currently the cause of 'attention deficit hyperactivity disorder' is in dispute. For the purpose of this collection, if the main reason why social services are involved is because the child is thought to have this disorder, then it should be included here.

If there is no medical diagnosis, or if the diagnosis is clearly framed in terms of family functioning, the 'Family Dysfunction' will be a more appropriate category.

Children with emotional and behavioural difficulties will present particular difficulties of classification. If there is a medically diagnosed condition attributed then the child should be included here. Otherwise, 'Family Dysfunction' should be used.

Possible sub-categories

Children with physical disabilities;
Children with sensory disabilities;
Children with learning disabilities (special educational needs);
Children with emotional and behavioural difficulties.

Figure 5: Continued.

3   Parental illness/Disability

Definition

Children whose main needs for services arises because the capacity of their parents or carers to care for them is impaired by disability, illness, mental illness or addictions.

Guide to inclusions and exclusion from this category

The key to inclusion to this category is that the parent has a diagnosable medical condition which is primary in limiting their parenting capacity and there is insufficient or no comprehensive help available other than through social services.

The medical conditions include seriously disabling mental illness, but in cases of episodes of reactive depression or anxiety accompanying acute family stress then the category 'Families in Acute Stress' should be used.

Children who are in need because their parent or parents have learning disabilities that reduce their parenting capacity should be included here.

This category should be used in the cases where the need for services arises out of parental alcoholism and drug taking which have been diagnosed as such by a doctor or specialist service.

It also includes the needs of 'young carers' who take on caring responsibilities for disabled or chronically ill parents.

In cases where these children are in need because the parents have 'personality disorders', but where there is doubt as to whether a clear medical condition exists, Family Dysfunction is the preferred category.

Possible sub-categories

Children with alcoholic parents;
Children with drug taking parents;
Children with acutely ill parents (short term);
Children being cared for by parents with learning disabilities;
Children being cared for by chronically disabled parent(s) but who are not taking responsibility for them;
Children being cared for by chronically mentally ill parent(s) but who are not taking responsibility for them;
Children assuming caring responsibilities for chronically ill or disabled parents.

4   Family in Acute Stress

Definition

Children whose needs arise from living in a family going through a crisis such that parenting capacity is diminished and some of the children's needs are not being adequately met.

Guide to inclusions and exclusion from this category

This category embraces those families that have got into difficulties but where the basic positive relationship between the parents and their children is not in question.

This would include families where the parenting capacity is normally good enough but who face family circumstances and environmental factors or events which undermine this capacity. This would include events such as:

- upheaval in family relationships;
- loss of employment;
- reduced income;
- adverse housing;
- loss of amenities important to the care of children;
- the death of a parent or other family member.

It would include the needs of children living in socially isolated and poorly resourced communities.

This would include a single parent who generally manages but occasionally needs additional help.

This would include a family that generally functions adequately but which has been rendered homeless.

This would include families which generally function satisfactorily facing a temporary 'explosion' by an adolescent member.

Figure 5: Continued.

Possible sub-categories
  Homeless family;
  Single parent;
  Death of parent/carer.

5 Family Dysfunction

Definition
  Children whose needs arise mainly out of their living in families where the parenting capacity is chronically inadequate.

Guide to inclusions and exclusion from this category
  This category should **NOT** be chosen if the primary reason for inadequate parenting capacity is parental illness or disability.

  This category includes those families where the low parenting capacity is at risk of, or actually, impairing the children's health and development.

  From the perspective of the child's experience, this category includes children who:
  • lack basic care;
  • do not enjoy consistent emotional warmth;
  • are under-stimulated;
  • are not given adequate guidance and boundaries;
  • who do not enjoy stable relationships with carers.

  From the perspective of the capacity of parents this category covers the inability of parents to provide the child with:
  • basic care
  • consistent emotional warmth
  • adequate stimulation
  • adequate guidance and boundaries
  • a stable relationship

  For inclusion in this category, parenting capacity must be a long term concern and not just a reaction to adverse circumstances. Within this category there will be degrees of severity in the extent to which the parenting capacity is inadequate.

  It will also include children for whom there is concern for their safety, as a consequence of family dysfunction, but there is not (yet) hard evidence of neglect sufficient to invoke child protection measures.

  This category could include the cases of children who are abandoned because the parent does not have the necessary parenting capacity to care for them.

Possible sub-categories:
  Currently none.

6 Socially Unacceptable Behaviour

Definition
  Children and families whose need for services arises primarily out of their children's behaviour impacting detrimentally on the community.

Guide to inclusions and exclusion from this category
  This would include children who demand services because they:
  • actually offend;
  • are considered to be at risk of offending;
  • are below the age of criminal responsibility but would otherwise be breaking the law;
  • are behaving in such a disorderly way that they cause alarm or disturb the peace.

  This would also include another group of children who create concerns within the community because they put themselves at unacceptable risk, for example:
  • children who truant
  • children who are sexually active

Figure 5: Continued.

This category would include the needs of children and young people being served by staff in a YOT paid from the SSD budget.

This category will also include children who are receiving services as part of the Crime Reduction Strategy in addition to or without Youth Offenders Teams involvement. However a referral made by a YOT for reasons that are not connected with the child's offending may indicate that another needs category should apply.

A defining factor for this category is that the children's behaviour 'pushes at the boundaries' of community acceptance. It has gone beyond the family.

Children for whom the primary concern is that they are thought to be, or are actually, involved in prostitution should trigger child protection measures and be categorised under Abuse or Neglect.

Possible sub-categories
disorderly behaviour
offending
truancy
unsafe sexual behaviour

7 Low Income

Definition
Children, living in families or independently, whose needs arise mainly from being dependant on an income below the standard state entitlements.

Guide to inclusions and exclusion from this category
This category is reserved for families or children whose special circumstances mean that their income is below the standard state entitlements.

It does not include people who are simply poor or who cannot manage on their entitlements.

It does include families who are asylum seekers and who do not have the means to provide adequately for their children.

It may include young people entering independence who, because of the rules relating to employment and training are eligible for full benefits, if there is no other reason for contact with social services.

Possible sub-categories
Asylum seeking families;
Non-habitually resident status;
'Independent' young people.

8 Absent Parenting

Definition
Children whose need for services arise mainly from having no parents available to provide for them.

Guide to inclusions and exclusion from this category
This category is reserved for the needs of children who simply do not have a source of parenting. It is completely neutral about quality of parenting because this bears no relationship to the need. If the need for services can be related mainly to adverse family circumstances or parenting capacity then another category should be chosen.

This category must not be used loosely for children looked after for whatever reason.

This category would include children whose needs arise because their parents have died, are lost, who sent them away from their families for 'good' motives or who have become separated from them as a consequence of civil or natural disaster or political events.

This includes unaccompanied asylum seeking children.

This could also include children in need simply because a parent has been imprisoned but the reason for the imprisonment bears no relation to the child being in need.

Figure 5: Continued.

Possible sub-categories
  Parents died;
  unaccompanied child asylum seekers
  separated from parents by natural or civic disaster or political events

9   Cases other than Children in Need

Definition
  Casework which is required for legal and administrative reasons only and there is no child in the case who is in need.

Guide to inclusions and exclusion from this category
This category captures work done by staff using children's budget resources but which is not a direct response to children in need.

This category is reserved for the following duties:
  • Inquiries for step-parent adoptions where the children are not in need.
  • Home study reports for inter-country adoptions or similar requests.
  • Requests for court reports in domestic or divorce proceedings in circumstances in which the children are not in need.
  • Subject access to files by adults who were looked after or received services as children.
  • Investigations of 'historical' allegations or complaints by adults who were looked after or received services as children.

Where residence order or post adoption order payments are made, this category should **NOT** be used and the children in question should be classified in one of codes 1–8.

Possible sub-categories
  step-parents adoptions
  inter-country adoptions
  court reports
  subject access to files
  historical allegations/complaints

taken to meet their needs better, and reduce the risk of social exclusion. Most children will not be 'vulnerable' throughout their whole childhoods, but will go through periods of vulnerability. This group includes, for example, children who have experienced poor socialisation through inadequacies in family life and in some cases destructive social support systems or social networks, such as peer relationships which lead them into trouble. Others may be identified relatively early in their pre-school or school careers, may be underachieving at school, or may be children with Special Educational Needs. The action needed may involve health visitors, school nurses, therapists, teachers and early years practitioners, education welfare service or educational psychologists, personal advisors/mentors, and family members, and sometimes, but not always, social workers.

• Children in need are defined in part III of the Children Act 1989. They may receive services provided through social services departments by virtue of this legislation. **They are, in the main, a subset of vulnerable children**.

This exploration of a threshold for the provision of a social work service raises many paradoxes. In reality, the framework will only probably achieve what it so determinedly set out to avoid i.e. that because the thresholds are so high and the completion of core assessments so time consuming and onerous, only high risk child protection cases are likely to be deemed appropriate to this level of work thereby allowing no services to be assessed, let alone receive services below the 'collapsed' and 'critical' criteria (Precey, 2001, personal communication).

There are direct implications for social workers and their managers in the discharge of their duties as they apply means testing to clients requesting a service they cannot afford to deliver. This affects staff morale which is low because of the growing disjunction between policy ends, means and resources and the ceaseless pressure of administrative changes. There is evidence to show that the recent changes have increased rather than reduced bureaucracy, and this often has the effect of distancing the agencies from their clients to the detriment of both (explored later in this chapter).

David Blunkett (2002) has recently acknowledged that the balance between crisis and preventive services is one of the most difficult questions facing work with children and their families. Most authorities found that it was difficult to transfer funds from child protection to family support, continuing to fund both, otherwise we run unacceptable risks with people's lives while waiting for preventive measures to take effect. In the short-term, however, all the new preventive initiatives like Surestart and Connexions are identifying levels of need which the acute services cannot cope with. So while universal initiatives fan out among the general population, highlighting individuals and families in crisis, and sowing the seeds of long-term improvements, the threshold for triggering intensive protection and support is continually being raised. Services for families in crisis are at the point of meltdown.

The barriers to information exchange between professionals

The issue of sharing information between professionals and agencies has been problematic for some time, and this has been brought to a head recently with the introduction of the Data Protection Act (1998), the Human Rights Act (1998) and the Caldicott Guardians.

Data Protection Act (1998)
The Data Protection Act 1998 (DPA) came into force on 1st March 2000 and implements the European Directive 95/46/EC, on the protection of individuals with regard to the processing of personal data and on the free movement of such data. It repeals the Data Protection Act 1984, Access to Personal Files Act 1987 and most of the Access to Health Records Act 1990. The DPA establishes a number of data protection principles that limit the reasons for which personal data may be obtained and specify how they may be used. A couple of points can be made here:

1. Staff must consider carefully the need to process personal data fairly and lawfully and should not do so until various conditions are met, such as compliance with a legal obligation or for the administration of justice for the exercise of functions conferred by any statute, for the exercise of functions of a Government Department or for the exercise of any other function of a public nature exercised in the public interest Schedule 2.
2. Where this refers to sensitive personal data, this must not be processed unless one of a number of conditions in Schedule 2 are met and also one of the conditions in Schedule 3, which includes that processing is necessary in order to protect the vital interests of the data subject or another person in a case where consent cannot be given by or on behalf of the data subject or the data controller cannot reasonably be expected to obtain that consent; or the processing is necessary to protect the vital interests of another person, in a case where the data subject had unreasonably withheld consent.
3. Where the disclosure of personal data is necessary in order to comply with a legal obligation imposed on the authority, then the consent of the subject data is not necessary. However, authorities should inform the subject that such an obligation exists and should, wherever possible, seek consent to disclose.
4. The interpretation of 'legal obligations' is unspecified but in order to broaden the capacity to share information between agencies below the child protection threshold, this is likely to be viewed broadly and embrace Section 17, 20 and 47.

The DPAs full requirements will be implemented subject to transitional periods (period one ends 23.10.01; and period two runs from 24.10.01 until 23.10.07).

Given that social services have to take a decision within 24 hours as to whether to carry out an initial assessment, and a maximum of seven days (less if there are child protection concerns) to complete the initial assessment, there is a need to gather a breadth of information quickly (from a range of sources) and in detail to help workers make a judgement as to what, if anything, needs to happen next. Good quality information is vital to assessment and decision-making. Research and experience have repeatedly shown that keeping children safe from harm requires professionals and others to share information. Often it is only when information from a number of sources has been shared and then put together that it becomes clear that a child is at risk of or is suffering significant harm (DoH, 1999). However, workers also need to be mindful of the legal duty of confidence, which applies equally to children and adults, and the rights to privacy enshrined in the European Convention on Human Rights, in particular Article 8 (see below for further details). The assessment framework states that personal information about children and families is subject to a legal duty of confidence and should not normally be disclosed without the consent of the subject. This means that permission should be sought before discussing a referral about a child or family with other agencies, unless to do so would put the child at risk. Workers trying to decide when information can be shared without consent have a fine line to walk. The law permits the disclosure of confidential information when this is necessary to safeguard a child from significant harm. The public interest in child protection may override the public interest in maintaining confidentiality. Disclosure should be justified in each case, according to the particular facts of the case (DoH, 1999). It seems abundantly clear, however, that if a child appears to be 'in need' under Section 17 of the Children Act 1989 but not suffering or likely to suffer significant harm (Section 47) there is unlikely to be a basis for acting without consent, as the public interest criteria would not be met. This creates real issues in terms of creeping cruelty cases such as neglect and emotional abuse where there is often no incident warranting a Section 47 enquiry and where the parents are unmotivated to give consent to further referrals and potential intervention. It also renders blanket automatic checks at referral unacceptable. The problem for workers is that they do not know what they do not know and for vulnerable children there may have to be a defined incident that changes the professional position. This is clearly an unfortunate position to put workers and children in.

What does seem clear is that workers in all agencies will have to seek consent to making referrals, unless this endangers children. They will have to be clear about why they are contacting other agencies or exchanging information and they must understand the legalities of the situation they are in. This will require practitioners in health, education and other agencies who come into contact with children to rethink the way they manage their concerns (Hendry and Horwath, 2000).

Human Rights Act (1998)

The Human Rights Act 1998 came into force in the United Kingdom on 2nd October 2000 and brings the rights set out in the European Convention of Human Rights into domestic law. As such, our courts must now interpret our laws as far as possible in a way which is compatible with convention rights. It creates a new form of unlawful conduct for public authorities – it will be unlawful for a public authority (local authorities, health authorities and trusts, the police) to act in a way that is incompatible with one or more of the convention rights.

The most significant is Article 8 which sets out a right to respect for private and public life, and one's home and correspondence and prohibits any arbitrary interference with this right by the State. The European Court of Human Rights (the Court) has recognised that the relationship between parent and child is a fundamental aspect of family life, which is not terminated by placing a child in care. A decision by a local authority to remove a child from his/her family and place him/her in care must thus be based on reasons that are relevant and sufficient in order to be Convention compliant. Accordingly, a care order must be used only as a measure of last resort and the measure must be no more than is necessary to protect the interests of the child concerned. Article 8 requires that as long as a care order is intended to be temporary it must always be guided by the ultimate aim of family reunion. This places a direct obligation on local authorities to fulfil a child's need for care and protection in a manner which allows him/her to maintain direct and frequent contact with family members (Kilkelly, 2001). Hale LJ in her judgement has given us a textbook and definitive analysis of the application and interpretation of Article 8 and said:

- Interference can only be justified in accordance with the law.
- It must be in the pursuit of legitimate aims provided for in the articles (which include protecting the child).
- The interference must be 'necessary in a democratic society', that is relevant and

sufficient and corresponding to a pressing social need.

There are some clear circumstances when a public authority can interfere: to protect rights and freedoms of others, to protect health or morals, to prevent disorder or crime, or in the interests of national security, public safety or economic well-being of the country.

In simple terms, both pieces of legislation require the consent of someone with parental responsibility to share information with and between agencies other than in cases of child protection. This clearly raises the potential for agencies to revert to the worrying practice of framing cases as child protection to allow the referral to be made, although this will not lead with any degree of certainty to it crossing the threshold for a continuing social work service. This inevitably raises problems for cases that fall in the compromised category, especially cases such as neglect and emotional abuse, as there is little prospect of the parents engaging in the process of assessment on a voluntary basis. There is also rarely an incident that would prompt a Section 47 child protection investigation and with it an ability to dispense with parental consent. This does raise an important issue about detailed local clarification on the circumstances when a Section 47 child protection investigation is to be conducted. For example, all anonymous referrals, when there are more than three enquiries to the child protection register in a twelve month period, in all circumstances when the police attend a domestic violence incident where there are children in the household, etcetera.

There is a worrying gap within the assessment documentation forms on information sharing issues. The initial referral form simply asks whether the family are 'aware' of the referral. This does not address three issues: the difference between informing and seeking consent; the need to get written consent and the time implications of this, not to mention considerations about literacy and translation; and the management of retraction of consent by the family as the process unfolds. An emerging issue with the breaking down of agency barriers (where health, social services and police work in the same team together, such as in the Youth Offending Teams) is one of what actually constitutes 'an outside agency'.

There is a potential that within the assessment process for professionals to infringe a person's right to a fair hearing (Article 6, Human Rights

Act, 1998). For example, any foster parents involved in more than short-term care of a child in need must be genuinely included in discussion on the child's future. They may be seen as having 'family life' rights under Article 8, and they also have civil rights (their registration) which can be 'determined' by social service decisions (Shaw, 2001). Decisions which involve the removal of children from their foster carers will need to be taken after all the information has been shared and the foster parents have been given the opportunity to be heard if they are objecting to the move (unless there is an emergency).

There is also a huge issue not just of consent for the families' information to be shared but also for material held by agencies to be available for other agencies. Health is especially worried about this, such as information about things such as HIV status, hereditary conditions, etc.

The idea of conflicts to information sharing between members of the family is also an issue, especially Gillick competent children and parents e.g. terminations, sexual orientation, etc., that young people or parents may not want other family members to know about but which may be relevant to the assessment. The issue of a separate location for such information to be stored outside the core assessment record frequently arises.

There is a clear expectation through the 'Working Together' guidance (DoH et al., 1999) that local agencies develop clear protocols for the inter-agency exchange of information and this is essential if operational staff are supported if they deviate from the rigid restrictions set down in the Data Protection legislation. There has to be some sensible way of continuing the process of information exchange as we have come to know it as it would lead to many tragedies if we could not record in the first instance any referral information below child protection that would allow a broad picture to be built up. In some respects, it is unfortunate that the legislation acts as a further barrier to any operational shift towards working effectively with children deemed to be 'in need'. Good practice supports the construction of detailed chronologies as the basis of formulating informed and potentially useful plans for intervention. For a detailed discussion on the implications of the Data Protection Act for social services, the reader is referred to DoH (2001b).

There are some further conflicts for those working with children and their families. We have a positive duty to seek to protect individuals from inhuman or degrading treatment (Article 3, Human Rights Act, 1998) and this reinforces the duties under the Children Act (1989) to step in to protect children from harm. At the same time we have a positive duty to respect family life and to respect the private life of individual adults and children under Article 8 Human Rights Act (1998). What is clear, however, is that it will not be possible to avoid interference with Article 8 rights in many cases, because of Children Act duties. The European Court has been realistic about the balancing of these rights when the professional making a decision can show they have looked at the matter on an individual basis, that they have acted lawfully and only as necessary, and they have acted proportionately: the steps taken are not a sledgehammer to crack a nut (Shaw, 2001). In this sense, local information-sharing protocols between the key agencies can set out clearly the occasions (such as neglect cases) where in order to properly assess and decide how to safeguard and promote a child's welfare, professionals will share information and this may need to be without an individual's consent. The Human Rights Act applies equally to the duties and discretions of workers within housing, education and health. Shaw argues that the watchword is proportionality – we need to judge what is a proportionate step when faced with choosing how to safeguard and promote the child's welfare, based on their professional skill and understanding. Where workers are able to work in partnership with parents that is good. Where they cannot, workers are not dis-empowered at all by the Human Rights Act: they are actively empowered to do what they must do to safeguard and promote the welfare of the child.

Howard (2001) reported on three landmark cases in which human rights considerations have effectively rewritten domestic law. These included cases where the local authority failed to take children into care and damages for wrongly taking children into care. Taken together, these cases demonstrate the resource implications, as courts demand more of local authorities. This will lead to more cases being transferred upwards – particularly those cases involving human rights arguments – and this will lead to cases taking much longer to be heard and much longer to be listed. The concept of drift re-emerges.

The Caldicott Guardians
The requirement for NHS organisations to appoint Caldicott Guardians of patient information is a product of the Government's commitment to implementing the recommendations of the Caldicott Committee's Report on the Review of Patient-Identifiable Information, published in 1997. Each Health Authority, Special Health Authority, NHS Trust and Primary Care Group should have appointed a Caldicott Guardian by no later than 31st March 1999. Ideally, they should be at Board level, be a senior health professional and have responsibility for promoting clinical governance within the organisation.

The Caldicott Committee had found that compliance with the full range of confidentiality and security requirements was patchy across the NHS. They developed a set of general principles governing patient information:

- Justify the purpose: every proposed use or transfer of patient-identifiable information within or from an organisation should be clearly defined and scrutinised, with continuing uses regularly reviewed by an appropriate guardian.
- Don't use patient-identifiable information unless it is absolutely necessary and there is no alternative.
- Use the minimum necessary patient-identifiable information: where use of patient-identifiable information is considered to be essential, each individual item of information should be justified with the aim of reducing identifiability.
- Access to patient-identifiable information should be on a strict need-to-know basis: only those individuals who need access to patient-identifiable information should have access to it and they should only have access to the information items that they need to see.
- Everyone should be aware of their responsibilities: action should be taken to ensure that those handling patient-identifiable information – both clinical and non-clinical staff-are aware of their responsibilities and obligations to respect patient confidentiality.
- Understand and comply with the law: every use of patient-identifiable information should be lawful. Someone in each organisation should be responsible for ensuring that the organisation complies with legal requirements (NHS Executive, 1999).

NHS organisations are intended to support the Guardian by:

- Developing local protocols governing the disclosure of patient information to other organisations (for guidance see NHS Executive, 2001).
- Restrict access to patient information within each organisation by enforcing strict need-to-know principles.
- Regularly review and justify the uses of patient information.
- Improve organisational performance across a range of related areas: database design, staff induction, training, compliance with guidance etc.

The issues raised by the Caldicott Guardian role are critical for health staff in frontline operational positions. Whilst social services will not necessarily accept referrals that are not child protection without parental consent, there is a concern that health staff will not refer cases at the Section 17 level. This raises major issues for neglect and emotional abuse cases.

The lack of fit between the assessment framework and 'Working Together'

Given that these documents were issued near simultaneously and are designed to dovetail with each other, it is with some surprise that they do not logically do so. For example, whilst there is an expectation that we move toward a 'children in need' approach, it is confusing and contradictory that the criteria for adding a child's name to the child protection register appears to have been relaxed. Under the previous guidance (DoH, 1991) there was a two-stage process when determining the appropriateness of registration. First, the circumstances of the case would have to fit into detailed definitions of physical abuse, sexual abuse, neglect or emotional abuse. The second stage was to show that there was a need for an inter-agency child protection plan to prevent or reduce the likelihood of any future harm materialising. In the new guidance (see DoH et al., 1999) there is only a need to show that a child has suffered or is likely to suffer significant harm (not defined) (see Calder, 2001b for a detailed discussion on this point) and then that there is a need for an inter-agency plan (not defined) (see Calder and Horwath, 1999 for guidance on this point). This could lead to a return to the pre-'Messages from Research'

practice of pushing cases down the child protection route to guarantee it crosses the threshold for social services intervention. In the service eligibility levels set out in Figure 3 earlier, all registered cases would fall into the critical category and procedurally would require a social-work led core assessment be completed. One can foresee some agencies requesting a child protection conference to get a case accepted by social services, and then seeking registration to guarantee a continued plan of intervention. This would clearly be an unfortunate experience for the recipient families.

There are some further issues raised between these two documents. Firstly, many local authorities are retaining their child protection recording forms but adapting them to the domains and dimensions because the ones accompanying the framework do not address risk. The danger is that social workers wait for the conference (to be held within 15 working days of referral) to commission the core assessment, thus reducing the assessment timeframe to 20 days (35 minus 15 days at conference). In other authorities, they removed their child protection forms to try and work with the assessment framework but have re-introduced them quickly when they found they did not work for them. Secondly, there is a danger of the proliferation of inter-professional meetings i.e. strategy meeting, a core assessment planning meeting at the start of a needs-led assessment, an initial child protection conference, a core group, a post-core assessment planning meeting, etc. The outcome of this is potential confusion and blurring of boundaries as well as an incredible amount of time commitment to convening or attending meetings.

There are further contradictions between the two documents. Firstly, whilst the framework advocates the use of professional judgement, 'Safeguarding Children' provides a significantly extended chapter on what needs to happen when we get it wrong (e.g. Part 8s). Secondly, there is a move away from child protection to children in need, but there is a significant extension of the catchment groups for the ACPC such as embracing domestic violence, strangers, etc. Thirdly, we have responsibility for young people who sexually abuse maintained by the ACPC yet at the same time they advocate exiting this group from the child protection system.

The lack of inter-governmental department liaison resulting in parallel ASSET guidance being issued

There are considerable content problems with the assessment framework (explored later in this chapter) that should have not been aggravated by the issuing of parallel core assessment guidance to the Youth Offending Teams. What is more worrying is the lack of cross-department discussion about content and fit, with the resulting problems for local practitioners in the application of both to some presenting cases. For example, where a young person has committed an offence, he is now more likely to have some involvement from YOT because of the prescriptive, interventionist approach. They are required to complete the detailed core assessment form pre-intervention and within 3 days. The sections and content headings are identified overleaf in Figure 6.

If the young person's behaviour is attributable to harm caused within the home or there has been a failure of the parents to protect or there are siblings in the home that need protecting, then the social services are also likely to be involved and will complete a core assessment of their own (set out earlier in this chapter). There is a potential duplication of task but using completely different sets of guidance, a significant difference in timescales, and also a conflict of terminology (risk versus need) explored later in this chapter. Calder (2001c) has articulated these difficulties in great detail.

One of the worrying findings from delivering the assessment framework training is that members of the Youth Offending Teams are not coming, perhaps because they have ASSET they distance themselves from the assessment framework, seeing it as nothing to do with them. The potential for confusion, duplication and a lack of 'joined upness' is colossal.

The critique continued

(b) The content

In this section I am drawing on materials developed by myself (Calder, 2000c and d; Calder, 2001d) in a quest to look at what needs to be addressed at a local level before there is any prospect of it becoming a useful framework for frontline practitioners. The following areas are the most obvious areas of concern:

- Ecological assessment: A three-sided square?
- Timescales: evidence-based madness?
- Paternalism not partnership: a role reversal?
- The deletion of the concept of risk and investigation: throwing the baby out with the bathwater?
- The limitations of an evidence-based practice approach in the child protection arena.
- NAF and the legal process
- Inclusive practice?
- The recording forms: to guide recording, assessment or both?
- Fragmented framework: where do you go for what?
- Determining outcomes: but where is the guidance?

Ecological assessment: well nearly . . .

Historically, each profession has developed their own theory of child abuse and neglect and adhered rigidly to it regardless of the presenting circumstances of a case. This is blinkered thinking and has led to a failure to offer a holistic framework within which respective theories could be located. The emergence of an ecological framework has offered the potential for conceptual unity across professions and professionals, although it has not explicitly been adopted or recommended to date. A shared knowledge base, originating from research is essential (Calder, 1992).

Ecology is a science, in which it explores how organisms interact and survive the environment in which they find themselves. It accepts that there are different levels in society where child maltreatment can occur – at an individual, family, community and society level. This approach is characterised by its prominent emphasis on the interaction between systems rather than on the properties and processes of any one system.

It allows for the dynamics of child abuse and neglect to be located in a framework which acknowledges that abuse frequently occurs in a socially unhealthy context, with factors such as isolation, poverty, and socially polluted environments acting as crucibles in which latent causal factors are identified (Calder, 1991). In my view, this has the potential as a comprehensive framework for organising knowledge of human behaviour as well as highlighting convergence among disciplines and integrating the diversity of theory, as seen in Figure 7. At one level, therefore the adoption of the ecological framework within the assessment framework is to be welcomed.

Figure 6: ASSET headings and content.

- **Living Arrangements:**
  - NFA
  - unsuitable
  - living with known offenders
  - disorganised chaotic
  - other
- **Family and Personal Relationships:**
  - Family/Carer Criminal Activity and Substance Abuse
  - Lack of communication or care/interest in YP
  - Inconsistent supervision and Boundary Setting
  - Abuse and violence
  - Bereavement or Loss
  - Difficulties with care of own children
- **Statutory Education:**
  - Education Provision
  - Special Educational Needs
  - Permanent Exclusion
  - Fixed Term Exclusion
  - Regular Truanting
  - Regularly Absent for other reasons
  - Bullied at school
- **Employment, Training and Further Education:**
  - Lack of Qualifications, skills or Training
- **Neighbourhood:**
  - Category
  - Crime 'Hotspot'
  - Drug Dealing/Usage
  - Lack of age-appropriate facilities
- **Lifestyle:**
  - Lack of age-appropriate friendships
  - Associating with predominantly pro-criminal peers
  - Absence of non-criminal friends
  - Non-constructive use of time
  - Participation in Reckless Activity
  - Inadequate legitimate personal income
- **Substance Use:**
  - Substance/Frequency
  - Practice which puts at particular risk
  - Substance misuse as positive/essential to life
  - Noticeable effect on education, relationships, daily functioning
  - Offending to obtain money for substances
  - Other link to offending
- **Physical Health:**
  - Health Condition which significantly affects everyday life functioning

- Physical Immaturity/delayed development
- Not registered with GP/lack of access to other services
- Health put at risk through own behaviour
- **Emotional and Mental Health:**
  - Emotions/thoughts which significantly affect daily functioning
  - Mental Illness
  - Other Emotional or Psychological Difficulties
  - Self Harm and Suicide
- **Perception of Self and Others:**
  - Difficulties with self-identity
  - Inappropriate self-esteem
  - General mistrust of others
  - Lack of understanding of others
  - Displays discriminatory attitudes
  - Sees self as an offender
- **Thinking and Behaviour:**
  - Lack of understanding of consequences
  - Impulsiveness
  - Need for excitement
  - Giving in easily to pressure from others
  - Poor control of temper
  - Inappropriate self-presentation
  - Destruction of Property
  - Aggression towards others
  - Sexually inappropriate behaviour
  - Attempts to manipulate/control others
- **Attitudes to offending:**
  - Denial of seriousness of behaviour
  - Reluctance to accept responsibility
  - Victims (empathy)
  - Lack of understanding about impact on family/carers
  - Belief that certain types of offence are acceptable
  - Belief that certain people/groups are acceptable 'targets'
  - Thinks further offending is inevitable
- **Motivation to Change:**
  - Some understanding of problematic aspects of behaviour
  - Some evidence of wanting to deal with problems
  - Understanding of consequences for self
  - Identifies reasons/initiatives to avoid offending
  - Evidence of wanting to stop offending

However, the ecological claims of the assessment model are compromised by its conflation of community and societal considerations into one 'domain' (family and environmental factors). By failing to set the child, their carers and their family/community environment into a wider socio-political context (i.e. a fourth domain), the model fails to prompt critical reflection on the influence of wider social trends e.g. gender roles; perceptions of child maltreatment; poverty; changes in family structure and work patterns; racism and other

Figure 7: An ecological framework (Calder and Waters, 1991).

Ecological levels	Levels of analysis/models
Ontogenesis/individual	Psychopathology
Family micro-system	Social-interactional
Community exo-system	Socio-situational
Cultural macro-system	Socio-cultural

forms of oppression; government policies regarding health, education, housing, social security. The omission of the cultural (societal) dimension detracts attention away from the sources of disadvantage that impact so detrimentally on children.

The cultural social macro-system comprises the set of cultural and social values that pervade and support individual and family life styles and community services in today's society. This level is often the invisible layer in theoretical models of child abuse, yet its influence is increasingly recognised as important in understanding the hidden forces that govern personal and institutional behaviours. Social and cultural factors can foster or mitigate stress in family life and such factors have achieved new importance in emerging models of child abuse. It is important to note that the wider society does not impact uniformly on individuals, families, and members of ethnic cultural groups.

The following are just selective examples of issues relevant at this level:

• Coleman (1997) explored the societal roots of sexual offending. It is an axiom that all sexuality occurs within a societal context, filled with assumptions, values, ideals, attitudes and beliefs. It is thus crucial to understand how culture spawns and maintains perpetrating behaviour within the juvenile population. It has certainly been abetted by the refusal to acknowledge childhood sexuality and the repression of sexuality during adolescence. The denial of the extent to which juvenile sexual offending is a problem has cultivated it. Society pays a price for silence about this group. Problems 'swept under the carpet' in one community only emerge in other locations with an additional set of victims. If we accept that sexuality is intuitive, natural and normal, then the logic evolves that there is a need to

educate. Similarly, if children are asexual, there is a need to re-educate. Any failure to openly discuss sexuality works against the juvenile offender who is often sexually naïve. Confusion about sexuality in general is a common trait of juveniles who sexually abuse and their families. This is aggravated by the current sex education curriculum in our schools. At the other extreme is the media who bombard children with distorted sex role images and inaccurate information about human sexuality. Children are exposed to vast amounts of sexual information through films, video games, television, movies and magazines. Embedded in the media messages is the impression that violence and sexual exploitation are normal parts of interpersonal relationships and are therefore acceptable. Sex education delayed until adolescence is threatened because of the weakened influence of the family. Adolescent males are commended for sexual encounters with older women. We clearly need to broaden our focus around juvenile sexual offending to include the social context in which these behaviours flourish. Exclusive focus on the other levels (individual, family, community) creates the situation where cultural forces are ignored. Yet child sexual abuse and adolescent perpetration are inter-twined with other problems in society and influenced by the culture of a society.

• If we were to look beyond sexual abuse, we would find a lack of clarity and consistency about the boundaries of acceptable physical chastisement of children. For example, physical chastisement is prohibited in state schools, but childminders may smack babies and very young children; the impact of poverty on children's developmental outcomes; or the appropriate age of leaving children unattended. We can refer to the concern raised by Kennedy and Wonnacott in Chapter 10 about the social factors that dis-able disabled children and the fact that child abuse and child protection are socially constructed phenomena. We cannot forget that social work practice has, and continues to be, affected by the threats of tabloid vilification.

I have argued elsewhere (Calder, 2000) that we need to shift the chosen triangle to a square to accurately reflect the ecological framework (see Figure 8 below), although I now feel it is more appropriate to have the societal and international issues circling the triangle to show how they represent an overarching influenc e on the three domains (see Figure 9 overleaf). There are some emerging views that an alternative construction of the square would be to have risk assessment as the fourth domain.

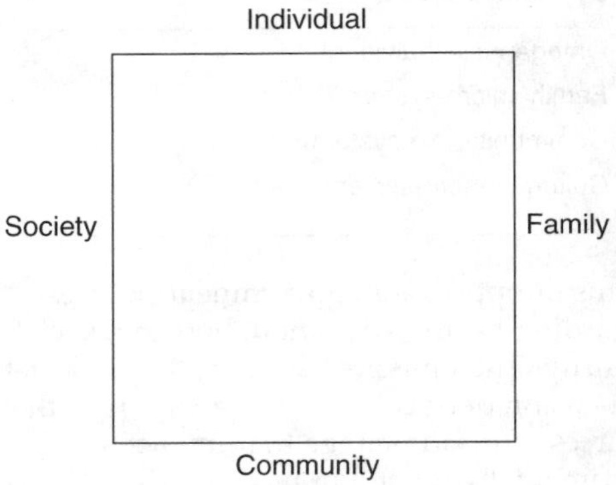

It is also helpful to acknowledge the place of the assessment framework within the broader political agenda. On the one hand we are aware that the government is committed to raising child welfare standards and they have used performance indicators as a mechanism to measure and demonstrate change in a very tangible way as well as playing the game with the Treasury to access monies through setting measurable targets. This does not consider whether the systems are able to deliver on these targets generally and those who fail may continue to fail, as they cannot break out of this cycle. At this level, I would conceive the framework as a process of management information through a professional process. A more positive spin would be to note the attempt to re-professionalise social work, re-igniting debates about training needs, what is a good assessment and good practice? This may be seen as an attempt to defend social work in the world of 'new labour' and try and find a new and credible niche/role for social work.

Caulkin (2001) usefully explored the issue of management being tied into set goals as being meaningless, counterproductive as well as leading to disaster. It systematically lowers quality, raises costs and wrecks systems, making them less stable and therefore harder to improve. Caulkin refers to the work of Deming 50 years ago who noted that if you give people targets and make their careers dependent on delivering them, they will likely meet the targets – even if they destroy the enterprise to do it. An organisation is a system and a system has a capability. If you have a

Figure 8: Squaring the assessment triangle (Calder, 2000).

stable system, there is no use to specify a goal. You will get whatever the system will deliver. A goal beyond the capability of the system will not be reached. If you do not have a stable system, there is no point setting a goal. There is no way to know what the system will produce: it has no capability. He argued we should eliminate quotas and numerical targets and substitute them with aid and useful leadership. Then, he argued, the patient can start to get better.

They do however offer 'quick fixes' for politicians and give the impression they are 'doing something' to address the issues within a given area.

What is also missing in the framework from government is any interaction between the different dimensions and the centrality of the worker if they are to engage with the client, motivate and then help them to change, managing any resistance offered. Shemmings (2000) makes reference to engagement but it is not in the body of the document and should be. The implications of engagement considerations is time consuming but not recognised within the prescriptions of the assessment framework. All these points are central to the ecological approach, demonstrated through the following guiding principles:

• The worker is holistic in his orientation, recognising that the ecosystem context is the foundation for every meaningful intervention into a troubled client system.
• The worker must place primary emphasis on relationships, recognising that every client is both part of a social environment for other

Figure 9: An ecological framework for assessment.

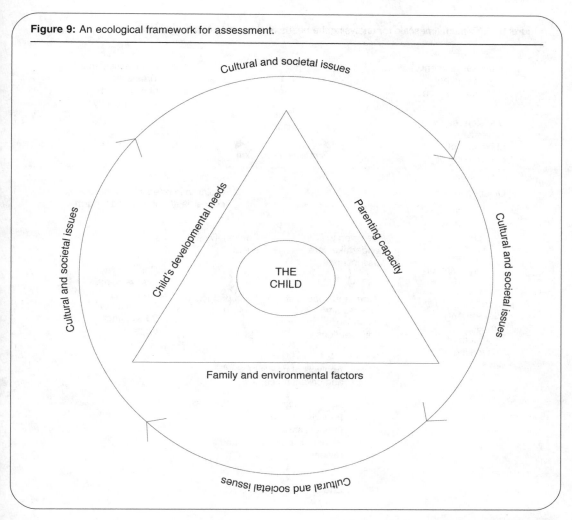

individuals and a participant with others in a variety of social contexts.

- The client unit is also a system-in-transformation through an evolutionary process of intervention.
- The worker must pay attention to his own place in the total ecology of the client's presenting situation, choosing an appropriate ecological niche from which to make some useful contribution (Maddock and Larson, 1995). For further discussions on the ecological approach, the reader is referred to Belsky (1980), Bronfenbrenner (1977) and Garbarino (1977).

These points are best taken up under the timescales set down by government for completing the assessments. This I term, 'evidence-based madness'.

Timescales: evidence-based madness?

The Orange Book (DoH, 1988) said that '(the timescale) will vary according to the complexity of the situation . . .' (p22). It did not specify exact timescales but it did acknowledge the many pressures on workers that tend to increase the time taken on assessments. These include engaging the family in treatment; working at the child's pace; the practical difficulties of involving other professionals in the assessment; and the courts' increasing insistence that recommendations are well argued and evidentially supported. The text was introduced at the time when the assumption was that workers needed a high degree of control over the parents to work effectively as many would be resistant to the work, untruthful and potentially violent to workers and children.

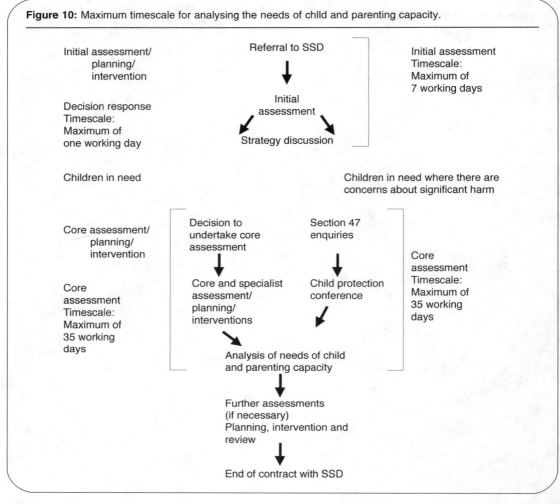

Figure 10: Maximum timescale for analysing the needs of child and parenting capacity.

Although we have shifted towards a partnership approach wherever possible, it is clear that this has the potential to expose children to great danger if applied uncritically (Calder, 1996). Partnership is not always a possibility with the child protection cases worked with above social service thresholds, but this is not accepted now as a reason to operate a flexible timescale for completing the core assessment.

The assessment framework sets down very rigid timescales for the completion of the required pieces of assessment (see Figure 10). This is problematic for two important reasons that I will explain in this section. Firstly, the family will be marginalised in a bid by agencies to comply with the mandated timescales. Secondly, the centrality of the worker in the process of engaging the client is made

significantly more difficult as the timescale does not allow for all the stages of the process to be attended to, thus reinforcing the first point.

Quite apart from the failure by government to model compliance with timescale when issuing rather belatedly the raft of guidance necessary for local authorities to consider strategies for implementation, the timescales are not 'evidence-based' as they require individual casework to be, but we have been reassured that they have been 'very carefully considered'!! I do not have a problem in principle with the drive to avoid drift in casework (so frequently identified in inspections and inquiries), but what I do find problematic is the reality that the timescales will dictate professional practice (given the link to standards and with it monies) to the point that families will be **done to** rather than **engaged with**, and this will create

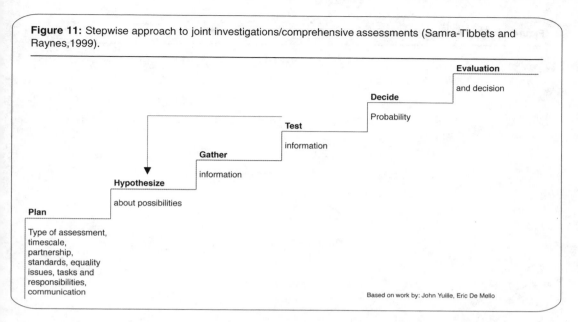

Figure 11: Stepwise approach to joint investigations/comprehensive assessments (Samra-Tibbets and Raynes,1999).

problems in terms of achieving optimal outcomes for children. This point warrants careful and detailed examination as it throws into question the principle of working **in partnership** with families and young people, and it also contradicts the principle that sees assessment as **an ongoing process** and not just a single event.

In the stepwise model of assessment (Samra-Tibbets and Raynes, 1999)(see Figure 11 and refer to Raynes in Chapter 7), it is clear that workers often skip the planning phase to progress to the information-gathering phase as invited through the assessment framework standardised forms (Cleaver and DoH, 2000). This is worrying as it means that the professional network has already accepted there is a problem that requires a solution, and they are moving into action-mode to process this. Unfortunately, a failure to spend time on the planning phase can lead to problems later. For example, there may be a professional difference of opinion about the risk, the plan or the strategies employed by particular workers; about professional roles and responsibilities; or about the level of partnership considered viable with the family. Whilst the planning stage is marginally allowed for (e.g. it is included in some of the training exercises in the Child's World) it does not feature at all in the document itself. Another side issue here is the lack of guidance in the assessment records to analysis. In fact, this is the only blank page of the core

assessment record and this is concerning since this is an area where social workers need the most help (judging by inquiry report findings and SSI inspection reports).

The area of engaging the family in the assessment process is an essential one that is often overlooked in our work, yet it can be essential to the outcome of any assessment work. Seabury (1985) identified engagement as the basic task of the social worker as it forms the basis of a working relationship. This can never be taken for granted and the worker must make a conscious, **persistent** and skilful intervention in order to facilitate relationship development. Workers have to pay attention to pre-contact details as attention to detail can pay dividends later. **Engagement is a process, not a set period of time.** It is a process of communication: an interactive process that gives, receives, and checks out meaning. We can never completely understand what another is saying, thinking and feeling, and we should not try and pretend otherwise (Compton and Galaway, 1999). The interactive nature of engagement, resistance and motivation (see Figure 12) between the worker and the client is an important consideration that is not represented pictorially within the new assessment framework. The triangle does not have any interactive dimensions suggesting it is a static model, and the worker does not appear. This is a significant and worrying omission that will be addressed in my reformulation later.

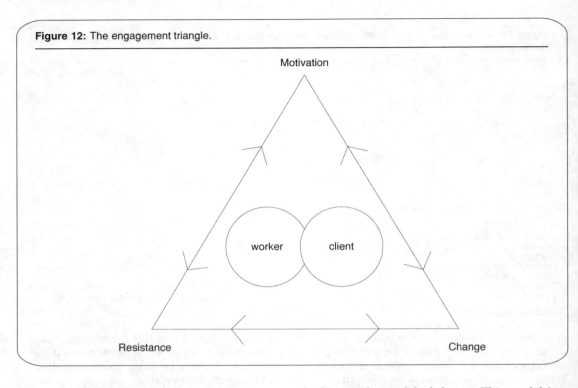

Figure 12: The engagement triangle.

In some circumstances, a short encounter between a social worker and a family may in itself be a problem-solving experience. However, if a working relationship cannot be developed, then it is unlikely that there will be any agreement on the child protection plan, and many children will not be protected (DoH, 1995). In child protection services, the target population is often the 'hard core' families where the initial relationship is usually characterised by a guardedness or reluctance to share information, avoidance and a desire to leave the relationship, or strong negative feelings such as anxiety, anger, suspicion, guilt or despair. It is clear, therefore, some degree of flexibility and creativity will be needed from the workers when attempting to engage the resistant client (see Calder, Peake and Rose, 2001 for a detailed exploration of this point). This process takes a **considerable amount of time** as well as skill and is not accommodated for within the timescales set down.

In order to start the engagement process, workers need to consider where the client is starting from, as there is frequently a discrepancy between professional and client starting points, which contribute to the problem, rather than serving to address and resolve it. This point can be made more clearly when

looking at the model of change. This model (see Figure 13 oveleaf) is very useful for setting out realistic plans of work at the outset, for setting attainable targets, and for reviewing what progress, if any, has been made. The model of change shows just how important it is for the professional to allow the client to move from pre-contemplation through to action (the start of the stepwise model) if there is to be any professional-family congruence about what needs to happen. Any failure to allow for this (and this is a very real issue with the timescales set down) sets the worker and the family up to fail. Given the worker should allow sufficient time in their assessment schedule to negotiate and hopefully create the necessary conditions for the client to engage in the work and effect some of the mutually agreed areas requiring change, workers do need to have some understanding of the important initial steps in the model of change. These are described below.

Precontemplation: This is where the individual is considering change far less than the professionals, who are often reacting to the presenting situation. Morrison (1995) pointed out that this phase is characterised by blaming others, denying responsibility, or simply being unaware of the need to change, e.g. depression. Whilst in this stage no change is possible.

Figure 13: A model of change (Prochaska and DiClemente, 1982; 1986).

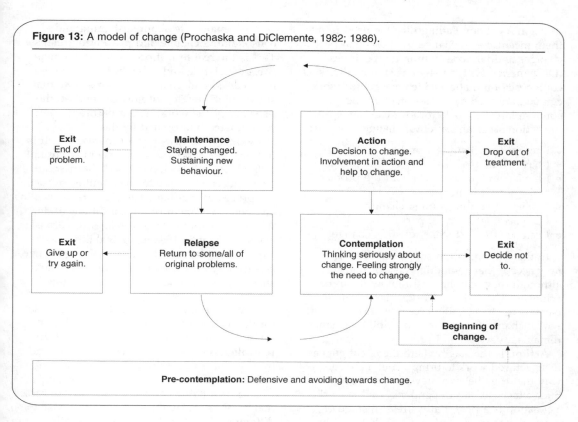

Individuals thus require information and feedback in order that they can raise their awareness of the problem and the possibility of change (Miller and Rollnick, 1991, p16). Pre-contemplation is the point at which the initial assessment takes place in order to ascertain, and hopefully enhance motivation to at least consider and contemplate, the need for change. Whilst the professionals enter the work at the action stage, the involuntary client is probably only in the pre-contemplation change. Such a combination cannot succeed as the two groups are at incongruent stages of change. There may also be a very different definition of the problem between the two groups. For the client, they are unlikely to be in a position to meaningfully engage in the proposed assessment work and a legal mandate often has to be sought.

DiClemente (1991) identified four categories of pre-contemplation. Reluctant pre-contemplators are those who through lack of knowledge or inertia do not want to consider change. Rebellious pre-contemplators have a heavy investment in the problem behaviour and in making their own decisions. The resigned pre-contemplator has given up on the possibility of change and seems overwhelmed by the problem. The rationalising pre-contemplator has all the answers but has discounted change as they have figured out the odds of personal risk, or they have plenty of reasons why the problem is not a problem or is a problem for others but not for them (p192–3).

Contemplation: Clients in this stage are most open to consciousness-raising interventions, such as observations, confrontations, and interpretations (Prochaska and DiClemente, 1986, p9). Through this process, their awareness of the problem increases, and they are then free to reject or adopt to change. The worker's aim is to tip the balance in favour of change (Miller and Rollnick, 1991, p16–7). Contemplation is often a very paradoxical stage of change. The fact that the client is willing to consider the problem and the possibility of change offers hope for change. However, the fact that ambivalence can make it a chronic condition can be very frustrating. It is the stage where many clients will be waiting for the one final piece of information that will compel them to change. The hope is that the information makes the decision for them. Failing this, we need to offer them incentives to change by looking at past changes and by accentuating the positives (DiClemente, 1991, p194–6). It is only after such contemplation that a viable contract for work can be made. There are six steps to the contemplation stage before we can move into the action stage and attempt change. They are:

- I accept that there is a problem.
- I have some responsibility for the problem.
- I have some discomfort about the problem and my part in it.
- I believe that things must change.
- I can see that I can be part of the solution.
- I can see the first steps towards change.

In the determination stage, the client may now accept that something has to change although they may be unsure how it can be achieved. The task for workers is to remove any barriers to change, and create an environment where change is a realistic possibility. Change remains a very painful process.

Action: Is the stage where the client engages in structured work to bring about a change, in a way that they believe they have determined. Such a tactic avoids dependency on the workers. Yet action is a potentially stressful stage of change as they can fail and feel that they have failed or been rejected. We need to plan for relapse and involve the wider family and the community networks, for it is they who are most likely both to spot the early signs of lapse, and who will provide the most day-to-day support (Morrison, 1995). This stage is where the individual is seen 'in action', implementing the plan. It is where they feel able to make a public commitment to action; to get some external confirmation of the plan; to seek support; to gain greater self-efficacy; and finally to create artificial, external monitors of their activity (DiClemente, 1991, p198–9). For the worker, they should focus on successful activity and reaffirm the client's decisions. They should point out that change is predictable where a person adheres to advice and the plan. The focus should be on learning, exploring and rehearsing ways of relating, thinking, behaving and feeling. All change is essentially a combination of these four basic human processes. This stage may take several months as new behaviour takes time to become established. At the end of the initial planning stage, the aim is to produce a longer-term plan of work.

Maintenance: Is about sustaining and consolidating change and preventing relapse. This is the real test. It occurs when the new ways of relating and behaving become internalised and generalised across different situations. They do not now depend on the presence of the workers, but become consolidated and owned by the individual/family as part of themselves. It is through this process that the client's sense of self-efficacy has been increased (Morrison, 1995). Successful maintenance builds on each of the processes that have come before, as well as an open assessment of the conditions under which a person is likely to relapse (Prochaska and DiClemente, 1986, p10). Stability and support will be essential to sustaining change, especially with the many families who have such poor experience of problem solving (Morrison, 1991, p96).

Relapse: The cyclical model of change allows for the reality that few people succeed first time round. Change comes from repeated efforts, re-evaluation, renewing of commitment, and incremental success. Relapse is thus part of, rather than necessarily hostile to, change. Change is a battle between the powerful forces that want us to stay the same, and our wish to be different (Morrison, 1991, p96). It usually occurs gradually after an initial slip (often due to unexpected stress), rather than occurring spontaneously (DiClemente, 1991, p200). It can lead to a loss of all or most of the gains, resulting in a giving-up and a return to pre-contemplation. This can be counteracted by the worker, giving feedback, on how long it takes to accomplish sustained change. They should aim to keep the change effort going rather than becoming disengaged and stuck. Morrison (1995) noted that where it is noted quickly enough, and help is urgently sought and available from friends, family or professionals, all is by no means lost. This may lead to further work through the contemplation stage.

The assessment of change is a very uncertain process, and is often very fragile where it is achieved. It is important that we acknowledge that change is very slow and, as such, workers need to set realistic expectations of involuntary clients so as not to personalise disappointment, experience frustration, impatience and feelings of failure. Few workers are effectively trained to deal with negatively charged emotional material, reluctance, or non-compliant behaviour (Ivanoff et al., 1994).

Resistance

Resistance is a natural response to the fear of change. A worker who understands that resistance is part of the interpersonal dynamics of a helping relationship will be able to help the client in the process of making the desire to change their own behaviour (Miller and Rollnick, 1991). By re-framing resistance as a feature of motivated behaviour, the workers can unlock an opportunity to help the client's change. Problems may occur when we try to use strategies, which are inappropriate to the client's readiness or attitude to change, or where the views and judgements of the workers are rejected by the family. Professionals need to acknowledge that resistance may peak during the assessment and planning phase of their intervention. A determination not to be overwhelmed, distracted, or immobilised by the parents' initial response is essential in establishing genuine emotional contact. Hostility can be diminished by being clear about tasks to be done and demonstrating a willingness to be flexible about matters that are negotiable. What is important here is an acknowledgement about the skills and the timescales needed to reframe resistance positively for the client to even consider engaging with the mandated assessment process, and which may well exceed the 35 days for the assessment itself. If we do not allow the client to move through the contemplation stage to action where the workers are often starting, then this incongruence will fuel client resistance and will often render any assessment done as partial, with little chance thereafter of engaging the client in any plan to address the concerns raised through the assessment process. An assessment of where the client is in the model of change is an essential first task for workers and this should inform the planning for the assessment itself.

Motivation and change

Motivation is not an attribute of the client but a product of the interaction of client, worker and environment. It is not a characteristic of the client's personality structure or psychological functioning. Morrison (1991) has argued that motivation comes from the interplay of internal and external factors and it is rarely the case that real change is accomplished only on the basis of personal motivation without the assistance of external reinforcement (p93). He provided us

with an excellent continuum of motivation to use with families to explore how it can be improved (see Figure 14).

This section is the crux of my reformulation of the assessment framework: the worker is central to engaging the client and this process requires we integrate the models of assessment and change (see Figure 15) to maximise the chances of partnership and with it probably better outcomes for children (Thoburn et al., 1995). As you can see from Figure 15, there is a tendency to start off with gathering information by professionals and this cuts-off over half of the process essential if we are to attempt to work in partnership with the client.

There are a few final points about the prescribed timescale that should be made. Adherence to the timescale and the completion of the core assessment document is not necessarily helpful for many reasons:

- There is a concern that we should lose the 7-day initial assessment period when child protection is the presenting concern given that the government cannot see any situation of this kind not requiring a core assessment. This would leave us with 35 and not 42 working days to do the task.
- The initial child protection conference is usually the commissioning forum for the core assessment and this is now only needed within 15 working days, which is likely to mean that the social worker will have needed to pre-determine and start the assessment before conference.
- There is no sequel core assessment document post-35 days. There is thus a void unless the child is within the 'looked after' system and the Assessment and Action Records (AAR) kicks in. Workers are unlikely to want to redo the core assessment as the actual structure and questions are unhelpful, too general, and do not allow sufficient space for supplementary comment, essential given the tick-box approach does not allow for any response to be contextualised.
- There is a great deal of confusion about the core assessment (record) and the legal process. What is an emerging pattern is that many authorities are not requiring the core assessment record be completed when there are multiple detailed reports being prepared for court. In some courts, they are setting their own parameters of assessment and not utilising the core assessment record.

Figure 14: A continuum of motivation (adapted from Morrison, 1991, p34).

Internal motivators

I want to change.
I don't like things as they are.
I am asking for your help.
I have resources to help solve this.
I think you can help me.
I think things can get better.
I have other support, which I will use to encourage me.
I accept that I am doing something wrong.
I accept what you say needs to change.
I accept that others are right (family, friends, community, agencies).
You defining the problem clearly helps.
I understand what change will involve.
I accept that if I do not change, you will take my children away.
I can change if you do this for me.
I'll do whatever you say.
I agree to do this so the family can be reconstituted.
It's your job to solve my problem.
You are my problem.
I am right and you are wrong.
I don't have any problems.

External motivators

- One has to wonder about the fit with the legal process given that a) the courts continue to request comprehensive assessments and do not accept the new core assessment documents as helpful and b) the timescale for hearing cases continues to exceed 12 and on many occasions 18 months and this renders the core assessment 35 day completion ridiculous. This is dealt with as a separate point later.
- The core assessment document lends itself more to needs-led assessments rather than child protection work, and thus the structure of the documents and the questions are unhelpful and even dangerous in that they do not begin to acknowledge never mind address the complexities of child sexual abuse (see Calder 2000 for a detailed exploration of this point).
- The sequential timeframe is inappropriate in some scenarios. For example, a young couple present themselves to social services and indicate they are expecting a child and the presenting concerns or history indicate the need for a pre-birth risk assessment. There is clearly a need to conduct a core assessment, but there has to be some discretion as to what point in the pregnancy this might be. There should be thus power to suspend the time frame.

- We have been directed forcefully in the past to carefully consider if and then how to intervene in cases of child sexual abuse, especially since the intervention with the child victim has to be sensitive, measured, at their own pace, and guided by their particular needs and wishes and feelings. This has implications for the time it takes professionals to respond and they cannot be dictated to by external factors such as timescales.

What is important is that we do not let the procedure drive the practice, but this is easier said than done. For example:

- There is considerable pressure from managers to fill in the forms and they in turn are being leaned on by senior management to hit Quality Protects targets, e.g. the Department of Health is suggesting that 60 per cent of assessments be done by timescales by 2002 and 85 per cent by 2003. The likely outcome from this is that the form will be completed rather than the assessment.
- In regional dissemination days organised by the Department of Health, any questioning about the timescales has been swiftly dealt with and very clear indications given that the 35 day core assessment timescale will be enshrined as a standard in the future, with

Figure 15: Integrating the child and worker processes.

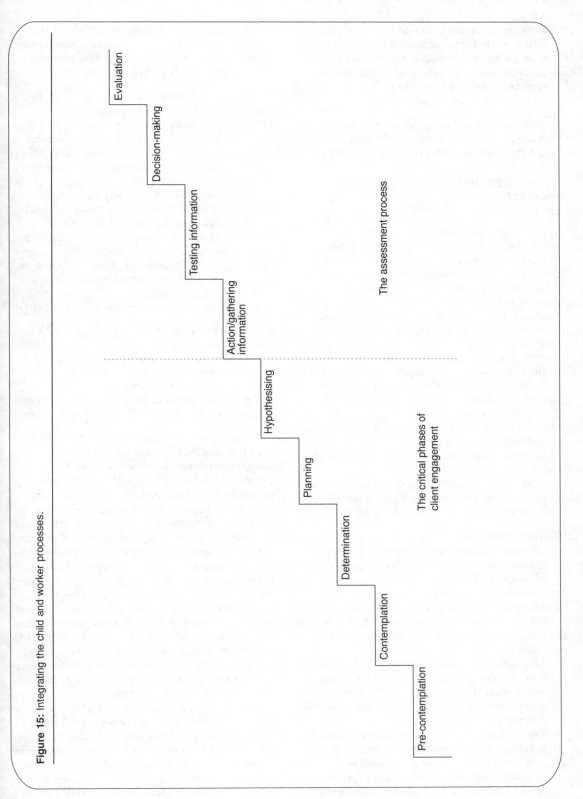

associated consequences for non-compliance. Rather than adopting such a confrontational position based on a national groundswell of concern, the Department of Health would have been better advised to review them since the concern is universal.

What we do need is a structure that encourages and facilitates reflective practice by social workers and other professionals. This is important as . . .

Paternalism not partnership: a role reversal?

Calder (1995) has pointed to the need to balance partnership and paternalism in any child protection work, rather than swinging the pendulum backwards and forwards between the two. With the emergence of the assessment framework we are likely to witness an operational shift towards paternalistic practice (with the emphasis on getting the job done) away from partnership practice so strongly advocated by government in recent years (DoH, 1995b). This is supported in part by the impact of the timescales on professional practice, but it is reinforced through the range of partnership models and the link between the restricted provision of a social work service with an alternative model of assessment. I will explain this point in more detail.

There are four possible models of partnership for professionals to choose from:

Calder (1995) identified four possible models of partnership to reflect how professionals can either work with, alongside or 'do to' the client:

1. The expert model: where the professional takes control and makes all the decisions, giving a low priority to parents view, wishes or feelings, the sharing of information, or the need for negotiation.
2. The transplant (of expertise) model: where the professional sees the parent as a resource and hands over some skills, but retains control of the decision-making.
3. The consumer model: where it is assumed that parents have the right to decide and select what they believe to be appropriate, and the decision-making is ultimately in their control.
4. The social network/systems model: where parents, children and professionals are part of a network of formal and informal development, and social support for the family and the child. They are capable of

supplementing existing resources via the facilitation of the social worker who should draw more on the extended family while complying with statutory requirements.

The danger is that workers revert back to the 'expert' model in order to prioritise the timescale above all other considerations. This fits well with the likely choice of assessment style selected by the worker. Smale et al. (1993) identified three possible models of assessment: the questioning model, the exchange model and the procedural model. The key difference between the models is in how power is used and the impact on the service user. Only the exchange model will empower the client to be fully involved as an equal partner in a process of negotiating the nature of 'their problem' and its possible 'solutions' through an appropriate 'tailor-made' response.

The *questioning model* assumes the worker:

• Is expert in people, their problems and in identifying needs.
• Exercises knowledge and skill to form 'their' assessment, identify people's needs.
• Identifies resources required.
• Takes responsibility for making an accurate assessment of need and taking appropriate action.

In this model, the professional gathers information from 'the client' and/or their carer(s), forms an assessment of their needs or problems and then works on a solution. The worker's behaviour is dominated by asking questions, listening to and processing the answers, using the information gained to form 'an assessment'. The questions reflect the worker's agenda, not other peoples. Enshrined in the questions asked will be implicit or explicit criteria or perceptions of the problems that people 'like the client' have, and a view of the resources available to meet them. In this model it is assumed that questions can be answered in a straightforward manner, or that the professional is able to accurately interpret what the client really wants even when they cannot or do not express it. The complexities of communication across cultural and other boundaries, such as race, ethnicity as defined by professionals, gender, class, disability or professional reference group and organisational allegiance, tend to be underestimated or even ignored. An 'accurate professional assessment' may be enough to identify 'need', but it is not enough if goals include increasing the choices of the people involved or maximising peoples potential. Additional skills are needed for work with people that empowers them to have as much control over their lives as possible and specifically enables them to exercise choice in how their needs may be met. The worker never has a monopoly of knowledge and can never replace the insight clients bring into their problems and themselves. People are, and always will be the expert on themselves, their situation, their relationships, what they want and need. They also bring a certain degree of control over their own behaviour that professionals will never have and so be able to influence the viability of the present and future relationships that underpin a plan of intervention. One can see that the framework set out in the 'orange book' (DoH, 1988) lends itself to this style of assessment. However, after much research, there was a shift from paternalistic to partnership-based practice, as characterised by the exchange model.

The *exchange model* assumes that people: are expert in themselves and assumes that the worker:

- Has expertise in the process of problem solving with others.
- Understands and shares perceptions of problems and their management.
- Gets agreement about who will do what to support whom.
- Takes responsibility for arriving at the optimum resolution of problems within the constraints of available resources and the willingness of the participants to contribute.

In the exchange model, the professional concentrates on an exchange of information between themselves and the client and others. The question and answer pattern of behaviour is avoided. The professional works to engage with the people involved either together or in series and each person's participation is negotiable. The behaviour of the professional is crucial in establishing the respect and the trust of others and will vary over time. Perceptions of the situation, its problems, availability of resources and the need for more, are shared. A definition of the 'problems', and their resolution or management, are arrived at as much through the initiative of the clients (and significant others) as by the professional (such as Family Group Conferences) and is often the product of interaction between them. The worker often negotiates with a range of people to get agreement about who should do what for whom rather than making 'an assessment' and organising a package of care or protection as the latter implies control. In this sense the professional can never be responsible for the whole package. Each participant is responsible for their own contribution, or lack of it.

Typically the professional will not lead the content of the dialogue because he or she will not know any more, if as much, as the other people about the situation, its problems, or what existing resources could contribute to 'the solution'. The professional follows or tracks what the other people say and communicate. To lead is to assume that the professional knows where to go and often this will go straight to a service-led response.

However, the assessor should be the expert in identifying the relationships between people. This includes understanding how the client's behaviour supports the current situation, and how this may be changed to support a different pattern of relationships so that the problem can be managed differently or even resolved. Professionals need to be able to recognise, understand and intervene in the patterns of relationships that precipitate and perpetuate social problems.

Although the theory underpinning the exchange model is supported by research studies, there are some potential problems with this approach:

- The communication of what people need and want is very complicated and has to include an exploration of, and take into account, the different assumptions of the two or more people involved, the different languages that they use, think and feel in, and the different levels of communication that exist.
- Communication across ethnic, racial, class, gender, professional, or other cultural boundaries needs particular care if preconceived assumptions and prejudices are not going to lead to misunderstandings or worse.
- People have their own ideas, beliefs and knowledge; they are not passive or neutral receivers waiting for messages. In practice, communicators enter into dialogues with people who interpret messages in accordance with their own assumptions and beliefs, which may or may not be the same as the communicators.

The exchange model can be a difficult, complex and time-consuming process for agencies, especially since the client has a greater say in the management of their situation. However, it is clearly much more likely to empower clients and create a framework for their engagement in the assessment and then the problem-solving process. It is also unlikely to allow workers to complete the assessment in the required timescale unless it is their only case. This is an important issue. I identified earlier that many social work agencies are establishing thresholds for the provision of services given the mismatch between likely need and available resources. This thus suggests that workers will be manoeuvred from the exchange to the procedural model of assessment.

In the *procedural model*, the goal of the assessment is to gather information to see if the client 'fits' or meets certain criteria that will make them eligible for services (see the discussion on threshold for a social work service earlier). Those defining the criteria for eligibility, in effect pre-allocating services for generally identified need make the judgement as to what sort of person should get which resources. The worker's task is to identify the specific people who match the appropriate degree of need defined within the categories of service available and to exclude those not eligible.

This model represents a variation to the questioning model where the professional is assumed to be the expert in identifying need. In the procedural model, it is assumed that the managers drawing up guidelines for workers have expertise in setting the criteria for resource allocation. To this extent they are experts in how problems should be managed and resources allocated.

In this model the worker will complete a referral form and/or an initial assessment with or without the client's involvement. Questions are asked and/or information gathered to answer each of the questions deemed relevant by those setting criteria for resource allocation. The information typically sought attempts to:

- Categorise the 'client'.
- Define the nature of the client's needs in the terms that services are offered, that is whether the client's needs make them eligible for services actually or potentially available.
- Gather information required for agency statistics to aid service planning.

Some of the issues such an approach raises include:

- The client's definitions of their problems or that of others may not be included.
- The client is not empowered by the process and they rarely get choices about the outcome
- Worker judgement beyond interpreting information and deciding on how to complete the necessary documentation is not required. They have little room for manoeuvre, acting as agents of their managers.
- The agenda is set by the agency and not the worker or the client.
- Clients may be labelled by workers to ensure they are eligible for a service.

The goal of the procedural model is legitimate when managers are responsible for the allocation of services to meet need within resource constraints placed upon them. It provides a quick, simple, practical and cost-effective approach of identifying clients who are eligible for available resources.

If the decision as to who gets what is grounded in professional judgement rather than on the available resources, then workers should use the questioning model.

The issue of partnership with children as well as the adults compounds the difficulties of the timescale as we are also expected to work at their pace and to employ techniques likely to empower them in the process. We also have a professional obstacle to overcome: transforming the worker view that working with children is a problem to be overcome rather than the basis of good practice (Calder and Horwath, 2000).

The deletion of the concept of risk and investigation: throwing the baby out with the bathwater?

In the most recently issued government guidance (DoH, 1999; 2000) terms such as 'protection', 'abuse' and 'risk' have largely been replaced by 'safeguard', 'promote', 'welfare' and 'need'. Indeed, 'need' is being promulgated as the central organising thesis for future social work policy and practice, with usage of the term 'risk' being eschewed and discouraged (Calder, 2000). This 'new language' may be promoted as being more muted, wider in meaning, less stigmatising, less confrontational and hence more appropriate to a partnership with families approach. They may even argue that the concept of risk is encapsulated within the broad-based concept of need. This change deserves a close analysis.

The government appears to be jettisoning the concept of risk and risk assessment in their latest guidance in favour of a needs-led assessment. This appears to be premised on a partial understanding in government of what a risk assessment is. The DoH assessment guidance of 1988 was built almost entirely on the notions of risk and dangerousness yet these do not appear to have been satisfactorily defined or applied in practice. This may be because it is a term which is often misused in social work because it focuses exclusively on the risk of harm, whereas in any other enterprise a risk equation also includes a chance of benefit resulting (Carson, 1994). Any risk assessment, should, therefore, be concerned with weighing up the pros and cons of a child's circumstances in order to inform decision-making as to what should happen with regard to intervention and protection. It involves examining the child and family situation to identify and weigh various risk factors (such as parents, family or other influences that increase the likelihood that a child will be harmed in a certain way), family strengths, family resources, and available agency services. This assessment information can then be used to determine if a child is safe, what agency resources are needed to keep the child safe, and under what circumstances a child should be removed from the family. This understanding of risk is one that is applied on a daily basis in their cases and most definitely in any case being presented to court.

The government appears to be deleting risk for several reasons: in the hope that by deleting risk the association with Section 47 child protection investigation will go, and to reinforce this the need to address enquiries pre-investigation is also restated; in the hope that workers will introduce the new concept of assessing and working with client strengths; and in the hope that workers will focus more on 'need'. Unfortunately, this is not convincing when there is repeated backtracking from needs-led assessments to a reminder that the child's safety is the primary objective of professional intervention. Workers will be conscious of the consequences of getting it wrong.

One of the more confusing issues is that at a time in which the government is moving away from notions of risk, there are huge developments in risk assessments emerging in the field of sexual abuse (see Calder, 2000 and 2001c for reviews) as well as a move towards risk management in most allied professions. There is also a concern for workers that all their

experience of 'risk assessments' in the past is redundant and should no longer be applied to cases. What they need is an up-to-date and accessible framework for assessing risk that they can use to guide their interventions (set out in Calder, 2000).

One of the key issues is where risk as a concept sits within the needs-led framework, particularly when the framework is failing to address child protection issues and many authorities are reintroducing their old documentation to supplement the framework records. This is now officially been looked at by the authors of the record who may consider 'developing some standardised child protection materials to support the integration of child protection procedures with the core assessment process' (Steve Walker, Personal communication, 7th August, 2001).

Donnelly (2001) explored the usefulness of the concept of risk as a way of thinking about possible future outcomes as an aid to social work planning. She concluded that rather than seeing the term as a 'hot potato' (difficult to handle and a history of already having 'burnt many fingers'), we should see it as part of our everyday life. We should thus see the term as 'an apt and essential feature of our language and its judicious usage, aided by an informed understanding, could enhance rather than undermine partnerships with families. I believe therefore that the framework represents an opportunity lost to define the concept of risk; to explain its chequered history; and to begin to educate social workers on its potential benefits and current limitations. Such an understanding becomes particularly salient when seeking to translate assessment conclusions into future hypotheses and casework plans: risk prediction is fundamental to needs-based planning' (p14) . . . it is difficult to identify how the framework or its materials can assist with risk prediction in seeking to determine whether a child is safe; how to deal with conflicting needs (e.g. siblings of different ages whose needs for permanency and contact may be very different); and in the translation of assessment conclusions into final plans (p19) . . . In failing to engage with the concept of risk, the framework has failed to provide social workers with significant technical information with which to inform their assessments (p20)'. By failing to address the concept of risk, the framework has failed to 'grasp the nettle' and so begin the process of re-definition, education and debate. Social

Table 1: Skills needed for evidence-based practice (Ramchandani et al., 2001, p60).

The ability to:
- Formulate an answerable question from a clinical or service issue.
- Search using bibliographical databases (such as Medline) and find short cuts to good quality evidence.
- Be confident in critically appraising research findings.
- Interpret and apply results for use in a particular clinical situation, or in developing service provision.
- Evaluate one's own clinical practice.

workers and their managers will continue to engage with risk but in the context of official guidance that has nothing specific to say on the subject. The consequences are likely to be a combination of 'best efforts' and 'untutored responses'. The framework misses the opportunity explicitly to advise on current understandings and the result is a perpetuation of a situation in which risk remains poorly understood and lacking in robust evidence. This has, and will continue to have, significant consequences for children and their families.

The limitations of an evidence-based practice approach in the child protection arena.

There is no agreed definition of evidence-based practice. Sackett et al. (1996) define it as the 'conscientious, explicit and judicious use of the current best evidence in making decisions about the care of individual patients', whilst Dartington Social Research Unit (1998) define it 'to mean social work undertaken by a range of people (not just professional social workers) which is grounded in good knowledge of the needs of children and families and what the best research has to say about what works for which groups of children and why. Increasingly, such analysis extends to the cost-benefit of different interventions. Evidence based social work should provide a common conceptual framework into which new ideas, new evidence and new projects can be fitted and implies a balance between the legal/moral, pragmatic, evidential and consumer influences on practice . . .' (p17).

It involves a number of skills (see Table 1 above) and the development of a process whereby new evidence can be found, examined and integrated into the provision of services to populations and the care of individual patients and their families (Ramchandani et al., 2001, p59).

Drawing upon his own experiences of working with social workers to implement such

approaches in Chapter 4, Hackett reflects upon the challenges and limitations of evidenced-based assessment. However, what follows here is offered as a more critical view.

The evidence-based movement argues:
- That practice is about accomplishing measurable changes in behaviour outcome ('what works'), based on clear objectives.
- That there exist a great number of well-constructed empirical research studies that can inform practice directly, so long as social workers have the necessary critical appraisal skills to assess these, and select the ones relevant for the case or cases in hand.
- That the methodology most appropriate for such studies is derived from quantitative social science, or (indirectly) from medical and health science, and rests on framing clear and testable hypotheses, and measuring concrete changes attributable to specific interventions.
- That social workers should be encouraged or required to build evaluation of the effectiveness of their work into their practice, to implement agency plans and policies, and to contribute to the dissemination and application of research outcomes. (Jordan, 2000, p206).

Jordan argues that criticism of this set of principles has focused on each of these elements, and on their combined application. Not all social work is concerned with short-term behavioural change; much manages adversity or decline. Objectives are inevitably complex, reflecting the political, moral and social context of human problems; hence social work involves uncertainty, confusion and doubt, often shared between workers and services users. Practice methods are seldom clear cut, and cannot be imposed; they need to be negotiated, paying attention to service-users' understandings of their needs and goals. If it is to empower and enable service users, social work must co-operate with them in research as well as practice, and qualitative methods are often more appropriate to such aims. The goal of analysing problems and deciding on interventions in line with the best available research evidence may in many instances be impracticable. The 'best evidence' of what works in medical and health care is usually taken to be based on randomised control trials, which are conspicuously lacking for the whole field of social care, partly for ethical reasons and partly because the conditions for such experimental research are seldom present. These arguments do not in themselves knock down the case for evidence-based approaches, but they do need to be acknowledged and worked with.

Evidence is therefore the new 'must have' in social care, not least because professional social workers need to know why they do what they do, and to be able to make their case confidently to colleagues from other disciplines such as health. But where is the evidence? Rickford (2001) points out that the most obvious source is fat books. Academic research evidence, at least for those of us outside the research industry, has a special authority. However, academics tell us that life is not that simple. In the first place there is not enough academic research to provide by itself a reliable basis for practice, largely because social work is barely 50 years old. Secondly, there is very little research evidence that is incontrovertible in terms of its implications for social work practice. Research is not simply a process of revealing an objective truth. Two people can interpret the results of the same study in totally different ways, and draw opposing conclusions about what it means. They may disagree about the weight of a piece of evidence and they can disagree about the interpretation and implications of research evidence. . Some studies may be too old or too small to be helpful, or they were carried out in the context of a different country. Often a study will show an association between two things – for example family poverty and child protection registration – but that doesn't necessarily mean one caused the other. A high proportion of people die in bed, but the Health Authority isn't advising us to sleep on the floor. Finally, research evidence is only one kind of evidence and is often only useful in conjunction with the experience and skill of an individual practitioner. Every situation in social care is different because each involves human beings and relationships between human beings, so off-the-shelf answers are never going to work. The recent spate of new initiatives and

pressures on workers is making it very difficult for them to step back and reflect on their practice. The managerialist culture of recent years has not fostered a climate which has encouraged them to do that. What is critical from agencies is to provide the context within which reflective practice can emerge (such as action research and access to the post-qualifying child care award for workers) and not simply to displace the expectation of evidence-based practice onto individual workers. The Social Care Institute for Excellence (SCIE) will attempt to set up a national 'knowledge base' on good practice which assesses and interprets evidence from users and staff as well as from academic literature. The way in which they go about it, say by viewing frontline staff as the experts, is essential if they are not to inherit another imposition from above that becomes another demand. It is also equally important that they draw upon people's expertise. The nature of the evidence in social research is more complicated than it is in scientific research. For example, you could not say adoption is good or bad. It depends on how it is applied and who experiences it. No two children and no two families are the same. The skill is in the interpretation and application of what we do know (Rickford, 2001b).

You can also argue against the view that more and more knowledge is the only solution to poor practice and in any event it only takes us so far down the process. For example, social work is as much a practical-moral activity as it is a technical-rational one. As such, workers use values and a range of rationalities when making their professional judgements. Evidence from research can assist workers in analysing risk and harm but this still leaves the social worker with the task of deciding which evidence is relevant to the case and then deciding which situations are harmful or risky. As Taylor and White (2001) highlight, 'an unquestioning dependence on external, pre-existing knowledge will not be sufficient in such circumstances, as it will offer neither conclusive proof nor categorical answers. It will not establish the right way to proceed . . . nor will it encourage a questioning and sceptical approach to a worker's own practice . . . In short, the worker will be faced with a number of possible interpretations leading to a range of options . . .' I believe that the assessment framework is a midpoint compromise between these two positions. On the one hand it clearly introduces a series of pro forma documents as part of a search for standardisation up and down the country, but it also leaves the worker with a void of material to apply it to the variety of practice situations they will encounter. The clear aim is to encourage the exercise of professional judgement by utilising an up-to-date evidence base. It is this latter point that is creating much anxiety in social work circles given that traditionally they have been steered clear of this by cautious legal advisors concerned that they would set themselves up to fail in any cross-examination.

Further examples of antipathy towards evidence-based practice include:

- Evidence-based practice has been taken to mean that practice should be based on the evidence of randomised controlled trials alone, and that all other practice is either not evidence based or of a lower quality. The hierarchy of evidence (see Table 2) compounds this impression. This narrow approach leaves many workers in a quandary as few systematic reviews exist.
- Practicing in an evidence-based way is time-consuming. For many workers, finding and appraising research to answer the operational questions is an activity that takes place outside the frontline work. Reaching a point where one can feel one has a satisfactory answer to a question can involve significant time spent searching databases and then retrieving and critically appraising several pieces of research. Gaining protected time to do this and apply the findings in practice, as well as to learn and develop the skills can prove difficult. For many, there will be an additional problem of access to libraries, computers and other information technology in the workplace (Ramchandani et al., 2001).
- There is a skill gap acting as a barrier to evidence-based practice. Workers need to learn the skills required to assimilate and appraise the evidence that is available (see Table 1). Many workers lack confidence in being able to search for evidence using electronic databases such as Medline and have not acquired skills in the critical appraisal of research. The development and practice of these skills require time and for many further training (Ramchandani et al., 2001). The spotlight is being brought to bear on training courses to examine what evidence is taught on social work courses and how will qualified social workers know the value of

Table 2: The traditional hierarchy of evidence (Ramchandani et al., 2001, p61).

Several systematic reviews of randomised controlled trials
Systematic review of randomised controlled trials
Randomised controlled trials
Quasi-experimental trials
Case control and cohort studies
Expert consensus opinion
Individual opinion

one piece of research in the context of any particular aspect of practice.

- Social workers often comment on how little of what they read is directly applicable to practice. Too often workers are presented with research in an unusable form yet they are expected to apply the findings as passive participants. There are clearly contrasting expectations of researchers and social workers that have to be addressed: social workers seek to apply general findings to particular cases whereas researchers seek to generalise from individual situations. Communication between researchers and social workers is hindered further by contrasting working practices. Researchers are inclined to hedge their findings – to the annoyance of workers who very often have to commit themselves to decisions that can have profound consequences for vulnerable children. On the other hand, there is a tendency for social workers to regard as extraordinary cases that researchers consider routine, and vice-versa (Bullock et al., 1998). Research is also often criticised by social workers for merely confirming what they already know, and in many cases they have furnished the researchers with the material to build their case.

'The promise of evidence-based social work may be short-lived. It would not be the first time that a challenge to social work had evaporated into the thin air from which it had momentarily emerged'
(Bullock et al., 1998, p18).

A model of professional knowledge for social work practice

Although there are concerns about the appropriateness of introducing an evidence-based approach into social work, ways need to be found to operationalise the concept. Drury-Hudson (1997) developed a useful model

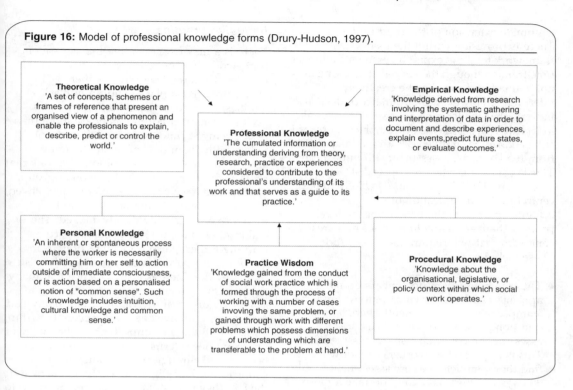

Figure 16: Model of professional knowledge forms (Drury-Hudson, 1997).

of professional knowledge for social work that articulates five main knowledge forms (see Figure 16): theoretical, empirical, procedural, practice wisdom and personal knowledge. These do not represent discrete categories as there is considerable overlap between each. For example, theoretical knowledge includes aspects of personal, practice and empirical knowledge forms, just as procedural knowledge integrates practice wisdom, theoretical and empirical knowledge forms. Research has demonstrated that theoretical and empirical knowledge forms are infrequently used in social work practice as workers are inclined to rely on practice wisdom, organisational policy and procedures, legislation and social work values as the basis of their practice.

'To allow social work to be continually defined on the basis of what social workers do, by virtue of a heavy reliance on personal knowledge forms and practice wisdom is likely to foster inconsistency in decision-making and reduce accountability in practice. It should not be too much to expect that professional social workers should keep abreast of current research trends and base their practice on an understanding of the nature, causes, and typical patterns of development of problems, and on interventions that have been evaluated as achieving positive outcomes. It is not enough

for social workers to rely upon their professional values, intuition or practice wisdom alone. Skilful and effective professional practice requires social workers to be knowledgeable about the research and theories applicable to a given area of practice or problem in order to make informed choices about the most effective course of action'

(Drury Hudson, 1997, p44).

The assessment framework and the legal process

Given that a large number of cases open to social workers will be within the critical or collapsed categories, there is also a likelihood that legal proceedings will be a feature of the case at some point in the process. This may not always be because of a need to remove, but it may be to share difficult decision-making with a third party. This may be fuelled by a professional concern that they are to exercise professional judgement based on the best available evidence, but if they get it wrong then they may well be pilloried for their (human) mistakes. This is evidenced by the expansion of the section in Safeguarding Children on Part 8 enquiries. Another driving force may be to seek specialist assessments within a legal framework that may absorb the costs as well as providing a legitimate extension of the rigid timescales. There is provision within the assessment framework to allow expert assessments a longer time frame although the specialist assessment is not defined and can thus be creatively interpreted. However, the framework does also indicate that whilst such assessments may take longer than the 35 days allowed, the core record still needs to be completed with the information from the specialist assessment still outstanding. This is confusing when the specialist assessment, by its very nature, is likely to be central to the identification of needs.

Quite apart from the benefits of the legal process, there are many limitations and areas of confusion that will require local resolution. These include:

- The core assessment documents do not appear to address the court request for a 'comprehensive' assessment! There is thus a question to be asked 'when is a core assessment a comprehensive assessment?' This is important as workers do not want to find they complete the core assessment within 35 days but then have to undertake a more detailed comprehensive assessment as defined by the court and which is clearly going to take a much longer time to complete.
- The core assessment documentation is single authorship and this does not conform with the legal process of requiring statements from all those who may be asked to give evidence. As such, the core assessment document, even when completed appropriately, will not be sufficient to use in court and will thus require additional statements to be prepared and lodged. This seems an unnecessary and time-consuming exercise when workers are over-stretched and few on the ground.
- The timescales for completing the core assessment and the final care hearing could not be further apart.
- There is a problem with using the assessment framework for children subject to criminal proceedings (especially young people who sexually abuse) given the even tighter timeframe set down for the YOT and the courts.
- The courts and the Guardian Ad Litems have not received much training on NAF and thus appear to be playing catch up through individual cases. Where training has taken place, the incredulity of the judges has been very noticeable (Precey, 2001).

Inclusive practice

There is a major concern that the assessment framework does not address white ethnic families (Chinese, Jews, etc.) as there is an over-emphasis on black children in black families, with no emphasis on refugee and asylum seeking children. There are more than 54,000 refugee children in the UK's schools today, with about 86% of them attending schools in Greater London. Studies indicate that refugee children, more than any other group, are likely to have parents who are unemployed, live in temporary accommodation and are therefore economically disadvantaged. These children, who themselves need support in learning English, also act as interpreters and advocates for parents who speak less English than they do. There is also evidence that many refugee children are targeted for bullying in school. Before their arrival in Britain many had experienced family separation, severe hardship, periods of living in camps, been at the mercy of unscrupulous intermediaries and sometimes been routed through three or four different countries in their flights to safety. On arrival in the UK, they may still feel insecure, unsure as to their safety, experience culture shock, be moved repeatedly, receive little counselling or professional support for their emotional needs, and assume a greater role within their family. In current political and media debates on asylum seekers, and particularly emotive discussions about 'bogus' refugees, refugee children and their needs are often invisible (*www.community-care.co.uk/cc archive*, dated 29.05.01).

In Kent, the number of children requiring the care of the local authority has almost doubled from around 1,500 to 2,800 in the past two years, largely because of unaccompanied child asylum seekers – a national issue that has received little public attention compared to the broader debate on asylum policy (Gilroy, 2001). Unaccompanied asylum-seeking children have the same essential needs as children everywhere. They also have the same rights to protection from abuse. These children are particularly vulnerable because they often have only a very limited understanding of the English language. Many have personally suffered or witnessed physical persecution and might be bereaved or deeply anxious about their families. Many have totally inaccurate expectations of their future in this country and they will all face substantial periods of uncertainty while their claim for asylum is being considered. The majority have no family or friends in this country and may be isolated from other members of their ethnic community. Attempts to place them with caring members of their own families or communities often run the risk of abuse given the problems associated with inadequate background checks.

Workers will thus need to generate their own assessment issues if working with such children. Gretchen Precey (unpublished) has indicated the following points for assessment:

- Economic disadvantage (parental unemployment/temporary accommodation).
- Trauma of experiences in country of origin.
- Post traumatic stress disorder (and associated mental health problems).
- Survivor syndrome.
- Unfamiliar with UK culture.
- Fear of further persecution in the UK.
- Frequent moves before obtaining permanent accommodation.
- Target of bullying at school.
- Acquiring competence in English is crucial to adjusting to life in the UK.
- High expectations of responsibility for other family members including parents.
- Act as interpreters and advocates for parents often with limited knowledge of English themselves.

The framework does not include children (no space on the documents for children to contribute until they are over 10 years of age) and there is conflict around timescale compliance and taking the time to include children (see Calder and Horwath, 2000 for some suggestions on how to be more proactive in this regard).

The framework is woefully inadequate for children with a disability and the reasons for this have been articulated well by Margaret Kennedy and Jane Wonnacott in Chapter 10. Whilst the Department of Health proudly note the support of disability charities in the assessment framework, it is now clear that they did so without any knowledge of the timescales or the inappropriateness of the recording forms in assessing the needs of disabled children and their families. The strength of feeling is high and we have seen the emergence of amended core assessment records to cover this group.

The framework creates a climate and culture where professional inclusion may become more problematic (see the obstacles to working together set out earlier in this chapter).

The recording forms: to guide recording, assessment or both?

There are a number of concerns emerging relating to the usefulness or otherwise about the purpose of the forms. If they are used as a guide to the conduct of individual assessments then they fail as the variety of different situations necessitates a specific rather than a vague or generalised structure. They might otherwise be seen as a document simply to record the assessment deemed appropriate by the social worker utilising their professional judgement. This might be helpful if the need to produce separate records of contacts is dispensed with.

Regan (2001) explored why the forms accompanying the framework hinder rather than help effective front-line work. She argued that managers and workers have been bracing themselves for yet another practice and organisation innovation in a climate of staff shortages, backlogs of unallocated work and the demand for social workers to attend compulsory post-qualifying training.

'Far from producing clarity and reducing uncertainty, new models of reform tend to produce a peculiar sort of unreason where organisational arrangements and procedures emerging from government reform bear little resemblance to situations routinely dealt with by social workers ... (the) framework ... presents social work agencies with yet another simulated model which prescribes structures of action in an idealised world and not in the grim complicated reality of the real world. In 'assessment world' social workers and other professionals are told how to plan for assessment – 11 steps (3.38) carry out the assessment eight steps (3.39) how to communicate with children – five steps (3.42). Embedded in the implementation of these 'steps' is social work the likes of which could only exist in fantasy ...'

(Regan: 2001).

Fragmented framework: where do you go for what?

The worker has to be familiar with the entire package (see Figure 17 above) if they are to have any chance of working within the guidelines. For example, in the assessment framework main text (DoH, 2000) it reproduces the developmental charts of Mary Sheridan (from 'the orange book') in the 1960s, thus suggesting that they should be used. However, in the training pack (The NSPCC and The University

Figure 17: The new assessment framework: a visual guide.

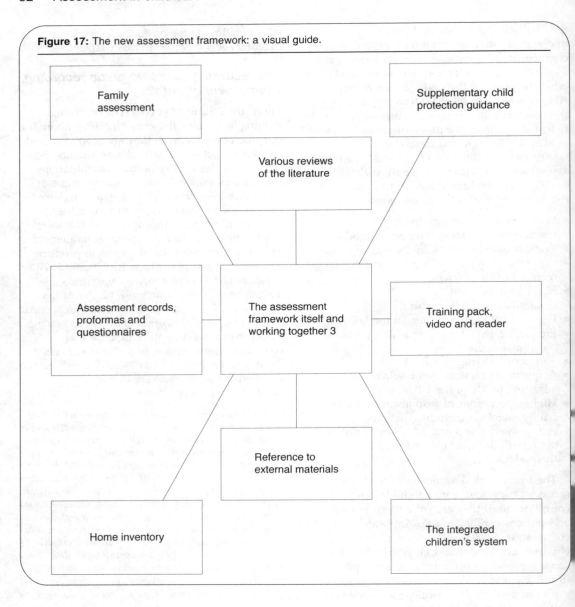

of Sheffield, 2000) there is material that quite rightly points to the concerns about this model and it attempts to provide some alternatives such as child observation, Piaget etc. This is confusing when you read the entire package, but is more worrying when you consider that few workers have access to, or time to read and digest, all the materials.

There is little attention paid to sexual abuse and this is worrying given the fact that 'the orange book' it replaces was so inadequate in this area. It is also of questionable value in cases of serious physical abuse.

Two detailed supplementary sets of assessment guidance: HOME (for assessing parent–child interaction) and Family Assessment have emerged since the framework was issued to formally compensate from some of the deficiencies, but these require specialist training and are family therapy grounded.

Determining outcomes: but where is the guidance?

One of the most consistent concerns being expressed by government is the collection of information without using it constructively to formulate plans. There remains considerably more guidance in this area in the orange book (DoH, 1988) and sets workers up as they not only have to assemble an evidence-based assessment, but also an evidence-based outcome measurement. The one excellent contribution comes in the form of Horwath and Morrison (2000) that addresses motivation, resistance and the model of change. These are essential building blocks to considering outcomes, but much more is needed. As I stated in Calder (1999);

> *'Outcome measures are important so that worker's can become aware of the impact of their actions and decisions on others. There needs to be a very clear differentiation between different kinds of outcome: professionals themselves need to develop outcomes so that they have clear expectations about what they are trying to achieve and also about what change has come about. This replaces the previous emphasis on process. Outcomes for young people are often set and reviewed by adults, and can be as simple as not re-abusing. We need to work with the knowledge that good outcomes to date have been linked primarily with parental commitment and a motivation to plan. Indeed, parental support for the work often provides a better mandate for the work than a legal one.'*

I strongly recommend reference to Parker et al. (1991) on looked-after children for an excellent discussion of such points.

What is deeply concerning about the assessment framework package is the overwhelming focus on compliance with timescales and completion of documentation rather than the outcomes for the child, which are noticeably absent.

The Department of Health (2001) guidance for co-ordinated service planning for vulnerable children and young people states clearly that their aim is to ensure that children and young people achieve the best possible outcomes. They provide a framework which shows how different planning requirements can be related and feed into each other. It proposes that planning activity can be unified within a consensus of shared objectives and agreed targets for improving the well-being of vulnerable children. This advisory guidance is issued jointly by the DoH, DfEE, DETR, HO, DCMS, HMT and Cabinet Office. It expects Chief Executives of Councils with Social Services Responsibilities, Local Education Authorities, and NHS bodies will act on its recommendations through joint planning. They

do note that the plans and the planning are important only insofar as they deliver better outcomes.

Adams (2001) in his report of SSI Inspections notes that attention to detail and resources are central to attaining outcomes. In his analysis, he found that the start of the assessment process be attended to appropriately as this was highly influential in determining the success of the overall outcome.

The reformulation

This chapter has highlighted concerns with the framework for assessment as introduced by the government, summarised in Figure 18 overleaf. These need exposing as a preface to remedial implementation strategies being mobilised. It is concerning that if we have a flawed framework, then workers have an uphill struggle to develop materials and skills to add flesh to the bones. The government have sketched an incomplete picture that they now want us to colour in. Figure 19 below embraces the worker as central to the process and with it interactive dimensions between the constituent parts of the framework.

Middleton (1997) has produced two useful tables for considering good and bad assessment practice (see Figures 20 and 21).

What is concerning is that the assessment framework does have the potential to lean workers towards the bad practice table, and their fear of reprisal for non-compliance and the lack of time for reflection will guide their interventions rather than them opting for a professionally balanced judgement. If we have a flawed skeletal framework, then how can we expect workers to add flesh to the bones?

What next?

At the time of writing this chapter, the Department of Health are moving swiftly to an integrated children's system aimed at providing an assessment, planning, intervention and reviewing model for all children in need under the Children Act 1989 (DoH, 2000c). Its development will bring together the assessment framework and Looking After Children System, so that the dimensions in the assessment framework will be common to work with all children in need and their families. It is designed to ensure that assessment, planning and decision-making leads to good outcomes for children. It will be interesting to see the process of consultation and implementation if the local

Figure 18: Summary of main concerns.

Limitations	Omissions	Conflicts
• There is no visual representation of any interaction between the three sides of the triangle.	• The centrality of the worker in the process: in terms of engagement, managing resistance, motivation and co-operation.	• No substantial evidence base in many areas of the work, such as children and young people who sexually abuse.
• The framework doesn't address circumstances such as serious physical abuse and sexual abuse.	• The triangle slices the fourth side off the ecological framework (society) and also misses out the two interactive components (meso- and exo-systems).	• Broadening remit of the work at a time when social services are narrowing down their remit through the production of thresholds for the provision of a social work service.
• The framework is very negative in that it says at one level it wants to move beyond the old model of reacting prescriptively in procedures to messages from child abuse tragedies, to a very loose framework that offers little guidance, promotes the use of professional judgement, but reinforces the negative findings of SSI inspections and says it will still not excuse workers if they 'get it wrong'.	• The child is too uni-dimensional and there is no reference on how to help the child engage with the process or to the issue of children's rights.	• The move to professional judgement by professionals but in the knowledge that they will be pilloried when they 'get it wrong'.
• The timescales set out are inserted as a response to allegations of drift, but they do not allow for trust to be built between either social worker and family, or social worker and other professionals either before or during the core assessment period. This is short-sighted since the dimensions of motivation, resistance and co-operation are interactive ones.	• There is no reference to the term risk assessment. There is a view that this is linked with Section 47 investigations and this is in conflict with the move to Section 17 work. This de-skills workers who have invested a great deal in using the concept. It also suggests a failure by the DOH to grasp the term in its entirety. It needs to weigh strengths against weaknesses to determine risk levels and whether this is manageable, and this is the essence of what the framework endeavours to achieve. This is in contrast to the development of more sophisticated and research-based risk assessment tools in the field of sexual abuse.	• Requirements of the Data Protection Act (1998) and the move towards a more needs-led assessment approach.
• The new working together and the assessment framework are being sold as partner documents, both moving us towards needs-led assessments (Section 17) from Section 47 investigations. This is not a seamless process and in fact there is a strong case to be made that the documents do not succeed in this goal. In fact, the system is moving in the opposite direction. At a time in which there are acute resource constraints upon social services departments, they are developing and implementing strict thresholds for service		• The complex and fragmented nature of the framework balanced against the need for operational clarity, particularly in light of the strict timescales.
• Provision that will maintain the status quo, in that the priority will be statutory duties and little or no focus for children in need, never mind prevention.		• Strict timescales for social workers when the DOH cannot meet their own deadlines for the publication of key materials.
• The documents take us back 10 years in terms of developing effective ways of working with parents and children, given that the over-focus on timescales precludes essential stages of the engagement process.	• There is no mention of the criminal process and thus we have a stand-alone document that ignores parallel documentation being developed in the criminal justice system, such as ASSET.	• The requirement for an evidence-based approach to the work set against a directive from legal advisors to stay clear of research in the court forum.

Figure 18: Continued.

Limitations	Omissions	Conflcts
• The framework firmly lays the primary and often exclusive responsibility for core assessments with the social services: failing to effectively model corporate responsibilities. • There is a naïve belief that assessments should be built on evidence-based materials. This assumes that there is an agreed and credible evidence base, and it does remove the critical analytical function needed to determine what information is both credible and useful in the work place. Research should not drive the work forward in isolation: that is dangerous. We know that practice is years ahead of research in the new areas we are required to deal with, such as young people who sexually abuse (see Calder, 1997; 1999c; 2001b and d).	• The focus of the guidance is principally on information collection and not on how, once collected, it should inform the decision-making process and planning. • A corporate approach to the construction and delivery of the assessment framework across government departments. • Clarity about what constitutes a good or bad assessment. • No model of the process of assessment as set out by Samra-Tibbets and Raynes (1999).	• The move towards greater skill use of workers in the assessment process against the shortage of qualified staff.

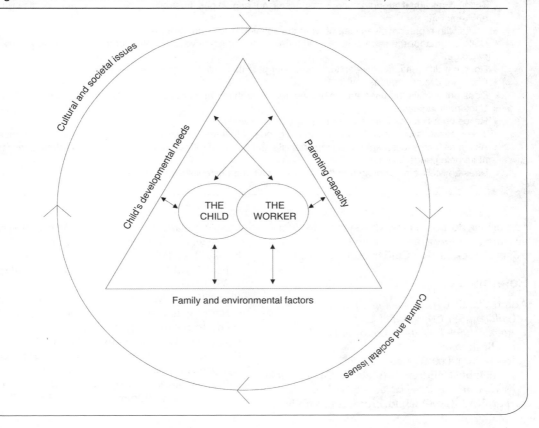

Figure 19: The assessment framework reformulated (adapted from Calder, 2000b).

Figure 20: Good assessment (adapted from Middleton, 1997).

Good assessment
- Starts with an open mind.
- Thinks about a range of options.
- Starts where the individual is involved and empowers the user as a partner.
- Does not put pressure on the user to choose the option the assessor wants or resources prescribe.
- Relates to their perceived problem and explores the reasons for it.
- Negotiations with the individual, and with existing and potential service providers, to find an acceptable and feasible solution.
- Puts the information in the context of its collection.
- Makes recommendations which relate to the information collected.
- Analyses the problem using the data.
- Makes arrangements for review.
- Explores the pros and cons of a range of solutions.
- Attends to how the user views the range of options and sees the match between options and the strengths of the user/circumstances.

Figure 21: Bad assessment (adapted from Middleton, 1997).

Bad assessment
- Diminishes the user.
- Lays difficulties at the door of the person, rather than having some appreciation of their circumstances.
- Leaves too much power in the hands of the assessor.
- Talks of individual strengths and weaknesses, not aspirations, frustrations, lack of resources or disabling environments.
- Starts with a preconceived idea of what the solution is, or what service may be required.
- Collects data for the sake of it, relating it neither to the perceived problem, nor the recommended care package.
- Does not differentiate between individuals but puts them all through the same process
- Does not explore options.
- Does not involve the user, and may even rely on a third party or observed data only.
- Uses no imagination.
- Relies on a tick box form as a crutch for unskilled workers.
- Takes services from a shelf or ready-made goods, rather than creates a custom-built individual response.
- Assumes the assessment has a long shelf-life and does not relate it to the time, place and circumstances of its being undertaken.
- Uses an MOT type approach to the person, against an established view of what is normal.

authorities do not believe this system to offer anything better or more streamlined than what exists at present (see Calder, forthcoming).

References

Adams, K. (2001) *Developing Quality to Protect Children: SSI Inspection of Children's Services August 1999–July 2000*. London: DOH Publications.

Adcock, M. (2000) Joined up Services for Vulnerable Children in England. *Clinical Child Psychology and Psychiatry*. 5: 4, 477–9.

Barker, R.W. (1996) Child Protection, Public Services and the Chimera of Market Force Efficiency. *Children and Society*. 10: 28–39.

Belsky, J. (1980) Child Maltreatment: an Ecological Integration. *American Psychologist*. 35: 320–35.

Blyth, E. and Milner, J. (1990) The Process of Inter-agency Work. In violence against children study group, *Taking child abuse seriously*. London: Unwin Hyman, 194–211.

Brechin, A. (2000) Introducing Critical Practice. In Brechin, A., Brown, H. and Eby, M.A. (Eds.) *Critical Practice in Health and Social Care*. London: Sage/Open University Press, 25–47.

Bronfenbrenner, U. (1977) Toward an Experimental Ecology of Human Development. *American Psychologist.* 32: 513–31.

Bullock, R., Gooch, D., Little, M. and Mount, K. (1998) *Research into Practice: Experiments in Development and Information Design.* Aldershot: Ashgate.

Calder, M. C. (1991) Child Protection: Core Groups: Beneficial or Bureaucratic? *Child Abuse Review.* 5: 2, 26–9.

Calder, M. C. (1992) *Towards an Ecological Formulation of System Maltreatment: Identifying the Casualties.* Unpublished MA dissertation, University of Lancaster.

Calder, M. C. (1993) Deferred Registration as a Deferred Partnership? *Panel news.* 6: 4, Dec. 12–21.

Calder, M. C. (1995) Child Protection: Balancing Paternalism and Partnership. *British Journal of Social Work.* 25: 6, 749–66.

Calder, M. C. (1999) A Conceptual Framework for Managing Young People Who Sexually Abuse: Towards a Consortium Approach. In Calder, M. C. (Ed.) *Working With Young People Who Sexually Abuse: New Pieces of the Jigsaw Puzzle.* Dorset: Russell House Publishing, 109–50.

Calder, M. C. (1999b) Towards Anti-oppressive Practice With Ethnic Minority Groups. In Calder, M. C. and Horwath, J. (Eds.) *Working for Children on the Child Protection Register: An Inter-agency Practice Guide.* Aldershot: Ashgate, 177–209.

Calder, M. C. (2000) *A Complete Guide to Sexual Abuse Assessments.* Dorset: Russell House Publishing.

Calder, M. C. (2000b) *Access to a Social Work Service in Salford: A Framework for Determining Eligibility.* Salford: Children in Need Project Implementation Team.

Calder, M. C. (2000c) *The New Assessment Framework: Advanced Practitioner Training.* Unpublished training pack. Salford CHIN and ACPC.

Calder, M. C. (2000d) *The New Assessment Framework: Origins, Content and Context.* Paper given to Child Care Programme, University of Salford.

Calder, M. C. (2001) Core Groups: A Review of the Literature. *Child Care in Practice.* 7: 1, 17–32.

Calder, M. C. (2001b) *Assessing Significant Harm: Research, Practice and Legal Issues.* Paper presented to Child Care Programme, University of Salford, April, 2000.

Calder, M. C. (2001c) Juveniles and Children Who Sexually Abuse: Frameworks for Assessment. (2nd Edn.) Dorset: Russell House Publishing.

Calder, M. C. (2001d) *The Assessment Framework and Safeguarding Children: A Critical Overview.* Paper presented to Child Care Programmes, University of Salford and University of Durham.

Calder, M. C. and Barratt, M. (1997) Inter-agency Perspectives on Core Group Practice. *Children and Society.* 11: 4, 209–21.

Calder, M. C. and Horwath, J. (1999) Policies and Procedures: A Framework for Working Together. In Calder, M. C. and Horwath, J. (Eds.) *Working for Children on the Child Protection Register: An Inter-agency Practice Guide.* Aldershot: Ashgate, 46–80.

Calder, M. C. and Horwath, J. (2000) Challenging Passive Partnerships in the Core Group Forum: Towards a More Proactive Approach. *Child and Family Social Work.* 5: 3, 267–77

Calder, M. C. with Peake, A. and Rose, K. (2001) *Mothers of Sexually Abused Children: A Framework for Assessment, Understanding and Support.* Dorset: Russell House Publishing.

Calder, M. C. and Waters, J. (1991) *Child Abuse or Child Protection: What's in a Name?* Paper presented to a one-day conference on child abuse for the Association of Psychological Therapies, University of York, 18 June 1991.

Calder, M.C. (forthcoming) Out of the frying pan and into the fire? The emergence of the Integrated Children's System.

Carson, D. (1994) Dangerous People: Through a Broader Concept of 'Risk' and 'Danger' to Better Decisions. *Expert Evidence.* 3: 2 21–69.

Caulkin, S. (2001) On Target for Destruction. *The Observer.* 5th Aug.

Charles, M. and Stevenson, O. (1990) *Multidisciplinary is Different!* Nottingham: University of Nottingham.

Cleaver, H. and DOH (2000) *Assessment Recording Forms.* London: The Stationery Office.

Coleman, H. (1997) Gaps and Silences: The Culture and Adolescent Sex Offenders. *Journal of Child and Youth Care.* 11: 1, 1–13.

Compton, B.R. and Galaway, B. (1999) *Social Work Processes.* (6th Edn.) Pacific Grove, CA: Brooks/Cole Publishing Company.

Corby, B. (1995) Inter-professional Co-operation and Inter-agency Co-ordination. In Wilson, K. and James, A. (Eds.) *The Child Protection Handbook.* London: Bailliere Tindall, 211–26.

Dartington Social Research Unit (1998) *Towards a Common Language.* Totnes, Devon: Dartington Social Research Unit.

DoH et al. (1999) *Working Together to Safeguard Children: A Guide to Inter-agency Working Arrangements to Safeguard and Promote the Welfare of Children.* London: The Stationery Office.

DfEE (2001a) *Children's Fund: Part One Guidance.* London: Children and Young People's Unit.

DfEE (2001b) *Children's Fund: Part Two Guidance.* London: Children and Young People's Unit.

DfEE/DoH (2000) *Guidance on the Education of Children and Young People in Public Care.* London: The Stationery Office.

DiClemente, C. (1991) Motivational Interviewing and the Stages of Change. In Miller, W. and Rollnick, S. (Eds.) *Motivational Interviewing.* London: Guilford Press.

DoH (1988) *Protecting Children: A Guide for Social Workers Undertaking a Comprehensive Assessment.* London: HMSO.

DoH (1991) *Working Together Under The Children Act 1989: A Guide to Arrangements for Inter-agency Co-operation for the Protection of Children from Abuse.* London: HMSO.

DoH (1995) *Child Protection: Messages from Research.* London: HMSO.

DoH (1995b) *The Challenge of Partnership.* London: HMSO.

DoH (1998) *Quality Protects: Transforming Children's Services.* LAC (98) 28. 11 Nov.

DoH (1998b) *Modernising Social Services.* London: The Stationery Office.

DoH (1999) *Framework for the Assessment of Children in Need and their Families.* Consultation draft. London: HMSO.

DoH (1999b) *Children in Need Guidance: Second Instalment.* London: DoH.

DoH (2000) *Children's Services Planning: Draft New Guidance.* London: DoH Social Care Group.

DoH (2000b) Data Protection Act 1998: Guidance to social services. London: DoH Publications.

DoH (2000c) *Integrated Children's System. Briefing Paper No1.* London: DoH.

DoH (2000d) Personal social services current expenditure in England: 1999–2000. London: DoH.

DoH (2001) *Fair Access to Care Services.* London: TSO. Also accessible from www.DoH.gov.uk/scg/facs

DoH et al. (2000) *Framework for the Assessment of Children in Need and Their Families.* London: HMSO.

DoH (2001) *Co-ordinated Service Planning for Vulnerable Children and Young People in England.* London: TSO.

Donnelly, A. (2001) *Recognising Risk and its Importance in Social Care Assessments of Children and Families.* Unpublished Project Report for the Post Graduate Certificate in managing public services. University of Birmingham: School of Public Policy.

Drury Hudson, J. (1997) A Model of Professional Knowledge for Social Work Practice. *Australian Social Work.* 50: 3, 35–44.

Garbarino, J. (1977) The Human Ecology of Child Maltreatment: A Conceptual Model for Research. *Journal of Marriage and the Family.* 39: 721–35.

Hallett, C. (1995) *Inter-agency Co-ordination in Child Protection.* London: HMSO.

Hendry, E. and Horwath, J. (2000) Can we Talk? *Community Care.* 2–8th Sept. 26–27.

Hill, M. (Ed.) (1999) *Effective Ways of Working with Children and their Families.* London: Jessica Kingsley.

Hood, S. (1997) The Purchaser/Provider Separation in Child and Family Social Work: Implications for Service Delivery and for the Role of the Social Worker. *Child and Family Social Work.* 2: 25–35.

Horwath, J. and Morrison, T. (2000) Assessment of Parental Motivation to Change. In Horwath, J. (Ed.) *The Child's World: Assessing Children in Need.* Reader. London: DoH, NSPCC and The University of Sheffield.

Howard, H. (2001) The Children Act and Human Rights. *Solicitors Journal,* 6th July, 626–7.

Ivanoff, A., Blythe, B. and Tripodi, T. (1994) *Involuntary Clients in Social Work Practice.* NY: Aldine de Gruyter.

Jordan, B. (2000) *Social Work and the Third Way: Tough Love as Social Policy.* London: Sage Publications.

Katz, I. (1997) *Current Issues in Comprehensive Assessment.* London: NSPCC.

Kilkelly, U. (2001) *The Human Rights Act 1998 and Children: Part 2.* London: National Children's Bureau Highlight no.183.

Lees, S. (1994) Talking About Sex in Sex Education. *Gender and Education.* 6: 3, 281–92.

Loxley, A. (1997) *Collaboration in Health and Welfare: Working With Difference.* London: Jessica Kingsley Publishers.

MacDonald, G. (2001) *Effective Interventions or Child Abuse and Neglect: An Evidence-based Approach to Planning and Evaluating*

Interventions. Chichester: John Wiley and Sons.

Maddock, J.W. and Larson, N. (1995) *Incestuous Families: An Ecological Approach to Understanding and Treatment*. NY: WW Norton and Company.

Margetts, T. (1998) Establishing Multi-agency Working with Sex Offenders: Setting up to Succeed. *NOTA News*. 25: 27–38.

Mathews, F. (1997) The Adolescent Sex Offender Field in Canada: Old Problems, Current Issues and Emerging Controversies. *Journal of Child and Youth Care*. 11: 1, 55–62.

McBeath, G. and Webb, S. (1990) Child Protection Language as Professional Ideology in Social Work. *Social Work and Social Sciences Review*. 2: 2, 122–45.

Middleton, L. (1997) *The Art of Assessment*. Birmingham: Venture Press.

Miller, W. and Rollnick, S. (1991) *Motivational Interviewing: Preparing People to Change Addictive Behaviour*. NY: Guilford Press.

Morrison, T. (1991) Change, Control and the Legal Framework. In Adcock, M., White, R. and Hollows, A. (Eds.) *Significant Harm: Its Management and Outcome*. London: Significant publications, 85–100.

Morrison, T. (1995) *Learning, Training and Change in Child Protection Organisations*. Keynote presentation to the National Child Protection Trainers conference, 15 March.

Morrison, T. (1996) Partnership and Collaboration: Rhetoric and Reality. *Child Abuse and Neglect*.20: 2, 127–40.

Morrison, T. (1997) Emotionally Competent Child Protection Organisations: Fallacy, Fiction or Necessity? In Bates, J., Pugh, R. and Thompson, N. (Eds.) *Protecting Children: Challenges and Change*. Aldershot: Arena, 193–211.

Morrison, T. (1998) Partnership, Collaboration and Change Under the Children Act. In Adcock, M. and White, R. (Eds.) *Significant Harm: Its Management and Outcome*. (2nd Edn.). Croydon, Surrey: Significant Publications, 121–47.

Morrison, T. (1998b) Managing Risk: Learning our Lessons. *NOTA News*. 25: 3–17.

NHS Executive (1999) *Protecting and Using Patient Information: A Manual for Caldicott Guardians*. London: NHS Executive.

NHS Executive (2000) *Information Sharing Protocols*. London: NHS Executive.

Parker, R., Ward, H., Jackson, S., Aldgate, J. and Wedge, P. (1991) *Looking After Children:*

Assessing Outcomes in Child Care. London: HMSO.

Prochaska, J.O. and DiClemente, C.C. (1982) Transtheoretical Therapy: Toward a More Integrative Model of Change. *Psychotherapy, Theory, Research and Practice*. 19: 276–88.

Prochaska, J.O. and DiClemente, C.C. (1986) Towards a Comprehensive Model of Change. In Miller, W.N. and Heather, N. (Eds.) *Treating Addictive Behaviours: Processes of Change*. NY: Plenum Press, 3–27.

Rai, G.S. (1994) Complexity and Co-ordination in Child Welfare Agencies. *Administration in Social Work*. 18: 1, 87–105.

Ramchandani, P., Joughin, C. and Zwi, M. (2001) Evidence-based Child and Adolescent Mental Health Services: Oxymoron or Brave New Dawn? *Child Psychology and Psychiatry Review*. 6: 2, 59–64.

Regan, S. (2001) When Forms Fail the Reality Test. *Community Care*, 25–31 Oct. 36–7.

Rickford, F. (2001a) A Knowing Silence. *Community Care*. 12–18th July, 22–3.

Rickford, F. (2001b) Make the Evidence Count. *Community Care*. 12–18th April, 18–9.

Roberts, R.E., Abrams, L. and Finch, J.R. (1973) 'Delinquent' Sexual Behaviour Among Adolescents. *Medical Aspects of Human Sexuality*. 7: 1, 162–83.

Sackett, D., Rosenberg, W., Gray, J. and Haynes, B. (1996) Evidence-based Medicine: What it is and what it isn't. *British Medical Journal* 312: 71–2.

Samra-Tibbets, C. and Raynes, B. (1999) Assessment and Planning. In Calder, M. C. and Horwath, J. (Eds.) *Working for Children on the Child Protection Register: An Inter-agency Practice Guide*. Aldershot: Arena, 81–117.

Schofield, G. and Thoburn, J. (1996) *Child Protection: The Voice of the Child in Decision-Making*. London: IPP.

Seabury, B.A. (1985) The Beginning Phase: Engagement, Initial Assessment and Contracting. In Laird, J. and Hartman, A. (Eds.) *A Handbook of Child Welfare: Context, Knowledge and Practice*. NY: Free Press, 335–59.

Sharland, E., Jones, D., Aldgate, J., Seal, H. and Croucher, M. (1996) *Professional Intervention and Child Sexual Abuse*. London: HMSO.

Shaw, B. (2001) *Awareness and Confidence: The Two Keys to Dealing With Human Rights Act*. London Borough of Ealing: Social Services and Education.

Smale, G., Tuscon, G., Biehal, N. and Marsh, P. (1993) *Empowerment, Assessment, Care*

Management and the Skilled Worker. London: HMSO.

Stainton-Rogers, W. (1989) Effective Co-operation in Child Protection Work. In Morgan, S. and Righton, P. (Eds.) *Child Care: Concerns and Conflicts: A reader.* London: Hodder and Stoughton, 82–94.

Stevenson, O. (1989) Multi-disciplinary Work in Child Protection. In Stevenson, O. (Ed.) *Child Abuse: Public Policy and Professional Practice.* London: Harvester Wheatsheaf, 173–203.

Taylor, C. and White, S. (2001) Knowledge, Truth and Reflexivity: The Problem of Judgement in Social Work. *Journal of Social Work.* April.

NSPCC and The University of Sheffield (2000) *The Child's World: Assessing Children in Need. Training and Development Pack.* London: The NSPCC.

Thoburn, J., Lewis, A. and Shemmings, D. (1995) *Paternalism or Partnership? Family Involvement in the Child Protection Process.* London: HMSO

Valios, N. (2001) Running on Empty. *Community Care.* 9–15 Aug. 20–1.

Valios, N. (2001b) Blame Game. *Community Care.* 15–21st Feb. 18–9.

Vince, R. and Martin, L. (1993) Inside Action Learning. *Management Education and Development.* 24: 2, 205–15.

Youth Justice Board (2000) *The ASSET Forms.* London: Home Office.

Chapter Three

Making Professional Judgements in the Framework for the Assessment of Children in Need and Their Families

Dr Anne Hollows

Making professional judgements lies at the heart of the application of the 'Framework for the Assessment of Children in Need and their Families'. This represents a significant shift in the relative importance of the professional task compared with the previous dominance of procedures, offering the potential to re-define social work as a professional occupation. This chapter explores what we mean by professional judgements and when judgements are made. It goes on to discuss theories about judgement making and shows how this should influence the sort of judgements we make. Finally it considers why judgement making represents a substantial challenge to practice with children and families. It is based on the literature of judgement making in a wide range of social policy settings and on the findings from a study of social work judgements in work with children and families.

What do we mean by judgement?

The precise meaning of judgement is difficult to establish in any professional process. For most researchers, as well as practitioners, it is entwined with the process of decision making. It is important to distinguish between the processes because, as we shall see later, when decisions are made, they are not always prefaced by judgement. Goldstein (1997) went some way to unpacking the distinction between judgement and decision making in saying that *judgement* described the ways in which people 'integrate multiple, probabilistic, potentially conflicting cues to arrive at an understanding of the situation' as opposed to *decision making* in which people 'choose what to do next in the face of uncertain consequences and conflicting goals' (p4).

This definition of judgement making, bounded neither by the scale of the question at issue, nor by any time frame, provides a helpful way of distinguishing the phenomenon of judgement making from decision making. In making judgements, we are combining different kinds of information from different sources and

sometimes, with only limited guarantees of truth. We expect social workers to make a judgement when there is a need to know how to proceed in a case. When social workers make a judgement, therefore, the starting point must be the collection of information, or data, about people and situations through their professional observations and enquiries, as well as from past information and information held by other professionals. We then expect that the social worker will analyse (or take apart) and synthesise (or re-assemble in a succinct way) the data, in order to reach an understanding of the situation. It is that judgement, or understanding, of the situation that is carried forward into the decision-making arena. Once at the decision making stage, the judgement will be a hostage to fortune as a range of conflicting values, experiences and professional imperatives come into play (see Dalgleish, Chapter 5). The implications of this are that when mistakes are described as 'errors of judgement' they may in fact be errors of decision making; a point we will return to later in the chapter.

The word 'judgement' in vernacular usage has connotations of dilemma, choice, and a fine line between competing views, as with the expression 'a judgement call' (drawn from tennis line calls). Judgement also implies a sense of wisdom (again in a close situation) as in the expression 'the judgement of Solomon'. But judgement also implies a level of individual responsibility, as in the expression 'to act upon one's own judgement'. 'Good judgement' is obviously an asset, while 'errors of judgement' are to be avoided. The diversity of shades of meaning attached to 'judgement' in the social work literature reflects that in the wider world. Within the social work literature it is suggested that judgement is a compilation of knowledge, skills, values and experience: a mixture of professional authority, including knowledge, experience and expertise; coupled with professional autonomy, meaning a capacity for independent thought and action, is one suggestion (Youll and Walker, 1995). A further suggestion is that judgement is the determining factor in the combination of structured sets of competencies to meet the needs of a single case, by an individual practitioner (Jones and Joss, 1995). Judgement is inextricably linked with professional expertise: Benbenishty defines the expert social worker as one who has 'superior ability in making judgements and decisions' (Benbenishty, 1992, 599). Judgement is therefore, to some extent, shrouded in a professional mystique, and linked with the notion of expertise in professional knowledge. This implied balance between the wisdom stemming from practice and wisdom from the knowledge base of the profession is at the heart of the theories about judgement making. Written into the Framework for the Assessment of Children in Need and their Families is the precept that assessments should be based on professional judgement and grounded in the evidence base.

When do we make judgements?

As noted above, judgements are generally made when we need to know how to proceed in a case. That means that in practice with children and families they are often made close to decision making points, such as intake, type of investigation, child protection registration or de-registration, care proceedings and permanency planning or re-unification. These decision points are often known as thresholds (Brandon et al., 1999), as they signify a point of transition to a different level of service. That means that the focus of the decision is on whether the improvement or deterioration of circumstances and responses in the case merits the decision in question: does the case need registration, for example, or can the children be returned home. In an Australian study, Scott has shown that judgements based around threshold points tend to focus on the information needed to make the decision (Scott, 1998). She noted that the judgement tended to incorporate the 'evidence necessary for statutory intervention . . . sometimes based on second guessing the Children's Court magistrate' (p85). As a result, while the judgement may include compelling evidence for a decision, it often achieves this at the expense of the more descriptive material which provides a sense of the overall issues in the case and the broad strategy for responding to the issues. This can pose problems both for the immediate decision, and for reviews of earlier decisions. If the focus of the judgement is

'what to decide to do', there may be only limited evidence to assist subsequent decision to change course, for example de-registration of registered child protection cases (Murray, 2001). The close links between procedural guidance and the thresholds outlined above also work against the development of analytical thinking and judgement making. Murray's (2001) study found many of the features identified in the past (Farmer and Owen, 1995) were present in the judgements presented to child protection conferences, in particular, lists of events instead of an analysis of issues.

In the best practice, judgements are made continuously, as recommended in the Framework for the Assessment of Children in Need and their Families. Of particular focus in such practice is the circular process whereby judgements about issues are followed by judgements about strategy and linked to a regular evaluation progress in the case. This model of practice, developed within the *Alameda Project* in California (Stein et al., 1978) provides clarity for social worker and service user alike. It enables a framework for practice in which a conversation could recur between worker and services user along the lines of:

> *This is what we are concerned about . . .*
> *This is what has to change . . .*
> *This is how we are going to help you to change . . .*
> *This is what may happen if you do not or cannot change.*

Alongside these major judgements, we make smaller, seemingly insignificant judgements on a day to day basis. These often amount to adjustments in our cumulative thinking or practice in a case. While this sort of process occurs in almost every aspect of professional and business activity, it is important to recognise that, over a period of time, such adjustments can result in a change on judgement about a case. Regular and systematic reviews of current thinking in relation to agreed prior judgements are an important way of checking on what I have termed 'judgement creep'. This may indicate that judgements are based on professional reflection and highly sensitive to small changes, but it may also signify a lack of control in the direction of a case.

How are judgements made?

The problem of error has come to dominate thinking and research about judgement making, with the expression 'error of judgement' offered as an explanation for most of the disasters within child welfare practice as well as in the wider world. Hammond describes the process of judgement making as one in which uncertainty is irreducible, error is inevitable and consequent injustice is unavoidable (Hammond, 1996) – not in every case but at least some of the time. While the error we tend to fear the most is that of failing to recognise a potentially dangerous situation, this is not the only concern. Jones notes the importance of studying false positive cases of child maltreatment 'as they can lead to great suffering. They have the potential to lead to unnecessary separation of child and parent, parental imprisonment, loss of job and reputation, quite apart from substantial distress to all concerned' (Jones, 2001). That does not mean we should avoid judgement making: to do so would be to make decisions without considering evidence. But it does mean that we should address judgement making as a serious task, and one which needs to be undertaken in full knowledge of the potential problems and pitfalls, including the possibility of error.

Theorists of judgement are, in general, polarised in their views of how judgements are best made. At one extreme are those who consider the judgement process lies at the heart of professional practice and combines the mystique of professional expertise with reflection on, and in, knowledge and practice (Schon, 1983). This approach to judgement making is known in the literature as *intuition*. At the other extreme are those who consider that judgement is far too complex a process to be trusted to the wit of individuals (Eddy, 1988). For these theorists, judgements require detailed and actuarially based formulae to provide rigour and avoid the many potential errors and biases (Kahnemann et al., 1982). Such an approach is sometimes described as *technical rationality*. This debate about judgement styles mirrors many of the tensions within social work today, including the pursuit of certainty (see, for example, Parton, 1998) and the nature of evidence for practice (see for example Sheldon, 2001; Webb, 2001).

Social workers, like other practitioners in clinical situations work on cues – aural, visual or previous test results. From these they make a mental model of the situation and decide how to apply their skills to it (Rouse and Morris, 1986). They then monitor the situation as they gain new information and insights and move towards making a judgement, and planning interventions (MacCrimmon and Wehrung, 1986). But there is evidence (Munro, 1995; 1996; 1998; Nurius and Gibson, 1990) that social workers are as prone as judgement makers in any other field to a number of heuristic errors (Kahnemann et al., 1982; Plous, 1993).

Nurius and Gibson, applying Kahnemann and Tversky's work to social work, consider that it is cognitive bias, in a variety of forms, that leads to distorted judgements (Nurius and Gibson, 1990). Plous has pointed to the ways in which experts may further contribute to error, by being unchallenged simply because they are experts (Plous, 1993). Munro, who has reviewed judgement making in a number of UK child death cases, helpfully identifies the particular issue of confirmatory bias in judgement making (Munro, 1995; 1996; 1998; 1999). Munro's work enables us to see that whatever the mechanism for bias, it is the tendency to seek confirming evidence for our beliefs within the judgement process that is most likely to lead to error. With this guidance, it is possible to suggest that the danger of making errors is to some extent linked with judgements being made alone, and unchallenged.

It is necessary to explore the theory of judgement making further to find some pointers to the potential for reconciling these apparently opposing ideas about professional judgement, in which the analytical framework of science is pitched against the art of intuitive practice.

The judgement making process

Hammond, a psychologist who has studied judgement for many years, was not convinced that the detailed technical rational approach of judgement making was error free either, and cited the scientist Richard Feynman's investigation into the Challenger space disaster as a prime example (Hammond, 1996, 35–9). He suggested that a reliance on technical rational approaches to judgement making, while generally accurate, could lead to sizeable errors simply by its very reliance on system and procedure at the expense of the sort of adjustments and allowances possible in intuitive reasoning. Fundamental to Hammond's reasoning was the notion that there are different kinds of judgements, made under different conditions and, therefore, applying different approaches to judgement making. The key aspects of difference noted by Hammond were

Figure 1: The Cognitive Continuum (adapted from Hammond, 1987).

Mode of judgement	Specific features
Intuitive judgements	Involve rapid, unconscious data processing; combine available information by 'averaging' it; low consistency; moderate accuracy.
Peer aided judgements, System aided judgement, Quasi experiment, Controlled trial	Involve intermediate, mixed or alternating features of analytical and intuitive judgements.
Analytical judgements	Involve slow conscious and consistent thought; usually quite accurate (with occasional large errors); apply more complex organising principles.

the time available, the kinds of knowledge available and the judgement task itself. He sought therefore to harness the potential of the extreme theorists by developing a *cognitive continuum* of judgement making (Hammond, 1987; 1996).

The *continuum* recognises that there are legitimately different approaches to judgement making from the rapid, on the spot processing of information and knowledge, known as intuition, to the detailed and analytical approach, sometimes using a form of experimentation. Hammond noted that clinicians would use a mode of judgement making which falls somewhere between the two points. This is based on the structural characteristics of the identified task, and the resources, particularly time, available. A less well structured task will lead to a more intuitive approach while a better structured task will lead to a more analytical or scientific approach. Less time available will lead to a more intuitive approach, while with greater time available we are more likely to apply analytical reasoning to the process. Six points are identified on this continuum: intuitive judgements, peer-aided judgements, system-aided judgements, quasi experiments, controlled trials and analytical judgements. Specific performance features apply to each judgement approach.

Unlike some authors in the field, who find no place for 'intuitive' judgement making (see for example (Kahnemann et al., 1982, Nurius and Gibson, 1990), Hammond recognises that some judgements have to be made, or at least started, in this way. He suggests that 'intuitive' judgement is appropriate, for example, where time scales are short, and where there is a high level of visual information in the presenting material. On the contrary, a clearly structured

task, with time available, will be an ideal situation for an analytical judgement. In between these points there will be a range of features coming into play. Wherever possible even the fastest judgements will benefit from some peer or management consultation. Reference to system aids will be available if they are the right aids for the task. Being able to try out ideas during judgement making will also be valuable, where time permits. What defines the expert judgement maker, according to Hammond (1996), is their ability to recognise the judgement task and to match it with the appropriate judgement style. They should also be able to articulate, clearly, the basis for their judgement. In short, this is just what is required by an Assessment Framework that envisages different kinds of judgements at different stages of the process. The greatest threat to the accuracy of judgements is likely therefore to be in the mismatch of task and judgement process.

In Hammond's terms there are three problems for the practitioner who is embarking upon judgement making:

- Should analytical or intuitive thinking, or a mixture be used in a particular clinical situation?
- How does the practitioner discover which kind of thinking to use?
- How is the appropriate thinking performed as well as possible?

Complex task structures
These involve cases where there are many relevant cues containing considerable relevant information, or where there are cues that may easily be predicted from each other an intuitive approach will generally be induced. Where a simple organising principle is known to apply

to the analysis of information, then again an intuitive approach will be likely to be applied. If it were known that the process of combining evidence is more complicated then more analytical reasoning would apply.

Ambiguity of content

Ambiguity of content induces a different cognitive approach. Here, prior knowledge and experience of techniques and their outcomes are critical to the selection of the mode of thinking. Where a complex organising principle is known to be available it is generally used. Where the circumstances and information are not those usually encountered, it may be harder to identify a particular organising principle. At this point intuition is generally relied upon, because the practitioner does not know how to weight and average the available cues.

Presentation of the task

Hammond's starting point is that tasks may be presented in ways that appropriately induce intuition, analytical reasoning or points between these poles. Hammond (1987) suggests that presentation in the form of a clear series of subtasks will lead to a more analytical response. He suggests that pictorial presentations of information, such as X-rays, or photographs of injuries, induce intuitive responses whereas quantitative data, presented objectively, induces a more analytical response. The identity of the presenter of the task may also influence the way the task is presented through the judgement making process. Research into the operation of the child protection system (Gibbons et al., 1995) showed that responses to referrals are often based on short cuts to judgement arising from *who* the referral comes from, rather than *what* the referral is about.

Response time

The permitted, or available response time will also influence the approach to judgement making. The quicker the response time needed, the more likely a practitioner will be to apply intuitive, rather than analytical techniques. It is of particular relevance to social work where it is common to speak of the 'bombardment rate' of cases. Here again, the weaknesses of less than expert practice are evident in social work (Gibbons et al., 1995).

Knowledge

This leads to a final point about the style of judgement used, namely the extent of knowledge in the area. Where the practitioner is on unfamiliar ground, they may not be aware of the current state of knowledge, or of the potential to apply an analytical approach. Conversely, practitioners with greater knowledge will be more aware of the availability and applicability of analytical approaches. The desirable level of knowledge must go further, demonstrating the ability to be more critical in interpreting the findings of analytical assessments. Intuitive judgement making because of lack of knowledge is likely to generate errors, but so is the uncritical application of analytical tools such as standard tests and scales.

Hammond's approach to judgement making is underpinned by the notion that many situations involve *multiple, fallible indicators*. By this he means information about a number of issues which may have greater or lesser truth. Judgements involving multiple fallible indicators are likely to be best made at the intuitive end of the scale while those involving infallible indicators will be best made at the analytical end of the scale. But here we begin to see the real potential of Hammond's continuum. The picture may not remain constant in a case, whether for judgements in general, or for a single judgement because knowledge will change. This applies both to the level of knowledge we have about the facts in a case, and to the practitioner's awareness of knowledge within the broad field of research and theory. While the early judgements in a case may well be intuitive, therefore, as knowledge about the case and about the research increases, so a more analytical approach may come into play. Application of the cognitive continuum within a case, or within practice as a whole, therefore has a dynamic aspect. Using the Cognitive Continuum enables practitioners to harness a range of approaches to judgement making in order to ensure that the acknowledged goals of efficacy, accuracy and consistency can be promoted. There are, however, other factors at work in the context of practice that may limit the achievement of these goals.

The context of judgement making

The difficulty of working within a number of conflicting goals such as managing scarce resources, media involvement and workload management have all been noted in research on judgement making (Einhorn and Hogarth, 1981; Stewart, 1993). It has been suggested that we apply a hierarchy of responses under time pressure. Under slight pressure their subjects maintained their strategies but tried to process information faster; under medium pressure they began to narrow their focus; but under severe pressure they abandoned their approach in favour of shortcuts (Payne et al., 1988). In further work they noted that time pressure impacted upon the selection of optimal short cuts (Payne, 1990). This raises the question of how people choose approaches to judgement making, and raises the issue of how accuracy and effort may be traded off in the selection of a judgement process.

One of the most commonly used anecdotal expressions to describe social workers' daily experience is the 'bombardment rate'. This constant pressure of new and difficult situations means that judgement is taking place in the context of Dalgleish and Hollows (2003). This means that while they are trying to track cues for one judgement, the social worker's attention will constantly be subject to interference. The social worker handling more than one case may find themselves trying to track two cases together. A study based on drivers' responses showed that greater risks were taken when tasks were performed concurrently and that interference increased risk taking potential (Horswill and McKenna, 1991). While risk taking may not always be inappropriate, the links with both increased stress factors and increased risk taking behaviour would be a cause for concern.

The impact of stress on the judgement making process is complex (Hammond, 1996). He chooses to focus on the disruptions to the task as one of the major stressors. A notable contribution to this is the 'Conflict Theory of Decision Making' (Janis and Mann, 1977). They found that stress generated an inability to deal with the conflicts that interfere with, and sometimes limit, the capacity to make a judgement. They described a number of behavioural features in judgement makers, which may have a particular resonance for social workers. Of particular note are:

Unconflicted adherence, in which new risk is discounted and the current strategy maintained without change.
Unconflicted change, in which a suggested new course of action is adopted uncritically,

without evaluation of the effectiveness of any prior strategy.

Defensive avoidance, in which conflict is avoided by procrastination, shifting responsibility to someone else or constructing wishful rationalisations to bolster the least objectionable alternative. Each of these is associated with incomplete and sometimes biased evaluations of information.

Hypervigilance, characterised by a frantic searching for ways out of dilemmas. Combined with time pressure, this can lead the judgement maker to seize upon hastily contrived solutions that seem to promise immediate relief. Emotional excitement and limited attention mean that the full range of consequences are ignored. In its most extreme state, there may be vacillation between unpleasant alternatives and panic.

Vigilance, in which there is a painstaking search for relevant information, relevant information is assimilated in an unbiased manner and alternatives are carefully appraised before a judgement is made.

The problem of individual affect and the judgement process has also been noted (Isen 1993). Positive affect can influence thought processes so that positive memories are cued into the judgement process. It may influence motivation to ensure that the judgement maintains a positive state. But it may also make them more risk averse, not wishing to provoke circumstances that would change their mood. This links with the concept of 'the rule of optimism' in social work (Dingwall et al., 1983) which has been a concern in a number of child death enquiries (see Reder, Duncan and Grey, 1993 p90, for more detailed discussion). Isen (1993) goes some way to explaining this when she notes that even a mild positive affect may lead people to mobilise material in the mind in a way which relates positive cues effectively. Thus by its very diversity and extent, the positive material tends to outweigh the negative. Some of the consequences of positive affect may have more subtle impacts on the judgement process. The desire to maintain the state of positive affect promotes helpfulness, generosity, responsibility and friendliness – characteristics that may contribute to the quality of interaction between social worker and client in ways that can be beneficial to the judgement. Positive affect is also identified as contributing to the ability to plan and organise work effectively.

Errors of judgement

Within the range of approaches to judgement making identified in the literature, it is clear that there is a preoccupation with error. The work of correspondence theorists (Kahnemann et al., 1982) has noted, under experimental conditions, errors which have also been observed in social work practice (Nurius and Gibson, 1990; Reder, Duncan and Grey, 1993; Gibbons, 1995; Munro, 1998; O'Sullivan, 1999; Dalgleish and Hollows 2003). Nurius and Gibson suggest a number of forms that error may take in social workers' judgements. Like Janis and Mann (1977), Nurius and Gibson also note the effect of mood on memory and judgement. The problem here is whether we can reduce error through applying a particular approach to judgement making, or whether, as Hammond (1996) categorically states, error is inevitable when judgements involve so much uncertainty. If it is logically impossible to eliminate error, then the issue of confirmatory bias (Munro, 1998; O'Sullivan, 1999) which makes it hard for an error to be corrected, is of critical importance and steps to avoid or reduce error will need to focus on developing disconfirmatory approaches.

The work itself combines with the organisational and context issues to exacerbate stress and distress and each of these can be a contributor to practice difficulties. The coherence theorists generally equate the incidence of these difficulties with the tendency to use intuitive approaches to judgement making. O'Sullivan (1999) equivocates, suggesting that the test of intuition should be 'whether it represents the use of skill and sound knowledge or a quick, and often erroneous, substitute for substantive processing of information' (p92). What appears to be the most serious challenge in intuitive judgement making is precisely its attraction for Schon: its elusive qualities that make it hard to articulate, but may deny it the transparency that should be a part of social work encounters with service users (Healy, 1998).

A robust approach to judgement making must enable practitioners to harness a range of approaches to judgement making in order to ensure that efficacy, accuracy and consistence can be promoted. We turn, next, to a consideration of how this could work within the Framework for the Assessment of Children in Need and their Families.

Making judgements in practice

As we have already seen judgement can be differentiated from decision making. Alongside the framework for practice defined by the Children Act 1989, there is a continuum of social work interventions with children and families, from the point of first referral onwards. Where interventions incorporate suspicions about harm, practice is based upon guidance provided by the Department of Health, designed to support inter-professional working (Department of Health et al., 1999; 1991) . This guidance generates a series of thresholds which form judgement points, concerning both the current concerns in the situation and the response most likely to secure the protection and well-being of the child.

The sense of a sequence of events applies whether a case is beginning from scratch, or within the process of working with an existing case, whether as a result of new circumstances, the recognition of more serious concerns in a case, or indeed positive responses to interventions. But as we have already seen, judgements that focus on the decision required at the threshold often avoid consideration of the broader needs and strategies in the case (Scott, 1998). Rather than making judgements in the broader areas of the child and family's circumstances, the consequent needs and risk and how to manage them, the participants in Scott's study focused their judgements on meeting, or not meeting, the procedural requirements of the threshold. Scott suggests that the 'uncertainty and anxiety evoked in the worker by the complexity of cases may increase the attraction of a predetermined response set' (1998, p. 86). Although the 'either, or' judgement may be superficially attractive, it raises the possibility of inconsistency and conflict. Differing value bases within and between agencies can contribute to this, both directly and through the emotional stress that derives from anticipating regret about the decision because of different decision thresholds (Dalgleish, 2000).

Alongside the judgements that can be seen as informing the statutory 'backbone' of social work practice with children and families, there will be a range of issues upon which a social worker will be required to make decisions within their everyday practice. Judgement implies consideration and it is not always easy to see the extent to which these everyday decisions are informed by consideration. While major judgements may be subject to scrutiny in the multi-professional arena, or at least in supervision, these day-to-day decisions are the stuff of social work practice: the essence of the relationship-centred work for which social workers have been trained. Brandon et al. (1999) describe this sort of practice as 'tenacious'; a constant adjusting of balance in cases in order to nudge the work with families and children in the right direction. This could include the use of the social worker's time, for example, the re-arrangement of priorities in the face of an unanticipated crisis in another case, how long to wait for a parent who is late for an appointment, dropping in unexpectedly on a family when in the area. It could include subtleties in the management of the relationship between social worker and family: the tone of voice used, looks and glances. Day-to-day adjustments in the management of a case may also fall into this category: a marginal extension or reduction in contact arrangements, for example, or in the support provided by an ancillary worker. This resembles the judgement making process described in the 'React' model of MacCrimmon and Wehrung (1986) enabling a constant evaluation and re-evaluation of response in relation to desired goals.

While there may be little tangible evidence of the rationale for these day-to-day judgements (Fook, et al., 1997), it would be a mistake to assume that there is an absence of theoretical consideration (Mullaly, 1993; Thompson, 1995). The difficulty is in establishing the base line constructs that may have informed the almost subliminal theorising of the social worker: constructs that will inform the process of making these judgements (Milner and O'Byrne, 1998; Thompson, 1995). Here, the concept of reflection-in-action (Schon, 1988) is of critical importance. This is indeed the basis for the judgements made in day-to day practice. Sheppard (1995; 1998; 1999) describes this as 'practice wisdom'. Although Mullaly (1993) suggests that practice wisdom may be seen by social workers as an alternative to theory, Sheppard's work suggests that it is closer to a fusion of theory, values and experience: the expertise that for Schon (1988) justifies the high value placed on intuitive judgements. The strength, or weakness, of such judgements is in the balancing of theory (including law), values and experience in the context of a particular case. This, in turn, needs to be grounded in a clear sense of the stage the case is at, and the goals of activity in the case.

Stein, et al. discuss the idea of 'purposeful planning' and describe the day-to-day judgement making resulting from the repeated setting and reviewing of targets with service users as a critical part of the ongoing process in a case (Stein et al., 1978). Their study found, however, that where social workers were not clear what changes had to be brought about to achieve required goals, the day-to-day process lacked a coherent direction. As a consequence, its achievements were limited. Conversely, the development of judgements around a clear route map of action in a case could be translated into short term tasks and goals.

The longitudinal study undertaken by Fook and colleagues (see Fook et al., 1994; 1997; 2000) adds to this picture of rudderless practice the finding that purpose and process are rarely clearly articulated, even by experienced workers. It is possible to see the lack of articulation as either a cause or a consequence of the lack of direction. In the absence of clear goals for interventions, the lack of articulation of process makes it difficult to challenge or to contribute to the social worker's judgement making. This in turn creates problems both for effective management and for effective participation or partnership, whether by service users or by colleagues from other agencies.

An organising framework for judgements

How then are judgements to be made and with what purpose? From the theory and from my own study of practice in judgement making, there seem to be several distinct, but inter-related kinds of judgements which practitioners should be making in cases.

Holding judgements
Holding judgements may be made at any stage of work in a case where a quick decision is needed. Most often they occur in the initial stages of work or at a point of crisis. The dominant features of holding judgements are to ensure safety, to create stability, and to endeavour not to reduce options in the longer term judgement making process (Munro, 1997), incorporated with fending off the 'something must be done' principle. Holding judgements are often made in intake and assessment work and by Emergency Duty Teams. One EDT worker told me that 'the main part of our job is

not to do anything . . . it is to stick a piece of plaster over something and say ' pop and see the doctor in the morning and get it looked at properly' '. The characteristic features of holding judgements are of speedy judgements involving multiple fallible indicators which may or may not have a bearing on the case (Hammond, 1996). Many of these indicators come as information from others (for example teachers, foster carers), and checking out the integrity of the statements is limited by time. Therefore considerable trust is invested in the relationship between the informant and the social worker. That could mean that interpretations of the statements are coloured by previous knowledge of the competency of the informant. It may explain the differential values placed on statements from particular professionals and from non-professionals in the early stages of judgement making as discussed in Gibbons (1995). The process of judgement making is intuitive, supplemented by consultation with peers, especially where the case is at a formal investigation stage (Hammond, 1996). There is rarely the opportunity for the development of a hypothesising approach within the judgement making. The availability of resources can militate against options within the holding judgement by leaving little or no scope for negotiation, while the conscious attempt to avoid reduction of options offers some safeguards to these judgements. In a fast moving period in a case, however, a series of holding judgements may result in a sort of creeping judgement, when a case gradually moves so far from the originally intended path that options are categorically changed.

Issues judgements

Issues judgements lie at the heart of a social worker's activities in a case. These judgements require a clear assessment of all the factors in the case, with an analysis of the issues raised in terms of the children's needs and the parents ability to meet those needs, set in the context of the environment of the child and family (Jack, 1997) and bearing in mind both vulnerabilities and strengths (Adcock, 1998; Jones, 1998; Department of Health, 2000). They should take into account not only the presenting problem or incidents but also the underlying circumstances. The Assessment Framework requires such judgements to be based on careful gathering of information, leading to an evidence based analysis. As a task, therefore, it matches judgement processes at the analytical, rather than the intuitive, end of the cognitive continuum (O'Sullivan, 1999). That requires time to be available (Hammond, 1996).

Time is in short supply at the beginning stages of work in a case. Judgements at this stage do indeed depend on the rapid, intuitive processing of multiple fallible indicators (Hammond, 1996). This is also, of course the process which is most likely to attract heuristic errors (Nurius and Gibson, 1990). Where these errors are absorbed into the mind set a worker has for thinking about the case, judgements may indeed move a long way from accuracy.

In one case in my study, the issues judgement made by the local authority at an early stage was that the mother needed help with parenting. This was a standard 'diagnosis' which just happened to match the first line of response to the situation, one of the standard 'packages' of support for children in need cases (about which both Wilding and Thoburn (1997) and Schofield (1998) raise concerns). This judgement appeared to omit any recognition of the fact that her parenting with her older children had been satisfactory. As the social worker was eventually able to establish, the real problem lay in the particular relationship of mother and child (the 'meaning of the child' (Reder et al., 1993)) because the circumstances around his birth – a deteriorating relationship with the child's father – led to her recall of childhood abuse. Mother in this case responded badly to all the interventions *because the interventions were based on the wrong judgement*. But mother's poor response led to further judgements that she was unable to respond to interventions and a strategy that viewed permanent separation of mother and child as the best option. This is a graphic example of the sort of accumulation of error noted by Nurius and Gibson (1990). It is important to note that when she took over the case, the social worker's first step was not to accept these judgements at face value, but to develop alternative hypotheses about the situation, to which she added an intuitive judgement about mother's determination. This suggested further possibilities with mother. At every stage she was checking out the situation, from her use of the 'test' for mother to explain things to her son, to her following up with the psychotherapist about mother's progress in therapy. Her approach ensured that any errors made in the emerging judgement would be swiftly recognised.

In another case it became gradually clear that mother's drinking, although problematic, was not the heart of the problem. The case would not be resolved by tackling mother's drinking alone. It was her cognitions and her understanding of herself as a parent that were critical to promoting change in the situation (Morrison, 2000). The gathering and synthesis of information required to reach this judgement took some time to be reached by two social workers who were constantly reviewing the evidence in the case.

Failure to make an issues judgement means that strategies may be as prone to error as those following a faulty issues judgement.

Strategic judgements

Strategic judgements involve the professional response to the issues. The whole gamut of knowledge and experience will come into play as the social worker considers how best to intervene (Clark, 1997; Wilding, 1997; Adcock, 1998; Jones, 1998). A clear understanding of the issues is critical to both the nature and to the pace of interventions. The outcomes of strategic judgements are likely to be packages of interventions, possibly involving a number of agencies, and sometimes they will form the basis of the care plan put to the court in proceedings.

Availability of resources may influence the judgement (Tunstill, 1997) but backed with a good issues judgement , the social worker has a much greater chance of influencing the allocation of resources. Complex strategic judgements, for example, about placing a large sibling group require prior consideration of all the related issues (Hollows and Nelson, 2000; Mullender, 1999; Wedge and Mantle, 1991). Issues about relationships between siblings are instrumental in making a strategic judgement that is as far as possible grounded in a desire to achieve equitable outcomes for all the siblings, rather than simply pragmatic in the sense of limiting aspirations to whatever is available. In my study, two social workers had succeeded in overturning policies at the highest level that would have led to sibling groups being separated to save money. They did this, in each case, by articulating evidence based judgements on the issues in the case which pointed to a different strategy.

Taken together, the issues judgement and the strategy judgement provide the basis for setting goals for practice and thereby assisting evaluation.

Evaluative judgements

In a dynamic assessment process, such as the Framework for the Assessment of Children in Need and their Families, judgement making does not simply cease once plans are clear. It is, on the contrary the engine of progress and review in the case. This requires an evaluation of both the issues judgement and the strategy judgement. Evaluating progress requires a positive appreciation of theories about change (Protchaska and DiClementi, 1982), and their implications for making evaluative judgements. One social worker said that it was important to understand whether one was working with change or 'just monitoring'. She adds ' there are times when monitoring is quite useful, but it can't go on too long . . . we did monitor on our visits but that wasn't why we were there . . . we were there to support change'. She was working with a mother who tended to binge-drink under stress, and in addition to a range of counselling interventions, a detailed written agreement negotiated how the mother would respond if she became stressed. So the question at issue was not whether mother would drink again, but whether she could remain a responsible parent at times of stress. This line of action complements the strong psycho-social arguments (Schofield, 1998) for the social worker's active engagement as part of the intervention and support package, rather than simply as instigator of it. Another social worker demonstrated a careful approach to evaluating her judgements in the case. An essential part of progress in the case was for mother to understand at least something of the consequences of her mental illness and to actively engage in strategies that reduced the impact it would have on her children's development. Mother was now co-operating with mental health professionals in a different way and, although it appeared that she was unlikely ever to be able to cope with full time care of all four children, a good enough outcome had been reached. Both these social workers were able to take a holistic view of progress. In each case the mothers concerned periodically phoned up and shouted or argued about the situation, but each of the social workers saw this as ventilation rather than part of an underlying hostility.

Some cautions

For those wary of the power and authority of professions, most notably the Thatcher government and its immediate successors, the potential for arrogance within professional expertise in general, and professional judgement in particular, were to be distrusted. In the mid-nineties, there were claims that judgement making had been effectively – and deliberately – ruled out of the social work task (Henkel, 1994; Pietroni, 1995). The evolution of new managerialism within social work involved a relentless pursuit of certainty through the use of protocols and procedures (Parton, 1998). Managers were concerned, above all else, to ensure that the unfettered judgements of individual social workers did not lead them to the front page of a newspaper as another tragedy unfolded (O'Neill, 1999). The managerial constraints on professional autonomy were instrumental in limiting the potential for judgement making.

This recent history is significant because within many agencies in social care there is still in place a culture that remains unfriendly to the basic tenets of judgement making. The Department of Health's Quality Protects programme, for example, re-emphasises scientific management and accountability. Grafted onto the pre-1997 system, it may have strengthened the pursuit of certainty through the achievement of prescribed targets and goals. As Pietroni says: 'There is . . . an intrinsic contradiction between the complexity of individual judgements that have to be made in practice, and the often lumbering organisational procedures through which practice guidelines are issued' (Pietroni, 1995, 36-7). The increasing regulation and bureaucratisation of social work has been noted by a number of authors (see for example Howe, 1992) and it has been recognised as directly inhibiting professional judgement (Sinclair and Carr-Hill, 1997). O'Neill (1999) notes that managers 'invite' social workers to make judgements and social workers may only exercise judgement when asked to do so.

Perhaps the greatest threat to the effective operation of the Framework for the Assessment of Children in Need and their Families is its implementation in a context which is ill prepared for judgement making, in terms of both management and organisation. The good supervision that is essential to good judgement making remains elusive (Hughes and Pengelly, 1997) and morale is generally agreed to be poor. And yet learning to make professional judgements not only lies at the heart of the Assessment Framework. It offers us the chance to reclaim the profession of social work from its critics and detractors, through making clearly articulated and evidenced judgements. Of even greater importance is the clarity and purpose, which it provides for our work with children and their families.

References and Bibliography

Adcock, M. and White, R. (1998) *Significant Harm.* (2nd Edn.), Croydon: Significant Publications.

Benbenishty, R. (1992) An Overview of Methods to Elicit and Model Expert Clinical Judgement and Decision Making. *Social Service Review.* 62: 599–616.

Brandon, M., Thoburn, J., Lewis, A. and Way, A. (1999) *Safeguarding Children with the Children Act, 1989.* London: The Stationery Office.

Clark, C. (1997) Competence, Knowledge and Professional Formation. *Issues in Social Work Education.* 16: 2, 45–56.

Dalgleish, L. (2000) Assessing the Situation and Deciding to do Something: Risk, Needs. and Consequences. *ISPCAN*, Durban.

Dalgleish, L. and Hollows, A.E. (2003) Making judgements and decisions about risk in child protection (forthcoming).

Department of Health, Home Office and Department for Education and Employment (1999) *Working Together to Safeguard Children.* London: The Stationery Office.

Department of Health, Home Office, Department of Education and Science and Welsh Office (1991) *Working Together under the Children Act 1989.* London: HMSO.

Dingwall, R., Eekelaar, J. M. and Murray, T. (1983) *The Protection of Children: State Intervention and Family Life.* Hemel Hempstead: Harvester Wheatsheaf.

Eddy, D. M. (1988) Variations in Physician Practice. in Elstein, J. D. A. (Ed.) *Professional Judgement.* Cambridge: Cambridge University Press.

Einhorn, H. J. and Hogarth, R. M. (1981) Behavioural Decision Theory: Processes of Judgement and Choice. *Annual Review of Psychology.* 32: 53–88.

Farmer, E. and Owen, M. (1995) *Child Protection Practice: Private Risks and Public Remedies.* London: HMSO.

Fook, J. (2000) 'Theorising from Frontline Practice', *Theorising Social Work Research*, Luton.

Fook, J., Ryan, M. and Hawkins, L. (1994) 'Becoming a Social Worker: educational implications from preliminary findings of a longitudinal study', *Social Work Education.* 13(2): 5–26.

Fook, J., Ryan, M. and Hawkins, L. (1997) Towards a Theory of Social Work Expertise. *BJSW.* 27: 399–417.

Gibbons, J., Conroy, S. and Bell, C. (1995) *Operating the Child Protection System.* London: HMSO.

Goldstein, W. M., and Hogarth, R.M. (1997) Judgement and Decision Research: Some Historical Context. in Hogarth, R. M. (Ed.) *Research on Judgement and Decision Making: Currents, Connections and Controversies.* Cambridge: Cambridge University Press.

Hammond, K. R., Hamm, R.M., Grassia, J. and Pearson, T. (1987) Direct Comparison of the Efficacy of Intuitive and Analytical Cognition in Expert Judgement. *IEEE Transactions on Systems, Man, and Cybernetics SMC.*17: 5, 753–70.

Hammond, K. R. (1996) *Human Judgement and Social Policy: Irreducible Uncertainty, Inevitable Error, Unavoidable Injustice.* New York: Oxford University Press.

Healy, K. (1998) Participation and Child Protection: The Importance of Context. *BJSW.* 28: 897–914.

Henkel, M. (1994) Social Work: An Incorrigibly Marginal Profession. in Becher, T. (Ed.) *Governments and Professional Education.* Buckingham: SHRE/Open University.

Hollows, A. and Nelson, P. (2000) Making Judgements About Sibling Groups: Equity or Pragmatism? *ISPCAN.* Durban.

Horswill, M. S. and McKenna, F. P. (1991) The Effect of Interference on Dynamic Risk Taking Judgements. *British Journal of Psychology.* 90: 189–99.

Howe, D. (1992) Child Abuse and the Bureaucratisation of Social Work. *The Sociological Review.* 40: 3, 491–508.

Hughes, L. and Pengelly, P. (1997) *Staff Supervision in a Turbulent Environment.* London: Jessica Kingsley Publshers.

Isen, A. M. (1993) Positive Affect and Decision Making. in Lewis, M. and Haviland, J. M. (Eds.) *Handbook of Emotions.* New York: Guildford Press.

Jack, G. (1997) An Ecological Approach to Social Work With Children and Families. *Child and Family Social Work.* 2: 109–20.

Janis, I. L. and Mann, L. (1977) *Decision Making: A Psychological Analysis of Conflict, Choice and Commitment.* New York: The Free Press.

Jones, D. P. H. (1998) The Effectiveness of Intervention. in Adcock, M. and White, R. (Eds.) *Significant Harm.* (2nd Edn.) Croydon: Significant Publications.

Jones, D. P. H. (2001) False Positives in the Field of Child Maltreatment. *Child Abuse and Neglect.* 25: 1395–6.

Jones, S. and Joss, R. (1995) Models of Professionalism. in Yelloly, M. and Henkel, M. (Eds.) *Learning and Teaching in Social Work.* London: Jessica Kingsley Publishers.

Kahnemann, D., Slovic, P. and Tversky, A. (Eds.) (1982) *Judgement Under Uncertainty: Heuristics and Biases.* Cambridge: Cambridge University Press.

MacCrimmon, K. R. and Wehrung, D. A. (1986) *Taking Risks: The Management of Uncertainty.* New York: The Free Press.

Milner, J. and O'Byrne, P. (1998) *Assessment in Social Work.* Basingstoke: Macmillan.

Morrison, T. (2000) *Lapse and Relapse.* Personal communication.

Mullaly, R. (1993) *Structural Social Work.* Toronto: McClelland and Stewart.

Mullender, A. (Ed.) (1999) *We are Family: Sibling Relationships in Placement and Beyond.* London: British Agencies for Adoption and Fostering.

Munro, E. (1995) The power of first impressions. *Practice.* 7: 3, 59–65.

Munro, E. (1996) Avoidable and Unavoidable Mistakes in Child Protection Work. *British Journal of Social Work.* 26: 793–808.

Munro, E. (1997) *Letter About Judgement Teaching.*

Munro, E. (1998) *Understanding Social Work.* London: Athlone Press.

Munro, E. (1999) Common Errors of Reasoning in Child Protection Work. *Child Abuse and Neglect.* 23: 8, 745–58.

Murray, J. (2001) *De-Registering Child Protection Social Work.* Sheffield: Sheffield Hallam University.

Nurius, P. S. and Gibson, J. W. (1990) Clinical Observation, Inference, Reasoning and Judgement in Social Work: An Update. *Social Work Research and Abstracts.* June: 18–25.

O'Neill, S. (1999) Social Work: A Profession? *Journal of Social Work Practice.* 13: 1, 9–18.

O'Sullivan, T. (1999) *Decision Making in Social Work.* Basingstoke: Macmillan.

Parton, N. (1998) Risk, Advanced Liberalism and Child Welfare: The Need to Rediscover Uncertainty and Ambiguity. *British Journal of Social Work.* 28: 5–27.

Payne, J. W., Bettman, J.R. and Johnson, E.J. (1990) The Adaptive Decision Maker: Effort and Accuracy in Choice. in Hogarth, R. M. (Ed.) *Insights into Decision Making: A Tribute to Hillel J. Einhorn.* Chicago: University of Chicago Press.

Payne, J. W., Bettman, J. R. and Johnson, E. J. (1988) Adaptive Strategy Selection in Decision Making. *Journal of Experimental Psychology: Learning, Memory and Cognition.* 14: 534–52.

Pietroni, M. (1995) The Nature and Aims of Professional Education for Social Workers: A Post-modern Perspective. in Yelloly, M. and Henkel, M. (Eds.) *Learning and Teaching in Social Work.* London: Jessica Kingsley Publishers.

Plous, S. (1993) *The Psychology of Judgement and Decision Making.* New York: McGraw Hill.

Protchaska, J. and DiClementi, C. (1982) Transtheoretical Therapy: Towards a More Integrative Model of Change. *Psychotherapy: Theory, Research and Practice.* 9: 3.

Reder, P., Duncan, S. and Grey, M. (1993) *Beyond Blame.* London: Routledge.

Rouse, W. B. and Morris, N. M. (1986) On Looking Into the Black Box: Prospects and Limitations in the Search for Mental Models. *Psychological Bulletin.* 100: 349–63.

Schofield, G. (1998) Inner and Outer Worlds: A Psychosocial Framework for Child and Family Social Work. *Child and Family Social Work.* 3: 57–67.

Schon, D. 1983 *The Reflective Practitioner,* Aldershot: Arena.

Schon, D. A. (1988) From Technical Rationality to Reflection in Action. in Dowie, J. and Elstein, A. (Eds.) *Professional Judgement.* Cambridge: Cambridge University Press.

Scott, D. (1998) A Qualitatve Study of Social Work Assessment in Cases of Alleged Child Abuse. *BJSW.* 28: 73–88.

Sheldon, B. (2001) The Validity of Evidence Based Practice in Social Work: A Reply to Stephen Webb. *British Journal of Social Work.* 31: 801–9.

Sheppard, M. (1995) *Care Management and the New Social Work: A Critical Analysis,* London: Whiting and Birch.

Sheppard, M. (1998) 'Practice Validity, Reflexivity and Knowledge in Social Work', *British Journal of Social Work.* 28: 763–81.

Sheppard, M. (1999) 'Reflexivity and the development of process knowledge in social work', *Theorising Social Work Research,* Brunel University.

Sinclair, R. and Carr-Hill, R. (1997) *The Categorisation of Children in Need.* London: National Children's Bureau.

Stein, T. J., Gambrill, E. D. and Wiltse, K. T. (1978) *Children in Foster Homes: Achieving Continuity of Care.* New York: Prager.

Stewart, A. L. (1993) An Investigation into Decision Making by Child Protection Workers. *Psychology.* Brisbane: University of Queensland.

Thompson, N. (1995) *Theory and Practice in Health and Social Welfare.* Buckingham: Open University Press.

Tunstill, J. (1997) Implementing the Family Support Clauses of the 1989 Children Act. in Parton, N. (Ed.) *Child Protection and Family Support: Tensions, Contradictions and Possibilities.* London: Routledge.

Webb, S. (2001) Some Considerations on the Validity of Evidence Based Practice in Social Work. *British Journal of Social Work.* 31: 57–79.

Wedge, P. and Mantle, G. (1991) *Sibling Groups and Social Work.* Aldershot: Avebury.

Wilding, J. and Thoburn, J. (1997) Family Support Plans for Neglected and Abused Children. *Child Abuse Review.* 6: 5, 343–56.

Youll, P. and Walker, C. (1995) Great Expectations? Personal, Professional and Institutional Agendas in Advanced training. in Yellolly, M. and Henkel, M. (Eds.) *Learning and Teaching in Social Work: Towards Reflective Practice.*

Chapter Four

Evidence-based Assessment: A Critical Evaluation

Simon Hackett

Introduction – the current context to evidence-based approaches in social work

There is currently considerable attention being paid within social work and social care to evidence-based approaches (Sheldon and Chilvers, 2000). Within the context of the Framework for Assessment, social workers are directed to ground their work in evidence (DoH, 2000). The Framework itself is designed to be 'evidence-based'. There is, however, a fierce debate about the validity and nature of such approaches in the social care field, with proponents (for example, Sheldon, 2001) engaging in a war of words with others (for example, Webb, 2001) who see the notion as limited in a social work context. In the midst of this unresolved debate, social workers may be left in an 'evidence-gap'-struggling to base their practice on the basis of incomplete and misleading ideas, lacking access to the 'evidence base' and confused as to the implications of moving to an evidence-based approach.

The lack of clarity about the *aims*, *process* and *implications* of evidence-based practice is amply demonstrated by a recent comment to me from an experienced childcare practitioner who was a candidate for the Post-qualifying Award in Child Care. This social worker explained to me that he had gone into a supervision session to be asked repeatedly and without warning what the 'evidence' was for his actions in relation to his cases. This question had never been posed to him in supervision before. He was slightly taken aback and could not answer these questions. When he stated that he had intervened in a certain way because he felt this to be the correct course of action, the supervisor replied that this did not matter any more and that the supervisor needed to record the *evidence* for the worker's actions. It is appropriate within the context of this chapter, which critically examines the notion of evidence-based assessment, to stop to ask what was going wrong in this encounter. The shift in demands upon the social worker had not been discussed beforehand either individually or at team level, nor had this been

accompanied by any training on the nature or implications of evidence-based approaches. Significantly, there not been any attempt on an organisational level to offer increased resources and access to the elusive 'evidence base'. The social worker left the supervision session feeling mystified and undermined, as if his years of experience and his professional judgement and opinion suddenly did not count any more. What was happening for the supervisor? One assumes that he had thought it necessary to change his previous supervisory practice in order to raise the quality of the service he offers to his team, as well as the quality of the team's practice. However, his persistent and uncritical use of the notion of evidence-based practice actually had a counter-effect. The worker ended up feeling defensive, demotivated and inadequate.

This chapter seeks to assist practitioners and managers in the challenges of grounding their work in evidence, examines some of the benefits and challenges of so doing and also offers practical advice and a framework for practitioners who wish to move to a more evidence-based approach within the context of their assessment practice.

Do social workers value 'evidence' as a basis for practice?

Much has been stated about the need for social workers to be better at grounding their practice in evidence. Are social workers really sceptical or dismissive about the need to integrate research findings into their practice or is the problem primarily about having the time and resources to access and contemplate research given the frenetic pace of social work practice? Of course, there are likely to be social workers in each agency who are, indeed, resistant and doubtful about evidence-based approaches. However, my experience of working with groups of social workers about this subject over a number of years is that most social workers recognise that it is an important area.

For the last two years I have been involved in a research project in the North East of England in which we have sought to work with teams of social workers from Durham Social Services Department to develop the idea of research-informed child care practice. The central aim of the research, which is ongoing, is to investigate whether the implementation of evidence based approaches can be seen to impact upon outcomes for children and families. The research has involved training each team in turn about the meaning of evidence-based practice and how to critically appraise and appropriately use research evidence in their practice. After this initial training, we have worked with teams over a six-month period in an attempt to assist them to locate and use appropriate evidence in their practice. At the beginning of the research project, I had expected that I could meet considerable resistance from social workers about the idea of using research, that practitioners might feel that their professional autonomy was being compromised, or just that there would be general cynicism about a group of researchers interfering in the realities of day-to-day practice. However, in all teams this has not been the case. There has been almost universal acceptance of the value of 'evidence' for practice. Social workers have persistently and openly acknowledged the importance of informing their practice with research findings. They have been aware of the dangers of approaches which rely on an individual's subjective judgements with no linkage to a wider frame of reference.

One overall message for me from this research is that there appears to be widespread support from social workers for the idea of using research evidence in practice. The problem does not appear to be that practitioners do not value research for practice, but more that they struggle to make use of research in their practice because of lack of resources and time, the restrictive nature of their organisations and the professional cultures within which they work. Table 1 summarises the work of one team when asked to identify for themselves the benefits or drawbacks of moving to a more evidence-based approach. The work of this group of social workers demonstrates very well some of the issues and dilemmas involved.

In my experience then, few social workers would wish to defend practice that has no apparent effect, is harmful or has been shown to be less effective than other approaches. However, the notion of evidence-based approaches in social work is not without its critics and there are many critical questions to be answered, such as:

- Should 'research' be the sole basis for developing or sustaining services? The research base may be incomplete or address issues of only marginal importance. Indeed, in many cases, the evidence may be conflictual and confusing.
- If we are relying on what has already been 'tried and tested' (and published) could this inhibit innovation and creative, new approaches that have not yet been subjected to research and publication?
- Can notions of evidence-based approaches, which gained prominence in the field of medicine, be adopted in social work. Whilst it might be relatively straightforward to devise tests to measure the effectiveness of a drug, can things as complex as human interactions, the essence of social work practice, be measured?
- Could reliance on research, especially the kind of research which is generally seen as the best 'evidentially', involving quantitative analysis and large sample sizes, devalue the importance of practitioner-user interactions or an individual user's perspectives?
- Is this approach politically motivated? For example, does paying attention to the effectiveness of interventions divert attention away from their casual influences?

Individual workers and teams need to consider their responses to these kinds of questions and to examine the implications for them in the debate engendered by arguments in favour and against.

What is evidence-based assessment?

Hill (1999) defines evidence-based practice by stating that 'good practice ought to derive from research evidence about either the *nature, causes* and *typical pathways* of social problems or about the *success of particular methods* to deal with those problems' (Hill, 1999, p20, my emphasis). Hill's statement, in my view, is of fundamental relevance to assessment practice. Each of the points above in emphasis links to a basic goal of assessment practice. Thus, assessment can be seen as a process in which information is gathered and analysed in order to:

- Examine the nature or characteristics of problems, presenting issues or unmet need.
- Understand the causes of the problems or issues at hand.

Table 1: Social workers' thoughts on the benefits and drawbacks of evidence-based approaches.

Social workers' thoughts – benefits of evidence-based approaches

- It might encourage a deeper level of reflective practice.
- We could use evidence to target resources more efficiently.
- It is helpful in that it could build increased professionalism.
- Looking at wider research findings could help clarify and inform our thinking.
- It might lead to new approach or confirm existing one.
- We might gain additional leverage or bargaining power when asking for resources, if we can demonstrate need arising from research evidence.
- The use of evidence could enhance our professional self-belief, confidence and professional autonomy.
- It could help us to review old and established approaches and to develop new ones.
- We could use it as a baseline to monitor our practice and achieve better outcomes.
- Use of evidence could help us to challenge our own and other people's assumptions about practice.
- We would be 'up-to-date' and this approach reflects current practice in a social context.
- We could use additional expertise to advise policy makers in our agency.
- It could help us present a particular case in court.

Social workers' thoughts – pitfalls of evidence-based approaches

- There is difficulty in applying research findings to practice where cultural difference is not reflected or is missing from the research or is at odds with the nature of children and families we are dealing with.
- There is always a dichotomy in research findings and always an opposing research- how do we know whether we are using the right findings?
- Research (and its interpretation) can be political in nature.
- It's not easy sometimes to know how to transfer research findings into practice.
- There is the problem of financial constraints- research findings might give clear indications about the best course of action, but we might not have that resource here.
- Analysis and interpretation of findings are subjective. There's no 'absolute truth' and we still need to use our own judgement.
- Some research can be inaccessible and beyond our understanding (e.g. statistics)
- We are dealing with individuals, not static inanimate objects.
- We work in a 'sort it now' crisis intervention culture where it is difficult to take time required to seek out relevant research.
- Could a focus on research evidence by a social worker disempower families and take away their level of self-determination?
- Agencies within the multi-agency network have their own perspectives which might not be in line with research evidence.

- Weigh up the likelihood of progression or the implications if the problems or issues persist, or if need remains unmet.
- Identify the most appropriate and effective way of solving the problems or meeting the need.

Figure 1 demonstrates how analysis of the 'evidence' is useful at all stages of the assessment process. Crucially, an evidence-based approach can help practitioners answer different kinds of questions at different stages within the assessment process.

There are key questions about the nature of *evidence*. For example, what counts as evidence? Should more weight in practice be given to a particular type of evidence? Are some types of evidence better than other kinds? The Assessment Framework suggests that sources of evidence could include:

- Relevant research findings.
- National and local statistical data.
- National policy and practice guidance.
- Social Services Inspectorate Inspection Standards.
- Government and local inspection, audit and performance assessment reports.
- Lessons learnt from national and local inquiries and reviews of cases of child maltreatment.

(DoH, 2000, p16).

This is a broad conception of the nature of evidence. Although this is welcome given the context of social work, care needs to be given to distinguishing and appraising the level and strength of such different types of evidence. This is not to say that one source of evidence should be valued to the exclusion of others, merely that

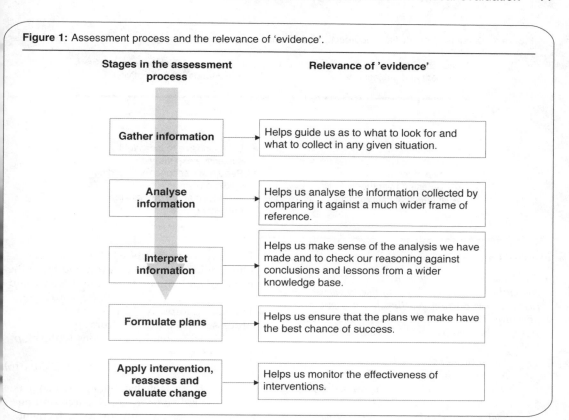

Figure 1: Assessment process and the relevance of 'evidence'.

Stages in the assessment process	Relevance of 'evidence'
Gather information	Helps guide us as to what to look for and what to collect in any given situation.
Analyse information	Helps us analyse the information collected by comparing it against a much wider frame of reference.
Interpret information	Helps us make sense of the analysis we have made and to check our reasoning against conclusions and lessons from a wider knowledge base.
Formulate plans	Helps us ensure that the plans we make have the best chance of success.
Apply intervention, reassess and evaluate change	Helps us monitor the effectiveness of interventions.

they may have different implications and should be seen as complementary rather than in competition (Brechin and Siddell, 2000). As Brechin and Siddell (2000) maintain, social workers frequently draw upon a range of different kinds of knowledge in their work, including empirical, theoretical and experiential, moving seamlessly between them. For example, in an assignment relating to intervention approaches and their empirical validity, most candidates on a local post-qualifying course in childcare described their intervention style as 'eclectic' and argued strongly in favour of this approach. Used effectively, the strength of such an approach is that it can harness the best methods from a range of theoretical standpoints and target them to those situations where they have the best chance of success. At worst, this approach becomes a 'mishmash' of theories, undistinguished and indistinguishable, with the 'eclectic' tag used to justify the uncritical application of approaches to situations where they are not suited.

Brechin and Siddell further (2000, p4) distinguish between three levels of knowledge:

- *Empirical knowledge*: the most explicit – where the practitioner responds on the basis of research evidence.
- *Theoretical knowledge*: public knowledge, but often used intuitively and informally – where the social worker uses theoretical frameworks into thinking about a situation or problem.
- *Experiential knowledge:* particularly hard to make explicit – where the social worker bases thoughts or actions on the basis of an experience base built up over the years

This is a useful conceptualisation and practitioners can usefully review and examine their use of these levels of knowledge within the assessment process. For example, I have used Exercise One, adapted from the work of Gibbs and Gambrill, (1995) in training social workers in evidence-based practice as a way of encouraging practitioners to make explicit the evidential basis for their practice. Completing this exercise often results in practitioners realising, sometimes with a degree of discomfort, that their 'intuition' alone may be dangerous basis upon which to respond in practice situations.

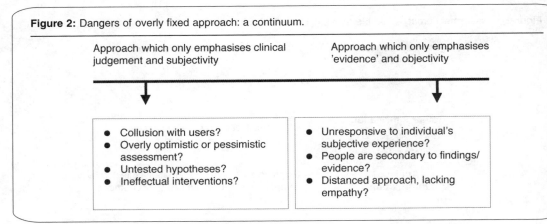

Figure 2: Dangers of overly fixed approach: a continuum.

Approach which only emphasises clinical judgement and subjectivity

Approach which only emphasises 'evidence' and objectivity

- Collusion with users?
- Overly optimistic or pessimistic assessment?
- Untested hypotheses?
- Ineffectual interventions?

- Unresponsive to individual's subjective experience?
- People are secondary to findings/ evidence?
- Distanced approach, lacking empathy?

Exercise One

- *Think about a case or practice situation you are currently engaged in. You may like to choose the case which is causing you the most anxiety or difficulty. Think about the following criteria and tick any that you have used in your decision making:*
  - ☐ *Your intuition about what would be appropriate or effective*
  - ☐ *Your experience of similar cases in the past*
  - ☐ *What fits your personal style*
  - ☐ *What colleagues or your supervisor have recommended from their experiences*
  - ☐ *What is usually done in your team or agency*
  - ☐ *What you know from reading professional literature*
  - ☐ *What the user, or other users, have said is helpful*
  - ☐ *The findings from empirical research*

What is expected of practitioners in completing evidence-based assessments?

The Assessment Framework addresses this question clearly. Practitioners are expected to:

- Use knowledge critically from research and practice about the needs of children and families and the outcomes of services and interventions to inform their assessment and planning.
- Record and update information systematically, distinguishing sources of information, for example direct observation, other agency records or interviews with family members.
- Learn from the views of users of services i.e. children and families.

- Evaluate continuously whether the intervention is effective in responding to the needs of an individual child and family and modifying their interventions accordingly.
- Evaluate rigorously the information, processes and outcomes from the practitioner's own interventions to develop practice wisdom.

(DoH, 2000, p16)

This is a formidable list, but one which makes it clear that judicious use of research findings should be combined with clinical judgement. Indeed, this is essential if practice is to be both effective and at the same time responsive to users' individual circumstances and needs, as demonstrated in Figure 2.

Therefore, in order to be consistent with its professional value base, social work needs to develop a form of evidence-based practice which combines and values both professional judgement and the user's experience, as well as knowledge from research. This point is made well in the Assessment Framework document itself:

The combination of evidence based practice grounded in knowledge with finely balanced professional judgement is the foundation for effective practice with children and families.

(DoH, 2000, p16)

Good practice, then, synthesises the best elements of professional experience, research evidence and the unique needs and experiences of the service user (Gomm and Davies, 2000).

Evidence-based approaches are therefore not merely an adjunct to approaches that rely upon clinical judgement, but may require a shift of focus and a number of discrete stages and tasks. Most challenging is the need for practitioners to actively **seek out**, **critically assess** and **apply** relevant research literature and findings throughout the different elements and stages of the assessment process:

> ... *evidence-based practitioners should themselves collect data systematically, specify outcomes in measurable terms and systematically monitor and evaluate their interventions.*
>
> (Hill, 1999, p20).

Thus (adapting Straus and Sackett, 1998), the steps involved in moving to an evidence-based approach include the following distinct stages:

- Commit oneself to evidence-based assessment.
- Ask an answerable question of practical relevance.
- Locate the best evidence related to your question.
- Critically evaluate the best evidence.
- Apply the results of your critical evaluation.
- Evaluate the outcome of your practice against goals.

Commit oneself to evidence-based assessment

It is clearly important as a first step in moving to a more evidence-based approach to assessment to think about the benefits and limitations on both a macro practice level (*how could my practice be enhanced overall ...*) and also to review the implications for individual cases (*how could my work with X be enhanced ...*). Examining the meaning of evidence-based practice and debating this with other colleagues within the context of a team's work is a good first step. Thinking about the 'benefits and pitfalls' debate and working through Exercise 1, as described above, can be done with good effect both individually, within supervision, and on a team basis.

Within our current research project it has been helpful to have a lead worker who is enthusiastic about the possibilities of evidence-based approaches and who can keep the emphasis on its development within a given team. However, the message from our research is that a team focus and distinct team 'space' to discuss cases in the light of research evidence is necessary. Therefore in our work with teams we developed the notion of 'practice development groups'. These have occurred at fortnightly intervals within each team and have involved all team members as well as the researchers. They have been chaired by the Team Manager and have sought to introduce a clear structure within which evidence-based approaches can be developed and discussed. We developed a standardised way of reviewing cases, evidence and goal setting within these meetings, as represented in Table 3 later in the chapter. Thus, practice development groups have functioned as a means by which social workers can share cases and outline particular questions and about which they would like to examine research evidence. A full-time researcher was employed to seek out relevant research requested by workers and to assist workers in the process of locating their own evidence. Social workers have then presented back to the wider team at Practice Development Groups their thoughts about the evidence identified for them and its implications for their practice. Such a co-ordinated and structured approach brings with it the need for additional time to hold meetings, however, several teams have reported that the process has encouraged them to stand back and reflect more carefully on their work. A number of Team Managers have reported that the process has had the overall benefit of streamlining the work of the team, making the interventions offered more effective and, overall, enabling them to increase their capacity to respond to referrals.

Ask an answerable question of practical relevance

We have found that it is vitally important for practitioners to ask specific answerable questions of the evidence base. At the beginning of the project, social workers would typically ask very general questions, such as 'how do you make contact better?' or 'what's the evidence on Munchausen's Syndrome by proxy'. Social workers have realised that unfocused and nonspecific questions often result in frustrated attempts to locate research findings or non-specific evidence which has limited value for them in their practice. Persistent use of the framework described in Table 3 has, however, enabled practitioners to become increasingly sophisticated (and realistic) about the nature of their requests, for example, 'is there any empirical evidence that describes the coexistence of physical abuse and Munchausen's syndrome by proxy within families.' Practitioners have also learnt to distinguish between the types of question that are most likely to be answerable, for example:

- *Assessment of influence of factors*: e.g.
  - What are the effects of a child living with a parent with schizophrenia?
  - What evidence is there to support various causes of sexually abusive behaviour?
- *Risk*: e.g.
  - What are the risks of an adolescent who has committed sexual abuse reoffending, and in what circumstances are such risks exacerbated?
- *Prognosis*: e.g.
  - What range of educational achievements can be anticipated for a child with Downs syndrome?
- *Effectiveness of interventions*: e.g.
  - What evidence is there to support the use of Solution Focused Therapy for school phobia?
  - What's the most effective intervention approach for behaviour problems in pre-adolescent children?
- *Prevention*: e.g.
  - Is screening for child abuse by health visitors cost effective?
  - Can pre-school intervention prevent behaviour problems at school?

Locate the best evidence related to your question

Locating relevant research to answer specific questions is enormously time consuming, even if one has relatively good access to research material. Where this is not the case, the process for social workers can be frustrating. Indeed, the most frequently stated difficulty for social workers within our current research has been the lack of access to empirical research. Whilst this situation is rapidly changing, with increasing amounts of peer-reviewed material being made available online, social workers are often party only to research summaries or abstracts, which give them a frustrating glimpse into potentially useful material but often nothing more. The advent of the Social Care Institute for Excellence (SCIE) is a huge step forward in this regard and is likely to help by creating and disseminating evidence of best practice guides in various aspects of social care. Despite such welcome advances, there is an urgent need for agencies to assist their social workers in developing evidence-based approaches by resourcing access to online

bibliographic databases and online peer-reviewed journals. Without this, the whole process of requiring social workers to ground their work in the best available research evidence is limited and limiting; like expecting a child to grow healthily without adequate nourishment.

Table 2, below, offers a brief introduction to some of the useful free online sources of information for practitioners which are available at the time of writing. As this is an area which is constantly changing, this list is offered as nothing more than a starting point and practitioners wishing to develop their evidence-based approach should routinely and regularly seek out new sources of evidence.

Once access issues are negotiated, social workers need to be given assistance where necessary to make use of available Information Technology. In our current research project, we have also found that it is important to encourage social workers to seek out evidence which is beyond the narrow confines of 'social work' research and to be open to the need to consult material from allied health, psychology literature, etc. This is ground that many social workers initially felt uncomfortable with, but the clear message is that many of the practice issues and questions asked were very complex and beyond the scope of the social work research base. In some instances, social workers have learnt that it is necessary to consult several distinct pieces of research evidence which, taken together, may go towards answering the question they have posed.

Critically evaluate the best evidence

Not all research is good research! For any one research finding, there is likely to be another which directly counters it. Research evidence needs to be critically evaluated and its limitations acknowledged. Evidence needs to be carefully appraised and the potential implications carefully drawn out. Practice that lurches from one approach to another simply as a result of the latest research study may be as dangerous as practice which is subjective and takes no regard to research evidence. Making sense of research information needs a different set of skills from those needed to locate it in the first place and social workers should be encouraged to develop these skills. 'Critical thinking' is a notion that can assist in making sense of evidence and its practice implications. Gambrill (1997) offers the following definition:

Table 2: A sample of online information sources.

Web URL	Description
http://www.scie.org.uk/	Social Care Institute for Excellence. Includes access to 'caredata' – an important social care database.
http://www.researchweb.org.uk/	Research web – supporting social work excellence for Scotland. Includes a knowledge forum and section on research into practice, as well as gateway to 'caredata'.
http://www.elsc.org.uk	Electronic library for social care. Includes 'knowledge bases' section.
http://www.swap.ac.uk/	**SWAP**ltsn – subject centre for Social Policy and Social Work -one of 24 discipline-based centres, which form the UK-wide Learning and Teaching Support Network.
http://www.jrf.org.uk	Joseph Rowntree Foundation. Includes a findings section from JRF funded projects at http://www.jrf.org.uk/knowledge/findings/
http://www.exeter.ac.uk/cebss	The Centre for Evidence-Based Social Services. Includes a useful publications section, with a number of papers on evidence-based approaches in social work, including Tony Newman's excellent publication *Developing Evidence-Based Practice in Social Care.*
http://www/chst.soton.ac.uk	Centre for Human Service Technology – a research, development and service centre for social work. Includes a useful section on 'research mindedness' in social work. Also access to a helpful social work information gateway at http://www.chst.soton.ac.uk/webconn.htm
http://www.ingenta.com	Ingenta. A collection of full text electronic journals. Searching is possible without registration, but full text availability of journal depends on e-journal subscriptions.
http://www.doh.gov.uk	Department of Health website, including access to DoH publications at <http://www.doh.gov.uk/scg/publist.htm> as well as Quality Protects Website at <http://doh.gov.uk/qualityprotects>
http://regard.ac.uk	Searchable database detailing research funded by the Economic and Social Research Council (ESRC)
http://www.sosig.ac.uk/	Social Science Information Gateway
http://bmj.com/	British Medical Journal, includes open access to all issues published since 1994

Critical thinking involves the careful examination and evaluation of beliefs and actions in order to arrive at well reasoned ones.

(Gambrill, p125).

Critical thinking, as it relates to evidence-based practice, therefore involves the careful examination of 'evidence' (whatever form the evidence takes), and the evaluation of findings in order that the practitioner arrives at informed and well reasoned conclusions which are likely to assist in meeting the needs of an individual or family. Many social workers need to learn how to critically think about research. This involves a careful balancing act. For example, many teams of social workers with whom we have worked in developing evidence based approaches have initially approached research almost reverentially. If something is in print, it must be right! At the same time, it is possible to be overly-critical about research, subjecting it to an impossibly tight critical evaluation to the point that potentially useful findings and implications are disregarded or missed.

The following are some examples of critical thoughts about research, derived from the work of Gambrill (1997):

- How do I know that the claims made as a result of the research are true?
- Who has presented it as accurate? Are vested interests involved? How reliable are the sources?
- Do the facts/perspectives presented stand up to scrutiny?
- Is there *evidence* that the *evidence* is reliable? How many critical tests have been performed? How have they been affected by bias? Have the results been replicated? How representative were the samples used?
- Have any facts or perspectives been omitted?
- Are there any other promising points of view? Have these been tested?
- Is the content potentially relevant?

- Is relevant literature referred to?
- Are concepts clearly defined?
- Are the data collection methods clearly described? Are they free of sample bias?
- Are measures valid and reliable?
- Is the study clearly described and is it accurate?
- Are the intervention methods clearly defined? Is it likely that the intervention caused the changes? Are there alternative explanations?
- Is the data analysis appropriate? Are there follow-up data?
- Can the findings be generalised to other situations?

Gomm and Davies (2000) suggest that it is important to distinguish between two separate questions in appraising research. The first is whether the research being presented is true in its own terms – in other words its internal validity. The second level is whether the findings might be relevant or true for other people in other contexts – in other words its external validity. Practitioners may also need to be able to distinguish levels of research reliability. Some studies have a high level of rigour and reliability and their findings may be regarded as conclusive. Others, however, may be less rigorous and findings may be at best indicative. For a fuller description of how to critically appraise evidence in health and social care, the reader is advised to consult the comprehensive and accessible edited text by Gomm and Davies (2000) and the excellent online guide to research mindedness for social work developed by the Centre for Human Services Technology at: *http//www.sws.soton.ac.uk/rminded/*.

Apply the results of your critical evaluation and evaluating outcomes

Having located evidence relating to specific assessment questions and having appraised it, the next stage of the evidence-based assessment process is to examine how the evidence helps to make sense of the specific questions asked about the user's position and, therefore, what interventions or recommendations are indicated in order to meet need or influence the situation as effectively as possible. In our research, we have used goal attainment scaling to encourage workers both to identify goals and appropriate indicators of these goals – either behavioural, skills-based or situational. The indicators of the

goals are important and workers should describe in clear terms what they are likely to see if the plan they have formulated to meet need has succeeded. As a general point it is better to set goals that are realistic and scaleable in discussion with the service user concerned. The resource implications of this process need careful consideration. For example, this has been an area of frustration for individual workers in some situations where they have felt that the 'evidence' indicates a very clear course of action, but the resources are not forthcoming to facilitate this. At intervals we have returned, within the context of practice development groups, to review progress in cases discussed at a team level and to examine how the evidence shaped the development of the work, as well as to what degree the envisaged goals were met.

Drawing the stages together

The framework offered below in Table 3 was developed as a protocol for casework discussion within our current research project, and offers a synthesis of many of the issues discussed in the preceding section. In practice this was an important tool for structuring discussion within our 'practice development groups' but it is equally appropriate to use this within the context of team discussions, individual planning and supervision, etc. as a way of orienting assessment and intervention practice within an evidence-based frame.

Summary. Does it work – would it work here?

As indicated above, our own research has represented an attempt to systematically introduce evidence-based practice in childcare teams and to measure the effect on outcomes.

As the project is ongoing, it is not possible to offer detailed findings of the research as yet, however, some key points have emerged to date, which may be important for other teams and individuals who are considering developing these approaches in relation to their assessment practice.

Firstly, in our experience, social workers have frequently used the opportunity to talk about their most troubling and complex cases. They have been more reluctant to discuss their 'run of the mill' cases. It may be that cases seen as less problematic were not viewed as needing

Table 3: A framework for evidence-based assessment.

(a) Personal details:	*To include:* • Name of service user • Gender and race • Family composition • Reason for referral/current involvement
(b) Define and prioritise service user's problems/issues in relation to user's position:	*To include:* • The likely origins of the problems • Patterns involved • Factors that maintain or exacerbate the problem, etc.
(c) Identify specific and answerable questions to be approached via research evidence:	• What evidence do we already know about? • What additional evidence might help to answer the questions . . . • Where might the additional sources of evidence come from . . .
(d) Evaluation of the evidence:	• What weight are we giving the evidence from different sources and why . . . • Distinguish between relevant/strong evidence and irrelevant/ weak evidence . . . • Quality and strength of evidence in relation to the specific questions posed . . .
(e) Planning and goals:	• What interventions/plans/proposals in relation to this user's situation emerge from the critical evaluation of the evidence? What needs to be done . . . • Frequency and duration of contact, etc . . . • What are the goals . . . • What are the likely outcomes if the plan works . . . • Resources implications . . .
(f) Review and outcomes (to be completed after interventions):	• What was done? • How did the envisaged plan work out? • How was the research evidence used in practice? • How far were the goals met? • What were the outcomes for the user/s, for you as the worker, for the department . . .

research evidence. It is nevertheless important to encourage evidence-based approaches across the board, not just in relation to problematic cases.

Secondly, the experience of our project suggests that the development and maintenance of evidence-based approaches within the context of a team's work needs considerable planning and an explicit focus. With support from the wider organisation and resources to match, each team in turn has embraced the project enthusiastically and has described a range of benefits from its involvement. These include a sense of increased professionalism and self-esteem, and confidence in multi-agency settings. Several team managers have described their view that the overall practice within the team had changed as a result, with practitioners better able to stand back and take a more reflective view. One supervisor described this as taking a less frantic but more productive' approach. However, there are pressures which

have made it difficult for teams to maintain this focus. Staff sickness and stress levels have had a direct bearing upon teams' abilities to sustain the approach, especially at the end of the formal research input. The whole process has worked well in teams with a relatively stable workforce and an established team identity, as well as a strongly committed Team Manager. The major dilemma for social workers remains where to get high quality, full-text and the most up-to-date research evidence and how to find time to appraise it.

Thirdly, a number of factors appear to be keys to success, both on an individual and a team level. Individually, social workers need to have a personal commitment to learn from research and integrate it into their thinking and practice. At the same time a practice context and team culture which supports this and appropriate access to the 'evidence' is vital. Newman (adapted from REAL, Research in Practice, 2001) suggests that teams will be more likely to

succeed in developing evidence-based
approaches if they:

• Are clear about why they are doing it.
• Start with a limited agenda – small successes
  are better than big failures.
• Recognise that progress will be slow.
• Identify and work on a specific and
  manageable topic.
• Work on an issue that arises regularly.
• Work on an issue that is important.
• Make the development of evidence-based
  practice a core activity not something
  'bolted-on'.
• Spread the load – don't just have a few
  'evidence based' experts in your team.
• Fit in with current organisational priorities,
  for example in relation to quality protects or
  best value.
• Identify administrative support, especially
  from someone with search skills, preferably a
  librarian.
• Enlist the support of line managers.
• Don't make excessive demands – set realistic
  timescales.

In conclusion, this chapter has described
some of the issues and possibilities in moving to
a more evidence-based approach to assessment
practice. In this regard, I would support the
emphasis within the Assessment Framework on
evidence-based practice and encourage
practitioners to be optimistic about the
possibilities of enhancing their assessment
practice through judicious and careful use of the
developing evidence base in childcare social
work and beyond. Evidence-based practice is
clearly not a panacea and, despite the best
intentions, efforts to consolidate practice in the
best available evidence can founder, or be
severely frustrated, in a number of regards,
especially due to the difficulty of access to
research and day-to-day pressures on
practitioners. Our experience suggests that the
process is often 'messy' and often does not yield
neat, easy answers to what are often complex
and intractable practice dilemmas. But, even in
situations where the evidence has confirmed
that there are no easy answers, social workers
have often reported that the process of
evaluating research has been useful and has
stimulated their thinking about the case. There
have been many positive and unforeseen
spin-offs from this process. For example, one
social worker described how she had discussed
research findings on the impact of parental

alcohol abuse on children with a parent who
had an identified alcohol problem. She said that
using the research findings helped shift the
focus away from the parent feeling that the
social worker was personally blaming of her to a
joint attempt to consider the messages from
other people in similar situations. The parent
was grateful that the worker concerned had
taken the trouble to find out about her problem
and they were both able to work together more
constructively. Another social worker described
how she had been able to have a conversation
with a paediatrician about the evidence on
Munchausen's Syndrome by Proxy. She felt that
she was taken seriously by this man for the first
time and, as a result, her views and overall
contribution to the case were more highly
valued. In turn, she felt her own level of
professional self-esteem had been raised. These
brief examples demonstrate well how, for users
and practitioners alike, evidence-based
approaches can offer a helpful additional tool
for enhancing practice and influencing
outcomes.

References

Brechin, A. and Siddell, M. (2000) Ways of
    Knowing. In Gomm, R. and Davies, C. (Eds.)
    Using Evidence in Health and Social Care.
    London: Sage/Open University Press.
Department of Health (2000) *Framework for the
    Assessment of Children in Need and their
    Families.* London: The Stationery Office.
Gambrill, E. (1997) *Social Work Practice: A Critical
    Thinker's Guide.* New York: Oxford University
    Press.
Gibbs, L. and Gambrill, E. (1995) *Critical
    Thinking for Social Workers: Exercises for the
    Helping Professions.* Thousand Oaks: Pine
    Forge.
Hill, M. (Ed.) (1999) *Effective Ways of Working
    with Children and their Families.* London: Jessica
    Kingsley.
Newman, T. *Developing Evidence Based Practice in
    Social Care. Locating, Appraising and Using
    Research Findings on Effectiveness.* Publication
    of the Centre for Evidence-based Social
    Services, http://www.ex.ac.uk/cebss/
Sheldon, B. (2001) The Validity of
    Evidence-based Practice in Social Work: A
    Reply to Stephen Webb. *British Journal of Social
    Work.* 31: 801-9.
Sheldon, B. and Chilvers, R. (2000)
    Evidence-based Social Care: A Study of Prospects

and Problems. Lyme Regis: Russell House Publishing.

Straus, S. and Sackett, D. (1998) Getting research findings into practice: Using research findings in clincal practice. *British Medical Journal*. 317: 339–42.

Webb, S. (2001) Some Considerations on the Validity of Evidence-based Practice in Social Work. *British Journal of Social Work*. 31: 57-79.

Chapter Five

Risk, Needs and Consequences*

Dr Lenard Dalgleish

Introduction

Assessment and decision making are core activities in child protection work. They apply across child welfare; from assessing whether a child is in need, to child protection intake, to re-uniting children and families. The nature and purpose of the assessments differ, as do the decisions they inform. There is tension between approaches to assessing children in need and for risk assessment. While there are similarities and differences in the approaches, the link between the assessment and the decision is not clear in these approaches. A model will be presented that links risk assessments and decisions by the idea that if an assessment of the situation is above a worker's threshold, then action is taken to manage the situation. Signal Detection Theory provides the theoretical base for the threshold concept in the model and methods for measuring the thresholds. In the model, different factors are assumed to influence the assessment of the situation and the threshold for action. Results from a content analysis of worker's statements about the consequences of decisions show that thresholds are influenced by qualitatively different factors to those used in the assessment of risk in a case. The model also accounts for inconsistencies between workers in their assessments of the situation and decisions. Results from research will show that differences in personal thresholds account for the great majority of disagreement between the workers. Implications for practice will be discussed especially where a supervisor and worker are in disagreement due to differing thresholds. Policy and practice implications about implementation of any approach to assessment (risk or needs led) will be discussed as will issues concerning the skills needed by child protection workers to undertake these assessments and make decisions.

Child welfare and child protection: Two sides of the same coin

There has been considerable debate and concern that child welfare has been overtaken by child protection. The perceived reason for this is the number of cases entering the child protection system (Costin, Karger and Stoesz, 1996; Department of Health, 1995; Schene, 1996; Thorpe, 1994). While I will be mainly referring to the UK and US literature, the issues are not confined to those countries.

In the UK the debate on child protection has been broadened so that child protection is viewed as one component of child welfare and the focus is more on identifying and meeting the needs of children, (Gray, 1998). The UK has recently introduced their 'Framework for the Assessment of Children in Need and Their Families', (DoH, 2000) and this states very clearly the goal of safeguarding and promoting the welfare of vulnerable children and provides guidance on how to achieve it. The word 'risk' is hardly used except that it discusses children who are suffering or are likely to suffer significant harm. Estimating the likelihood of amount of harm in the future is a risk assessment. Very little guidance is given on how the information collected during an assessment is integrated to provide such a risk assessment. However, they do state that 'determining who is in need, what those needs are, and how services will have an effect on outcomes for children requires professional judgement' (DoH, 2000, p5).

Wilson and Morton (1997) cite Barth (1995) who asserted that (in the US) policy makers and experts have come to an agreement in recent years that child safety is the 'superordinate' child welfare goal. Wilson and Morton (1997) further state;

'A few years ago the question being debated was whether a commitment to helping families and to family preservation was congruent with a coercive child protection investigative process. Currently, the question is whether children can be effectively protected by a child welfare system with commitments to family preservation and re-unification following out-of-home placement' p6.

Wilson (1997) has argued that a 'tunnel vision' approach concerned with child maltreatment fails to place children in the broader context of

*A version of this chapter was presented at the 2000 ISPLAN Congress i Durban, South Africa.

their families and to promote a child's total well-being and future development.

While there has been some discussion about the goals of child welfare, the fact is that a great majority of states in the US have implemented risk assessment systems of a variety of types, (Baird, Wagner, Healy, and Johnson, 1999; Schene, 1996).

Assessing children in need and risk assessment: The tensions

These two approaches, one focussing on assessment of needs and the other on the assessment of risk, differ in the goal of the assessment. However, they do have at least one similarity and some other differences.

Risk assessment systems consist of a number of types, matrix models, empirical predictor models (actuarial), and consensus models amongst others (Baird, Wagner, Healy, Johnson, 1999; English and Pecora, 1994). They vary considerably in the amount and detail of information used to arrive at the risk assessment. We will consider just two risk assessment systems; the Structured Decision Making System's Family Risk Assessment of Abuse and Neglect (FRAAN) (Baird, Wagner, Casky, and Neuenfeldt, 1995) and the Washington Risk Assessment Matrix (WRAM) (Washington State SDHS, 1995). Two systems for the assessment of needs are the UK Assessment Framework (DoH, 2000) and the Child Well-Being Scales, (CWBS) (Lyons, Doueck, Koster, Witsky and Kelly, 1999; Magura and Moses, 1986). There are a great many systems I could have compared and I chose these four to highlight the issues I want to discuss. A full review would uncover many more distinctions among the various approaches.

The two types of systems are similar in that both imply that it is useful to be structured and systematic. That is, they all ask the worker to gather information and organise it in some systematic way. In general they cover a variety of assessment factors about nature of the harms, the child, the family and the environment.

They differ in how comprehensively they assess the situation. The FRAAN model uses answers to twelve quite particular questions to arrive at a risk assessment which is a weighted sum of the answers. Proponents argue that answers to these questions have been found statistically to be most predictive of

re-occurrence of abuse. The WRAM, the CWBS and the UK Assessment Framework use a consensus approach in which the items were derived from the general findings from the empirical literature combined with practice wisdom. The WRAM uses ratings on 31 items under eight groupings with the user forming a final risk rating. The CWBS consists of 43 behaviour rating scales, under four dimensions with total scores also calculated. The UK Assessment Framework has 20 broad dimensions listed under three domains with no scaling of overall assessment. Cox and Bentovim (2000) suggest how to measure some of these dimensions using a pack of questionnaires and scales. How much information is enough? In 1997, I invoked the dictionary definition of 'good' when comparing risk assessment approaches (Dalgleish, 1997). The definition is: Satisfactory in quality, genuine, sound, sufficient and competent. It is pertinent because it suggests that only sufficient information needs to be gathered to inform the assessment whether it be of risk or needs. The FRAAN is the least comprehensive and the UK Assessment Framework the most. The FRANN is the most specific and the UK Assessment Framework is the most general.

They differ in the way the information is aggregated to form the overall assessment. FRANN uses an actuarial approach where the answers to the questions are weighted with empirically derived weights and summed to provide a numerical score. The CWBS has a total score across the scales. The WRAM asks the user to form an overall assessment of risk. The UK Assessment Framework doesn't ask the user to summarise their overall assessment and just provides a way of organising the case information needed for an assessment.

They differ in the degree of professional judgement (discretion) allowed or encouraged. The UK Assessment Framework encourages workers to use their professional judgement. The FRAAN allows minimal discretion with supervisors able to override the total score (Hetherington, 1997).

They differ in how they link the assessment to decisions about action. The FRAAN has preset cutpoints. For example, if the total risk score is between 9 and 18, it is a high risk case and the response is predetermined. These are linked to levels of service, the differential response. The cutpoints have been derived from statistical analyses. In the implementation of the CWBS

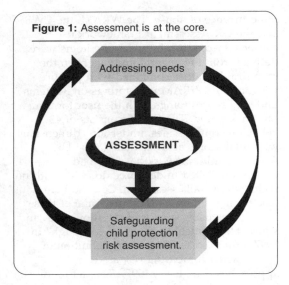

Figure 1: Assessment is at the core.

education etc.). The WRAM, like the FRAAN links level of risk to level of service, (English, 1992) with the cutpoints being determined by the agency. The UK Assessment Framework states that the 'purpose of the assessment is to identify the child's needs within their family context and to use this understanding to decide how best to address these needs' (Department of Health, 2000, p62). When discussing whether action is needed to protect the child, no explicit threshold is defined for significant harm or likelihood of significant harm. The issue of thresholds, who sets them and their impact is a major theme of this chapter.

Assessment is at the core

Across these approaches, the biggest similarity is that assessment is their core even though it is more comprehensive in some and the focus of the assessment changes. My view is that both are essential and linked. One should not do one without the other.

Hardiker, Exton and Barker (1999) developed a grid for looking at the twin approach of safeguarding and promoting welfare at different levels of intervention. I have extended this to illustrate that assessment is at the core of these

discussed by Lyons et al. (1999), threshold scores were 'identified for each item on the scales as an indicator that a situation is serious enough to warrant ongoing agency services absent of other factors and regardless of total score.' The agency negotiated the threshold scores internally (supervisors, workers) and externally (other agencies, police, health,

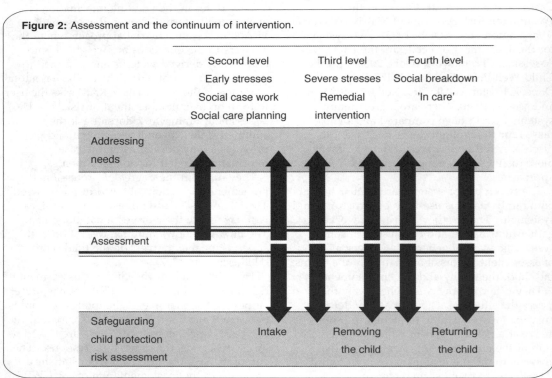

Figure 2: Assessment and the continuum of intervention.

twin activities along the continuum of intervention. While there are 'named' key decision points along the continuum for risk, we don't have such a vocabulary for needs. However, the needs of the child and family and the services required differ across the intervention continuum. Addressing the assessed needs of children occurs before child protection issues may be evident is shown and is one approach to prevention. At each key decision point along the continuum, both risk assessments and assessment of needs are performed and they inform each other. These occur at the key decision points and at re-assessments in between to monitor risk and needs. It is in the addressing of the needs that the risk to the child is managed.

Assessment and decision making is a difficult task

While assessment of the situation and organising that information is the core task, deciding whether to take action is difficult too. These assessments and decisions are based on information that is often unclear, noisy and uncertain. They are sometimes made under time pressure in a highly emotional atmosphere. They are influenced by the experiences and history of the decision maker. This complex and

challenging work usually occurs in a highly charged context with:

- Structural constraints – scarcity of resources, staff shortages or high staff turnover, little or insufficient supervision, heavy caseloads.
- Intense media interest and commentary.
- Political and public accountability and examination.
- Working with clients who are often involuntary.
- Working with a degree of unpredictability of outcomes.

However, even with the best possible information many cases are not clear cut as to the appropriate response. These are the 'grey area' cases caused by complex, unclear, ambiguous or unreliable information and cause workers to be hesitant as to the consequence of potential for errors. Decisions in these circumstances can be characterised as decision making under uncertainty.

A model for assessment and decision making

In a number of papers (Dalgleish, 1990; Dalgleish and de Michele, 1995; Dalgleish and Newton, 1995), I have developed a general model for risk assessment and decision making

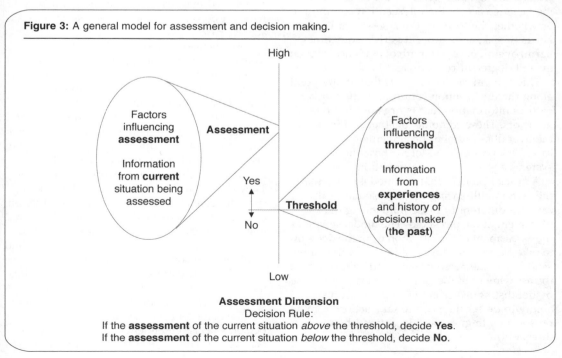

Figure 3: A general model for assessment and decision making.

High

Factors influencing **assessment**

Information from **current** situation being assessed

Assessment

Yes

Threshold

No

Factors influencing **threshold**

Information from **experiences** and history of decision maker (**the past**)

Low

Assessment Dimension
Decision Rule:
If the **assessment** of the current situation *above* the threshold, decide **Yes**.
If the **assessment** of the current situation *below* the threshold, decide **No**.

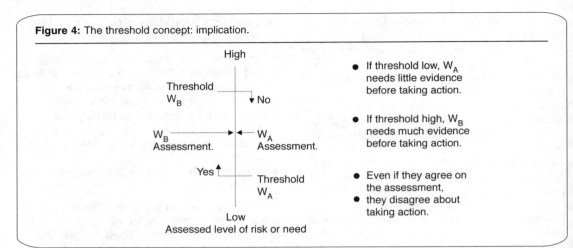

Figure 4: The threshold concept: implication.

- If threshold low, W_A needs little evidence before taking action.

- If threshold high, W_B needs much evidence before taking action.

- Even if they agree on the assessment,
- they disagree about taking action.

(RADM) in child protection. It has been successfully applied to the removal and reunification decisions. The RADM model is a special case of the General Assessment and Decision Making model. This general model incorporates an approach for assessing the situation from the available information and an approach for deciding what to do. It links assessments and decisions by the idea that if an assessment of the situation is above a worker's threshold, then action is taken to manage the situation. The name given to the assessment may change across the intervention continuum or whether the focus of the assessment is on needs or risk; sometimes it is risk, sometimes harm, overall need, strength of evidence or even overall degree of concern.

This general model suggests that at any point along the intervention continuum, the worker gathers information that is organised into a set of factors. These combine together and influence the overall assessment or judgement about the case. This part is a model for how the four systems aggregate case information.

A crucial point is that the model states that the factors influencing the assessment of the case are different to those influencing the placement of the threshold. The model separates the assessment of the situation from the decision to take action. This threshold is like a line in the sand and is the personal standard against which the assessment of the situation is evaluated. The model distinguishes between the person's ability to detect the need to take action from a person's willingness to take action (their threshold).

The threshold concept and inconsistency in decision making

The notion of a threshold for action is not new. Much is made of it in the UK Messages From Research (Department of Health, 1995). They state, 'Professionals see parenting behaviour on a continuum but they have the additional duty to decide whether to intervene and, if so, how. To do this they must draw a threshold; this involves deciding both the point beyond which a behaviour (or parenting style) can be considered maltreatment and the point beyond which it becomes necessary for the state to take action', p15.

Rossi, Schuerman and Budde (1996) researched agreement among child protection experts and workers in their decisions about court referral on substantiated abuse and neglect cases. They found there was considerable inconsistency in the decisions of workers and experts with similar cases treated quite differently by different respondents. They also found similar patterns of case factors in predicting decisions across workers and experts. They state 'our data indicate that the lack of consistency may largely be a matter of different decision thresholds held by different decision makers. By and large, workers appear to take into account the same pieces of information and combine these data in similar ways. So the 'scales' they use are similar: it is the cut points that differ' (p85–86). They term this their 'common scale, varying thresholds' hypothesis.

The position of the threshold defines a person's decision tendency or willingness to take action. This is 'in place' before they get any

Table 1: Agreement on the decision to visit the child and family between Worker 1 and Worker 2 over the 100 case vignettes.

		Worker 2		
		Visit (Yes)	Not Visit (No)	Total
Worker 1	Visit (Yes)	17	77	94
	Not Visit (No)	0	6	6
	Total	17	83	100

specific information about a case and so is independent of the case information. To illustrate, assume that risk is the assessment dimension. If their threshold is low, then they would take action even if they assess a case to have low risk. These people have a decision tendency towards taking action. If their threshold is high, then they would take action only if the risk assessment is high. They have a decision tendency to not take action. Consequently, even if two people agree on the amount of risk or evidence in a case, they may disagree about the course of action because their thresholds differ.

Decisions in child protection, for example the intake decision, are made under uncertainty. A psychological theory that describes performance of decision making under uncertainty is Signal Detection Theory (SDT; Swets, 1992) which dates from the 1950s (Tanner and Swets, 1954). SDT had its origins in the application of statistical decision theory to human observers, particularly that of radar operators. This theory has had wide application, from laboratory studies on tone detection (Ryder, Pike and Dalgleish, 1974) and recognition memory, (Pike, Dalgleish and Wright, 1977) to radiologists detecting abnormalities in X-rays, (Swets and Pickett, 1982) and to child protection decision-making (Dalgleish, 1988; Baumann, 1997). SDT provides methods for measuring thresholds for an individual.

I want to illustrate the importance of threshold in explaining inconsistency in decision making. In 1999 we conducted two studies on decision making at intake. The aim of the first study was to provide operational definitions of the factors influencing both the assessment of the case and the threshold for action. Dalgleish, Elliott, Smith and Sultman (1999) reported the results of the first study and I will discuss the main findings later. The second study provided data to illustrate the importance of the threshold. One hundred and two workers from the Queensland Department

of Families, Youth and Community Care participated. Based on the results of the first study, we constructed 100 hypothetical vignettes representing cases notified to the Department. Each worker considered each case and decided whether the case warranted a visit or not. They also rated the case on a nine-point overall degree of concern scale.

We will focus on two workers because they had such large differences in threshold. The threshold for W1 was 3.1 on the nine point scale and the threshold for W2 was 7.4. They were selected because they were equally good at distinguishing cases that should be visited from those that should not be visited. They also used the overall degree of concern (risk) scale in the same way with highly similar mean ratings, 4.3 and 4.7, and the same case factors predicting their assessments of the cases. The correlation between their assessments of overall concern over the 100 cases was 0.75 and this shows the similarity in assessment. However, Table 1 shows they agreed on whether to visit the child on just 23 per cent of cases. It is clear that W1 recommended a visit to the child in many more cases (94 per cent) than W2 (17 per cent). Cohen's Kappa is a measure of agreement corrected for chance and is .03 for this pair of workers. This is a very low level of agreement and very much lower than that reported by Rossi et al. (1996). These results support the 'common scale, different threshold' hypothesis of Rossi et al. (1996).

Influences on the threshold for action

If case factors do not influence the threshold, then what does? In any decision made under uncertainty, if a person takes action, there may be an error or if they don't take action there may be an error. 'Damned if you do or damned if you don't' is one way to express this duality of error. McMahon (1998) wrote a book about child protection workers with this as its title. There are these two types of error and two types of

Table 2: Four-fold table showing the duality of error for the intake decision.

	'Appropriate decision'	
	Should have taken action Should have visited	Should **NOT** have taken action Should **NOT** have visited
Actual decision: **Yes** Visit family	**Hit** True positive	**False Alarm** False positive Damned if you **do**
Actual decision: **No** Visit family	**Miss** False negative Damned if you **don't**	**Correct No** True negative

correct response. This can be seen in the fourfold table (Table 2). (Although, one doesn't often hear the expression 'Praised if you do and praised if you don't'!) As an example consider the intake decision. This is the decision to visit the family to assess the concerns raised by some notifier.

The first study had a focus on the factors influencing the threshold. Basically, in the first study we interviewed 20 experienced child protection workers from the Queensland Department of Families, Youth and Community Care. After introducing the fourfold table, we asked them to write down all the consequences they could think of for each of the four possible outcomes of the decision. They did this for five stakeholders in the outcome (the child, the family, the worker, the agency, the community/society). Participants were instructed to list in each cell of the table the consequences for each stakeholder that would result from the worker's decision to make their decision an Initial Assessment (Yes; Visit Family). There could be positive and negative outcomes that would come from an amalgam of all the cases in their experience for that particular decision. Participants were informed that they could have had direct or indirect experience with these cases.

Signal Detection Theory posits that decision makers place their threshold so as to maximise utility. The utilities are the values attached to the consequences in each of the four outcomes. In applying this theory to child protection decision making, we assume that workers are aware of the consequences for each of the four outcomes for each stakeholder. This is why we directly asked them to provide this information. Furthermore, we are interested if there are similarities across workers in the types of consequences they name.

To check this, a content analysis of the statements of the consequences was performed. This was done for each stakeholder in the decision, the child, the family, the worker, the agency and the community or society. Statements that were similar in meaning were grouped and a general statement that conveyed the meaning of the category was developed. Table 3, from Dalgleish et al. (1999) shows the most frequently mentioned category for each outcome for each stakeholder. The number of statements in that category together with the total number of statements is also shown.

From Table 3, consider the stated consequences for the inappropriate outcomes, Misses and False Alarms, across stakeholders. A person sets a threshold in an effort to guard against these outcomes. However, given the irreducible uncertainty, (Hammond, 1996), in the task of deciding whether to investigate, the possibility of making an error cannot be avoided. Now, workers do not value these consequences the same. Based on their history and experiences, some may wish to avoid False Alarms more than Misses and others wish to avoid Misses more than False Alarms. That is, the consequences of the different outcomes are valued differently. Not only that, but different people strike different balances. This influences where their personal threshold for action is placed.

We developed a questionnaire from the content analyses. This questionnaire listed four consequences for each outcome for each stakeholder. We asked each of the 102 workers in the second study to rate the importance or value of the consequences.

The responses of W1 and W2 to this questionnaire help explain the large differences in their threshold. Table 4 shows the means ratings of importance of the consequences for

Table 3: Summary of most frequently cited category of consequences by stakeholder and outcome.

Stake-holder	Outcome	Category of consequences	Number/total number
Child	Hit	The child is protected from abuse/harm by way of intervention; the child feels safe; the child feels others also care about their welfare.	28/107
	Miss	As the risk of harm is not identified, there is risk of ongoing or more severe harm to the child (the child is not protected/safe).	22/82
	False Alarm	The child is unnecessarily interviewed. This may lead to fear, anxiety, defensiveness and resistance to disclose harm in the future.	15/72
	Correct No	The child's life is not disrupted as the child stays with their family and is secure in their surroundings. There is no trauma for the child, such as embarrassing and invasive interviews.	15/41
Family	Hit	The family is supported and can be assisted to develop strategies that are more effective. Family functioning improves and children are protected from abuse.	23/92
	Miss	The family continues in dysfunctional patterns of abuse behaviours, with members at risk of harm. The family unit may break down.	27/68
	False Alarm	The family is intruded upon unnecessarily which may cause paranoia, anger, defensiveness, stress and a lack of trust. The family's attitude toward the department may be damaged.	19/76
	Correct No	The family remains intact and continues to resolve their own issues adequately. The family is unaware of the department's involvement.	14/46
Worker	Hit	The worker feels satisfaction having made an accurate assessment and this affirms their child protection intervention skills. The worker is positively regarded by line mangers, team leaders and staff.	26/85
	Miss	The worker feels guilty, responsible and inadequate for not taking action, and suffers decreased self esteem and increased stress.	26/85
	False Alarm	The worker feels guilty for unnecessarily disrupting the family and intruding into their life. The worker has to pacify distressed families.	16/76
	Correct No	The worker feels good about himself or herself and good casework is confirmed. The worker feels competent and relieved, and is praised by other staff noticing the decision.	16/43
Agency	Hit	The Agency reputation is enhanced. There is positive media coverage and public support for the Agency.	23/71
	Miss	The Agency is seen as incompetent, ineffective and is blamed for inaction.	28/69
	False Alarm	The Agency is publicly criticised and blamed and suffers poor morale There is a negative media response with bad public image.	12/58
	Correct No	The department is using resources effectively and efficiently.	12/69
Community/ Society	Hit	The community is stronger, safer and there is decreased violence and disruption to families. Society will have better functioning members who can contribute more fully.	19/60
	Miss	The community lacks confidence in the department and is angry. The community does not know who to turn to.	24/72
	False Alarm	There is anger toward the department and an environment of distrust. The department is viewed as intrusive and is feared.	21/53
	Correct No	There is no disruption or intrusion into families lives, so a sense of autonomy of families within the community is maintained.	7/31

these two workers for the child and family as stakeholders. For the Child as Stakeholder, W1 valued the consequences of a Miss much higher than a False Alarm whereas for the Family as Stakeholder, W2 valued the consequences of a False Alarm higher than a Miss. W1 wishes to

Table 4: Threshold from the vignette task; mean ratings of importance of consequences for 'Misses' and 'False alarms', and percentage of child protection items endorsed.

		Child as stakeholder		Family as stakeholder		
	Threshold	Miss	False alarm	Miss	False alarm	Balance of worker's focus
W1	3.1	8.25	4.75	8.00	6.00	84%
W2	7.4	6.00	4.50	2.75	7.50	32%

avoid Misses for the Child and W2 wants to avoid False Alarms for the Family and they have set their thresholds accordingly.

Statements about the relative balance of the values of consequences are in the literature. As an example, Krugman (1985) stated his values clearly. 'I believe the costs to children of not reporting are much higher than the risks of a social evaluation. Henry Kempe said it best, 'No child ever died of a social work evaluation – many have died because we didn't get one'.' These are clear statements of the desire to avoid misses. No doubt there were equally strong statements about the desire to avoid false-alarms after the United Kingdom's Commission of Inquiry into the removal of children in Cleveland (UK), Butler-Sloss, (1988).

In the literature, there has been tension between a child protection focus and a family preservation focus, (e.g. Wilson and Morton, 1997). This tension is present for individual workers too. We developed a questionnaire that contained 19 pairs of statements: one was consistent with a child protection focus and the other with a family preservation focus. The items were a mix of general value statements and practice principles. Two example pairs were:

A   The state has a responsibility to protect children.
B   Families are the best place for children to achieve their full potential.

A   Work should be focussed on keeping the family together.
B   The client is the child and all other work is secondary.

Workers were asked to indicate which member of the pair they endorsed. Table 4 presents the percentage of child protection focus items endorsed for W1 and W2. This indicates that W1 had a strong focus towards child protection and these values and practice principles are consistent with their threshold placement. W2 had a strong family preservation

focus and this consistent with their threshold placement.

In summary, we have shown that differences in threshold are critical in explaining inconsistency in decision making in child protection. Not only that, but the factors determining a worker's threshold are their values and the value that they attach to the consequences of their decisions. Thresholds are not determined by case factors. Using the General Assessment and Decision Making model and its theoretical basis, a worker's threshold can be measured and made explicit and the influences on their threshold also elicited. These enable workers to gain access to those influences on their decision making that are difficult to articulate since they are not a function of the case information.

Implications for policy and practice: Thresholds

Resolving decisional conflict

Decisional inconsistency arises when two workers differ in their threshold for action and both their assessments of the situation fall between the two thresholds, see Figure 4. This means that they would recommend different courses of action. If they are a worker and their supervisor then they are in conflict and have differences of opinion. If they do not differ or do not differ by very much in their assessment of the current case, it is not useful exploring aspects of the current case. This is a difficult difference of opinion to resolve because the locus of the differences is not in their assessment of the case. What is useful is for each to be able to explain the bases for their threshold for action. Their experiences and history have led them to have different thresholds. It is not easy for a person to suddenly change the values they attach to consequences generally. Nor would it be good for them to change their values for each case that is in dispute. Sometimes, if one of the people is a supervisor, they can say that they will take the decision. While the worker's decision is overruled, they know that it is not their professional judgement that is being devalued. That is, the supervisor has taken responsibility for the decision but the worker's assessment about the amount of risk or evidence of need in the case has been respected. This also implies that supervisors and their workers need training in how to make explicit where their thresholds are and why.

Separating the assessment of the situation in a particular case from the decision about whether that situation is acceptable to the decision maker has these implications. When discussing the assessment, focus on the case characteristics. When discussing whether to take action because the situation is unacceptable, focus on the experiences and history of the decision maker.

When a worker makes a decision that later turns out to be an error, a Miss or a False Alarm, unpleasant consequences follow (e.g. Horwath, 1995). If they do not get appropriate support, then these consequences will be viewed as punishment. This has the effect of rapidly changing that person's threshold for action in the direction of minimising the possibility of making that error again. So if they did not take action and they should have, for later cases their threshold will be lower and they would be more willing to take action. Not only is this interpreted as protecting more children but it also protects the worker from 'punishment'. Research from Signal Detection Theory has shown that punishment, changing the cost/benefit structures for the outcomes, does not improve a person's ability to detect the need to take action, it changes their willingness to take action.

Differential response: Who sets the thresholds?

Differential response is matching the priority for services to the risk assessment. In the structured decision making systems such as FRAAN and the South Australian version of it (Hetherington, 1997), cases are assigned a priority at intake based on cut-points and an actuarial scoring system. After a home visit and a risk assessment, there is a clear and consistent link between the assessed level of risk and the levels of intervention and service from the department and other agencies (Hetherington, 1997, p25). This implies that thresholds are preset for different levels of service. In an actuarial

approach, thresholds are determined from a statistical analysis. (See Lyons, Doueck and Wodarski (1996) for examples of the results of such statistical analyses). Statistical programmes for classification use only the base rates or prior probabilities for classification. This can result in obtaining a relative proportion of Misses and False Alarms that neither policy makers nor workers may want. These computer programmes just do not know how to include the values attached to the consequences of each outcome in the fourfold table. Making these values explicit at the personal, policy and societal level is difficult because no matter what threshold is set, errors of either type are possible and someone will suffer as a consequence, (Hammond, 1996).

What happens when the worker's threshold doesn't agree with the agency's system? I suspect there are at least two reactions. The worker could subvert the system by 'fitting the case information' to arrive at a decision consistent with the worker's decision. There is evidence from the second of our 1999 studies that if a worker perceives the agency taking less action than they want them to, then the worker has high scores on Emotional Exhaustion and Client Depersonalisation as measured by the Maslach Burnout Inventory. That is, morale and worker health and performance are affected.

Implications for policy and practice: Implementation of assessment systems

There are a number of issues concerning implementation of any structured assessment system. The ones I will address are whether the system is a management tool or a practice tool; the comprehensiveness of the system and that implementing a system involves organisational change.

In South Australia's structured decision making system (similar to FRAAN), Hetherington (1997) states 'The system is based on three main premises:

1. The information needed to make good case decisions is the same information that supervisors and managers need in aggregate.
2. Assessment and case planning tools should be as easy to understand and use as possible and should not create additional paperwork.
3. The system should provide accessible management data for evaluation, planning, research and budgeting'.

The latter point is crucial but it only indirectly impacts on the practice of workers. In the implementation of CWBS, Lyons et al. (1999) reports that there was a philosophical shift away from an administratively driven MIS to a service oriented system. The results were that the quality and quantity of information flowing to the frontline improved. The first point is debatable, since I think workers need more comprehensive information on record to use as a practice tool. The information for case decisions should be able to be transformed into the management information system.

The second point really concerns the comprehensiveness and perceived workload of the system. Ease of understanding and use does not mean the system needs to be overly simplistic. However, there is a tension here. If a comprehensive system has better quality information, then for a well implemented and used system, there is likely to be fewer errors of both types. This is an increase in system accuracy. On the other hand, if the comprehensive model is not used by workers because the workers think it is all too difficult and they abandon using it, the consequence is that there may be more errors of both types. So implementation of systems is critical. DePanfillis (1996) used Lewin's Field theory analysis to discuss and outline useful ways of implementing change in social service organisations. Doueck, Bronson and Levine (1992) also discuss implementation issues in child protection services.

Implications for policy and practice: Competencies and skills of workers

While the threshold is important, it is crucial that the decision is informed by the best possible assessment. All the approaches to risk assessment and assessment of needs assume that the workers are competent and have sufficient knowledge. Competency tests and lists of competencies have been developed in many places. I have seen some examples of this and I am sure there are many more. In Illinois, workers need to pass a competency test and in Scotland, there is a list of core competencies. Australia has also developed competency standards for training child protection workers, (Community Services and Health Training Australia, 1998).

The release of the UK Assessment Framework was accompanied by a considerable array of specially commissioned training materials, (NSPCC and University of Sheffield, 2000). The UK Assessment Framework document states, 'This Guidance has an expectation that staff who work directly with children and families and those who supervise and manage this work are knowledgeable, confident and able to exercise professional judgement' (Department of Health, 2000, p86).

Viewing assessment as the core of both assessment of needs and risk assessment implies that training in assessment is crucial. This not only means training in whatever assessment tool has been implemented, since they are the way the case information is organised and summarised, but also training in the skills to collect good quality information. To collect good quality information means having good skills and knowledge about, for example, interpersonal skills and child development. My hunch is that the more comprehensive the assessment tool, the deeper and more extensive the training needs to be.

Sharpening up assessment skills is only part of the picture in the General Assessment and Decision Making model. Such training will lead to more consistent assessments of the situation but will not improve consistency in decision making. There also needs to be training about the threshold. This includes training of workers and supervisors in:

• The threshold concept.
• Use of tools to make explicit threshold placement.
• How to make explicit the influences of the experience and history of the person and the value positions they hold.
• Tools for supervision including the resolution of decisional conflict.

The research reported in this paper is part of a larger research project that includes training on threshold.

Events such as a fatal child abuse case have a large effect on all who have contact with the child. Horwath (1995) details the effects of such cases on staff and makes suggestions for training. While there are lessons to be learned about assessment from reviews of child deaths, (e.g. Sanders, Colton and Roberts, 1999; Reader, Duncan and Lucy, 1993), a very large effect would be to greatly lower the threshold for action. In training on thresholds, this effect may be modified by getting workers to also focus on the costs of false alarms across the range of stakeholders.

However, workers and their supervisors are not the only ones with thresholds for action. Consider the following quote from the Queensland Child Protection Strategic Plan, 2000-2003. This is one of seven principles underlying the child protection system.

Appropriate levels of intervention: Government has a responsibility to ensure the child protection intervention occurs to the extent necessary to ensure the safety and well being of children and young people whilst causing the least disruption to family relationships. This is achieved through access to a range of child protection services that are timely and responsive to the level of need.

In this quote the delicate balance between the desire to avoid Misses and False Alarms is evident, but where the balance may lie is not made explicit. People who determine such policy have in mind some thresholds for action. There could be training for policy makers to make explicit their thresholds and training in how to communicate them to staff in agencies and the community.

Conclusions

I have argued that assessment is at the core of both the assessment of children in need and risk assessment. While there are tensions between the approaches, both are necessary in child protection work. They differ on a number of aspects. A model of professional judgement which links the assessment of the situation to decisions using the idea of personal thresholds was able to account for inconsistency in decision making. Thresholds are influenced not by the case information but by the values placed on the consequences by the decision maker. However, where people put their thresholds and why they do can be made explicit and used to resolve conflict in decision making. It is vitally important that the decision making be informed by the best possible assessment of the case. That is, work should not cease on developing better tools to improve the skills and ability of child protection workers. However, because of irreducible uncertainty in the environment, (Hammond, 1996), there will always be the need for the exercise of professional discretion. This means that thresholds and what drives them for child protection workers, agencies, policy makers and legislators will need to be addressed.

I would like to thank the participants in the study for their enthusiastic contributions. I would also like to thank Louise Earnshaw, Michelle Heron and Will Coventry for conducting the interviews, testing and assisting with the analyses. Birch, Carroll and Coyle donated movie passes and Stuart's Range Wines donated wine to participants. We thank them for their support. The research was supported by an Australian Research Council, Strategic Partnership with Industry, Research and Training Grant ARCL007G/99 and by Queensland Department of Families, Youth and Community Care.

References

Baird, C., Wagner, D., Casky, R. and Neuefeldt, D. (1995) *Michigan Department of Social Services Structured Decision Making System*. Madison, WI: National Council on Crime and Delinquency, Children's Research Centre.

Baird, C., Wagner, D., Healy, T. and Johnson, K. (1999) Risk Assessment in Child Protective Services: Consensus and Actuarial Model Reliability. *Child Welfare*. 78: 6, 723–48.

Baumann, D.J. (1997) Decision Theory and CPS Decision Making. In Morton, T.D. and Holder, W. (Eds.) *Decision Making in Children's Protective Services*. Atlanta, GA: Child Welfare Institute.

Butler-Sloss, E. (1988) *Report of the Inquiry Into Child Abuse in Cleveland, 1987*. London: HMSO.

Costin, L.B., Karger, H.J. and Stoesz, D. (1996). *The Politics of Child Abuse in America*. New York: Oxford University Press.

Community Services and Health Training Australia Ltd. (1998). *Child Protection, Juvenile Justice, Statutory Supervision National Competence Standards*. Canberra: Author.

Dalgleish, L.I. (1988) Decision Making in Child Abuse Cases: Applications of Social Judgement Theory and Signal Detection Theory. In Brehmer, B. and Joyce, C.R.B. (Eds.) *Human Judgement: The SJT View*. North Holland Elsevier.

Dalgleish, L. (1990) *Assessment of Perceived Risk in Child Protection: A Model, Some Data, and Implications for Practice*. Presented at the First International Conference on Risk Assessment. Leicester, England, August.

Dalgleish, L.I. (1997) *Risk Assessment Approaches: The Good, the Bad and the Ugly*. Presented at the 6th Australasian Conference on Child Abuse and Neglect, Adelaide, October.

Dalgleish, L. I. and de Michele, E. (1995) *Risk Assessment and Decision Making in Child Protection.* Presented at the 5th Australasian Conference on Child Abuse and Neglect, Melbourne.

Dalgleish, L.I. Elliott, A., Smith J. and Sultman, CM. (1999) *Assessment and Decision Making at Child Protection Intake.* Presented at the 7th Australasian Conference on Child Abuse and Neglect, Perth, October.

Dalgleish, L. I. and Newton, D. (1996) *Reunification: Risk Assessment And Decision Making.* Presented at the 11th International Congress on Child Abuse and Neglect, Dublin.

DePanfillis, D. (1996) Implementing Child Mistreatment Risk Assessment Systems: Lessons From Theory. *Administration in Social Work.* 20: 41–59.

Department of Health (1995) *Child Protection: Messages from Research.* London: HMSO.

Department of Health (2000). *Framework for the Assessment of Children in Need and Their Families.* London: The Stationery Office.

Department of Health, Cox, A. and Bentovim, A. (2000) *The Family Assessment Pack of Questionnaires and Scales.* London: The Stationery Office.

Doueck, H.J. Bronson, D.E. and Levine, M. (1992) Evaluating Risk Assessment Implementation in Child Protection: Issues for Consideration. *Child Abuse and Neglect.* 16: 637–46.

English, D. J. (1992) *Prediction in Child Protection: Research Results From Two Studies.* Presented at the Ninth International Congress on Child Abuse and Neglect, Chicago.

English, D. J. and Pecora, P. J. (1994) Risk Assessment as a Practice Method in Child Protective Services. *Child Welfare.* 73: 5, 451–73.

Gray, J. (1998) *Development of a Needs-led Framework for Assessing Children and Families in England and Wales.* Presented at the 12th International Congress on Child Abuse and Neglect, Aukland.

Hammond, K.R. (1996) *Human Judgement and Social Policy: Irreducible Uncertainty, Inevitable Error and Unavoidable Injustice.* New York: Oxford University Press.

Hardiker, P., Exton, K. and Barker, M. (1999) The Prevention of Child Abuse: A Framework for Analysing Services. In Stevenson, O. (Ed.) *Childhood Welfare in the UK.* Oxford: Blackwell.

Hetherington, T. (1997) *Child Protection in South Australia: A New Approach.* Adelaide: Department of Family and Community Services.

Horwath, J. (1995) The Impact of Fatal Child Abuse Cases on Staff. Lessons for Trainers and Managers. *Child Abuse Review* 4: 5, 351–5.

Krugman, R.D. (1985) Where You Stand Depends on Where You Sit: The Need for Improved Skills in Evaluating Children and Families. *American Journal of Diseases of Children.* 139: 867–8.

Lyons, P., Doueck, H.J. and Wodarski, J.S. (1996) Risk Assessment for Child Protective Services: A Review of the Empirical Literature on Instrument Performance. *Social Work Research.* 20: 143–55.

Lyons, P., Doueck, H.J., Koster, A.J., Witsky, M.K. and Kelly, P.L. (1999) The Child Well-being Scales as a Clinical Tool and a Management Information System. *Child Welfare.* 78: 2, 241–58.

McMahon, A. (1998) *Damned if You Do, Damned if You Don't.* Aldershot: Ashgate.

Magura, S. and Moses, B.S. (1986) *Outcome Measures for Child Welfare Services: Theory and Applications.* Washington, DC: Child Welfare League of America.

The NSPCC and University of Sheffield (2000) *The Child's World: Assessing Children in Need Training and Development Pack.* London: The NSPCC.

Pike, R., Dalgleish, L. and Wright, J. (1977) A multiple-observations Model for Response Latency and the Latencies of Correct and Incorrect Responses in Recognition Memory. *Memory and Cognition.* 5: 5809.

Reader, P., Duncan, S. and Gray, M. (1993) *Beyond Blame: Child Abuse Tragedies Revisited.* London: Routledge.

Rossi, P.H., Schuerman, J. and Budde, S. (1996) *Understanding Child Maltreatment Decisions and Those That Make Them.* Chicago: University of Chicago, Chapin Hall Center for Children.

Ryder, P., Pike, R. and Dalgleish, L. (1974) What is the Signal in Signal Detection? *Perception and Psychophysics.* 15: 47982.

Sanders, R., Colton, M. and Roberts, S. (1999) Child Abuse Fatalities and Cases of Extreme Concern: Lessons From Reviews. *Child Abuse and Neglect.* 23: 257–68.

Schene, P. (1996) The Risk Assessment Roundtables: A ten-year Perspective. *Protecting Children.* 12: 4–8.

Swets, J. A. (1992) The Science of Choosing the Right Decision Threshold in High Stakes Diagnostics. *American Psychologist.* 47: 522–32.

Swets, J.A. and Pickett, R.M. (1982) *Evaluation of Diagnostic Systems: Methods From Signal Detection Theory.* New York: Academic Press.

Tanner, W.P. Jr. and Swets, J.A. (1954) A Decision Making Theory of Visual Detection. *Psychological Review.* 61: 401–9.

Thorpe, D.H. (1994) *Evaluating Child Protection.* Buckingham: Open University Press.

Washington State Department of Social and Health Services, Division of Children and Family Services, (1995). *Risk Factor Matrix Guide.* Seattle, WA: Author.

Wilson, D. and Morton, T.D. (1997) Issues in CPS Decision Making. In Morton, T.D. and Holder, W. (Eds.) *Decision Making in Children's Protective Services.* Atlanta, GA: Child Welfare Institute.

Wilson, D. (1997) Emerging Issues. In Morton, T.D. and Holder, W. (Eds.) *Decision Making in Children's Protective Services.* Atlanta, GA: Child Welfare Institute.

Chapter Six

Risk and the Framework for Assessment

Alan Cooper

This chapter attempts to answer a question that many have raised with respect to the DoH (2000a) *Framework for the Assessment of Children in Need and their Families* – where is the consideration of 'risk' within the Framework's system? The answer given here is that there is a complex system of risk analysis buried deep in the Framework's structure, but that the full formal articulation and use of it would be impossibly demanding. However, it is perhaps worth trying to explicate the system even if it cannot easily be consciously used.

Supplementary and more easily wielded risk models are already available that can complement the Framework's apparent deficit. Nevertheless, in the final analysis, the most important aspect of the Framework is the emphasis it places on the impact of parenting and family and environmental factors on the child's development.

This paper also looks at how social work judgements are made (including risk judgements), the vexed question of the 'probability' component to risk, error theory in child protection and the issue of why intervention programmes are not (when they should be) intrinsically part of the overall calculation of risk when deciding on Child Protection registration.

The reader is warned that the analysis provided here is not easy – it will demand close reading and refers to 'risk' in a way that may be unfamiliar to some readers from a social work background. I offer no apology for the requirement of the reader to think in depth, as my contention is that risk in social work has long been inadequately examined and explicated.

Risk and the Framework for Assessment

What is risk in Child Protection? Why is it important? How is it that we make mistakes in some cases which, from the benefit of hindsight, seem to have been predictable? What are the components of risk and risk analysis? These are important questions demanding answers.

Whilst many practitioners have welcomed the advent of the *Framework for the Assessment of Children in Need and their Families* (DoH 2000a), it has being criticised for 'not taking risk into account'. For example, Martin Calder makes this criticism (p6) in his recent book *The Complete Guide to Sexual Abuse Assessment*. At one level this is true. There is not any obvious mechanism of risk assessment within the Framework apparatus. At another level, it can be argued that this criticism misconstrues the Framework.

Risk and 'need'

Rather than focus on 'risk' the DoH has chosen to emphasise that social workers must exercise professional judgement in determining child need. This is to be done by comparing the effects on 7 dimensions that encapsulate the child's development with the impact of 6 dimensions of parenting capacity and 8 dimensions of family and environmental factors (see Chapter 2).

The child is at the centre of the triangle to symbolise that the entire assessment is about the child.

The application of professional judgement to determine need and do something about it requires that all practitioners develop extensive knowledge and skills in:

- Applying theory and knowledge to determine levels of harm relative to norms of behaviour, intentionality and circumstance and in reference to possible negative impacts on child development.
- Assessment of need should take place within a culturally and socially sensitive framework of anti-oppressive and anti-discriminatory practice.
- Framing estimates of the future probability of harm in terms of future outcomes where:
  - (Hypothesis) no intervention occurs.
  - (Hypothesis) intervention is considered. There might be several possible hypothesised interventions.
  - Levels of co-operation and motivation to change are determined.

– Intervention is ongoing and evaluated against clearly specified outcomes.
• Applying methods of intervention to effect change and having the ability and flexibility to evaluate and change the method or manner of intervention when needed.

This means that a thorough knowledge of child development is essential, as is knowledge of social work related theory (e.g. Attachment Theory) and of anti-oppressive and anti-discriminatory practice that inform us of normal and abnormal development within the contexts of culture and disability.

Deficits in child development, parenting capacity and family and environmental factors, as well as strengths, are all identified in terms of 'standards' that are rarely, if ever, fully articulated[1] – they are the 'norms' we use (usually unconsciously) to apply value judgements as to whether a behaviour, an intention, a facility (e.g. why a guard for a fire?) is present or not, or in 'excess,' or is 'deficient'.[2] This is an exercise in pure normative based (value) judgement, whether the judge is a member of the public, a social worker, a health visitor using median based centile charts, or the foremost paediatrician in the country. This is why cultural knowledge and sensitivity is so vitally important, as well as knowledge of relative frequency based 'normative' checklists across the range of human development, behaviour, social circumstances and cultures. Furthermore, we should be guided in our normative-based 'valuations' by a sound understanding of and genuine commitment to social work ethics.

The value (need) component of 'risk'

Where there is 'need' there exists risk. 'Risk' is a concept which is totally incoherent unless it is understood in terms of being composed of judgements concerning a possible outcome having both *value and probability* (see Figure 1 and Rescher, 1983).

The 'value' component can be positive or negative.

The identification of any human need is intrinsically a normative based value judgement.[3] Since we are talking about need, the value is negative. The concept of need implies a possible 'harm' or 'impairment' which we can associate with a possibility of future occurrence within a definite timescale (of concern to us) and which might further result in an avoidable

Figure 1: The value/need components of risk.

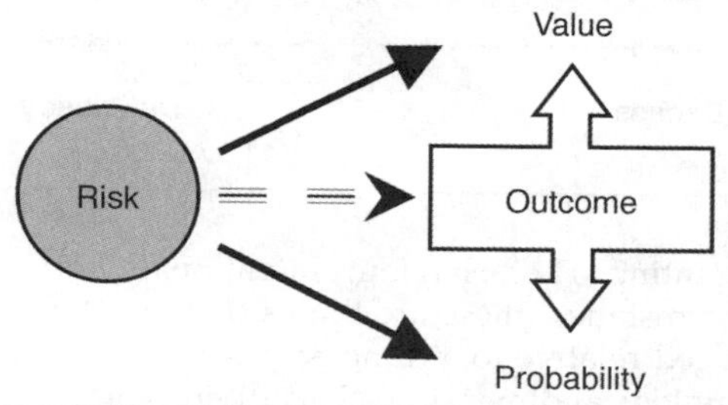

heightening of the need if there is a failure to meet the need.

In social work, we are sanctioned by legislation to make judgements on whether something is harmful or constitutes impairment. Whenever we do this, we make a value judgment relative to the 'norms' for this culture in terms of its legally preferred normative standards. We are enjoined to take fully into account the norms of other cultures but, at the end of the day, we must judge relative to the preferred set of norms, e.g. the law and its precedents and the bodies of knowledge (theory and research) that are accessed to guide the evolution of legal and professional standards. The set of norms that frame our attitudes and responses is forever changing – although the abuse of children has always been with us (Corby, 1993).

The assessment of need and value judgements

A useful way of assisting the judgement of need is the application of the scaling methodology successfully used in Brief Therapy interventions (Kim Berg, 1988; Hawkes et al., 1998). All value judgements can be referenced to scales, which at one end encompass the normal and at the other the seriously abnormal. Such 'scales' are entirely subjective aids to assessment. However, the point of using them is that they can demonstrably show others the subjective 'value' placed on this or that item.

Another way of doing this is to use part of the conceptual apparatus of Axiological Value Theory (Figure 3) to illustrate areas of normal 'acceptability' which is equated with 'good enough parenting'. Behaviour, intentionality[4] or circumstance[5] and which are abnormally in 'excess' (too much of it) or 'deficient' (not enough of it) are equated with 'unacceptable'

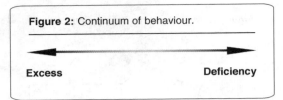

Figure 2: Continuum of behaviour.

Excess   **Deficiency**

parenting. The behaviour, intentionality or circumstance (these are things that exist) is judged relative to a dimension known as the 'ontological dimension'. This dimension is scaled on a continuum having at opposite ends areas of 'excess' and areas of 'deficiency' (Figure 2).

The light area in the middle of the arrow is the 'normal range' of behaviour, intentionality and circumstance that is defined by our experience, theory, knowledge and culture.

Any 'item' of behaviour, intentionality and circumstance is amenable to a judgement of normality or harm (excess or deficiency) in relation to a 'value dimension' overlaid on to the ontological dimension. This value dimension is simply a scale of 'goodness' or 'badness,' or for our purposes 'acceptability' or 'unacceptability,' with respect to how the need or harm is perceived (Figure 3).

The subjective placing of, say, behaviour X on the scale must be evidenced and argued.

The whole point about the use of knowledge, research and theory is to enable the evidencing of judgements. Without this, the judgement is arbitrary and likely to be grossly unfair. When assessing a service user, you have to *show* how, say, behaviour X is 'deficient' at the point where you place it. Indeed, without using knowledge and theory, it is possible that you would not be able to make a reasoned judgement at all. 'Facts' tend to be meaningless unless 'interpreted' through some relevant system of understanding. Furthermore, your scaling can then be readily disputed by parents or constructively used as a means of securing agreement and evaluating progress via intervention.

The technical apparatus of Axiological Value Theory (Figure 3) underlies the graphical representation of Figure 9 'The Sphere of Normative Acceptability'. It must be emphasised that the pictorial representation of the 'fuzzy' area (the 'fuzzy mist' of acceptability, as we might call it) of normative acceptability is a modelling device for illustrative purposes only.

Note: Axiological Value Theory originally derives from Aristotle's Nichomachean Ethics. For a modern introduction see Nicolas Rescher (1969) Introduction to Value Theory (New Jersey, Prentice Hall).

Figure 3: Value and axiological value theory.

Behaviour/intentionality/circumstance for each dimension

Acceptable

Excess

Deficiency

Area of normative acceptability

Unacceptable

Value (judgement) mapping of parental capacity, child need or environmental circumstance on each dimension

The probability component of risk

Probability is measured on a scale from 0 to 1. Traditionally, 0 is taken to mean: 'no chance of something happening' and 1 is taken to mean: 'it is certain to happen'. In either case, there is *no risk*. If something isn't going to happen then to speak of risk is nonsense. If it is certain that something will happen then to speak of risk is nonsense.

These considerations are relative to a timescale that is pertinent to the risk we are examining. In child care work this would normally be a maximum of 18 years (usually much less) at any one time. A probability is (technically) expressed as a number *between* 0 and 1. For example, tossing a coin and expecting 'heads' has a probability of 0.5 – one half of the two possible chances which together add up to the 'certain' 1. We 'scale' a risk by estimating where it would be on a scale of 0 to 1 (easier if you use a 0 – 100 scale and state estimates in terms of percentages %.) The 0.5 example used above becomes 50%. I shall return to the crucial subject of probability later.

Risk relations

A 'risk relation' is simply a logical connective asserting that something 'a' is a risk to something 'b'. This is symbolised 'aRb'. It does not say how or why 'a' is a risk to 'b' – it simply states the relation of a to b in terms of risk. In practice, suppose that you identify domestic violence as having a negative emotional effect on a child. In the schemas to follow we use 'a' to denote an element from the domain of child development, 'b' to denote an element from the domain of parenting capacity, and 'c' to denote an element from the domain of family and environmental factors. Thus, the example given is expressed as: if the domestic violence (b) continues you might perceive that there is an ongoing risk (R) of emotional harm (a) to the child = (bRa).

In general, the detailed analysis of an evidenced risk relation contains the elements of both a value judgement and probability judgement. The value judgement is framed in reference to the behaviour, intentionality or circumstance and its perceived 'unacceptability' in relation to the probable harm it is judged likely to cause.

Models of risk

There are several different models of risk available to social work staff to help them assess levels of risk. Among the better known are Brearley (1982); Greenland (1987); DoH Orange Book (1988); Browne and Saqi (1988); Dalgleish and Drew (1989); Stone (1992) and, more recently, Hagell (1998) and Samra-Tibbetts and Raynes (1999). The Greenland, Browne and Saqi, Stone and Hagell models are based on the actuarial model (relative frequency based checklists). The DoH Orange Book is based around specific question sets used to elicit information. The Brearley, Dalgleish and Drew and Samra-Tibbetts and Raynes models provide various frameworks for the analysis of perceived risks in order to facilitate judgement about overall risk.

Checklists are notorious for restricting risk perception to the items on the checklist and for the statistical solecism of predicting against the group (no controls) from which the information is drawn. The Orange Book has been criticised for encouraging intrusive and narrow questioning. Samra-Tibbetts and Raynes offer a marked improvement on the Orange Book and within their model they utilise Brearley's model to aid the risk analysis. Brearley distinguishes between situational risks (what he calls hazards) and dangers – but the value of this distinction is questionable and the analysis overall is completed at a (macro) high level. Dalgleish and Drew offer a sophisticated model which asks the assessor to examine various areas of family life and assess risk within these areas before moving on to making a judgement about the overall risk in terms of magnitude (negative value) of harm and probability. However, none of these models provide a sufficiently detailed and systematic child-focused structure facilitating the identification of 'risk relations' to guide the assessment.

The biggest problem with all of these models is that they do not encourage comparative analyses of risks and strengths symmetrically – positive benefit to and from, or negative harm to and from, at all levels of the analysis. In the table below, positive 'risk' is termed 'benefit' and 'weakness' is framed as negative 'risk'.

Strength or Weakness	From	To
Risk –	Parent (carer)	Child
Benefit +	Parent (carer)	Child
Risk –	Child	Parent (carer)
Benefit +	Child	Parent (carer)

Risk −	Family and environment	Child
Benefit +	Family and environment	Child
Risk −	Child	Family and environment
Benefit +	Child	Family and environment
Risk −	Parent (carer)	Family and environment
Benefit +	Parent (carer)	Family and environment
Risk −	Family and environment	Parent (carer)
Benefit +	Family and environment	Parent (carer)

Symmetry is analysed as *risk to* (+ or −) someone or something and *risk from* (+ or −) someone or something. This must then be comparatively summarised in terms of an assessment of overall level of risk considered asymmetrically – *as risk to the child.*

The framework as a model of risk

One very good reason for the DoH failure to provide a detailed system of risk assessment within the Framework is that it would be *formally* extraordinarily complicated. The articulation of risk measures within a system like the Framework would require that *formal* risk measurement takes place as a calculation not simply between three domains (Parenting Capacity, Child Development and Family and Environment) but also between the *evidenced* mitigating strength of each of the dimensions of each of the domains against weaknesses (Figure 8). This would correspond to, for each dimension of each domain (6 × 7 × 8) = 336 'dimensions' of risk having to be formally articulated each and every time an assessment is completed.

Technically, even this huge figure is only a general picture as the precise ascertainment of risk represents the analysis of 'risk relations' within each dimensional set. Each set can be thought of geometrically as a triangle connecting one dimension within each domain to one dimension within the other two domains (Figure 8). The number of possible sets is 336. The set of 'risk relations' is characterised by dimensional dyads aRb, bRa, cRb, bRc, aRc, cRa, and the summative system triple set R(abc), and is the number of relations (seven) that are possible over and within each set of three dimensions (Figure 8). The summative system triple R(abc) corresponds to a 'dimension' of risk (Figure 8). As noted, there are 336 such 'dimensions'. The 'value' of each system triple R(abc) can be positive +, negative −, or neutral 0. Each dimensional dyad is two elements of a system triple R(abc) comparison set, that is to say, two dimensions of a possible three examined in terms of risk impacting either way a to b, b to a, c to a and so on. Thus far, we find that the overall number of dyad risk relations is 6 and, therefore (6 × 336) = 2,016 is the total possible number of 'risk relations' at the dimensional level in the Framework.

As we have seen above, a risk relation aRb specifies that there is a risk perceived to be associated with 'a' in relation to 'b'. In terms of the Framework apparatus this is characterised in Figure 4.

Although, at the end of the day, we treat the overall discerned 'risk' as an asymmetrical relation – risk to the child – in terms of the detailed assessment, we cannot forego the symmetrical analysis of the possible dyad comparisons ('risk to and risk from' dimension to dimension (see Langan, 2001, p9)) because, for example, an 'irritable child' ('a' of aRb) (Health Dimension) might represent an ongoing

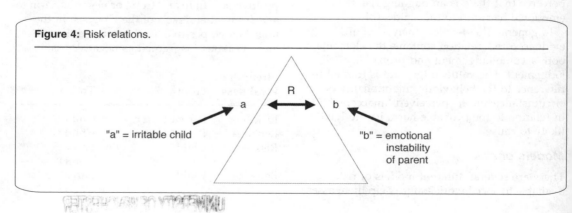

Figure 4: Risk relations.

"a" = irritable child   R   "b" = emotional instability of parent

Figure 5: The detail mapping of risk relations.

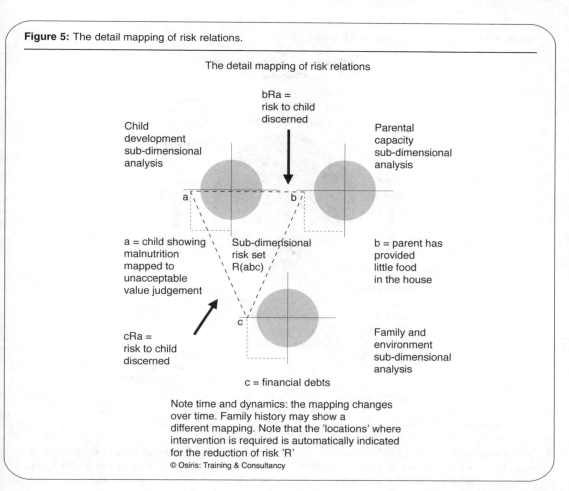

The detail mapping of risk relations

bRa =
risk to child
discerned

Child
development
sub-dimensional
analysis

Parental
capacity
sub-dimensional
analysis

a

b

a = child showing
malnutrition
mapped to
unacceptable
value judgement

Sub-dimensional
risk set
R(abc)

b = parent has
provided
little food
in the house

c

cRa =
risk to child
discerned

Family and
environment
sub-dimensional
analysis

c = financial debts

Note time and dynamics: the mapping changes
over time. Family history may show a
different mapping. Note that the 'locations' where
intervention is required is automatically indicated
for the reduction of risk 'R'
© Osiris: Training & Consultancy

stress factor for a parent. In this sense, the child's whining might be seen as a 'risk' to parental stability of mind ('b' of aRb) (Emotional Warmth Dimension). This in turn is represented by a possible 'mirror risk' to the child of parental annoyance and expressed verbal irritation or it can flip to[6] (Ensuring Safety Dimension) physical harm = b_2Ra. The task would then be to sum all these relational risks within each comparison set (this is a sum over the dimensional system triple R(abc) to produce an overall risk assessment for that particular comparison set. In turn, all the comparison sets are summed likewise to produce an overall assessment of risk. It is not suggested here that by the term 'summed,' numerical weights are placed upon the discerned risks, but 'weighting' of some sort will be *consciously* or *unconsciously* applied both in terms of value (harm) and probability (likelihood of the harm occurring).

However, this is only part of the story: each dimension is itself analysed in terms of many possible sub-dimensions. For example, consider the number of possible aspects of the dimension 'Stimulation' in the domain of 'Parenting Capacity'. Each risk relation R has a value (represents a normative based judgement) which can be positive, negative or neutral. Negative = possible 'harm' (Figures 3, 5 and 6). A negative might be cancelled via *mitigation* (Stage 4, Figure 7) to create a neutral valuation in each case. An example of this might be 'parent doesn't engage in any play' for the child = bRa. This is valued as 'negative value,' = −. This is *mitigated* by grandmother (family and environmental factors domain) always providing sufficient play with the child = cRa. This is valued as 'benefit' = +. If all other dyads in this set are valued as neutral, or no harm = 0, this particular sub-dimensional risk set might then be valued overall as

Figure 6: Sub-dimensional assessment mapping.

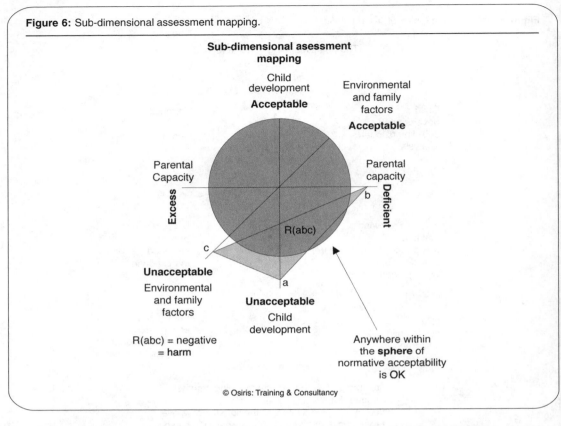

Sub-dimensional asessment
mapping

Child development
Acceptable

Environmental and family factors
Acceptable

Parental Capacity

Excess

Parental capacity

Deficient

b

R(abc)

c

a

Unacceptable
Environmental and family factors

Unacceptable
Child development

R(abc) = negative
= harm

Anywhere within the **sphere** of normative acceptability is OK

© Osiris: Training & Consultancy

R(abc)=0=no risk. But if grandmother is unlikely to be around in six months time there then might be a predictable future negative impact on the child. Determining what strengths are present also enables credit to be genuinely given and (much more difficult to achieve even if you know how) can enable the features of strengths to be utilised within interventions to help address weaknesses.

The reality of trying to figure out what some of these (technically present) risk relations might actually mean in practice would be a nightmare, albeit many are 'edited out' as not relevant anyway. Nevertheless, and for the purposes of illustration, it is useful to have 'fun with numbers' through explicating the sheer complexity of this type of risk analysis system. For example, on pages 19, 21 and 23 of the DoH Framework (2000a) publication, lists of factors are provided that help workers identify some of what these 'sub-dimensions' might be. Depending on how you count them, you will find approximately 53 for child development, 45 for parenting capacity and 55 for family and environment.[7] This observation requires that there be two

applications of the summative system triples R(abc). It is applied once at the lower level of sub-dimensional analysis (see Figure 6) and again at the higher level of dimensional analysis (both applications are depicted in Figure 7).

If we place the sub-dimensional numbers into the combinatorial dimensional comparison formula, you will see that we potentially need to examine $(53 \times 45 \times 55) = 131{,}175$ sub-dimensional comparison sets R(abc) and when this is multiplied by the dimensional dyad risk relation sets, we find that there are $(6 \times 131{,}175) = 787{,}050$ risk relations overall.[8] I am sorry to say there is no truth in rumours that the DoH is working on computer implants for social workers.

Figure 7 illustrates the overall process of the Framework risk analysis. However, this is a static picture. The dynamic characteristics of risk and how any kind of intervention (including the assessment process) affects change can be shown by adapting Figure 5 to illustrate how the judgement of harm can shift over time through family history and possible 'future history' (imagined possible worlds

Figure 7: The process of risk analysis using the framework apparatus.

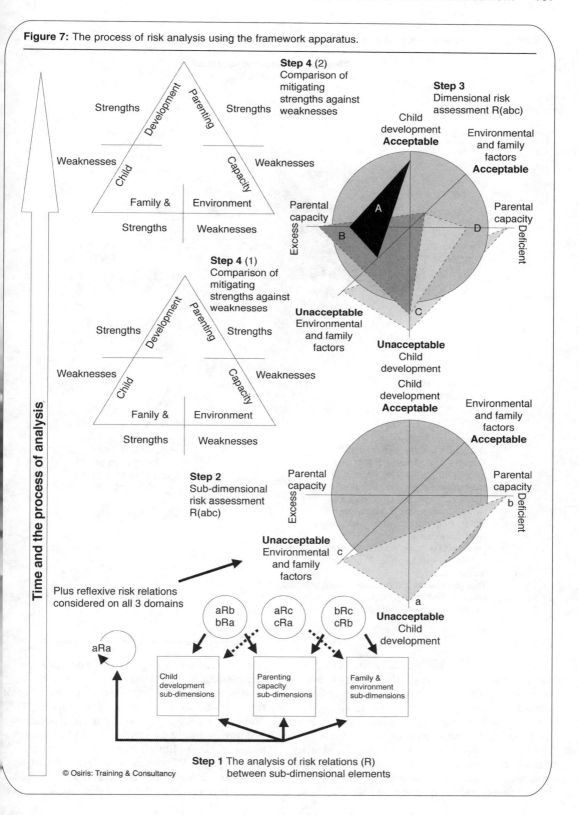

© Osiris: Training & Consultancy

Step 1 The analysis of risk relations (R) between sub-dimensional elements

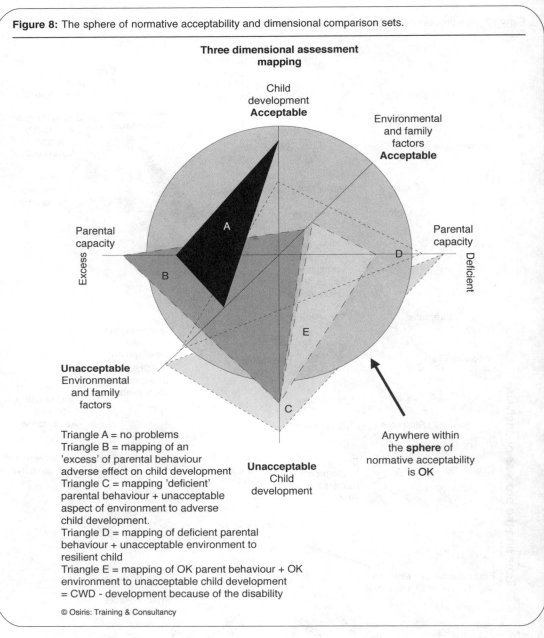

Figure 8: The sphere of normative acceptability and dimensional comparison sets.

Three dimensional assessment mapping

Child development **Acceptable**

Environmental and family factors **Acceptable**

Parental capacity

Excess

Parental capacity

Deficient

A

B

D

E

C

Unacceptable Environmental and family factors

Unacceptable Child development

Anywhere within the **sphere** of normative acceptability is OK

Triangle A = no problems
Triangle B = mapping of an 'excess' of parental behaviour adverse effect on child development
Triangle C = mapping 'deficient' parental behaviour + unacceptable aspect of environment to adverse child development.
Triangle D = mapping of deficient parental behaviour + unacceptable environment to resilient child
Triangle E = mapping of OK parent behaviour + OK environment to unacceptable child development = CWD - development because of the disability

© Osiris: Training & Consultancy

where intervention has partially succeeded – a 'time series'). Furthermore, this analysis can readily help identify the type of intervention regarding what needs to be done to correct 'unacceptable' behaviours, intentionalities or circumstances. This would be with a view to reduce the magnitude of harm associated with risk 'R' in terms of its impact 'a' on the child. This analysis can be done with any one sub-dimensional comparison or collections of

sub-dimensions through to full analytical dimensional comparison.

Another aspect of importance is the matter of reflexive (between elements of the same domain) risk relations. For example, a child who is anorexic might be considered to be at risk in terms of $a1$ emotion/behaviour causing self-harming risk R'^9 to health a_2. But this sort of risk relation might be considered as self-reflexive within the *same* dimension, to say

$a_{1a}Ra_{1b}$ – read as 'health issue 1a impacting in terms of risk to health 1b'. These reflexive risks can occur within any dimension of any domain and represent another layer of complexity within the analysis.

The micro assessment of risk (Figure 7) takes place at Stages 1 and 2 but with an application of Stage 4 on each sub-dimensional triple R(abc) (Figures 5 and 6). The overall macro assessment of risk is derived from Stages 3 and 4 of the process depicted in Figure 7. The R(abc) functions must also act as additional 'rank ordering' functions applied at stages 1 and 2, and 3 and 4, to select those risk relations most prominent in terms of 'harm' and the 'likelihood of harm'. In practice, most Framework risk assessments will be carried out at the dimensional macro stages 3 and 4 level. But if the micro-analysis has not been thorough, major risks may remain undetected or diminished in significance[10] and they will not feature in the final assessment.

Given that there are at least 131,175 sub-dimensional comparison sets R(abc) and *at least* (6 × 131,175) = 787,050 dyad risk relations overall at the sub-dimensional level, it will be appreciated that it would be easy to miss one or several.

It is important to emphasise that the identification and analysis of risk relations is the *very heart of risk analysis* no matter what the subject area. The analysis produces sets of results which are used summatively (appropriate here are the R(abc) functions) to assess risk. In the real world of practice there is no doubt that social work staff are risk analysts whether they like to think of themselves this way or not. Much of social work risk analysis is carried out intuitively[11] and, for the most part, accurately. This is a tribute to the power of the human mind. It is a little like a chess game between a computer and a chess grandmaster. The computer has to follow the programme and examine each and every move for several ahead, tens of thousands of them. The grandmaster sees 'strategic patterns' in the play and plays with strategic intentionality. Good social workers, knowledgable in theory, research and practice, also see 'patterns' in family cases. However, even chess grandmasters lose games. When a game is lost it is because of a failure to 'see' the significance of an opponent's move and its contribution to the game's patterns. This 'blindness' is the equivalent of an undetermined risk relation. Later in this paper, I shall examine the subject of organisational and judgement errors which lie at every turn in this process and which are all too ready to befuddle and bedevil workers undertaking risk assessment.

Reasons for the framework

It is speculation, but I suspect that the DoH has deliberately suppressed the overt risk assessment issues of the Framework for four main reasons:

1. The urgent need for the Framework was shown by the research underpinning Messages from Research (DoH, 1995) which clearly showed that the child protection process was being massively overused. Most cases (76%) going through the Section 47 process were being filtered out before case conference and, of these, many were Section 17 and yet received no service. Hence the Framework is principally designed to encourage 'refocusing' away from the child protection route into more use being made of Section 17.

2. Further evidence for change was provided by SSI inspections that showed (as Maureen Stone (1992) and Peter Reder et al. (1993) had found) that there was no systematic approach taken to assessment and it was often of poor quality and haphazard. Other research (from Parker (1980, 1991) through to the LAC system launch of 1995 and Utting et al. *People Like Us* (1997)) showed that the care system was radically failing a significant proportion of children and young people and the general need for clear identification of problems and outcome evaluation was paramount (hence the *Modernising Social Services* (DoH, 1998) and the 'Quality Protects' initiative).

3. It can easily be seen that if the 'buried' risk system of the Framework were to be openly and 'officially' formalised, its complexity would automatically flow as a consequential requirement and its credibility for practical field use would be impaired. It is necessary to note that the Framework does not preclude the use of supplementary risk models such as Brearley (1982) or Dalgleish and Drew (1989).

4. The fourth and most important reason of all – the Framework is a comprehensive system for assessment designed to uncover the *impact* on the child of family behaviour and circumstances when other risk oriented assessment models can lead all too easily to focussing rather too much on the parents and their 'risky' behaviour and lose sight of the child.

The probability component of 'risk'

It is important to remember that 'risk' is *not* a Section 47 Children Act measure alone but is just as prominent within Section 17 of the Children Act in terms of the level of potential 'impairment' or 'harm'. But it doesn't stop there. The Framework is intended as a *dynamic* model. Therefore, any calculated set of 'risks' is not static, but evolve over time. As intervention is succeeding or not succeeding (according to stated outcome and evaluation measures of the Intervention Plan) the level of risk is going up or down – it is a dynamic which is dependent on the interplay of parental co-operation and motivation and the resources brought to bear on the problem. It is disappointing to note that the standard Initial and Core Assessment forms have no provision to record change within the period of the assessment.

Determining the probability of possible outcomes is something from which social work seems to shy away. There are many reasons for this, among which is the lack of understanding as to the nature of risk (usually seen as sets of risk factors to do with harm), the lack of Risk Management Policies (not the same as Child Protection Procedures)[12] and the level of 'risk adversity' shown by the media.

Nevertheless, there is no escape from trying to determine probability within risk situations unless the strategy adopted (as it usually is) is that of the automatic: 'there is 100% probability of harm unless we are shown otherwise'. Here the judgement taken is that there has been (negative value) harm based on determined fact and that this means that there will be 100% (certain) chance of further harm unless it is demonstrated to the SSD that this will not be the case. This strategy results in registration on the Child Protection Register (CPR) for many families. I call this the 'certainty strategy'. I doubt that this 'certainty strategy' will ever be overthrown, especially in a climate of public inquiries and the vilification of social work. This will likely mean that the 'refocusing' intentionality of the Framework is ultimately doomed to failure.

Whether the above is true or not, estimates of the probability component of risk are required if we are to approach the subject of risk assessment professionally. It might continue to be the case (because of the fear of catastrophic harm) that the 100% 'certainty strategy' of knee jerk registration doesn't change. Given that we

are exposed to life and limb risks this isn't so surprising. However, the vast majority of cases eventually come off the CPR by reason of successful intervention. This means that the probability of harm, in most cases, was never fully 100% given the co-operation/motivation of the parents and the successful intervention utilised. In other cases, children are deregistered by coming into the care system.

'Working together' and the 'certainty strategy'

The main culprit in the illogicality referred to above as the 'certainty strategy,' is the DoH publication (1991, revised 1999) *Working Together to Safeguard Children*. This document is about as 'anti-Framework' as it is possible to be whilst pretending otherwise. The problem is articulated by paragraph 5.64 which speaks of the Case Conference consideration of harm and risk and which goes on in paragraph 5.66, to say: 'If a decision is taken that the child is at continuing risk of significant harm and hence in need of a child protection plan . . .' So the exhortation (and the longstanding practice of most departments) is that consideration of harm done or likelihood of harm being done is enough to cause registration on the CPR. This bizarre emphasis puts the cart before the horse and ensures the registration of children who (probably) should not be registered at all. It helps ensure a 'risk averse' mindset throughout the land because the *efficacy of intervention plans cannot be considered until after the registration decision is taken.*[13]

It is an incontrovertible fact that most children do come off the CPR within two years – so *something* has worked. Most do not return to the CPR, so something has *worked well*. Unless it was *just the fact* of being on the CPR ('punishment mentality'), then the CPR cannot be the sole determinant of interventive success.

The scaling of 'risk'

In social work we are often confronted by cases in which we are certain that something unacceptable will happen and will remain present if we don't do something about it and intervene. In such a case, we are not really talking about risk in terms of the probability of harm. Rather, we are talking of the perceived certainty of harm[14] and, at the same time, looking toward a probability of no harm (or less harm) given success in our intervention.

In my view, this is the only rational justification for the 'certainty strategy' referred to above. The problem we are left with is what sense does it make to speak of a probability of something not happening? It makes perfect sense, as in the case of it being highly probable (odds on bet) that you will not win the National Lottery this weekend.

But this stance *demands that we examine and critically evaluate intervention strategies* in terms of probabilities of success or otherwise. Furthermore, the estimation of probability on a % scale of 0 to 100 is every bit as subjective and fuzzy'as the 'valuing' of intentionality, behaviour or circumstance that determines the value' part (the harm) of any identified risk. We take, for convenience and it is all we have, risk factor checklists as 'objective'[15] measures which will inform or guide our estimations of harm.

For example: it is likely we would ask Probation to provide a risk assessment on this problem:

For untreated male sex offenders (offending against boys) there is a 40% recidivism rate of sex offending.
(Beckett, 1994).

This 'fact' is derived from such checklists and he studies that contributed to the checklist, or more usually the quoted checklist itself is our evidencing'. But this particular man, facing you right now (suppose you are the Probation Officer), might be a future 'false positive' with no intentionality to re-offend and will not, as a matter of future fact, re-offend. However, the problem with the checklist (used on its own) is that it demands you place a 100% certainty on the likelihood of re-offending. Several things will tell against the likelihood of this – an assessment of his history, attitudes, intentionality (includes motivation) and time.[16] But assessments of intentionality are very difficult. If he lies (as people intent on sexual re-offending do) and his lying remains undetected, the assessment is fatally flawed. But what if you are 'reasonably convinced' he is not lying and seems genuinely motivated and committed to an ongoing therapy programme?

What does 'reasonably convinced' actually mean in terms of probability? This is a real problem, not a fanciful one. The London Business School once conducted a series of exercises on how 250 business executives used 'probability' expressions.[17] The results indicated fairly close agreement on such terms as 'quite certain' (expressive of high probability) but a wide variation of the use of such terms as 'possible'.[18] Not surprising, you might say, but still the problem remains.

What if you use the term 'reasonably certain' as expressing about 50:50 in terms of probability (50% chance of sex offence and 50% chance of no sex offence)? You cite your evidence to the Case Conference and people are impressed, but you tell no one (this is common) of the probability (the %) that you are thinking of as corresponding to your phrase 'reasonably certain'. In other people's eyes your use of the term 'reasonably certain' has been unconsciously translated to mean 'quite certain' (highly probable) that this person won't re-offend. Maybe you even had an unconscious bias that you wanted this to happen given your findings and you presented these in a way that 'swayed'[19] your audience. But suppose you had actually drawn the scale:

10%	20%	30%	40%	50%	60%	70%	80%	90%	100%

Now you have to tick exactly what you mean when you say 'reasonably certain'. This results in a different story for people. Now there is a 50% chance that he *will* re-offend and your unconscious bias is uncovered for all to see. This interpretation (or the non-offending alternative) should result in the correct determination that there is a high risk of re-offending and the ultimate test can only be time.[20]

The essentials of estimating the probability component of risk

- Knowledge of relative frequency based checklists of risk factors. e.g.

There is approximately a 50% chance of violence given a male convicted of serious violence and who has recently been engaging in violent fantasies.
(Monahan et al., 2000).

Checklists are rarely much better than around 80% reliable (Browne, 1995) so 'false positives' (people identified as abusers but which haven't/won't abuse) and 'false negatives' (abusers which don't show up) will always get through. The former group is of concern because of the severe stress Child Protection enquiries place on families (Farmer, 1993; Cleaver and Freeman, 1995). Nevertheless, checklists might be full of faults, but they are still the indispensable guides to alertness and informing our judgement on risk issues.

- Accurate and ongoing assessment of levels of co-operation and motivation.

This is really crucial and is often ignored or woefully incomplete in risk assessments. But it is a dynamic. Some parents are not in the least co-operative and motivated in the early stages of child protection work. How would you be if your parenting were called into question? And yet this means that a seven week based risk assessment addendum (containing an assessment of co-operation and levels of motivation) to a Core Assessment is perhaps not likely to be wholly accurate. Our experience in training social service staff leads us to the view that knowledge of assessing motivation, in particular, seems fairly weak (Morrison, 1991). Knowledge of intervention strategies to improve motivation seems virtually non-existent.[21]

- Knowledge of the effectiveness (relative frequencies of success) of intervention strategies measured against clearly identified outcomes (goals).

This is an area where social work is really in the mire. Furthermore, social work has almost forgotten about intervention (as opposed to assessment) and some newly qualified workers have even said to us that this is 'not our job'. But again, the concept of 'risk' cannot be coherently used to inform any action unless you have some idea of the efficaciousness of what it is that you plan to do. There are relatively few cases that are so serious and so evidently dangerous that you immediately plan total separation. And yet even here, you will be calling upon research knowledge and professional experience allowing predictions of catastrophic harm to say (preference value judgement) that the child would be *better off* in permanent care or adopted.

There are many reasons why our profession is poorly served with effectiveness studies. Yet it is with intervention methods that we should be primarily concerned, for it is these that make the difference in most cases. Intervention methods should be empirically testable in terms of success and be capable of stating procedurally in a step-by-step fashion. It is possible to say that Cognitive – Behavioural based approaches represent the most likely route to success in certain defined situations; but even here, this is much too broad a brushstroke to be really informative[22] and psychodynamically based approaches have much to say which is highly

pertinent (e.g. Allen, 2001; Fonagy, 2001; Hill, 1999).

However, what we *really* want to know is: *Exactly* what *method* is best used *with this* problem, in terms of achieving *what outcome* and with *what likelihood* of success (the reduction of expected harm) and given *this level of co-operation* and *this level of motivation during timescale* X?

So where are our 'checklists' for successful interventions? And all this says nothing about the competence of the practitioner to build and effectively utilise rapport[23] and to be able to actually use the selected method, and then to be competent enough to evaluate the intervention, and then, if it doesn't work – to do something different.[24]

The timescale and outcome components of risk analysis

Besides conveniently forgetting the details of how risk might be incorporated into the Framework apparatus, the DoH pays insufficient attention in its Framework publications to the dynamic time-based aspect of 'assessment through intervention'. I have used this phrase to emphasise my belief that intervention (whatever it is) should be treated as an intrinsic component to the assessment of risk.

Framing a timescale does require knowledge of the probable efficaciousness of interventions. It also requires that outcomes be well specified and framed in language which allows for verification or refutation. To this end, practitioners would be best served by adopting the *sensory-based language* advocated in the 'well-formed outcome' model of Neuro-Linguistic Programming (NLP). This model for outcomes is based on sound behavioural principles. It encourages taking into account matters of 'secondary gain' and ecological issues and stipulates the framing of an evidence procedure for testing results.

The well-formed outcome model (Hall and Belnap, 1999)

- The outcome should be stated in the positive – what is wanted – NOT what is not wanted (you can't test for what doesn't exist). This will need to be agreed by you and the service user.
- The outcome *must* be demonstrated in sensory experience – what would you and others see, hear, feel (and possibly taste and smell) when the outcome is realised. This provides for an

evidence procedure to test for achievement of the outcome.

- The outcome *must* be appropriately specified and contextualised. In what context should the outcome appear? When should it occur? When shouldn't it occur?
- The outcome should be initiated and maintained by the individual – you are not conditioning rats or pigeons, you must work in partnership and agree/negotiate outcomes. No agreement necessitates a differently specified outcome.
- The process to achieving the outcome must be 'do-able' – each step needs to be framed in chunks which are achievable and evaluated in terms of sensory experience.
- The outcome should be ecological in effect – it must maintain (not fragment) the homeostasis (balance) of the system. This means that any secondary gain attached to an unwanted behaviour must be taken into account and solutions factored in. If this isn't done – the proposed change programme will probably fail.
- The outcome *evidence procedure* must be time-scaled and a review date set. The timescale must be realistic, but be framed in reference to the paramountcy of the child's needs.

This model is more usefully prescriptive in terms of empirically testable requirements than other generalistic (much too vague and high level) outcome framing models such as the 'ASPIRE' model of: Assessment, Planning, Intervention, Review and Evaluation. It is also more useful than the 'SMART' model of: Specific, Measurable, Acheivable, Reviewable and Timescaled insofar as it gives real meaning to the required steps.

Figure 9 is a representation of the Essentials of Risk Assessment and attempts to illustrate that the overall assessment of 'risk' in social casework is a comparative judgement involving six elements: the *co-operation* and *motivation* of the service user, the *probability* of something happening which is seen as harmful, the *magnitude (negative value)* of the harm, the *likelihood of success of the intended intervention package* in terms of *what specified* outcome and the *timescale* of the intervention.

Figure 9 highlights the difference between Framework based risk assessment where the intervention package should be an integral part of the risk assessment and the *Working Together* version, Figure 10 where the intervention

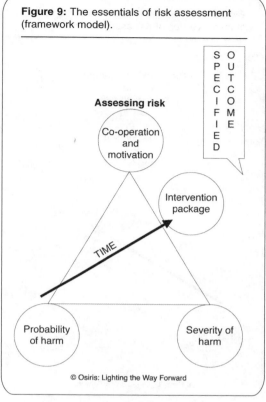

Figure 9: The essentials of risk assessment (framework model).

© Osiris: Lighting the Way Forward

package is not considered at all (prior to registration and in cases that have not been prior worked).

I advocate the simultaneous use of 9 and 10 in all risk assessment situations.

Risk and objectivity

Developing an estimation of the probabilities associated with possible harms and interventions is a professional duty. Because of the inherent problems of working with uncertainty, despite any amount of 'normative-based' theory and knowledge at our disposal, our judgements on probabilities are essentially subjective and tentative. The *only way* we can 'objectify' our judgements is to evidence them and share them. This same principle of evidencing and sharing applies equally to our value judgements regarding levels of harm or impairment. Using scaling methodology with clients and colleagues during meetings and supervisions and frankly stating our evidence in support of our value (harm and strengths) and probability judgements makes this 'objectification' process easier and fairer. More

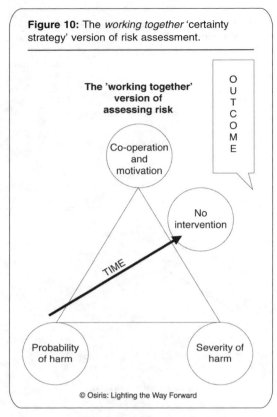

Figure 10: The *working together* 'certainty strategy' version of risk assessment.

The 'working together' version of assessing risk

OUTCOME

Co-operation and motivation

No intervention

TIME

Probability of harm

Severity of harm

© Osiris: Lighting the Way Forward

importantly, our judgements are open to challenge and refutation. Please note that it is 'refutation' which is key to the whole process and not 'confirmation'.[25]

I believe that the process of 'peer aided judgement' (Simmonds, 1998) should be adapted and elevated to the status of the *key scrutiny system* for all Child In Need and Child Protection casework. But the process needs to be manifested at all stages of assessment and intervention and the 'peers' should be extended to include parents, child (if of an age and understanding) managers, case conferences, meetings and core group work. This would be aided at the assessment stage if, instead of the virtually useless 'yes/no' tick boxes[26] of the Core Assessment, ready-to-use scales set against the Core Assessment questions are available for social workers to scale their judgements.[27]

Mistakes and risk: error theory in social work

The literature on how people can make mistakes when confronting risk situations is vast.[28] For some strange reason hardly any of this research

is ever quoted in social work texts.[29] And yet, as Stone (1992) and Reder et al. (1993) noted, we keep making the same mistakes. So what does go wrong? Is it failures of individual competence or something much wider that is at issue? I would speculate that it is the latter.

DipSW and much of post qualification training do not touch the deeper aspects of risk. I often find that qualified social workers cannot even give a basic definition of risk, let alone think about how probability and value judgements connect to risk and assessment. And then there is the fact of the non-existent risk management policies (see footnote 25) and the absence from many departments of effective workload management schemes in conjunction with staff shortages. Most important of all: I also believe that the sheer complexity of risk analysis has *never* been fully appreciated in social work.

Howitt (1992), in his critical book on the child protection process, noted that social work has yet to develop an 'Error Theory' in terms of the meta-level analysis of mistakes. Certainly, there have been a great abundance of inquiries. Despite the publication of several studies (DoH, 1982, 1991; Reder et al., 1993; Hagell, 1998; Reder and Duncan, 1999) examining the lessons from these inquiries there has hardly been any attempt to link the findings of social work research with the enormous literature on judgement mistakes and risk errors outside of social work.

In my study of risk literature (both social work and outside of social work) I would submit that most mistakes uncovered by inquiries fall into the categories identified and listed below,[30] although this listing is not presented as exhaustive. Furthermore, in principle, I believe that this list is as applicable to risk management in adult social work as it is to child protection work.

Organisational errors

- Procedural error – policies and procedures not followed.
- Checklist fixation bias, including over reliance and fallacy of the base rate error.
- No risk management policy: no guarantees for support, training or workload management within the context of working to policy and procedures. No senior management group that regularly monitor and record organisational risks.
- Inter-agency failures of communication: not sharing/comparing information.

- Intra-agency failures of communication: Adults and children and families not sharing/comparing information.
- Inter-agency tensions/role confusion: can cause assessment paralysis.
- Assessment paralysis: groups cannot agree on problem or intervention strategy.
- Resource tensions: the right intervention is not available or is deficient.
- Media fear and paranoid risk adversity: lowers risk threshold – more CPR registrations and children in care.
- Management withdrawal/isolation: distance from staff and refusal to take case accountability – causes poor morale/staff tension – raises organisational risk.
- Management offers poor quality supervision: management inadequacy of knowledge and skills, uncaring attitude toward staff – raises organisational risk.
- Management/staff tension: poor morale, workplace stress and conflict.
- Workload stress and 'burn out'. (associated with inadequate staffing and poor or non-existent workload management).
- Inappropriate allocation (inexperienced and inadequately trained staff).
- Inadequate knowledge and training on theory and research informing assessment.
- Inadequate training on 'what works' in terms of interventions and evaluation.
- Inadequate training on risk and risk management.

Judgement errors

- Non-existence error: (not seeing or talking to the child).
- Outcome (goal) error: non-specificity or confusion over framing outcomes.
- Templating error: mindset fixed on mistaken definite descriptions concerning a person's behaviour, intentionality, circumstances or culture.
- Attribution error: false ascription of intentionality.
- Availability error: false belief that information is complete.
- Contrition bias: believing the best in the face of evidence.
- Diminishment bias: reducing the significance of important information.
- Confirmation bias: falsely believing that hypotheses should be confirmed and finding 'confirmation' at every turn.

- Ratcheting error: the upshot of confirmation error – the case is 'magnified' or 'diminished' out of all proportion and the reality cannot easily be recovered.
- Logical reasoning errors: e.g. Affirming the consequent.

These items apply as much to Managers as to front line staff.

There is insufficient space in this paper to examine these errors in detail. Many of the items listed under 'organisational errors' are almost self-explanatory. However, whilst most of these organisational factors work negatively to heighten the probability of things going dramatically wrong for the service user and the organisation, media fear tends to work against service users and their families because the organisation adopts a strongly 'risk averse' philosophy and children come into the care system unnecessarily or unjustly. Indiscriminate use of checklists (checklist fixation) is associated with misplaced faith in their efficacy (Beckett, 2001). This is what Pride (1987) and Howitt (1992) have railed against in their polemics against the child protection process.

The lack of risk management policies that guarantee staff adequate training, effective workload management and conditional support when things go right and when they go wrong is simply inadmissible. The tendency of management to avoid taking full and unequivocal accountability at all times, including when something goes wrong is hardly conducive to building staff morale. On a more positive note, the strong emphasis placed on effective 'working together' by the DoH (1999 and 2000a) will hopefully impact more and more progressively on all agencies involved in the assessment process. Sadly, it would seem, the DoH has forgotten intervention and its critical role in risk management (Regan, 1992). One would have thought that when such an august body as the Royal Society notes the importance of risk management and offers a definition:

The making of decisions concerning risks and their subsequent implementation . . . flows from risk estimation and risk evaluation.

(Royal Society, 1992).

The reference to 'implementation' would automatically be taken to mean that it is continually necessary to assess and evaluate risk during intervention. On this understanding, intervention cannot be divorced from the assessment of risk at any time and should be part of the initial assessment relative to the set of possible hypothesized outcomes. This set is inclusive of the assessment of risk without any specific outcome-intended intervention and with (various possible) interventions.[31] (See Figures 9 and 10).

Judgement errors are almost certain to occur to most people at some time and in some place. They are therefore of enormous importance to managers and practitioners. Nevertheless, to judge from my own experience, few managers and practitioners have heard of them. Outcomes are often framed in language that is not permissive of testing. Several fatal abuse inquiries have shown that belief system 'templating' has led directly to signs and symptoms being ignored or 'diminished' in significance. The child 'not existing' and therefore not seen is well documented in several inquiries. Errors of false attribution (falsely believing something of someone); errors of availability (incomplete information falsely treated as complete when deciding action), errors of contrition (wanting to believe the best in the face of evidence) all seem to occur with regularity. The error of diminishment entails the 'reduction' of the significance of information: for example, the fatality of Lauren Wright (2001, Norfolk SSD) where the Team Manager was reported to have unfortunately delayed an indicated urgently needed visit because one had been planned for a few days time. The error of confirmation bias is the tendency to look for 'proof' of hypotheses instead of refutation, which in turn can lead to 'ratcheting' where the favoured hypothesis is elevated to a state of unchallengeable sanctity. Lastly, logical reasoning fallacies such as affirming the consequent are connected to checklist fixation errors. For example, the 'anal dilation' reasoning error of Cleveland exemplifies this fallacy: Anal sex abuse causes anal reflex dilation in some cases (statistical finding) – this is a legitimate conclusion from observation. Anal reflex dilation (singular case) indicates sex abuse – this inference is not legitimate as the case may be a false positive and the dilation caused by something else.

Most of these judgement errors are intimately related to each other and psychologically driven. They derive from ignorance, anxiety, fear, racism or uncertainty about working with people of other cultures, but all occur within the context of the ethos and pressures of the organisation. The organisation should always bear the responsibility.

Social work educators neglect the deeper understanding of risk to the great peril of social work. There is much more to the assessment of risk than risk factor checklists which seem to constitute the sum total of what most students and social workers ever remember being taught both at DipSW level and above.

Conclusion

The identification of child need is facilitated within the Framework by making a series of comparative judgements about the impact on the child of parental deficit / strengths and family and environmental deficits / strengths (these are the triangle 'comparison sets' of Figure 8). The detailed formal analysis of risk is logically possible within the Framework apparatus but represents a colossal mind-boggling enterprise. And yet this enormously complex task refers to a 'risk reality' (the world in which the child lives) that is independent of *any* system facilitating a risk analysis. The risks can be thought of as 'in there somewhere' whether you use the Framework system or some other system to uncover them.[32]

The *quality* of a risk analysis system is indicated by the number of 'risk relations' capable of being uniquely specified within the system. The *usability* of a system is a trade off between its quality and its ease of use. The analysis provided here of the 'hidden' risk analysis system of the Framework serves only to highlight, through the logical and numerical analysis of the Framework's 'risk analysis' structure, just how fantastically complex risk analysis can be within the field of child protection, or indeed, any other area of social work. The advocated need to incorporate intervention into the assessment right at the start (from referral on) further complicates matters.

An alternative to the Framework's hidden risk structure might be to facilitate risk analysis by applying a supplementary risk model such as Brearley (1982) or Dalgleish and Drew (1989)[33] to the dimensional elements of the Framework and the derivations of mitigated or non-mitigated deficit / strengths of the dimensional comparisons. This may be less threatening and easier to use, but carries its own inherent risk of focussing on parental 'risky' behaviour and excluding the impact on the child. Furthermore if risk relations are left unexamined (as they will be – who can possibly examine *at least* 787,050 in 35 days?)[34] the assessment is not complete and the assessor is inevitably vulnerable to 'Availability Error'. The assessment of risk is a complicated business and the price exacted by complexity is very high.[35] This remains the unadulterated truth no matter how child protection systems might be organised.

Nevertheless, much more needs to be done in terms of managers' and social workers' appreciation and understanding of the nature of risk. Education and training on risk in social work need to become deeper and more broad-based than looking just at child abuse signs and symptoms and adult risk indicators, essential though this is. Until and unless the DoH defuse their own time bomb and reconcile the radically mismatching *Working Together* with the *Framework*, nothing much will happen with regard to ending the dominance of the 'certainty strategy' in child protection. Case Conferences at 15 days from the point of Section 47 decision will cement rather than weaken this strategy. The continuance of its dominance will possibly result in us remaining embedded in time-constrained assessment and interventive competence will further diminish and atrophy.

Notes

1. An example of written normative standards is scholastic tests such as the Department of Education and Employment, e.g. Standard Assessment Tests. Another example of normative checklists for *abnormal* behaviour would be the checklists of DSM IV: Diagnostic and Statistical Manual of Mental Disorders: American Psychiatric Association.

2. The DoH seems not to like the term 'deficient,' but 'abnormal' or 'bad' are much worse. Nevertheless, the word 'deficient' is not, as the DoH says, particularly empowering. More suitable language would need to be used when working with service users.

3. Interestingly, this flies in the face of the simplistic (and dangerous) interpretation of the ethic of universal 'non-judgementalism' in social work. Indeed, I advocate here that the concept is incoherent unless it is understood as a necessary ethical *intentional* stance toward the client. The concept is usually understood (but unfortunately not always) in this way.

4. 'Intentionality' is used in this paper as in philosophical psychology, to denote 'object of mind'. A discussion on this is to be found in Rescher (1969) and John Searle (1992) Chapter 8.

5. 'Circumstance' is here used as a shorthand for 'Family and Environmental Factors'.

6. Catastrophe Theory can provide a useful graphical model of this behaviour. See Woodcock and Davies (1978). Further, the graphical representations of the 'cusp' and 'butterfly' catastrophes can be utilised to model 'risk ready' and 'risk averse' intervention pathways and to illustrate the associated patterns of risk endemic in either option. These various aspects will be explored in a forthcoming paper: *Working Together, Partnership and Games People Play.*

7. In training exercises, social workers consistently identify substantially more sub-dimensions than those listed for illustrative purposes by the DoH. Specialist assessments will generate yet more.

8. This type of risk analysis system generates these sorts of numbers automatically. If we had four domains instead of three and another set of, say, six dimensions to work with, the required comparative sets rise to $6 \times 7 \times 8 \times (6 \text{ extra dimensions}) = 2,016$ and the number of possible risk relations rises accordingly.

9. The letter 'R' is here shown in a different typeface to indicate a reflexive 'risk relation'. There is *at least* $7+6+8=21$ such Framework reflexive relations and many more per individual case – especially regarding CWD cases.

10. See 'Diminishment Error' and 'Availability Error' in later section on Error Theory.

11. Of relevance here are naturalistic models of judgement and decision-making. See Klein (1996) and Beach (1997).

12. See Audit Commission Report: (2001). A Risk Management Policy is at a level higher than particular sets of procedures and should operate at a more global perspective. For example, ensuring adequate workload management. I would argue that it should guarantee adequate training on risk and risk issues and offer support (not suspension) for staff following procedures and having attended stipulated training programmes.

13. This also raises the probability of non-cooperation as game theoretic analysis can show. Interestingly, the 'risk decision

model' (Figure 10) of *Working Together* is at complete variance with every other published mainstream naturalistic or classical model of decision insofar as intervention (protection plan) is left to a later decision process. See forthcoming paper: *Working Together, Partnership and Games People Play*.

14. It is not uncommon to treat judgements of 'high probability' as 'certain' in most circumstances.

15. Of course, they are not really 'objective' – all real world probabilities (human observer) are essentially subjective in the Bayesian sense (see footnote 20).

16. On no account is it here intended to portray a very complex analytical task as simple – this section is concerned only to illustrate probability estimation.

17. Reported by Moore (1995). Some decision models, e.g. the Delphi model, insist that ALL decision-makers undergo prior training in the use of such 'risk' words.

18. Alan Cooper and Judith Tuck (Osiris Training & Consultancy) have informally replicated these results with more than 140 social work staff.

19. This is reminiscent of the 'Availability Error' of Amos Tversky and Daniel Kahneman (1974)

20. This scaling methodology can assist to reflect the results obtained by formal Bayesian analysis of prior + expected probability as would be quickly seen if the expected probability of offending had been scaled at 10% and the prior (checklist) probability had been given as (near) 100%. However, this is beyond the scope of this paper. Bayes' probability theorem (and the mathematician Brandon Carter's amazing use of it) is frighteningly well explained by John Leslie (1998) in his *The End of the World*. Alternatively, see Plous (1993). However, while I seriously doubt that formal Bayesian analysis is a practicable option for social workers, it is certainly necessary to build in to social work practice the Bayesian principle of constant risk evaluation feedback loops during all interventive (including assessment) work.

21. The DiClemente and Prochaska *Comprehensive Model of Change* championed by Morrison (1991) and by the DoH (2000b) is a worthwhile tool for assessment and intervention strategy. Nevertheless,

practitioners might explore the many and varied patterns for supplementing motivational change. See, for example: Bandler (1985), Andreas et al. (1996), Bodenhamer and Hall (1997), Hall and Belnap (1999). Hall et al. (2001) discuss the DiClemente and Prochaska model in terms of supplementary interventions.

22. Brian Sheldon (1995) has long championed Cognitive – Behavioural intervention, although the traditional approach favoured by Sheldon tends to be more behavioural than cognitive. Nevertheless, the behavioural method of 'Shaping' can be enunciated in an easy stepwise way and is eminently testable throughout the entire process of intervention.

23. Good rapport is the key to doing anything at all with people: See Andreas et al. (1996).

24. One of the maxims of Brief Therapy and NLP.

25. This the guiding principle formulated by Karl Popper (1959) and is applicable to any enquiry.

26. For example, on a visit to test for 'Emotional Warmth' you observe 10 minutes warmth and 50 minutes of coolness. Have you observed 'warmth?' Yes? No? What if you see half and half? What then? Of course, the report can expand, but so much easier to scale in the first place.

27. The DoH propriety scales released with the Framework are best used as additional casework aids to assessment. Most do not have reliability measures attached.

28. See Plous (1993) for an easy and entertaining guide through some of these common human errors.

29. There are exceptions: For example, Howitt (1992) and Strachan & Tallant (1997)

30. This listing is derived from many sources other than those already referred to in the text and footnotes. Amongst these are: Baron (1994), Bernstein (1996), Kaplan (1996), Klein (1996) Beach (1997), O'Sullivan (1999) and Connolly et al. (2000) and numerous other articles and studies I have read over the years.

31. The importance of 'therapeutics' in terms of intervention is emphasised by Morrison (1991).

32. I am aware that social de-constructionists would argue that it is the risk analysis system itself that constructs 'the risks,' but whilst having some sympathy with this

view, I maintain that a child who is being abused is being harmed in a sense relative to what *might have been* (adapting across the board the 'similar child' test of the Children Act, Threshold Criteria, Section 31(10)) no matter the model we actually use to articulate estimates of the degree of harm and the likelihood of harm the child may suffer.

33. Dalgleish and Drew utilise a nine-step risk assessment matrix to accompany their model. This matrix is probably too ambitious in terms of its attempted precision and perhaps should be collapsed into three or four (approximate) divisions in order to help define levels of risk.
34. Determining the value and probability aspects of just one risk relation per minute, every minute, would take 31 days and 23 minutes based on a 7 hour day (working solidly on one case with just one child) and this is not including any kind of comparative analysis or overall summative risk assessment.
35. The complexity is simply the result of our subject being concerned with the most (by a very long way) complex objects known in the universe – human beings. In comparison, a half-dozen Cray supercomputers running in parallel would give about the intellectual equivalent of a slug – but this might insult slugs everywhere.

References

Allen. J. (2001) *Traumatic Relationships and Serious Mental Disorders*. New York: Wiley.

Andreas, et al. (1996) *NLP: The New Technology of Achievement*. London: Nicolas Brealey.

Aristotle *The Nichomachean Ethics* (any edition).

Audit Commission Report (2001) *Worth the Risk: Improving Risk Management in Local Government*. London: Audit Commission.

Bandler, R. (1985) Going for It. In Andreas, C. and Andreas, S. (Eds.) (1985) *Using Your Brain for a Change*. Moab Utah, Real People Press.

Baron, J. (2nd edn.) (1994) *Thinking and Deciding*. Cambridge, CUP.

Beckett, C. (2001) Social Workers Knew. *Professional Social Work*, Dec. 3.

Beckett, R. (1994) Assessment of Sex Offenders. in Morrison, T. et al. (Eds.) (1994) *Sexual Offending Against Children: Assessment and Treatment of Male Abusers*. London: Routledge.

Berg, I. K. (1988) *Family Preservation: A Brief Therapy Workbook*. George, E. (Ed.) London: BT Press.

Bernstein, P. L. (1996) *Against The Gods: The Remarkable Story of Risk*. New York: Wiley.

Beach, L. R. (1997) *The Psychology of Decision Making: People in Organisations*. London: Sage.

Bodenhamer, B. and Hall, L. M. (1997) *Figuring Out People: Design Engineering with Meta-programs*. Carmarthen: Anglo-American.

Brearley, C. P. (1982) *Risk in Social Work*. London: Routledge.

Browne, K. D. (1995) Predicting Maltreatment. in Reder, P. and Lucey, C. (Eds.) (1995) *Assessment of Parenting: Psychiatric and Psychological Contributions*. London: Routledge.

Browne, K. D. and Saqi, S. (1988) Approaches to Screening Families at High Risk for Child Abuse. in Browne, K. D. et al. (1988) *Early Prediction and Prevention of Child Abuse*. Chichester: Wiley.

Calder, M. C. et al. (2000) *The Complete Guide to Sexual Abuse Assessment*. Dorset: Russell House Publishing.

Cleaver, H, and Freeman, P. (1995) *Parental Perspectives in Cases of Suspected Child Abuse*. London: HMSO.

Connolly, T. et al. (2000) *Judgement and Decision Making*. Cambridge: CUP.

Corby, B. (1993) *Child Abuse: Towards a Knowledge Base*. Buckingham: OU Press.

Dalgleish, L. and Drew, E. (1989) The Relationship of Child Abuse Indicators to the Assessment of Perceived Risk and the Decision to Separate. *Child Abuse and Neglect*. 13: 491-506.

DoH (1982) *Child Abuse: A Study of Inquiry Reports 1973–1981*. DoH.

DoH (1988) (Orange Book): *A Guide for Social Workers Undertaking a Comprehensive Assessment*. DoH.

DoH (1991) *Child Abuse: A Study of Inquiry Reports 1980–1989*. DoH.

DoH (1995) *Messages from Research*. DoH.

DoH (1998) *Modernising Social Services*. DoH.

DoH (1999) *Working Together to Safeguard Children*. DoH.

DoH (2000a) *Framework for Assessing Children in Need and their Families*. DoH.

DoH (2000b) *The Child's World: Assessing Children in Need: Trainer Modules 1 to 4 and Reader*. DoH, NSPCC and University of Sheffield.

DSM IV (1994) *Diagnostic and Statistical Manual*

of *Mental Disorders*. Washington: American Psychiatric Association.

Farmer, E. (1993) The Impact of Child Protection Interventions: The Experiences of Parents and Children. in Waterhouse, L. and Stevenson, O. (1993) *Child Abuse and Child Abusers*. London: Jessica Kingsley.

Fonagy, P. (2001) *Attachment Theory and Psychoanalysis*. New York: Other Press.

Greenland, C. (1987) *Preventing CAN Deaths: An International Study of Deaths due to Child Abuse and Neglect*. London, Tavistock.

Hagell, A. (1998) *Dangerous Care: Reviewing the Risks to Children From Their Carers*. London: Policy Studies Institute/Bridge Child Care Development Service.

Hall, L. M. and Belnap, B. (1999) *The Sourcebook of Magic: A Comprehensive Guide to the Technology of NLP*. Carmarthen:, Crown House.

Hall, L. M. et al. (2001) *The Structure of Personality: Modelling 'Personality' Using NLP and Neuro-semantics*. Carmarthen:Crown House.

Hawkes, D. et al. (1998) *Solution Focused Therapy: A Handbook for Health Care Professionals*. Oxford: Butterworth/Heinemann.

Hill, M. (Ed.) (1999) *Effective Ways of Working with Children and their Families*. London: Jessica Kingsley.

Howitt, D. (1992) *Child Abuse Errors: When Good Intentions Go Wrong*. London: Harvester Wheatsheaf.

Kaplan, M. (1996) *Decision Theory as Philosophy*. Cambridge: CUP.

Klein, G. (1996) *Sources of Power: The Study of Naturalistic Decision Making*. New Jersey: Lawrence Erlbaum.

Langan, J. (2001) *The Risk Factor. Professional Social Work*. Dec. 2001, 9.

Leslie, J. (1998) *The End of the World*. London: Routledge.

Monahan, J. et al. (2000) Developing a Clinically Useful Actuarial Tool for Assessing Violence Risk. *British Journal of Psychiatry*. 176: 312-9.

Moore, P. (1995) *The Business of Risk*. Cambridge: CUP.

Morrison, T. (1991).) Partnership, Collaboration and Change Under the Children Act. in Adcock, M. and White, R. (Eds.) *Significant Harm: Its Management and Outcome*. Croydon: Significant Publications.

O'Sullivan, T. (1999) *Decision Making in Social Work*. London: Macmillan.

Parker, R. (Ed.) (1980) *Caring for Separated Children: Plans, Procedures and Priorities*. London: MacMillan.

Parker, R. et al. (1991) *Looking After Children: Assessing Outcomes in Child Care*. London: HMSO.

Plous, S. (1993) *The Psychology of Judgement and Decision Making*. New York.

Popper, K. (1959) *The Logic of Scientific Discovery*. London: Routledge.

Pride, M. (1987) *The Child Abuse Industry*. Winchester: Crossway.

Reder, P. et al. (1993) *Beyond Blame: Child Abuse Tragedies Revisited*. London: Routledge.

Reder, P. and Duncan, S. (1999) *Lost Innocents: A Follow-up Study of Fatal Child Abuse*. London: Routledge.

Regan, S. (2001) When Forms Fail the Reality Test. *Community Care*. 25–31 Oct.

Rescher, N. (1969) *Introduction to Value Theory*. New Jersey: Prentice Hall.

Rescher, N. (1983) *Risk: A Philosophical Introduction to the Theory of Risk Evaluation and Management*. Washington: UPA.

Royal Society (1992) *Risk: Analysis, Perception, Management*. London.

Samra-Tibbets, C. and Raynes, B. (1999) Assessment and Planning. in Calder, M. C. and Horwath, J. (1999) *Working for Children on the Child Protection Register*. Aldershot: Arena.

Searle, J. R. (1992) *The Rediscovery of the Mind*. London: MIT Press.

Sheldon, B. (1995) *Cognitive Behavioural Therapy: Research, Practice and Philosophy*. London: Routledge.

Simmonds, J. (1998) Making Decisions in Social Work: Persecuting, Rescuing or Being a Victim. in Adcock, M. and White, R. (Eds.) *Significant Harm: Its Management and Outcome*. Croydon: Significant Publications.

Strachan, R. and Tallant, C. (1997) Improving Judgement and Appreciating Bias Within the Risk Assessment Process. in Kemshall, H. and Pritchard, J. (Eds.) (1997) *Good Practice in Risk Assessment and Risk Management 2*. London: Jessica Kingsley.

Stone, M. (1992) *A Model for Risk Assessment in Physical Abuse/Neglect*. London.

Tversky, A. and Kahneman, D. (1974) Judgement Under Uncertainty: Heuristics and Biases. in Connolly, T. et al. (2000) *Judgement and Decision Making*. Cambridge: CUP.

Utting, W. et al. (1997) *People Like Us*. London: HMSO.

Woodcock, T. and Davies, M. (1978) *Catastrophe Theory*. New York: Dutton.

Part Two: Child Care Assessments in Specific Areas

Chapter Seven

A Stepwise Process of Assessment

Barry Raynes

Introduction

This chapter provides an update from Samra-Tibbets and Raynes (1999) in light of the Assessment Framework. The reader should be aware of the following position statements from Reconstruct which influence the chapter:

- In practical terms the Assessment Framework falls into three areas; the triangle, the forms and the questionnaires and scales. Reconstruct's view is that the triangle is straight-forward, three broad headings (domains) divided into twenty sub-headings (dimensions) and it has been well received by inter-agency groups over the past year. The disadvantage of the triangle is that it is not ecological in design or function leaving the child fragmented into the twenty dimensions (discussed in detail by Calder in Chapter 2). Guidance accompanying the framework stresses the interdependency of the dimensions and the effect that they have on one another. Unfortunately in practice guidance has less impact than forms.
- The forms themselves are divided into age groups which, immediately, duplicates one of the problems already associated with the Looked After Children materials which is that the forms are not appropriate for children with disabilities.
- Some of the questions in the core assessment forms are invasive and inappropriate for child protection cases. Unfortunately these type of questions are best avoided if working with children who are in need but not at risk. Of course local practice will dictate how, when and why certain questions can be avoided but this practice contradicts the framework's aim to reduce the distinction between 'in need' and 'at risk from significant harm'.
- Reconstruct's main criticisms of the forms is not the questions per se, after all nobody could define a set of questions which would work with all eventualities, but the lack of

attention to analysis and the inadequate care planning system included at the back.
- Once the information has been collected the worker is invited to add their analysis via a blank page. There is no guidance relating to how that information should be analysed or presented. Consequently the information can remain separated and un-ecological.
- The care plan structure at the end of the core assessment forms, a series of linear tables, continues the separation of dimensions and implies that each objective has a separate task thus denying the fact that one task can meet many objectives. There is no room for target setting, measurement of success or monitoring.
- The questionnaires and scales are a motley crew of what happened to be available; poorly produced and, in places, not proof read. They relate to eight different areas, there is no comment as to why these areas were chosen. Some of the questionnaires and scales are undeniably helpful, some printed incorrectly and some, plainly insulting to families. The 'parental daily hassles' scale is usually appreciated by workers and families. It lists a variety of behaviours that parents, irrespective of class, race or circumstance can find difficult. It is thus neutral enough to provide a helpful introduction to a detailed discussion about how difficult children's behaviour can be. The 'alcohol' and 'adolescent well-being' scales contain typing errors which mean that they are unusable. The 'family activities' questionnaire, in stark contrast to the parental daily hassles scale is eurocentric and classist containing, memorably, the question 'How many times in the last six months has your family attended a county show?'
- Some local authorities have instituted their own approaches based on the framework. Throughout this chapter I intend to address, where possible, these inadequacies in the system drawing upon ideas from workers, researchers and trainers.

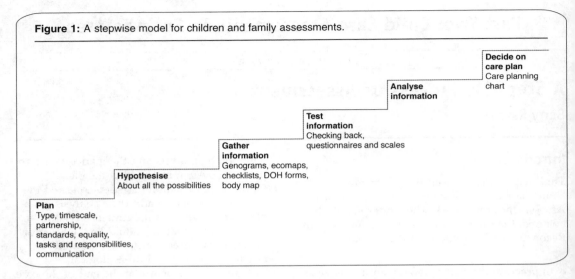

Figure 1: A stepwise model for children and family assessments.

Decide on care plan
Care planning chart

Analyse information

Test information
Checking back, questionnaires and scales

Gather information
Genograms, ecomaps, checklists, DOH forms, body map

Hypothesise
About all the possibilities

Plan
Type, timescale, partnership, standards, equality, tasks and responsibilities, communication

The process of assessments

The Framework repeats the mistakes of earlier assessment systems by focusing on information-gathering and not on the process of assessments, the route from referral to care plan. Reconstruct has developed a model based on work by Eric DeMello and John Yuille, called 'stepwise' (see Figure 1). This illustrates the steps which the assessment team need to follow to produce an effective assessment and, more importantly, a care plan. The remainder of this chapter describes those steps and follows through the process of assessment.

The planning stage

Where a group of professionals, particularly those who do not regularly work together, are to jointly undertake an assessment, they need to agree not just how they will assess the family but also how they will work together effectively. In our experience workers tend to concentrate on the tasks they need to undertake in respect of the child and the family, but spend little time considering how they will maximise the groups' combined skills and knowledge, and support and complement one another's work. In addition, consideration should be given to developing strategies for resolving difficulties and differences of opinion.

The type of assessment required

The initial child protection conference should give directions to the assessment team regarding the areas to be addressed in an assessment. In practice, assessment teams may only receive very general directions or be requested to 'do a core assessment' and so need to agree in detail what areas require assessment. Group members will also need to clarify what is meant by an assessment. To a teacher, the request for an assessment of a child may have a very different meaning to the expectations of social services. Many professionals are still not familiar with the assessment framework.

The time scale

Time scales for some assessments have been set within the framework itself allowing staff seven days to complete an initial and 35 days to complete a core assessment. It would be a mistake to presume that these are the only types of assessments and other risk assessments and specialist assessments should be clear with regard to timescales. Everyone involved, including the family, should be clear about how long the assessment will take and what is expected of them at different stages. This is important for the following reasons:

- Decisions about the child should not be unnecessarily delayed.
- The family will feel more empowered if they have a clear understanding of the time parameters and when decisions are likely to be taken.
- Professionals contributing to the assessment need to be clear about how long they have for information gathering, when and where to provide information and when and how this will be evaluated.

Measuring parenting skills

It is important that the family and the professionals involved in an assessment know what indicators will be used to evaluate the family i.e. what is a reasonable level of parenting for the children in this particular family and how this will be measured.

There will not always be a consistent view within the assessment team. Agreement will need to be reached on what is a 'good enough' level of parenting so that the family can understand what is expected of them, what they will have to do to meet those targets, and what are likely to be the thresholds for de-registration or, in some cases, legal action.

In cases where these issues have not been discussed and some level of consensus reached, assessment teams can become split and unable to function, assessments can be flawed and decision making impaired. If dissension remains within the group, supervisory input or an early return to conference will be required. The process of discussing this issue will, in itself, be helpful to the group in planning their intervention with the family.

Partnership

Another area where assessment teams require a consistent approach is the level of partnership which can be safely achieved with the family. Research by Thoburn, Lewis and Shemmings, (1995) states that:

> *Whilst failure to work in partnership can sometimes be attributed to aspects of the case itself or characteristics of family members, differences between cases where family members were informed, involved and consulted and those where they were not were almost always attributable to either agency policy and procedures or the social work practice, or both together.*

Thus there is a ladder of partnership (see Figure 2) and families will be on a different 'step of the ladder', depending on the characteristics of the case and the stage which the case has reached in the child protection process.

It is also true to say that different professionals will be working with the family at different levels of partnership. This should be identified and consideration given to the role that these professionals should then play.

At the beginning of an assessment the professionals will need to consider how best to engage the family, and on what stage of the ladder. There will always be cases where the family refuse to engage, and a small number

Figure 2: A ladder of partnership.

Full partnership – shared working but not necessarily equality

Participation – influencing what is going on

Involvement – being present

Consultation – asked for opinions

Keeping fully informed – information provided

No partnership

where to attempt to actively involve a family could put a child further at risk. These issues have been discussed in detail by Calder (Chapter 2) and Calder et al. (2001).

Assessment team professionals will also need to regularly jointly assess how effectively they are working in partnership, whether they are all working at a similar level, and what is the highest level of partnership they can achieve without jeopardising the welfare of the child.

Equality issues

Of course the impact of equality issues needs to be considered throughout the assessment process. I include this here because if it is not planned into the assessment, there will be no opportunity of introducing it later. When one considers that anti-discriminatory practice is; empathy, allowing children and families to explain their circumstances to you, addressing imbalance of power, considering the role that the identity of the worker plays in the process, considering issues of strength as well as weakness, checking out beliefs and hypotheses, being trustworthy and honest, attempting to improve partnership working at all stages of the process, combating power imbalances in the system, ensuring that institutionalised abuse is limited, appropriately using resources and systems to protect and promote children's health and development and understanding the effect of your professional power then it seems that a failure to work in an anti-discriminatory manner is, in itself, a failure of the social work service. How else should one work with children and families?

A good assessment will address the following questions of equality.

- Do family members need particular resources e.g. accessible venues, loop systems, child care facilities, ethnically sensitive play equipment?

- How will the race and gender of the workers impact on the assessment? Can family members be better engaged by using certain workers? Will consideration be given to race and gender when tasks are allocated to assessment team professionals?
- What child rearing skills are expected of the family – are they based on euro-centric norms?
- Is the assessment focusing on women – can men who are significant to children be engaged? Farmer and Owen (1995) have noted that where children were least well protected professionals were working almost exclusively with the mothers, whilst the dangers were frequently from their male partners. Intervention, thus, had little impact.
- Are there issues which require specialist input to assess certain aspects of the family e.g. parents with mental health problems and learning disability?
- Does any member of the family have a first language which is not English. If so, can the assessment be carried out in that language? If not, it is likely that the assessment will provide an inaccurate picture, thereby putting service users at a disadvantage and children at risk.
- If there are no workers who can undertake the assessment in the appropriate language an interpreter must be used. Check out that the interpreter has the same first language as the family/service user and is acceptable to the family. Ensure the same interpreter can be used throughout the assessment, and involve them in all planning meetings so that they understand the tasks and processes involved.

Bandana Ahmed, 1990, also suggests the following issues to consider:

- Have you acknowledged the fact that all assessments of black clients require recognition of racism and its effects whether covert or overt?
- What steps have you taken to critically examine your values and perception of black families?
- How do you ensure that your assessment is not based on negative stereotypes of black families?
- Do you usually define the needs of black clients or ensure your assessment is based on

their experience and reality? How do you ensure your assessment is based on their experience and reality?

- Do you assess the strengths of black clients, their families and communities as well as their weaknesses, problems and needs?
- Can your assessment make clear distinctions between clients' possible control of personal problems and external constraints beyond their control? What are the distinctions?
- Do you fit black clients' needs in your assessment or vice versa?
- Are you fully aware of racist outcomes your assessment may have on black clients? Identify and list any possible outcomes that may be racist.
- Can your assessment empower black clients? How?

For a detailed discussion on strengths-based assessments, the reader is referred to Calder (1999).

Communication

Most communication between professionals is channelled through the key worker. Information is passed verbally or in writing to that one social worker. Of course, concerns about further harm must always be relayed direct to the key worker, or, in their absence, to a previously agreed person, but if all information is passed through that one person the dynamic outlined below occurs.

The key worker is in control of the information and takes decisions: the other professionals merely provide the information. This dynamic can result in key workers being overloaded, while other professionals feel marginalised or have a lesser investment (Calder, 2001). It can also be a dangerous dynamic, because, when the pivotal worker is absent, inter-agency communication is more likely to break down (Calder, 2001; Reder et al., 1993).

Assessment teams need to have rules about how they communicate. Could sub-groups take responsibility for completing parts of an assessment, and feed back their overall findings to the key worker? What responsibility does every member of the assessment team have for ensuring that action will be taken to protect a child?

To conclude this section, planning is essential to a good assessment, and should address the process of working together as well as the task of assessing the family. For a detailed discussion

Figure 3: Communication.

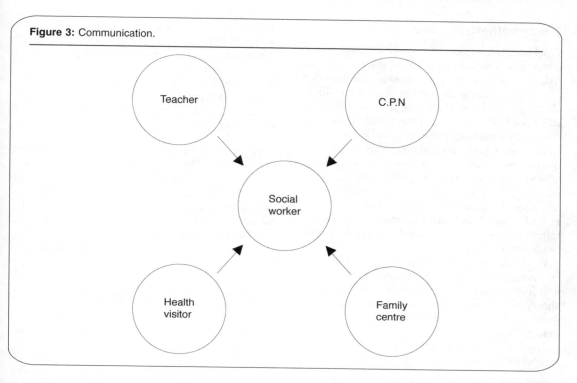

around this issue, please refer to Calder and Horwath (1999).

Setting up checklist

Horwath (2000) has edited a book which I would recommend be made available to practitioners as well as the wider training pack (DoH, NSPCC and The University of Sheffield, 2000). The pack produces a series of checklists which fits our stepwise model. The first of these, entitled 'setting up and beginning', is included below.

Setting up and beginning

- What questions require answering through the assessment, what are the issues and what are the likely consequences for the child's health and development of the present situation?
- Is the child safe, now? Has there been or is there risk of significant harm?
- Who is most worried about this child or family – does any one else have concerns; are they the same? Who is requesting this assessment?
- Who is involved – which children, family members, workers, agencies, court?

- Has the family been assessed before and for what purpose?
- Are there any special considerations?
- What is the family's first language, culture, religion or identity?
- Are any family members disabled? What is their main communication method?
- Is there a need for an interpreter?
- Who can help best understand and work with this family?
- Are there any likely or possible barriers to carrying out this assessment?
- Is there agreement with the family and between family members about the need for and purpose of the assessment?
- Is there agreement within the professional group about the need for and purpose of an assessment?
- Is there agreement about respective professional roles and responsibilities, what information will be shared and who has lead responsibility?
- Are other types of assessment concurrent?
- Are there adequate resources to carry out the assessment?
- Is the worker competent and do they possess the necessary knowledge and experience to carry out the assessment working to the Framework?

The hypothesising step

Workers often remain narrowly focused on proving or disproving whether the immediate risk still exists and fail to consider the broader picture. The assessment team should consider all the possibilities regarding the harm that the child could be suffering, both within their family and the wider community. Each hypothesis should be addressed and only discounted when there is clear evidence to do so. Explicitly hypothesising about all possibilities ensures that every possibility is considered, assessment team members' attitudes and biases are addressed and the family can clearly understand what concerns the workers may have.

While this stage has been placed at the beginning of the assessment process in stepwise, it is important to recognise that this process should be repeated when any new evidence comes to light which may challenge previously held views.

The following case scenario illustrates the importance of hypothesising.

> *Sylvia is a young woman with four children under the age of six, their ages are 1, 3, 4 and 6. The six-year-old, Amanda, has a learning disability and receives respite care.*
>
> *Yesterday, 7 p.m. at bath time, a member of staff at the respite care unit noticed a red mark which looked like a hand imprint at the top of Amanda's leg. When asked about it she said that 'mummy smacked her'. Sylvia had previously phoned the unit to say that Amanda had a nappy rash which had left a mark at the top of her legs.*

Various hypotheses which could be made about this case are that:

- Sylvia has smacked and injured Amanda and regularly does so because she dislikes and does not want to care for this child.
- Sylvia has smacked and injured Amanda and is likely to do this again because she is under considerable stress.
- Sylvia has smacked and injured Amanda because she is under stress but is unlikely to do this again if she receives support.
- Sylvia has smacked and injured Amanda, but has never done so before and is unlikely to do so again.
- Another adult within the family has smacked and injured Amanda.
- Another adult within the community e.g. school, respite care unit has smacked and injured Amanda.

- Another child has injured Amanda.
- Amanda is being sexually abused and the mark has resulted from her being forcibly held down.
- The red mark has been caused by an accidental injury or rough handling.
- The red mark is the result of a self-injury.
- The red mark is a nappy rash.

All of these, or a combination of some of them are possible. The reason why Amanda stated her mother had smacked her if this was not the case, would need further assessment. But whatever has happened, this family is likely to be under considerable stress, and deserve a service which considers all possibilities and provides an appropriate and holistic response to their needs.

The information gathering step

Information for the assessment should be gathered from all adults who are significant to the child, plus, of course, from the child. The assessment team will need to be clear about their reasons for approaching people. Members of the extended family, people who are not relatives but act as carers e.g. childminders or friends, workers in voluntary community organisations and other professionals can all provide valuable information, but parents need to be aware that they are being asked to contribute and issues of confidentiality will need to be addressed.

There are a range of tools available to assist workers in gathering information, and some are outlined in this section. Many of the tools can be used equally well with adults and children, but will need to be adapted to meet particular needs e.g. the age and understanding of the child, the abilities of parents with learning disabilities. For babies and young children or children with severe learning disabilities who have limited or no language skills detailed observation using specialist workers e.g. nursery nurses can provide invaluable information.

Genograms

The use of genograms (or family trees) is becoming more common in many agencies but their use is sadly still not universal. Genograms are particularly good for working with families to clarify complex relationships, to indicate gaps in knowledge and to make visible intergenerational and life cycle issues. They can be used to gather information and to work therapeutically.

As they can be powerful in raising painful and suppressed memories, it is important to explain what a genogram is and what it is likely to raise before undertaking this task. Some of the symbols used can have a considerable but unintentional impact. For example the use of X to symbolise the death of a family member may be very hurtful. Family members should be asked what symbols they would wish to use.

Workers sometimes avoid genograms because they feel the result often looks a mess, or the family structure is so large that they have difficulty drawing it on one sheet of paper. But this misses the main point of the exercise which is to help the family provide information which they think is important and assist them to see patterns and gain insights. Once the process is completed a neat version can be produced.

It is recommended that before using genograms workers should draw and discuss their own genogram not only to learn how to structure them but to experience the feelings which they can raise.

Ecomaps

Additional information can be gained from ecomaps. At the moment this tool is used even less often than are genograms. These focus on the relationships children and family members have not only with their relatives but with significant others like friends and pets, with organisations such as schools and family centres and with pastimes and activities. Information can be gained on who, and what, are important to each family member, whether relationships are supportive or stressful and the extent of their support systems.

Ecomaps should not be seen as a static record of the child or families eco-system. Family relationships change – children may feel hostile towards a parent one week and have resolved the conflict the following week. Therefore ecomaps should be undertaken on a number of occasions to map the changes.

It is preferable, particularly when working with children not to draw ecomaps on paper but to use moveable objects to represent their ecosystem. Play people can be used or cardboard circles on to which can be drawn happy, sad and angry faces. The child can then choose the appropriate play person or face to represent themselves and the people or things they are identifying as significant and be able to move them around to indicate what their feelings are and how they can change.

This type of approach is empowering as it gives children and families greater control over the information-giving process, it can provide information that a structured question and answer session would not illicit, and may help families to gain insights and to self-assess their own situations.

Inter-agency incident chart

The Inter-agency Incidents Chart (see Figure 4) is an essential tool for recording information gathered about the possible harm to a child.

Reder et al. (1993) noted that workers involved in assessing families 'often did not have available to them a framework within which to organise information and observations about the family or consider their implications'.

Figure 4: Inter-agency incident chart.

Date	Incident	Explanations given by carer and service user	Advice given	Action taken

The authors were struck that in a large number of the child death cases they reviewed events were considered in isolation from each other and so the accumulating evidence of the risk was not observed and no coherent overview or strategy emerged.

Inter-agency incident charts provide a brief, chronological record of each incident during a child's life which has led a professional to believe that the child may be suffering harm, the date when it occurred, who noted the incident, brief explanations by both the child and the carer, and what action was taken.

They should be kept at the front of files of all workers involved in an assessment and:

• Provide an easily accessible record of all significant incidents.
• Make visible patterns of harm e.g. The duration and severity of the harm.
• Whether incidents are increasing or decreasing in frequency, specific periods of high risk.
• Enable assessment team members to compare the information they have about incidents and explanations given and note whether there are inconsistencies.
• Help workers not to become single incident focused; ensure that multiples of similar single incidents that happen over a short period of time and are observed by different professionals are all recorded and not erroneously seen as a single incident.
• Provide an index based on dates to help workers locate the fuller records.
• Can be attached to the final assessment report, thus providing the conference or court with information that is clearly formatted.

Many social services departments use incident charts (usually called critical incidents) but fail to realise that their greatest value is as an inter-agency information tool. A good process will allow room for contributions from all agencies. These charts can be completed at assessment team meetings, conferences, planning meetings and reviews.

The time clock
Professionals need to be clear about when the child is at risk because families face different stresses at different times of the day. There is a danger that observations of how a family functions may cover a narrow window of time. The team of inter-agency workers should

organise their assessment sessions at different times to obtain as broad an overview as possible.

Using clock faces (see Figure 5) workers should record with the family what happens throughout the 24 hour day. When this work is undertaken with young children or parents with learning disabilities symbols can be used to indicate the time of day rather than numbers. Families may function very differently at weekends so this must also be assessed.

Additionally this tool is valuable in assisting workers at the service planning stage to identify the key times to provide resources.

A further area of thought highlighted by the 'time clock' is that of interaction with working fathers. Continual assessment visits during 'working hours' will disenfranchise working fathers more from the assessment.

The testing and evaluation step
The testing and evaluating stage of an assessment is particularly important, but often given limited attention. Workers frequently use most of the time allotted to the assessment to gather information and produce a report which details this but fails to evaluate the information or draw conclusions.

Although post-registration assessment work is an inter-agency task it is usually the social worker who evaluates the information, and consequently members of the assessment team from non-social work agencies are not involved in this process. This is not good practice as inconsistencies, different interpretations of evidence gathered and differences of opinion may only come to light as the report is being presented to conference or court.

Parents also need to be involved in this process, and arranging assessment team sessions to jointly test and evaluate the findings will ensure that parents are given a forum in which to understand, discuss and contribute to the conclusions that are being reached before the report is produced.

The risk assessment checklist
Those involved in evaluating information will need tools to assist them. The Risk Assessment Checklist (see Figure 6) can be used by individuals in their assessment work and as a basis for joint discussion within the assessment team. The checklist asks a series of questions which will assist workers to consider the type

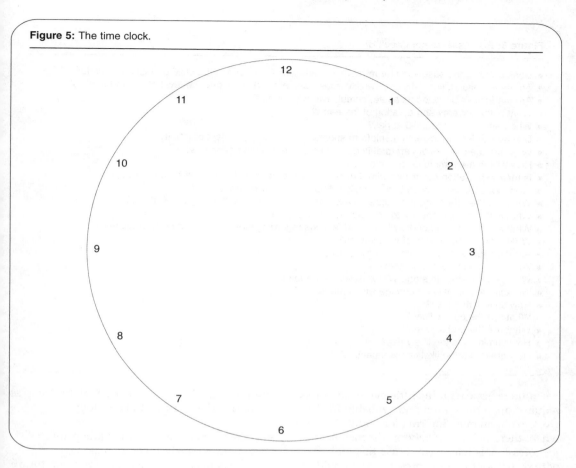

Figure 5: The time clock.

and level of harm a child may be suffering, the possible effects of that harm, the likely outcomes of intervention, the safety factors in the child's environment and the potential for change within the family.

Associated with the checklist are a range of tools, some of which have already been covered at the information gathering stage. Tools like the incident chart will help to answer very clearly questions such as 'Are the injuries/incidents acute/cumulative/episodic' and 'What is the severity and duration of the harm?' Genograms and ecomaps can assist discussions on 'What does the child mean to the family?' and 'What are the strengths and weaknesses of the family?'. Further tools associated with the checklist are outlined in the following section.

Can the level of risk that has been identified be safely and satisfactorily reduced by the voluntary provision of services? If so intervention and services outside of the formal child protection process should be the preferred option.

Continuums

Some questions in the checklist can be difficult to answer e.g. 'Did the injuries or incidents result from spontaneous actions, neglect or intent?' Workers may feel they have insufficient evidence or there are differences of opinion. Families may have made a statement which workers are not sure whether to believe or not.

The continuum is a tool to assist discussions about such issues. Simply draw a horizontal line to represent the continuum; as an example, anxiety about whether an injury could have resulted from poor supervision or from intent.

Poor supervision _____ Intent

Each professional places a cross on the line to indicate where their 'gut feelings' tell them they are between the two possibilities. This will clarify whether all the professionals hold a similar opinion, one worker is seeing the case differently or the group is completely split. The reasons why professionals may disbelieve the family, hold different views or feel anxious

Figure 6: Risk Assessment Checklist.

- Does or could the suspected harm meet the definitions of abuse in the child protection procedures?
- Are there cultural, linguistic or disability issues which could impact on the level of risk to the child?
- Are the injuries or incidents acute, cumulative or episodic?
- What is the severity and duration of the harm?
- When and how is the child at risk?
- Did the injuries or incidents result from spontaneous actions, neglect or intent?
- What are the parents or carers attitudes and response to your concerns?
- How willing are they to co-operate?
- Is their explanation consistent with the injuries or incidents (Is there need for a medical)?
- What does the child mean to the family? What role does the child play?
- What are the effects on the child's development? What may be the long term effects?
- What is the child's reaction to and perception of the harm?
- What are the child's needs, wishes and feelings regarding intervention and likely outcomes?
- What may be the effects of intervention?
- Are the injuries or incidents likely to re-occur?
- What are the protective factors?
- What are the strengths and Weaknesses of the family?
- What is the potential for change within the family?
- How safe is the child?
- What are the possibilities?
- What are the probabilities?
- How imminent is the likely risk?
- How grave are the likely consequences?

when there appears to be little evidence of risk requires open discussion and probably further work to obtain more information about the areas where there is high anxiety or dissension.

Professionals may wish to use this tool with or without parents present, but should always share their final conclusion with the family.

Model of change

The final tool in this section looks at the potential for change within the family and is explained by Martin Calder in Chapter 2. Assessments tend to focus on the action stage when families are receiving a high level of support which enables them to function more effectively. But the assessment must also consider the maintenance and relapse stages. Families need to have strategies for maintaining new behaviour when they have less support and may meet resistance from friends and other family members who may not want them to change.

The analytical step

Analysis and decision making checklist

The Child's World (DoH, NSPCC and the University of Sheffield, 2000) has a further checklist for this step. It is worthwhile checking

this out at the beginning of the analytical step as it informs the work that needs doing.

- Is the assessment providing adequate evidence to analyse before making judgements leading to decisions about future actions?
- Is the worker distinguishing between fact and opinion?
- Is there reasonable cause to suspect that a child is suffering, or is likely to suffer, from significant harm?
- Has the assessment revealed significant unmet needs for support and services?
- If the decision is not to provide services, this is itself a decision. What is the next step?
- Is the worker able to evaluate evidence drawing on his / her understanding of theory; for example, child development?
- Is the worker drawing on knowledge of research?
- Is the worker informing the family (including the children) of the outcome and recommendations arising from the assessment?
- Is the supervisor ensuring that rigour and challenge form part of their supervision?
- Is the supervisor able to ask questions, to challenge and probe where necessary? This

Figure 7: The child's protective environment.

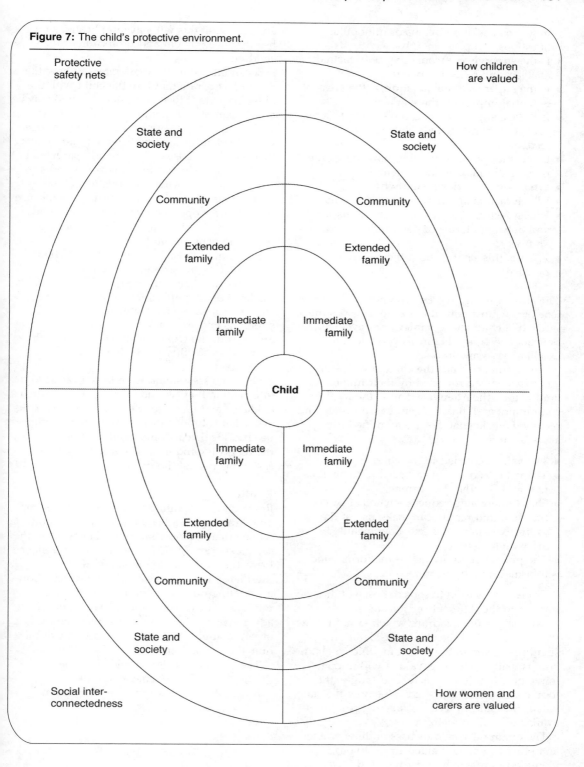

Protective
safety nets

How children
are valued

State and
society

State and
society

Community

Community

Extended
family

Extended
family

Immediate
family

Immediate
family

Child

Immediate
family

Immediate
family

Extended
family

Extended
family

Community

Community

State and
society

State and
society

Social inter-
connectedness

How women and
carers are valued

may mean asking obvious or unpopular questions.

- Is the supervisor encouraging both factual analysis and reflective practice?
- Is the supervisor able to address the areas of potential impact on the worker?
- Is there a supervisory agreement in place that allows for constructive challenge and feedback?
- Is the supervisor evaluating how the worker is currently making judgements?
- What is given priority and why?
- Which factors are marginalised and why?
- Which factors are causing most discussion and debate in terms of determining priority and why?
- What is this saying about their current practice?

The child's protective environment
One of the most critical issues to assess is the safety of a child and a framework developed by Boushel (1994) (see Figure 7) provides an excellent assessment tool.

This framework has the child at the centre of an ecosystem, surrounded by their immediate family, then the extended family, the local community and, finally agencies from state and society. Four key factors are identified for assessment:

- The value accorded to the child.
- The value and status accorded to the child's mother and other key carers.
- Social interconnectedness – whether or not the child and family can make use of the protective safety nets and how included they are with society.
- The protective safety nets – the formal and informal sources of protection.

Professionals need to consider each of these in relation to the different sections of the ecosystem. In the quadrant which examines the value accorded to the child consideration should be given to the extent to which a child both is valued and feels valued within their immediate family , the extended family, the local community, school etc. plus how the state values the child in terms of making resources available for their welfare.

The quadrant which focuses on how women and other carers are valued raises issues identified in research by Farmer and Owen (1995) i.e. that if carers' welfare needs are not adequately addressed by family, community

and state that this will have implications for the health, development and protection of their children.

Social interconnectedness refers to how the networks operate that link the child with the different parts of their ecosystem. A child may be poorly parented at home, but if they are able to easily access good support from relatives, peers, youth leaders, school etc., they will fare better than a child who is similarly poorly parented but has little or no access to support networks.

The protective safety net relates to how individuals in the child's ecosystem would use the networks operating between them to take action and alert the appropriate agencies to protect the child from harm.

By shading in each of the sixteen sections, dark shading for strong, no shading for non-existent, a pattern emerges. This can show the level of support which exists within the child's protective environment, where the strengths and weaknesses are, whether there are gaps in the worker's knowledge, and the areas where further work should be undertaken.

Once the assessment team have evaluated the information they should be able to order their evidence and reach conclusions about the risks and what solutions there may be for meeting needs. This discussion should take place before the report is produced. The following tools assist this part of the process.

Resilience
Research is continuing into what makes some people able to weather adversity and misfortune while others become hurt and damaged by the same experiences. The 'International Resilience Project' used the following definition. 'Resilience is a universal capacity which allows a person, group or community to prevent, minimise or overcome the damaging effects of adversity'. The following act as useful indicators of vulnerability and resilience in terms of the domains of the framework.

The project has also provided further thoughts which may enable a worker to consider the resilience present in children.

Child

Sources of vulnerability	Sources of resilience
Young age	Higher IQ
Disability	Good attachment
Earlier history of abuse	Good self-esteem

Parent-carer

Sources of vulnerability	Sources of resilience
Domestic violence	Social support
Serious substance misuse	Positive parental childhood
	Good parental health

Chronic serious psychiatric illness	Good relationship with sibling
	Education
	Work role

Family and environment

Sources of vulnerability	Sources of resilience
Run down neighbourhood	Committed adult
Poor relationship with school	Good school experience
	Strong community
Weak fabric of social support	Good services/supports
Poverty	
Social isolation	

I Have

- People around me I can trust, and who love me no matter what.
- People who set limits for me so I know when to stop before there is danger or trouble.
- People who show me how to do things right by the way they do things.
- People who want me to learn to do things on my own.
- People who help me when I am sick, in danger or need to learn.

I Am

- A person people can like and love.
- Pleased to do things for others and show my concern.
- Respectful of others and myself.
- Willing to be responsible for what I do.
- Sure things will be all right.

I Can

- Talk to others about things that frighten me or bother me.
- Find ways to solve problems I face.
- Control myself when I feel like doing something not right or dangerous.
- Figure out when it's a good time to talk to someone or take action.
- Find someone to help me when I need it.

Further issues

- The child has someone who loves them unconditionally.
- The child has an older person outside their home they can talk to about problems and feelings.
- The child is praised for doing things on its own.
- The child can count on their family being there when needed.
- The child knows someone they want to be like.
- The child believes things will turn out all right.
- The child does endearing things that make them liked.
- The child believes in power greater than seen.
- The child is willing to try new things.
- The child likes to achieve.
- The child feels that what they do makes a difference to what happens.
- The child likes itself.
- The child can focus on a task, and stay with it.

Resilience and protection

Completion of Boushel's 'protective environment' and consideration of the child's resilience can be plotted on the following 2 × 2 matrix (DoH, NSPCC and The University of Sheffield, 2000) (see Figure 8).

In this model the child is plotted depending upon their resilience and protective

Figure 8: Resilience/vulnerability matrix.

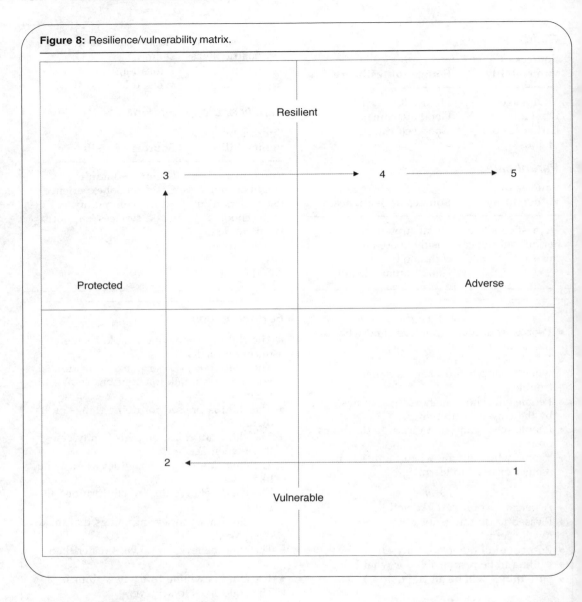

environment. Position (1) represents a vulnerable child living in very adverse circumstances. The ideal quadrant is top left but it is not possible to make that move in one step. Typically the child may be removed to a foster home or another member of the family, which is represented by the move to (2). However the child's own resilience will only improve if their carers and the professionals around them are able to work with the child directly on issues of self-confidence, self-reliance and identity. If successful the child then moves quadrant to (3). If the child returns home either in a planned or unplanned way they will now be at (4) or (5)

depending upon how much the family has been able to improve their own situation.

A model for risk assessment

This tool is a set of questions produced by Paul Brearley for analysing the evidence regarding risk to a child. By considering the possible dangers and then dividing the hazards i.e. the things that might cause the danger to occur, into two types – predisposing and situational – workers and the family are helped to examine the processes which may lead to a child being harmed and actions which could cause or prevent situations from becoming dangerous. This model also focuses on strengths in family and community networks which can be used to reduce risk and also gaps in information i.e. what the professionals have not been able to find out during the assessment.

1. List the dangers in this case
- *A danger is something you want to avoid, so what possible events would you fear in these circumstances? Rank these dangers in order of their significance.*

2. List the hazards in the case
- *A hazard in this context is something which might result in a danger being realised. Something that helps to bring about the circumstances you want to avoid.*

3. Divide the hazards into two:
a) Predisposing hazards
b) Situational hazards
- *A predisposing hazard makes the danger more likely. It is something that creates vulnerability, though it may need to be activated by something else, perhaps a situational hazard.*
- *A situational hazard is something that happens, and which has an immediate effect directly related to the danger*

4. List what you consider to be strengths in this case
- *Strengths are those factors whose effects counteract the danger, and make it less likely to become a reality.*

5. Identify the additional information which you believe to be necessary.
- *Evaluating the information you already have may indicate that there are some important gaps in your knowledge, gaps which should be filled (if possible) before a final assessment is arrived at.*

6. Indicate the decisions you feel should be taken.

For each stage of the analysis, try to answer the question WHY?

The care planning stage

The forms leave little space for detailed report writing. I worked with a group of social workers in Birmingham. We examined reports in the light of some of the principles inherent in the framework; child centred, involves the family, builds on strengths and protective factors, is rooted in child development, ensures equality, covers inter-agency issues and is evidence

based. The following guide, draws upon their material.

A guide to writing reports for core assessments
Introduction and background
You need to introduce the report by outlining the reasons for it and the legal framework. If for Court you should add your qualifications and dates obtained and make further reference to 'Reporting to Court under the Children Act' published by HMSO.

The introduction should contain a list of concerns (if relevant) and some consideration of the need for change allowing the reader to consider these issues throughout.

The introduction should include a short, relevant history of the family and should finish with a chronology of significant events. All comments here about relevant history should be elaborated upon later in the report.

It is appropriate to include a genogram of the family.

Details of the plan that has been followed need to be given. This will include details about the process including number of visits, who was invited to be present, who was present, observations of interaction, behaviour etc.

Be careful to distinguish between fact and opinion. You could describe here tools used and the research that informed the work.

You need to outline contact with other professionals and consideration of the impact that you and other worker's identities may have on the assessment.

You should clearly set out how this report fits with other reports (which, if relevant, should be contained as appendices).

Engaging with the child and family – ensuring the work is child centred and involves the family.

It is essential that assessments are not 'done' to families but that they are fully involved and engaged. Questions to consider before you begin include:

- How will I ensure that families are as comfortable with the process as possible – venue, timing, individual needs, etc.?
- How will I share information with the family and child?
- What will happen if there are disagreements between professionals or with the family.

Any direct work you undertake should be age appropriate. It is important to describe how you worked with the children and be clear about why you worked in that way.

Remember to look at each child individually and write individual pen pictures. Look at their individual understanding of history, events and the impact on them. Ensure you represent and understand their wishes and feelings.

Try to use the child's own words where appropriate but clearly indicate they are quotes (i.e. '. . .').

Give clear, thorough general information on child/ren. How do they present? Their personality, physical appearance etc.

In order to involve the family, eco-maps can be useful as can genograms (see Introduction).

You should consider the family in relation to the child, the immediate family, extended family, friends, neighbourhood, school/nursery etc.

List your methodology and explain why you used a variety of approaches (e.g. individual sessions, joint sessions, joint visits with other professionals.) Include where the sessions were held, and why, (e.g. home, family centres, office, children's homes).

Make sure that you express views of all involved in the assessment regardless of whether you agree with those views or not.

List the number of contacts had with each member of the family.

Builds on strengths and protective factors
You must ensure that the report is balanced, identifying where individual's strengths lie and considering whether these can be developed and how. You should consider strengths in the wider family network and community that could be used to support the children and their family. Consider children individually – remember some children are more resilient than others due to a wide range of factors including support which other children in the family may not have access to:

● Highlight positives of people involved.
● Highlight these first.
● Remember that negative things can change.
● Set targets for improvements but don't be rigid with deadlines unless to not be rigid would further harm the child/ren.

Consider how well the family has done given their circumstances: dealing with issues such as poverty, racism, poor housing, educational attainment etc.

Look for tasks that the family are good at e.g. engaging in open and honest communication with the social worker, good basic care, etc.

Ensure that you include family culture, routines, etc.

When you are carrying out the assessment help the child and their parents to identify strengths.

Avoid pathologising and stereotyping but do not minimise risks and negative indications. Be positive but not over optimistic.

Rooted in child development
You need to consider where the child's development is compared to where it should be. Use the framework dimensions as guidance and seek advice from other professionals.

Use evidence of research in child development and child development milestones.

Also gauge parents' understanding of this and their attitude to their child's development.

Ensures equality
You should consider all power issues that will be having some effect on the family, their ability to interact with the community and professionals.

This should include; race, gender, disability, class, income, educational attainment, sexuality, as well as issues such as the power imbalance between professionals and the public.

Note any fear that the family may have felt regarding the consequences of the assessment.

Use family member's words where relevant – again clearly marked (i.e. '. . .')

If not in the introduction consideration could be given regarding the effect of the identity of the worker/s upon the assessment.

Check through the assessment with the family before it is finished to allow them to correct misinformation and suggest language and words which they are happier with. Of course it is your report and you have the final decision about what is written.

Inter-agency issues
You must ensure that you liaise with other professionals involved with the child and the family. To work effectively you must have a good knowledge of other agencies, their roles and responsibilities.

You need to gain information about the relevant professional's input and their assessments. You should be clear about any specific areas you want them to address. Ensure all areas in respect of multi-agency links are highlighted.

You should share information with other professionals about the SSD assessment and ensure joint working. Together you can identify if there are any gaps in knowledge.

If there is disagreement between professionals you should describe this in the assessment and consider its effect on it.

Within the report cite other relevant agencies. If there are a number of professionals involved it may help to draw a diagram

A good report will show time/dates when liaison takes place with other agencies.

Make sure you list previous assessments from SSD and other agencies.

Always be clear about who was doing what, why and how.

Evidence based
When carrying out the assessment always make sure that you check out information to ensure that facts are correct.

This should include information that supports your hypotheses as well as information that argue against them. It should also include information from other professionals.

If possible, get corroboration for self reports, talk to other people, carry out observations of relationships, child management, boundaries etc.

    e.g. Check school attendance, clinic attendance
          Test out hypotheses
          Make sure you are objective

Ensure that you make a clear distinction between first hand information and hearsay evidence.

Ensure that you can identify actual events to support any view that you take. Be prepared to accept that there could be contrary conclusions.

Do not make assumptions. Any statements you make must be supported by dated examples.

You should use research to support findings and underpin your recommendations. Ensure that research is clearly and consistently referenced throughout the report.

Any statements you use from the child, family or others need to be clearly sourced, and use quotation marks and ascribe the statement to the person who said it.

Concentrate less on historic events and more on current events.

Ending/conclusion
Your *Analysis* must make sense.

There should be a summary of the factual information and the thought process involved in reaching your recommendations.

Again references should be made to Department of Health research as a minimum and, if you choose, further research that supports your analysis.

Make sure you use information from the assessment to form conclusions.

There should be a logical flow and the analysis should point to conclusions and recommendations. Refer back to evidence when drawing conclusions. There should be no contradictions. Ensure that the assessment is consistent.

To help clarify your reasoning you can summarise information at the end of each section if it is a long report.

In your recommendations ensure that you reflect on the assessment, looking at positives, negatives, weaknesses, strengths and changes in a balanced way.

Any recommendations you make must be clear, provide a list of them.

Measure what the situation is against what the situation should be.

Consider a prognosis of change (i.e. how likely is change?). Importantly consider how long can the child/ren wait for change – if they can wait at all?

If you are considering care proceedings always provide evidence that the threshold criteria having been met.

The care planning step

Care planning process
Figure 9 (with a completed example) enables the development of thinking from assessment of need to care plan. Needs are identified and written as objectives in the first box. (Be careful to set these objectives at a suitable level, not too high 'improve quality of life' not too low 'institute a toileting regime' but somewhere in the middle 'to remain at home safely'). Workers then consider possible solutions which should include family strengths and universal children's services (toy library) as well as statutory services. It is important to be creative. For example a service-led response to a child with speech delay is likely to be a referral to speech therapy whereas, as the diagram example shows, there are a range of solutions

Figure 9: From assessment of need to care plan.

Objectives

To reduce child's language delay

Possible solutions

To improve child's language through language development programmes.

To assist mother to stimulate and talk to her child by addressing her depression and providing her with parenting knowledge and skills.

to provide play opportunities,
- with other children and with other adults.

To encourage adults in the child's informal support network to spend more time with the child.

Medical checks regarding possible physical problems.

Possible resources

Speech therapy

Family centre, direct work with child/parents

Mental health services
Parenting classes
Parent's support group

Playgroup
Parent and toddler group
Play workers to visit the child at home

Section 17 money to enable contact with extended family

Targets

To reduce delay from 12 months to 6 months in 1 year.

Bedtimes to be good times with stories read by parents

Monitoring arrangement

Reports on outcome of language evelopment programme
Discussion with and observation of parents
Liaison with medical health services
Observation visits of child in play provision and at home
Discussion with extended family
Feedback on medical examinations and treatment

Figure 10: Outline care plan format.

Overall description of the issues to be addressed and the broad objectives to be achieved.

Objectives

Measurements

Monitoring arrangements (how, by whom)

Task	Person/Agency	Frequency	Timescale

which could draw upon both formal and informal resources, be cost-effective and are often more empowering. Once the resources have been identified thought needs to be given to the targets and monitoring arrangements. How will you know when you are being successful and how will you find out? These should reflect the objectives, e.g. the child's speech improving, not the process, e.g. did the child go to speech therapy?

Care plan system
The final pages of the assessment framework core assessment forms contain tables which relate to care planning. The problem with this part of the framework's process is that, having sub-divided the situation into twenty dimensions these pages fail to bring everything back together again. Not very ecological!

The linear nature of the design implies that there is one outcome per objective whereas this is not the case, one objective can have a number of desired outcomes and one outcome can measure a number of objectives. Also objectives cannot be limited to one domain. Take, for example 'to improve the relationship between

parents and child', this must be a fairly common objective. Which dimensions should it be in? basic care?, ensuring safety?, emotional warmth?, stimulation?, guidance and boundaries?, stability?, family's social integration?, wider family?, family history and functioning?, emotional and behavioural development?, identity?, family and social relationships?, social presentation? It would be easier to list which dimensions it wouldn't be covered in. I therefore recommend the following format designed by Reconstruct which does not mention domains and dimensions as these have no part to play when considering the ecological nature of the child's world.

A good care plan will differentiate between high and low level objectives, will set measurements against these objectives, will list tasks and who will carry them out and identify systems for monitoring success. Our care plan format (see Figure 10) allows the assessment team to pool the information gleaned from the assessment, consider the situation as a whole and identify, via the care planning process described above, objectives, tasks, targets and monitoring arrangements.

A guide to good care planning

1. If written correctly needs and objectives are the same thing.
2. Objectives must be needs led and must not mention services.
3. Objectives should not be set too 'high' (vague and long term) nor too 'low' (precise and short term).
4. Separate tasks from objectives.
5. Use family and universal services as well as more focused services.
6. Write what will be done.
7. Each objective should have at least one measurement.
8. One measurement can measure more than one objective.
9. Measurements should combine both 'hard' (measurable) and 'soft' (less tangible) elements.
10. There should be specific arrangements for monitoring progress.

Conclusion

In this chapter I have described a process, rather than a framework, of assessments based around a 'stepwise' model. It is this model that workers need to use to build sound assessment practice rather than uncritically applying the Framework for Assessment. Indeed, although the framework is a vast improvement on the 'orange book' (DoH, 1988) it is unlikely to stand the test of time without adaptation. There is a worrying void in the framework when it comes to analytical and planning tools in the core assessment records and their unsuitability for use with disabled children. I hope that the publication of this book along with other work will encourage the development of improved resources to help professionals in the difficult task of identifying need and risk and appropriately improving the situation of children and families.

References and bibliography

Ahmed, B. (1990) *Black Perspectives in Social Work*. Birmingham: Venture Press.

Boushel, M. (1994) The Protective Environment of Children: Towards a Framework for Anti-oppressive, Cross-cultural and Cross-national Understanding. *British Journal of Social Work*. 21: 2 173–90.

Brearley, P. (1982) *Risk and Social Work*. London: Routledge.

Calder, M. C. and Howarth, J. (Eds.) (1999) *Working for Children on the Child Protection Register: An Inter-agency Practice Guide*. Aldershot: Arena.

Coleman, R. and Cassell, D.(1995) Parents who Misuse Drugs and Alcohol. In Reder, P. and Lucey, C. (Eds.) *Assessment of Parenting: Psychiatric and Psychological Contributions*. London: Routledge.

DoH (1988) *Protecting Children*. London: HMSO.

DoH (1995), *Looking After Children Forms*. London, HMSO.

DoH, (1995b) *Child Protection: Messages from Research*. London: HMSO.

Falkov, A. (1996) *Fatal Child Abuse and Parental Psychiatric Disorder: An Analysis of 100 ACPC Case Reviews*. London: HMSO.

Farmer, E. and Owen, M. (1995) *Child Protection Practice: Private Risks and Public Remedies*. London: HMSO.

Harper, N. (1996) *Children Still in Need: Refocusing Child Protection in the Context of Children in Need*. London: NCH Action for Children.

Katz, I. (1997) *Current Issues in Comprehensive Assessment*. London: NSPCC.

McBeath, G. and Ibb, S. (1990) Child Protection Language as Professional Ideology in Social Work. *Social work and Social Sciences Review*. 2: 2, 122–45.

McGaw, S. and Sturmey, (1994) Assessing Parents With Learning Disabilities. *Child Abuse Review*. 3: 36–51.

Phillips, M. and Dutt, R. (1990) *Towards a Black Perspective in Child Protection*. London: Race Equality Unit/ NISW.

Reder, P., Duncan, S. and Gray, M. (1993) *Beyond Blame: Child Abuse Tragedies Revisited*. London: Routledge.

SSI (1993) *Inspecting for Quality: Evaluating Performance in Child Protection*. London, HMSO.

Thoburn, J., Lewis, A. and Shemmings, D. (1995) *Paternalism or Partnership? Family Involvement in the Child Protection Process*. London: HMSO.

Chapter Eight

A Child Concern Model to Embrace the Framework

Lynne Jones and Tom O'Loughlin

Introduction

All child care systems in England and Wales operate within the same legislative framework and are advised by similar pieces of Government Guidance. But this new guidance does not create the direct and immediate change that the government desires. Instead it is translated and implemented via a sieve that is made up of existing systems, resources, local history and research and current inter-agency relationships. So in effect we have over a hundred different child protection systems within the country, all of which will assimilate guidance in slightly different ways (PIAT working group, 2001).

This chapter describes one system's assimilation of *Child Protection: Messages from Research* (DoH, 1995) and the subsequent development and implementation of a Child Concern Model, which has been adopted by the inter-agency network in Bolton. This Model, which was our response to the refocusing agenda, became the cornerstone of the implementation of the Assessment Framework (DoH, 2000). Within Bolton, the Assessment Framework has been integrated into the Child Concern Model, which informs all inter agency child care work and has been accepted by all agencies. The major challenges faced in this development, the practical problems and the areas that worked well will all be explored in this chapter.

Historical context

This model provides a simple framework for safeguarding and promoting the welfare of children in need. It contains a continuum of involvement, ranging from support to protection. It was developed in response to the following publications and pieces of guidance:

Seen but not Heard (DoH, 1994) which raised concerns about systems concentrating resources on children in need of protection and failing to offer support and services to children in need at a lower level of vulnerability.

Children Still in Need, Refocusing Child Protection in the Context of Children In Need (NCH 1996) which was commissioned by the Association of Directors of Social Services to further the debate for change. It made the following suggestions about the way forward: Systems need to:

• Improve child protection processes.
• Achieve more integrated children in need services.
• Promote more effective use of existing resources within child care organisations, and how.
• Develop a wider range of family support services.

By far the most influential document was *Child Protection: Messages From Research* (DoH, 1995), an overview which summarised the main messages from 20 research projects on child abuse and protection. More than half of these studies were commissioned by the Department of Health in the wake of the Cleveland controversy. The document strongly advocated a better balance between child protection and family support activity.

The key messages from this research were:

• That the best outcomes for children and families are achieved when cases are categorised as 'children in need' when there may be minor protection issues.
• That, except in the most extreme cases, child abuse should not be defined by single abusive incidents.
• That generally children suffer more long term difficulties from living in unfavourable environments, (i.e. low warmth, high criticism) than from single abusive incidents.
• That scarce resources are squandered in the investigation of large numbers of abusive incidents which result in almost half of the families receiving no protective or supportive services.
• Whilst this emphasis on investigation ensures that children are protected it leaves families traumatised, alienated by the process and unsupported.

The document highlights the need for:

- A wider perspective on child protection.
- Sensitive and informed professional/client relationships.
- An appropriate balance of power between participants.
- Effective supervision and training of social workers.

in addition to 'services, which enhance children's general quality of life (p45)'.

It recommends that Children in Need of Support and their families (S17 Children Act 1989) be prioritised and that Children in Need of Protection (S47 Children Act 1989 referrals) be treated with a 'lighter touch'. Enquiries should be undertaken to assess need rather than a concentration on the investigative, forensic approach to reports identifying concerns about children.

Surprisingly the report was launched in a blaze of publicity via the radio, television and national press. What wasn't surprising were the sensational headlines which castigated social workers for their practice, e.g. 'Stop witch hunts that split families' (*Daily Express*), 'Social workers add to family distress in sex abuse cases' (*The Times*), both 22 June 1995. All reports ignored the very positive message within the overview report that children in Britain were protected from abuse at the hands of their parents.

These publications were part of a national focus on early intervention in children's lives, which at the time was reflected by Government policy, mainly in the area of Youth Justice but more recently in the plethora of initiatives such as Early Years Partnership, Sure Start, Connexions and the Children's Fund.

The local context

Like most child care systems, Bolton had developed a multi-agency policy for categorising the various degrees of 'children in need' within the borough in 1994. The framework identified three levels of vulnerability with indicators to help workers assess which level children and families reached. The document interpreted need narrowly, with Levels 2 and 3 primarily relating to children in need of protection. This policy helped agencies to be clear about their concerns, have a common understanding of need and consequent eligibility for services. Although the policy was adopted by the key agencies in the borough (Health, Education and Social Services)

it was not promoted well, used inconsistently and not widely understood.

The above documents and subsequent media coverage (particularly in respect of *Messages From Research*) had a significant impact on child care practice, especially social work practice, in Bolton. We began to see a reduction of the use of formal child protection systems and a greater reliance on an informal 'child in need' approach. The numbers of Initial Child Protection Conferences reduced from 135 in 1994/95 to 115 in 1996/97 and the numbers of children on the register similarly declined from 184 to 154 respectively. It became evident that this change of emphasis by social workers created anxieties for other agencies who relied heavily on the child protection system. At the same time Department of Health Guidance and Working Together (DoH, 1991) remained unchanged. The local Area Child Protection Committee (ACPC) policies and procedures were also unchanged but were being interpreted more 'liberally' than prior to 1995.

The refocusing process

All changes in childcare systems, whether internally motivated or in response to external guidance, should be seen and viewed as a process and not an event. Within the last few years, the importance of including managers, staff and users in the change process has become more and more evident. We attempted to include as many people as possible within our change process.

The 'refocusing roadshows'

It was in response to the concerns about change and the desire to address the issues raised in the publications that, in October 1996, the ACPC agreed to host a series of multi-agency roadshows. These attempted to ensure that staff in all agencies were familiar with the key messages from the research studies and to receive feedback on what needed to change locally to try to refocus our practice.

The roadshows were held in small venues across the Borough and presented by representatives from Health, Education, Police, Probation, SSD and the voluntary sector. Those attending were workers who regularly came into contact with each other e.g. social workers, day care workers, health visitors, school nurses, headteachers and designated teachers, education social workers, drug workers and family support staff. This encouraged open and frank discussions about the strengths and weaknesses of the system we were operating and some clear messages about what needed to change.

The messages from these practitioners included:

- The need to try to standardise responses to concerns about children across the borough and in all organisations. Workers were concerned that thresholds were applied differently by teams and workers within Social Services Department and indeed by other professionals, e.g. health visitors and schools.
- The need for specific help in determining responses to what they called the 'grey areas': those cases that were not easily identified as either child protection or family support work, e.g. neglect and emotional abuse.
- The need to include some professional discretion in the child protection system, which was perceived to be absent.
- The view that agencies needed to have more ownership of 'children in need' of support and that a system similar to that of child protection would be needed to ensure a consistent multi-agency response to these families.
- The need to minimise duplication in systems, e.g. social workers having to complete assessments of families referred by other professionals for services from SSD (Health Visitors referring children for services from Social Services Departments family centres), children and families being in several systems at any one time e.g. Looked After Children, Child Protection and Family Support, which was not considered to be the most effective use of resources. (This caused confusion for children and families who were invited to a myriad of meetings to discuss the same issues and built up resentment between professionals who felt their skills and judgement were in question).
- The need to respond to children reported as in need of protection and that only children on the register received any services from the SSD.
- The need for a common language, and clearly prescribed processes in respect of children in need of support.

On the positive side the feedback highlighted:

- The good working relationships between agencies in the borough especially around children in need of protection. This was felt to be as a result of the excellent ACPC training programme, geographical advantages, i.e. a clearly defined, compact borough council, the existence of a specialist child protection team and good relationships between practitioners who are committed to multi-agency work.
- A keenness to be involved in any work which would improve outcomes for children and their families.
- A recognition of the pressures on staff in all organisations and the need to ensure that scarce resources are used to benefit those most in need.
- An optimistic approach to change. Workers felt that the systems in Bolton were very positive and that we would be building on existing good practice and evident goodwill.
- An acknowledgement that we should strive for minimum intervention in families' lives to assist in accessing appropriate services.

The strategic study group

Following the Roadshows, a Social Services Department (SSD) Strategic Study Group was established with the aim of ensuring that services for **all** children in need throughout the continuum, from support to protection are provided in a way which would:

- Encourage the best outcomes for children and families.
- Make the most effective and creative use of resources.

The strategic study group was made up exclusively of social services staff from all levels of the Children's Division. This was a surprising start to a process that relied so heavily on major contributions, understanding, support and ultimately agreement from all agencies and organisations. However, because of the Department's key role, we wanted to involve workers from all service areas to ensure as wide a debate as possible. This would include 15 representatives from the Department, and to include representatives from other agencies would make the group too big.

One key to the success of the group was the encouragement and support of senior officers in the Department and the establishment of a North West Refocusing Group (with representatives from the majority of North West authorities) which developed a framework to structure the debate and encourage shared learning. In addition Bolton, Wigan and

Cumbria Authorities entered into an agreement with the National Children's Bureau to assist us in the process by appointing a Development Officer whose primary task was to work with first line managers and their teams to develop practice and to share learning across the authorities.

Throughout the process Bolton were active participants in the refocusing agenda, hosting the first regional conference for the North West Group on 21 February 1997, contributing to subsequent conferences held in Chorley (September 1997) and Kendal (1998) and sharing and learning with other local authorities nationally.

The group was an excellent catalyst for initial ideas of how to develop the work and was very useful in testing out our current practice. The group undertook the exercise recommended in Messages From Research, 'True For Us': The child protection process: criteria for decision making (p103).'

Four cases were selected for analysis using the following criteria:

- Referred but not investigated.
- Investigated but not conferenced.
- Conferenced but not registered.
- Conferenced and child registered.

Each case was examined to determine:

- What criteria were used to reach the decision.
- What needs were assessed in the enquiry.
- What support services, if any, were offered to the family.

The findings confirmed that in the past there had been a great deal of consensus about the criteria for reaching decisions at each stage of the child protection process. However, due in part to the change of emphasis within the department, a broader range of interpretations were being used and the new consensus was proving more difficult to find. As interpretations and subsequent responses were not standardised within the department; understood by colleagues in other agencies; or underpinned by guidance or procedures.

The findings also indicated that, in some circumstances, decision making focused on the abusive activity and not the broader needs of the family (although this was thought largely due to resource issues).

One example arose of workers using a 'lighter touch' in a traditional child protection case. The outcomes of this case were very positive. We suspected that these would not have occurred if the child protection route had been used. This case also highlighted the issue of 'worker protection' where old procedures had been interpreted very widely.

The lack of any system for managing multi-agency services to children in need who fall outside of the child protection system was also identified and the lack of any agreed multi-agency approach to assessing need in families was evident. It was clear that we needed to develop policy, procedures and systems in line with the changing emphasis, but at the same time it would also be necessary to encourage and promote the development of a wider range of family support services as part of the process.

The group also recognised the need to not erode the strengths of the child protection system;

- to develop any change from a wide debate between people who do the work, managers, users, carers and elected members and to be incremental, systematic and outcome oriented.
- The Group produced a snap shot of activity in several service areas to produce information relating to activity at the two polar points on the continuum of need, (ie support and protection). This would include:
- looked after children
- family support centres
- family day care
- advice and assessment (short term first contact teams of field social workers)
- children and families (long term field social work teams)
- children with disabilities
- child protection unit (specialist assessment and therapy team)

This work reassured the group that valuable support services were provided to children and families in need of support not only within the Department, but from many statutory and voluntary organisations in the Borough. It emphasised the difficulties experienced in providing for local community needs, particularly for Asian families who were seriously under represented in support service activities, but who did figure in the much more intrusive child protection services and in the Looked After population. The work also underlined the tensions that exist in providing a comprehensive response at the highest level of vulnerability (child in need of protection) and the awareness that if services were provided at an earlier stage (child in need of support), it is possible that the demand for these intensive, intrusive, sometimes damaging and always costly services would lessen.

Multi-disciplinary task groups

With the benefit of these conclusions, the Strategy Group set up eight multi-disciplinary practice/task groups in 1977. These involved representatives from Education and Arts Department, Leisure Department, Housing Department, Health, Community and Hospital Trusts, Voluntary Organisations, Police, Community Drugs Team, Probation and the Social Services Department.

Three of those task groups were instrumental in developing the Model. The other five concentrated on promoting and encouraging the development of family support services, integrating children's services, improving access to services by Minority Ethnic Communities and empowering families through the development of Family Group Conferencing.

This chapter will concentrate on the work of the three groups who were tasked with addressing the policy and practice issues raised by the multi-disciplinary groups at the roadshows and through the SSD Strategic Study Group. (It is important to note that the groups initially had no notion of a model of work, that this evolved naturally during the process of tackling the specific areas identified, i.e. assessment of need, consultation and thresholds).

The three groups were keen to build on existing good practice, policies and procedures and used existing multi-agency forum to consult on the work. The chairs of the three task groups met on a regular basis to share learning, ensure the work progressed in a complementary fashion and that duplication was avoided, and it was through these meetings that the Model was conceived.

The consultation task group

This group had the task of encouraging more ownership of children in need who were identified as being at the lower levels of vulnerability. The group determined that this could be achieved in part by introducing a formal consultation stage into the referral processes for all agencies. Initially the group focused on referrals to SSD who were perceived

to be the agency who most frequently refused to take ownership of children in need at the lower levels of vulnerability. This was quickly broadened as the group recognised the need for advice and guidance for workers from a wide range of professions and organisations.

The assessment of need task group

This group was tasked with reviewing and revising the 'Child in Need' document developed in 1994, developing guidance in respect of assessments and reviewing the process of accessing services

The thresholds task group

This group was tasked with developing guidance on the threshold of entry into the 3 levels of vulnerability described earlier. The aims of the group were to:

- Assist in standardising responses across the borough in all agencies.
- Provide a Framework for all staff to understand the challenge of refocusing, in action, in Bolton.
- Assist in clarifying the 'grey areas' of concern.
- Provide security for staff and children and families in applying professional discretion to child protection processes.
- Consider the issue of duplication within systems.

The group reviewed the existing policies, procedures, guidance and practices and recognised:

- The lack of a systematic approach to those children in need and their families who fell short of being determined children in need of protection.
- The lack of guidance about what circumstances constitute child abuse warranting investigation (enquiry).
- That significant resources were being wasted through duplication of effort.

The group developed the idea of multi-agency 'child in need' meetings for complex cases which fell short of the threshold for child protection systems, and reinforced the need for wide ownership of these by recommending that the meetings were convened, chaired and noted by the agency with the concern.

The group determined that duplication could be minimised if children who had been removed from home due to abuse were not placed on the Child Protection Register. The group proposed to continue to hold initial conference on all children but not to register if there were no plans to reunite the family.

The group also proposed discretion in the child protection system to not conference children who had experienced abuse in specific circumstances e.g. an isolated incident, admitted by the perpetrator and a request for services to minimise risk. The proposal ensured safeguards for children, families and staff.

The proposals of all three groups were routinely consulted on with staff teams of the agencies represented, the Area Child Protection Committee and the Joint Strategy Team (the body in the borough who are responsible for developing the Children's Services Plan). On reflection a major flaw in the process was the lack of user involvement. A small number of user groups were consulted on specific aspects of the proposals but this was ad hoc and had little effect on the outcome.

The Child Concern Model

The Child Concern Model was simply a joined up version of the three groups' work, but became much greater than the sum of the three parts. The proposed model was presented to the strategic partnerships in the town and met with favourable responses and then a programme of workshops was developed to share the proposals with a wide range of professionals and receive their feedback. The documents were subsequently amended in line with this feedback.

The whole process was slow, taking 18 months from inception to fruition. It was very labour intensive and, like all successful inter-agency work, undertaken by committed individuals, with a named individual to lead on the task. The importance of allies in key positions in organisations who were committed to the development was key to success.

The process involved almost 100 representatives from a wide range of statutory and voluntary agencies, regular task group meetings and consultation exercises involving more than 900 staff and volunteers. The key decision making fora were involved in the process and consulted throughout. The process was exhaustive but clearly key to successful acceptance and commitment to the child concern approach.

The final version (see Figure 1) was launched and implemented in May 1998 through multi-agency briefing sessions. The model advocated that organisations begin with a more holistic assessment of the child's needs within the family context and only move onto a child protection enquiry if that is indicated.

The model prescribed four steps to be taken when there were any concerns that a child may be in need:

1. Assess the extent of need.
2. Assess the level of vulnerability (indicated by the level of unmet need).
3. Assess which needs must be met as a matter of priority.
4. Access the most appropriate, least intrusive, services to meet these needs.

The model introduced the concept of a continuum of concern and built on revised levels of need/vulnerability which encouraged a stronger multi-disciplinary approach so that:

- Duplication in assessments and service provision could be avoided.
- there could be better targeting of multi-disciplinary services.
- children in need across the continuum from support to protection influenced budgeting priorities.
- a basis for joint commissioning for services could be developed.

Our initial framework of assessment

The Child Concern Model is based on good inter-agency assessments. Three stages of assessment were identified:

1. **Request for Service**
   This was described as the initial process undertaken by every agency that receives a request for a service involving a child who might be a child in need. A request for service may be met at this stage – possibly by giving advice or referring to another service or forwarding for a higher stage assessment. Request for leaflets, information about services such as childminders, welfare rights, schools, housing possibilities, leisure and health facilities, are examples of service requests dealt with at this stage.
2. **Intermediate Assessment (Screening)**
   This involved gathering some basic information to enable the assessor to determine areas of need and identify the appropriate service. The request for a service may be dealt with at this stage or the case

Figure 1: Child concern model.

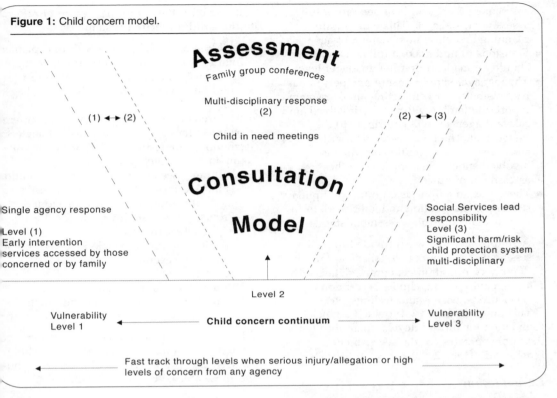

may be referred for a full assessment. A request for Family Day Care Service, a short term difficulty resolved through payment under Section 17, application for help with school meals, or a request for guidance on feeding an infant, might be examples of services provided with this stage of assessment.

. Full Assessment

In cases where the needs are complex, where there appears to be risk of harm, or a danger of family breakdown or an adverse affect on the child's health or development, a child would be referred for a full assessment. The decision to embark upon a full assessment, which would usually have a multi-disciplinary component, would be taken at Team Leader level in the Social Services Department and the equivalent management level in other organisations.

Some basic guidance on the process was developed:

• Work in partnership. Be clear with families about what will happen during and after the assessment process. Involve families fully in all processes.

• Encourage self-referral whenever possible.
• Link assessed need to appropriate service(s) quickly without intrusion or unnecessary information gathering. Only convene child in need meeting or any form of meeting when this is essential and has a clear purpose.
• Try to avoid duplication i.e.: redirecting a family to another agency when the advice, information or guidance on referral process can be satisfactorily given by yourself.
• Ensure children/families have a copy of assessment reports and action notes of meetings concerning them.
• Assessments should always determine the level of vulnerability (if any).
• Staff must seek permission from the child/family before requesting confidential information from another agency.
• Staff will often seek information by telephone. Information should be shared as required to assess need.
• When any stage of assessment has been made, staff should explain the structure or method they have used to make that assessment.
• In complex cases where the child/family's needs cannot be identified or satisfactorily linked to services by stages (1) and (2)

assessment there will be a need for a full assessment, stage (3). This will require planning and close involvement of agencies.

- Decisions to undertake a full assessment should be made at first line manager level.
- The manager should ensure one person has responsibility for completing an assessment report, the family will be fully involved, and relevant agencies will contribute to the assessment. The person completing the assessment report should co-ordinate involvement of other agencies in the assessment of outcomes.
- There was an emphasis on multi-disciplinary sharing of information and joint work in the intermediate and full assessment stages.

A simple checklist was provided for full assessments to encourage a holistic approach, i.e. family composition genogram, details of the referral, environment, child's perception of his/her needs, wishes and feelings, etc.

This initial framework provided a crucial foundation for further development through to the implementation of the Assessment Framework (DoH, 2000).

Consultation

Consultation is key to the model and was instituted in a more formal way. It is available to any worker from all related agencies. If professional advice about work to be undertaken by the consultee is given then this is recorded and a copy sent by the consultant to the person asking for advice.

The Child Concern Model relies upon the availability of positive consultation between all agencies. It provides an opportunity for those working with the child and family to access additional knowledge and expertise in order to explore a concern. Consultation is not seen as a way of transferring ownership of a 'problem' (unless this is the agreed outcome of discussion). If the case is particularly complex it may be necessary to agree that ongoing consultation is appropriate. In such cases it is preferable if the same person could offer the agency consultation on each occasion.

We recognised that in some cases it is difficult to decide whether a child needs a single agency preventive response (Level 1 vulnerability), or multi-agency assessment – Section 17 (Level 2 vulnerability), or child protection – Section 47 enquiry (Level 3 vulnerability) (see Figure 2). The following criteria were developed to help

staff establish the appropriate point of **referral to the child protection system**:

- Children or young people with unexplained injuries, suspicious injuries, or where there an inconsistent explanation of the injury.
- Children or young people who have alleged abuse.
- Children or young people who have suffered or are suffering specific incidents of neglect emotional abuse that are impairing or will impair their development, e.g.:
  – Failure to seek necessary medical attention
  – Failure to thrive that has been investigated medically and no organic cause found.
  – Problems associated with carers' lifestyle – e.g. chaotic drug use.
  – Children or young people involved in one serious or several lesser incidents of domestic violence.
  – Vulnerable children who are left alone.
- Where there are serious concerns about the risk of significant harm to an unborn child.

In the revised guidance currently being printed this list has been extended to include children and young people who sexually abus and those abused through prostitution.

Child in need meetings

Child in need meetings were developed to provide a structure for inter-agency meetings and collaboration when a protective response was not required. Guidance in respect of the meeting was provided as follows:

- Staff need to ensure that meetings with the child/family are not replicated and kept to a minimum with a clear purpose. If the family are already involved in multi-disciplinary meetings with a child welfare purpose, effort should be made to avoid repetition.
- Apart from child protection enquiries the agency with the most involvement with the child/family raising the requirement for a meeting should convene the meeting either by telephone or letter.
- The family should be fully consulted and in agreement.
- The meeting should **only** involve staff with a direct and relevant involvement with the child/family. If ongoing consultation is being provided by Social Services it may be appropriate for a Social Worker to attend.
- The meeting should not be held without the full involvement of the family, the

child/young person of an appropriate age and members of the extended family or involved friends.

• The venue does not need to be formal but the most convenient place to meet for a confidential discussion. It could be the family home if this is appropriate.

• The meeting should be chaired by a member of staff from the agency raising the need to meet. He/she completes a pro-forma which will then be circulated to all in attendance and those who need to be aware of the plan.

• A Child In Need meeting should consider how the plan agreed for the child/family is evaluated as to its effectiveness. This may be by arranging further meetings within a timescale or leaving it open to anyone involved to propose a meeting if this is thought necessary.

A pro-forma was developed to provide structure to process and record the meeting. From these meetings multi-disciplinary action plans are drawn up to meet the child's needs which could be reviewed and amended as necessary.

Access to services

A further area of work was to encourage all child welfare service providers to be explicit about access to their service and referral arrangements. The guidance and training explained that child need assessed at Level 1 should be met by the agency identifying the concern or via services accessible from others. If all available services had been provided, the needs remained unmet and concern persisted, then the level of vulnerability increased to Level 1/2 and consultation should be sought from the most appropriate agency.

If through consultation and advice from others the worker is unable to meet the need identified and the concern persists then the level of vulnerability is increased to Level 2. It is at this point that if the assessment indicates the need for an inter-agency response that a Child in Need meeting should be convened and an multi-disciplinary Action Plan (and review if necessary) be developed.

If the child's needs are not met through the plan, concern persists and assessment indicates the need for protection, Social Service Department should be consulted and a decision made in respect of a child protection enquiry. If the assessment is to undertake child protection enquiries the child is deemed to be at Level 3.

Clearly the process is not always incremental, the first contact with a family may indicate that a child is in need of protection and then quite properly a referral should be made directly to SSD. Similarly children can enter the continuum at any level and move up or down depending on their assessed need and access to services.

The model built on the existing good practice within the Borough, however, it was recognised that it would inevitably require review and amendment, and members of the JST and the ACPC agreed to undertake the task after a 12 months operational period.

Review of the model

The review identified the difficulties in retrieving consistent information from diverse systems across many agencies. However it gave us some very important messages.

For the main part those who were aware of the model felt that it was helpful. However, despite extensive training and publicity many workers were still unaware of its existence. This was particularly true of schools and the voluntary sector, who have many staff and volunteers and whose lines of accountability are more fragmented.

Some organisations questioned the status of the model, expressing the view that they had not been involved in its development and therefore felt it had been imposed. There were pockets of staff in organisations who struggled to apply the model and others who were passionate about its benefits. Some organisations felt that the guidance could be clearer, particularly in respect of thresholds, when to convene Child in Need meetings and the recording of Consultation.

There was some concern about the lack of administrative support to operationalise the model and a lack of confidence of some workers to chair and note multi-agency Child in Need meetings, which were viewed by the vast majority as extremely helpful in sharing concerns and accessing support services with children and families.

The review recommended that the model be formally recognised by chief officers of all child care organisations, that a comprehensive awareness training programme be developed and that the guidance and procedures be reviewed and clarified. These actions were delayed whilst we waited for the (long promised) publication of *Working Together to*

Figure 2: The three levels of vulnerability.

Level 1

Features	Possible Indicators to be determined by assessment
Children from households where the Carers are under stress which may affect their child's health and development. Children whose health and development may be adversely affected.	– Children with isolated, unsupported carer(s). – Families with a high number of children or more than two under five. – Children of parents with mental or physical health difficulties. – Young carers. – Children who present management problems to their parents. – Children in families where there is poor hygiene. – Children identified by schools as requiring additional educational support. – Children who have started involvement in criminal activities. – Children involved in contact/residence disputes. – Children of parents involved in substance misuse. – Children of parents where there has been some domestic violence. – Children starting to have unauthorised absences from school. – children experimenting with drugs/substances.

Level 2

Features	Possible indicators to be determined by assessment
Children whose health or development is being impaired or there is a high risk of impairment.	– Child with emotional/behavioural disorder. – Disabled children. – Children regularly absent from school. – Children beyond parental control. – Homeless young people. – Children with chronic ill health or a terminal illness. – Children whose parents, through extreme poverty are unable to meet their basic needs. – Children previously on the Child Protection Register or siblings of a child on the Register. – Children in families where there has been one serious incident of domestic violence or several lesser incidents. – Children in families where parents/carers have substance dependency. – Children/young people with substance dependency.

Level 3

Features	Possible indicators to be determined by assessment
Children experiencing significant harm or where there is a likelihood of significant harm. Children at risk of removal from home.	– Children subject to proceedings in the Family Court. – Children on the Child Protection Register. – Children from families experiencing a crisis likely to result in a breakdown of care arrangements. – Children whose parents are unable to provide care whether for physical, intellectual, emotional or social reasons. – Children whose behaviour is sufficiently extreme to place them at risk of removal from home, eg. Control issues, risk taking, dangerous behaviour, involvement in prostitution. – Children who disappear or are missing from home regularly or for long periods. – Children in households where parents/carers have all of the following problems: mental health, substance dependency and domestic violence.

Safeguard Children (DoH, 1999) and the *Framework for the Assessment of Children in Need and their Families* (DoH, 2000).

The ACPC agreed that the Child Protection Handbook should be replaced by a Child Concern Handbook which addresses all children in need, not just those who were in need of protection. We were also keen to ensure that the next set of guidance for workers would be more helpful, more accessible and more comprehensive.

Integration of the Child Concern Model With the Assessment Framework

When the Framework for the Assessment of Children in Need and their Families was introduced in April 2000, there was an emphasis on Social Services Departments carrying a lead role in the assessment of need. The Framework also expressed the importance of involvement of other agencies. Initially we were concerned that the Framework might undermine the Child Concern Model. This related primarily to interpretation of the lead role of Social Services. In particular, there was a desire to preserve the work that had been undertaken in developing and acknowledging the assessment skills of other departments and agencies. Additionally the Framework that had already been developed had enabled children and families to be linked to services below the child protection threshold without having to route the referral through Social Services.

A decision was taken at senior level in the Department at the outset to preserve, as much as possible, the benefits of the Child Concern Model in the implementation of the Assessment Framework. Two implementation groups were set up: one internal involving several sections of the children and families division and the second a multi-disciplinary group involving other key agencies. Both reported to the Joint Strategy Team.

Additionally a social worker was seconded for two days a week for six months to help with the task of implementation. The manager responsible for implementation also had access to a regional Greater Manchester group for advice and support.

There was considerable consensus from other departments and agencies that the major positives of the Child Concern Model should be maintained. A detailed action plan was developed which covered all the areas required

for implementation. The Assessment Framework demanded that the Social Services Department be extremely clear about their threshold for cases that should be referred to SSD for direct involvement.

The first task was to review and update the threshold criteria and to embrace the new timescale requirements of the Assessment Framework (described by Calder in Chapter 2).

Having achieved clarity for this threshold with other agencies, the Social Services Department needed to ensure that there was a satisfactory arrangement in place in accordance with the Assessment Framework for assessments of need below this threshold.

The reviewed Child Concern Model was changed in accordance with the new arrangements. The existing three levels of vulnerability were considered again and the indicators were brought up to date in accordance with practice and knowledge developments. The definitions of the levels of vulnerability remained the same.

Initially the main issue causing confusion was responsibility for assessing children at vulnerability Level 2 'children whose health or development is being impaired or there is a high risk of impairment'. There was general agreement that Social Services did not need to be involved with children at the lowest level of vulnerability and that they would always be involved with those at the highest. Initially we believed that all children considered to be at 'Level 2' vulnerability would need to be referred to Social Services (to benefit from the new assessment forms, assessment tools and skills and standardised approach promoted by the Framework). However, in tracking through individual cases at this level there were clear examples of cases where this seemed inappropriate. An example would be a child with an emotional/behavioural disorder recognised and identified by a school or a health professional. The Child Concern Model encourages these agencies to discuss with parents and access an appropriate service directly to meet the need.

We established that Social Services would only need to get involved with children at Level 2 vulnerability if the child and family were isolated from any agencies already involved who could help assess need and refer to appropriate services. Also if the child had been referred to appropriate services but were not taking up or benefiting from that service and

Figure 3: Revised child concern model.

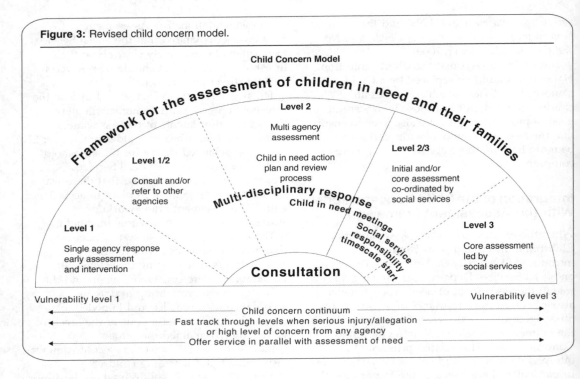

there were concerns that health and development continued to be impaired.

There was considerable discussion with other agencies which eventually led to the following criteria or threshold for Social Services involvement. Children whose health or development is being impaired or there is a high risk of impairment **and** they do not have access to appropriate services or they are not benefiting from help being provided.

This quickly became known as Level 2/3. There was general satisfaction with this threshold. Whilst Social Services had dropped their threshold for involvement from Level 3 cases the new criteria preserved the principles of the Child Concern Model in relation to the ability of other agencies to access services. (Figure 3)

The integrated model is underpinned by the following principles:

- The child's welfare and safety is paramount.
- All agencies must demonstrate commitment to effective multi-disciplinary processes for all Children in Need and not just those in need of protection.
- The Assessment Framework gives Social Services 'lead' responsibility for assessments of Children in Need. In managing this 'lead'

role, the skills and knowledge of other agencies will be fully utilised.
- Inter-agency collaboration must seek to avoid duplication and unnecessary intrusion into family life.

The threshold for Section 47 enquiries was reviewed and updated, involving a task group of staff. Clearer guidance on situations that warrant a Section 47 enquiry was the outcome.

The Multi-Disciplinary Implementation Group then worked to develop a single multi-agency referral and assessment form (Appendix 1) that could be used by all agencies for cross referrals below the threshold for Social Services involvement. This form was developed based on the three dimensions in the Assessment Framework described by Calder in Chapter 2.

The form was developed in two parts. Part one provided a structure for collecting factual information and simple referral details. It was felt that the completion of part one would be sufficient for staff helping families access services at the lowest level of vulnerability. Part two provides a format for collecting more assessment information and is similar to the format for initial assessments but briefer and simpler. The staff are asked to complete part two in addition to part one for children who are considered to be at Level 2 vulnerability. This enables information on children and families to be collected using a common structure and language in accordance with the Assessment Framework.

If concerns about the child persisted or they passed the threshold for Social Services involvement requiring initial and possibly core assessments the information that had already been recorded at an earlier stage could be utilised and built on rather than duplicated and repeated. Also, when appropriate, staff from agencies could help with the initial assessment process co-ordinated by Social Services.

In addition, a protocol was developed in consultation with other agencies and signed up to by all child welfare agencies in Bolton. The Joint Strategy Team accepted both the protocol and the multi-agency referral and assessment form and were keen to ensure that adequate audit and monitoring arrangements were in place.

The integrated Child Concern Model was launched in October 2000 with briefing sessions for 850 workers. In addition specific sessions were held focusing on the Assessment Framework attended by 300 workers who are involved with children assessed at vulnerability Levels 1 and 2.

A one day multi-disciplinary training course focusing on the use of the multi-agency referral and assessment form and the skills needed to gather information for assessments, completing analysis and linking children and families to services has been developed. This course has been repeated six times during the year.

Finally the guidance on how to use the model and the framework has been incorporated into our new *Child Concern Handbook* (Bolton JST and ACPC, 2000). What follows are the parts of the guidance which help practitioners assess where children and families are on the model.

Levels of vulnerability

The Children Act 1989 necessitates a process where priorities of child need can be identified. Three levels of vulnerability have been developed locally to achieve this:

Level 1:
- Children from households where the carer(s) is/are under stress which **may** affect their child's health and development.
- Children whose health and development may be adversely affected.

Level 2:
- Children whose health or development **is** being impaired or there is **a high risk** of impairment.

Level 3:
- Children **experiencing significant harm** or where there is a likelihood of significant harm. Children at risk of removal from home.

We developed the following indicators to help staff undertaking assessments establish the appropriate vulnerability level. The lists are not exhaustive.

We also developed the following flow chart to describe how children should move between the different levels of vulnerability.

What to do if you are concerned about a child
Vulnerability Level 1
Make an early assessment of the child/family. If possible, meet the need from within your own agency or access a service from an appropriate agency, using Part 1 of the multi-agency referral and assessment form.
Needs Not Met or Concern Persists
↓
Vulnerability Level 1/2
If early assessment shows multiple needs and your agency would benefit from assistance with meeting these needs, identify appropriate agency, seek consultation and/or refer to other agencies/organisations for services. Completing as much of Part 2 of the multi-agency assessment form as appropriate.
Needs Not Met or Concern Persists
↓
↓
Vulnerability Level 2
If early assessment indicates the need for an inter-agency response, complete Parts 1 and 2 of the multi-agency referral assessment form, call a Child in Need Meeting and draw up an Action Plan to meet need.
Needs Not Met or Concern Persists
↓
↓
Vulnerability Level 2/3
If the child/family are not appropriately linked to services and/or are not benefiting from the help provided, refer to Social Services who will co-ordinate the initial and/or core assessment using the Framework.
Needs Not Met or Concern Persists
↓

Vulnerability Level 3

Social Services will undertake a child protection enquiry to assess the level of need for protection. Social Services will facilitate a core assessment.

Remember: Fast track to Level 3 if there are serious protection concerns. Offer services in parallel with assessments – do not wait until the assessment is completed to provide services and refer to Social Services for an Initial Assessment if you cannot link the child/family to services or they are not benefiting from the help provided.

Audit

An annual audit system has been developed with a form (see Appendix 2) to be completed by all services. The Joint Strategy Team has responsibility for the overview of the integrated model. The first audit will take place in April 2002. Quality assurance and control systems have been developed, e.g.

- Random sampling of assessments/files.
- Audits of children conferenced, but not registered.
- Case reviews.
- Independent research from University of Northumbria.

Conclusions

The Child Concern Model which has been operational since May 1998 was Bolton's response to the refocusing challenge to achieve a better balance between family support and child protection. The Model put us in a strong position to implement the Assessment Framework building as it does on this challenge to ensure 'that referral and assessment processes discriminate effectively between different types and levels of need and produce a timely service response'

Our initial concerns that the Framework could effectively reduce the multi-agency collaboration around children in need was unfounded. The agreed threshold for social services lead in assessing need is set at Level 2/3 i.e.

Children whose health or development is being impaired or there is risk of impairment and they do not have access to appropriate services or they are not benefiting from the help being provided.

Our Quality protects indicators have shown some positive outcomes for children and

families as a result of the integrated model, i.e.: a steady reduction in the number of repeat referrals of the same need within a 12 month period and a high number of assessments which produce clear service plans for children/families.

The numbers of children on the Child Protection Register have reduced from 185 in 1995 to 91 in 2001. Our numbers of children looked after in the same period have fallen from 304 in 1995 to 275 in 2001.

The integrated model has preserved a simple straightforward process for linking children and families to appropriate services without delay, duplication or bureaucracy.

The development and consolidation of work with other welfare agencies/staff so that they have confidence in their own assessment skills has been maintained and strengthened by specific training. Further support through clear procedures and protocols – a single multi-agency referral and assessment form, a mutual consultation service and the structure of child in need meetings has helped maintain this multi-disciplinary approach.

Commitment to the child concern approach has continued in the face of considerable change in most agencies. The model in many ways is a multi-disciplinary team approach (particularly for Social Services, Education, Health and when necessary the Police), but without the workers being located together. It will be interesting to see whether co-location, as is being considered now by many local authorities, would further improve the service and outcomes for children.

The timescale targets for assessments have proved difficult, particularly with core assessments. The main difficulties have related to families with large sibling groups requiring individual forms for each child causing repetition; whilst separate forms were also having to be completed for children subject to Child Protection Conferences, the first LAC review and Care Proceedings.

In response to this we developed a draft family form avoiding this duplication. A pilot of the form was evaluated prositively.

References

DoH (1994) *Seen But Not Heard*. London: HMSO.
DoH (1995) *Child Protection: Messages from Research*. London: HMSO.
DoH (1999) *Safeguarding Children*. London: TSO.

DoH et al. (2000) *Framework for the Assessment of Children in Need and Their Families.* London: TSO.

NCH (1996) *Children Still in Need, Refocusing Child Protection in the Context of Children in Need.* London: NCH.

PIAT (2001) *Report from the Working Group on the Implementation of Working Together and the New Assessment Framework.* Leicester: PIAT.

Platt, D. (not dated) *Initial Social Work Assessments of Need following the Refocusing Initiative.* Report to Bolton Metro Social Services Department.

Appendix 1

Multi-agency referral and assessment form

Copies of the guidance notes, form and audit form are available from the Assessment Framework Implementation Group, The Woodlands, Manchester Road, Bolton, BL3 2PQ, telephone 01204 337464.

Chapter Nine

A Framework for Assessing Parenting Capacity

Simon Hackett

Introduction

The assessment of parenting is a notoriously, and perhaps inherently, value-laden area of child welfare practice (Jones, 2000; Daniel, 2000; Budd and Holdsworth, 1996). Practitioners who are making judgements about other people's parenting need a sound conceptualisation of parenting which is grounded in the best available research evidence and theoretical knowledge. Such a conceptualisation has to be broad enough to embrace the dynamic nature of parenting tasks across a child's lifespan, the challenges of and threats to effective parenting, and the processes and mechanisms that link parental behaviours and child developmental outcomes. It is therefore vital that practitioners are both alert to the impact of their own values and also ask themselves the following core questions at all stages of the assessment process:

- On what am I basing my judgements about people's parenting?
- What factors am I emphasising?
- What are the implications of emphasising these factors?

This chapter therefore seeks to help practitioners to develop an evidentially-sound conceptualisation of parenting and to offer some guidance as to how parenting can be assessed, exploring and building upon the notion of parenting capacity embodied in the DoH (2000a) *Framework for Assessment for Children in Need and their Families*. I start by discussing the concept of parenting capacity, before going on to explore the dimensions of parenting suggested by the DoH. I then offer an integrative model for the assessment of parenting capacity which builds upon the DoH triangular model. This includes a functional model of parenting assessment which encourages practitioners to examine the fit between parenting behaviours and child need. Attention is also given to research into parenting styles. In the final section of this chapter, the focus shifts to the process and content of assessments of parenting capacity, with practical guidance as to what to include in parenting capacity interviews and observations.

The concept of parenting capacity

One of the key concepts within the DoH Assessment Framework is the notion of 'parenting capacity'. This is highlighted as one of the three sides of the Assessment Triangle, alongside the child's developmental needs and family and environmental factors. In my view, this is not merely a change in terminology, but embodies a fundamental conceptual shift in thinking in relation to the assessment of parenting issues. Surprisingly, the defintion of the term 'parenting capacity' is not, however, given a great deal of attention within the Assessment Framework document itself, nor indeed the accompanying Practice Guidance. However, it is perhaps most clear what is intended through the statement:

Children's chances of achieving optimal outcomes will depend on their parent's capacities to respond appropriately to their needs at different stages of their lives.
(DoH, 2000b, p9).

It is important to open up 'parenting capacity' and to explore some of the key elements associated with the term. In my view, it is a more helpful construction than the notion of 'good enough parenting' which has been a core aspect of professional language and practice in this area previously. In essence, practitioners are now encouraged to move away from assessing whether someone's assessed level of parenting is 'good enough' in any given situation to a broader and more dynamic view of their capacity to meet their children's needs within their familial, social and environmental contexts. This conceptual shift has many important practice ramifications.

One of the problems with viewing parenting as 'good enough' or 'not good enough' is that it suggests that parenting can be seen, and indeed assessed, outside of its environmental and developmental context. In other words, evaluating a person's parenting as 'good enough' has tended to be used to imply that this is likely to be persistent over *time* and *place*. It may also suggest that being a 'good enough' parent is a characteristic inherent to that person.

However, it is clear that parenting is a much more complex, fluid and contextual endeavour. A person can clearly offer good parenting to a particular child in one situation and less optimal in others. Indeed, a parent may offer a very good level of care and attention to a child in one dimension of a child's development, but highly problematic in another. The notion of 'good enough' parenting also implies that there is an identifiable and accepted level of parenting that is 'good enough', beneath which professionals should intervene. Whilst there are clear examples of parenting practices that do, indeed, fall well beneath what most people would consider acceptable, in practice most cases fall into a more difficult grey area where practitioners need to balance risks and strengths and contemplate the course of action most likely to enhance outcomes for the child and family.

Seeing parenting as either 'good enough' or 'not good enough' *for a child* at least ties the notion of parenting to a child's developmental outcomes, but this is in itself an incomplete conceptualisation. As a parent, it may be that my children are meeting or exceeding their developmental milestones. This might have something to do with my activities or behaviours, but equally it could mean that I have all the necessary material resources to give my children to enable them to thrive within the context of the cultural aspirations set for them within our society. On the other hand, it could mean that my children are easy to parent and do not have a range of particular needs which would test or exceed my own parenting resources. Thus, according to this conceptualisation, a parent in 'easy circumstances' could be considered to be a good enough parent yet have less well developed parenting skills than a highly skilled and emotionally responsive parent in a difficult situation, whose children have multiple and complex needs. This is depicted in Figure 1.

The dynamic nature of parenting capacity

The notion of *parenting capacity* goes beyond the limitations of this 'good enough' conceptualisation. Parenting capacity suggests that parenting is a dynamic process, involving a range of factors and influences. As made clear in the Assessment Framework (DoH, 2000a, 2000b) there is no one perfect way of parenting children. Indeed, research shows pervasive differences in parenting practices and beliefs

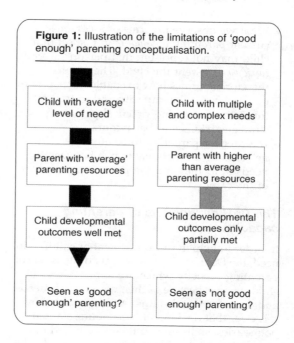

Figure 1: Illustration of the limitations of 'good enough' parenting conceptualisation.

Child with 'average' level of need

Child with multiple and complex needs

Parent with 'average' parenting resources

Parent with higher than average parenting resources

Child developmental outcomes well met

Child developmental outcomes only partially met

Seen as 'good enough' parenting?

Seen as 'not good enough' parenting?

associated with socioeconomic class, race, ethnicity, religion and other human differences and these factors 'do not exert direct effects on families resulting in 'better' or 'worse' parenting, but rather research suggests that people of different groups have different experiences which make them different people, both in their beliefs and values and in their behaviours' (Budd, 2001, p3). Furthermore, Rutter (1974) highlights how 'good parenting requires certain permitting circumstances. There must be the best necessary life opportunities and facilities. Where these are lacking even the best parents may find it difficult to exercise these skills' (cited DoH, 2000b). Similarly, Cleaver (2000) identified that not all children are equally vulnerable to adverse consequences of parental problems. Thus, as suggested within the Assessment Framework, evaluating a person's parenting capacity cannot be done without reference to the level and range of needs presented by the child and the wider situational, environmental and cultural factors within which the parenting takes place. In short, the implications of moving to this conceptualisation of parenting capacity include an awareness that:

- A person's *capacity* to parent a particular child can fluctuate according to a whole range of factors, which might make it more or less likely that the child reaches its developmental outcomes.

- What we observe in terms of a person's current parenting *behaviours* in respect of a child may not represent that person's overall *capacity* to parent the child. The emphasis therefore becomes how to enable the parent to develop her or his capacity and to translate this into specific and practical parenting strategies, skills and behaviours.
- In order for parenting to be effective, there needs to be a functional match between the needs of a child and the parenting resources of the carer.

The DoH dimensions of parenting capacity

In order to help in the assessment of children in need, the DoH has highlighted six dimensions of parenting capacity which are applicable to all children, irrespective of their age, specific needs and developmental status. As suggested above, it is clear that the kind of behaviours, standards, boundaries, skills and strategies required of a parent in respect of her or his children need to be considered as fluid over time. For example, to implement the rules with regard to road safety that are sensible and necessary to ensure appropriate safety for a toddler would be developmentally inappropriate, if not developmentally damaging, for most teenagers. Thus, the dimensions of parenting capacity described in the Assessment Framework are very broad and need to be seen within the context of the developmental span of childhood and adolescence. Nonetheless, it is clear that 'basic competence in each parenting dimension is required throughout childhood and adolescence in order to meet the developing person's needs' (Jones, 2000, p203). The six core dimensions of parenting capacity are the provision of:

- **Basic care**, including food, drink, warmth, shelter, appropriate clothing, personal hygiene.
- **Safety and protection from harm and danger**, including protection from unsafe adults/children, self-harm, recognition of hazards and dangers associated with the home and external environment.
- **Emotional warmth**, including the child's needs for secure, stable and affectionate relationships, appropriate physical contact, comfort, warmth.
- **Stimulation**, including appropriate levels of interaction, communication, facilitation of play.

- **Guidance and boundaries**, including modelling appropriate behaviours and emotional regulation, effective discipline, behaviour shaping.
- **Stability**, including continuity of care and stability of attachments, consistency of emotional warmth and of response.

          (DoH, 2000a, p21)

One overall difficulty faced in assessing parenting capacity is the lack of a minimum standard of competency within these dimensions. Although the dimensions are proposed as elements of adaptive parenting – and by association the lack of these qualities would constitute a parenting deficit – for the most part these broad qualities have not been translated into valid and empirically tested behavioural indicators (Budd and Holdsworth, 1996). The DoH has attempted to address this by offering examples within its Assessment Records of both positive and negative examples of parenting within each of the six suggested dimensions of parenting capacity, matching these to the proposed dimensions of child need at various developmental stages. Thus, for example, within the 'emotional and behavioural development' dimension of need for a child aged between three and four years old, the following four examples are offered with regard to parenting capacity in relation to 'emotional warmth':

- Child is comforted when distressed.
- Child is exposed to frequent criticism or hostility.
- Child is encouraged to talk about fears and worries.
- Parent takes pleasure in appropriate physical contact with the child.

Practitioners are asked to tick 'yes' or 'no' to each of these statements and offer clarification of the strength or 'issue identified'. However, it is difficult within this model to know how much weight to ascribe to each individual factor or how the individual factors might interact with others within the same or different dimensions of need to impact upon parenting capacity as a whole. For example, it is not inconceivable for a child to be routinely comforted when distressed (clearly an identified strength) and yet also subject to criticism and hostility (seen as an 'issue'). What sense of this mixed picture are we to make? How strong would the level of 'comfort when distressed' need to be in order to compensate for the level of 'criticism/ hostility'? Therefore, whilst the individual parenting factors to examine in assessment under this model are clearly stated, practitioners need to go beyond the framework to examine the mechanisms that might operate between dimensions and identified factors in order to influence the child's development.

Assessing parenting capacity: an integrative framework

As highlighted above, the notion of parenting capacity offers an opportunity to conceive of parenting as fluid and multi-dimensional. The dimensions of parenting offered are helpful in organising the collection of information relating to parenting practices and linking these to the core elements of child need. A further step, however, is the provision of an integrative framework of assessment of parenting capacity which helps practitioners to consider the interactions between the identified factors and which assists practitioners in reaching conclusions and offering interventions to enhance parenting and to meet child need.

Belsky (1984) proposes that competent parenting is multiply determined and suggests that influences can be categorised into three general categories of influence:

- The parent's characteristics.
- The contextual sources of support (e.g. the partner or marital relationship, support from the wider social network).
- The child's characteristics (e.g. temperament and child's behavioural responses to the parent).

Furthermore, Belsky maintained that these three factors exert a different level of influence, with the *parent's characteristics* the most significant factor, followed by the *context of support* and with the *child's characteristics* as the least influential factor. Whilst it has been presumed that parents influence children and that parenting strongly impacts upon children's developmental outcomes, at times this has been seen to be a 'one-way street'. There is, however, strong evidence that parenting practices can be powerfully driven by children, their temperaments, personalities and needs, etc. (Maccoby, 2000). Whilst the degree of influence is an ongoing matter of debate and further research, the clear message for practice is that assessment of parenting capacity has to involve

assessment of the nature of the relationship between parent and child and the 'relational fit' between the child's need and the competencies of the parent. Indeed, 'parenting' does not exist outside of the context of a relationship. It is not just what parents have by way of parenting attitudes, values and skills, but it concerns how these are expressed and translated into behaviours within the context of the parent–child relationship. This notion is supported by various authors, including Bogenschneider et al. (1997) who suggest adding to Belsky's model a fourth category concerning the 'goodness of fit' between characteristics of the child and parent.

It is also clear that the degree of influence exercised by parents over outcomes for children varies according to the child's developmental stage. For very young children, parents are usually the primary influences on biologically driven developmental change. As children grow, and particularly in adolescence, parental influence tends to decline and the influence of peers and the external world becomes more significant. Additionally, and also in favour of assessments of parenting capacity which examine the notion of 'goodness of fit' between parent and child, it is clear that children with different predispositions elicit correspondingly different reactions from their parents (Maccoby, 2000). Thus:

> There is reason to believe that there are forces motivat-ing children to differentiate themselves from their siblings, and these may counterbalance, or transform, the effects of parental inputs that might otherwise function to make them the same. Of course, some of the differentiation between siblings can come directly from differential treatment by the parents, or it can stem from differential reactions by different children to the same parental inputs.
>
> (Maccoby, 2000, p17).

Maccoby (2000, p3) therefore suggests that assessments of parenting should seek to address the three following core and interlinked elements:

- **Familial risk factors** (in other words, aspects of family functioning related to the development of internalising or externalising behaviours or poor developmental outcomes in children);
- **Social conditions** that affect parenting practices (e.g. how well the child is monitored, etc.); and
- **Parenting behaviours as mediators** of the connections between societal risk factors and

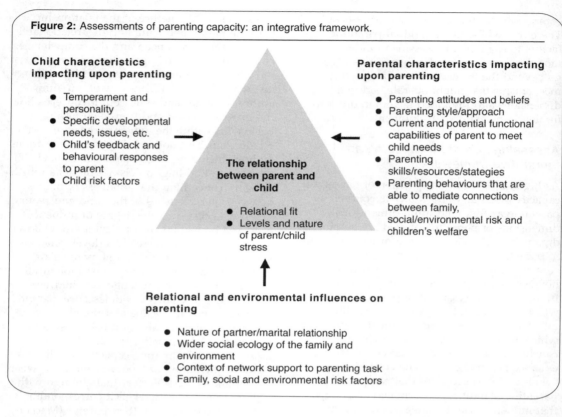

Figure 2: Assessments of parenting capacity: an integrative framework.

Child characteristics impacting upon parenting

- Temperament and personality
- Specific developmental needs, issues, etc.
- Child's feedback and behavioural responses to parent
- Child risk factors

The relationship between parent and child

- Relational fit
- Levels and nature of parent/child stress

Parental characteristics impacting upon parenting

- Parenting attitudes and beliefs
- Parenting style/approach
- Current and potential functional capabilities of parent to meet child needs
- Parenting skills/resources/stategies
- Parenting behaviours that are able to mediate connections between family, social/environmental risk and children's welfare

Relational and environmental influences on parenting

- Nature of partner/marital relationship
- Wider social ecology of the family and environment
- Context of network support to parenting task
- Family, social and environmental risk factors

children's adjustment (e.g. how well a parent's behaviours help cushion the impact of a child living in poverty).

The following model seeks to take the frameworks offered by both Belsky and Maccoby and to transpose them into the Assessment Triangle in order to produce an integrative framework for assessing parenting capacity. Thus, I have depicted the notion of the parent-child fit as the product of both the child's and adult's characteristics, influenced also by the context of environment support or risk. This integrative model, represented in Figure 2, is offered as a guide for the practitioner in relation to areas to cover within assessment alongside the six specific dimensions of parenting capacity offered in the DoH Framework.

Understanding the interaction between factors within the integrative model

Having identified a conceptual model within which to assess parenting capacity, it is important to look at the mechanisms operating between the proposed dimensions. Van Bakel and Riksen-Walraven (2002) used Belsky's

conceptualisation of parenting to examine the links between parenting and development of one year old children. They investigated the inter-relationship between the three domains of *parental characteristics, the context of stress and support* and *child characteristics* in a sample of 129 Dutch families. They found that where all three domains were intact, there were almost always positive outcomes for children. However, interestingly, where one domain was weak, the other two appeared to **buffer** the level of parenting. In other words, parenting competence in the face of a child with complex needs or difficult temperament may remain intact if the parent's own support needs are met and if the parent's own capabilities are relatively high. Similarly, where parental characteristics are problematic, (for example where parents have unresolved issues from their backgrounds), outcomes can remain positive if child and environment characteristics are positive. However, crucially in van Bakel and Riksen-Walraven's study, where any two (or more) of these three domains were weak, this was a strong predictor of poor outcomes for children. This suggests that, in conducting parenting capacity assessments, we should look carefully not only at the individual dimensions of parenting capacity suggested, but at the interactive effects of the identified factors.

Another important message concerns the relative effectiveness of different kinds of support as a factor influencing parenting. In van Bakel and Riksen-Walraven's (2002) study, as in previous research, there was considerable evidence that high levels of marital support and satisfaction were associated with skilful parenting. This appeared to hold true for mothers and fathers, as well as in culturally diverse populations and remained the case even after parental characteristics had been controlled for. Thus, the quality of marital or partner support was consistently found to be a stronger predictor of parenting competence than network support, and wider network support was not found to fully compensate for a lack of spousal support and satisfaction. The clear message, therefore, is that we need to look very carefully at the context of any marital or partner relationship within the course of parenting assessments as this is likely to be an important factor in influencing overall parenting responses. This may require practitioners to go beyond the Assessment Framework and its recording forms, where the emphasis appears to be very much centred on the parent-child dyad and the wider environmental or social context. In my view, the quality and nature *specifically* of the parents' relationship (of course where there are two parental figures) should be included as a core element of the assessment of parenting capacity.

Assessing the notion of the child-adult fit

Budd (2001) emphasises a functional approach to assessment of parenting which focuses on:

- The current and potential functional capabilities of the parent to meet the needs of the specific child.
- The nature of the relationship between parent and child.
- The developmental needs of the child.
- Wider social ecology of the family and environment.

This is a helpful model which emphasises everyday behaviours and skills that make up parenting or 'what the caregiver understands, believes, knows, does and is capable of doing related to childrearing' (Budd, 2001, p3). This approach, she maintains, has the advantage of focusing constructively on identifying parenting strengths and areas of adequate performance in contrast to deficit models. Budd conceptualises parenting adequacy as the fit between the *parent's functioning* and the *child's needs* on two distinct levels:

- The connection between a child's developmental needs and the parent's caregiving skills.
- The connection between the parent's competence to care for his or her own needs and for the child's needs (2001, p5).

She develops this into a matrix which is designed to offer practitioners a working framework for organising and integrating information both about parenting functioning and the nature of the parent-child fit. The model:

... focuses on the link between the parent's independent functioning in particular domains and his/her competence in caregiving functioning. Deficits in a parent's adaptive skills in, for example, the cognitive domain may affect childcare abilities in the same domain (e.g. ability to teach the child) or in another domain (e.g. ability to read medicine labels and care for child when ill).

(2001, p5).

Both areas are considered in relation to the broad domains of physical, cognitive and social/emotional development. The matrix is depicted below in Figure 3, together with illustrative examples taken from Budd (2001, p6).

Parenting styles research and its use in parenting capacity assessment

A useful addition to the ideas on parenting capacity described in the Assessment Framework is the wider research evidence on overall parenting styles. This is important for practitioners *assessing* parenting, as well as for those seeking to *intervene* to enhance parenting capacity following an assessment which highlights parenting deficits. For example, as well as helping to address one particularly problematic parenting response, it is vitally important to keep the broader parenting picture in focus. Indeed, this is consistent with a strengths approach to assessment. A parent may have difficulties in one or two micro level areas, but the overall parenting picture may be generally positive.

A significant amount of work in the developmental psychology field over the last

Figure 3: Assessing the parent–child fit.

Dimensions of child need	Examples of functional parenting skills	Examples of functional parenting deficits
Physical care	e.g. takes child for injections	e.g. fails to gain medical treatment for head lice
Cognitive	e.g. provides activities or toys for child	e.g. leaves child alone and in cot for long periods of time
Social/emotional	e.g. shows warmth and affection towards child	e.g. loses temper at child for minor accidents or mistakes

Area of parent competence	Examples of adaptive skills/deficits in parent's independent functioning	Examples of how deficits in independent functioning may impact upon parenting
Physical care	e.g. shops and prepares regular meals/ often goes hungry	e.g. feeds child irregularly because of lack of food in the house
Cognitive	e.g. exercises judgement/fails to consider the consequences of actions	e.g. has unrealistic child-rearing beliefs
Social/emotional	e.g. has a social network/is isolated and mistrustful of others	e.g. prevents child from having social contact with peers

four decades has been done to research overall parenting approaches and styles which may contribute to optimal developmental outcomes for children. This work consistently identifies that parental acceptance, non-punitive disciplinary practices based on reasoning, and consistency in childrearing are each associated with positive developmental outcomes in children. This constellation of factors, characterised on the one hand by high levels of parental involvement in a child's life and of behavioural monitoring, whilst at the same time parental acceptance, trust and allowing the child psychological autonomy, has become known as 'authoritative parenting'. This has been envisaged as the most positive and helpful of one of four broad parenting styles (Baumrind 1971; 1989 and Maccoby and Martin, 1983) which can be conceptualised on two dimensions:

- *Demandingness* – the extent to which parents show control, maturity demands and supervision in their parenting.
- *Responsiveness* – the extent to which parents show emotional warmth, acceptance and involvement.

Figure 4 describes the relationship between these two dimensions and the four parenting styles.

Authoritative parenting
This form of parenting is characterised by demandingness and responsiveness on the part of parents. Thus, authoritative parents typically have a high level of involvement in the life of their children, communicate actively and openly and have clear expectations of their children, including relatively high levels of behavioural

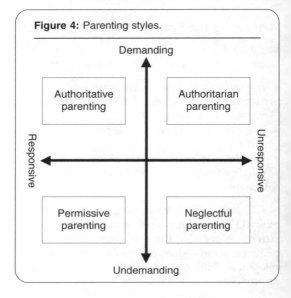

Figure 4: Parenting styles.

control and monitoring. However, at the same time, they encourage psychological autonomy, are trusting and display acceptance. This mixture of firm and clear expectations and boundaries has been strongly linked to the development of a whole range of developmental competencies, including childhood social adjustment, high level of school performance and strong engagement in school and other networks (Weiss and Schwartz, 1996), as well as positive attitudes, empathy and high levels of self-esteem (Thompson et al., 2002). In particular, the use of 'positive' or 'gentle' reason based strategies in disciplining and managing children's behaviours has been seen to increase the level of child compliance and decrease behavioural problems (Gray and Steinberg, 1999). Gray and Steinberg (1999) examined the independent and joint contributions of three core dimensions of authoritative parenting (parental involvement, autonomy granting and structure) in a large sample of 8,700 14–18-year-olds. They found that these three components not only function independently to positively influence developmental outcomes in young people, but that there is also a significant interactive effect between them. They conclude that 'teens report the healthiest psychosocial development when they also perceive that their parents grant a high level of psychological autonomy, stay actively involved in their teen's life, and establish firm standards for behavior' (1999, p. 584). Whilst there have been some suggestions that authoritative parenting is a white, middle-class conception, the evidence in support of the concept appears compelling. Gray and Steinberg (1999) claim that no large-scale studies have indicated that non-authoritative parenting has more beneficial effects on adolescent development than authoritative parenting, regardless of the population studied.

Authoritarian parenting

This style of parenting is characterised by parents who are demanding, but not responsive towards their children. Parents who are authoritarian place a high level of control and demands upon their children, but are generally less trusting and less engaged with their children than authoritative parents. As opposed to authoritative parenting, parental controls are more adult than child focused (Maccoby and Martin, 1983) and open communcation between parent and child is limited. Frequently

discipline is physical and based on confrontation. This approach to parenting has been linked to a range of potential outcomes for children, including impaired learning and problem-solving abilities and increased dependence on adult control and guidance (Hess and McDevitt, 1984) and decreased psychological autonomy (Barber, 1994). The over-use of confrontational strategies based on the assertion of parental power has been seen to be ineffective in promoting internalised compliance in children (Grusec and Goodnow, 1995), especially if such strategies are imposed without discussion. Aunola et al. (2000) found that adolescents who had experienced authoritarian parenting were more likely to deploy maladaptive strategies, particularly passive behaviour and a lack of use of self-enhancing attributions, which are indicative of learned helplessness.

Permissive parenting

This approach to parenting is characterised by parents who are responsive but undemanding. Parents who are permissive, like authoritative parents, are warm, accepting and have child-centred attitudes and approaches. However, unlike authoritative parenting, permissive parenting is characterised by non-demanding parental behaviour and a general lack of parental control. Parents operating using such an approach frequently do not require mature behaviour from their children, but allow them to behave autonomously and independently. Again, a number of possible child outcomes have been linked to permissive parenting approaches. As there are fewer maturity and control demands placed on children, their self-regulatory abilities may be under-developed and they may demonstrate higher levels of impulsivity. Experiencing this parenting style has also been linked to academic underachievement in children (Onatsu-Arvilommi and Nurmi, 1997).

Neglectful parenting

Neglectful parents are those who are neither responsive to, nor demanding of, their children. In general, they tend not to support the child's self-regulation and this is combined with an overall lack of monitoring and supervision. Whilst such parents have a non-controlling attitude, this is combined with overall under involvement in their children's lives. Emotionally and practically, such parents are often absent when needed. Such a parenting approach has been linked to a range of problematic outcomes for children, including high impulsivity, particularly low levels of academic achievement and poor levels of self-esteem and self-regulatory abilities (Maccoby and Martin, 1983; Aunola et al. 2000).

Using the parenting styles model within assessment of parenting capacity

The categories of parenting style described above can provide a useful reference point for practitioners engaged in parenting capacity assessments, however, a number of caveats are needed.

Firstly, it is important not to 'pigeonhole' parents into one category, or expect that their responses at all times and in all circumstances will be indicative of a particular parenting style, thereby writing off their potential to develop an alternative approach to parenting issues. Many of us would like to claim that we are authoritative parents, but know full well that there are examples of our parenting behaviours that fall within the permissive, authoritarian or neglectful styles. In other words, despite our ideas about how best to parent children, we often fail to live up to our own expectations in the face of a whole range of pressures and difficulties. However, the research evidence does indeed suggest that parents' responses to their children broadly fall within one of the four categories described (Aunola et al. 2000; Thompson et al., 2002). For example, Thompson et al. (2002) investigated behaviours indicative of authoritative and authoritarian parenting in a group of mothers with 10-year-old children and found a complete lack of overlap between the use of physical punishment and use of reasoning, with only one person mentioning both responses. Therefore, whilst these very general and broad groupings should not be seen as either inborn or necessarily fixed character traits of parents, they do appear to be useful in articulating some key and broad-based differences between parents in relation to their parenting approaches and beliefs, and indeed, these differences do appear to be linked to differential outcomes for children.

A second caveat is that the model could be used to promote a unidirectional view of the influence between parenting practices and outcomes for children. There is, however, as has been discussed above, compelling evidence that parenting practices may be substantially influenced, if not determined, by children.

A third caveat, relating to the difference between authoritative and authoritarian parenting, is that there is some evidence to suggest that the potentially negative impact of a number of 'non-ideal' disciplinary practices can be mediated by the degree of consistency and emotional responsiveness offered by a parent. In Thompson et al.'s (2002) study, authoritarian parents who used physical punishment were no more likely to have children with behaviour problems. Authoritative parents who used reasoning were no more likely to have children without behaviour problems. But crucially, parents who failed to follow up on threats were more likely to have children at greater risk aged eight years than those who did not. This appears to give some important messages about diversity in parenting approaches in that in this study a range of parenting responses was linked to outcomes within the normal developmental range for children, yet this diversity was not represented on an individual level as parents tended either to engage in authoritative or authoritarian practices. Given this, the use of praise appeared to provide a buffer for the use of physical discipline. Thompson et al. conclude that 'parental inconsistency, a characteristic often linked to childhood problems, rather than physical punishment may be the key factor in the development of problems' (Thompson et al. 2002, p154). They hypothesise that the damaging effects of parenting style on children may not be the use of a particular strategy, nor the strictness of its use, but the emotional context within which the strategy is conducted.

In summary, the parenting styles model is limited in its 'diagnostic' ability. However, the evidence associated with the benefits of the cluster of factors within the authoritative type is such that the model is a powerful way of assessing and articulating how parenting behaviours can be amended to the benefit of both the parent and child. It is all too easy for parents to fall into counter-productive or negative patterns of behaviour towards their children, often based on the parenting models that they themselves experienced as children. Practitioners can use knowledge of parenting styles to anchor and link the individual factors they identify through attention to the DoH dimensions of parenting capacity, in order to identify how a person's overall approaches to parenting can be enhanced. Derived and

Table 1: Assessment of Parenting Style Checklist.

Authoritative parenting *Look for examples where* *the parent:*	• Praises the child for good behaviour. • Reasons with the child after misbehaviour. • Explains consequences of child's behaviour. • Gives child expectations before activity. • Shows patience with child. • Apologises if he or she is wrong. • Channels child's negative behaviours into acceptable alternatives.
Authoritarian parenting *Look for examples where* *the parent:*	• Uses physical punishment. • Screams at child. • Uses punishment more than reason. • Tells off child as an attempt to improve child's behaviour. • Responds with intense anger when child misbehaves. • Puts child alone without explanation.
Permissive parenting *Look for examples where* *the parent:*	• Gives in to child's tantrums. • Ignores child's misbehaviour. • Allows child to annoy others. • Finds it difficult to discipline child. • Bribes child to comply.
Neglectful parenting *Look for examples where* *the parent:*	• Is frequently unavailable, either physically or emotionally. • Does not respond to expressions of child need. • Appears unconcerned at child's problematic behaviour or at dangers to child. • Does not give child structure or appropriate levels of responsibility.

adapted from the work of Thompson et al. (2002), Table 1 offers some ideas about the range of indicators which can be used to distinguish parenting typologies. As with any behavioural checklist, this list should be used with caution and with regard to context, age of child, child's specific needs, etc.

Conducting parenting capacity assessments – process and content issues

Relatively few studies have investigated how parenting assessments are conducted in practice. In a North American study of 190 mental health assessments concerned with child welfare and children at risk, Budd (2001) found that assessments of parenting were usually completed in a single session and generally used few sources other than parent self-report. The majority did not consider previous reports or information and they rarely included parent-child observation. The relationship between the parent and child was also overlooked. In addition, the assessor often neglected to describe the parent's caregiving qualities and only noted perceived deficits. Budd and Holdsworth (1996) raise a number of important points in the assessment of parenting,

including the need to be aware of situational influences on the assessment process, as well as the importance of asking specific questions at the outset of the process. Taken together, these points help to highlight a number of important process and content issues which should underpin assessments of parenting capacity. In particular, such assessments should:

• Be specific about the aims and questions to be answered.
• Use historical information and reports with care.
• Be aware of situational influences that can distort the assessment process and findings.
• Be based on multiple sources of information including direct observation of parent-child interaction.
• Offer parents specific opportunities to reflect upon their parenting in interviews.
• Address both strengths and deficits in parenting and family functioning.

• Be specific about the aims of the assessment and the questions to be answered

When conducting an assessment which seeks to evaluate a person's parenting capacity, it is important to be as concrete and specific as possible at the outset about the particular questions that will hopefully be addressed within the assessment. Thus, practitioners should consider the following questions to help orient their assessment around specific concerns or issues (Budd and Holdsworth, 1996):

– What specifically do you want to know about the parent's functioning?
– What problems or events give rise to concerns (and whose concerns are these)?
– What specific outcomes or options will be affected by the findings of the assessment? So, rather than simply asking 'what is the potential of this person as parent for the children . . .'a more useful and specific question might be 'what strengths and deficits does this person have in terms of her/his ability to adequately care for these three young children'.

• Use historical information and previous reports with care

Some practitioners express caution as to the use of previous reports or historical information from files as part of the assessment process for fear that past reports have been biased or incomplete, or that they reflect problems and issues that are either no longer present or have little bearing upon current parenting functioning. As social work files may be extensive or contain information compiled by many practitioners over long, but fragmented, periods of time, concerns about the fairness and accuracy of such data are often justified. Scrutiny of historical files and documentation can often reveal incomplete or missing information, a host of unevidenced and value-laden statements and decision-making which is not transparent. At the same time, the predictive value of past behaviour is well established in a range of aspects of human functioning where patterns of escalating behaviours are often seen, such as in entrenched patterns of criminality or sexually abusive behaviour in adults. In such circumstances, it is well established that the best predictor of future behaviour is past behaviour and to disregard documented historical information would therefore be both unwise and dangerous. Whilst previous reports about parenting difficulties should therefore not be seen to be indicative of an inability to change, it is obviously important to look carefully at any previous assessments to look for patterns of behaviours or concerns. Budd and Holdsworth (1996) suggest that

assessors should 'avoid making assumptions about the impact of past events on parents' current functioning unless current corroborative evidence exists' (1996, p6). The question is less whether previous reports should be scrutinised, and more what should be done with the information gleaned from them. There is an enormous difference, therefore, between using past reports destructively as fuel to discredit or undermine a parent and using them constructively to identify approaches and intervention strategies that appear to have been either particularly effective or unhelpful for the person or family concerned in the past.

One of the most difficult aspects concerning historical information is the role that previous negative life events, such as a parent's own history of being abused, may play in influencing or shaping an individual's own parenting practices. This is an area which can easily lead to the pathologisation of the many individuals who have survived childhood adversity and have developed resilient and adaptive coping and positive parenting skills. Thus, whilst a range of studies have suggested a *correlation* between a history of childhood abuse and a range of future parenting difficulties (Meron, 2001), *causal* mechanisms are difficult to establish and there is little empirical support for the notion of direct intergenerational transmission of abuse. Whilst the evidence relating to this debate cannot be analysed in depth here, it is clear that survivors of childhood abuse are not destined to become abusive parents by dint of their own experiences. However, it is the case that many parents in difficulty have themselves experienced very poor models of parenting in their own childhoods and need support in seeking out other models for their own parenting. Budd and Holdsworth conclude that past experiences of abuse or trauma should therefore be regarded as 'potential risk factors that bear investigation as part of parenting assessments' (1996, p6).

• Be aware of situational influences that can distort the assessment process and findings

The assessment of parenting capacity is particularly vulnerable to situational influences which can mean that observations made in the course of assessments range from an overly positive or overly negative account of an individual's parenting capacity. The stress of professional intervention can easily disrupt or distort a parent's responses and, indeed, the stress of the assessment process can be falsely assumed to be indicative of the level of parenting stress. As Budd and Holdsworth (1996) highlight, 'some parents appear more impaired than they actually are, whereas others appear literally too good to be true' (p5). The kind of situation factors can impact in a number of different ways, including:

- *Changing the interactions observed between parent and child.* The interaction and parental behaviours can appear stilted and false or mechanistic. If this is the case, practitioners need to examine carefully how far this is influenced by the situational context of the assessment, or how much this is reflective of how the parent generally responds to the child.
- *Affecting the nature of information given by parents in interview.* Some parents are keen to present themselves in a socially desirable light which can mask underlying difficulties and result in an overly-optimistic view, whilst others may find the assessment process so stressful that they are not able to give an accurate picture of their competence in a particular parenting task, and this can lead to assessments that fail to highlight strengths or are overly pessimistic.
- *Changing the nature of responses given by parents to tests or questionnaires.* The administration of parenting questionnaires or psychometric measures is more common in psychological evaluations than it is in social work assessments, although a range of very useful questionnaires has been provided by the DoH as part of the Assessment Framework pack. Budd and Holdsworth highlight how practitioners should interpret parenting measures with caution due to 'potential subject-reporting biases, limited information about normative responses with minority populations, and lack of research on predictive validity'. (1996, p8).

Overall, it is important for practitioners who are making judgements about parenting issues to be sensitive to the impact of the assessment process itself upon parenting practices and family situations. Budd and Holdsworth (1996) suggest that practitioners should take steps to minimise the impact of potentially biasing effects of the assessment process on family members by:

- Observing interactions as far as is possible in a natural setting (i.e. the family home) or, where this is not feasible, in a structured environment which is comfortable for family members, has adequate resources and is familiar.
- Observing family interactions over multiple occasions.
- Including the entire family in observations.

• Use multiple sources of information including direct observation of parent-child interaction

The nature of a person's parenting occurs within the context of daily interactions with her or his children, rather than in discussion with a social worker. Therefore, assessment of parenting should use multiple sources of information, including focused interviews with parents, use of questionnaires and assessment tools *and* observation of parent-child interactions. The Assessment Framework document states that 'children's responses and interactions in different situations should be carefully observed wherever possible, alone, with siblings, with parents and/or caregivers or in other settings as children may 'hide or suppress their feelings in situations which are difficult or not safe for them' (DoH, 2000a, p. 43). In addition to this, assessments of parenting capacity should include direct observation because parents too may present differently in interview than in the course of daily interactions with their child.

Observation is often presumed to be an easy thing to do, but is in fact fraught with complications and dilemmas. How much interaction should we observe? Should we focus on a wide range of parent-child interactions, or examine a more narrow range in order to comment on particular aspects of parenting capacity which may be of concern? How should observations be recorded or interpreted? Is our clinical judgement sufficient or should we be using standardised parenting-specific measures – and if so, what might these be? Budd and Holdsworth (1996) caution against the potential for over-generalising or misinterpreting findings from clinical observations and suggest that competent observation requires:

- Training in methods of structuring the observational situation.
- Preparation of family members for the interaction.

Table 2: Core elements in observing parent-child observation in assessments of parenting capacity.

Parent behaviour patterns
- How does the parent structure interactions through instructions, toys or activities?
- How does the parent show understanding or misunderstanding of the children's developmental level?
- How does the parent convey acceptance or approval of the children's behaviour (praise, descriptive feedback, physical affection)?
- How does the parent convey disapproval of children's behaviour (criticism, negative commands, threats, physical means, etc.)?
- Does the parent notice and attend to the children's physical needs (e.g. hunger, bathroom, safety risks, etc.)?
- Is the parent responsive to children's initiations via verbalisations, facial expressions and actions?
- How does the parent respond to children's disagreement or expressions of their own opinions? To what extent are disagreements allowed?
  Does the parent follow through with their instructions or rules?
- Does the parent spread attention fairly across children if more than one child is involved?
- How far does the parent focus on the children? Does the parent appear distracted, withdrawn, or bored during the observation (e.g. watching TV rather than responding)
- Is there any evidence of problematic statements or attributions (e.g. asking the child if they love the parent, making negative comments about family members [or foster carers], using inappropriate adult language, etc.)?

Child behaviour patterns
- To what extent do the children appear at ease around the parent (e.g. smiling, playing and verbalising versus remaining silent, distant or fearful)?
- Is there evidence of the child initiating interactions with the parent?
- Are there any examples of developmental, emotional or behavioural difficulties that require different parenting strategies than those offered by the parent?
- How far do the children respond to the parent's initiations by showing interest and acceptance of the parent's attention?
- Do the children disagree with the parent or express their own opinions?
- In what ways do the children show affection and interest towards the parent?
- What topics do the children bring up in conversation with the parent (e.g. do they report activities in foster care, talk about other family members, etc.)?

- Selection of relevant behaviours and sequences to monitor based on previous research.
- Recording (formally or informally) identified events and behaviours.
- Interpretations of findings in comparison to other parents and children.
                    (Budd and Holdsworth, 1996, p10).

They state that their own work in reviewing assessments of 'at risk parents' suggests that practitioners are often prone to overstating the findings of their observations, inferring parental qualities based on selective child behaviours and failing to mention the limitations of the observations. They conclude that, whilst parent-child observations are crucial to the process of parenting assessment, misuse of observational procedures 'may do more harm than good by lending an appearance of credibility to a poorly conducted evaluation' (1996, p10).

Such a critique sets a high standard for practitioners to plan and conduct their observations with care. Although the process and content of observations will need to be determined by the context and in collaboration with family members concerned, Table 2, taken and adapted from Budd (2001, p. 12), suggests a range of core elements to assist practitioners in the observation of parent-child interactions, separating out both parent and child behaviour patterns.

- **Give parents specific opportunities to reflect upon their parenting in interviews**
'Parenting capacity', as I have described earlier in this chapter, is helpful as an overarching theoretical framework within which a person's beliefs about parenting and children, approaches to parenting tasks, and parenting behaviours or responses are assessed. Although these factors interact with each other to inform a person's parenting capacity, there may be inconsistencies and tensions between the individual elements. For example, a person's overall parenting beliefs (what it means for an individual to be a parent, how they approach

parenting, etc.) may be in contrast to that person's observable parenting behaviours. Thus, in interviews with parents about parenting issues it is helpful to break down the constituent elements of 'parenting' into a set of distinct, albeit overlapping, areas for exploration, comprising:

- *Parenting beliefs*: This area includes parents' attitudes and beliefs about parenting and parenthood, their understanding of children's needs and children's development. It is helpful to discuss parents' beliefs about child-rearing practices and how the models of parenting that they themselves have experienced as children may be consistent with, or different from, the models they have adopted.
- *Parenting strategies:* This includes parents' ideas about how to respond to their children in certain situations, as well as the way that they deal with macro level parenting tasks, such as the strategies they have to discipline their children, manage difficult behaviour, etc.
- *Parenting style:* As discussed above, this concerns parents' overall style of parenting.
- *Parenting behaviours*: This includes parents' micro level behaviours towards children, their specific behavioural responses to children's needs, discussion of observed interactions, as well as parents' self-report about behaviours that have been helpful or unhelpful in the past in a range of given circumstances.

It is not possible to draw up a standard interview schedule to be used within all assessments of parenting capacity as each family situation brings with it distinct areas which will need to be given specific attention. Practitioners should clearly orient the format of their interviews of parents with attention to issues of engagement and collaborative working, empowerment and recognition of the inherent stress of professional involvement in parenting issues. Issues of diversity, particularly around culture and race, gender, sexuality and disability, are commonly bound up with notions about 'normative' or 'adequate' parenting and need close attention. Practitioners should negotiate with parents a commonly understood, shared language about parenting issues. Whilst flexibility and diversity of approach is necessary, Budd (2001) provides a helpful framework for practitioners to help structure and focus the exploration of parenting issues within an assessment interview, which I have adapted and added to in Table 3.

• Address both strengths and deficits in parenting and family functioning

One of the key changes within the discourse of parenting assessment has been the shift from deficit-based models, in which attention was paid to identifying parenting problems and risks, to a more strengths-based approach, where a parent's strengths or competencies are acknowledged (DoH, 2000a). For the purposes of assessing parenting capacity, a focus on strengths and competence is clearly vital in helping parents to see that parenting problems do not constitute all of their life and that, however entrenched the 'problem', they as individuals are always more than their problems (Saleebey, 1997). At the same time, there have been concerns expressed about the move to strengths-based models, including strong criticisms expressed about the deletion of the concept of risk within the Assessment Framework (see Calder in Chapter 21 of this volume; Calder, 2002). A particular matter of confusion is how much weight should be given to strength in the face of an identified difficulty and how the mechanisms that operate between, and mediate the relationship amongst, individual risk and protective factors actually work.

Strengths-based assessment practice is not simply the opposite of deficit models. Indeed, ignoring deficits in parenting or family functioning, being overly optimistic about situations of risk and putting a positive gloss on people's real-life difficulties would be dangerous to children (who may be harmed or denied opportunities to meet developmental targets) and disrespectful to parents (whose real and painful problems remain). The essence of a strengths-based approach to parenting issues is therefore not to disregard problems, but to conceive of strengths as a key part of resolving difficulties. Despite the myriad of difficulties that may exist, every parent is likely to have some strengths, assets or resources. Problematic parenting practices may indeed present risk to children's development, however identifying and facing these may be a source of opportunity and change. Such strengths-based constructions are particularly important given that most assessments of parenting capacity are borne out of concern. In short, it is necessary for practitioners to 'assess parenting strengths and potential resources in the family's environment and to delineate these positive features along

Table 3: Core elements of parenting assessment interviews.

Purpose of assessment and confidentiality.	• The parent's understanding of the reason for the assessment and its potential outcomes. • Developing an agreed and clear awareness of the limits of confidentiality and the parent's rights of challenge, etc.
The child's developmental history and any parenting concerns.	• The parent's perspectives and version of events. • The parent's views of the credibility of any external concerns and level of personal responsibility for events. • The parent's view of how events or child's developmental issues have impacted on their own life and parenting.
Services received to date relating to allegations or parenting concerns. **Parent's current living situation.**	• The nature and helpfulness of professional intervention previously (e.g. relationships with health visitors, parent's perspectives on how any past intervention plans or advice have assisted or not, etc.). • The nature, stability and environmental circumstances of residence. • People in the home and their specific needs (extent to which other people's needs or issues may impinge upon an individual parent's ability to meet a specific child's need). • The nature of the parents' relationship- where two parents are present. To include: levels of support, division of parenting tasks and roles, etc. • Employment or school status. • Physical health of people in the home. • Substance use. • Mental health. • Social support network.
Parent's personal background.	• Family of origin – continuity and discontinuity of relationships and why. • Parent's own early health and development. • Childrearing and disciplinary experiences whilst growing up. • Educational history. • Significant life events (e.g. trauma, abuse or neglect, moves, criminal history, etc.). • Cultural and religious identity. • Significant partner relationships and break-ups.
Children and parent–child relationship.	• First experiences as a parent. • Pre- and postnatal history of the children. • Time spent as caregiver. • Perceived strengths and weaknesses as a parent. • Current relationship with children. • Specific needs, fears or considerations about children's welfare. • Views of how the children are doing now. • Things parent would like to do for the children and their views on their ability to provide these things.
Parent's hopes and expectations for dealing with parenting concerns.	• What the parent would like to happen. • What would be best for the child in their view. • Views on what the children would like to happen. • What services or changes does the parent feel are needed to help achieve the desired outcomes? • The views of the parent on the likelihood of being able and willing to make needed changes. • Barriers to achieving the desired outcomes. • Consequences if desired outcomes are not achieved.

with weaknesses as part of the report' (Budd and Holdsworth, 1996, p12)

Summary

This chapter has sought to identify some of the key aspects relating to the assessment of parenting capacity, outlining a range of theoretical models, research evidence and practical frameworks to complement the ideas presented within the DoH Assessment Framework model. This is a difficult and somewhat controversial area of practice, which brings our own values and personal experiences into sharp focus as practitioners. The ideas presented herein should therefore be taken, used and developed in practice. As such, no theory should ever be regarded as complete (Hackett, 2000; Preston-Shoot and Agass, 1990). It is necessary for us to seek out the best available evidence to support our practice, whilst at the same time remaining sensitive to the individual narratives and struggles of parents and children in circumstances of adversity. This remains a formidable challenge.

References

Aunola, K. Stattin, H. and Nurmi, J.-E. (2000) Parenting Styles and Adolescents' Achievement Strategies. *Journal of Adolescence.* 23: 205–22.

Barber, B. (1996) Parental Psychological Control: Revisiting a Neglected Construct. *Child Development.* 67: 3296–319.

Baumrind, D. (1971) Types of Adolescent Life-styles. *Developmental Psychology Monographs.* 4: 1, (pt 2).

Baumrind, D. (1989) Rearing Competent Children. In Damon, W. (Ed.) *Child Development Today and Tomorrow.* San Francisco: Jossey-Bass.

Belsky, (1984) The Determinants of Parenting: A Process Model. *Child Development.* 55: 83–96.

Budd, K. (2001) Assessing Parenting Competence in Child Protection Cases: A Clinical Practice Model. *Clinical Child and Family Psychology Review.* 4: 1, 1–18.

Budd, K. and Holdsworth, M. (1996) Issues in Clinical Assessment of Minimal Parenting Competence. *Journal of Clinical Child Psychology.* 25: 1, 2–14.

Bogenschneider, K., Small, S. and Tsay, J. (1997) Child, Parents and Contextual Influences on Perceived Parenting Competence Among Parents of Adolescents. *Journal of Marriage and the Family.* 59: 345–62.

Calder, M.C. (2002) A Framework for Conducting Risk Assessment. *Child Care in Practice.* 8: 1, 7–18.

Cleaver, H. (2000) When Parents' Issues Influence their Ability to Respond to Children's Needs. In Horwath, J. (Ed.) *The Child's World. Assessing Children in Need.* DoH/NSPCC/University of Sheffield.

Cleaver, H. and Freeman, P. (1995) *Parental Perspectives in Cases of Suspected Child Abuse.* London: HMSO.

Daniel, B. (2000) Judgements about Parenting: What do Social Workers Think They are Doing? *Child Abuse Review.* 9: 91–107.

DoH (2000a) *Framework for the Assessment of Children in Need and their Families.* London: HMSO.

DoH (2000b) *Assessing Children in Need and their Families. Practice Guidance.* London: HMSO.

Hackett, S. (2000) Sexual Aggression, Diversity and the Challenge of Anti-oppressive Practice. *Journal of Sexual Aggression.* 5: 1, 4–20.

Hess, R. and McDevitt, T. (1984) Some Cognitive Consequences of Maternal Intervention Techniques: A Longitudinal Study. *Child Development.* 55: 2017–30.

Jones, D. (2000) The Assessment of Parental Capacity. In Horwath, J. (Ed.) *The Child's World. Assessing Children in Need.* DoH/NSPCC/University of Sheffield.

Maccoby, E. (2000) Parenting and its Effects on Children: On Reading and Misreading Behavior Genetics. *Annual Review of Psychology.* 51: 1–27.

Maccoby, E. and Martin, J. (1983) Socialization in the Context of the Family: Parent-child Interaction. In Mussen, P.H. (Ed.) *Handbook of Child Psychology.* New York: Wiley.

Meron, A. M. (2001) Predicting the Child-rearing Practices of Mothers Sexually Abused in Childhood. *Child Abuse and Neglect.* 25: 3, 369–87.

Onatsu-Arvilommi, T. and Nurmi, J.-E. (1997) Family Background and Problems at School and in Society: The Role of Family Composition, Emotional Atmosphere and Parental Education. *European Journal of Psychology of Education.* 12: 315–30.

Preston-Shoot, M. and Agass, D. (1990) *Making Sense of Social Work. Psychodynamics, Systems and Practice.* London: Macmillan.

Saleebey, D. (1997) The Strengths Approach to Practice. In Saleebey, D. (Ed.) *The Strengths Approach in Social Work Practice.* White Plains: Longman.

Thompson, M.J.J. et al. (2002) Parenting Behaviour Described by Mothers in a General Population Sample. *Child Care, Health and Development.* 28: 2, 149–55.

Van Bakel, H. and Riksen-Walraven, M. (2002) Parenting and Development of One-Year-Olds: Links with Parental, Contextual and Child Characteristics. *Child Development.* 73: 1, 256–73.

Chapter Ten

Disabled Children and the Assessment Framework

Margaret Kennedy and Jane Wonnacott

Introduction

The Assessment Framework for Children in Need and their Families (DoH, 2000) could make a significant positive impact on practice with disabled children and their families. For the first time a government document has been published with detailed advice and guidance relating to disabled children. The detailed chapter in the practice guidance (DoH, 2000) on assessing the needs of disabled children and their families is essential reading for all those conducting such assessments. This chapter does not aim to reproduce this but, rather, to put the whole assessment process in context, and to highlight some of the questions that will need to be asked if this framework is to improve practice with disabled children. How effective this model is will rely significantly on the political and individual mindsets of participants in the process, as well as individual practice skills. This chapter draws on information obtained from a survey of disability teams, in depth discussion with a group of team managers and experience of running many training courses with disability workers. It aims to explore the complex issues impacting on the assessment process for disabled children and to consider how the Framework may be developed and used effectively, bearing also in mind that there may be constraints within the Framework which may provide a number of challenges.

The policy context

One of the key principles underpinning the framework is that we should be grounded within an ecological approach. Such an approach requires assessments to understand the needs of the child 'within the context of the child's family (parents or caregivers and the wider family) and of the community and culture in which he or she is growing up' (DoH, 2000). Context is therefore of great importance, and it is equally important for those conducting assessments to be aware of the context within which the assessment process is taking place. Failure to do this will result in assessment

practice which is at best narrow in its approach and at worst dangerous. The context surrounding the assessment process for disabled children can be very complex and in this chapter we aim to identify the range of factors that might be influencing the systems surrounding the process. Each tier will have a different power dynamic and hence influence on the other systems. These are represented in Figure 1.

The ecological model has been used extensively by Cross and Westcott (1999), Kennedy (1989), Sobsey (1994) and Wonnacott and Kennedy (2001) to further understanding about the inequalities experienced by disabled children and how these can contribute to an increased incidence of abuse. Research into abuse incidence (Crosse et al., 1993; Sullivan et al., 1997) indicates that the overall incidence of abuse for disabled children ranges from 1.6 to 3.9 more than that for non-disabled children (see Table 1 overleaf).

These figures are very significant and it is important that the ecological approach promoted within the Assessment Framework helps us to address not only structural issues such as poverty but also the values and attitudes which allow disabled children to be so vulnerable. These values and attitudes are played out within all settings but will not be adequately addressed at team and individual levels unless the policy context is supporting assessment practice within a social model perspective. The guidance to the framework by Marchant and Jones (2000) was rooted in the social model; however, this is not reflected consistently throughout the documentation, which allows confusion to arise. For assessments to be effective they need to be supported consistently within a social model framework at all levels.

The social model is a way of understanding the position of disabled people and children in the world in which they live. This model was conceived by disabled people (Morris, 1999; Oliver, 1999) as a way of challenging the accepted premise that disabled people were 'defective' and therefore needed to change.

Figure 1: Power dynamic influences.

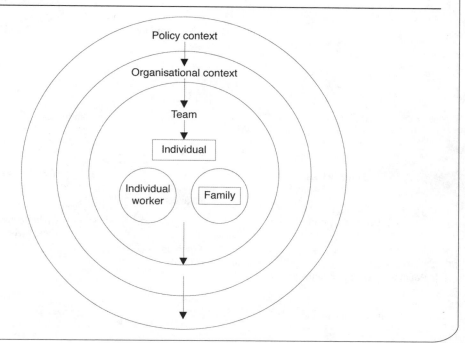

Historically, disabled people have been portrayed negatively (Shakespeare, 2000) within literature and the media, leading to a view that to be disabled was a 'bad' thing which needed to be either eradicated or remedied. Thus the medical model (sometimes now referred to as the 'individual' model) became the established approach towards disabled people. The individual model thus aims to change disabled people via medical intervention rather than changing the disabling barriers within society. Thus the ecological model, correctly implemented, would address these disabling barriers, including attitudes and values which portray disabled children as a 'burden' on their families and communities. The ecological model does not prevent us addressing the needs of the child in relation to their impairment, but it does

emphasis balance and will move us away from the 'defective' mindset.

Since values and attitudes are an integral part of looking at the situation of disabled children it is crucially important to acknowledge how this is reflected in our use of language. The meaning of 'disabled children' is quite different to the phrase 'children with disabilities'. The former is describing the social model, where there are disabling barriers and the child is 'dis-abled' by society, whereas the latter uses the word 'disability' to describe the child's impairment. Disabled people have consistently argued for the social model use of language. This is correctly used in the guidance to the assessment framework but not elsewhere. The 'individual' (medical) model use of language is used throughout the 'Children in Need' definitions

Table 1: Likelihood of abuse of disabled children.

Type of maltreatment	Crosse et al. (1993)	Sullivan and Knutson (1997)
Neglect	1.6 times as likely	3.8 times as likely
Sexual abuse	1.8 times as likely	3.1 times as likely
Physical abuse	2.1 times as likely	3.8 times as likely
Emotional maltreatment	2.8 times as likely	3.9 times as likely

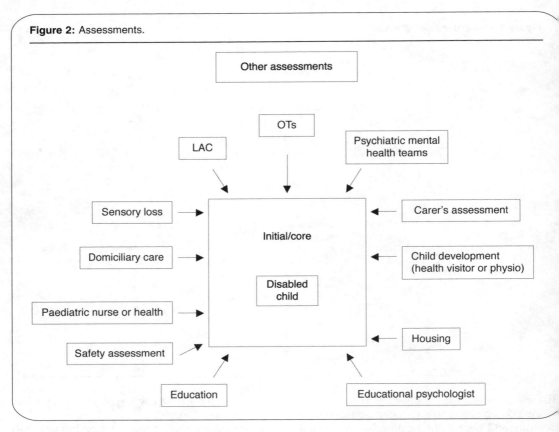

Figure 2: Assessments.

(DoH, 1999), thus ignoring the political dimension of prejudice and discrimination which should be acknowledged and addressed when undertaking any assessment. This might not have happened had the social model been fully understood by these writers.

A key plank of the policy context in relation to the Framework is the imposition of timescales for assessment. A survey of 72 children's disability teams (Kennedy and Wonnacott, 2001) found that there was general concern about how these timescales could be met for disabled children, particularly those with complex needs. For example, one respondent said 'We need to gather and collate more information than the timescales for an initial assessment would suggest'. Another respondent commented, 'Timescales are restrictive – it takes time to communicate with some children'. In depth discussions over three days with team managers of eight disability teams revealed similar concerns, particularly in relation to the quality of work that could be undertaken within the required time frames. Often disabled children and their families are involved in numerous

assessments (see Figure 2) and these may be happening within timescales at variance with the Assessment Framework. If the Framework i to be effective it must take account of these othe assessments and may not be able to do this within the timescale required since they may still be ongoing.

In addition to this, those working with disabled children are working within a comple legislative frame work with requirements for a range of assessments (Figure 3). For example, the recent Carers and Disabled Persons Act 200 makes provision for a person with parental responsibility for a disabled child to request a assessment of his or her ability to care for that child, where the Local Authority is satisfied tha it could provide services under section 17 of th Children Act 1989. There is inherent a possible conflict of interest between the focus of the assessment frame work on the child's needs an the focus of carers' legislation on the carers' needs. How this is worked out in practice will depend on the skill of the social worker in achieving the right balance between the two processes.

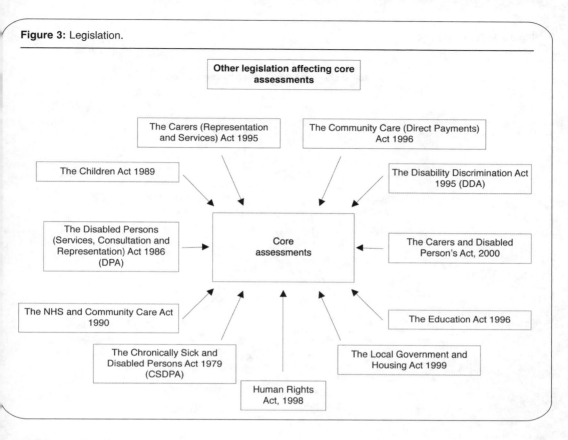

Figure 3: Legislation.

Other legislation affecting core assessments

The Carers (Representation and Services) Act 1995

The Community Care (Direct Payments) Act 1996

The Children Act 1989

The Disability Discrimination Act 1995 (DDA)

The Disabled Persons (Services, Consultation and Representation) Act 1986 (DPA)

Core assessments

The Carers and Disabled Person's Act, 2000

The NHS and Community Care Act 1990

The Education Act 1996

The Chronically Sick and Disabled Persons Act 1979 (CSDPA)

The Local Government and Housing Act 1999

Human Rights Act, 1998

The organisation context

Messages from Research (1995) identified a valuable model to describe the way in which thresholds influence whether or not a child enters the child protection system. Although these related to child protection they have equal relevance to other situations where decisions are being made about interventions in a child's life. Where any thresholds are in operation the question must be asked whether these operate differently for different service users and exclude specific groups. Operating differently has been an historical feature of work with disabled children and has usually resulted in their increased risk being overlooked, based on the myth that they would not be harmed. The focus of work with disabled children and their families has been on 'need' whereas work with non-disabled children has focused on 'risk'. The assessment framework, as a response to research which is based on work with non-disabled children, aims to shift the emphasis to need and, in doing so, may risk ignoring the unmet needs of disabled children to be kept safe (see Figure 4).

An additional factor that may lead to risk being ignored for disabled children within the assessment framework is that the framework 'inclines towards the view of abusing parents as being helpless and poor – doing their best in difficult circumstances' (Dale, Green and Fellows, 2001). Not all referrals of disabled children fall into this category and this, combined with the tendency to feel sorry for parents of a disabled child, may push the threshold yet higher. The position that should be reached is one where both need and need for protection is adequately addressed for child populations.

Using the Messages from Research model, it is not hard to see why the threshold may be higher for disabled children (see Figure 5).

The legal and moral concerns have been discussed above in terms of the social model and complex legal framework. In addition, the Children Act 1989 has led to the notion that disabled children are 'children first', which has tended to lead workers to ignore the implications of impairment or disabling barriers.

Figure 4: Protecting children.

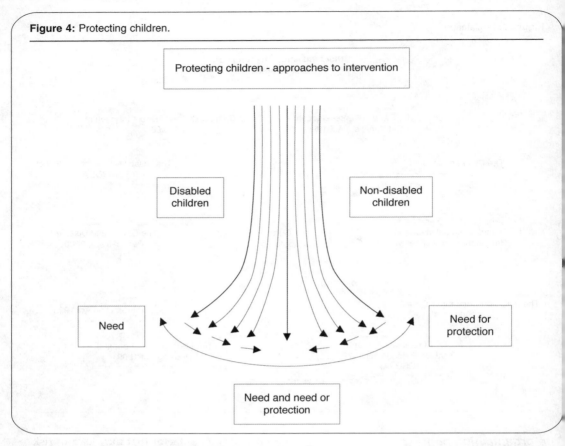

The pragmatic concerns are perhaps the greatest influence on the organisational context. From our discussions with disability team managers it is clear that the definition of 'disabled child' varies from agency to agency as does the criteria for inclusion on the disability register. The operation of the register is not consistent, with some Local Authorities refusing to operate any register at all, whereas others use registration as a pre-requisite for assessment. Being included on the register may therefore not mean an assessment is automatically done.

The second Analysis of the Quality Protects Management Action Plans (Council for Disabled Children, Oct. 2000) expressed concerns that although many authorities are continuing to work around definitions of 'disabilities' and their eligibility criteria for services, little consensus has emerged. One authority noted the concerns of parents of children with moderate levels of impairment who were no longer eligible for services. The timescales required by the assessment framework may increase pressure on providers to narrow which

disabled child 'fits' the eligibility criteria in order to meet their targets and to cope with large numbers of disabled children, without the staff in the teams to serve them.

The Assessment Framework is not explicit regarding criteria for undertaking a core assessment. Local Authorities are clear that they cannot undertake core assessments on all open cases and in many cases it would be inappropriately intrusive to do so. To assist front line workers many Local Authorities have established criteria for doing a core assessment. Out of 72 Disabled Children's teams we surveyed, the majority either *had* developed criteria or were in the process of doing so. Where criteria had been developed, they could be grouped as follows:

1. All cases who met the criteria for allocation within the disabled children's team (one person commented that this was the view of her principal officer, but it was impossible to put into practice so unofficial criteria were operating).

Figure 5: Thresholds.

Thresholds (Messages from Research) influenced by:	Issues for disabled children:
• Legal/moral concerns	• Not valued/excluded • Legal action difficult • Myths
• Pragmatic concerns	• Who is included under 'disabled child'? • Difficulties in defining abuse • Time consuming nature of interventions • Communication issues (e.g. Blissymbolics/sign language) • Resources e.g. accommodation • Negative attitudes
• Outcomes for children	• Little research on outcomes for disabled children
• Parent/child concerns	• Lack of balance between parent/child concerns • Wishes and feelings of disabled children not abtained

2. Where the child required a service.
3. Where the child was receiving an accommodation service.
4. Children with complex needs/larger packages of care.
5. Child protection concerns.

The variation in criteria between Local Authorities is unlikely to facilitate equitable service delivery for disabled children.

A further organisational issue is who exactly will be responsible for assessments where there is a disabled child. Problems may begin at the referral stage. There are several ways in which referrals for disabled children may be dealt with; these include:

a. All referrals going to a general assessment team, who will immediately pass disabled children to disability teams.
b. All referrals going to general assessments teams who will conduct initial assessments and refer disabled children requiring core assessment to disability teams.
c. All referrals for disabled children going to disability teams.

There are dangers with a and b above. In relation to immediate transfer, this may exacerbate inconsistencies in threshold criteria since social workers inexperienced in working with disabled children may not take account of the specific complexities of the child's condition in applying the criteria. Lack of understanding of complexities will also impact on initial assessment, for example, where there are the additional communication issues for those children who do not use voice but use augmentative communication systems or sign language. If they recognise they do not have adequate skills they may refer quickly to disability teams but if they mis-assess they may not offer a service at all.

There are further complications where child protection (safeguarding) issues are also identified. We have identified several models (see Figure 6).

The first model, where safeguarding activities are located in general assessments teams whilst disabled children's teams focus on promoting welfare, is unlikely to achieve integrated assessment and planning. This model goes against the spirit of the framework, which is clear that the ongoing assessment is not a separate or different activity to child protection enquiries and processes. Splits can lead to information being lost or misinterpreted, and concerns about abuse originating in disability teams may not be seen as a priority by assessment teams (children and family teams). Where such a structure exists, disability workers regularly report to us that when they refer disabled children regarding safeguarding issues they have received a lower priority rating.

The second model involves a degree of co-working between the two teams when concerns are identified about the safety of the disabled child. In such a model, social workers from children and families teams are viewed as the child protection (safeguarding) experts, with specialist input in relation to the disabled child coming from the disability worker. If such a

Figure 6: Practice models.

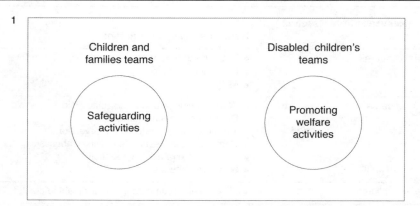

1

Children and families teams

Disabled children's teams

Safeguarding activities

Promoting welfare activities

Unlikely to achieve integrated assessment and planning

2

Children and families teams

Disabled children's teams

Safe-guarding activities

Promoting welfare activities

Integrated assessment and planning *possible*

3

Disabled children's teams

Promoting welfare

Safeguarding activities

Integrated assessment and planning *probable*

model is to be effective, the power dynamics between the two teams must be considered, as specialist disability workers report that they are regarded as 'inferior', which interferes with the assessment of the child since the disability workers' views are sometimes not valued.

The third model, which involves disabled children's teams being responsible for both safeguarding and welfare activities, may be more effective in delivering a service which is fully integrated and meets all the child's needs. There is an argument that the disability worker is not sufficiently trained or skilled to work in this way, yet it is rarely questioned whether the children and families worker has the required expertise to assess the needs of disabled children. This is a discriminatory anomaly.

The organisational context is a significant influence on the effectiveness of inter-agency collaboration which is a key component of the new framework. There are two historical features that have underpinned the work with disabled children. On ACPCs they have been represented by 'health', which has narrowed the focus of their needs to that of their impairment alone.

Additionally, different organisational systems are developing within the social care field which will directly impact on the assessment process and particularly as it affects disabled children. Already some social services departments have merged education and social services functions, which may facilitate effective integrated assessments but may not necessarily be positive for disabled children who need assessments that take account of their impairments. The alternative arrangements that 'health' be the lead agency where disabled children are concerned will also not be satisfactory as this may be a retrograde step into a heavy emphasis on the medical (individual) model as described above, just at the time when the social model is becoming more understood and accepted. As these developments begin there will be a need for very careful watching as to how new structures may affect the service to disabled children.

Team context

The concept of the team in relation to assessment practice needs careful definition. Traditionally, teams have been thought of as a group of people who work for the same agency, line managed by the same person, working together to achieve objectives set by the organisation. Often these teams have been made up of people from the same professional discipline, although there have always been some notable exceptions particularly in the mental health field. In the recent past the notion of the multi-disciplinary team as the preferred means of service delivery has gained ground and we have, for example, seen the

establishment of Youth Offending Teams, which bring together police and probation officers, social workers, education and health staff. This model is also developing within many teams working with disabled children, in an acknowledgement of the importance of effective multi-disciplinary working with children whose needs are likely to be met from a variety of sources. The imperative for assessments of children in need to be the responsibility of social services, but multi-agency in their approach, can fit well with this model.

As well as the *actual* team, assessments will be carried out by the *virtual* team (Chicenski, 2001). That is, a team of people who are not managed by the same person, or are not from the same agency but are engaged together in one particular task – the assessment of a child's needs. The make up of this team will vary from assessment to assessment. The potential for conflicts within this team having an adverse effect on the assessment should always be taken into account. The impact of the dynamics of professional systems on child care practice has been well documented in relation to child abuse (Reder, Duncan and Gray, 1993; Reder and Duncan 1999) and, since the professional system surrounding a disabled child is invariably even more complex, due attention must be paid to the inter-relationship between the dynamics of the system and the assessment process.

The virtual team

Questions that must be asked in relation to the virtual team are:

- Who is in the team?
- Are their roles clear?
- What is their value base?
- Is the professional hierarchy affecting the assessment?

Who is in the team?

Before embarking on any assessment it is important to consider who is best placed to give the information that is required and assist with the task of analysis. Services may well need to be provided during and after the assessment process and these may be delivered by a wide range of statutory and voluntary agencies. It is likely that assessments involving disabled children will include a large number of people who are potentially part of the team and the task of facilitating effective working together will require time and skill.

One issue that also needs attention is whether or not the parents of the child have become part of this virtual team. Whist it is important to work with children and their parents during any assessment, there is a danger that where disabled children are concerned, boundaries will become fudged and the parents will lose their separate identity. This process of 'professionalising parents' presents dangers for the child and puts an unfair burden onto parents. For professionals who do not have the necessary skills to communicate directly with the child, it is tempting, and more comfortable, to work closely with the parents and assume that this will give all the necessary information about the child's needs. When this happens, the child may become lost in the system and plans built around the needs of the parent rather than those of the child. Parents' and child's needs are, of course, often inextricably bound together, and meeting the needs of the parent will go a long way towards meeting the needs of the child. Indeed, most parents will want services that are specifically focused on the child's needs. However, this is not always the case and it is important that the professional team is able to stand back and keep a firm eye on the child. The child focused approach of the assessment framework should go a long way towards ensuring that this happens. Beware teams who give parents the label 'carer'. Children need parenting, not just caring – a fact that often appears to get lost when we work with disabled children.

Are team roles clear?

One complaint made by families who have had contact with social services is that they are asked the same questions by many different people. This is even more likely where disabled children are concerned due to their contact with large numbers of professionals. Role confusion amongst professionals can put unnecessary strain on families, and can also leave children vulnerable and unprotected (Reder, Duncan and Gray, 1993). The more people that are involved, the more likely it is that someone will think that someone else is taking responsibility for certain tasks. These tasks may be the very ones that focus on the safety needs of the child. For example, others in the professional team may believe that because social services are involved any issues that relate to the protection of the child will be dealt with, and that any niggling concerns that they have about the care of the

child must be wrong. The worker from a social services disability team may well be inexperienced in child protection work (although this should not be assumed) and be relying on others to raise any concerns. The assessment framework presents a real opportunity for effective planning at the beginning of the assessment: planning based on a common language which clarifies roles and expectations, and is understood and agreed by the child and their parents.

What is the team's value base?

We have already highlighted the importance of values and the social model of disability in work with disabled children and their families. Workers are likely to be approaching the assessment task from different perspectives in relation to this, hence risking the emergence of another dangerous dynamic highlighted in child death enquiries, that of polarisation:

> In this pattern of interaction a schism developed between two groups of workers and over time, two subsystems of the network emerged whose points of view progressively diverged ... although communication within the groups was often satisfactory, information or ideas were rarely exchanged between them and the families usually received contradictory messages from different sources.
>
> (Reder, Duncan and Gray, 1993, p72)

The stage is set for polarisation to occur where those working together have not made explicit the value base which underpins their work (see Figure 7 overleaf). The honest exploration of differences can help to ensure that all are aware of the influences on the assessment process and take steps to ensure that these do not affect the ability of the whole to focus on the needs of the child. Assumptions should never be made that all are either aware of, or practising within, the social model. It is also dangerous to operate from the stereotypical notion that social workers will be operating from a social model and doctors from a medical model. Our experience of running many multi-agency training courses is that there are doctors who work clearly within a social model framework and many social workers who do not.

Is the professional hierarchy affecting the assessment process?

The virtual team will comprise workers from a range of professionals, all of whom have a

Figure 7: Value base of assessments.

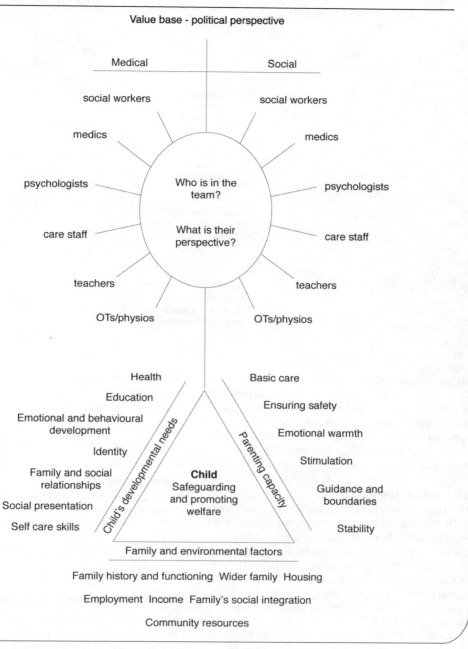

Value base - political perspective

Medical | Social

social workers — social workers

medics — medics

psychologists — **Who is in the team?** — psychologists

care staff — **What is their perspective?** — care staff

teachers — teachers

OTs/physios — OTs/physios

Health | Basic care
Education | Ensuring safety
Emotional and behavioural development | Emotional warmth
Identity | Stimulation
Family and social relationships | *Child's developmental needs* | **Child Safeguarding and promoting welfare** | *Parenting capacity* | Guidance and boundaries
Social presentation | Stability
Self care skills

Family and environmental factors

Family history and functioning Wider family Housing

Employment Income Family's social integration

Community resources

perceived place in the professional hierarchy. There is a danger in such situations that those who are perceived to be most powerful will be those who are most influential in the assessment process. These are not necessarily the people who know the child best. This phenomenon, referred to as *exaggeration of hierarchy*, has been noted in the child abuse literature (Reder, Duncan and Gray, 1993) and can been seen to be clearly operating in the disability field (see Figure 8).

Residential workers on our training courses have often noted that they are marginalised within an assessment, yet they have vitally

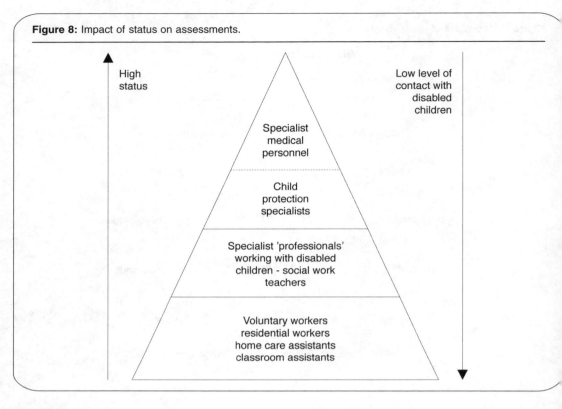

Figure 8: Impact of status on assessments.

High status

Low level of contact with disabled children

Specialist medical personnel

Child protection specialists

Specialist 'professionals' working with disabled children - social work teachers

Voluntary workers residential workers home care assistants classroom assistants

important information to contribute. Throughout any assessment, it is important to check that those who know the child best are being heard; often it is the volunteer or residential worker who may have a lowly status in the eyes of others but will have most to contribute.

The actual team

The team of workers within the social services with responsibility for carrying out assessments of need is likely to be located within the children and families section of the department, and may or may not be a mixture of social workers and other professionals such as occupational therapists and psychologists. Our survey of 72 disability reams identified the following in Table 2:

We have already commented on the range of possible structures that might be in place in order to deliver the service, particularly in relation to child protection. As well as organisational structures there are several important factors within the team context which will influence the effectiveness of assessment work with disabled children. These include the dynamics of the interface with the rest of the

Table 2: Team composition.

Team composition

Social workers only	8/72
Included occupational therapists	26/72
Included psychologists	3/72
Included assistant social workers	32/72
Included various others including volunteers, project workers etc.	35/72

department, workload and staff skills training and supervision.

The dynamics of the interface

What is crucial is how this team is viewed by others in the department and how the workers within it feel about themselves. 'We feel like second class citizens' is all too often the cry from social workers working within disability teams. It is interesting to note that in the training video in the Child's World training pack (University of Sheffield, NSPCC and DoH, 2000) a non-specialist worker was allocated to an assessment of a disabled child, based on the assumption that the disability team would not have the skills to undertake an assessment which involved child protection issues. This assumption is not borne out by our survey, in which approximately 50 per cent of disability teams were doing their own child protection work.

We have frequently heard workers in disability teams say that they feel that they are 'bottom of the heap' in the same way that their clients are. There are instances where social workers within disability teams are paid less than their counterparts in other teams, even where they are expected to undertake child protection enquiries. What does this say about the value that is placed on disabled children? There seems to be the view in some departments that work with disabled children is the 'easy option' whereas the reality is that it is extremely complex and demanding work.

Managing the interface is particularly important when work with one family spans team boundaries. As the delivery of the social work service becomes increasingly more specialised, it is possible that more than one worker will be visiting the family. For example, the worker from the disability team may be visiting in relation to the disabled child whilst another social worker may be working with another child in the family who has behavioural problems, and a family centre may be providing parenting support. Whilst specialisation should ensure a high quality service, the dangers inherent in a specialised system must not be overlooked. Too often we have heard of situations where the disability workers, because of their perceived lower status, do not feel that their views are given value. This has involved the disability worker identifying serious child care concerns which are not taken seriously by other teams in the system. Consequently the needs of the disabled child may be overlooked. Where such split working occurs, and there are concerns about the standard of care being given to a disabled child, it is absolutely vital that the disability worker's voice is heard and given due weight.

Team rivalries, particularly over resources, can prevent an approach which works on the basis of respect for everyone's contribution to the process and aims to understand the needs of the family as a whole. The challenge is to ensure that our systems provide the specialist knowledge and skills required for a high quality service, whilst at the same time promoting an approach within which teams can work together in an atmosphere of trust.

Senior managers need to ensure that strategies are in place to develop such an approach, but unfortunately the split between disability teams and the rest of children's services may go right to the top. Joint meetings and training events where perceptions of each other can be shared at all levels within departments are important if children are not to be lost in the chasm that can so easily develop between teams.

Workload

From our survey of disability teams it is clear that workers carry heavy caseloads, often in excess of workers in other teams. The average number of open cases within disability teams was 227, with an average caseload of 38.5 per social worker. Due to the nature of the work there is likely to be less throughput, with cases remaining open longer. Some of these cases may require minimal intervention but many are extremely complex and time consuming. The very nature of the work requires collaboration with a large number of people. From our discussions with team managers it is clear that often the only way to manage is to cut corners. For example, in one Local Authority, children receiving respite care are not reviewed under the LAC system, and many others are developing strict eligibility criteria to ration the number of assessments. This will result in only those disabled children with complex needs receiving a service.

If this is the case, how is the Assessment Framework to be managed? Various models seem to be emerging. One model is that in all cases where a referral involves a disabled child, an initial assessment is undertaken by the disability team. In some cases, this is linked with an assessment for inclusion on the disability register. Following an initial assessment, a care package will be agreed if appropriate, and core assessments will then only be completed on a relatively small number of children who meet strict criteria. Another model involves all children who are receiving any service that has cost implications receiving a core assessment. In these situations the initial assessment may be skipped altogether. Another variation is for a generic assessment team to undertake an initial assessment and pass to the disability team only those children who meet specific criteria. All these ways of managing

Table 3: Implications of various assessment regimes.

Assessments	Advantages	Disadvantages
Initial assessments by disability team on large numbers/core assessments on a few.	Disabled children are likely to be seen by someone who understands their impairment and how their needs might be met. Concerns about care of the child may be more likely to be picked up by a specialist worker	Not doing core assessments may mean that more subtle information, discovered over time, may be missed. This could prove dangerous if this information relates to safeguarding welfare.
Initial assessments skipped. Core assessments for all children requiring a service with cost implications.		Could be unnecessarily intrusive Workload could become unmanageable. Focus becomes 'cost' not the child.
Initial assessments by non-specialist teams. Children meeting specific criteria passed to disability team.		Many children's needs will not be addressed. A lack of disability awareness could lead to misattribution of information.

workload have implications that need careful consideration (see Table 3).

What is clear is that equity of service for disabled children will not easily be achieved simply by the introduction of the Framework. Where the task appears impossible departments and teams will respond by finding their own solutions which may or may not meet the needs of disabled children in their area.

Staff skills training and supervision

It goes without saying that those undertaking assessments should be skilled in the task. The Framework requires a positive shift towards putting the child centre stage and, for many of those working with disabled children, that means that they cannot rely on parent focused work. They need to be able to communicate with the child, and this may involve developing new skills. Their understanding of child development may also need to be extended, and training opportunities will need to be in place. It is not uncommon for staff to complain that very few courses are put on for disability teams by central training units, and it is often down to the teams themselves to fight for the resources required.

Good assessments will be underpinned by training, which includes consideration of the research knowledge. This will be harder for those working with disabled children than workers with other child populations, as research information on outcomes for disabled children is limited. Such research that has been

carried out in the UK has been funded by the charitable sector (Cooke, 1999). The Department of Health funded overviews of research which accompany the framework (Cleaver, Unell and Aldgate, 2000; Jones and Ramchandani, 1999 and Ryan, 2000) do not include information on disabled children.

A challenge for supervisors within disability teams may be the multi-professional nature of the team. 28 of the 72 teams included workers from professional backgrounds other than social work, and most had at least one worker without a social work background. The challenge for supervisors is to ensure that the professional development needs of all the team are met and that all staff receive additional professional consultation as required.

The individual context

The 'children first' principle has largely been responsible for delaying a more comprehensive analysis of the needs of disabled children. There have been three very damaging repercussions:

1. From this principle came the accepted (to non-disabled people/professionals) medical model (individual model) term, 'children with disabilities'.

Children	with	Disabilities
1st	(split)	2nd

Here, there was an attempt to relegate to secondary consideration; 'Disability' (meaning impairment). This phrase ignored the Social Model construction where the word 'disabled' is used to describe the disabling barriers in society that dis-able the child or adult. The medical (individual) model continues to use the word 'disability' to describe the child's impairment, despite the considerable attempts by disabled people to have the social model embraced by all professionals. The 'children first' principle has therefore promoted the medical (individual model). The 'children first' principle has therefore been a dis-abling barrier to full acceptance of disabled children and all that it implies **politically.**

2. The 'children first' principle has also been responsible for a very unhelpful 'split' (see above) separating a child from their impairment. Thus the identity formation so crucial to self-esteem and confidence becomes compromised and confused. 'Disability' (meaning impairment in this model) becomes a 'bad' word that must be a secondary consideration. It implies the important part is 'child' with the unpleasant (unmentionable) part being 'disabled'. It is difficult to know how disabled children can feel positive about themselves when this split is encouraged or emphasised. Ignoring the impairment is damaging to identity formation and it is not something we do for children from ethnic minority groups who must cope with racism. It is important for disabled children to come to know they are living in a disabling environment that is discriminatory towards them. They must know the concept of 'oppression' and must identify their many difficulties as probably more likely from this oppression and discrimination, invariably not coming from their impairment (which the medical model promotes).

3. The 'children first' principle may have been responsible for the lack of efficient, sufficient and effective services to children who had additional requirements brought by impairment, and not 'allied' to the 'children' part of the principle. It may lead to us not looking closely enough at these additional requirements, such as computer-aided communication systems, as they are often complex and costly. It then becomes politically expedient that disabled children and their parents come to feel that the 'problems' are attached to the child's impairment, rather than the disabling barriers (service provision). It is paradoxical that 'looked after' children may have a budget for computers, so that they can compete with their peers, while providing computer-aided communication systems for disabled children becomes a battleground for parents of disabled children. Such an anomaly must be considered discriminatory. We know one local authority where a four-year-old non-voiced child was assessed for a computer-aided communication system; by the age of nine, she still had not got one. In five years she has had no means to alert anyone to danger, pain or distress.

When the 'children first' principle was instituted to help practitioners to focus on the disabled child's needs as a child, this was important, as practitioners could not focus on the child, only on the child's **impairment.** Now the pendulum has swung too far and practitioners are not focusing enough on the child's **identity** as a **disabled** child, and all that it means to live in a discriminatory world.

We must adopt the social model which looks more at the child's identity formation as a disabled child, at the discrimination and oppression they face, and the poor service provision that has come out of that discrimination. The reality is that disabled children are unique and essentially different children with specific needs. Meeting these needs requires practice with individual children and their families to be sensitive, flexible and creative.

Implementing the Framework in practice

The Framework outlines the principles that should underpin our practice. How can we ensure that these guiding principles are played out in the assessment process?

Child centred

Historically assessments with disabled children have primarily focused on the parents' support needs. This may encourage workers to have a 'feel sorry for attitude' towards parents because of the apparent burden of their disabled child. This is child centred practice which focuses negatively on the child rather than looking at positive features. One of the outcomes of this model has been the tendency to view parents as 'heroic carers' and the child as a passive recipient of their care. This dis-empowers the

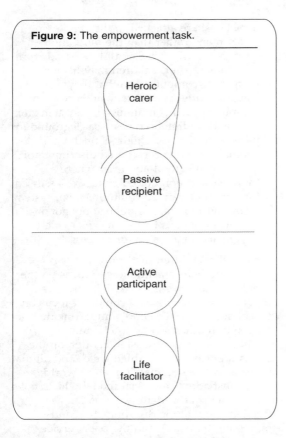

Figure 9: The empowerment task.

Heroic carer

Passive recipient

Active participant

Life facilitator

child and stifles growth and development. The parent role is compromised as they are seen as carers rather than parents. An alternative model may be more helpful (Figure 9). In this model the parent is seen as a facilitator of the child's life encouraging the child to be an active participant in their own life and in the world. The Assessment Framework is ideally suited to promoting such an approach.

Rooted in child development

Disabled children have often been perceived as having a different developmental route. This allows workers to overlook critical emotional and psychological developmental tasks, such as developing a sexual identity. Whilst disabled children may reach developmental milestones differently, their needs are exactly the same.

Those undertaking assessments with disabled children must ask themselves the following questions:

- Am I familiar with what should be expected for any child this age in terms of physical, emotional and behavioural development?

- Do I understand how the impairment impacts on this child's development?
- Am I wrongly attributing developmental delay to impairment?

Participants on training courses have noted that, for example, lack of self-care skills may have little to do with the child's impairment and more to do with the under expectations of them by others.

Ecological in their approach and ensuring equality of opportunity

The paradigm illustrated in Figure 10 may help practitioners to view disabled children more holistically, more ecologically as emphasised by the new assessment framework.

This triangle simply shows that disabled children are, of course, children; however, they have additional requirements brought by impairment (the condition or illness of the child), as well as those aspects in life stemming from discrimination and oppression that lead to disabling barriers. It is incumbent on the assessor to analyse all three sides of the below triangle when using the new assessment framework.

Involves working with children and families

Disabled children and their families are very familiar with professional contact. Since they were born disabled, children have been subject to myriad assessments and interventions. Parents have had longstanding involvement with dealing with the impact of the numbers of professionals involved, and have often

Figure 10: Adapting the assessment framework for disabled children.

Impairment

Disabling barriers

The disabled child

Children

developed coping mechanisms. It is easy to assume that the assessment now required will therefore not have an appreciable impact on the disabled child and their family. In fact, the converse may be the case: they may feel this to be one too many intrusions. The language of the assessment such as 'parenting capacity' might well seem offensive to parents of disabled children, who have approached social services for provision of basic needs. This can be exacerbated when they discover in some cases that the assessor has no experience in disability. A comment in our survey from one team manager: 'In other instances an otherwise well functioning family has to make contact with social services in order for their child to access services which would automatically be available to any other child in the community. In these instances I feel a core assessment is intrusive and inequitable for the disabled child'. The child, too, may feel that this assessment is just another one to see what they cannot do, and both child and parent may resent having to go over the same ground as with other workers.

The assessor should be aware of this history and how it might impact on this new relationship. Great sensitivity and honesty is required.

Working with disabled children requires an ability to communicate with them in their preferred method. The assessor will need to be aware of very specific communication methods such as Blissymbolics, Rebus, Makaton and British Sign Language, and how using these systems will make a marked difference. Where children are not using any recognised system, people well known to the child may help the assessor interpret facial expressions, behavioural patterns and demeanour. Recent publications and videos will be of great assistance in this task, and should be required reading for all workers undertaking assessments with disabled children. (Joseph Rowntree Foundation, Triangle and NSPCC, 2001; Marchant and Martyn, 1999; Marchant et al., 1999; Morris, 1998; NSPCC, 1997; Triangle, 1999). These skills will be needed throughout the process, not just at the information gathering stage. Careful thought will need to be given as to how to feed back the results of the assessment to children in an accessible format; simply giving them a copy of the assessment documentation may not be appropriate.

Involving disabled children in the process will therefore require careful planning in a number of areas, for example, thinking carefully about the time of day that is chosen to see the child. Disabled children may be very tired at certain times of day or be affected by medication. Being aware of the possible implications of the child's condition, such as epilepsy and the effects of stress on their impairment or illness.

Build on strengths as well as identify difficulties

There is a particular mindset in relationship to disabled children that focuses on the perceived 'deficits' and what they cannot do. Successful implementation of the framework will involve a shift in this mindset. Workers need to be careful, and conscious that the design of the Department of Health forms may mean a picture emerges of a child who cannot do very much, as many questions have largely been based on attainment and achievement where the child has both physical and intellectual capacity. Anecdotal evidence from workers is that using these forms with disabled children can lead them to feel failures.

In our survey one worker asked, 'What is the impact on parents and children who will have to give lots of negative answers?'

When using the Framework in training with disability workers we have found that there is a tendency to over-focus on the health and education aspects and to emphasise in these categories what the child cannot do. Just because the child is disabled, it does not mean that the health category should be the main focus of attention; nor does it mean that disability is a health issue. It is very important to ensure that all dimensions are given equal weight and that the strengths that are evident within the disabled child and family are recognised and used to inform planning.

Inter-agency in their approach to assessment and the provision of services

It is important that parents and disabled children feel that they have some control of the process. Professionals become very used to working in the virtual team and sharing information, without always liaising with the child and family. This is a danger for all children, but may be particularly so for disabled children where there are strong inter-agency links. The Assessment Framework presents an opportunity for parents and children to have a clearer picture of roles and responsibilities

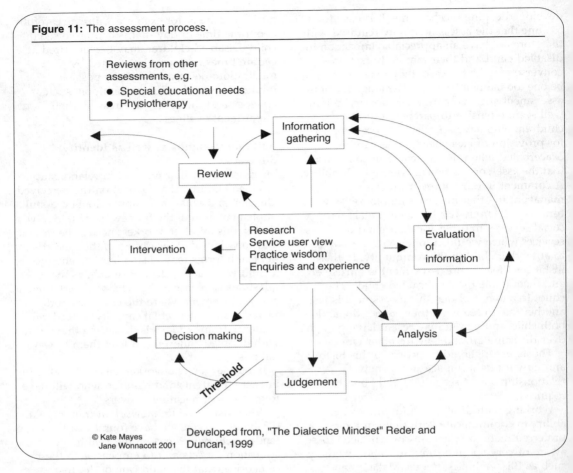

Figure 11: The assessment process.

Reviews from other assessments, e.g.
- Special educational needs
- Physiotherapy

Information gathering

Review

Research
Service user view
Practice wisdom
Enquiries and experience

Evaluation of information

Intervention

Analysis

Decision making

Threshold

Judgement

© Kate Mayes
Jane Wonnacott 2001

Developed from, "The Dialectice Mindset" Reder and Duncan, 1999

within the multi–disciplinary team. The need for planning is stressed by the Framework and this should be an opportunity to help parents and children fit together the jigsaw of the professional system in order to see the whole picture.

A continuing process not a single event and carried out in parallel with other action and providing services

Disabled children are more likely to have professionals involved over a longer period of time and to be subject to numerous assessments and reviews. It is important that the Framework feeds into the reviewing process and that the assessments are constantly updated. Using a circular model (Figure 11) to understand the assessment process, we can see how the review stage is important in updating the assessment and that it is an opportunity to include information from other reviews that are taking place as a result of other assessments.

The lives of disabled children may be subject to a number of fluctuating circumstances. As well as being affected by common life events such as divorce, moving house or school, they may have degenerative conditions or require repeat hospitalisations. Some disabled children may also have disabled parents who also have fluctuating needs. Assessment processes need to be flexible enough to cope with these situations, and assessments must be regularly updated.

Grounded in evidenced-based knowledge

Although there is not an extensive UK research base in relation to disabled children and the protection from harm (with the exception of Cooke, 1999; Kennedy, 1989; Westcott, 1993) we can draw on some important international authors (Crosse et al., 1993; Sobsey, 1994). With regards to welfare issues we have more relevant studies (Morris, 1998, 1999; Oswin, 1991; Prewitt, 1999; Beresford, 1994). Other important literature has also contributed to our knowledge

Table 4: Outcomes for disabled children.

Practice principles	Outcomes for disabled children
Child centred.	• Child feels valued, respected and part of the process. • Child's parents are used to inform decision making, planning and intervention. • Child has a positive self-identity as a disabled person.
Rooted in child development.	• Services are relevant to the different developmental milestones relevant to the child's impairment, and under- and over-expectation is guarded against.
Ecological in their approach and ensure equality of opportunity.	• Disability barriers are recognised, noted and addressed throughout the process. • Parents and child (as appropriate) have an understanding of the political process of discrimination and oppression. • The child has positive self-identity as a disabled person ('It's OK to be disabled'.)
Involve working with children and families.	• Records are stored with disabled child and family in appropriate, accessible formats. These are used as part of the child's life story. • Child and family will feel the process as empowering and has resulted in gains to the quality of their lives. • Assessment is not perceived as intrusive or insensitive.
Build on strength as well as identify difficulties.	• Child can move beyond feeling 'defective' to identifying their contribution to the world, and feel a sense of fulfilment. • Whole family feel non-stigmatised and an acceptable family unit. • Risks to the child are identified and plans put in place to keep the child safe.
Inter-agency in their approach to assessment and provision of services.	• Services are not duplicated causing confusion. • Families do not feel overwhelmed and fatigued by assessments.
Continuing process, not a single event and carried out in parallel with other action and providing services.	• Services meet the child's needs at the right time, and are responsive to crises, growth and development, and deterioration. • Disabled children and their families feel supported through difficulties without intrusions into every day family life.
Grounded in evidence-based knowledge.	• Child and family feel confident and trusting of worker.

base (Kennedy 1995, 1990; Kennedy and Gordon, 1993; Ward, 1997; Westcott and Cross, 1996).

Qualifying, post-qualifying and in-service training are important forums for the dissemination of this information, and it is a concern that many social workers report that DipSW courses rarely incorporate this body of knowledge about disabled children and that, once qualified, opportunities to access this knowledge base continue to be limited.

If all this is put into practice, what will the outcomes for disabled children be? Table 4 above attempts to give some indicators of the positive benefits that could arise if the framework is used in a way that take properly into account the needs of disabled children.

In summary

We believe that the Framework offers advantages over previous assessment models for disabled children as long as the numerous factors affecting the process are taken properly into account (see Figure 12).

A disabled child is not simply a 'child' but a child which has the additional issues of impairment and disabling barriers (see Figure 10). Organisations and individuals must grasp this opportunity to move the Framework forward so that the disabled child's life is truly enhanced. In our experience taking the opportunity to reflect on the specific needs of disabled children in the context of the framework has highlighted both the limitations as well as the opportunities. We have discovered that continuing evaluation of how the framework can 'fit' for disabled children will be an ongoing and important process.

The base of this triangle accepts that disabled children have the emotional, psychological, and practical care needs as all children. It includes all of the developmental needs as per new assessment framework. At this point then, disabled children differ not at all from non-disabled children.

Figure 12: Factors affecting the assessment process.

Communications issues

- What system does the child use?
- Do I need an interpreter?
- What does the child's behaviour tell me?
- What do I need to do to understand what the child is telling me?

Values

- What do I feel about disabled people?
- What stereotypes/ prejudices inform my thinking?

Feelings

- Do I feel sorry for the child's parents? If I do, have I lost sight of the child?
- Do I feel sorry for the child? If I do is there a danger of patronising, rather than empowering, them?

Knowledge and skills

- What do I know about the child's impairment?
- Do I have the necessary communication skills?
- Is my child protection knowledge sound and up to date?
- Do I have access to research findings in relation to needs/risk/outcomes for disabled children?

Thresholds

- Would I feel this situation is acceptable for a non-disabled child?
- Has the assessment taken account of both need and possible risk?

Disabled children and the assessment process

Family's perception of the process

- Are the family clear about the purpose of the assessment?
- Have the parents become part of the professional system? If so, does this compromise their ability to parent the child or affect the child's safety?
- Is the process inappropriately intrusive – would parents of a non-disabled child be assessed to receive basic services?

Child's perception of the process

- Does the child understand the nature and purpose of the assessment?
- Does the child see evidence that people are interested in their point of view?
- Is the process inappropriately intrusive?

Worker's previous involvement with the family

- How do the family perceive me? Could our past relationship compromise this assessment?
- Have I developed a collusive relationship with the parents?

Relationships with colleagues

- Are we all operating from a social model perspective? If not, is there a danger of misinterpretation and polarisation?
- Are we all clear about our roles?
- Are those with most knowledge of the child respected and listened to by others in the system?

Agency context

- Am I letting knowledge of resources influence my judgement?
- Am I receiving supervision which challenges my thinking and promotes a good analysis of the child's needs?
- Is work with disabled children valued within the organisation?

Societal context

- How are disabled children valued and how far does this affect what is happening for this child?

© Kennedy and Wonnacott 2001

The left side of the triangle (Figure 10) 'impairment' includes aspects that must be addressed for a satisfactory assessment. This includes a careful analysis of the child's physical condition and what is thus required. Not only physical condition, however, as it is also essential here to consider such things as; positive identity formation which might manifest itself in the expression, 'It's OK to be disabled'. There must also be a specific focus on the development of independence, autonomy, choices, decision-making, and control of their lives. Specific questions could be:

1. How does this child's impairment impact on this child's life?
2. Does the child have everything they require in relation to their impairment?
3. Does the child feel positive about themself?
4. Does the child's impairment hinder their development of autonomy, independence, choice, decision-making and control of their life?

The right side of the triangle; 'disabling barriers' looks at the discrimination and oppression that the child is experiencing in it's life right now. This might be from bullying in a mainstream school to lack of a suitable communication system. Unfortunately, this has been a very threatening concept to social workers and service providers. For doing this properly highlights both service provision and attitudes and values. It requires the worker to analyse whether the lack of effective service provision could be called discrimination/oppression. It is the 'naming' that is problematical.

Within this category the following might be addressed:

1. Bullying of disabled children within mainstream school.
2. Poor service provision.
3. Negative attitudes of social workers, teachers, medical personnel, parents and carers towards the disabled child.
4. Stereotyping of disabled child.
5. Lack of access to criminal justice system (for abused disabled children).
6. Exclusive education services/ low expectations.
7. Emphasis on 'perfection', thus heavy medical surgical/therapeutic intervention, beyond the emotional/psychological endurance of the disabled child.

8. Denigration or rejection by family or peers. 'I wish I never had her'.
9. Infringements of human rights.

It is at this point that we must stress the need for social workers working with disabled children to have a thorough and extensive understanding of the European Human Rights legislation now enshrined in British law.

References

Beresford, B. (1994) *Positively Parents: Caring for a Disabled Child.* York: Social Policy Research Unit.

Beresford, B. (1997) *Personal Accounts: Involving Disabled Children in Research.* York: Social Policy Research Unit.

Chicenski, K. (2001) *The Interface Between Adult Substance Misuse Services and Local Child Care Teams.* Unpublished Conference Paper.

Cleaver, H., Unell, and Aldgate, J. (2000) *Children's Needs: Parenting Capacity.* The Stationery Office.

Cooke, P. (1999) *Final Report on Disabled Children and Abuse.* The Ann Craft Trust, Nottingham University.

Council for Disabled Children (2000) *Second Analysis of the Quality Protects Management Action Plans: Services for Disabled Children and Their Families.* London: National Children's Bureau.

Council for Disabled Children (2000) *Management Action Plans (MAPS).*

Cross, M. and Westcott, H. (1996) *This Far and No Further: Towards Ending the Abuse of Disabled Children.* Birmingham: Venture Press.

Crosse, S.B., Kaye, E. and Ratnofsky, A.C. (1993) *A Report on the Maltreatment of Children with Disabilities.* Washington, DC: National Center on Child Abuse and Neglect.

Dale, P., Green, R. and Fellows, R. (2001) Risk Radar. *Community Care.* 21–27 Jun.

DoH (1995) *Child Protection: Messages from Research.* London: HMSO.

DoH (1999) *Safeguarding Children.* London: TSO.

DoH (2000a) *Framework for the Assessment of Children in Need and Their Families.* London: The Stationery Office.

DoH (2000b) *Framework for the Assessment of Children in Need and Their Families. Practice Guidance.* London: The Stationery Office.

DoH, NSPCC and The University of Sheffield (2000c) *The Child's World: Assessing Children in Need.* London: TSO.

Jones, D.P.H. and Ramchandani, P. (1999) *Child Sexual Abuse: Informing Practice From Research.* Oxford: Radcliffe Medical Press.

Joseph Rowntree/Triangle/NSPCC (2001) *Two Way Street: Training Video and Handbook About Communicating with Disabled Children and Young People.*

Kennedy, M. (1989) The Abuse of Deaf Children. *Child Abuse Review.* 3: 1.

Kennedy, M. (1990) The Deaf Child who is Abused: Is there a Need for a Dual Specialist? *Child Abuse Review.* 4: 2, 3–6.

Kennedy, M. (1995) The Perception of Abused Disabled Children. In Wilson, K. and James, A. (Eds.) *The Child Protection Handbook.* London: Balliere and Tindall.

Kennedy, M. and Gordon, R (Eds.) (1993) *The ABCD Pack: The Abuse of Children Who Are Disabled Resource and Training Pack.* ABCD Consortium, Leicester: NSPCC.

Marchant, R. et al. (1999) *Listening on All Channels: Consulting with Disabled Children.* Brighton: Triangle.

Marchant, R, and Martyn, M. (1999) *Make it Happen: Communicating with Children. Communication Handbook.* Brighton: Triangle.

Marchant, R. (1991) Myths and Facts About Sexual Abuse and Children with Disabilities. *Child Abuse Review.* 5: 2, 22–4.

Marchant, R. and Jones, M. (2000) Assessing the Needs of Disabled Children and Their Families. In DoH (2000) *Assessing Children in Need and Their Families: Practice guidance.* London: The Stationery Office.

Morris, J. (1991) *Pride Against Prejudice.* London: Women's Press.

Morris, J. (1998) *Still Missing? The Experience of Disabled Children and Young People Living Away From Home.* London: Who Cares? Trust.

Morris, J. (1999) *Space for us: Finding Out What Disabled People and Young People Thinking About Their Placements.* London: London Borough of Newham Social Services Department.

NSPCC (1997) Turning Points: A Resource Pack for Communicating with Children (1997).

Oliver, M. (1999) *Understanding Disability: From Theory to Practice.* London: Macmillan.

Oswin, M. (1991) *They Keep Going Away: A Critical Study of Short Term Residential Care Services for Children with Learning Difficulties.* The King's Fund.

Prewitt, B. (1999) *Short Term Break, Long Term Benefit: Family Based Short Term Care for Disabled Children and Adults.* The University of Sheffield/Joseph Rowntree Foundation.

Reder, P. and Duncan, S. (1999) *Lost Innocents: A Follow Up Study of Fatal Child Abuse.* London: Routledge.

Reder, P., Duncan, S. and Gray, M. (1993) *Beyond Blame: Child Abuse Tragedies Revisited.* London: Routledge.

Ryan, M. (2000) *Working With Fathers.* Oxon: Radcliffe Medical Press.

Shakespeare, T. (2000) *Help.* Birmingham: Venture Press.

Sobsey, D. (1994) *Violence and Abuse in the Lives of People with Disability: The End of Silent Acceptance?* Paul Brookes Publishing.

Sullivan, P.M. and Knutson, J.F. (1998) *The Association Between Child Maltreatment and Disabilities in a Hospital-based Epidemiological Study.* NY: Pergamon Press.

Sullivan, P.M. and Knutson, J.F. (1997) *Maltreatment and Disabilities: A School Based Epidemiological Study.* St Joseph's Service League Centre for Abused.

Triangle (1999) *Tomorrow I go: What You Told Us about Dorset Rd.* Brighton.

Ward, L. (1997) *Seen and Heard: Involving Disabled Children and Young People in Research and Development Projects.* Joseph Rowntree Foundation.

Westcott, H. (1993) *Abuse of Children and Adults with Disabilities.* London: NSPCC.

Wonnacott, J. and Kennedy, M. (2001) A Model Approach. *Community Care.* 8–14 Mar.

Wescott, H. and Cross, M. (1996) This Far and No Further; Towards Ending the Abuse of Disabled Children. BASW/ Venture Press.

Chapter Eleven

A Framework for Assessing the Physical Abuse of Children

Dr Neil Frude

The nature of child physical abuse

The physical abuse of children is not a 'disorder' and cannot be 'diagnosed' or 'treated' (although the injurious *effects* of such abuse can be diagnosed and treated). Physical abuse is a social phenomenon and a social problem, and an abusive incident is a particular type of *event*. Definitions vary, but physical abuse is often defined as 'an injurious assault on a child by a parent or caregiver'. Various criteria are proposed for what constitutes an assault, and what constitutes an injury. At one extreme, some would apply the term 'physical abuse' only to cases which lead to permanent physical injury, while others would include incidents which result in minor bruises. At the other extreme, there are many who argue that any use of physical punishment methods, including a slap, should be labelled 'physical abuse'. When this position is adopted, one consequence is that a clear majority of parents qualify as 'child abusers', because the majority of parents have administered physical punishment to their children (Daro and Gelles, 1992; Knutson and Selner, 1994; Nobes and Smith, 1997). When 'lenient' criteria are used to define physical abuse, very high incidence rates are to be expected. When more stringent criteria are used to identify 'an injurious assault', the incidence becomes correspondingly smaller. Major variations in the reported incidence of physical child abuse tend to reflect differences in definitional criteria at least as much as any substantive differences in the facts being reported.

There have been many attempts to explain why some parents injure their children. Some accounts have focused on cultural norms or social circumstances, and others have focused on the personality (or in some cases, the possible psychopathology) of the abuser. Over the past twenty years, however, there has been a growing consensus that the most appropriate and useful accounts are those which consider physically abusive assaults on children primarily as acts of aggression (Dolz, Cerezo and Milner, 1997; Frude, 1980).

Such an analysis draws upon our knowledge of human aggression to explain physical child abuse. In the simplest terms, it maintains that an abusive assault occurs when a parent is enraged by some action of the child, is uninhibited in expressing this anger, and does so in an extreme and injurious fashion. This analysis is not appropriate to every single case of child physical abuse, but it does appear to be applicable to the vast majority of cases.

A distinction is commonly made, in the field of human aggression, between 'hostile aggression', which results from anger, and 'instrumental aggression' in which aggressive acts are carried out in order to gain a particular payoff. The aggression of the hired assassin, the mugger, the soldier in combat, and the violent bank robber do not stem from the assailant's anger with the victim but from hoped-for gains (or, in the case of the soldier, from having a job to do). Certain types of family violence often do have a strong instrumental element, including marital violence (Frude, 1994), but child abuse is rarely instrumental. There is generally little to be gained from injuring a child, other than the child's fearful compliance.

While physical child abuse is almost always the result of a hostile (rather than an instrumental) attack on the child, there are rare, but noteworthy, exceptions to the general rule. For example, it has been reported that in certain countries in which some families survive entirely on the proceeds of begging, children are sometimes deliberately maimed or handicapped so that they will be more pitiable, and hence more profitable, as beggars. The disfiguring injuries which result from such strategic actions are clearly the result of instrumental aggression. Another example of such premeditated aggression is provided by the case of Brian Stewart, a hospital laboratory aide in Missouri who was arrested and charged in 1998 having injected his baby son with HIV-contaminated blood. Estranged from the boy's mother, it appeared that his aim was to kill the child so that he would avoid having to pay for child support.

Other unusual and instrumental forms of physical abuse include sadistic or torturous abuse (Bowdry, 1990; Goodwin, 1993), ritual abuse and Munchausen syndrome by proxy. Frude (1996) has discussed the difficulties involved in defining and identifying ritual abuse and has argued that this should not be regarded as a separate category of child abuse. He argues that abusive ritual acts are best regarded as cases of physical abuse, or sexual abuse, or psychological abuse (or any combination of these), committed *in the context* of some ceremony or rite. The very existence of 'satanic abuse' remains an issue of extreme controversy (Bottoms and Davis, 1997; La Fontaine, 1997; Sinason, 1994).

Munchausen syndrome by proxy is a form of emotional abuse and sometimes severe physical abuse in which the child's caretaker (in most cases, the mother) repeatedly presents the child for medical treatment and gives false reports of symptoms (sometimes substantiating the story with fabricated evidence) (Donald and Jureidini, 1996). The perpetrator usually begins to invent false illnesses early on in the child's life. In the past decade over 200 cases of the syndrome have been documented in the UK (Loader and Kelly, 1996; Neale et al., 1991).

It needs to be stressed that instrumental violence towards children, sadistic abuse, ritual abuse and Munchausen by proxy are all atypical forms of physical abuse. In the vast majority of cases the aggression which leads to the child being injured results from anger, and the aggression is spontaneous rather than premeditated. What leads to the majority of injurious attacks is extreme anger, invariably triggered by some behaviour of the child. In terms of its psychological antecedents, abusive behaviour is not qualitatively different from less extreme forms of behaviour shown by most angry parents. The majority of parents hit their children occasionally and almost all sometimes shout at their children. We need to understand why some angry parents attack their children with such force that they severely injure, or even kill, their children.

Even in abusive families, an injurious incident is likely to occur only once or a few times during the child's life. Thus the phenomenon of physical abuse is unlikely to be explained by focusing exclusively on characteristics such as the parent's personality or social situation, which remain relatively constant over many months or even years. Such characteristics may be associated with an increased risk of injury, but they need to be integrated into a model which ultimately focuses on the abuse incident. Understanding the incident invariably entails an appreciation of the interaction between the parent and child in the hours, minutes and seconds before the assault. The purpose of this chapter is to explore further this interactional view of child physical abuse.

The interactional view of child physical abuse

The vast body of research on child physical abuse has revealed several hundred factors associated with a greater or lesser probability that a child will be physically abused. Some of these factors relate principally to the parents, some to the child, and some to the family circumstances. The most powerful single predictor of whether a child will be injured by a parent is the fact of such abuse having occurred previously. The probability that a child will be injured is also high when the parent is regularly aggressive towards the child. The more severe the aggression, the more likely it is that the parent will one day injure the child. Thus 'customary high aggression' by a parent towards a child signals that the child is at relatively high risk of being injured. The likelihood of serious injury is related not only to the frequency but also to the form of aggression generally used. Thus if punches to the head are customary, the danger of serious injury will be much greater than if customary attacks take the form of slaps to the buttocks.

There is thus an association, or a probability link, between customary high aggression and an injurious attack. When we examine factors that are closely associated with customary high aggression, and may help to establish such a parental style, we are beginning to establish a probability chain. 'Customary high-level aggression' would seem, in particular, to be associated with a frequent occurrence of serious disciplinary encounters that tend to escalate so that the parent loses control. If a parent is involved in frequent attempts to control a child's behaviour, and if these attempts meet with little success, then the parent may regularly engage in serious aggressive actions towards the child.

A further step back in the causal chain involves examining the antecedents of frequent and difficult disciplinary encounters. Why do some parents engage in frequent disciplinary confrontations with their children, or with one particular child in the family? A number of factors can be identified as probable precipitants of frequent and ineffectual disciplinary encounters. Some involve aspects of the child's behaviour, some involve the parent's general style of interaction with the child, and some focus specifically on the parent's disciplinary behaviour. Briefly, the evidence to be presented suggests that frequent and harsh discipline often reflects a child's disturbed behaviour (especially aggressiveness and non-compliance), critical and 'blame oriented' parental attitudes, poor child management skills, and a child's imperviousness in the face of parental requests, demands and punishments. Furthermore, these factors are likely to be associated with a parent–child relationship which is distant and mutually antagonistic.

The analysis presented here traces a causal probability chain from the event of an injurious assault back through a series of antecedents. This 'retrospective' account can be reconfigured so that we trace the causal analysis 'in prospect'. Thus we can first identify certain aspects of a parent–child relationship which are likely to lead to disciplinary problems, and then consider how such problems might escalate in seriousness and lead to the customary use of dangerous aggression. The analysis might end at this stage, with the assumption that frequent serious aggression will be associated with a high probability of an eventual injurious attack. But it would also be useful to be more specific, and to attempt to explain how a particular injurious incident might arise on a particular day and at a particular time.

This chapter provides a prospective analysis of the type outlined. We will first consider aspects of the parent–child relationship which may be distal antecedents of abuse. We will then consider the kinds of problematic disciplinary encounters that are likely to escalate, so that the parent is frequently highly aggressive towards the child, before focusing specifically on the aggressive or abusive incident.

The parent–child relationship

Many research studies have now identified a number of aspects of parent–child interaction which differentiate groups of abusing (or 'high-risk-for-abuse') families and non-abusing families. Comparisons of the interaction styles within these two groups of families indicate significant differences across a wide range of characteristics. Before reviewing the relevant evidence, it is important to consider the nature and significance of findings from this type of research. The studies examine the characteristics of parents, children, and the parent–child relationship, in non-abusive (or 'low-risk') families and abusive (or 'high-risk') families and, in many cases, report statistically significant differences between the two types of family on various characteristics. However, even when there is such a difference there may be a considerable degree of overlap between the groups. Results may be interpreted by the casual reader as indicating a 'sharp contrast' between abusive and non-abusive families and this may reinforce the idea that abusive families are qualitatively different from other families in their behaviour and relationships. In fact, many abusive families are not at all 'extraordinary'. No single characteristic (and indeed no combination of characteristics) can be used as a 'marker' to differentiate between abusive and non-abusive families and we need to avoid the tendency to caricature abusive families by overstating the degree to which they are similar to one another or different from other families.

There are also limits to the degree that any characteristic which differentiates the groups can be said to be predictive of abuse. Many families that display the interactive styles that are found more frequently in abusive than in non-abusive families will not themselves be abusive. Finally, it must be acknowledged that comparison studies of the type generally undertaken in the abuse field are able to identify only associations between variables. Although there is a natural tendency to conclude that such variables play a causal role in precipitating abuse, in many cases it would be equally plausible to suggest that the particular style of parent–child interaction may have developed as a result of abusive, 'sub-abusive' or 'pre-abusive' actions. It is highly likely, for example, that child characteristics that reflect earlier episodes of parental aggression may act as triggers for abusive acts. Most of the studies so far undertaken in this area are able to provide only synchronic (or 'snapshot') accounts of what are undoubtedly long narrative affairs.

The parent brings to the relationship with the child a personal history, a personality, a set of attitudes and expectations, and a current lifestyle. The child, too, brings many individual characteristics. The relationship which develops between them, however, emerges in a highly dynamic and interactive way, with each individual changing constantly in response to the other's behaviour. To a large degree, the parenting behaviour of any parent is determined by the behaviour of the child, while a child's behaviour is substantially determined by the parenting that he or she has experienced. Although this interdependency means that it is often impossible to identify the parent's and the child's separate contributions to their interaction, it is still reasonable to maintain a distinction between what the parent does and what the child does. Such an account, in terms of behavioural topography ('who does what'), should not however be taken as reflecting any particular pattern of causal antecedents. A particular aspect of a parent's current parenting style, for example, may well reflect the child's past behaviour more than it reflects the parent's 'original' parenting disposition. Similarly, a child's behaviour may reflect how he or she has been treated by the parents more than it reflects any behavioural tendency that is 'intrinsic' to the child.

Parent characteristics

Unresponsiveness and the absence of warmth

Abusive parents tend to focus less attention on their children and to be less responsive to them, compared to other parents (Diaz et al., 1991). They spend less time looking at their children, for example, and speak less to them (Burgess and Richardson, 1984; Fontana and Robison, 1984; Starr, 1980). Such parents also exhibit particularly low rates of positive behaviours such as showing physical affection and praising good behaviour (Kelly, 1983). Reid (1983) found that abusive parents reported significantly less playful teasing and less humour in their interactions with the child than did non-abusive parents, and Bousha and Twentyman (1984) indicated that abusive mothers expressed approval of their children less often than did non-abusive mothers.

Observational studies of interaction between abusive parents and their children have demonstrated a lack of warmth in the parent–child relationship. Reid (1983), for example, found that observers who watched abusive parents interacting with their children judged these parents as enjoying their children significantly less than non-abusive parents. This impression is supported by studies which have

shown that, compared with non-abusive families, abusive parents were less satisfied with their children, and perceive child rearing as more difficult and less enjoyable than other parents (Trickett and Susman, 1988).

A preponderance of negative responses

It thus seems that abusive parents tend to exhibit a general low level of positive child-directed or child-responsive behaviour. When they do direct their behaviour towards the child, it is often inappropriate and negative in tone. Dolz, Cerezo and Milner (1997) found that high-risk mothers displayed more negative behaviours towards their children than non-abusive mothers, and DiLalla and Crittenden (1990) found that abusive parents were often hostile in their attitude and behaviour towards the child.

Burgess and Conger (1978) found that abusive mothers displayed, on average, a 60 per cent higher rate of negative actions (e.g. complaints and threats) compared to non-abusive mothers.

A hostile attitude towards the child

It is clear that some abusive parents have a generally hostile attitude towards children or a specific dislike of their own child (DiLalla and Crittenden, 1990; Milner et al., 1995). Herrenkohl and Herrenkohl (1979) examined parents' attitudes towards abused children and their non-abused siblings, and found that those who had been abused were described by the parents in predominantly negative terms and were seen more negatively than their siblings.

Parents' lack of empathy

A lack of empathy by abusing parents has also been revealed by various research teams (Acton and During, 1990; Milner et al., 1995). Letourneau (1981) suggested that in some cases the lack of empathy may reflect a parent's own history of being abused as a child.

Aversion to child behaviours

Some abusive parents have an aversion to particular normal child behaviours (such as the messy eating typical of two and three-year-olds). A number of studies have demonstrated the tendency for such parents to become physiologically aroused and stressed when viewing videotapes of child and infant behaviours that most parents find relatively innocuous. Thus Frodi and Lamb (1980) showed videotapes of infants crying and smiling to groups of women while they monitored their physiological responses. After each section of the tape the mothers were asked to describe their feelings. It was found that abusive mothers tended to respond somewhat aversively not only to the crying infants but also to the smiling infants. Some of the abusive mothers reported extreme feelings of anger and annoyance in response to tapes of crying infants. In another study, Wolfe et al. (1983) asked abusive and non-abusive parents to rate the degree of stress they experienced in response to various scenes of child behaviours and found that abusive parents tended to report stress in response to significantly more scenes than other parents (including some scenes which had been included in the belief than they would be 'non-stressful').

Criteria for judging behaviour as 'bad'

There is now a solid body of research evidence indicating that abusive parents tend to be over-inclusive in the child behaviours that they judge to be 'inappropriate' or 'naughty'. Wood-Shuman and Cone (1986) showed abusive, at-risk and control mothers videotapes of children aged from six months to seven years in various situations (e.g. involving a child disobeying a command, crying, refusing to go to bed, and playing quietly). The results showed that the abusive mothers tended to rate even innocuous child behaviour in a negative way. These authors suggested that the abusive mothers tended to be 'blame oriented', and they speculated that, for some of them, a history of childhood abuse meant they had never managed to establish an appropriate distinction between 'good behaviour' and 'bad behaviour'. They also comment that mothers who remain relatively isolated will have few opportunities to learn how other mothers judge children's behaviours or to establish reasonable expectations of how children will behave.

Other studies which have found that abusive parents are especially likely to identify a child's behaviour as problematic include those reported by Bradley and Peters (1991), who suggested that abusive parents are hyper-reactive to anything that might constitute misbehaviour, and Chilamkurti and Milner (1993), who found that high risk mothers tend to evaluate conventional and personal transgressions as significantly more wrong than those in a low risk group.

When a parent categorises a broad range of child behaviour as 'bad', or has particularly strict criteria for deciding whether a child's actions are 'acceptable', this will increase the frequency with which a child's actions provoke an aversive or angry parental response and are seen to call for disciplinary intervention or to deserve punishment. A low threshold for judging that a child has been 'naughty', 'insolent' or 'unruly' may reflect a general critical and unfavourable view of the child, but will also serve to strengthen the view that the child is habitually bad and particularly difficult to manage (Wahler and Dumas, 1984).

Unrealistic expectations and standards

One reason why abusive parents may judge their own child's behaviour to be 'bad' or 'defective' may be that they are applying standards of behaviour that are inappropriately high for a child of that particular age (Rosenberg and Repucci, 1983; Stern and Azar, 1998; Twentyman and Plotkin, 1982). A lack of knowledge about normal child development may well lead to unrealistic expectations of how clean, obedient and polite their own child should be, as well as how advanced the child should be with regard to toilet training, speech, mobility and motor skills. Research shows that some abusive parents have extremely high expectations of their children in terms of both their obedience and their achievement levels, and are angered by what they take to be the child's defective and reprehensible behaviour (McKenry et al., 1991; Schellenbach et al., 1992). The development and maintenance of unrealistic standards among some abusive parents may be partly explained by the fact that many of these families have relatively little contact with other people, have little social support, and mix with other young families very infrequently (Kinard, 1996).

Parents' Attributions

Parental responses to children's behaviour reflect the parents' interpretations of the meaning of the behaviour, and when a child is judged to be doing something 'naughty' or 'bad', the emotional impact on the parent, and the parent's behavioural response, will reflect assumptions about *why* the child is misbehaving. Call (1984) and Stern and Azar (1998) have provided examples of the rather extreme interpretations that parents sometimes make of ordinary child behaviours. An infant's crying may be seen as a sign of 'defiance' or 'greediness', for example, while turning away from the breast or bottle may be regarded as a deliberate rejection of the parent.

Parents differ considerably in their attributional style, and their style predicts the degree of anger and annoyance they feel in response to child misdemeanours (Bugenthal, Blue and Cruzcosa, 1989). Johnston and Patenaude (1994) showed that parents who judge their children's disruptive behaviour as deliberate and internally caused exhibit stronger negative reactions than those who regard such behaviour as uncontrollable and externally caused. There is now a good deal of evidence to show that many abusing parents have a negative bias in the attributions they make about their children's behaviour (e.g. Acton and During, 1990; Bradley and Peters, 1991; Golub, 1984; Oldershaw et al., 1989; Stern and Azar, 1998). Such parents tend to attribute misbehaviour to stable factors and to judge the child as being deliberately naughty and intentionally harassing. Furthermore, they are less likely to 'make excuses' for the child, or to take account of any circumstances which might serve to mitigate the child's responsibility. Milner and Foody (1994) compared the impact of mitigating information on attributions for positive and negative child behaviours and showed that high-risk-for-abuse mothers took relatively little account of the mitigating circumstances compared to low risk mothers.

Attributions of intentionality and defiance, not only to clearly disruptive behaviours but even to normal, innocuous and age-appropriate behaviours, are likely to increase the frequency with which a parent believes that discipline is called for and may increase the harshness of any punishment given to the child. Furthermore, negative attributions of specific actions may eventually lead to a general view of the child as especially naughty and difficult to control, and such a view will in turn strengthen the bias towards interpreting the child's actions in the worst possible light (Bugental et al., 1989).

Child behaviour
Although many abusive parents have a somewhat distorted view of the child, it cannot simply be assumed that their negative experiences of the child are entirely the result of their own perceptual biases and distortions. Some children are more vulnerable to abuse than other children and, as a group, children who are especially at risk are liable to be 'objectively' more aversive, more 'naughty', or

more strong-willed than other children (Crockenberg, 1987; Forehand and Long, 1996; Kinard, 1995). It is highly likely that much of their disturbed behaviour results from a history of parental mishandling and abuse, rather than being intrinsic to the child, but this is of marginal relevance when we are considering how the child presents to the parent and how the parent is likely to respond. Abusive parents are unlikely to recognise their own responsibility for the child's aggressiveness or naughtiness, and even if they did they would be unlikely to consider this in mitigation (Milner and Foody, 1994). Their attributional bias is likely to persuade them that the fault lies solely with the child and reflects the child's intrinsic unruliness (Bugental et al., 1989).

Developmental difficulties
Certain developmental difficulties and delays, as well as particular behaviours, may adversely affect the development of the parent–child relationship, and may increase the likelihood of physical abuse. Some babies settle comfortably into the arms of the caregiver, whereas others are awkward or 'floppy'. Some babies are more socially responsive (and thus 'rewarding') than others, and some are more easily soothed. It would seem likely that the parent's response to a comfortable, responsive and easily soothed baby would be more positive than to a floppy, unresponsive and 'unsoothable' infant. Such factors have been suggested as highly significant for understanding the abuse of young infants. Heinicke (1984), for example, describes differences in 'infant soothability' as being particularly relevant. Other infant variables which appear to be important include sleep pattern and characteristics of the child's crying (frequency, pitch and loudness, for example).

Infants who have been abused tend to have been less healthy than other children, and have had more illnesses in the first year of life (Friedrich and Boriskin, 1976). A relatively high proportion also show decreased muscle tone and significant developmental delays in sensory motor skills (Oates et al., 1979; Schilling and Schinke, 1984). In addition, both mental and physical handicap have long been established as important risk factors for abuse (Friedrich and Boriskin, 1976; Starr et al., 1984). While some of these characteristics may be intrinsic to the child, some are likely to be the effects of suboptimal (or even abusive) parenting. Whatever their origin, they are likely to make the parent less appreciative of the infant and they may make the child particularly difficult to care for. These effects may render children who have early developmental difficulties particularly vulnerable to parental assault.

Behavioural symptoms

Martin and Beezley (1977) found that older abused children exhibited a number of behavioural symptoms, including tantrums, enuresis, opposition, compulsivity, hypervigilance and pseudo-mature behaviour. Perry and Doran (1983) reported that abused children were more cautious, shy and anti-social. Kinard (1995) found that both mothers and teachers rated abused children as exhibiting more behaviour problems than non-abused children, and concluded that intervention strategies must address the children's behavioural problems as well as the mother's behaviour.

A child who is unattractive, lacks physical robustness, or is developmentally delayed may be a source of particular anxiety and distress for the parent. Some parents of such children will be disappointed with their offspring, and resentful of the fact that their child is less than perfect. Poor health, handicap or disturbed temperament may mean that a child is relatively unresponsive to the parent while also making extra care demands on the parents' time, effort and finances. The parents may feel less proud of such a child than they would of a 'perfect' child, and the additional problems they experience in dealing with the child's special difficulties may lead to anxiety, depression, guilt, frustration and anger. Some parents respond to the challenge by investing extra vigour and devotion into their parenting and develop a deep respect and love for the child. Others, however, find it particularly difficult to develop a loving relationship with their 'impaired' offspring. For the parent who is resentful of the child, and has failed to develop a close relationship with him or her, any peculiarities of the child's appearance or behaviour which signal the child's disability may be a continuing source of frustration and annoyance, and in some cases they will elicit a particularly intense anger which may eventually result in an injurious assault on the child.

Children's aggression

Many parents find it difficult to respond in a controlled and appropriate way to a child who is being overtly aggressive, whether the aggression is directed towards the parents themselves, other adults, or other children. In attempting to explain the parent's 'here and now' response to the aggressive child, the underlying cause of the aggression is largely irrelevant. It may well be that much of the aggression observed in abused children results from frustration, parental mishandling and the imitation of the parents' own aggressive responses. More relevant is the fact that abusive parents are likely to attribute their child's aggression to 'internal' and 'stable' factors and to regard it as a sign of the child's general hostility and 'nasty nature'.

Many abused children do appear to be particularly hostile. Evidence of this comes not only from parents' reports of their children's behaviour but also from observational studies conducted both in clinics and in the home. In a review of several relevant studies, Patterson (1982) and Trickett and Kuczynski (1986) showed that aversive behaviour is reliably higher in abused children, and Main and Goldwyn (1984) concluded from their analysis of studies of young (1–3-year-old) abused children that many appeared to find it difficult to control their aggression. Burgess and Conger (1977) found more fighting and conflict among siblings in abusive than in non-abusive families, and Straus (1983) also showed that abused children exhibited a high degree of aggression towards their siblings. Seventy-six per cent of the abused children in his sample had repeatedly and severely assaulted a sibling during the 12 month period covered by the study, compared to 15 per cent of those whose parents used no physical punishment or violence.

Reid et al. (1981) found that youngsters in high-risk-for-abuse families displayed increased rates of both extremely aversive behaviours (such as hitting and threatening others) and mildly obnoxious behaviour (such as whining and teasing). Correlational analyses show that the more aversive the behaviour shown by the child, the more frequently the parents engaged in aversive behaviour (Reid et al., 1982). This finding is of course open to a number of alternative causal interpretations.

George and Main (1979) found that in a play situation abused children more often hit, slapped and kicked their peers. They also assaulted or threatened to assault their caregivers four times as frequently as controls and were markedly more avoidant of the friendly overtures of both peers and caregivers. Whereas children in the control groups tended to show sadness, concern or empathy when they observed the distress of a peer, none of the abused infants ever showed such empathic responses. Instead, the abused children tended to respond to peer distress by showing disturbed behaviour patterns including fear, anger or physical abuse. Thus some of the abused children reacted to peer distress with aggression and apparent malice. Sroufe (1983) also found that many abused children are hostile and isolated at school, lack empathy, and tend to respond maliciously to peer distress.

Children who are highly aggressive, whatever the origin of their aggressiveness, would seem particularly likely to attract an aggressive response from a parent. This can partly be explained with reference to the phenomenon of behavioural reciprocity – just as a kind act tends to elicit kindness from the recipient, so hostility tends to elicit hostility. A child's aggression is also likely to be regarded by a parent as a particularly heinous offence that calls for strong, immediate disciplinary action.

Parent–child interaction

It is clear that an abusive assault on a child rarely takes place in the context of an 'ideal' parent–child relationship and that relationships between abusing parents and their children are often chronically disturbed. Although we may make an analytical distinction between 'the parent's contribution' and 'the child's contribution' to problematic interactions, the parent and the child each play a major part in determining (and, often, in disrupting) the other's behaviour. Gaensbauer et al. (1980) wrote of the 'lack of sensitive and contingent reciprocity between mother and infant' in many abusive families. Children's behaviour is largely shaped by parental responses, but children also have their own intrinsic behavioural style. The notion that a child begins life as a passive *tabula rasa* has long been discarded (Schaffer, 1977; Stafford and Bayer, 1996; Thomas et al., 1970;). Children are individuals from the moment of birth, and their character has profound effects on how their parents feel about them and behave towards them. Thus the infant acts as a stimulus for the parents' behaviour as well as responding to parental actions.

If we were to attempt to trace the origins of the difficulties in the relationships between

abused children and their parents we would need to consider the biological characteristics of the infants, the parents' own childhood experiences, and the attitudes of each parent. Belsky and Isabella (1985) found that it was possible to predict how men and women would adjust to parenthood from their self-reports of their own childhood history. Belsky (1993) noted a consistent finding across several research studies indicating that individuals in happier marriages, and those with a supportive network of family and friends, tend to provide more nurturant and less punitive care for their children.

Main and Weston (1982) found that women who had apparently been rejected by their mother in childhood tended to reject their own infants, and that a mother's rejection is related to the degree to which the infant avoids her following brief separations. These authors suggested that a mother's rejecting behaviour may lead the child to develop a syndrome of avoidance, hostility and lack of feeling for others, and that such behaviour by the child is likely to further antagonise the mother.

There is clearly a complex story to be told about the antecedents of poor parent–child relationships, but the main concern here is not to consider these antecedents but rather their consequences. If the quality of the relationship is poor, then one effect of this may be to create special problems when parent and child are in conflict or when the parent attempts to control and discipline the child. If the general relationship is poor, if parent and child have little mutual affection and little mutual understanding, then such occasions are likely to be fraught with difficulty. The discipline issue is evidently of special importance, for many serious aggressive and abusive incidents arise in the context of disciplinary confrontations.

Discipline

We would expect there to be more frequent and more hostile disciplinary confrontations when the quality of the relationship between the parent and the child is relatively poor. These confrontations may then escalate so that aggressive attacks become relatively common, and this will increase the probability that the child will one day be injured in an attack.

Many of the features commonly found in the parent–child relationships within abusive families are particularly relevant to the generation and progression of disciplinary encounters. Children in such relationships are often more difficult to control, less compliant and more aggressive than other children. Thus their behaviour is often likely to be annoying not only to the parents, but to other people as well – Kinard, 1995). Some parents also find many aspects of children's behaviour aversive and regard a wide range of behaviours as 'bad' or 'regressive'. They are also likely to blame the child and to make uncharitable attributions about why he or she has 'behaved badly'.

As a result of their children's behavioural characteristics and their own judgemental biases, some parents will frequently see the child's actions as calling for disciplinary action. There is evidence of a high frequency of disciplinary encounters on a day-to-day basis within families in which a child is eventually injured. Reid et al. 1981), for example, found that abusive parents reported a higher density of discipline problems than other parents, and Majonis (1991) also reported evidence of a high rate of general disciplinary conflict in abusive families.

Such problems may not always result in physical punishment, but might lead to a high rate of screaming and verbal abuse which contribute to a high level of ambient aggression. In a study of child-rearing violence in a national sample, Hemenway et al. (1994) showed a positive relationship between verbal and physical discipline, so that parents who yell at their children frequently also tend to hit them frequently. The same conclusion was reached by Reid et al. (1982) who found that parents who express their anger more openly, as evidenced by yelling, disapproval, humiliation etc., are also likely to be physically abusive towards their youngsters.

Escalation of disciplinary encounters

Disciplinary skills
Not only do abusive families engage more frequently in disciplinary encounters but these tend to last longer and to escalate in severity. Again there are a number of contributory factors. It seems that abusive parents tend to be less skilled in discipline management, that abused children are less compliant and less easily controlled, and that a norm of harshness develops in the parents' punishment style.

Reid et al. (1981) found that abusive mothers were less successful in terminating the problem behaviour of their children by normal disciplinary means. These authors suggest that this lack of success tends to undermine the abusive mother's confidence that she is able to control the child. The resulting uncertainty then has further adverse effects on the development and performance of disciplining skills. In a review of relevant studies, Kelly (1983) also concludes that abusive parents tend to display high rates of ineffective behaviour (for example, failing to notice the child's good behaviour, frequently threatening punishment, and issuing many unclear and inconsistent commands). Further evidence of low management skills has been provided by a number of other workers, including Kadushin and Martin (1981) and Herrenkohl et al. (1983). Effective discipline involves not only responding to undesirable behaviours but also positively reinforcing good behaviour, and especially compliance. Schindler and Arkowitz (1986) reported that abusive mothers in their sample reinforced compliance significantly less often than controls.

For children who are deprived of positive interaction, even 'negative attention' (shouting, threatening, hitting, etc.) may prove reinforcing and strengthen the behaviour it is intended to check (Miller, 1980; Patterson, 1982). Descriptions of abusive families provide evidence that many of these parents do inadvertently reinforce their children's continued misbehaviour (Kelly, 1983).

Parental disciplining skills develop partly by a process of trial and error learning. Parents learn how to best control the child by witnessing how the child responds to various forms of request, goading, bribery, threat and punishment. Thus disciplinary skills develop during interactions with the child and reflect the child's response patterns as well as parent behaviours. The fact that many abused children appear to be especially attention-seeking, relatively immune to positive goading, and non-complaint (Bousha and Twentyman, 1984; Schindler and Arkowitz, 1986) means that such children may be especially poor in 'training' their parents in effective disciplinary skills.

Parental anger
The problem with discipline may be amplified by the fact that abusive parents tend to respond more aversively to a disciplinary failure than would other parents facing a similar problem. Reid (1983) asked abusive and non-abusive parents to complete 'discipline report forms' each day. These reports included information

about the most significant disciplinary confrontation of the day, and about how much anger the parents had experienced. Parents in the abusive group reported feeling significantly more angry during a typical discipline confrontation. Abusive parents' increased anger in response to child misbehaviour has also been reported by Kolko (1996); Lesnik-Oberstein et al. (1995); and Trickett and Susman (1988).

Some of the factors which might help to explain why these parents become more angry have already been identified. They find many child behaviours aversive, for example, and they tend to blame the child inappropriately. However, many abusive parents also face difficulties in other areas of their lives which may also increase their general level of hostility and bitterness (Whiteman et al., 1987). Patterson (1982) showed that depression and other emotional problems decrease the extent to which parents are able to handle discipline problems, and Schinke et al. (1986) point to the role of stress as a trigger for anger and interpersonal violence. These authors also draw attention to the fact that the important stresses which affect day-to-day behaviour are not just the major life events such as bereavement or divorce but also the 'hassles' of everyday life. Some such hassles will stem from the child's behaviour, but some will originate in other areas. If everyday hassles lead to anger then a child may become the unfortunate target of any resulting aggression. Many case studies of abusive behaviour illustrate such an effect. In a study reported by Scott et al. (1982), for example, careful interviews revealed that most instances of a mother's violent behaviour towards her child occurred when disagreements with her boyfriend led her to become angry. The role of marital conflict in precipitating abuse has been identified by, among others, Reid et al. (1981) and Straus (1980).

There is a clear positive relationship between the degree of anger felt by parents and the severity with which they are likely to punish a child. Peterson et al. (1994) found that different situations evoked differing amounts of anger and different degrees of physical punishment. The child behaviours that made mothers most angry resulted in the highest use of physical discipline. Similar findings were also reported by Golub (1984).

Harsh punishment methods

A large body of evidence indicates that abusive parents tend to use harsh punishment methods

in the normal course of disciplining (Kolko, 1996; Patterson, 1982; Reid, 1978; Whipple and Richey, 1997). In a behavioural observation study, Reid et al. (1981) found that many abusive parents engage in frequent serious aversive acts towards the child. The high-risk mothers hit their children four times as frequently as non-abusive mothers and issued substantially more threats. Overall, parents in the abusive families exhibited ten times as many aversive behaviours towards their children as non-abusive parents. Similarly, when Reid (1983) asked parents how many times they punished their children and what types of punishment they employed, he found much more physical discipline reported by abusive parents than by non-abusive parents. Furthermore, the abusive parents reported the use of more serious and abusive forms of physical force in their day-to-day disciplining. Thus both observation and self-report data indicate the frequent use of harsh disciplinary methods by abusive parents. Trickett and Kuczynski (1986) found that abusive parents tended to use punishment as their disciplinary strategy regardless of the type of child misbehaviour involved.

Reid (1986) found that abusive mothers were not only more likely to engage in aversive interchanges with their children than other mothers but that the likelihood of an aversive interchange escalating to aggression was also markedly higher for these mothers. Reid also reported that disciplinary episodes involving abusive mothers extended significantly longer than those involving non-abusive mothers.

Why should some parents develop harsh styles of discipline? One relevant factor is the parent's attitude to child control. Some parents maintain that 'a smack is the only thing s/he understands' and, when a child is aggressive, some parents feel that 'aggression deserves to be met with aggression' (Kelley, 1990). Those who have a history of having been beaten themselves as children, and are relatively isolated from other parents, may have odd ideas about what constitutes 'normal' or 'acceptable' levels of punishment. Several studies have suggested that abusive parents tend to believe that strong discipline is necessary to control a child (Chilamkurti and Milner, 1993; Kelley, 1990; Schellenbach and Guerney, 1987). Non-abusive parents who express a positive attitude towards the use of power assertive methods also tend to use harsher forms of punishment in the ay-to-day disciplining of their children (Frude nd Goss, 1979). Studies of the 'desensitizing' ffects of exposure to violence (Berkowitz, 1962) uggest that people whose parents were ggressive towards them (or towards each ther) may have become tolerant of violence. In ddition, such early experiences may have elped to establish the belief that physical methods of disciplining are acceptable and normal'. It is not surprising, therefore, to find that parents who were abused as children tend o use more severe methods of discipline than ther parents (Herrenkohl et al., 1983).

The main reason why some parents use harsh isciplinary measures, however, may relate to heir history of attempts to discipline the child. Most disciplinary acts are attempts to curtail ngoing behaviour which the parent finds versive or judges to be 'naughty' – they are ttempts at controlling the immediate situation. A child who stops behaving badly in response o a request or a reprimand will reinforce the arents' use of such a strategy and will ncourage the parent to use the same approach n subsequent occasions. If mild and reasonable ttempts at control prove ineffective, however, he parent may progress to harsher attempts to ontrol the child, and an escalation may occur which will then continue until an effective form f action is finally found. Parents will differ in he rate at which they ascend the 'disciplinary arshness hierarchy', and in how far they are repared to go, but the level will also be partly etermined by the response of the child. Children differ in their compliance, their ensitivity to different forms of punishment, and he speed with which they habituate to mildly versive disciplinary acts. They may acclimatise o particular forms of punishment, so that a hout which is initially sufficient to bring about ontrol may have little effect at a later stage. Because abusive parents are often more punitive han other parents, their children may habituate o low-level punitive controls more rapidly, hereby increasing the risk of escalation (Kelly, 983).

The process by which violence is shaped by he rewards and punishments which follow ggressive behaviours has been well described by Patterson (1982). He described a 'coercive' amily cycle in which both the parents and the hild engage in escalating rates of aversive behaviour towards one another. According to Patterson's Coercion Theory, inconsistent punishment and positive reinforcement for

anti-social behaviours will tend to produce an escalation of hostility. In such a situation, Patterson suggests, both parties will make hostile attributions concerning the other's malevolent intent. The parents' hostility may act as a stimulus to further child misbehaviour, rather than an effective control, and the situation may then instigate a vicious circle which spirals into extreme violence.

Thus certain types of difficult parent–child relationships tend to produce frequent and harsh disciplinary encounters which may escalate to violence. We now need to focus more closely on how specific incidents arise which are so extreme that they lead to a child being injured.

Discipline and abuse

Most injurious assaults on children by their parents arise in the context of what can be broadly recognised as 'disciplinary encounters'. Schindler and Arkowitz (1986) suggest that abusive behaviour is often triggered when a parent is frustrated by a series of non-compliant behaviours by the child. The abusive attack, they suggest, is a coercive attempt to induce compliance following the parents' frustration at the fact that other attempts at control have proved ineffective. Majonis (1991) also found that abuse invariably occurred in the context of disciplinary encounters, and Kelly (1983) maintains that parents who rely on physically punitive controls run a relatively high risk of eventually injuring the child in the course of their attempts at discipline. Reid (1986) also made a similar point, again using a probability argument:

> For a parent who reports spanking his or her child on the average of once every three days . . . who makes a practice of using threats in his or her attempts to control the behaviour of the children, it is simply a matter of time before a discipline confrontation will escalate into violence.
>
> (op cit., p247).

In their interactional analysis of abusive incidents, Kadushin and Martin (1981) also focus on disciplinary encounters and describe many instances in which disciplinary encounters led, through 'chains of escalating coercion', to attacks on a child which resulted in the child being injured. They found that a large proportion of abusive parents reported that the intention of the attack had been to control the child, and that many of these parents regarded the use of strong physical measures as legitimate when 'no other form of discipline is effective'.

The aggressive/abusive incident

So far, we have considered some of the factors that may increase the risk that a child will be subjected to an aggressive attack. However, although a poor parent–child relationship and harsh disciplinary measures may be considered as 'necessary conditions' for the occurrence of an injurious attack, they are clearly not 'sufficient conditions'. A comprehensive understanding of abuse must include a detailed analysis of the nature of abusive *incidents* (Frude, 1980). In order to facilitate such an analysis, a five-stage model of hostile aggressive incidents was formulated as a framework for understanding incidents of physical child abuse (see Figure 1). Briefly, the model can be described in the following way. Hostile aggressive incidents occur when situational events are judged (or 'appraised') in such a way that the person becomes sufficiently angry and, in the absence of effective inhibitory forces, expressed this anger as aggressive behaviour.

Following this model, abusive incidents are seen as more likely to occur when there are frequent situational triggers (e.g. an infant's prolonged crying or aggressive actions by the child), when the parent tends to appraise the child's behaviour as 'bad' (and to attribute the bad behaviour to 'defiance' or 'malevolent intent'), when the parent has a propensity to become extremely angry very quickly, when he or she has few inhibitions against being violent towards the child, and when the form of aggression used is particularly harsh and dangerous. Much of the evidence reviewed earlier in this chapter has a clear relevance to

one or more of the stages in the model. We will now consider further evidence, much of which comes from clinical accounts of specific abuse incidents, to illustrate how these various factors may contribute to an attack on a child.

Situation
In almost all cases of physical child abuse, the attack is triggered by some action of the child. Parents do not attack the passive, sleeping child. Typically, the trigger is prolonged crying or screaming, in the case of babies, or, for older children, some act of defiance or 'naughtiness'. A number of the home observational studies reviewed above found that parents who physically abuse their children do experience their children's behaviour as particularly annoying, and while much of their annoyance reflects inappropriate judgements of the child, there is some evidence to indicate that a number of vulnerable children are judged by objective observers as being disruptive, aggressive, 'strong-willed', or in other ways difficult to manage. At-risk children also tend to be somewhat less compliant than other children and may seek attention by engaging in transgressive behaviours.

Kadushin and Martin (1981) provide a detailed analysis of child abuse incidents. The results of their study with 66 families led the authors to conclude that the behaviour of children and adolescents contributes to, precipitates and, in some cases, 'causes' abuse: 'In every instance, the chain of interactions which finally culminated in physical abuse begins with some behaviour manifested by the child and perceived by the parent as aversive' (op cit., p148). Thomson et al. (1971) also found that most abusive incidents were 'provoked' by the child; they cite crying, wetting, refusing to eat and such acts of naughtiness as lying and stealing as examples of triggers to physical attacks. Similarly, Herrenkohl et al. (1983) studied the records of 328 abusive families, and concluded that physical abuse is invariably a response by the parent to some 'objectionable' behaviour by the child – refusal to comply with requests, fighting, etc. They add that most of the behaviours which appear to trigger an attack are fairly commonplace in the normal course of child-rearing.

Schmitt (1987) also emphasised the fact that innocent child behaviours such as those related to colic, night waking, separation anxiety, normal exploratory behaviour, normal

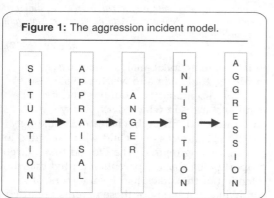

Figure 1: The aggression incident model.

SITUATION → APPRAISAL → ANGER → INHIBITION → AGGRESSION

egativism, and normal poor appetite, can rigger dangerous or even deadly abuse for the hild living in a high-risk family. On the other and, Terr (1970) quoted examples in which an ttack had apparently been precipitated by xtreme acts of naughtiness, including an ncident in which clothes were cut to pieces and ne in which a child defaecated into a laundry asket full of clean clothes. Several other uthors have also provided evidence indicating nat most abuse incidents begin as attempts to ontrol misbehaviours and that the situation scalates when the parent's ability to control the hild is directly challenged – for example by a hild 'deliberately' disobeying a command Peterson et al., 1994; Wolfe et al., 1982).

The presence of a situational trigger is ndicated in aggressive incidents at all levels of eriousness. Thus, in a survey of non-abusing nothers, Frude and Goss (1979) reported that ncidents reported by these mothers as having enerated a high level of anger were always ssociated with some environmental trigger. Jone of the mothers in this survey reported eeling aggressive towards the child 'for no eason'. And at the other end of the severity pectrum, in a study of fatal incidents of abuse, cott (1973) reported that each one of 29 fathers nprisoned for killing his child claimed that the atal incident had been precipitated by an specially annoying behaviour by the child.

There is, then, a great deal of consensus about he importance of specific trigger events in rovoking the abuse incident. If such an event is ndeed a 'necessary condition' for abuse ccurring then it would follow that preventing he trigger from occurring would prevent the buse. However, the event which triggers ggression is often of a type so common, and so rdinary', that it would be unrealistic to magine that such triggers could be avoided or liminated altogether.

Appraisal

he way in which a situation is judged is a major leterminant of its emotional impact. A judgement hat a crying baby is 'screaming deliberately', for xample, will typically generate much more anger han the judgement that the crying indicates that he baby is in pain. Evidence cited earlier in this hapter indicated that abusive parents tend to ppraise their child's behaviour in negative ways. They judge many kinds of behaviour to be 'bad', hey are 'blame oriented', they attribute deliberate nd malevolent intentions to the child, and they

have unrealistic expectations of the capabilities of young children. In addition, they experience many child behaviours as aversive. These tendencies are evident in case reports of specific abuse incidents. Thus one abusive mother told the NSPCC (Baher et al., 1976): 'I couldn't stand to hear a child scream, it went right through me.' Others reported feeling physically nauseous when they saw their child eating messily. One mother, disturbed by her baby's crying during her favourite television soap opera, felt that the child was intent on spoiling her enjoyment of the programme. In an example from another study, a baby's 'look' was given a sinister interpretation: 'He looks at me as if to say 'Just you try and feed me' (Brandon, 1976). Another mother reported: 'When he cried all the time . . . it meant he didn't love me, so I hit him' (Steele and Pollock, 1968).

Anger

Abusive parents tend to appraise situations in a negative and uncharitable way, and this means that they are likely to become more angry with their children than other parents. In addition, many abusive parents are particularly quick-tempered and flare up easily when faced with a difficult or unruly child (Azar, 1986; Reid, 1983). Anger may accumulate over a series of successive incidents, and case evidence indicates that abuse often occurs on an especially difficult day, when a sequence of annoying events has provoked the parent to a highly aroused state. A classic example of such a scenario is provided by Steele and Pollock's (1968) case of 'Larry':

> After losing his job, Larry told his wife; she immediately walked out on him, leaving him alone with the baby. When the baby started to cry, Larry was unable to find the feeding bottle. Looking everywhere, with the cries of the hungry baby becoming louder and louder, Larry became totally frustrated. Finally, unable to satisfy the baby's hunger, his temper exploded and Larry beat the child severely.

The build-up of anger is also affected by a broad range of factors, including extreme tiredness, noise, and the consumption of alcohol, all of which appear to play a critical role in some incidents of abuse.

Inhibition

Anger, even if it is extreme, is not always expressed as overt aggressive behaviour, and most people are able to control their aggressive impulses when they judge that it would be dangerous or inappropriate to act aggressively. External situational elements that may act as powerful inhibitors to aggression include the presence of other people who would be witness to any aggressive act and a target person who is judged as having the power to retaliate strongly. Internal inhibitors include moral attitudes which maintain that physical aggression (for example, against a young child) is wicked.

Thus inhibitions reflect both situational circumstances and the individual's beliefs and values. The relevance of both of these aspects to physical child abuse is illustrated in parents' reports of extreme situations in which they did *not* attack their child. Thus in a study by Frude and Goss (1980) non-abusive mothers were asked to account for the fact that they had not assaulted their child when they had felt their anger to be almost beyond control. Some reported that they had taken the child outside the home, where other people's presence would be likely to have an inhibiting effect, while others brought to mind and then focused on the seriously damaging effects that might result from an attack on the child.

A low level of inhibition against hitting a child dangerously may reflect the attitude that strong discipline is justified and necessary for controlling some children. Such attitudes are sometimes evident in parents' explanations of why they attacked and injured their child. Inhibitions against beating the child may also be lowered by a parent's lack of empathy for the pain that a child will suffer by being beaten.

Because abusive parents frequently use highly aggressive behaviour towards the child they may become desensitised to such action – their inhibitions are likely to be reduced through a process of habituation. The process of escalation has been extensively documented by Patterson, and is also evident in many first-hand reports by parents:

> The first time I hit her it was only a small blow and I cried all the rest of the day. I swore to myself I'd never lift a finger to her again. But it was only a few days after when she drove me mad with her crying and I hit her even harder. It sort of escalated, I hit her a bit harder each time.
>
> (Renvoize, 1978).

Even those parents who do have relatively strong inhibitions against beating their child may lose control over their aggressive impulses when their anger reaches an extreme. Individuals differ in the degree to which they are able to marshal their inhibitions and control their impulses, and in an early review of the characteristics of abusing parents, Parke and Collmer (1975) concluded that one of the most striking and consistent of findings was the general difficulty that such parents had in controlling their aggressive impulses.

Aggression
Abusive parents tend to use dangerous forms of aggression, some of which are modelled on the punishment methods they experienced themselves in childhood (Gelles, 1979). Their aggressive behaviour towards the child may also have been shaped by earlier responses of the child, and the severity of punishment may have escalated over time.

The form of aggression used obviously plays an important part in determining the nature and extent of any injuries sustained by the child. Parents tend to develop general habits with regard to their method of disciplining their children, and in circumstances of extreme anger the habitual method may be used in a more exaggerated form. Those who are used to shouting at their children may scream and yell and those who usually slap the child may slap more severely, and perhaps on a more vulnerable part of the body. Several other factors also help to shape the form of aggression. For example, the aggressive act may be an exaggerated attempt to gain the child's compliance. A pillow may be held against the face of a screaming child to stifle the noise, or a young child who won't eat may be force-fed, with the spoon being pushed into the mouth so harshly and roughly that it is clearly serving as a weapon.

Some abusive actions seem to have a symbolic content. For example, Young (1964) reported the case of a father who rubbed pepper into the genitals of a little girl who had been 'touching herself'. The classic punishment for profanity – washing the child's mouth with soap and water – has a similar symbolic significance, and cases have been reported in which this kind of transgression has been punished by forcibly introducing noxious substances such as chilli sauce and caustic soda into the child's mouth. Other abusive actions are directly retaliatory – the parent matches an aggressive action of the child in form, but with increased severity. Thus a child who tugs at the hair of a sibling may have handfuls of hair pulled out (often with the parent asking: 'How do *you* like it?').

metimes, a parent will make use of anything
hand which could serve as a weapon, and
ch 'opportunism' can explain why children
e sometimes burned with cigarettes or with an
on.

plications for treatment

though it is beyond the scope of this Chapter
review the various approaches to the
eatment and prevention of physical child
use, the analysis presented clearly has many
plications for both types of intervention. Thus
e view of physical abuse as multifactorial and
terogeneous suggests that there may be many
fferent ways in which it can be treated and
evented, and that different forms of
tervention may prove most effective for
fferent families.

The analysis also suggests that many abusive
milies are characterised by chronic difficulties
the parent–child relationship, and this
plies that a resolution of these longer-term
oblems would decrease the risk of an abusive
cident occurring. Several approaches to
erapy have been shown to be useful in
riching the parent–child relationship,
cluding family-based and
gnitive-behavioural therapies. The parent
ight be taught, for example, to monitor their
vel of positive interaction and to increase the
equency with which they encourage and
aise the child.

A parent who has an aberrant view of child
velopment (with unrealistic performance
pectations, for example) may be provided
ith a more reasonable and accurate view of the
rms for child behaviour through an
ducational programme. Discussing children's
haviour with a therapist or with other parents
ould give parents with special problems a
tter insight into their children's behaviour,
d expose them to alternative interpretations
such behaviour. Other parents might also act
useful models when their friendly, close
arenting style reflects a positive and realistic
sponse to children.

The stresses of parenting (which may
timately prove dangerous to the child) may be
duced in a number of ways. One of these is by
lping parents to understand their child better
d to develop skills in handling the 'ordinary
oblems' associated with sleeping and feeding,
r example. Additionally, many abusive
arents have a very low opinion of themselves

as parents, and suitable interventions may
enable them to develop an appropriate pride in
their parenting. Another strategy for reducing
parental stress involves providing practical help
with housing, economic and marital difficulties;
and another focuses on reducing social isolation,
for example by providing drop-in centres and
day-care facilities, and helping with the
establishment and continuation of
parent-and-toddler groups in the community.

Other forms of intervention focus more
specifically on the type of interaction that may
be the immediate precursors to an attack. For
example, various types of intervention may be
used to help parents deal effectively with
disciplinary situations. Parents who find specific
child behaviours highly aversive may be helped
by desensitisation treatment. Professionals, or
other parents, can help to change at-risk
parents' views of what child behaviours are
age-appropriate, 'normal', and excusable and
thus promote a more reasonable categorisation
of children's behaviours as 'good' and 'bad'.
Such interventions should reduce the frequency
of disciplinary encounters. Other intervention
strategies would focus on increasing the
parent's skills in making discipline more
effective, so that such encounters are less harsh,
less prolonged and less likely to escalate to
abuse. Approaches which focus on such goals
are likely to promote consistency in discipline
and to teach specific skills such as the use of
distraction techniques and 'time out'.

Interventions may also attempt to challenge
parents' pro-punishment attitudes and to deal
with the belief that failing to punish a
transgression severely will 'spoil' the child.
Parents may be informed of the disadvantages
and dangers involved in the frequent use of
physical punishment and shown more effective
and less hazardous methods of controlling the
child's behaviour.

Finally, the aggression incident model
suggests that injurious abuse might be
prevented by interventions aimed at changing
the parent's behaviour when there is immediate
danger of abuse. Parents may be taught
'emergency tactics' for use on such occasions.
The model indicates that there are several stages
at which there may be opportunities to break
the progression from the trigger situation to an
aggressive response. At the situation stage the
parent might cope by avoidance (for example,
leaving the room in which the child is
misbehaving) or by controlling the child's

behaviour in some non-abusive manner. At the appraisal stage, the parents might use imagery or self-statements to 'reframe' and thus 'defuse' the situational trigger. Thus parents faced with a screaming baby may be encouraged to repeat a verbal formulation designed to neutralise the situation (for example: 'He is not doing this deliberately; he doesn't understand; all babies behave this way sometimes'). With respect to the anger stage, a number of effective strategies are used to promote self-control, including relaxation, self-distraction, deep breathing, and the use of self-statements designed to help the person maintain control (for example: 'calm down – take it easy – hold on') (Kolko, 1996; Novaco, 1975).

An explosive outburst of aggression may be avoided if the individual has developed strong inhibitions against extreme physical acts. Attempts to strengthen a person's inhibitions may involve identifying dangers associated with extreme aggression (for example, legal sanctions, or the child being taken into care). Factual information about the dangers of particular forms of aggression (for example, the fact that severely shaking the child may produce diffuse brain damage or a whiplash injury) will sometimes be sufficient to inhibit a parent's use of such behaviour. At-risk parents can also be taught to replace self-statements which attempt to justify the use of harsh aggression towards the child (such as 'he deserves this' or 'he has asked for it') with statements that will foster a more charitable appraisal (e.g. 'he doesn't mean anything by it'), or reduce anger (e.g. 'I ought to just calm down') or strengthen inhibition (e.g. 'What would my mother say'; 'He's just a fragile baby, I must not damage him'). If such strategies are developed and rehearsed in a therapeutic context they may prove effective even when the immediate danger of abuse is very high. There is evidence that many parents use such strategies, to good effect, when they feel that they pose a threat to their child (Frude and Goss, 1979).

Conclusions

The probability that a parent will abuse his or her child increases substantially if the relationship between the parent and child is poor. A poor relationship is likely to stem partly from parent characteristics, partly from characteristics of the child and partly from specific difficulties in the relationship which develops between parent and child. These difficulties give rise to disciplinary problems, with frequent clashes which tend to escalate in severity. The level of aggression tends to escalate and may eventually result in an attack which causes serious injury to the child.

Hostile verbal and physical interactions tend to occur frequently in the day-to-day interactions between abusive parents and their children. Abusive parents' aggressive behaviour towards their children can be seen as a response to situational triggers. The situation-response link is mediated by negative appraisals, high anger and low inhibitions against the use of strong physical methods of discipline and control.

Although research has revealed many statistically significant differences between groups of abusive and non-abusive families, no characteristic reliably separates families in which a child has been injured from those in which no child has ever been injured. Thus abusive parents and abused children should not be considered 'a breed apart' from non-abusive parents and non-abused children (Main and Goldwyn, 1984). The psychological processes that lead to extreme parental assaults are not qualitatively different from those which lead most parents to become angry with and at least shout at their children. Belsky (1987) remarked that 'child abuse and neglect should not be regarded as distinct entities but rather as cases of parenting gone awry which are lawfully related to relationship processes in non-dysfunctional families'. Straus (1983) also emphasised that the same factors are involved in child abuse and 'ordinary physical punishment' – 'violence is violence, irrespective of the severity of the attack' (op cit., p231).

Thus it appears reasonable to regard families as ranged along a continuum of abuse risk, with certain families (including those in which abuse has previously occurred) close to the 'dangerous' extreme. Thus the relevance of the analysis presented in this chapter is not confined to 'high-risk' families. It is important to understand everyday 'sub-abusive' violence against children, not only because such violence may escalate to injurious child abuse, but also because lower levels of violence towards children may result, directly and indirectly, in pernicious and long-lasting psychological effects (Graziano, 1994).

References

ton, R. G. and During, S. (1990) The
Treatment of Aggressive Parents: An Outline
of a Group Treatment Program. *Canada's
Mental Health*. 38: 2–6.

zar, S., Robinson, D., Hekimian, E. and
Twentyman, C. T. (1984) Unrealistic
Expectations and Problem-solving Ability in
Maltreating and Comparison Mothers. *Journal
of Consulting and Clinical Psychology*. 52: 687–91.

zar, S. T. (1986) A Framework for
Understanding Child Maltreatment: An
Integration of Cognitive Behavioural and
Developmental Perspectives. Special Issue:
Family Violence: Child Abuse and Wife
Assault. *Canadian Journal of Behavioural Science*.
18: 340–55.

her, E., Hyman, C., Jones, C., Jones R., Kerr,
A. and Mitchell, R. (1976) *At Risk: An Account
of the Work of the Battered Child Research
Department, NSPCC*. London: Routledge and
Kegan Paul.

lsky, J. (1987) Child Maltreatment and the
Emergent Family System. Paper presented at
Conference of the Society for Reproductive
and Infant Psychology, Leicester, March.

lsky, J. (1993) Etiology of Child Maltreatment:
A Developmental-ecological Analysis.
Psychological Bulletin. 114: 413–34.

lsky, J. and Isabella, R. A. (1985) Marital and
Parent Child Relationships in Family of
Origin and Marital Change Following the
Birth of a Baby: A Retrospective Analysis.
Child Development. 56: 361–75.

rkowitz, L. (1962) *Aggression: A Social
Psychological Analysis*. New York:
McGraw-Hill.

ottoms, B. L. and Davis, S. L. (1997) The
Creation of Satanic Ritual Abuse. *Journal of
Social and Clinical Psychology*. 16: 112–32.

ousha, D. M. and Twentyman, C. T. (1984)
Mother-child Interactional Style in Abuse,
Neglect and Control Groups: Naturalistic
Observations in the Home. *Journal of Abnormal
Psychology*. 93: 106–14.

owdry, C. (1990) Toward a Treatment-relevant
Typology of Child Abuse Families. *Child
Welfare*. 69: 333–40.

radley, E. J. and Peters, R. D. (1991) Physically
Abusive and Non-abusive Mothers'
Perceptions of Parenting and Child Behavior.
American Journal of Orthopsychiatry. 61: 455–60.

randon, S. (1976) Physical Violence in the
Family: An Overview. In Borland, M. (Ed.),
Violence in the Family. Manchester: Manchester
University Press.

Bugental, D. B., Blue, J. and Cruzcosa, M. (1989)
Perceived Control Over Caregiving
Outcomes: Implications for Child Abuse.
Developmental Psychology. 25: 532–9.

Burgess, R. and Richardson, R. (1984) Coercive
Interpersonal Contingencies as a Determinant
of Child Maltreatment. In Dangel, R. F. and
Polster, R. A. (Eds.) *Parent Training:
Foundations of Research and Practice*. New York:
Guilford Press.

Burgess, R. L. and Conger, R. D (1977) Family
Interaction Patterns Related to Child Abuse
and Neglect: Some Preliminary Findings.
Child Abuse and Neglect. 1: 269–77.

Burgess, R. L. and Conger, R. D. (1978) Family
Interaction in Abusive, Neglectful and
Normal Families. *Child Development*. 49:
1163–73.

Call, J. D. (1984) Child Abuse and Neglect in
Infancy: Sources of Hostility Within the
Parent-infant Dyad and Disorders of
Attachment in Infancy. *Child Abuse and
Neglect*. 8: 185–202.

Chilamkurti, C. and Milner, J .S. (1993)
Perceptions and Evaluations of Child
Transgressions and Disciplinary Techniques
in High and Low Risk Mothers and Their
Children. *Child Development*. 64: 1801–14.

Crockenberg, S. (1987) Predictors and Correlates
of Anger Toward and Punitive Control of
Toddlers by Adolescent Mothers. *Child
Development*. 58: 964–75.

Daro, D. and Gelles, R. J. (1992) Public Attitudes
and Behaviours With Respect to Child Abuse
Prevention. *Journal of Interpersonal Violence*. 7:
517–31.

Diaz, R., Neal, C. and Vachio, A. (1991)
Maternal Teaching in the Zone of Proximal
Development: A Comparison of Low and
High Risk Dyads. *Merrill-Palmer Quarterly*. 37:
83–107.

DiLalla, D. L. and Crittenden, P. M. (1990)
Dimensions of Maltreated Children's Home
Behaviour: A Factor Analytic Approach.
Infant Behaviour and Development. 13: 439–60.

Dolz, L., Cerezo, M. A. and Milner, J. S. (1997)
Mother-child Interactional Patterns in High
and Low Risk Mothers. *Child Abuse and
Neglect*. 21: 1149–58.

Donald, T. and Jureidini, J. (1996) Munchausen
Syndrome by Proxy: Child Abuse in the
Medical System. *Archives of Paediatric and
Adolescent Medicine*. 150: 753–8.

Fontana, V.J. and Robison, E. (1984) Observing Child Abuse. *Journal of Paediatrics*. 105: 655–60.

Forehand, R. and Long, N. (1996) *Parenting the Strong-willed Child*. Chicago, IL: Contemporary Books.

Friedrich, W.N. and Boriskin, J.A. (1976) The Role of the Child in Abuse. *American Journal of Orthopsychiatry*. 46: 58–90.

Frodi, A.M. and Lamb. M.E. (1980) Child Abusers' responses to Infant Smiles and Cries. *Child Development*. 51: 23–41.

Frude, N.J. (1980) Child Abuse as Aggression. In Frude, N. (Ed.) *Psychological Approaches to Child Abuse*, London: Batsford.

Frude, N.J. (1994) Marital Violence: An Interactional Perspective. In: Archer, J. (Ed.) *Male Violence*. London: Routledge.

Frude, N.J. (1996) Ritual Abuse: Conceptions and Reality. *Clinical Child Psychology and Psychiatry*. 1. 59–77.

Frude, N.J. and Goss, A. (1979) Parental Anger: A general Population Survey. *Child Abuse and Neglect*. 3: 331–3.

Gaensbauer, T.J., Mrazek, D.A. and Harmon, R.J. (1980) Emotional Expression in Abused and Neglected Infants. In Frude, N.J. (Ed.) *Psychological Approaches to Child Abuse*. London: Batsford.

Gelles, R.J. (1979) *Family Violence*. Beverly Hills, CA: Sage.

George, C. and Main, M. (1979) Social Interactions of Young Abused Children: Approach, Avoidance and Aggression. *Child Development*. 50: 306–18.

Golub, J.S., Espinosa, M., Damon, L. and Card, J. (1987) A Videotape Education Program for Abusive Parents. *Child Abuse and Neglect*. 11: 255–65.

Goodwin, J.M. (1993) Sadistic Abuse: Definition, Recognition, and Treatment. *Dissociation: Progress in the Dissociative Disorders*. 6: 181–7.

Graziano, A.M. (1994) Why we Should Study Subabusive Violence Against Children. *Journal of Interpersonal Violence*. 9: 412–9.

Heinicke, C.M. (1984) The Role of Pre-birth Parent Characteristics in Early Family Development. *Child Abuse and Neglect*. 8: 169–81.

Hemenway, D., Solnick, S. and Carter, J. (1994) Child-rearing Violence. *Child Abuse and Neglect*. 18: 1011–20.

Herrenkohl, E.C. and Herrenkohl, R. (1979) A Comparison of Abused Children and Their Non-abused Siblings. *Journal of the Academy of Child Psychiatry*. 18: 26–9.

Herrenkohl, R. and Herrenkohl, E.C. and Egol B.P. (1983) Circumstances Surrounding the Occurrence of Child Maltreatment. *Journal of Consulting and Clinical Psychology*. 51: 424–31

Johnston, C. and Patenaude, R. (1994) Parent Attributions of Inattentive-overactive and Oppositional-defiant Child Behaviours. *Cognitive Therapy and Research*. 18: 261–75.

Kadushin, A. and Martin, J.A. (1981) *Child Abuse: An Interactional Event*. New York: Columbia University Press.

Kelley, M.L., Grace, N. and Elliott, S.N. (1990) Acceptability of Positive and Punitive Discipline Methods: Comparisons Among Abusive, Potentially Abusive, and Non-abusive Parents. *Child Abuse and Neglect*. 14: 219–26.

Kelly, J.A. (1983) *Treating Child-abusive Families Intervention based on Skills-training Principles*. New York: Plenum.

Kinard, E.M. (1995) Mother and Teacher Assessments of Behaviour Problems in Abused Children. *Journal of the American Academy of Child and Adolescent Psychiatry*. 34 1043–53.

Kinard, E.M. (1996) Social Support, Competence, and Depression in Mothers of Abused Children. *American Journal of Orthopsychiatry*. 66: 449–62.

Knutson, J.F. and Selner, M.B. (1994) Punitive Childhood Experiences Reported by Young Adults Over a 10-Year Period. *Child Abuse and Neglect*. 18: 155–66.

Kolko, D.J. (1996) Clinical Monitoring of Treatment Course in Child Physical Abuse: Psychometric Characteristics and Treatment Comparisons. *Child Abuse and Neglect*. 20: 23–43.

La Fontaine J.S. (1997) *Speak of the Devil: Tales o Satanic Abuse in Contemporary England*. Cambridge: Cambridge University Press.

Lesnick-Oberstein, M, Koers, A.J. and Cohen, L (1995) Parental Hostility and its Sources in Psychologically Abusive Mothers: A Test of the Three-factor Theory. *Child Abuse and Neglect*. 19: 33–49.

Letourneau, C. (1981) Empathy and Stress: How They Affect Parental Aggression. *Social Work* 26: 383–9.

Loader, P. and Kelly, C. (1996) Munchausen Syndrome by Proxy: A Narrative Approach t(Explanation. *Clinical Child Psychology and Psychiatry*. 1: 353–63.

Main, M. and Goldwyn, R. (1984) Predicting Rejection of her Infant From Mother's

Representation of Her Own Experience: Implications for the Abused-Abusing Intergenerational Cycle. *Child Abuse and Neglect.* 8: 203–17.

Main, M. and Weston, D. (1982) Avoidance of the Attachment Figure in Infancy. In Parkes, C.M. and Stevenson-Hinde, J. (Eds.) *The Place of Attachment in Human Behaviour.* New York: Basic Books.

Majonis, J. (1991) Discipline and Socialization of Children in Abusive and Non-abusive Families. *Child and Adolescent Social Work Journal.* 8: 203–24.

Martin, H.P. and Beezley, P. (1977) Behavioural Observation of Abused Children. *Developmental Medicine and Child Neurology.* 19: 373–87.

McKenry, P. C., Kotch, J. B. and Browne, D. H. (1991) Correlates of Dysfunctional Parental Attitudes Amongst Low-income Adolescent Mothers. *Journal of Adolescent Research.* 6: 212–34.

Miller, K.L. (1980) *Principles of Everyday Behaviour Analysis,* (2nd edn.) Monterey, CA: Brooks/Cole.

Milner, J.S. (1994) Assessing Physical Child Abuse Risk: The Child Abuse Potential Inventory. *Clinical Psychology Review.* 14: 547–83.

Milner, J.S. and Foody, R. (1994) The Impact of Mitigating Information on Attributions for Positive and Negative Child Behaviour by Adults at Low and High Risk for Child-abusive Behaviour. *Journal of Social and Clinical Psychology.* 13: 335–51.

Milner, J.S., Halsey, L.B. and Fultz, J. (1995) Empathic Responsiveness and Affective Reactivity to Infant Stimuli in High and Low Risk for Physical Child Abuse Mothers. *Child Abuse and Neglect.* 19: 767–80.

Neale, B., Bools, C. and Meadow, R. (1991) Problems in the Assessment and Management of Munchausen Syndrome by Proxy Abuse. *Children and Society.* 5: 324–33.

Nobes, G. and Smith, M. (1997) Physical Punishment of Children in Two Parent Families. *Clinical Child Psychology and Psychiatry.* 2: 271–82.

Novaco, R. (1975) *Anger Control: The Development and Evaluation of an Experimental Treatment.* Lexington, MA: D.C. Heath/Solidus/Lexington Books.

Oates, R.K. and Bross, D.C. (1995) What Have We Learned About Treating Child Physical Abuse? A Literature Review of the Last Decade. *Child Abuse and Neglect.* 19, 463–73.

Oldershaw, L., Walters, G.C. and Hall, D.K. (1989) A Behavioural Approach to the Classification of Different Types of Physically Abusive Mothers. *Merrill-Palmer-Quarterly.* 35: 255–79.

Parke, R.D. and Collmer, C.W. (1975) Child Abuse: An Interdisciplinary Analysis. In Hetherington, E.M. (Ed.), *Review of Child Research and Development, Volume 5.* Chicago: University of Chicago Press.

Patterson, G.R. (1982) *Coercive Family Process.* Eugene, OR: Castalia.

Perry, M.A. and Doran, L.D. (1983) Developmental and Behavioural Characteristics of the Physically Abused Child. *Journal of Clinical Child Psychology.* 12: 32–4.

Peterson, L., Ewigman, B. and Vandiver, T. (1994) Role of Parental Anger in Low-income Women: Discipline Strategy, Perceptions of Behaviour Problems, and the Need for Control. Special Issue: Impact of Poverty on Children, Youth, and Families. *Journal of Clinical Child Psychology.* 23: 435–43.

Reid, J.B. (1983) *Final Report: Child Abuse: Developmental Factors and Treatment.* Grant No. 7 ROI MH37938, NIMH, USPHS.

Reid, J.B. (1986) Social Interactional Patterns in Families of Abused and Non-abused Children. In Zahn-Waxler, C., Cummings, E.M. and Lanotti R. (Eds.) *Altruism and Aggression: Biological and Social Origins.* Cambridge: Cambridge University Press.

Reid, J.B. (Ed.) (1978) *A Social Learning Approach to Family Intervention, Volume 11: Observation in Home Settings.* Eugene, OR: Castalia.

Reid, J.B., Patterson, G.R. and Loeber, R. (1981) The Abused Child: Victim, Instigator, or Innocent Bystander? *Nebraska Symposium on Motivation.* 29: 47–68.

Renvoize, J. (1978) *Web of Violence.* London: Routledge and Kegan Paul.

Rosenberg, M.S. and Repucci, N.D. (1983) Abusive Mothers: Perceptions of their own and their Children's Behaviour. *Journal of Consulting and Clinical Psychology.* 51: 674–82.

Schaffer, H.R. (1977) *Studies in Mother-infant Interaction.* London: Academic Press.

Schellenbach, C.J. and Guerney, L.F. (1987) Identification of Adolescent Abuse and Future Intervention Prospects. *Journal of Adolescence.* 10: 1–12.

Schellenbach, C. J., Whitman, T. L. and Borkowski, J. G. (1992) Toward an Integrative Model of Adolescent Parenting. *Human Development.* 35: 81–99.

Schilling, R.F. and Schinke, S.P. (1984) Maltreatment and Mental Retardation. In Berg, J.M. (Ed.) *Perspective and Progress in Mental Retardation, Volume I.* Baltimore, MD: University Park Press.

Schindler, F. and Arkowitz, H. (1986) The Assessment of Mother-child Interactions in Physically Abusive and Non-abusive Families. *Journal of Family Violence.* 1: 247–57.

Schinke, S.P., Schilling, R.F., Barth, R.P., Gilchrist, L.D. and Maxwell, J.S. (1986) Stress-management Intervention to Prevent Family Violence. *Journal of Family Violence.* 1: 13–26.

Schmitt, B.D. (1987) Seven Deadly Sins of Childhood: Advising Parents About Difficult Developmental Phases. Special Issue: Child Abuse and Neglect. *Child Abuse and Neglect.* 11: 421–32.

Scott, P.D. (1973) Parents who Kill their Children. *Medicine, Science and the Law.* 13: 12–6.

Scott, W.O.N., Baer, G., Christoff, K. and Kelly, J.A. (1982) Skills Training for a Child Abusive Parent: A Controlled Case Study. Unpublished manuscript, Mississippi Medical Center.

Sinason, V. (Ed.) (1994) *Treating Survivors of Satanic Abuse.* London: Routledge.

Sroufe, L.A. (1983) Infant Caregiver Attachment and Patterns of Adaptation in Preschool: The Roots of Maladaptation and Competence. In Perlmutter, M. (Ed.) *Minnesota Symposium on Child Psychology, Volume 16.* Hillsdale, NJ: Lawrence Erlbaum Associates.

Stafford, A. and Bayer, C.L. (1993) *Interaction Between Parents and Children.* Newbury Park, CA: Sage.

Starr, R.H. (1980) Towards Prevention of Child Abuse. In Harel, S. (Ed.) *The At-risk Infant.* Amsterdam: Excerpta Medica.

Starr, R.H., Dietrich, K.N., Fischoff, J., Ceresnie, S. and Zweier, D. (1984) The Contribution of Handicapping Conditions to Child Abuse. *Topics in Early Childhood and Special Education.* 4: 55–69.

Steele, B.B. and Pollock, D. (1968) A Psychiatric Study of Parents Who Abuse Small Children. In Kempe, C.H. and Helfer, R.E. (Eds.) *The Battered Child.* Chicago: Chicago University Press.

Stern, S.B. and Azar, S.T. (1998) Integrating Cognitive Strategies Into Behavioural Treatment for Abusive Parents and Families With Aggressive Adolescents. *Clinical Child Psychology and Psychiatry.* 3: 387–403.

Straus, M.A. (1980) Social Stress and Marital Violence in a National Sample of American Families. In Wright, F., Bain, C. and Rieber R.W. (Eds.) *Forensic Psychology and Psychiatry. Annals of the New York Academy of Science.* New York: New York Academy of Science.

Straus, M.A. (1983) Ordinary Violence, Child Abuse and Wife Beating: What do They Have in Common? In Finkelhor, D., Gelles, R.J., Hotaling, G.T. and Straus, M.A. (Eds.) *The Dark Side of the Family.* Beverly Hills, CA: Sage.

Straus, M.A. and Kantor, G.K. (1994) Corporal Punishment of Adolescents by Parents: A Risk Factor in the Epidemiology of Depression, Suicide, Alcohol Abuse, Child Abuse, and Wife Beating. *Adolescence.* 29: 543–61.

Terr. L. (1970) A family Study of Child Abuse. *American Journal of Psychiatry.* 127: 125–31.

Thomas, A., Chess, S. and Birch, H.G. (1970) The Origin of Personality. *Scientific American.* 223: 102–9.

Thomson, E.M., Paget, N.W., Bates, D.W., Mesch, M. and Putnam, T.l. (1971) *Child Abuse: A Community Challenge.* New York: Henry Stewart and Children's Aid and Society for the Prevention of Cruelty to Children.

Trickett, P.K. and Kuczynski, L. (1986) Children's Misbehaviours and Parental Discipline Strategies in Abusive and Non-abusive Families. *Developmental Psychology.* 22: 115–23.

Trickett, P.K. and Susman, E.J. (1988) Parental Perceptions of Child-Rearing Practices in Physically Abusive and Non-abusive Families. *Developmental Psychology.* 24: 270–6.

Twentyman, C.T. and Plotkin, R.C. (1982) Unrealistic Expectations of Parents Who Maltreat Their Children: An Educational Deficit That Pertains to Child Development. *Journal of Clinical Psychology.* 38: 497–503.

Wahler, R.G. and Dumas, J. (1984) Changing the Observational Coding Styles of Insular and Non-insular Mothers: A Step Towards Maintenance of Parent Training Effects. In Dangel, R.F. and Polster, R.A. (Eds.) *Parent Training: Foundations of Research and Practice.* New York: Guilford Press.

Whipple, E.E. and Richey, C.A. (1997) Crossing the Line From Physical Discipline to Child Abuse: How Much is Too Much? *Child Abuse and Neglect.* 21: 431–44.

Whiteman, M., Fanshel, D. and Grundy, J.F. (1987) Cognitive-behavioural Interventions

Aimed at Anger of Parents at Risk of Child Abuse. *Social Work*. 32: 469–74.

Wolfe, D.A., Fairbank, J.A., Kelly, J.A. and Bradlyn, A.S. (1983) Child Abusive Parents' Physiological Responses to Stressful and Non-stressful Behaviour in Children. *Behavioural Assessment*. 5: 363–71.

Wolfe, D.A., St Lawrence, J., Graves, K., Brehony, K., Bradlyn, D. and Kelly. J.A. (1982) Intensive Behavioural Parent Training for a Child Abusive Mother. *Behaviour Therapy*. 13: 438–51.

Wood-Shuman, S. and Cone, J.W. (1986) Differences in Abusive, At-risk for Abuse, and Control Mothers' Descriptions of Normal Child Behaviour. *Child Abuse and Neglect*. 10: 397–405.

Young, L. (1964) *Wednesday's Child: A Study of Child Neglect and Abuse*, New York: McGraw-Hill.

Chapter Twelve

A Framework for Assessing Neglect

Bill Stone

Introduction

It might be said that child neglect is the litmus test for the new Assessment Framework (DoH, 2000). In other words, the extent to which the Assessment Framework enables and empowers child care professionals to get to grips with the rising tide of child neglect gives a good indication as to the success or otherwise of the whole ambitious enterprise. Back in 1988 previous Government Guidance on Comprehensive Assessments recognised the difficulties:

> Neglect rarely comes to the attention of social workers through a precipitating incident. Social workers often have lengthy involvements with chronically neglecting parents but find it difficult to make judgments about the standards of parental care and the effect these can have on the child's safety and development. The neglected child needs the same structured and rigorous approach to assessment and treatment as any other abused child.
>
> (DoH 1988, p7–8).

However, one of the things that has become apparent since this guidance was published is that the problems of emotional abuse and neglect demand a rather different response from the narrow, incident-based, forensic approach embodied in the 'Orange Book'.

Child welfare professionals have been struggling for years to develop an approach to assessment which does justice to the multi-dimensional and long term nature of child neglect (see, for example Minty and Pattinson, 1994; Stone, 1998). They have found the daily bombardment of incident-driven cases a distraction from the possibly more serious and certainly more worrying cases of neglect which have a tendency to remain at the bottom of their pile of 'cases pending assessment'. As is often the case, the urgent is given priority over the important and, in the absence of a precipitating crisis, our response to neglected children often amounts to little more than worried concern. The 'neglect of neglect' within the child protection arena has been so often commented upon that it has almost become a cliché yet, the fact remains that the way in which child

protection procedures have been implemented has made it difficult to pay attention to the needs of neglected children. In a frantically busy access and assessment team where the rule of thumb at the duty desk is: 'If there's blood on the carpet we'll do a visit!' (as part of a Section 47 investigation) – what hope for neglected children?

It is nevertheless true that child neglect, as a category of child maltreatment, has remained a very significant problem. Department of Health analyses of Child Protection Register statistics consistently show neglect as the largest single category of abuse. When compared with the other main categories of abuse (physical abuse, sexual abuse and emotional abuse), neglect amounts to between 30 per cent and 40 per cent nationwide – and this percentage has been steadily rising since the mid-1990s (DoH, 2000b). Bearing in mind the fact that these Child Protection Register figures represent the most serious cases where children have been assessed as being at risk of serious harm, the problem of child neglect is demonstrably a major challenge for child protection agencies. However, when the focus is broadened out to include children in need as the refocusing debate has encouraged us to do (DoH, 1995; Jones and O'Loughlin, Chapter 8), the extent of the problem of child neglect becomes massively greater.

The implementation of the Assessment Framework therefore represents an exciting opportunity for practitioners working in the field of child neglect. It promises a new, holistic needs-led approach which moves on from the deficiencies of previous models. In relation to possible neglect it offers a clear structure for assessing the needs of children and parents' and carers' abilities to meet those needs within a particular social and environmental context. Dubowitz et al. (1993) proposed a broad conceptual definition of neglect in the following terms: 'Child neglect occurs when a basic need of a child is not met, regardless of cause(s)'. If this definition is accepted then a framework for assessment which majors on children's needs, parenting capacity and the social and environmental context promises to be an invaluable tool for practice.

In this chapter the Assessment Framework will be subjected to a critical analysis specifically as it relates to child neglect to see whether this promise has been achieved.

A conceptual framework for neglect

The new Working Together (DoH, 1999) and the Assessment Framework (DoH, 2000) represent a paradigm shift in conceptualising child welfare. Jenny Gray, who has lead responsibility at the Department of Health for the implementation of the Assessment Framework, has described the new approach as requiring a 'sea change' in thinking. The challenge of the Assessment Framework, both at a conceptual and a practice level, should therefore not be underestimated. With regard specifically to child neglect there has been a marked absence of theorising and research (Stone, 1998) and practice has been developed in an anecdotal, ad hoc fashion. In the absence of clear thinking and cogent analysis practitioners rely on their gut instincts: child neglect is defined as 'enough is enough!' Such intuitive responses, whilst not without some value, are not sufficiently robust and credible to serve as a foundation for professional practice. The field of child neglect undoubtedly stands in need of **evidence based** research and practice knowledge. Any conceptual map, therefore, which offers a way through the daunting complexities of the subject is particularly welcome.

One of the primary claims made by the Assessment Framework is that it should lead to **child centred** assessments. This is a key criterion in relation to child neglect. One of the big challenges in assessing families where there are concerns around child neglect is that the carers are frequently very needy themselves and may monopolise the assessor's attention to the detriment of the child. Parents who are preoccupied with their own unmet needs may be psychologically unavailable to their own children and this, in some cases, is the underlying dynamic in child neglect (Polanski, 1981). The struggle to maintain a focus on the child and the child's needs is therefore of critical importance in neglect. The Assessment Framework, by placing the child at the centre of the triangle, should help to remind practitioners of the Children Act principle that the child's interest is the paramount consideration.

Another key conceptual theme in the Assessment Framework is that assessments should be **ecological** in their approach. This ecological approach has much to commend it to professionals working with neglect because their daily practice constantly reminds them that child neglect is a social problem as well as a problem for individual families. There is a strong association between neglect (especially low level neglect) and socio-economic deprivation. Neglected children are often children whose parents are struggling to cope on inadequate incomes, in substandard housing, on sink estates, where the schools are vandalised and the teachers demoralised. Such children are often being neglected as much by official agencies as by hard-pressed parents (Parton, 1995). Child care professionals know from experience that the quality of social and family support can make the difference between a child's needs being met or not. It is important therefore when conducting assessments to do justice to these other dimensions rather than just concentrating on the psychological dynamics within a particular family. The Assessment Framework, by providing the domain 'Family and Environmental Factors', signals the importance of these wider, social factors and encourages assessors to take them into account.

Dubowitz (1999) argues for an ecological approach to child neglect in the face of the complexity and interconnectedness of human behaviour. He states:

> A systems approach helps clarify the complexity we face in understanding the interplay of biological, psychological, social and cultural forces in neglect. An ecologically grounded systems approach helps us discover connections that might otherwise remain invisible.
>
> (p4).

In an exploratory study of child neglect focusing on practitioners' perspectives, I found that neglect is a complex and multi-faceted phenomenon which cannot easily be defined. Out of 35 different factors identified by practitioners as being possibly significant in defining neglect, the mean score for the number of factors reported as being significant per individual case in the sample was 18.5 (Stone, 1998). This means that any assessment of a family where there are concerns around neglect needs to take into account this multiplicity of factors. A simple, one-dimensional assessment will not be able to adequately represent the **multi-factoral nature** of neglect. From this point of view the Assessment Framework, derived as it is from ecological thinking, may help assessors to get a handle on the complexity of neglect.

Dalgleish in Chapter 5 identified that the framework is very broad in focus and this is a potential strength when applied to neglect. Its ecological approach enables the insights of sociology as well as those of psychology and medical science to be incorporated into an integrated, holistic assessment. The triangle is easily understood as a diagrammatic representation of this approach to assessment and, in this respect, the Assessment Framework as a conceptual map is very helpful and offers the possibility of significantly enhancing our understanding of child neglect.

The Assessment Framework assumes a working knowledge of normal **child development** to be used as a benchmark against which to measure concerns about a child's welfare. Because of the ill defined nature of neglect and the associated dangers of prejudice and subjectivity, this basic understanding of child development is vitally important where there are allegations of neglect. Without some awareness of developmental milestones and appropriate expectations for children at various ages and stages of development, the assessor will be hard put to substantiate neglect. Similarly, knowledge of child development is critical to any assessment of a child's needs as those needs change according to the child's age and maturity (Daniel, Wassell and Gilligan, 1999).

Another associated area of knowledge which assessors require in order to make sense of what is going on in families where children are being neglected is **attachment theory**. Although attachment theory is not enunciated as one of the underpinning principles it is frequently referred to in the pack accompanying the framework (DoH, NSPCC and The University of Sheffield, 2000). A working knowledge of the difference between secure and insecure attachment can be very helpful in understanding neglectful relationships between children and care givers. The observational skills that are central in analysing the character and quality of attachment relationships can play a very useful role in assessments where neglect is an issue (Tanner and Turney, 2000). At the very least a basic understanding of the concept of attachment should underline for practitioners the importance of paying close attention to parent-child relationships when conducting

assessments of potential child neglect. These issues are explored further by David Howe in Chapter 21.

The Orange Book has been widely criticised for promoting a style of assessment which effectively disempowered service users by its narrow, forensic approach. Parents who were being investigated following allegations of child abuse felt that they were not listened to (Cleaver and Freeman, 1995). The Assessment Framework, by contrast, claims to **build on strengths** as well as identify difficulties and thus seeks to promote genuine **partnership practice**. The Assessment Framework does, on the face of it, appear to allow more room for respectful consultation with parents and carers. It is less prescriptive and interrogatory and acknowledges that the subjects of assessment are themselves experts in their own lives. King (2000) states:

> If the guidance is followed, children and families will be participants in an assessment process they can understand and be more ready to commit to, and which will be conducted in a therapeutic way.

Although the Framework and accompanying guidance and research (Ryan, 2000) emphasises the importance of **engaging men** in the assessment process, this is a particularly difficult and contentious matter with regard to neglect. Turney (2000) explored the gendered nature of care and implications for our understanding of its absence, neglect. She states:

> The feminising of neglect readily leads to a concentration on the role of mothers and a corresponding downplay of the role of men within neglecting families. (p54).

It is too easy for practitioners to either collude with this focus on mothers or simply to assume that any male presence in the household will be at best marginal and at worst dangerous to children. In this respect the Assessment Framework can only point out the pitfalls and signpost good practice.

There is guidance in the Assessment Framework on working with black children and families but a gap with respect to other ethnic groups. The concept of cultural competence is useful here and has been helpfully applied to neglect by Korbin and Spilsbury (1999). Similarly the Assessment Framework has little to say about children with a disability (see Chapter 10 by Kennedy and Wonnacott). Genuinely **inclusive practice**, in these and other reas, will need to be supported by ongoing raining and supervision if the Assessment ramework is to live up to its stated principle of nsuring equality of opportunity.

The Assessment Framework emphasises the mportance of **making professional judgements** nd this is crucial in assessing neglect because, t the end of the day, assessing neglect is about orming a judgement about 'good enough care'.)ne of the worries about any framework for ssessment is that it will be used by ard-pressed practitioners as a short cut to a lecision which has not been properly thought hrough and which is not substantiated by the vidence. Because neglect is, almost inevitably, a oosely defined category indicative of concerns bout child care, it needs to be approached in a udicious, measured way. An allegation of reglect is not like physical abuse, which leaves a ruise or a disclosure of sexual abuse. Neglect is problematic because it is about an absence of are rather than deliberate or malicious naltreatment. Neglect is often demonstrated only in retrospect by its consequences in the levelopment of the children who have experienced it.

Building a case for neglect demands a core ssessment of the child and family's circumstances. This assessment needs to include he **time dimension**, both in terms of a proper nistory or chronology of the past as well as a projection into the future. Children's needs are not static. They follow a certain trajectory and one of the most intellectually challenging aspects of forming a professional judgement depends on he ability to hypothesise about future outcomes. With regard to the family history there are many neglecting families that have been known to nany different agencies over a lengthy period of time, 'Paul' in Islington being a classic example The Bridge Consultancy, 1995). All too often assessments (and this is almost bound to be the case for initial assessments) simply attempt to provide a snapshot of need at one particular point in time. This is likely to be counter productive for cases of chronic neglect. Assessments of neglecting families are likely to produce plans of intervention which are naïve and ineffective unless the family history is given due weight. The famous 'rule of optimism' has not sunk without trace – it is still alive and well and offering great comfort to professionals working with neglecting families!

Finally, in this section, it must be noted that the concept of **risk** would appear to have been completely expunged from the Assessment Framework. Presumably somebody has decided that risk with all its associations is simply incompatible with the whole idea of needs-led assessments and therefore the concept is ignored or reconstructed as 'in need of protection' (Stone, 2000). The unpalatable reality however is that, whatever words are used, a significant number of children are in real danger for their lives. The number of children who die each year as a result of abuse and neglect is hotly contested. However, the NSPCC regularly quote the figure of fifty children per year in their publicity and they reckon that this is a serious underestimate of the true figure. Although it is rare (but not unknown) for a child to die solely as a result of neglect, chronic neglect is almost always a major concern in fatal abuse. Whilst it would be misleading to argue that these children are particularly representative of children who are at risk of significant harm (still less children identified as being in need) it would be foolish to imagine that child welfare professionals should lower their guard.

There is a wealth of learning, painfully accrued, from many tragic child deaths in situations of serious abuse and chronic neglect, which we cannot afford to ignore when conducting assessments (Reder and Duncan, 1999). The case of Victoria Climbie is just one recent and particularly pertinent example. There is quite clearly a difference, conceptually and practically, between risk assessment and need-led assessment but to completely jettison all notions of risk and dangerousness seems misguided in this context.

An operational framework for neglect

In this section a number of operational issues will be considered which arise out of the implementation of the Assessment Framework. These issues are discussed in other chapters in this book, particularly by Martin Calder in Chapter 2, so the discussion here is restricted to the implications for child neglect.

One of the most fundamental aspects of the Assessment Framework is that it promises a coherent approach to promoting the welfare of children while safeguarding them from harm. It is designed to enable a comprehensive assessment of a child's family circumstances whether that child is thought to be at risk of harm or in need of support and help. The Assessment Framework, in line with the new

Working Together, assumes that all children in need will be offered an assessment (an initial assessment at least) of a generic nature. This has got to be a positive development in terms of responding to neglect. I have talked to many health visitors, social workers and teachers who have children within their professional remit who show signs of possible neglect. They worry about these children and they may even talk about them with colleagues or discuss them in staff meetings but they don't know what to do. The children who cause so much worry do not fit easily into an incident-based child protection system, which has an orientation towards crisis intervention.

The Assessment Framework is only part of a much bigger agenda for Children's Services, which is about refocusing services in the direction of family support and early intervention. There have, as yet, been few studies looking at the bigger picture and asking whether broadly based assessments of children in need are, in fact, leading to supportive interventions in cases which would otherwise receive a child protection investigation. In a small scale study which examined this question Platt (2001) reaches a cautiously optimistic conclusion. One of her findings is of particular importance with regard to neglect. In the sample of cases she looked at it was found that:

> Neglectful care or harm to the emotional wellbeing of a child was an actual or potential issue in 100 per cent of the cases where concerns relating to possible child abuse had cropped up (i.e. about half of the sample).
> (op. cit. p146).

Although there is a widespread consensus that such cases are better handled outside of the child protection system (Gibbons, 1995; Thoburn, 2000) the study revealed that:

> Practice may fall short when higher priority for social work services is given to children on the child protection register. This might lead to a case of neglect, for example, being 'pended' and not receiving a service for several months, simply because it has been managed in a different, albeit appropriate way.
> (p146).

If cases which attract the label of child protection (however appropriate or otherwise this label may be) continue to be fast-tracked in this way one has to be cautious about how far the refocusing agenda has been progressed.

Martin Calder, in Chapter 2, outlines some of the obstacles to working together in a multi-agency way and these obstacles are very pertinent in cases of child neglect. Where there is disagreement about levels of seriousness and the **threshold** for assessment between different agencies, multi-agency working becomes almost impossible.

Glennie (2001) talked about her experiences of an action research project commissioned by a Midlands ACPC. The project was focused on working together in cases of serious child neglect and comprised a number of practitioners from different child care agencies. In the practitioner focus groups one of the pre-occupying questions to which the participants constantly returned was the question of thresholds for intervention. Is the threshold a personal one, a gut reaction felt by an experienced professional when confronted with a particular family? Is the threshold an agency threshold, defined by the particular agency's procedures and protocols? Or is the threshold cross-agency, agreed between agencies and spelt out in local procedures and inter-agency practices? Clearly, in the absence of a threshold for assessment which is agreed across the different child care agencies in a particular locality there is ample room for disagreement and conflict which has the potential to paralyse inter-agency working with children who may be experiencing neglect.

Because an evaluation of the seriousness, or likely seriousness, of neglect in any particular case is a matter for professional judgment there needs to be a proper assessment of the circumstances *before* such a decision about seriousness can be made. This is one reason why the threshold for assessment is critical. Clearly there has to be some room for discretion as it is utterly impossible to spell out in minute detail precisely what evidence is needed before an assessment is justified as that is the purpose of the assessment! So the threshold for assessment will need to be set at a level which picks up at least some of the 'indeterminate cases' as these are precisely the cases which require assessment. These are also the cases that tend to get missed by social workers who are being bombarded on a daily basis with 'heavy end' child protection work.

Turney and Tanner (2000) argued for a definition of neglect which does justice to the relational aspects of neglect, namely that neglect is about the breakdown, or absence, of a relationship of care. If this understanding of neglect is adopted, it follows that the relationships established between a neglecting parent and the workers in the core group is of the greatest importance. Empowering reluctant parents to engage in the assessment process is a crucial aspect of this work, as is partnership in subsequent therapeutic interventions. To stress the importance of **relationship-based practice** (is this simply another word for what used to be called 'casework'?) may call for a different, and less dismissive, take on dependency and a shift from managerialism to the management of practice.

One area in which the drive for efficiency, closely associated with public sector modernisation, has impacted the implementation of the Assessment Framework very directly, is in the rigid **timescales** which have been issued with the Framework (see Chapter 2 for details). Whether or not any relaxation of these timescales may be allowed in the future the principle remains clear: performance will be measured against these timescale targets. There are at least two reasons why this approach is difficult to apply to neglect cases. One is to do with the nature of child neglect as a complex, multi-faceted and often chronic problem. The other is to do with the nature of the assessment process, which requires families to engage in the process through building trusting relationships with those professionals who are doing the assessment. These difficulties may relate more specifically to a Core Assessment but, where there are concerns around emotional abuse and neglect, it is questionable whether an Initial Assessment would be of much value. I suspect that, at least in the more serious cases of child neglect, a Core Assessment may usually be required.

This criticism is related to a further problem of implementation, namely the perception among front line practitioners that the Assessment Framework means 'more forms to fill in'. The distortion of a potentially empowering and liberating professional development into merely a barren, form-filling exercise would be a disaster for neglected children as well as for child care professionals. Yet hard pressed practitioners, already weary with the increasing volume and pace of change, may be tempted to react negatively and defensively to something which has so many challenging ramifications for their practice.

Using the Framework in neglect cases

The dimension **Child's Developmental Needs** allows the assessor to present a balanced picture of how the child is progressing in terms of his or her overall development. In particular, the developmental delay associated with neglect, which may reveal itself in delayed speech and language development and general socio-emotional immaturity, should be picked up here. Other professionals have a crucial imput into the assessment at this point, particularly the health visitor in commenting on the child's health needs and the (nursery) teacher, if appropriate, on their educational needs. A child's identity needs have to do with its sense of self and the associated concept of self-esteem which is so central to a child's emotional development. One of the most damaging dynamics in neglect is the child's perception that no one really cares about them so it doesn't matter where they are or what they're doing.

Of the seven domains outlined in this dimension of the framework many overlap with each other and with other domains from other sides of the triangle. This is a function of the fact that children's development is a holistic process and each aspect is held in a complex, mutually interacting, relationship with every other aspect. This makes using the Assessment Framework a challenging and creative task particularly because the child's needs have to remain at the centre. My experience of conducting and evaluating assessments in a Court context leads me to conclude that this dimension is often the one which is most lacking. It is not unusual to read lengthy and detailed accounts of the various problems (intra-familial and external) experienced by families without any proper consideration of the impact of these on the child who is caught up in these problems and conflicts. The dimension 'Child's Developmental Needs' should help to ensure that the impact of these problems on the child's overall development is a key part of the comprehensive assessment.

The dimension **Parenting Capacity** looks at the extent to which the child's parents or carers are effectively meeting the child's identified needs. In terms of child neglect it is important to consider whether there are any obstacles which get in the way of parental capacity and militate against the meeting of the child's needs. There is a growing body of evidence which suggests that parental mental illness, parental alcohol and drug misuse and domestic violence may all be contributory factors in child neglect, although it is important always to look at these issues in terms of their effect on the children concerned (Cleaver et al., 1999). It is widely acknowledged that neglecting parents have many unmet needs of their own (Stevenson, 1998; Stone, 1998), but it is important when conducting assessments of parental capacity to distinguish between the needs of the parents and the needs of the child. One possible intervention may indeed be to offer some support to the parents around their unmet needs but the needs of the child must have priority. Equally, any intervention should be congruent with the child's time scale: children can't wait indefinitely for parents to get their lives sorted.

In neglecting families it often seems to be the case that the parents are so preoccupied with their own distress and unhappiness that they are not physically or psychologically available to their children. Their own problems become so overwhelming that the child's needs for basic care, safety, emotional warmth, stimulation, guidance and stability are overlooked. In some cases it is not that the parents necessarily lack the capacity to provide for the child's needs, it is simply that this happens in such a haphazard and unpredictable way that the child is at the mercy of the chaos which surrounds such families. The manner in which the child's care giver meets the child's needs is therefore also significant, if the care given is erratic and inconsistent then this also should be noted.

When conducting a Framework Assessment it is important, at some stage, to undertake some direct observation of the parent/s and child together. What is required is not an in-depth analysis of attachment patterns but some good quality observations of parents and children interacting together. This will provide evidence of the *process* of care giving which will support (or possibly challenge) analysis of professional records and statements from the carers themselves.

The dimension **Family and Environmental Factors** enables the assessor to locate this particular family within a wider family and socio-economic context. This is very important in neglect as there are strong associations between child neglect and other wider issues and concerns such as social exclusion and child poverty. Clearly a child's basic need for warmth, shelter, clothing and food may be compromised within a family that is homeless, for example. However, as with parenting capacity, it is important to distinguish between the economic conditions themselves and the

effect of these on the children as they are mediated by the parents' care giving. It is emphatically not the case that all parents who experience material hardship are 'poor parents' in the sense of lacking the capacity or willingness to meet their children's needs. What has been demonstrated in research though is that neglecting families are often socially isolated and find it difficult to take advantage of such community resources as may be available (Dubowitz, 1999).

The **Family Pack of Questionnaires and Scales**, which have been issued with the Framework guidance, are of some value in relation to assessment of neglect. Used properly they can provide valuable evidence to be incorporated into the Core Assessment although, as with the other forms, there is a danger of gathering information for its own sake. However, from the point of view of neglect, it is disappointing that there are no scales or questionnaires which specifically address the quality of child care, nor any which attempt to include information about the various factors which are known to be associated with child neglect. There is also a danger that parents and carers in potentially neglecting households will overestimate their abilities as carers and therefore produce results which are over-optimistic. It is vitally important that those undertaking assessments balance the information they gather from self-report scales and questionnaires against careful observation, the views of other professionals and a full history.

Practical guidance for assessing neglect cases

Rose (2001) set out the following detailed guidance for professionals conducting a core assessment of neglect cases that is consistent with the government triangle. The proposed framework has been divided into six sections:

1. The guidance for professionals in collating and organising the information they already have and identifying possible gaps: **Action by professionals**.
2. The guidance for areas of the assessment relevant for the whole family: **The family.**
3. **Adults:** areas of strengths and difficulties that relate specifically to the carers.
4. The interplay of the child and the parent's relationship: **Parent/child**.
5. **The child**: which reviews how the child presents and functions within the family.

This is rightly the longest section of the assessment framework.

6. Finally, an area frequently missing in assessments which explores **the child's own perception of their experience**.

It is not expected that each family giving cause for concern would require an assessment covering all areas. Some of the framework applies more readily to concerns in relation to neglect and some to emotional abuse. The aim is that professionals are able to identify at what level their assessment is at (refer to process diagram) and to use the framework or parts of the framework to facilitate and focus their involvement. Where an assessment is being done at a higher level, it is anticipated that the tasks are shared according to professional role. For example, the expertise of the health visitor would be best placed to gather and evaluate information relating to development and nutrition, teachers to education, presentation etc.

It is important to recognise that an assessment is not a static event, it should be a fluid process through which change can occur. It is important therefore that professionals evaluate their involvement and are clear with families about the expectations for change, the timescales within which it needs to occur and how it may be measured. Towards the end of the pack there are some practical pro-formas which can be photocopied and used in work with families.

1. Action by professionals

When concerns are raised about a family in situations of emotional abuse or neglect, an important starting point for each professionals is to review the information they hold and to produce a chronology.

Any need identified for further assessment of the family should be informed by this information and, where appropriate, that of other agencies:

a. *Chronology* (to include)
    – house moves
    – missed appointments
    – no access visits
    – attendance at school/nursery
    – requests for support
    – specific incidents (i.e. inappropriately dressed)
    – missing meals, recurring head lice
    – use of A/E

    – referrals from other agencies/public
    – meetings held
    – domestic violence incidents known

b. *An early medical* by community paediatrician of all the children in the family to provide a baseline. This will be important in evaluating the progress that any intervention may achieve.

c. *Professionals meeting* often occurs before concerns reach the child protection threshold. This ensures that the chronology reflects the range and level of involvement as well as the relative success of previous interventions:
    • clarify concerns
    • agree support/roles
    • timescales and review

In beginning an assessment with the family, it is important to structure the areas that need to be covered into separate but intersecting components.

The areas of assessment identified in this practice are consistent with the DoH triangular model and might be represented on the triangle in the following way:

2. The family – process of assessment with the family

Information should be gathered and reviewed in the areas identified below. Interventions tried to improve physical standards should be monitored in relation to:

• The parents ability/willingness to change.
• The length of time improvements are sustained.
• Recognition of the adults need to change/impact on the children.
• Willingness to accept appropriate support.

a. *The environment*
    • Family structure
      – including extended family
      – significant supports
      – evaluation of quality of support they provide
      – family movements
    • Living conditions
      – description of home
      – neighbourhood (e.g. proximity, shops, health centre, buses etc.)
    • Child centredness of home
      – safety
      – toys/books
      – furniture, bed/bedding

– hygiene
– nutritional needs met
- Financial situation
  - earnings/benefits
  - management of money
  - budgeting

b. *The family*
- Family background
  - employment/education history
  - relationships –their parents
  - siblings
  - family strengths and weaknesses
  - own experience of being parented
  - similarities/differences in experiences to way brought up
  - expressions of affection and care within family
  - family unit and closeness
  - convictions
- Marital relationships
  - length of relationship
  - mutual support and help in every day tasks
  - communication and affection
  - role distribution re: child rearing
  - alcohol/substance misuse
  - history of violence and abuse
- Physical and emotional presentation
  - physical and psychological health (including treatment)
  - depression/moods
  - apathy and dissatisfaction
  - current stresses in family (and their perception of them)

3. Adults

The adults are most importantly those who have a primary care role for the children, and therefore may include co-habiting partners, extended family members as well as birth parents.

Iwaniec (1999) breaks down the assessment of a child's quality of care at home to include the following areas:

a. *Physical care of the child*
- Is the child appropriately dressed for the weather?
- Is the child's clothing clean?
- Is the child's clothing regularly changed?
- Is the child washed and bathed?
- Is hygiene at home reasonable?
- Is a cot/pram/bed available and clean?
- Are sleeping arrangements appropriate?
- Is the room warm?

- Is safety observed, such as fire, electric points, sharp objects, medicine, chemical substances etc?
- Are supervision and guidance for the child provided?
- Is medical attention provided when the child is not well?

b. *Nutrition*
- Is the child regularly fed?
- Is the child given enough food?
- Is the child given appropriate food?
- Is the child handled patiently during feeding/eating?
- Is the child encouraged to eat?
- Is the child encouraged to develop their own skills?
- Is there reasonable flexibility in the feeding/eating routines?
- Is there evidence of anger, frustration, and force feeding during the feeding/eating period?
- Is the child punished for not eating?
- Is there awareness that the child is too thin?
- Is there concern about the child's well-being?
- Is there evidence of seeking help and advice?
- Is there evidence of responding to help and advice?

c. *Child rearing practices*
- Use of discipline e.g. range, consistency, appropriateness.
- Unrealistic expectations (too much or too little).
- Supervision and guidance.
- Clear and fair rules and routines.
- Interest in the child and the child's well being.
- Affection, warmth, support (examples).
- Appropriate teaching life-skills and tasks.
- Willingness to learn and to change.

4. Parent/child interactions

This information should be obtained through direct observation and interview. It should cover:
- How much physical/emotional contact with child.
- Quality of parental contact with child.
- Nature of parents-child interaction.
- Expressed parental attitudes towards the child.
- Emotional maturity between child's parents (do they love each other etc.).

- Sense of belonging and togetherness.
- Sense of security and the child's freedom of expression and movements.
- Affection towards the child.
- Commitment to and protection of the child.

5. The child

Adults Perception, Observation and Experience of: (Parents and Professionals)

a. *Birth*
   - prematurity, low birth weight
   - special care, addiction
   - planned/preparation

b. *Attachment*
   The theory: No individual can be understood apart from the relationship in which they live. The kind of person we are forms and arises in our social relationships. The type of self we are depends upon the quality of those relationships; and the way we manage new and present relationships, depends upon those we have experienced in the past.

   For children where there are concerns about emotional abuse and/or neglect, the theory and understanding of attachment is crucial to our evaluation of the child and their parenting.
   In considering attachment, the most important factor is to have the ability **to see the world from the child's point of view**.
   Howe identifies five styles of adult interaction with children:

1. Controlling – overt hostility: physically abrupt, rough, angry, impatient.
2. Controlling – covert hostility: ignores child moods/wishes, demonstrates pseudo-sensitivity, child's feelings are not important or are devalued by the parent.
3. Unresponsive: distant, unavailable, disinterested.
4. Sensitive: responses are alert and attuned to the child.
5. Inept: behaviours from all four; can't maintain a coherent pattern of sensitivity or sustain over time.

   In parallel to this, Howe suggests that children have three ways of responding in relationships:

1. Difficult (including crying, grimacing, rejecting proffered toys or refusing to engage with parents).

2. Passive (i.e. vacant facial expressions, failing to respond to adults, reluctant to play).
3. Co-operative (enjoys social intercourse, turn taking, responds to adult interest).

   Mary Ainsworth explored how this then shapes the types and qualities of attachment relationships between parents and children:

- Secure attachments: – strong feeling of self confidence and self worth.
- Insecure-avoidant attachments: – children don't see out physical contact, generally wary,

  play inhibited, little discrimination with whom they interact. Parents fail to recognise or are indifferent to the child's signals and needs.
- Insecure – ambivalent or resistant attachments: – seek contact but don't settle when receive it, resist attempts to pacify. Demand parental attention and angrily resist it, nervous of new situations often reflects inconsistent, insensitive care though not hostile and rejecting.
- Insecure and disorganised attachments: – show confusion and disorganisation for the child, their parents are experienced as frightening or frightened therefore not a source of safety and comfort.
- Non-attachments: – profound developmental impairment, difficulties controlling impulses and feelings or aggression.

   With the theory in mind, the task is to gather information in order to clarify the need, the appropriate intervention and evaluate the change. For the child, the assessment should include using an observational checklist. Gathering examples make the concerns clear to parents, professionals and courts alike. The observations should cover the following areas:

Conscience development

- May not show normal anxiety following aggressive or cruel behaviour.
- May not show guilt on breaking the laws or rules.
- May project blame onto others.

Impulse control

- Exhibits poor control, depends upon others to provide external controls on behaviour.
- Exhibits lack of foresight.
- Has poor attention span.

Self-esteem

- Is unable to get satisfaction from tasks well done.
- Sees self as undeserving.
- Sees self as incapable of change.
- Has difficulty having fun.
- Doesn't attempt new tasks.

Interpersonal interactions

- Inappropriate affection and trust.
- Lacks trust in others.
- Demands affection but lacks depth in relationships.
- Exhibits hostile dependency.
- Needs to be in control of all situations.
- Has impaired social maturity.
- Stops making demands on parents.

Emotions

- Has trouble recognising own feelings.
- Has difficulty expressing feelings appropriately, especially anger, sadness and frustration.
- Has difficulty recognising feelings in others.

Cognitive problems

- Has trouble with basic cause and effect.
- Experiences problems with logical thinking.
- Appears to have confused thought processes.
- Has difficulty thinking ahead.
- May have impaired sense of time.
- Has difficulties in learning.

Developmental problems

- May have difficulty with auditory processing.
- May experience delays in personal social development.
- May have inconsistent levels of skills in all of the above areas.

c. *Early child rearing management*
    - feeding and eating
    - sleeping
    - persistent loud crying
    - boundary setting

d. *Child's development and growth*

The theory: The table overleaf provides a guide to judging the needs of children and young people at particular ages. It is important to be aware that it is very generalised.

It is important to remember that where there are concerns about a child's failure to thrive,

Health visitors in Salford have a detailed process for assessment and access to a specialist service. A child's health and development will need to take account of:

- special needs
- developmental physical and emotional delays
- failure to thrive, organic/non-organic

e. *Education*
    - punctuality/tiredness
    - appearance
    - relationships
      - adults
      - peers
    - behaviour
      - within class
      - unstructured times (i.e. play time)
    - independence
    - concentration
    - ability
    - achievement of potential
    - contact/involvement with parents
    - strengths
    - difficulties
    - responses to adults
      - difficult
      - positive
      - co-operative

f. *Child's behaviour*
    Schools and nurseries will be vital in assessing and monitoring both children's behaviour and emotional presentation outside of home. These guidelines may be useful in defining and evaluating the areas of concern:

- non compliance or overly compliant
- self harming and destructive behaviour
- disturbed eating behaviour
- poor self control, short concentrating span
- unresponsiveness, attention seeking
- irritability
- aggressive/hostile
- atypical sleeping patterns

g. *Child's emotional presentation*
    - fear, severe inhibitions and apprehensions
    - detachment, depression and sadness
    - unhealthy attachment (see b)
    - soiling and wetting
    - passivity
    - child's attractiveness to parents
    - child's interaction with other
    - appropriateness
    - unusual fantasising/escape from reality

6. The child – perception of experiences

(Again nurseries and schools will be vital in providing information and in monitoring these areas.)

The child's experience of their parenting is the most significant factor in emotional abuse and neglect, and yet, it is often the area about which there is little information. What does exist tends to be adult assumptions about what the child experiences other than the words of the child themselves.

Information directly from the child

It is increasingly clear that children/young people need to be given the opportunity to express their experiences directly in the assessment process. It is envisaged that both social workers, schools, nurseries and family centre workers may all have a part to play in facilitating a child/young person to give us insight into their experience.

These handlings are intended as areas to explore how children see themselves. These are linked to DoH Action and Assessment Records.

Health:

May include child's experience of their health needs, e.g. bedwetting:

- Are they upset, do they feel they receive reassurance.
- Is the bed changed, by whom.
- Is it referred to in the family as a put down, etc.

Education:

(e.g. I'm the cleverest in my class, but I'm rubbish at reading.)

Identity:

This may look at their experience of difference in their house, involving:

- race
- gender
- disability
- culture
- sexuality

Parenting:

- fair
- closeness
- safe

Important/positive relationships:

- within family
- with adults (i.e. teachers etc.)
- with peers

Feelings:

- 'how do I feel?'
- 'how do I show it?/'how do others know what I feel?'
- 'what helps me cope with them?'

Conclusions

The Assessment Framework should work well in cases of neglect since it is the parental failure to meet the child's needs that raises concerns. Neglect does remain a subjective area of practice, and so developments such as the Graded Care Profile (next chapter) can allow some objectivety to be injected.

References

Cleaver, H., Unell, I. and Aldgate, J. (1999) Children's Needs – Parenting Capacity: The Impact of Parental Mental Illness, Problem Alcohol and Drug Use, and Domestic Violence on Children's Development. London: The Stationery Office.

Cleaver, H. and Freeman, P. (1995) Parental Perspectives in Cases of Suspected Child Abuse. London: HMSO.

Daniel, B., Wassell, S. and Gilligan, R. (1999) Child Development for Child Care and Protection Workers. London: Jessica Kingsley.

Depanfilis, D. (1999) Intervening With Families When Children are Neglected. In Dubowitz, H. (Ed.) Neglected Children: Research, Practice and Policy. Thousand Oaks, Ca.: Sage Publications, 211–36.

DoH (1988) Protecting Children: A Guide for Social Workers Undertaking a Comprehensive Assessment. London: HMSO.

DoH (1995) Messages From Research. London: HMSO.

DoH (2000) The Framework for Assessing Children in Need and Their Families. London: TSO.

DoH (2000b) Children and Young People on Child Protection Registers Year Ending 31st March 1999. London: HMSO.

Dubowitz, H. et al. (Eds.) (1999) Neglected Children: Research, Practice and Policy. Thousand Oaks, Ca: Sage Publications.

Dubowitz, H., Black, M., Starr, R. and Zuravin, S. (1993) A Conceptual Definition of Child

Neglect. Criminal Justice and Behaviour. 20(1): 8–26.

Gibbons, J, Conroy, S. and Bell, C. (1995) Operating the Child Protection Register. London: HMSO.

Glennie, S. (2001) Working Together With Neglect: Developing Appropriate Inter-agency Practice. Presentation Given At BASPCAN Conference, Sheffield, 25th June 2001.

Glennie, S., Cruden, and Thorn, (1998) Neglected Children: Maintaining Hope, Optimism and Direction. Nottingham: ACPC.

Gray, J. (2001) The Framework for the Assessment of Children in Need and Their Families. Child Psychology and Psychiatry Review. 6: 4–10.

Iwaniec, D. (1995) The Emotionally Abused and Neglected Children. Chichester: John Wiley and Sons.

King, M. (2000) The Future is Bright But no Longer Orange: The New Framework for the Assessment of Children in Need and Their Families. Representing Children. 12: 4, 288–93.

Korbin, J. and Spilsbury, J.C. (1999) Cultural Competence and Child Neglect. In Dubowitz, H. (Ed.) op cit, 69–88.

MacDonald, G. (2001) Effective Interventions for Child Abuse and Neglect. Chichester: John Wiley and Sons.

Minty, G. and Pattinson, G. (1994) The Nature of Child Neglect. British Journal of Social Work. 24: 733–47.

Parton, N. (1994) Neglect as Child Protection: The Political Context and the Practical Outcomes. Children and Society. 9: 67–89.

Platt, D. (2001) Refocusing Children's Services: Evaluation of an Initial Assessment Process. Child and Family Social Work. 6: 2, 139–48.

Polansky, N., Chalmers, M.A., Buttenweiser, A. and Williams, D.P. (1981) Damaged Parents: An Anatomy of Neglect. Chicago: The University of Chicago Press.

Reder, P. and Duncan, S. (1999) Lost Innocents. London: Routledge.

Rose, K. (2001) Practice Guidance on Assessing and Monitoring Emotional Abuse and Neglect. Salford ACPC.

Ryan, M. (2000) Working with Fathers. Oxford: Radcliffe Medical Press.

Stevenson, O. (Ed.) (1998) Child Neglect: Practitioner's Perspectives. Oxford: Blackwell Science Limited.

Stone, B. (1998) Child Neglect: Perspectives. London: NSPCC.

Stone, B. (2000) Words That Mask the Meaning. Community Care. 17th February 2001.

Tanner, Y. and Turney, D. (2000) The Role of Observation in the Assessment of Child Neglect. Child Abuse Review. 9: 337–48.

The Bridge Consultancy (1995) Paul: Death Through Neglect. London: The Bridge Consultancy Service.

The Bridge Consultancy (1999) Neglect and Developmental Delay: Part 8 Case Review Overview Report. Caerphilly: ACPC.

Thoburn, J., Wilding, and Watson, (2000) Family Support in Cases of Emotional Abuse and Neglect. London: HMSO.

Turney, D. (2000) The Feminising of Neglect. Child and Family Social Work. 5: 47–56.

Chapter Thirteen

The Graded Care Profile: A Measure of Care

Dr Prakash Srivastava, Richard Fountain, Patrick Ayre and Janice Stewart

Introduction

Judging the quality of care received by a child is an essential component of any assessment in a child welfare or child abuse context. However, experience shows us that such judgements may be highly subjective and prone to bias, both individual and systematic. The Graded Care Profile offers a standardised framework for assessment which allows the component parts of quality of care to be separately assessed against predetermined criteria. It is founded upon bipolar scales, encouraging the identification of strengths as well as weaknesses. By allowing the highlighting of specific deficiencies, it facilitates cost-effective, targeted intervention in place of the generic, all-embracing, 'one-size-fits-all' approaches so often encountered in this field.

A key feature of the GCP is that it is not profession-specific and can be used by staff of all the key agencies involved, providing a shared understanding and common frame of reference. The framework has proved to be very easy to use, experienced practitioners needing only two hours training to become competent in its use. Early evaluations have suggested that it is popular both with professionals and families and that it is regarded as having significant advantages over the assessment methods formerly employed.

The Graded Care Profile: a measure of care

There is evidence to suggest that for any given genetic makeup, developmental outcome will vary depending on environmental feedback. Environmental feedback plays an important role in determining the elaboration of neuronal structure and organisation, and the differentiation of cellular, molecular and biochemical functions which mediate physiological responses. Once fully organised and set, these form the biological basis for the acquisition of skills and functions – the process of learning (Prechtl, 1984). Stimulation in the form of exposure to intellectually challenging but enjoyable interaction enhances the capacity to learn within the genetic ceiling. The reverse is also true (Greenfield, 1994). The environment starts exerting this type of influence in foetal life and continues for a variable period after birth.

During early maturational stages, the environment not only helps to determine the potential for cognitive development, it also influences the development of speech and language (Taitz and King, 1988) and modulates emotional well-being through the effect of warm tactile nurturing on synaptogenesis in the limbic system of the brain. Thereafter, environment influences the relationship between achievement and potential through its effect on emotional and motivational factors and cognitive behaviour. Therefore, any child, whatever their genetic endowment, may achieve sub-optimal development if exposed to adverse environmental care.

The effect of an adverse environment on children has been studied mainly in the context of neglect, which tends to be assessed subjectively and often has a high threshold for recognition (Ayre, 1998a; Fitzgerald, 1995). In practice, especially within health, there has been a growing feeling based on experience that children suffer harm at a level of neglect falling below that threshold. Therefore, the need was perceived for a tool which could quantify different levels of care for use in the community inside and outside the child protection context. The Graded Care Profile (GCP) scale was conceived to fill this void. This development was particularly timely since historic difficulties in intervening in milder forms of neglect have been considerably alleviated by the arrival of the Children Act 1989 (s17) and more recently by the preventive focus encouraged by the refocusing debate (Ayre, 1998b; Department of Health, 1995; Parton, 1997) and represented in the *Framework for the Assessment of Children in Need and their Families* (Department of Health et al., 2000).

In assessing care, it is essential that we attempt to be as objective as possible. A carer may be poor or rich, educated or uneducated, but may still be equally caring. Therefore, any

Table 1: The assessment of carer commitment within the GCP.

Grades of care	1	2	3	4	5
Description	Child first	Child priority	Child – adult at par	Child second	Child last

tendency to extrapolate quality of care from these attributes alone will inevitably produce flawed assessments. It is equally inappropriate to estimate the level of care from a child's appearance alone. In the search for a tool, the focus needs to be on the process of caring. This is the principal objective of the Graded Care Profile (GCP) scale.

There are three major components of the care milieu – parenting/care giving, the social and familial context, and the attributes of the child. Of these, parenting/care giving must be regarded the single most important factor in ensuring that the child develops successfully to adulthood. Parents or carers are biologically attuned to care for a child in their care, displaying what Donald Winnicot (1957) has described as 'a thing called love'. It is an instinctive attribute that carers possess distinct from other attributes that they may have. Different carers may have different capacities for caring (or strength of instinctive care) but the net care delivered depends upon its interaction with other contributory factors. Whatever initial strength of caring instinct one may have, it can be further enhanced by the positive influence of supportive social or familial circumstances or a child who is easy to care for, and eroded when these factors are negative.

Basing an assessment on various combinations of such factors, Belsky (1984) proposed eight theoretical grades of final outcome of the caring process. In practice, however, it would be difficult to make such fine judgements as to be able to distinguish reliably between all eight levels of care. In a well known prospective cohort study, one of the areas studied by Miller et al. (1960, 1974) was the effect of care on the long-term outcome in children. For this purpose care was assessed to be in three categories – satisfactory, unsatisfactory, and variable. For the GCP, it was decided to take a middle path and to seek to identify five qualitative grades of care for each element of assessment. By way of illustration, the descriptors used to assess commitment of the carer are presented in Table 1.

The next task was to isolate the areas of care to which this approach could be applied. For

this purpose, Maslow's (1954) hierarchy of human needs had a strong appeal. It captured all the elements of human needs which must be met to proceed towards self-actualisation. It was adopted as a basis for the GCP not so much for its hierarchical structure as for the mutual exclusivity and exhaustiveness of its component parts. Four main domains or areas of care were identified: *Physical Care, Safety, Love* and *Esteem*. In order to make this approach to assessment workable in practice, these major categories needed to be subdivided into 'sub-areas' and some of the sub-areas into 'items', which could be aligned with normal professional observation. In making these sub-divisions, every effort was made to ensure their factor alignment with respective 'areas' based on established psychological principles (Mussen et al., 1990; Rutter, 1985). Five grades of care could then be applied to each 'item' or 'sub-area'. For each 'item' or 'sub-area', a brief description of each of the five grades of care was drawn up, relying heavily on evidence of the impact of adverse care on children drawn from a range of published research findings.

On completion, the whole framework was written up in booklet form and printed as a manual to guide users on how to obtain scores for the aspects of care which they were assessing. In order to facilitate the collation of scores, a specialist record sheet was devised. All the scores for individual elements of assessment are transferred to the reverse of the record sheet. The aggregated score for the main 'areas' and 'sub-areas' can then be calculated and recorded on the front side of the record. This side of the record sheet also has a box, which allows the user to highlight 'items' or 'sub-areas' scoring particularly poorly for the follow up re-scoring after a period of intervention. It is possible to denote any individual element of assessment by using a simple notation consisting of three characters – capital letter for an 'area', a number for a 'sub-area', and a lower case letter for an 'item'.

When the design of the scale had been completed, a field trial of inter-rater agreement was completed in order to check its reproducibility and user-friendliness. Samples

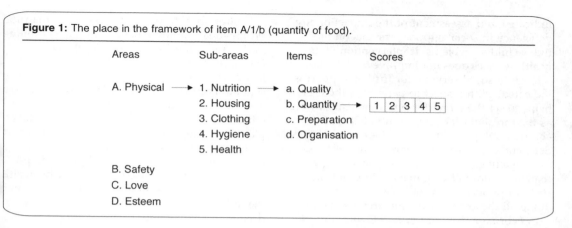

Figure 1: The place in the framework of item A/1/b (quantity of food).

Areas	Sub-areas	Items	Scores
A. Physical ⟶	1. Nutrition ⟶	a. Quality	
	2. Housing	b. Quantity ⟶	1 2 3 4 5
	3. Clothing	c. Preparation	
	4. Hygiene	d. Organisation	
	5. Health		
B. Safety			
C. Love			
D. Esteem			

were drawn from children on a child protection register under the category of neglect and from children in the community not on any register to get a fair spread of scores. The same cases were scored by two professionals (Health Visitor v. nursery nurse; Health Visitor v. social worker) independently. Their inter-rater agreement was assessed by weighted kappa; user friendliness was assessed by considering scoring time and completeness of scoring. An almost perfect level of agreement was achieved in 'Physical' ($k=0.899$; $CI=0.8850–0.948$), 'Safety' ($k=0.894$; $CI=0.854–0.933$), and 'Esteem' ($k=0.877$; $CI=0.808–0.946$) areas, and a substantial level in the area of 'Love' ($k=0.785$; $CI=0.720–0.849$). The mean time taken for scoring was 20 minutes per case (range 10–30 minutes). Of a total of 108 cases scored, the area of 'safety' was not scored in three cases. All areas were scored in the rest of the cases. Those who used the GCP more often took considerably less time to score (Srivastava and Polnay, 1997)

A pilot study of the scale was conducted by a social worker as the subject of her dissertation for the degree of Masters in Social Sciences in 1997. The social workers in her team were asked to use the scale on children for whom neglect was a concern. This was followed by a focused interview. The findings reinforced the initial impression of user-friendliness and highlighted that the process was objective, gave a useful snapshot of care, captured transients in care (in one case showing good grades of care when the carer was not drunk but poor otherwise), and covered many important aspects of care in all cases regardless of initial allegation (Smith, 1997).

Health Visitors undertook a second pilot study in 1998 in order to look at the feasibility of use in daily practice. Fifteen Health Visitors participated by employing the scale in cases where care neglect was suspected. They reported that it was fairer and more objective than their own previous assessment methods. At times, they found that the assessment outcomes surprised them, especially in cases where they had developed empathy with the carer because of prolonged association. Because it profiled the care of an individual child by a named carer, it was found that it picked up many important areas which could otherwise have been missed. For example, in one family different children scored differently with the same carer and different carers scored differently with the same child.

One of the profile's major strengths was that it enabled identification of specific areas of weakness, thus promoting targeted intervention in place of the ill-focused, scatter-gun approach which often characterises the response to a more general label of 'poor standard of care'. By virtue of being a bipolar scale, it was able to capture both positive and negative aspects of care. This helped to engage carers by acknowledging their strengths as well as their weaknesses. It was possible to plan gradual achievable improvement in areas, sub-areas, or items where care was deficient, rather than working on a total transformation right from the outset. Regular re-scoring was undertaken to assess progress.

It is intended that where relevant concerns are identified within the health services, the GCP should form one aspect of a three dimensional assessment – assessment and management of the main referral problem (developmental delay, emotional and behavioural problems, failure to thrive, soiling etc.), assessment of parenting using the GCP by the Health Visitor if indicated and assessment of the impact of any deficiency in social support systems on the index child's problems. If intervention by the health services does not improve the situation, a referral to social services for further support is indicated. With respect to parenting, the GCP helps to set the target for improvement as well as the threshold for referral. It is felt that children living in situations where parenting is deficient are potentially more vulnerable and more likely to be abused or seriously neglected than are children living in situations deficient in social support systems only (where carers are doing all they can in difficult circumstances).

In February 1999, Luton ACPC formally adopted the GCP as the primary basic assessment tool to be used by agencies working with families where neglect of children is of concern. As part of the agreed procedures for multi-agency collaboration, Health Visitors undertake GCP assessments wherever there are concerns relating to the quality of parenting. The assessment assists them in prioritising their work and in detecting issues of neglect which should trigger a referral to Social Services for intervention. The GCP assessment is submitted in support of a referral to Social Services and represents a baseline against which future progress can be measured. Within Social Services, the GCP is used by both social workers and family centre workers to reassess families referred and to measure change in the quality of care. Instances where the scoring is 4 or 5 on more than two consecutive assessments trigger a strategy meeting held under child protection procedures to decide on action to be taken. The GCP is also used as an ongoing monitoring tool as part of the protection plan in relevant cases.

The use of the GCP has helped child protection and child welfare services to refocus their attention to address neglect on a more even footing with physical and sexual abuse. The absence of a clear measure and common understanding of neglect has in the past contributed to the difficulties experienced by professionals when dealing with families where concern about care levels develops cumulatively over time and where obvious physical manifestations may be lacking (Ayre, 1998a; Fitzgerald, 1995; Iwaniec, 1995; Wattam, 1997). In Luton, over 75% of children on the Child Protection Register are currently registered for reasons of physical or emotional neglect and the GCP is the primary framework for identifying support services and interventions required.

In support of the GCP process, more than 150 professionals in Luton have undertaken training in the use of the Grade Care Profile since February 1999. Initially, the training targeted health visitors, social workers and family centre staff but has been extended to include voluntary agencies, teachers and education welfare officers. In addition, briefing sessions have taken place for magistrates, lawyers and county court judges explaining how the GCP contributes to assessments completed for legal proceedings.

The GCP has been used extensively by health and social services staff for some 15 months and the following key elements of the process have been identified as important:

- *Assessment in partnership*
  The assessments are undertaken with parents/carers who contribute their own evaluation of levels of parental care. Wherever possible, children and young people are assisted to contribute their own perceptions.
- *User-friendly process*
  Both professionals and families find the method and the resulting assessment understandable and credible. The user-friendliness of the process is evidenced by the fact that it has been found that experienced professionals are competent and confident to implement it after only two hours' training.
- *Identification and evaluation*
  Preparing a balanced assessment which addresses both the strengths and the weaknesses of parental care poses a considerable challenge for child welfare professionals (Ayre, 1998a). The GCP promotes and enables an even-handed approach to this task. At the same time, it offers a means of early identification of neglect and informs the need for preventative intervention.
- *Baseline assessments*
  The GCP provides a means of measuring care levels at a particular point in time and in specific circumstances. For example, it allows the comparison of care levels when the carer is under the influence of drink/drugs and when they are sober/drug free. Subsequent assessments can be compared with the baseline assessment in order to measure change over time.
- *Relatively objective, value free assessment*
  The statements and scoring process employed in the GCP are much less subjective than the

free-form approaches to assessment usually adopted. Consequently, assessment outcomes are less likely to reflect directly the personal values of the professionals involved. Experience to date suggests that the evaluations of domain sub-areas by parents tend to concur with those of the professionals.

● *Links with the Framework for the Assessment of Children in Need and their Families (Department of Health and others, 2000)*
The Graded Care Profile can be used at three stages of assessment. It can play a part in pre-referral assessments that inform referral to Social Services and also in initial assessments that need to evaluate parental care levels. Where core assessments are being undertaken, the GCP can contribute to assessment of the parenting capacity dimension of the new framework.

Having become firmly established within its local area as the primary tool employed in assessing the quality of care within families when neglect is of concern, further developments are in hand. Consideration is currently being given to extending this structured approach to the assessment of care levels of foster carers, either during the registration process or during on-ongoing placement reviews, and within residential establishments. Further evaluation is planned, consisting of two phases. The first is a short-term research project currently being undertaken to establish the extent of usage and perceived effectiveness of the GCP. The findings of this research will assist in consideration of any modifications or adjustments to procedure or practice which may be required and will inform the final development of the second phase of the evaluation, a longitudinal study focusing on outcomes. There has been considerable interest in the framework from relevant organisations across the British Isles and it is understood that a number of agencies have now adopted it as an assessment tool.

References

Ayre, P. (1998a) Significant Harm: Making Professional Judgements. *Child Abuse Review.* 7: 330–42.

Ayre, P. (1998b) The Division of Child Protection From Child Welfare. *International Journal of Child and Family Welfare.* 3: 2, 149–68.

Belsky, J. (1984) The Determinants of Parenting: A Process Model. *Child Development.* 55: 83–96.

Department of Health (1995) *Child Protection: Messages from Research.* London: HMSO.

Department of Health, Department for Education and Employment and Home Office (2000) *Framework for the Assessment of Children in Need and Their Families.* London: Stationery Office.

Fitzgerald, J. (1995) *Paul: Death Through Neglect.* London: The Bridge Child Care Consultancy Service.

Greenfield, S. (1994) *Journey to the Centre of the Brain.* Royal Institution Christmas Lecture, London: BBC Education Developments.

Iwaniec, D. (1995) *The Emotionally Abused and Neglected Child.* Chichester: Wiley.

Maslow, A. (1954) *Motivation and Personality.* New York: Harper and Row.

Miller, F. et al. (1960; 1974) *Growing up in Newcastle upon Tyne.* London: The Nuffield Foundation, Oxford University Press.

Mussen, P.H. et al. (1990) *Child Development and Personality.* 7th edn. New York: Harper Collins.

Parton, N. (Ed.) *Child Protection and Family Support: Tensions, Contradictions and Possibilities.* London: Routledge.

Prechtl, H. (1984) *Continuity of Neural Functions From Pre-natal to Post-natal Life: Clinic in Developmental Medicine.* Oxford: SIMS, Mac Keith Press.

Rutter, M (1985) *Child and Adolescent Psychiatry.* 2nd edn. Oxford: Blackwell.

Smith, C. (1997) *Pilot of Graded Care Profile in Practice.* Unpublished MSS dissertation.

Srivastava, O.P.and Polnay, L. (1997) Field Trial of Graded Care Profile (GCP) Scale: A New Measure of Care. *Archives of Diseases in Childhood.* 76: 337–40.

Taitz, L.S.and King, J.M. (1988) A Profile of Abuse. *Archives of Diseases in Childhood,* 63: 1026–31.

Wattam, C. (1997) Can Filtering Processes be Rationalised? In Parton, N. (Ed.) *Child Protection and Family Support: Tensions, Contradictions and Possibilities.* London: Routledge, 109–25.

Winnicot, D. (1957) *The Child and the Family.* London: Tavistock.

Appendix 1 The Graded Care Profile (GCP) Scale

A qualitative scale for measure of care of children

Introduction

The Graded Care Profile (GCP) scale was developed as a practical tool to give an objective measure of the care of children across all areas of need. Other scales in this field at best indicate whether the care environment is neglectful or not by comparing a score in a case with a reference score worked on a sample. A given care case could be bad in one area and not so bad or even good in another. This scale was conceived to provide a profile of care on a direct categorical grade. It is important from the point of view of objectivity because the ill effect of bad care in one area may be offset by good care in another area.

Instead of compartmentalising care into neglectful and non-neglectful this scale draws on the concept of a continuum. It has long been recognised that mothers are naturally disposed to care for, and nurture their children to adulthood (Winnicott, 1957; Brimblecombe, 1979). However, the net care delivered is the product of interaction of the carer's disposition to care (caring instinct) with socio-familial circumstances, carer's attributes other than caring disposition and child's attributes. It can be enhanced if interacting factors are positive or eroded if negative. Thus, in the same case, care can vary if circumstances change. Based on different combinations of this interaction Belsky (1984) proposed eight grades of care on a bipolar continuum, best when all factors are positive and worst when negative. This scale is based on actual care by giving a grade to what the carer is doing in the way of caring without taking separate account of other factors. If those factors actually influenced the care then they are

reflected in the same. Belsky's eight grades seemed difficult to work in practice. A practical approach was found in a long term prospective cohort study of children and families (Miller et al., 1960; 1974). Here, care was categorised in three grades; **satisfactory** – if families provided everything that the child needed and making extra effort if required, **unsatisfactory** – if there was clear disregard for the child mixed with cruelty, and **variable** – if it was unpredictable.

In this scale there are five grades based on levels of commitment to care. Parallel with the level of commitment is the degree to which a child's needs are met and which also can be observed. The basis of separation of different grades are outlined in Table A1.

These grades are then applied to each of the four areas of need based on Maslow's model of human needs – physical, safety, love and belongingness and esteem. This model was adopted not so much for its hierarchical nature but for its comprehensiveness. Each area is broken down into sub-areas, and some sub-areas into items, for ease of observation. A record sheet shows all the areas and sub-areas with the five grades alongside.

To help obtain a score, a coding manual is prepared which gives brief examples (constructs) of care in all sub-areas/items for all the five grades. From these, scores for the areas are worked as per instructions.

Items and sub-areas are based on factors which have been shown to bear relation to child development. Care components relating to the items and sub-areas are based more on intuitive than learnt elements (skills) keeping the interest of child uppermost as some skills themselves could be controversial and ever changing (e.g. nursing babies on their backs). This should minimise scores being affected by culture, education, and poverty, except in extreme circumstances.

Following its design, a field trial was conducted to assess its user friendliness and

Table A1.

	Grade 1	Grade 2	Grade 3	Grade 4	Grade 5
Level of care	All child's needs met	Essential needs fully met	Some essential needs unmet	Most essential needs unmet	Essential needs entirely unmet/hostile
Commitment to care	Child first	Child priority	Child/carer at par	Child second	Child not considered
Quality of care	Best	Adequate	Equivocal	Poor	Worst

inter-rater reliability. It was found to be workable, user friendly. and gave a high inter-rater agreement. The inter-rater acreement was a measure of its consistency in getting the similar grade by different independent raters on the same case. Almost perfect level of agreement was achieved in the area of physical care $(k = 0.899$; 95% CI = 0.850–0.948), safety $(k = 0.894$; 95% CI = 0.854–0.933), and esteem $(k = 0.877$; 95% CI = 0.808–0.946), and a substantial level in the area of love $(k = 0.785$; 95% CI = 0.720–0.849). The mean time taken for scoring was 20 minutes (range 10–30) (Srivastava and Polnay, 1997).

It is a descriptive scale. The grades are qualitative and on the same bipolar continuum in all areas. Instead of giving a diagnosis of neglect it defines the care showing both strengths and weaknesses as the case may be. It provides a unique reference point. Changes after intervention can be demonstrably monitored in both positive and negative directions.

In practice it can be used in a variety of situations where care of children is of interest. In child protection it can be used in conjunction with conventional methods in assessment of neglect and monitoring: in other forms of abuse it can be used as an adjunct in risk and need assessment. Where risk appears low but care profile is poor it will safeguard the child by flagging up the issues, if it is good it will relieve any anxiety that there might be. Where risk is high and care profile is also poor it will strengthen the case and care will not be a forgotten issue, but if it is good it should not be used to downgrade the risk on its own merit as yet. In the context of children in need, it can help identify appropriate resources (depending on area of deficit) and target them. In the context of child health it can be used to identify care deficit where there is concern about growth, development and care, post-natal depression, repeated accidents, or simply where care is the sole concern.

Uniforrn care profile (same grade of care in all areas) poses less of a problem in decision making than uneven care profiles. From intervention point of view it gives a point of ocus. More work and experience is needed to know the true significance of uneven profiles.

Finally it should be remembered that it provides a measure of care as it is actually delivered irrespective of other interacting actors. In some situations where the conduct

and personality of one of the parents is of grave concern a good care profile on its own should not be used to dismiss that fact. At present it brings the issue of care to the fore for consideration in the context of overall assessment.

References

Belsky, J. (1984) The Determinants of Parenting: A Process Model. *Child Development.* 55: 3–96.

Winnicott, D. (1957) *The Child and the Family.* London: Tavistock.

Brimblecombe, F. (1979) *Child Rearing: Fashion or Science?* Inaugural lecture. Exeter: Exeter University.

Miller, F. J., Court, S. D. and Knox, E. G. (1960) *Growing up in Newcastle-upon-Tyne.* London: OUP.

Miller, F. J., Court, S. D., Knox, E.G. and Brandon, S. (1974) *The School Years in Newcastle-upon-Tyne.* London: OUP.

Maslow, A. H. (1954) *Motivation and Personality.* New York: Harper and Rowe.

Srivastava, O. P. and Polnay, L. (1997) Field Trial of Graded Care Profile: A New Measure of Care. *Archives of Disease in Childhood.* 76: 337–41.

Acknowledgements

This work has been supported by the Luton and Barnsley Child Protection Committees, particularly the sub-groups on neglect. The field trial was supported by the staff of Barnsley Communitv and Priority Services NHS Trust, Barnsley Social Services Department and Barnsley LEA (especially nursery staff), Luton Social Services and Bedfordshire and Luton Community NHS Trust. We are indebted to all of them.

Dr Leon Polnay, Professor in Community Paediatrics, University of Nottingham

Dr Om Prakash Srivastava, Consultant Community Paediatrician, Bedford and Luton Community NHS Trust

Instructions

The Graded Care Profile (GCP) is a new design which gives an objective measure of care of a child by a carer. It is a direct categorical scale which gives a qualitative grading for actual care delivered to a child taking account of commitment and effort shown by the carer. Personal attributes of the carer, social environment or attributes of the child are not accounted for unless actual care is observed to be affected by them. Thus, if a child is provided with good food, good clothes and a safe house GCP will score better even if the carer happened to be poor. The grades are on a five point bipolar (extending from best to worst) continuum. Grade one is the best and five the worst. This grading is based on how carers respond to the child's needs. This is applied in four areas of need – physical, safety, love and esteem. Each area is made up of different sub-areas: and some sub-areas are further broken down into different items of care. The score for each area of made up of scores obtained for its items. A coding manual is prepared giving brief examples of constructs for the five grades against each item or sub-area of care. Scores are obtained by matching information elicited in a given case with those in the coding manual. There is a system of notation by which each item or sub-area can be represented. This is taken advantage of in designing the follow-up and targeting intervention. Methods are described below in detail. It can be scored by the carers themselves if need be or practicable.

The Profile has two main components the **Record Sheet** and the **Coding Manual**.

The Record Sheet

It is printed on an A4 sheet with 'areas' and 'sub-areas' in a column vertically on the left hand side and scores (1 to 5) in a row of boxes horizontally against each sub-area. Next to this is a rectangular box for noting the scores for the area which is worked from the scores in sub-areas (described later). Adjacent to the area score, there is another box to accommodate any comments relating to that area. At the top there is room to make note of personal details, date and to note who the main carer is against which the scoring is done. At the bottom there is a separate table designed to target items or sub-areas where care is particularly deficient and to follow them up.

On the reverse side of the record sheet there is a full reference scheme which accommodates the entire system down to the items. It is for the reference and the record as it is not feasible to keep a coding manual with each case each time scoring is done. A capital letter denotes an 'area'. Numerals denote a 'sub-area' and a small letter denotes an 'item'. For example, A/1a = area of 'physical' care sub-area

'nutrition' for this area/item 'quality' for this sub-area; meaning quality of nutrition for physical care.

The coding manual

The coding manual which is incorporated here next to the instructions is laid out according to the reference system described above. There are four '**areas**' – physical, safety, love and esteem which are labelled as – **A, B, C** and **D** respectively. Each area has its own '**sub-areas**' which are labelled numerically – **1, 2, 3, 4** and **5**. Some of the '**Sub-areas**' are made up of different '**items**' which are labelled as – a, b, c, d. Thus unit for scoring is an 'item' or a 'sub-area' where there are no items. For example, the score for 'nutrition', one of the five sub-areas of the area of 'physical' care, is worked from scores obtained for four of its items – quality, quantity, preparation and organisation. For some of the sub-areas or items there are **age bands** written in bold italics. Apparently, only one will apply in any case. Stimulation, a sub-area of the area 'esteem', is made up of 'sub-items' for age bands 2–5 years and above 5 years.

Instructions for use

Fill in the relevant details at the top of the record sheet. The Main Carer is the person these observations mainly relate to – one or both parents as the case may be, a substitute carer or each parent separately if need be. Make note of it in the appropriate place at the top right corner of the record sheet.

For prescriptive scoring it is necessary to do a home visit to make observations. In that case carry a check list of sub-areas and items to ensure that they are covered during the visit. Alternatively, carry the coding manual itself and if feasible, share it with the carer. It can also be used retrospectively where already there is enough information on items or sub-areas to enable scoring. Carers using it for themselves can simply go through the manual.

View the situation

- So far as practicable use the *steady state* of an environment and discount any temporary insignificant upsets e.g. no sleep the night before.
- Discount effect of *extraneous factors* on the environment (e.g. house refurbished by welfare agency) unless carers have positively

contributed in some wa y – keeping it clean, adding their own bits in the interest of the child like a safe garden, outdoor or indoor play equipment or safety features etc.
• Allowances should be made for *background factors* which can affect interaction temporarily without necessarily upsetting steady state e.g. bereavement, recent loss of job, illness in parents. It may be necessary to revisit and score at another time.
• If carer is trying to mislead deliberately giving wrong impression or information in order to make one believe otherwise – score as indicated in the manual (e.g. 'misleading explanation' – grade five for PHYSICAL Health/follow up or 'put an act showing care' – grade five for LOVE Carer reciprocation), otherwise score as if it is not true.

Obtain information on different items or sub-areas

A) Physical
. *Nutritional (a) quality (b) quantity (c) preparation and (d) organisation.* Take a good and skilful history about the meals provided including nutritional contents (milk, fruits etc.), preparation, set meal times, routine and organisation. Also note carer's knowledge about nutrition, note carer's reaction to suggestions made regarding nutrition (whether keen and accepting or dismissive). Observe for evidence of provision, kitchen appliances and utensils, dining furniture and its use without being intrusive. It is important not to lead as far as possible but to observe the responses carefully for honesty. Observation at meal time in natural setting (without special preparation) is particularly useful. Score on amount offered and the carer's intention to feed younger children rather than actual amount consumed as some children may have eating/feeding problems.
2. *Housing (a) Maintenance (b) Décor (c) facilities.* Observe. If deficient ask to see if effort has been made to remedy, ask yourself if carer is capable of doing it themselves. Discount if repair or decoration is done by welfare agencies or landlord.
3. *Clothing (a) Insulation (b) Fitting (c) Look.* Observe. See if effort has been made towards restoration, cleaning, ironing. Refer to the age band in the manual.
4. *Hygiene.* Child's appearance (hair, skin, behind ears and face, nails, rashes due to long term neglect of cleanliness, teeth). Ask about practice. Refer to age band in manual.

5. *Health Opinion sought (b) follow-up (c) Surveillance (d) Disability.* See if professionals or some knowledgeable adults are consulted on matters of health, check about immunisation and surveillance uptake, reasons for non-attendance if any, see if reasons can be appreciated particularly if appointment does not offer a clear benefit. Corroborate with relevant professionals. Distinguish genuine difference of opinion between carer and professional from non-genuine misleading reasons. Beware of being over sympathetic with carer if the child has a disability or chronic illness. Remain objective.

(B) Safety
1. *In Presence (a) Awareness (b) Practice (c) Traffic (d) Safety features.* This Sub-Area covers how safely the environment is organised. It includes safety features and career's behaviour regarding safety (e.g. lit cigarettes left lying in the vicinity of child) in every day activity. The awareness may be inferred from the presence and appropriate use of safety fixtures and equipment in and around the house or in the car (child safety seat etc.) by observing handling of young babies and supervision of toddlers. Also observe how carer instinctively reacts to the child being exposed to danger. If observation not possible, then ask about the awareness. Observe or ask about child being allowed to cross the road, play outdoors etc. along the lines in the manual. If possible verify from other sources. Refer to the age band where indicated.
2. *In Absence.* This covers child care arrangement where the carer is away, taking account of reasons and period of absence and age of the minder. This itself could be a matter for investigation in some cases. Check from other sources.

(C) Love
1. *Carer (a) Sensitivity (b) Response Synchronisation (c) Reciprocation.* This mainly relates to the carer. Sensitivity denotes where carer shows awareness of any signal from the child. Carer may become aware yet respond a little later in certain circumstances. Response synchronisation denotes the timing of carer's response in the form of appropriate action in relation to the signal from the child. Reciprocation represents the emotional quality of the response.
2. *Mutual Engagement (a) Overtures (b) Quality.* IT is a dyadic trait inferred from observing

mutual interaction during feeding, playing, and other activities. Observe what happens when the carer and the child talk, touch, seek out for comfort, seek out for play, babies reaching out to touch while feeding or stop feeding to look and smile at the carer. Skip this part if child is known to have behavioural problems as it may become unreliable.

Spontaneous interaction is the best opportunity to observe these items. See if carer spontaneously talks and verbalises with the child or responds when the child makes overtures. Note if the pleasure is derived by both the carer and the child, either or neither. Note if it is leisure engagement or functional (e.g. feeding etc.).

(D) Esteem

1. Stimulation. Observe or enquire how the child is encouraged to learn. Stimulating verbal interaction, interactive play, nursery rhymes or joint story reading, learning social rules, providing developmentally stimulating equipment are such examples with infants (0–2 years). If lacking, try to note if it was due to carer being occupied by other essential chores. Follow the constraints in the manual for appropriate age band. The four elements (i, ii, iii and iv) in age band 2–5 years and 5+ years are complimentary. Score in one of the items could suffice. If more items are scored, score for which ever column describes the case best. In the event of a tie choose the higher score (also described in the manual).

2. Approval. Find out how and how much child's achievement is rewarded or neglected. It can be assessed by asking how the child is doing or simply by praising the child and noting the carer's response (agrees with delight or neglects).

3. Disapproval. If opportunity presents, observe how the child is reprimanded for undesirable behaviour, otherwise enquire tactfully (does she throw tantrums? How do you deal if it happens when you are tired

yourself?) Beware of discrepancy between what is said and what is done. Any observation is better in such situations e.g. child being ridiculed or shouted at. Try and probe if carer is consistent.

4. Acceptance. Observe or probe how carer generally feels after she has reprimanded the child or when the child has been reprimanded by others (e.g. teacher), when child is underachieving or feeling sad for various reasons. See if the child is rejected (denigrated) or accepted in such circumstances as shown by warm and supportive behaviour.

Scoring on the manual

Make sure your information is factual as far as possible. Go through the constructs in the order – (sub-areas and items) as in the manual. Find the construct which matches best, read one grade on either side to make sure, then place a tick on that construct (use pencil which can be erased and manual reused). The number at the top of the column will be the score for that item or sub-area. Where more than one item represents a sub-area, use the method described below to obtain the score for the sub-area.

Obtaining a score for a sub-area from score in its items

(a) Read the score for all ticks for different items of a particular sub-area: if there is a clear mode but none of the ticks are beyond three (3) score the mode for that particular sub-area. To score on the record sheet encircle the appropriate score box against the sub-area (Table A2).

(b) Obtaining a Score for an 'area' from a score in its constituent sub-areas: same as 6a.

(c) If there is even a single score **above** point 3, score that point regardless of mode.

This method helps identify the problem even if it is one sub-area or item. Its primary aim is to safeguard child's welfare while being objective. Besides, if mathematical computation like calculating the mean are done to obtain a common score it will not be

Table A2:

Nutrition	1	2	3	4	5
Quality			✓		
Quantity		✓			
Preparation		✓			
Organisation		✓			

Score for Nutrition would be 2.

ossible to refer to an item or sub-areas which gave a
oor score in order to target it which is an advantage
ith this scale. This is why it has been left as a
ategorical scale.

Transferring the score onto the Record Sheet

ransfer all scores down to the items from the
oding manual to the reverse side of the record
heet which is titled 'Full Reference Scheme'.
Having worked on the score for the sub-areas
which have items, transfer the scores for all
ub-areas on record sheet in the front by
ncircling the appropriate corresponding score
ox. Then is the time to work the score out for
he areas and note it down in corresponding
oxes.

Comments

This column in the record sheet can be used for
flagging up issues which are not detected by the
scale but may be relevant in a particular case.
For example, a child who is temperamentally
difficult to engage with (in the 'manual
engagement' a sub-area of 'love') or a parent
whose overprotectiveness gave rise to concern
(may score better in the sub-area of
'disapproval' in 'area' of esteem). These may
need separate expert evaluation.

Targeting

If the care is of poor grade in an item or
sub-area, it can be picked up for targeting by
noting it in the table at the bottom of the record
sheet by using the reference system. A better
score can be aimed at after a period of
intervention. By aiming for one grade better will
place less demand on the carer than by aiming
for ideal in one leap.

Record Sheet   **Graded Care Profile (GCP) Scale**

Name (Child)_____ Main Carer/s_____

Date of Birth _____   Rater's Name_____

Unit Number _____   Rater's Signature_____

Date of Scoring _____   Other Identification Date _____

Area	Sub-Area	Scores					Area Score	Comments
A Physical	1. Nutrition	1	2	3	4	5		
	2. Housing	1	2	3	4	5		
	3. Clothing	1	2	3	4	5		
	4. Hygiene	1	2	3	4	5		
	5. Health	1	2	3	4	5		
B Safety	1. In Carer's Presence	1	2	3	4	5		
	2. In Carer's Absence	1	2	3	4	5		
C Love	1. Carer	1	2	3	4	5		
	2. Mutual Engagement	1	2	3	4	5		
D Esteem	1. Stimulation	1	2	3	4	5		
	2. Approval	1	2	3	4	5		
	3. Disapproval	1	2	3	4	5		
	4. Acceptance	1	2	3	4	5		

Targeting Particular Items of Care:
Any item with disproportionately high score can be identified by reference to the manual as: capital letter for an 'area', numerals for the 'sub-area', and small letter for an 'item', (A/1/b = physical-nutrition-quantity).

	Targeted items	Current score	Period	Target score	Actual score
1					
2					
3					
4					
5					

FULL REFERENCE SCHEME:

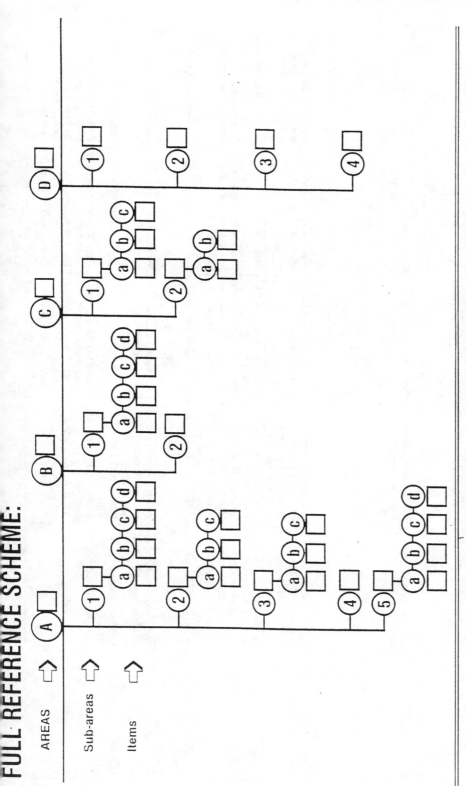

This is the scheme representing all 'items' (represented by small letters); 'subareas' (represented by numericals), and 'areas' (represented by capital letters). These are printed in circles.

Scores are to be noted in boxes adjacent to corresponding 'items'. 'sub-areas' and 'areas'. This represents the entire record as in the manual, for full reference.

A   AREA OF PHYSICAL CARE

Sub-areas	1	2	3	4	5
1. Nutrition					
A. Quality	Aware and proactive; provides excellent quality food and drink.	Aware and manages to provide reasonable quality food and drink.	Provision of reasonable quality food inconsistent through lack of awareness or effort.	Provision of poor quality food through lack of effort only occasionally of reasonable quality if pressurised.	Quality not a consideration at all or lies about quality.
B. Quantity	Ample.	Adequate.	Adequate to variable.	Variable to low.	Mostly low or starved.
C. Preparation	Painstakingly prepared and cooked.	Well prepared, always accommodating the child's needs.	Preparation infrequent and mainly for adults, child sometimes accommodated.	More often no preparation, if there is child's need or taste not accommodated.	Hardly ever any preparation, child lives on snacks and cereals.
D. Organisation	Meals elaborately organised, seating, timing, manners.	Well organised, often seating, regular timing.	Poorly organised, irregular timing, improper seating.	Ill organised, no clear meal time.	Chaotic, eat when and what one can.
2. Housing					
A. Maintenance (See also B/1/D)	Additional features benefiting child, double glazing, child care etc.	All essential amenities, effort to maximise benefit for child if lacking due to practical constraints.	No additional features but well maintained.	In disrepair, amenable to self-repair.	Dangerous dis-repair, amenable to self repair, (exposed nails, live wires).
B. Décor	Excellent, child's taste specially catered for.	Good, child's taste accommodated	In need of decoration but reasonably clean.	Dirty.	Dirty and filthy, bad odour.
C. Facilities	Essential and additional amenities, central heating, shower and bath, play and learning facilities.	All essential amenities, effort to maximise benefit for child if lacking due to practical constraints.	Essential to bare, no effort to maximise benefit to the child who shares equally.	Essential to bare, adult first and child if any left (e.g. blanket).	Child dangerously exposed or unprovided.

NOTE Discount any direct external influences like repair done by other agency, but count if the carer has spent loan or grant on house or had made any other personal effort towards house improvement.

	1	2	3	4	5
3. Clothing					
A. Insulation	Well protected with high quality material garments.	Well protected even if with cheaper material garments.	Adequate to variable weather protection.	Inadequate weather protection.	Dangerously exposed.
B. Fitting	Excellent fitting and design.	Proper fitting even if handed down.	Fitting somewhat improper.	Clearly improper fitting.	Grossly improper fitting.
C. Look age 0-5	Newish, clean, ironed.	Effort to restore any wear, clean, ironed.	Repair lacking, usually not quite clean or ironed.	Worn, somewhat dirty and crumpled.	Dirty, badly worn and crumpled, odour.
D. Look age 5+	As above.	As above, odour if bed wetter, not otherwise.	Worse than above unless self-helped. If younger (under 7) gets relatively better clothes.	Same as above unless self helped. Even under 7 same as above.	Same as above, no means even of self help by the child.

A AREA OF PHYSICAL CARE (CONT.)

Sub-areas	1	2	3	4	5
4. Hygiene					
Age 0 to 4	Cleaned, bathed and groomed regularly.	Regular, almost daily.	Irregular but often, less so with older toddlers.	Occasionally bathed but seldom groomed.	Seldom bathed or clean.
Age 5 to 7	Some independence at above tasks but always helped and supervised.	Reminded and provided for regularly, followed and helped if need perceived.	Irregularly reminded and provided but not followed.	Reminded only now and then, minimum supervision.	Not bothered.
Age 7+	Reminded, followed, and helped regularly.	Reminded regularly and followed if lapses.	Irregularly reminded, even provision not consistent.	Left to their own initiatives. Provision minimum and not consistent.	No concern.
5. Health					
A. Opinion sought	Not only on illnesses but also other genuine health matters proactively and with sincerity preventative.	From professionals/ experienced adults on matters of genuine and immediate concern about child health.	On illness of any severity or frequent disgenuine consultation or medication.	When illness becomes moderately severe (delayed).	When illness becomes critical (emergencies) or even that ignored.
B. Follow up	All appointments kept. Rearranges if problems.	Fails one in two appointments due to doubt about their usefulness or due to pressing practical constraints.	Fails one in two appointments even if clear benefit for reasons of personal inconvenience.	Attend third time after reminder. Contest its usefulness even if it is of clear benefit to the child.	Fails a needed follow up a third time despite reminders. Misleading explanations.
C. Surveillance	Visits in addition to schedules. Up to date with immunisation unless genuine reservations.	Up to date with scheduled surveillance unless exception or practical problems.	Omission for reasons of personal inconvenience, take up if persuaded.	Omissions because of carelessness, accepts if accessed at home.	Clear disregard of child's welfare, frustrates home visits.
D. Disability/chronic illness (3 months after diagnosis of illness)	Compliance excellent (any lack due to difference of opinion).	Any lack of compliance is due to pressing practical reason.	Compliance is lacking from time to time for no pressing reason (excuses).	Compliance frequently lacking for trivial reasons, very little affection, if at all.	Serious compliance failure, medication not given, can lie, inexplicable deterioration any affection is put on.

Compliance = availing professional advice at any venue and carrying out advice given.

B   AREA OF CARE OF SAFETY

Sub-areas	1	2	3	4	5
1. In Presence					
A Awareness *Please refer to the item 'D' (Safety Features) and the note below it.*	Keep awareness of safety issues how ever remote.	Aware of important safety issues.	Poor awareness and perception except for immediate danger.	Oblivious.	Not bothered.
B. Practise Pre-mobility age	Very cautious with handling and laying, seldom unattended.	Cautious whilst handling and laying, frequent checks if unattended.	A bit precarious handling, frequently unattended when laid within the house.	Handling precarious unattended even during care chores (bottle left in mouth).	Dangerous handling, left dangerously unattended during care chores like bath.
Acquisition of mobility	Constant vigilance and effective measures against any perceived dangers when up and about.	Effective measures against any imminent danger.	Measure taken against imminent danger of doubtful efficacy.	Ineffective measures if at all, improvement from mishaps soon lapses.	Inadvertently exposes to dangers (dangerously hot iron nearby).
Infant school	Close supervision indoors and outdoors.	Supervision indoors, no direct supervision outdoor if known to be at a safe place.	Little supervision indoors or outdoors, intervenes if in appreciable danger.	No supervision intervenes after mishaps which soon lapses again.	Minor mishaps ignored or the child is blamed; intervenes casually after major mishaps.
Junior and senior school	Allows out in known safe surroundings within appointed time checks if goes beyond.	Can allow out in unfamiliar surrounding if thought to be safe and in knowledge, reasonable time limit. Checks if suspicious.	Not always aware of whereabouts outdoors believing it is safe as long as returns in time.	Not bothered about daytime outings, concerned about late nights in case of child younger than 13.	Not bothered despite knowledge of dangers outdoors-railway lines, ponds, unsafe building, or staying away until late evening or night.
C. Traffic Age 0-4	Well secured in the pram, harness, or walking hand clutched with child's pace.	3-4 year old allowed to walk but close by, always in vision, hand clutched if necessary i.e. crowd.	Infants not secured in pram.4 year old expected to catch up with adult when walking, intermittent glance back if left behind.	Babies not secured, 3-4 year olds left far behind when walking or dragged with irritation.	Babies unsecured, careless with pram, 3-4 year old left to wander and dragged along in frustration when found.
Age 5 and above	5-10 year old escorted by adult crossing a busy road walking close together.	5-8 year old allowed to cross road with a 13+ child: 8-9 allowed to cross alone if they reliably can.	5-7 year olds allowed to cross with older child but below 13 simply watched: 8-9 crosses alone.	5-7 year old allowed to cross a busy road alone in belief that they can.	A child 7 crosses a busy road alone without any concern or thought.

B   AREA OF CARE OF SAFETY (CONT.)

Sub-areas	1	2	3	4	5
1. In Presence					
D. Safety Features *Note: This item along with other safety provisions which are not a fixture like a bicycle helmet, safety car seats, sports safety wear etc. can be used to score for item 'A' (Awareness of safety).*	Abundant features, gate, guards, drug lockers, electrical safety with garden pond and pool etc.	Essential features – secure doors, windows and any heavy furniture item, safe gas and electrical appliances, drugs and toxic chemicals out of reach, smoke alarm. Improvisation and DIY if cannot afford.	Lacking in essential features, very little improvisation or DIY (done too casually to be effective).	No safety features. Some possible hazard due to disrepair (tripping hazard due to uneven floor, unsteady heavy fixtures, unsafe appliances).	Definite hazard for disrepair – exposed electric wires and sockets, unsafe windows (broken glass), dangerous chemicals carelessly lying around.
2. In Absence					
Safety	Child is left in care of a vetted adult, never in sole care of an under 16.	I=Out of necessity a child aged 1-12 is left with a young person over 13 who is familiar and no significant problem, for no longer than necessary. Above arrangement applies to a baby only in an urgent situation.	For recreational reason leaves a 0-9 year old with a child aged 10-13 or a person known to be unsuitable.	For recreational reason a 0-7 year old is left with an 8-10 year old or an unsuitable person.	For recreational reason a 0-7 year old is left alone or in company of a relatively older but less than 8 year old child or an unsuitable person.

C   AREA OF CARE OF LOVE

Sub-areas	1	2	3	4	5
1. Carer					
A. Sensitivity	Anticipates or picks up very subtle signals-verbal or nonverbal expression or mood.	Comprehends clear signals-distinct verbal or clear non-verbal expression.	Not sensitive enough-stimuli and signals have to be intense to make an impact e.g. cry.	Quite insensitive-needs repeated or prolonged intense signals.	Insensitive to even sustained intense signals or aversive.
B. Response synchronisation timing	Responses well synchronized with signals or even before in anticipation.	Responses mostly synchronized except when occupied by essential chores.	Not synchronized for own recreational engagement, synchronized if fully unoccupied or child in distress.	Even when child in distress response delayed.	No responses unless a clear mishap for fear of incrimination.
C. Reciprocation	Responses complimentary to the signal. Both emotionally and materially, can get over stressed by distress signals from child. Warm.	Material responses (treats etc.) lacking but emotional responses warm and reassuring.	Emotional reciprocation warm if in good mood (not burdened by strictly personal problem) otherwise flat.	Emotional reciprocation brisk, flat and functional, annoyance if child in moderate distress but attentive if in severe distress.	Aversive/punitive even if child in distress, acts after a serious mishap mainly to avoid incrimination, any warmth or remorse deceptive.
2. Mutual Engagement					
A. Overtures	Bilateral but overtures more by carer.	Bilateral-equally by both. Positive overture even if child is defiant.	Overtures mainly by child, sometimes by carer, negative if child's behaviour is defiant.	Mainly unilateral overture by the child, seldom by the carer.	Child appears resigned or apprehensive and does not make overtures.
B. Quality	Frequent pleasure engagement mutual enjoyment, carer may seem to enjoy a bit more.	Quite often and both enjoy equally.	Less often engaged for pleasure, child enjoys more; carer passively participates getting some enjoyment at times.	Engagement mainly functional, indifferent when child attempts to engage for pleasure, child can derive some pleasure (attempts to sit on knee, tries to show a toy).	Aversive to pleasure overtures if any, child resigned or plays on own, carer directed engagement only.

CAUTION: If child has temperamental or behavioural problems, scoring in this mainly quality sub-area item can be affected unjustifiably. Scoring should be done on the basis of score in some area 'carer' (C/1) alone and problem noted as comments.

D   AREA OF CARE OF ESTEEM

1. Stimulation

Sub-areas	1	2	3	4	5
0-2 years	Ample and appropriate stimulation (talking, touching, looking).	Enough and appropriate intuitive stimulation but less of commercial equipments.	Inadequate and inappropriate, baby left alone while carer pursues own recreation; sometimes interacts with baby.	Baby left alone while pursuing own pleasure unless sought badly by the baby.	Absent-even mobility restricted (confined in chair/pram) for carer's convenience. Irate if sought by baby.
2-5 years					
Interactive stimulation (talking to, playing with, reading stories and topics)	Plenty and good quality.	Sufficient and of satisfactory quality.	Variable-adequate if totally otherwise occupied.	Deficient-even if totally unoccupied.	Nil
Toys and gadgets (items of uniform, sports equipment, books etc.)	Elaborate provision.	Provides all that is necessary and tries for more, improvises.	Essentials only. No effort to improvise if unaffordable.	Lacking on essential.	Nil, unless provided by other sources-gifts or grants.
Outings (taking the child out for recreational purposes)	Frequent visits to child centred place locally and away.	Enough visits to child centred place locally occasionally away	Child accompanies carer whatever carer decides, usually child friendly places.	Child simply accompanies or locally e.g. shopping, plays out doors in neighbourhood.	No outings for the child, may play in the street but carer goes out e.g. to pub with friends.
Celebrations (seasonal and personal)	With pomp and zeal.	Equally zealous but less pompous.	Mainly seasonal low key personal (birthdays).	Only seasonal-low key to keep up with the rest.	Even seasonal absent or dampened.
5+ Years					
Education	Active interest in schooling and support at home.	Active interest in schooling, support at home when free of essential chores.	Maintains schooling but little support at home even if has spare time.	Little effort to maintain schooling or manly for other reasons like free meals etc.	Not bothered or can even be discouraging for other gains.
Sports and Leisure	Well organised outside school hours e.g. swimming, scouts, etc.	All affordable support.	Not proactive in finding out but avails local opportunities.	Child avails by self effort, carer not bothered.	Not bothered even if child is unsafe/unhealthy pursuit.
Peer interaction	Facilitated and vetted.	Facilities.	Supports if a peer is from a friendly family.	Child finds own peer, no help from carer unless reported to be bullied.	Not bothered.
Provision	Elaborate e.g. sports gear, computers.	Well provided and tries to provide more if could.	Under provided.	Ill provided.	No provision.

NOTE: *Whichever describes the case best should be ticked as the score; in the event of a tie choose the higher score.*

D   AREA OF CARE OF ESTEEM (CONT.)

Sub-areas	1	2	3	4	5
2. Approval	Talks about the child with delight/praise without being asked; generous emotional and material reward for any achievement.	Talks fondly about the child when asked, generous praise and emotional reward, less of material praise.	Agrees with others praise of the child, low key praise and damp emotional reward.	Indifferent if child praised by others, indifferent to child's achievement which is quietly acknowledged.	Negated if the child is praised, achievements not acknowledged, lack of reprimand or ridicule is the only reward if at all.
3. Disapproval	Mild verbal and consistent disapproval if any set limit is crossed.	Consistent terse verbal, mild physical, mild sanctions if any set limits are crossed.	Inconsistent boundaries or methods terse/shouts or ignores for own convenience, mild physical and moderate other sanctions.	Inconsistent shouts/harsh verbal, moderate physical, or severe other sanctions.	Terrorised. Ridicule, severe physical or cruel other sanctions.
4. Acceptance	Unconditional acceptance. Always warm and supportive even if child is failing.	Unconditional acceptance, even if temporarily upset by child's behavioural demand but always warm and supportive.	Annoyance at child's failure, behavioural demands less well tolerated.	Unsupportive to rejecting if child is failing or if behavioural demands are high. Accepts if child is not failing.	Indifferent if child is achieving but rejects or denigrates if makes mistakes or fails.

NOTE: *If the style of parenting (over protective, permissive to foster independence, authoritarian) or type of values instilled is of concern, please make a note in the corresponding comment box on the record sheet.*

Chapter Fourteen

A Framework for Assessing Emotional Abuse

Dr Celia Doyle

Introduction

Emotional abuse has been explicitly recognised in the UK as a form of mistreatment requiring state intervention since 1980 when Government guidelines recommended the inclusion of emotional abuse on child protection registers (DHSS, 1980; Fogarty, 1980).

State intervention in the protection of children is inevitably fraught with difficulty, not least because as expounded by Hallet (1995) child abuse is a social construction. Societal problems can be regarded as those issues which come to prominence as a result of 'groups asserting grievances or making successful claims for attention and resources' (Hallet, 1995, p23). A social problem emerges as such when powerful people in society agree to define a phenomenon as problematic. However, different powerful sectors may interpret the evidence differently and view the phenomenon as more or less problematic. Over the years this has been clearly shown in some instances of physical abuse; one person's maltreatment is another person's justifiable chastisement (e.g. Shumba, 2001).

In emotional abuse, because there are no clear signs of injury or sexually exploitative incidents, the possibilities for dissent, fluctuating thresholds and different interpretations of information are legion. Furthermore, there are some distinctive characteristics of emotional abuse which makes intervention even more complex than in other forms of abuse.

This chapter aims to provide suggestions for assessment and intervention in cases of emotional abuse, particularly where this is the main or sole form of abuse. It will address some of the key issues relating to emotional abuse such as characteristics, definition and manifestation. It will then relate emotional abuse to the Framework for Assessment (DoH, 2000) and beyond.

Characteristics of emotional abuse

First, because emotional abuse is not characterised by physical signs, with the exception of associations with psychosocial short stature (see Iwaniec, Chapter 14) nor by incidents of sexual exploitation, it can be difficult to assess and define.

Furthermore, emotional abuse has a number of other distinctive features. It has been suggested (Glaser, Prior and Lynch, 2001) that two of these are: that it refers to a relationship rather than an event, and it does not require direct contact. But these are open to dispute because there is little difference in relationship terms between a parent who deliberately burns, starves or rapes a child and one who forces a child to watch the torture of a beloved pet. Furthermore, while many types of emotional abuse do not require immediate physical contact neither does starvation nor forms of sexual abuse such as voyeurism or pornographic photography.

There are however several other, more clearly distinctive, features of emotional abuse. The first is that it is the only form characterised by both acts of omission and commission. In sexual and physical abuse there have to be identifiable acts committed by perpetrators. In physical neglect there are unmistakable omissions by people responsible for a child's care. Some emotional abuses, such as terrorising threats or verbal denigration, lie at the commission end of the continuum whereas ignoring and passive rejection reside at the omission end. But most types (e.g. locking a child in a dark cupboard) involve both damaging actions and failure to give 'good enough' care.

Because of this complex blend of commissions or omissions it may be difficult to identify a 'perpetrator'. Take the following case description:

Both parents completely ignore their five children aged 1–6 years old. They are packed to bed at 6.00 p.m. and have no toys or entertainment . . . The mother who has given birth almost every year for the past six years is struggling to cope in a two-bedroomed council house with very little money and is asking for help. The father will not allow her to have any assistance but will not help her himself. He will not accept 'charity' but will not work or go on any employment schemes, conse-quently family finances have been cut.

(Doyle, 1998, p198).

In this instance it is unclear whether responsibility rests with the mother, father or a society that condemns a family of eight to poverty and inadequate housing.

Another distinctive feature of emotional abuse is that it underpins all other forms of abuse (Brassard and Gelardo, 1987; Claussen and Crittenden, 1991; Navarre, 1987). In an authoritative paper, Hart, Binggeli and Brassard (1998) write, it 'appears to be the core component of most of what is considered child abuse and neglect and to occur more frequently than any other form of maltreatment' (p49). However, unlike all other forms it can exist in the absence of other physical abuse and neglect and sexual exploitation; Jellen, Mc Carroll and Thayer (2001) call this 'primary emotional abuse'.

Emotional abuse in families is not a homogeneous entity. In some instances families love and care for all their children except one child who, like a Cinderella figure, is rejected by the parents. In other families, all the children are loved but the parents are so fearful of losing control that they impose a rigid regime, a closed system, in which it is hard for the children to develop emotionally. In some instances the children are grossly controlled and over-protected. For example:

A boy aged eight soils and wets himself in school because he does not know how to go to the toilet on his own. He is always dressed in very warm clothes, which he cannot take off even for PE. He is not allowed to go swimming with the school in case he catches cold. He cannot stay for school dinners or eat while in school in case he chokes.

(Doyle, 1998, p196).

Other parents have generalised, but substantial, difficulties with relationships, which can be chaotic and ambivalent or sadistic and exploitative. In these situations the children will be subjected to fundamentally the same relationship deficiencies as everyone else in the parents' lives.

Another characteristic of emotional abuse is explained by Lachkar (2000) 'Physical abuse is usually cyclical and intermittent, whereas emotional abuse is often continuous and omnipresent' (p75). Physical and sexual abuse can clearly stop if the child or perpetrator leaves home or the perpetrator is persuaded or forced to desist. Similarly, purely physical neglect can become insignificant if an alternative carer provides necessities or the child reaches

financial and physical independence. However, as Doyle (1998) in a survey of adult survivors of emotional abuse found, emotional abuse often persists long after the victim leaves home and is an independent adult. When asked at what age the emotional abuse stopped less than half said during childhood or on leaving home. Some 33% said it was still continuing. For example:

Zoe, who is now a grandmother herself, is still verbally abused when she visits her mother. Her father has died and her mother keeps declaring that Zoe should have died instead of her father.

(Doyle, 2001, p397).

A final problem, particularly in terms of inter-professional communication and literature searching, is differences in terminology. Navarre (1987) observed 'In professional literature the terms psychological abuse, emotional abuse and mental cruelty have been used interchangeably' (p49). Much USA literature refers to 'psychological maltreatment' (e.g. Brassard, Germain and Hart, 1987). O'Hagan (1993, 1995) argued the case for a distinction to be made between 'emotional' and 'psychological' abuse. However, the term 'emotional abuse' has been adopted by UK procedural and register systems (DoH, 1999). It is an appropriate descriptor because it conveys to both professionals and the general public the essence of the impact on the child.

Definition

Intervention and research into emotional abuse is beleaguered by claims that there is no operational definition. This is not surprising given that emotional abuse is a socially constructed problem. Several works are entirely devoted to the issue of definition (Bersharov, 1981; Haugaard, 1991; McGee and Wolfe, 1991a, 1991b). In some senses this is true and, as identified above, this form of abuse has certain characteristics which mean that definition, intervention and research is far from straightforward.

However, a search of the literature produces a number of serviceable definitions. One of the most functional is that provided by Hart, Germain, and Brassard (1987) which states that emotional abuse consists of:

. . . acts of omission and commission which are judged on the basis of a combination of community standards and professional expertise to be psychologically damaging. Such acts are committed by individuals, singly or collectively, who by their characteristics (e.g. age

status, knowledge, organizational form) are in a position of differential power that renders a child vulnerable. Such acts damage immediately or ultimately the behavioural, cognitive, affective or physical functioning of the child.
(p6).

A first strength of this definition is that it acknowledges the importance of social and cultural contexts (community standards) as well as professional judgement. Secondly it acknowledges that an essential component is the abuse of power. Thirdly and perhaps most importantly it moves away from the idea that the treatment of children is only abusive if there are long term developmental effects, something which it is often very difficult to prove. Instead, behaviours which cause immediate damage, such as degradation, humiliation or anguish, are also deemed abusive.

Manifestation

Although many commentators argue that emotional abuse is hard to define, most people know what is meant by the term. In a study by Thoburn, Wilding and Watson (2000) parents of abused children were able to provide examples of emotionally abusive behaviour, such as 'not showing them any affection or giving them praise' (p62). Parents in their study also recognised racial harassment and adult conflict witnessed by children as forms of emotional abuse. Burnett's (1993) American study showed a substantial consensus among the 1,285 respondents about which vignettes constituted emotional abuse. Similarly, Haj-Yahia and Shor (1995) in a contrasting cultural setting, that of West Bank Arab students, found the highest degree of consensus (94.8 per cent) over the vignette that described emotional abuse.

It appears therefore rather counter-productive to insist on a precise definition of what is after all a socially constructed problem and instead ask 'what is emotional abuse?' in terms of its manifestation. Here again, the debate is beset by esoteric discussions on the precise categories of emotionally abusive behaviour. If emotional abuse is a construct then any categorisation is an even more evident construct. Categorisation is merely an attempt to bring order to a mass of otherwise diverse data. The categories provided in Figure 1 are therefore a convenient way of summarising and conveying information.

The examples in Figure 1 are from (1) the emotional abuse category of child protection registers and (2) those respondents of a survey who identified themselves as survivors' of childhood emotional abuse (see Doyle, 1997a; 1998). The categories also follow the framework for identifying needs provided by Maslow (1970).

Ecological framework

Ecological theory subsumes individualistic and societal causal theories. It draws on the concepts of systems but unlike General Systems theory applied to families (see Jackson and Weakland, 1961; Lask, 1987) there is the imagery of nests. An 'individual's environment, particularly a child's environment, can be understood as a series of settings each nested within the next broader level from the microenvironment of the family to the macro-environment of the society' (Garbarino and Gilliam, 1980, p79).

Garbarino has conducted extensive research into emotional abuse (e.g. Garbarino, 1978; Garbarino and Garbarino, 1986; Garbarino, Guttmann and Seely, 1986; Garbarino and Kostelny, 1992; Garbarino and Vondra,1987) and has for many years embraced an ecological approach to understanding this form of maltreatment. Garbarino and Gilliam (1980) not only use the imagery of nests but also make a distinction between 'sufficient conditions' and 'necessary conditions'. 'Sufficient conditions' are multifarious factors in both the family and wider society, such as caregiver vulnerabilities or oppressive macrosystems and discriminatory social policies. They identify just two 'necessary conditions': social isolation, and the misuse of power.

Social isolation can occur because of the failure of community networks to support the family and/or because of the parents' refusal or inability to use support networks. However, an important feature of emotional abuse identified in Doyle's (1998) research was how often emotionally abused children, not just their parents, suffered substantial isolation.

The misuse of power is fundamental to all forms of abuse (see Doyle, 1997b) and the use of ecological theory enables the assessor to examine not just the misuse of power within the family but also the social/cultural environments which permit this abuse of power.

A power analysis is complex. First, as Handy (1985) has illustrated there are different forms of power: physical, resource, position, expert, personal and subversive. Similarly, Michael

Figure 1: Emotional abuse categories.

Fear inducing *(failure to meet safety/security needs)*
Fear inducing includes terrorising such as holding a child hostage, killing or injuring a loved relative or pet in front of the child and making severe threats. It can also include creating insecurity by, for example, frequently leaving young children with different, strange carers.

Survivor statement: 'my father would make stabbing movements towards our eyes saying "I could kill you". He stuck cigarettes into himself and cut himself in front of us saying he was indestructible . . . he would sit there with a knife waiting for one of us to move.'

Tormenting *(failure to meet safety/security needs)*
Tormenting is the deliberate creation of mental anguish, especially by maliciously denying one child something others in the family have, or vicious teasing.

Survivor statement: 'when it came to birthdays and Christmas, the other two (his brothers) had presents and parties. I was lucky if I got a card'.

Rejecting *(failure to meet belonging/love needs)*
This can be active rejection, telling children they are unloved and unwanted, or passive rejection, which is ignoring or the absence of any demonstration of affection, particularly when other children in the family may be receiving these demonstrations.

Register example of passive rejection: 'the children, aged six months and two years, have to sit in darkness and when anyone visits they are always 'asleep'. The mother ignores them until it is time for her to feed or dress them as if she were taking them out of a box.'

Isolating *(failure to meet belonging/love needs)*
This includes both social isolation and segregation within the home such as locking away for long periods.

Register example: 'the girl, aged 12, has to put her nightdress on straight after school so she cannot play with friends and is ashamed if anyone visits'.

Degrading *(failure to meet esteem needs*
This encompasses verbal denigration and abuse as well as humiliation in public.

Survivor statement: 'I was well-built as a child and my father would say "you've a backside like a cow". Once he took me to a potato weighing machine for a public weighing and subjected me to ridicule.'

Corrupting *(failure to meet esteem needs)*
Corrupting refers to involving children in criminal activities, rather like latter day Oliver Twists, or exhortations to abuse others.

Register example: 'the boys were taught that they should fight the police and hit girls. They were encouraged to steal from shops. In the foster-home they were surprised the foster carers were buying items rather than stealing them.'

Inappropriate roles *(failure to meet needs for fulfilment)*
The broadest category, it includes burdening with adult responsibilities or, conversely, over-protecting and infantilising. It also includes making a child the family scapegoat or a weapon in family disputes.

Register example: 'a girl aged six years has to clean herself up if she is sick or wets herself. She has to look after her parents and is the household drudge.'

Foucault (1980) argued that power circulates within society rather than being top-down i.e. associated with a hierarchical structure, and power can be used for good or ill.

Many researchers debate how far intent is an essential component of emotional abuse with Bourton (1991) and Covitz (1986) arguing that emotional abuse is often unintentional while Garbarino (1978) maintains intent is a key feature. However, intent is irrelevant. Rather the

essential questions are: Who in the situation holds power? Who misuses it? In a register case (Doyle, 1998), a father, who slit the throat of a mother while the child cuddled up to her, probably had no intention to harm the child but was clearly abusing his physical power and subjecting his son to emotionally abusive trauma. Parents naturally have, or are given, most forms of power – physical, resource, position, expert and personal – over their children with the expectation that they will use that power wisely and to the benefit of those children. Abuse occurs when parents misuse or fail to use this power.

Ecological theory however also directs the assessor to look at other dimensions of power. Parents can be substantially disempowered either by inequalities in society or by misfortune. A good example is that of young carers. In some cases unjust burdens of responsibility are placed on children by parents, who are emotionally abusive because they refuse to make use of support services regardless of their children's welfare. However, in many other instances the parents are substantially disempowered by illness or disability. There are inadequate support services and the parents have no option but to depend on their children. Such young people can be viewed as emotionally abused, but by 'society' rather than by their parents.

Similarly, societal racism can have disempowering effects and result in what might be perceived as emotional abuse. Gibson and Lewis (1985) explain that, as young black British people, particularly in poorer economic areas, experienced racist attacks and the unsympathetic attentions of the police, their parents became 'paralysed with fear when their children were out of sight' (p80). The consequent restrictions imposed by the parents were seen by the young people as oppressive and conflicts ensued.

Before leaving the ecological model, the adoption of a four-sided model which includes the cultural/societal dimension (see Calder, Chapter 2) is essential in understanding and assessing emotional abuse. Doyle (1997a, 1998) found that emotional abuse was more likely to occur in families facing multiple external and internal stressors. The extent of emotional abuse rose as stressors on the family rose. Similar findings have been made by Coulton, Korbin, Su and Chow (1995); Garbarino and Kostelny (1992), and Krishan and Morrison (1995). Social policies, cultural change and economic pressures can all lead to stress which can impair the functioning of vulnerable families.

Finally, cultural influence is an important consideration for those who work in the field of child protection. Britain could be described as a society in cultural transition. Many families, especially those affected by migration and refugee-status, will be encountering substantially changing cultural contexts.

Furthermore, all families will be affected by shifting views on child welfare as international and European perspectives impact on UK practice, law and social policy. A useful paper by Roer-Strier (2001) 'proposes guidelines to both parents and professionals for the prevention and reduction of risk associated with cultural differences, conflicts and misinterpretations' (p231). The author argues that societies have an image of the 'adaptive adult' for that society and adopt child rearing practices which will ensure that the children become constructive members of that society. In a stable, homogenous society the image of adaptive adulthood and consequent child care practices will remain constant across generations. In a rapidly changing, heterogeneous society some of the practices will no longer be adaptive. The important message for practitioners is that there is a need to share views on images of 'adaptive adults' with parents. 'Clarification of the similarities and differences may further provide professionals with a basis for offering alternative strategies and utilise community support systems in cases they continue to perceive as maltreatment' (p239).

The Framework for Assessment of emotional abuse

This section examines aspects of the Framework for Assessment in terms of the areas to be assessed in relation to what is currently known about emotional abuse especially where it is the sole or 'primary' form of abuse.

Child's developmental needs

Health

Almost by definition, emotional abuse is unlikely to be identified through physical signs and symptoms of ill-health, with the exception of non-organic failure to-thrive (see Iwaniec, 1995; Iwaniec, Chapter 14). Furthermore, many emotionally abused children appear to be in excellent physical health. Nevertheless, there are some health-related factors.

First, there may be signs of self-harm which actually, or will potentially, damage the child's health. In Doyle's (1998) study, 14 per cent of the registered children attempted suicide or made serious attempts to harm themselves, including children as young as 6 years old. Permanent injuries can occur because of failed attempts at suicide such as jumping from heights, drugs overdoses, hanging or cutting wrists. Pearlman (1998) noted 'survivors may loathe, detest or rage against themselves. These feelings are often manifest in destructive behaviours directed against one's own body' (p13).

Research indicates a substantial link between emotional abuse and a range of eating disorders, including anorexia nervosa, bulimia and over-eating, (Witkietz and Dodge-Reyome, 2000). Doyle (1998) found that while most failure-to-thrive children were allocated to the 'Neglect' register category, 17 per cent of children in the Emotional Abuse section had eating disorders including over-eating.

Escape from the harsh realities of emotional abuse and rejection can result in substance abuse. In Doyle's study one child aged six was recorded as 'drinking excessively'. In some instances the parents provide access to drink and drugs. In the study by Glaser et al. (2001) it was noted 'a child, aged seven years, was mis-socialised, on the basis of being given alcohol and exposed to . . . drugs, including cocaine' (p25).

Inappropriate treatment where emotional factors rather than physical ones predominate can constitute a form of emotional abuse. For example, a teenager forced to wear nappies and crawl on the floor as part of a 'regression therapy' was viewed by conference members as emotionally abused (Doyle, 1998) Similarly, Munchausen syndrome by proxy (see Precey, Chapter 16) can be viewed as a form of psychological maltreatment.

Education

Problems relating to education and schooling appear to be a key feature of emotional abuse. In Glaser et al.'s (2001) study 25 per cent of the registered children were either absent from school or persistently late, while in Doyle's (1998) study the figure for non-school attendance was 21 per cent. The reasons for non-school attendance can vary from children whose truancy was ignored by parents to those who were deliberately kept off school.

Account, however, has to be taken of wider environment and cultural factors. Different cultures have different priorities in relation to education. One white survivor recalled how her mother opposed her going to grammar school and university on the basis that they were a working class family and did not need 'fancy' education (Doyle, 1998). All British-based children have a right to the same educational opportunities regardless of culture, class or creed. But there are different dynamics in relation to parents whose culture may influence their view of the education on offer and those who deliberately keep children at home to meet their own emotional needs.

Generally, Doyle found 62 per cent of registered school-age children had some education-related problems including vulnerability to bullying by peers or refusal to try anything new because of the fear of failure. Glaser et al. (2001) found that substantial numbers of emotionally abused children were underachieving educationally. Other studies show similar findings (Crittenden, Claussen and Sugarman, 1993; Milling Killard, 2001; Starkey, 1980).

There is also the issue of emotional abuse in school from both peers and staff (Krugman and Krugman, 1984). Nesbit (1991) explored the issue of the emotional abuse of learning disabled children in school. For a child suffering psychological maltreatment at home the effects of supplementary abuse at school may be profound.

Nevertheless, for those children able to attend school where the educational environment is caring and encouraging, school can provide a sanctuary. For example from the register cases one key worker commented of a girl aged 6 years 'bright and behaviour good in school although sometimes distressed. School is a safe haven' (Doyle, 1998, p210).

Identity

In emotional abuse, especially rejection and denigration, there are substantial risks to the child's identify and self-esteem. Repeatedly, studies have shown that psychological maltreatment is among the most damaging to the child's sense of self-esteem (e.g. Briere and Runtz, 1990; Iwaniec, 1995; Rohner and Brothers, 1999) 'Sexual abuse and psychological maltreatment were the types of maltreatment most strongly related to trauma symptomatology and self-depreciation' (Higgins and McCabe, 2001, p268).

Emotionally abused black children face double jeopardy. Sanchez-Hucles (1998) noted that young children exposed to societal racism, which is itself a form of emotional abuse, 'develop a poor sense of positive identity, competence, belonging and security' (p73). When this is combined with denigration and abuse in the home then the negative effects on the self-esteem and identity of black, Asian and other children subjected to societal racism are likely to be profound.

Family and social relationships

One important factor is that families in which emotional abuse occurs, as mentioned earlier, are not a homogenous group. The main difference is between those families were one child is singled-out for mistreatment and those where all the children are abused in more or less equal amounts.

In many of the 'singled-out' situations the families appear to be unexceptional and may be very similar to other families in the area. They might not appear to be subjected to very much stress and other children in the family may well thrive and appear happy and contented. Warm caring relationships are likely to be observed between the parents and other children in the family. Only careful observation will reveal anything amiss. Often clues can be gained from questions about apparent peripheral subjects such as the toys children have, their bedroom décor, and parties and presents on birthdays. They will reveal that the 'singled-out' child is being subjected to discrimination and rejection. The cause may well be traced back to bonding problems, a significant death or tragedy at the time of the child's birth or the child representing a hidden part of the family history. For example 'Luke was conceived while his 'father' was away working and was a constant reminder to both parents of his mother's adultery. His brothers received affection, approval and treats from which he was excluded' (Doyle, 2001, p391).

In other families, relationships are relatively chaotic. All the children suffer as the parents show alternating over-concern then indifference. The emotional care of all the children is inconsistent and ambivalent. Often they are left with ever-changing, temporary carers. Relationships between the parents and extended family members are fraught, while relationships with neighbours, friends and professionals tend to be polarised. The same person may be regarded as 'virtue personified' one moment and 'evil incarnate' the next. Here, care has to be taken not to confuse the scapegoating of one child in this situation with the 'singled-out' child described above where alleviation of the difficulties or the removal of the child will often lead to a noticeable improvement in family functioning. In the family with chaotic and generally ambivalent relationships, removal of the scapegoat will simply lead to the production of a new family scapegoat.

In marked contrast, are those families characterised by rigid, inflexible relationships. Here the parents appear to be fearful of losing control. Professionals are regarded with suspicion, and interference in family life is hugely resented. All the children in the family are subjected to a punitive, oppressive regime in the home. For example, 'Kate came from a wealthy, white service family. Her father was domineering, ruling by fear and insisting on absolute, unquestioning obedience' (Doyle, 2001, p391).

Finally, there are families that may appear to be unexceptional but which contain a seriously damaged individual in a position of power. Often this person is a parent but in some families might be a grandparent or an elder sibling. This figure is more often seen in sexual abuse cases but can be apparent in families where there appears to be no sexual exploitation. Often the damaged individual is a bully, skilled at manipulating relationships and may well present as charming, plausible and eloquent. Frequently professionals find it difficult to evidence or articulate their concerns about these people. They often have a 'gut feeling' that something is amiss. An example of this type of abuse of power was given by Roy who 'witnessed extreme violence from his father towards his mother, which often led to her hospitalisation. His father maintained Roy was a worthless waste of space 'a fat slob' and would make him engage in repetitive tasks for several hours' (Doyle, 2001, p392)

These distinctions in family relationships should not be used as rigid classifications. They are however helpful guides to understanding and assessing the general patterns of social and family relationships. Furthermore they illustrate that a clue to family relationships may be gained by professionals reflecting on the way they are made to feel by key people in the family.

Social presentation

Many emotionally abused children show no particular difficulties with social presentation. However, there are some possible indicators.

The first is that 'singled-out' children may appear to be more shabbily dressed, more withdrawn or attention seeking, and less confident than their siblings. However, care is needed because despite sharing the family genetic inheritance and the same environment, siblings often have remarkably different temperaments. One child may be naturally scruffy and attention-seeking, while the rest of the family are quiet and neat.

Professionals can also be alert to those children who are too well-behaved, too tidy, too meticulous about their appearance. Kate, mentioned above, expressed astonishment that no one had noticed that she and her brother had perfect manners in public and would sit still for ages without speaking, moving or daring to go to the toilet.

In one register case (Doyle, 1998) the school was alerted to problems because of the extreme distress a young girl showed if her shoes became scuffed, if her clothes became slightly marked or if she lost a hair ribbon. Her behaviour in school was described as 'too good'.

Emotional and behavioural development

Emotional abuse almost by definition is likely to have an adverse impact on emotional development. The Framework for Assessment does not serve children who suffer emotional abuse well because it does not offer an adequate structure for the assessment of emotional need. Instead, the basic human needs model initially offered by Maslow in 1970 is particularly useful. Hart et al. (1998) write that Maslow's model 'has been supported as having particularly strong explanatory and heuristic value for psychological maltreatment' (p29).

Assuming that carers are not physically neglectful and physiological needs are being met the primary emotional need is a sense of safety and security. All the main commentators on children's psychosocial development point to the importance of a sense of security, whether this is Maslow's (1970) 'safety needs', Erikson's (1965) 'trust versus mistrust' or Bowlby's (1965) 'secure attachment'. It is perhaps no surprise that in Doyle's (1998) study 'fear inducing' behaviour was present in 95 per cent of the registered cases, while 71 per cent of the emotional abuse survivors in the survey said that they were made to feel insecure. An important associated factor for assessors to consider is that in abusive families, children who are not the primary victims of abuse live in constant fear for their abused parent or sibling and in case the abuse is suddenly directed towards them. Therefore in situations of child abuse or domestic violence all children present

in the family should be considered to be the victims of emotional abuse.

Insecurity almost inevitably means that emotionally abused children do not develop a strong sense of belonging. Furthermore passive or active rejection and ignoring (present in 86 per cent of the register cases in Doyle's study) further compound the children's feelings that they are unlovable; 'internalisation of the self as described by the abuser's word and behaviours also result in confusion and profound self-loathing' (Pearlman, 1998, p11). However, it is not just the abuser's behaviour which can impair the child's sense of love and belonging. Many children with 'care careers' are emotionally abused by the 'system'. They have had so many changes of foster or substitute carer that they have no one they feel truly loves them and they have no sense of belonging. This has been a particular problem for black children with white substitute carers. Many have felt that they are not fully accepted by either the white or black communities. More generally, the need to understand one's origins and roots in order to give a sense of belonging is important for many people.

Esteem needs are part of developing a sense of self-worth which was discussed in the section on identity. One of the problems in emotional abuse is that the harm to the child's self-esteem may be insidious. As Pearlman (1998), discussing abuse victims' developing sense of self-loathing, noted:

> When the abuse is emotional but not physical these same feelings may emerge, but without the physical evidence the child may feel s/he requires to make sense of them. Emotionally abused children (and then adults) may feel like they are crazy or making it up, they are set apart from others by their secret shame, yet unable to understand why they feel so bad, so angry, so different. (p11).

Finally, rather than using Maslow's actualisation, Doyle (1998) preferred to substitute fulfilment. This is firstly in terms of objective assessment. Has a child fulfilled their full potential? Are they meeting their milestones? Are they able to benefit from educational opportunities? It is also in terms of an internal sense of fulfilment. For example, in Doyle's (1998) study, Zoe, who had spina bifida, was constantly frustrated in her secondary school where she was not allowed to undertake physical activities in case she had an accident and her parents sued the school.

Self care skills

Emotional abuse may not adversely affect children's self-care skills. However, children who have over-developed care skills may be emotionally abused, as in the case of the 6-year-old girl who had to clean herself up when she was sick or wet (Doyle, 1998, p195). Similarly, like the eight-year-old boy who could not even wipe his bottom, lack of self-care skills in an able child suggests over-protection.

However, diverse cultures will encourage different self-care skills at different ages. For example, Solberg (1990) writes that in Norway, children of working parents look after themselves and younger siblings after school from about 10 years, In the UK the acceptable age is nearer 12 to 14 years. Professionals again have to be sensitive to the cultural norms of each family.

Parenting capacity

Basic care

Emotional abuse may be combined with physical neglect but in those cases where emotional abuse is the sole form there may be no problems with basic physical care. However, there may be subtle clues in the basic care which indicate emotional abuse. First, there are instances where the care of some children seems to be 'mechanical'. It is efficient but devoid of pleasure and playfulness. Secondly the care might be almost too good. The children appear to be fashion mannequins or their home is too clean or too tidy. For example: the 'family's maisonette is kept in an immaculate state and no toys are allowed because of the mess they might make' (Doyle, 1998, p160).

Ensuring safety and stability

In cases of emotional abuse it makes sense to link ensuring safety with providing stability because the key area, as already discussed in the earlier sections, is meeting children's security needs.

It must however be remembered that there can be the colloquial 'too much of a good thing'. The over-protective parent who is attempting to keep the child totally safe is emotionally abusive. This is because the parent is conveying fear to the child, fear that the outside world is a totally dangerous place. The parent is also damaging the child's self-esteem because the message being conveyed is 'you cannot be trusted to look after yourself'.

Emotional warmth

This appears to be a common sense proposition and it would seem that it would be easy to detect the absence of warmth in emotional abuse cases. However, practice shows that this is not the case. First, in cases of over-protection the parents are not cold and critical but very much the opposite. However, the cloying entrapment of an overpoweringly protective and morbidly anxious parent can be every bit as abusive as cold criticism.

There is also the issue of the cultural expression of emotional warmth. Edwards (2001) highlights the very different expressions of emotion between cultures. British fathers of the early twentieth century were often very formal and rather distant with their children but nonetheless very caring.

Stimulation

Often again there are no problems with stimulation and children's cognitive and educational development. However, problems with education have been discussed and with children who are ignored and rejected there may be no attempt to stimulate them or help them develop cognitively.

However, again care has to be taken to appreciate different cultural perspectives. A colleague (Lena Roberts, personal communication, 17/9/01) recounted how an associate, researching the use of educational play materials among families with pre-school children, noticed in some impoverished Bangladeshi families no evidence of any such materials. The researcher initially made the assumption that educational play materials were not valued by these families. However, closer inquiry revealed that such resources were so highly valued by the families that, rather than lying around the house, they were kept safely in boxes when not being used because the families could not afford for them to be destroyed by casual use.

Guidance and boundaries

Often emotionally abusive parents are characterised by either a substantial lack of boundaries and guidance or rigidity and overly strict boundaries. In these rigid families there is no guidance rather there are a series of edicts and commands.

Family and environmental factors

Family history and functioning and wider family

Abuse in the background of the parents can be an important factor. Of those cases where the parental background was known, 88 per cent of the mothers and 77 per cent of the fathers had suffered at least one form of abuse during their childhood (Doyle, 1998). However care has to be taken when making assumptions about the 'intergenerational transmission of abuse'. Survivors often make a conscious effort to avoid repeating the behaviour of their abusive parents.

The study also showed that unlike sexual abuse and some physical abuse in which there can be a clearly identified 'non-abusing parent', often in cases of emotional abuse both parents are emotionally unavailable. In Doyle's (1998) study there were profound differences in allocation of responsibility for the abuse between the register cases and the survivor survey. Only 17 per cent of fathers were deemed to have sole responsibility in the register cases, whereas this rose to 36 per cent in the survivor reports. Interviews with the survivors indicated that in many instances one parent, often the father, was the main emotional abuser while the other parent was either ineffectual or a powerless co-victim.

Examining the wider family, the study showed that grandparents were frequently so involved with the dynamics of the family or so distant that they were rarely a source of help for the victims. However, aunts and uncles were particularly important. Sometimes these were not direct kin but were honorary 'aunts' such as close neighbours or the mother's best friend. These aunts seemed to be able to stand aside from the various family conflicts and emotional tensions and focus on the victimised child. Even from a distance, or with only intermittent contact, they could play a major role in enhancing the abused child's self-esteem. One aunt for example lived abroad but would send her niece gorgeous underwear. This conveyed a symbolic message 'your parents may not be able to see it but underneath you are really beautiful'.

Income, housing and employment

Doyle's study showed that emotional abuse can occur in families with no apparent material stressors. In one registered family the father was a wealthy businessman with a time-share in Florida.

Stress was likely to feature in the register cases because families experiencing material and personal difficulties are likely to be referred to professionals who are in a position to identify emotional abuse. It is therefore necessary to turn to the population survey for an indication of whether stress is higher in families in which emotional abuse occurs in comparison to those in which it does not.

Khamis (2000) who explored emotional abuse in Palestinian families found 'Economic hardship in regard to parents' inability to fulfil child's needs was a significant risk factor for psychological maltreatment' (p1055). This is similar to Doyle's (1997a) survey in which the 'emotionally abused' respondents were significantly more likely to have had financial problems than non-abused ones. However, as Khamis intimates, it is the parental perception of insufficient income or financial problems, as well as any objective measurement of poverty, that is important.

Doyle (1998) also found that emotionally abused respondents were significantly more likely to have encountered accommodation problems. However, accommodation was not always a key problem. For example 18 per cent of the registered families were in owner occupied houses.

Employment, occupation and class are not clear indicators of emotional abuse as 34 per cent of the emotional abused respondents' parents and 17 per cent of the registered cases were from the Registrar General's professional and managerial classes I and II. Nevertheless, parents who have less occupational security and less power in the economy appear to be more vulnerable. Furnell, Dutton and Harris' (1988) study showed over half of the referred cases were class V. In Doyle's study 38 per cent of the register cases were in classes IV and V and a further 25 per cent on long term state benefits. In the survey 21 per cent of parents of the emotionally abused group were in classes IV and V compared to only 11 per cent of the non-abused group.

Family's social integration and community resources

As pointed out by Garbarino and Gilliam (1980) social isolation is a key component of emotional abuse. Doyle (1998) found that nearly half (45 per cent) of registered families had little nstructive social support. In many cases olation is due to circumstances, such as a mily moving to a new community or eographical isolation. For others community apports are alienating or inadequate.

However, as noted, social isolation can be due the fact that the key adults in the family have rofound problems with relationships. Their nbivalence and inconsistency towards the ildren is mirrored in their relationships with her adults including voluntary or professional elpers. In some instances one adult in the mily will be determined to remain in control nd manipulate power to meet their own needs. orking with such adults is extremely difficult. horburn et al. (2000) concluded 'an important inority of cases will need a longer-term, elationship-based casework service' (p201). ne of the difficulties facing practitioners is that is those very cases – where children suffer om parental inability to form trusting, on-exploitative relationships – that need such ong-term intervention, and yet the parents have ifficulty relating not just to their children but to rofessional helpers as well. Therefore the hances of social workers making and naintaining such relationships, while not mpossible, are unquestionably difficult and motionally demanding.

Further reflections on the Assessment Framework

Prevalence, policy and implications for hresholds

The recognition of, and response to, a social problem is influenced by many factors including he economic situation, the prevailing political nd moral philosophy, and demographic changes. Another important factor is the perceived magnitude and extent of a problem. If, for example, one or two people are homeless hey can be catered for individually but when a high proportion of families have no home then housing policies might be tailored to address these families' plight.

Because of the implications for social policy of the extent of a problem and because even by the mid-1990s there were no published studies of the prevalence of emotional abuse in the UK, Doyle (1998) conducted a survey in three different UK populations: young undergraduates, helping professionals and mature students on 'Access' courses. The results are presented in Figure 2.

Figure 2: Prevalence of emotional abuse.

The prevalence rates were:

Emotional abuse	
Undergraduates	21%
Professionals	33%
Access students	45%
Total emotional abuse	**29%**
Total physical abuse	14%
Total sexual abuse	9%

The prevalence rate for physical abuse in Doyle's study is comparable to the UK rate of 16 per cent estimated by Creighton and Russell, 1995. The 9 per cent rate for sexual abuse in Doyle's study is similar to that of the 10 per cent calculated by Baker and Duncan (1985). It would therefore seem that the prevalence rate of 29 per cent for emotional abuse could be a useful guide given that the other prevalence rates in the study accorded with other accepted estimates.

As La Fontaine (1990) pointed out, 'the recognition of a serious social problem need not depend on the percentage of those affected being exact to the last decimal point' (p47). However, the prevalence estimate indicates that emotional abuse is widespread.

It is evidently impractical to register a quarter of the child population. Much emotional abuse could be prevented if there was effective service provision at Level 0 and Level 1 (see Calder, Chapter 2, Figure 3). It is perhaps incumbent on welfare professionals to critically examine how children are viewed in UK society. Are they respected or objectified, for example? How many editors and lecturers challenge references to the child as 'it' in text books (e.g. Gross, 1992; Hayes, 1994) or in social work student assignments?

The main problem with the virtual abandonment of the discourse of risk is that the real risks to children posed by emotional abuse will not be recognised. In Doyle's survey, 10 per cent of respondents recorded so many negative and damaging experiences that their exposure to maltreatment is irrefutable. Several recorded attempting suicide. Therefore, although emotional abuse is rarely viewed as life-threatening, there are evident risks to life. Some UK commentators (e.g. Hawker, 1995) suggest that there should only be an investigation agency for criminal assaults against children. Because emotional abuse rarely involves criminal assaults, its victims are unlikely to receive protection under this proposal. The severest 10 per cent of cases in the study amply demonstrate the need for emotional maltreatment to be a registerable form of abuse whose victims require child protection services.

In theory, the refocusing to a needs-led assessment rather than investigations should benefit children suffering from primary emotional abuse. However, unlike physical and sexual abuse there are rarely serious, acute episodes, nor is there an unequivocal link between cause and negative effect as in physical neglect. Emotional abuse, which of all the forms of abuse is the most damaging to self-concept and emotional development, requires skilled, energetic assessment and proficient, carefully planned intervention. However, as Thoburn et al. (2000) point out, demonstrating harm in emotional abuse cases is difficult. Therefore, intervention is likely to be no higher than 'Level 3, Compromised' or 'Level 2, vulnerable' (see Calder, Chapter 2, Figure 3). There is the danger that emotional abuse cases will be filtered out of receiving social work services altogether.

Interagency working

There are particular problems in interagency working in cases where emotional abuse is the sole form because of the different roles and powers of the various welfare professions. The recognition of physical abuse and neglect was spear headed by the powerful male-dominated medical profession and, because serious physical assault and serious neglect are criminal offences, a second powerful male-dominated profession, the police, became centrally involved. Child sexual abuse took longer to be acknowledged. Finkelhor (1984) argued this was because doctors were less involved since 'few victims of sexual abuse show any medically significant traumas' (p10). Nevertheless, medical examinations are often required and many types of sexual abuse constitute a criminal offence, therefore again the medical profession and the police have a central role in such cases.

Emotional abuse, existing in the absence of physical or sexual assault, rarely involves criminal actions and it only indirectly enters into the domain of the medical profession. Hobbs (1992), for example, argued that

paediatricians have a central role in child abuse but does not mention emotional abuse in his review of child protection issues.

Emotional abuse, in all but its most florid manifestations, is predominantly the concern of the female-dominated and arguably less powerful professions of social work, nursery nursing, primary school teaching and health visiting. These are the professionals in a position to observe day-to-day child-parent interaction but whose voices are less likely to be heard. Unlike physical or sexual assault, which might be referred directly to the police or hospitals, concerned lay people will refer their concerns about emotional maltreatment to social work agencies, local school or nursery staff or community nurses. Doyle (1998) found 51 per cent of emotional abuse referrals came to social services department directly from family members and neighbours, while a further 18 per cent were from schools and health visitors. In Glaser et al. (2001) the figures were similar, 45 per cent from family members and 14 per cent from schools and health visitors.

Without doctors and the police using their power to advocate on behalf of emotionally maltreated children, physical abuse and neglect and sexual exploitation are likely to be prioritised above cases of primary emotional abuse.

Beyond the framework

Making an assessment is essential and valuable. However the assessment is only part of intervention. There is little point in spending time simply collecting and evaluating information without planning and implementing intervention.

Once emotional abuse has been identified professionals have to decide what to do about it. With physical and sexual abuse the first and obvious action is to stop the physical or sexual assaults. In cases of physical neglect the immediate and obvious action is to ensure that the children are nourished, clean, healthy and physically safe. In emotional abuse there is rarely such clarity about aims and priorities.

With other forms of abuse, removal of the children from home in the most serious or intractable instances should automatically improve matters by ensuring that the children are safe from assault or neglect. But in emotional abuse the act of removal may compound the children's sense of rejection and abandonment. This does not mean that removal is never appropriate in emotional abuse cases but it is only rarely a satisfactory solution.

Ezzell, Cupit Swenson and Brondino (2000), who investigated the importance of support for physically abused children, wrote 'If a child has few supportive relationships, interventions that target enhancing children's social support network may be beneficial' (p649). Doyle's (1998) research suggested that this is also true in cases of emotional abuse. A possible intervention therefore is to develop and strengthen those sources of help that can enhance the child's esteem and provide a sense of trust and security. These are discussed in detail in Doyle (2001) but are summarised in this section.

Much of the focus of work in abuse cases is ensuring the child is well supported by the 'non-abusing parent'. But the emotional needs and relationship difficulties of both parents in emotional abuse cases may be such that they are unable to reach out consistently to their children. Glaser et al. (2001) noted 'In all but two of the two-carer families both carers were identified as abusers' (p14). This is very much in line with the findings of Doyle (1998, 2001) where interviewed survivors said that neither parent was emotionally available or supportive.

Siblings are often important although some parents, particularly the rigid, controlling ones, use a divide and rule policy. Where siblings already support each other or can be helped to assist each other, they are of considerable importance and the potential for mutual support always needs to be assessed.

A major support or life-line for the overwhelming majority of the children in Doyle's (2001) study were 'aunts' in the widest definition of the term. Some were the parents' siblings but others were family friends or neighbours. It seems that a caring figure who, unlike grandparents, do not become embroiled in the family tensions but are close enough to understand them can send powerful messages to children that they are valuable people, worth spending time, resources and effort on.

School teachers and peer-group friends were also principal forms of support. This concurs with Milling Kinard's (2001) finding; 'For some maltreated children the school environment may serve to enhance their self-perceptions, particularly if they receive approval and support from teachers and peers' (p41).

For some otherwise unloved children, pets can give unconditional love. One survivor explained:

From about the age of 5 to 20 I had a dog. He was a brother and a friend. He was my world. I used to dress him up ... Dad was very cruel to him and beat him badly. I could comfort him. It meant I wasn't the only one to be badly treated. I did not feel so guilty.
(Doyle, 2001, p396).

Ascione (1998) who has researched extensively the relationship between pets and abuse writes that one of the problems of using shelters in domestic violence cases is that it 'entails separating children from buffers in their environment (e.g. toys, pets)' (p131). Accommodation or removal into care may similarly involve 'separation from beloved pets, who may be significant sources of psychological support and attachment' (p131).

Finally, the value for emotionally abused children of play, toys and play therapy should not be underestimated. One survivor said 'we were desperate for someone to listen to us, play therapy would have been wonderful' (Doyle, 2001, p395).

In Doyle's (1998, 2001) studies a recurrent theme was the escape into an imaginary world through toys and books. Some toys like 'Big Teddy' were rather like pets, giving the children unconditional love and an understanding ear.

Conclusion

A careful use of the Assessment Framework will help to identify children who are being emotionally abused as the primary form of abuse and could help professionals to address their needs. However, the recognition that emotional abuse occurs in a huge diversity of families, the use of Maslow's needs framework and the assessment of children's 'life-lines' or supports are all essential if, in accordance with the aspiration of the Department of Health (2001, pviii), the assessment is to prove effective in 'securing the wellbeing of' emotionally abused children.

References

Ascione, F.R. (1998) Battered Women's Reports of Their Partners' and Their Children's Cruelty to Animals. *Journal of Emotional Abuse.* 1: 1, 119–33.

Baker, A.W. and Duncan, S.P. (1985) Child Sexual Abuse: A Study of Prevalence in Great Britain. *Child Abuse and Neglect.* 9: 4, 457–68.

Besharov, D.J. (1981) Toward Better Research on Child Abuse and Neglect: Making Definitional Issues an Explicit Methodological Concern. *Child Abuse and Neglect.* 5: 383–90.

Bourton, A. (1991) No Intention to Abuse: Recognising Emotional Abuse. *Journal of Law and Practice.* 2: 1, 45–50.

Bowlby, J. with Ainsworth, M. (1965) *Child Care and the Growth of Love.* (2nd edn.). Harmondsworth: Penguin.

Brassard, M.R. and Gelardo, M.S. (1987) Psychological Maltreatment: The Unifying Construct in Child Abuse and Neglect. *School Psychology Review,* 16: 2, 127–36.

Brassard, M., Germain, R. and Hart, S. (Eds.) (1987) *Psychological Maltreatment of Children and Youth.* New York: Pergamon Press.

Briere, J. and Runtz, M. (1990) Differential Syptomatology Associated With Three Types of Child Abuse Histories. *Child Abuse and Neglect.* 14: 357–64.

Burnett, B.B. (1993) The Psychological Abuse of Latency Age Children: A Survey. *Child Abuse and Neglect.* 17: 4, 441–54.

Claussen, A.H. and Crittenden, P.M.(1991) Physical and Psychological Abuse: Relations Among Types of Maltreatment. *Child Abuse and Neglect.* 15: 5–18.

Coulton, C.J., Korbin, J.E., Su, M. and Chow, J. (1995) Community Level Factors and Child Maltreatment Rates. *Child Development.* 66: 1262–76.

Covitz, J. (1986) *Emotional Child Abuse: The Family Curse.* Boston: Sigo.

Creighton, S.J. and Russell, N. (1995) *Voices from Childhood.* London: NSPCC.

Crittenden, P.M., Claussen, A.H. and Sugarman, D.B. (1993) Physical and Psychological Maltreatment In Middle Childhood and Adolescence. *Development and Psychopathology.* 6: 145–64.

Department of Health, Home Office, Department for Education and Employment. (1999). *Working Together to Safeguard Children.* London: The Stationery Office.

Department of Health (2000) *Framework for the Assessment of Children in Need and Their Families.* London: The Stationery Office.

Department of Health and Social Security (DHSS) (1980) *Child Abuse: Central Register Systems.* LASSL (80) 4, HN (80) 20.

Doyle. C. (1997a) Emotional Abuse of Children: Issues for Intervention. *Child Abuse Review.* 6: 330–42.

Doyle. C. (1997b) Protection Studies: Challenging Oppression and Discrimination. *Social Work Education.* 16: 2, 8–18.

Doyle, C. (1998) *Emotional Abuse of Children: Issues for Intervention.* Unpublished doctoral thesis, University of Leicester.

Doyle, C. (2001) Surviving and Coping With Emotional Abuse in Childhood. *Clinical Child Psychology and Psychiatry.* 6: 3, 387–402.

Edwards, D. (2001) Emotion. In Wetherell, M., Taylor, S. and Yates, S.J. (Eds.) *Discourse Theory and Practice.* London: Sage, 236–46.

Erikson, E.H. (1965) *Childhood and Society.* Harmondsworth: Penguin.

Ezzell, C.E., Cupit Swenson, C. and Bronding, M.J. (2000). The Relationship of Social Support to Physically Abused Children's Adjustment. *Child Abuse and Neglect.*24: 5, 641–51.

Finkelhor, D. (1984) *Child Sexual Abuse: New Theory and Research.* New York: The Free Press.

Fogarty, M. (1980) Emotional Abuse to be Included in Registers. *Social Work Today.* 12: 1, 4.

Foucault, M. (1980) *Power/knowledge.* Brighton: Harvester.

Furnell, J.R.G., Dutton, P.V. & Harris, J. (1988) Emotional Abuse Referrals to a Scottish Children's Panel Reporter Over Five Years. *Medical Science Law.* 28: 3, 219–26.

Garbarino, J. (1978) The Elusive 'Crime' of Emotional Abuse. *Child Abuse and Neglect.* 2: 89–99.

Garbarino, J. and Garbarino, A.C. (1986) *Emotional Maltreatment of Children.* (2nd edn.) Chicago: National Committee for the Prevention of Child Abuse.

Garbarino, J. and Gilliam, G. (1980). *Understanding Abusive Families.* Lexington, Mass: Lexington Books.

Garbarino, J., Guttmann, E. and Seely, J.W. (1986) *The Psychologically Battered Child.* San Francisco: Jossey Bass.

Garbarino, J. and Kostelny, K. (1992) Child Maltreatment as a Community Problem. *Child Abuse and Neglect,* 16: 4, 454–64.

Garbarino, J. and Vondra, J. (1987). Psychological Maltreatment: Issues and Perspective. In Brassard, M.R., Germain, R.B. and Hart, S.N. (Eds.) *Psychological Maltreatment of Children and Youth.* New York: Pergamon Press. 25–44.

Gibson, A. and Lewis, C. (1985) *A Light in the Dark Tunnel.* London: Centre for Caribbean Studies.

Glaser, D,, Prior, V and Lynch, M.A. (2001) *Emotional Abuse and Emotional Neglect:*

Antecedents, Operational Definitions and Consequences. York: BASPCAN.

Gross, R.D. (1992). *Psychology: The Science of Mind and Behaviour* (2nd edn.) London: Hodder & Stoughton.

Haj-Yahia, M. and Shor, R. (1995) Child Maltreatment as Perceived by Arab Students of Social Science in the West Bank. *Child Abuse and Neglect*. 19: 10, 1209–20.

Hallet, C. (1995) Child Abuse: an Academic Overview. In Kingston, P. and Penhale, B. (Eds.) *Family Violence and the Caring Professions*. London: Macmillan, 32–49.

Handy, C. (1985) *Understanding Organisations*. (3rd edn.) Harmondsworth: Penguin.

Hart, S.N., Binggeli, N.J. and Brassard, M.R. (1998) Evidence for the Effects of Psychological Maltreatment. *Journal of Emotional Abuse*. 1: 1, 27–58.

Hart, S.N., Germain, R.B. and Brassard, M. (1987) The Challenge: To Better Understand and Combat Psychological Maltreatment of Children and Youth. In Brassard, M., Germain, R.B. and Hart, S.N. (Eds.) *Psychological Maltreatment of Children And Youth*. New York: Pergamon Press. 3–24.

Haugaard, J.J (1991) Defining Psychological Maltreatment: A Prelude to Research or an Outcome of Research? *Development & Psychopathology*. 3: 71–7.

Hawker, M. (1995) Let's Scrap the Guidelines. *Professional Social Work*. Aug, 4.

Hayes, N. (1994) *Foundations of Psychology*. London: Routledge.

Higgins, D.J. and McCabe, M.P. (2000) Relationships Between Different Types of Maltreatment During Childhood and Adjustment in Adulthood. *Child Maltreatment*. 5: 3, 251–60.

Hobbs, C. (1992) Paediatric Intervention in Child Protection. *Child Abuse Review*. 1: 1, 5–18.

Iwaniec, D. (1995) *The Emotionally Abused and Neglected Child*. Chichester: Wiley.

Jackson, D.D. and Weakland, J. (1961) Conjoint Family Therapy. *Psychiatry*. 24: 34–45.

Jellen, L. K., McCarroll, J.E. and Thayer, L.E. (2001) Child Emotional Maltreatment: A Two Year Study of US Army Cases. *Child Abuse & Neglect*. 25: 5, 623–39.

Khamis, V. (2000) Child Psychological Maltreatment in Palestinian Families. *Child Abuse & Neglect*. 24: 8, 1047–61.

Krishan, V. and Morrison, K.B. (1995). An Ecological Model of Child Maltreatment in a Canadian Province. *Child Abuse & Neglect*. 19: 1, 101–14.

Krugman, R.D. and Krugman, M.K. (1984) Emotional Abuse in the Classroom. *American Journal of Development and Cognition*. 138: 284–6.

Lachkar, J. (2000) Emotional Abuse of High-Functioning Professional Women: A Psychodynamic Perspective. *Journal of Emotional Abuse*. 2: 1, 73–92.

La Fontaine, J.S. (1990) *Child Sexual Abuse*. Cambridge: Polity Press.

Lask, B. (1987) Family Therapy. *British Medical Journal*. 294: 203–4.

Maslow, A.H. (1970) *Motivation and Personality*. (2nd edn.) New York: Harper Row.

McGee, R.A. and Wolfe, D.A. (1991a) Psychological Maltreatment: Toward an Operational Definition. *Development & Psychopathology*. 3: 3–18.

McGee, R.A. and Wolfe, D.A. (1991b) Between a Rock and a Hard Place: Where Do We Go From Here in Defining Psychological Maltreatment? *Development & Psychopathology*. 3: 119–24.

Milling Killard, E. (2001) Perceived and Actual Academic Competence in Maltreated Children. *Child Abuse and Neglect*. 25: 1, 33–46.

Navarre, E.L. (1987) Psychological Maltreatment: the Core Component of Child Abuse. In Brassard, M. Germain, R. and Hart S. (Eds.) *Psychological Maltreatment of Children and Youth*. New York: Pergamon Press, 45–58.

Nesbit, W. (1991) Emotional Abuse: Vulnerability and Developmental Delay. *Developmental Disabilities Bulletin*. 19: 2, 66–80.

O' Hagan, K. (1993) *Emotional and Psychological Abuse of Children*. Milton Keynes: Open University Press.

O' Hagan, K. (1995) Emotional and Psychological Abuse: Problems of Definition. *Child Abuse and Neglect*. 19: 4, 449–62.

Pearlman, L.A. (1998) Trauma and the Self: A Theoretical and Clinical Perspective. *Journal of Emotional Abuse*. 1: 1, 7–26.

Roer-Strier, D. (2001) Reducing Risk for Children in Changing Cultural Contexts: Recommendations for Intervention and Training. *Child Abuse and Neglect*. 25: 2, 231–48.

Rohner, R.P. and Brothers, S.A. (1999) Perceived Parental Rejection, Psychological Maladjustment, and Borderline Personality Disorder. *Journal of Emotional Abuse*. 1: 4, 81–95.

Sanchez-Hucles, J.V. (1998) Racism: Emotional Abusiveness and Emotional Trauma for Ethnic Minorities. *Journal of Emotional Abuse.* 1: 2, 69–88.

Shumba, A. (2001) The Epidemiology and Etiology of Reported Cases of Child Physical Abuse in Zimbabwean Primary Schools. *Child Abuse and Neglect.* 25: 2, 265–78.

Solberg, A. (1990) Negotiating Childhood: Changing Construction of Age for Norwegian Children. In James, A. and Prout, A (Eds.) *Constructing and Reconstructing Childhood.* London: Falmer Press.

Starkey, S.L. (1980) The Relationship Between Parental Acceptance-Rejection and the Academic Performance of Fourth and Fifth Graders. *Behaviour Science Research.* 15: 67–80.

Thoburn, J., Wilding, J. and Watson, J. (2000) *Family Support in Cases of Emotional Maltreatment and Neglect.* London: The Stationery Office.

Witkietz, K. and Dodge-Reyome, N. (2000) Recollections of Childhood Psychological Maltreatment and Self-reported Eating Disordered Behaviours in Undergraduate College Females. *Journal of Emotional Abuse.* 2: 1, 15–29.

Chapter Fifteen

A Framework for Assessing Failure-to-Thrive

Professor Dorota Iwaniec

Introduction

The Framework for Assessment of children in need (DoH, 2000) has been issued by the Government with the intention of providing holistic, child-centred, much more targeted help for children based on assessment of their developmental needs. The Assessment framework is multi-dimensional, informed by research findings and evaluation of 'what works best in practice'. Ecological theory was adopted emphasising the importance of taking into consideration the child's individual family, community, and society in general when assessing both problems and needs.

A good understanding of child development is required in order to make appropriate judgement as to whether the quality of child care is good enough to meet a range of different and complex developmental needs which have to be addressed during each stage of the child's life. The philosophy of the Framework aims to redirect assessment attention from the risks and blame culture to the developmental attainments or lack of appropriate progression for the child's chronological age, to suitable provision of services for those who require help. Additionally, it is rightly argued that the 'wait and see' approach needs to be avoided when dealing with cases where evidence suggests a poor prognosis for change in parenting, thus promoting quicker decision-making to avoid escalation of presenting problems leading to significant harm. There is emphasis on providing better distribution of resources for all children in need, and to narrow the gap between protection and family support.

This chapter will deal with the assessment of children who fail-to-thrive generally, and specifically with those whose growth and developmental failures are associated with psycho-social aetiology. A range of factors relevant to failure-to-thrive, which are indicated in the Assessment Framework triangle, will be described and supported by the research findings. Some assessment instruments, developed by the author over the years, will be provided. Not all assessment factors will be

dealt with as children who fail-to-thrive are young, mostly infants and toddlers, so some aspects are not that relevant for their age.

Special emphasis will be given to identification of the major problems associated with failure-to-thrive (FTT) based on research findings and practice outcomes. Issues, such as measurement of physical growth, provision of nutrition, feeding problems and feeding style, a child's individual characteristics and interaction between carers and child, attachment and relationships, and demographic factors, will be discussed.

What is Failure-to-Thrive?

During the first year after birth human growth is quicker than at any other time during childhood, decreasing rapidly until the end of the third year, then continuing at about one-third of its post-natal rate until puberty. However, not all children grow at the same rate and there are many different reasons for this.

Some children might fail-to-thrive because of illnesses, some because they are not given sufficient food, some because of being neglected or abused, some because of acute feeding difficulties (or their carers' lack of understanding of children's nutritional and nurturing needs), and others from being rejected and under-stimulated or living in a poor, deprived environment. There is seldom one factor which determines failure-to-thrive. The aetiology is multi-factorial.

It is often said that the size of the parents will determine the size of the child: in other words, if parents are small they will produce a small child; and when they are tall (or at least one of them is) they will tend to have a big child. However, we need to remember that some of those parents might have failed-to-thrive as children and therefore have not reached their genetic potential because of under-nutrition or all round deprivation. It is advisable to take a good social history of parents, exploring their childhood, so some light is shed on their early health, development, and welfare.

Let us look then at how failure-to-thrive is

Figure 1: Profile of children who fail-to-thrive.

Failure-to-thrive
- child falls below the 3rd percentile in weight often in height and head circumference

Physical appearance
- small, thin, wasted body, thin arms and legs, enlarged stomach, thin, wispy, dull and falling hair, dark circles around the eyes

Characteristic features
- feeding-eating problems
- vomiting, heaving
- refusal to chew and swallow
- diarrhoea
- frequent colds and infections

Insecure attachment
- tense when in the mother's company;
- does not show interest and pleasure when with the mother or carer;
- does not show distress when mother leaves

Developmental retardation
- motor development
- language development
- social development
- intellectual development
- emotional development
- cognitive development

Psychological description and behaviour
- sadness, withdrawal, and detachment
- expressionless face
- general lethargy
- tearful
- frequent whining
- minimal or no smiling
- diminished vocalisation
- staring blankly at people or objects
- lack of cuddliness
- unresponsiveness
- insecure attachment
- passivity

Problematic behaviour and psychological description
- whining and crying
- restlessness
- irritability
- sadness, withdrawal, and detachment
- general lethargy
- minimal or no smiling
- poor vocalisation
- staring blankly at people and objects
- lack of cuddliness
- unresponsiveness
- passivity
- apprehension
- anxiety

---

defined and how it can be identified and assessed.

Failure-to-thrive is defined in many ways, but fundamentally it is failure to grow in terms of weight, height, and head circumference, in a healthy and vigorous way, and failure to develop in the psychosocial way according to the child's chronological age. It is conceived as a variable syndrome of severe growth-retardation, delayed skeletal maturation and problematic psychomotor development, which are often associated with illnesses, nutrition inadequate for normal growth, acute feeding difficulties (including motor-oral problems), disturbed mother-child interaction and relationship, poor parenting, neglect, insecure attachment, family dysfunctioning, depression, social isolation, and poverty (Drotar, 1991; Frank and Zeisel, 1988; Iwaniec, Herbert, and McNeish, 1985a).

Failure-to-thrive is normally diagnosed within the first two years of life, although its effects and consequences can be observed much later than this. Estimates of prevalence have varied from as many as 10 per cent of the deprived children seen in outpatient clinics in both urban and rural areas to 1 per cent of all paediatric hospitalisations (Bithoney and Newberger, 1987). McMillan (1988) estimated that FTT probably affects 1–3 per cent of the child population at any time.

Some children may fail-to-thrive because of an organic or medical condition. A direct predictable link can normally be observed between the course of the illness and the child's growth patterns (e.g. after a successful course of treatment or an operation the child's growth pattern will gradually stabilise and return to normal). But, although nearly all childhood illnesses result in growth failure to some extent, there may also be more subtle organic problems which, if not taken into account, may lead to making wrong assumptions. These include oral motor difficulties and pre-natal factors. However, it is estimated that less than 5 per cent of all FTT is due solely to organic disease (Wright and Talbot, 1996; Wynne, 1996).

Most of the children who fail-to-thrive come into the category of non-organic FTT. They are physically healthy, but their environment and quality of parenting may be inadequate and stressful to promote appropriate growth and development. The range of triggering factors is quite wide including neglectful parenting, deficiencies in child-rearing knowledge, maternal depression and lack of social and emotional support, immature personality, mental illness, and learning difficulties. Factors contributing to non-organic failure-to-thrive are varied and complex and need to be studied separately and together as there is seldom one factor responsible for triggering the problem and prolonging it.

Failure-to-thrive is generally defined in terms of growth. When children are under-nourished they fail to gain weight. After a while their growth in height also falters. On growth charts they drop below the third or fifth percentiles of weight or height. Most children are diagnosed as failure-to-thrive when their weight or height percentiles are low; others are diagnosed when their growth crosses percentile lines downwards. Under-nutrition also impairs brain growth, so the head circumference is measured as well.

Children who fail-to-thrive as infants are found to be at high risk of developmental delays, personality problems, abuse and neglect, and even death. The effect of early malnutrition may be extensive, given the rapid period of growth, particularly brain growth, which occurs during the first five years of life (Wynne, 1996). Slow weight-gain in infancy can also lead to subsequent stunting of growth. If successful and appropriate intervention does not take place at an early stage, failure-to-thrive may lead to the distortion of the parent–child relationship, serious attachment disorders, disturbed behaviour, and developmental impairment, especially in cognitive and emotional areas. These effects may be long-lasting persisting into adulthood as well as to the next generation (Iwaniec, 2000).

Psychosocial short stature (emotional stunting of growth)

Children with a long and severe history of failure-to-thrive are almost always rejected, emotionally abused, and cruelly treated by their families. They are labelled as psychosocial short-stature, thought to stem from emotional abuse or hostility experienced at home. Children who come into this category of failure-to-thrive are those who are exceptionally short and remain stunted for a considerable time, although there is no obvious organic reason for their poor growth. Weight is normally below that expected for the height. The child might appear well-nourished, but that may be deceptive because neither weight nor height is normal for the chronological age (Skuse, 1989). It is believed that children exposed to severe stress and emotional adversity may be stunted in growth and that functioning of growth-hormone secretion could be arrested. Once the child is removed from the stressful environment, growth and development quickly accelerate, but if returned to the same environment a marked deterioration becomes evident and behaviour worsens (Iwaniec, 1995; Skuse et al., 1996). Serious attachment problems resulting in rejection and physical abuse were found in Iwaniec's 1983 study. She argued that failure of professionals to detect and deal with FTT children at the onset of the problem can lead to serious emotional and physical abuse and neglect, often resulting in care proceedings.

There are striking behavioural characteristics of these children, such as bizarre eating patterns, disturbed toileting, destructiveness, defiant hostility and self-harming behaviour, and abnormal sleeping patterns. Distorted behaviour around food tends to emerge at the older toddler stage, although early history is of under-eating, and is expressed in two ways: by either an excessive hunger drive, hoarding and searching for food at night, eating non-food items, eating quickly and voraciously to the point of gorging and vomiting; or by poor appetite, food faddiness, and refusal to eat. When pressed to eat they tend to heave, store food in their mouths, and chew and swallow with difficulty.

Attachment between these children and their mothers is usually anxious/avoidant and

Figure 2: Psychosocial short stature.

Growth retardation
Child's weight and height and head circumference below expected norms.

Physical appearance
Small, thin, short legs.
Enlarged stomach.
Disproportionate body build.

Characteristic features
Bizarre eating behaviour, excessive eating, an obsessive preoccupation with food, hoarding food, begging food from strangers, eating non-food items, searching for food during night and hiding, scavenging food from waste-bins, voracious eating, gorging and vomiting. Some children eat little as a result of chronic malnutrition.

Attachment disorder
- mutually antagonistic relationship
- active rejection
- hostile or extremely poor mother-child interaction
- addressing mother as "miss", "lady" (elective mutism)
- lack of proper stranger anxiety
- insecure avoidant attachment

Development retardation
Language
Social
Motor
Intellectual
Cognitive
Emotional
Toilet-training

Behaviour
Bizarre eating pattern (over-eating), soiling, wetting, smearing, defiance, demanding, destructiveness, whining, fire-setting, screaming, aggression, short-attention span, poor sleeping, head-banging.

Psychological description
Withdrawal, expressionless face, detachment, depression, sadness, minimal or no smiling, diminished vocalisation, refusal to speak to mother, staring blankly at people or objects, unresponsiveness, lack of cuddliness.

relationships are mutually antagonistic. Discipline is harsh and cruel and may involve frequently withdrawing food as a punishment for a minor misbehaviour and making a hungry child watch others eat. Locking up a child in the bedroom for a long time, or getting rid of a favourite toy is quite common (Iwaniec, 1995).

Disturbed behaviour, poor developmental and school performance attainments, as well as poor social adjustment, have been reported over the years by many researchers (Blizzard and Bulatovic, 1993; Powell et al., 1967).

It is believed that acute stress affects growth hormonal functioning and that the excessive eating of some of these children is a reaction to cope with stress. It is argued that excessive appetite is not simply a response to food restriction (which often happens) but is more associated with ongoing emotional stress. It is also proposed that a proportion of these children showing under-eating behaviour is stunted because of chronic nutritional deficiencies (Skuse et al., 1996).

Characteristics associated with families of children who fail-to-thrive are given below:

- poverty
- increased levels of family stress
- low levels of maternal education

- lack of knowledge about parenting
- poor social support
- high levels of dietary restraint in carers
- maternal depression
- low parental self esteem
- distorted perception and attitudes towards the target child
- physical and emotional distancing from the child
- limited interaction with the child
- finding the child difficult to manage and enjoy
- insecure attachment

Figure 2 provides a tabulated overview of these issues.

Dimensions of child's developmental needs

General overview

Human development is viewed in terms of the accomplishment of crucial socialisation tasks. Those tasks will be learned and skills acquired if the socialising agents such as parents create an atmosphere and opportunities for the child to learn to the best of its ability. Parents, however, if they are to meet children's socialisation tasks, require complex parenting skills and physical and emotional resources to fulfil those obligations.

Failure-to-thrive demonstrates itself in different ways and in varying degrees, from lack of care and provision of basic physical needs to lack of attention to stimulation and encouragement of optimal growth and development. It also manifests itself by failure to provide love, a sense of security, belonging to the family, a feeling of being wanted and appreciated, recognised and praised for achievements, educated and guided towards social competence, being given the opportunity to explore the environment and learn from new experiences. As they seldom are praised their development of self-esteem is poor. Some children are simply difficult to feed and to care for, which can lead to disturbed interaction between the caregiver and the child.

From the time of birth infants can signal information about their needs. Where the mother perceives the signal accurately and responds appropriately, the mother-infant relationship is said to be characterised by synchrony, which facilitates the baby's development and is a source of satisfaction to the mother. It is postulated that those children whose parents respond to their signals of communications promptly and appropriately throughout infancy, develop confidence in their parents' availability and will have the security to use them as a base from which to explore their environment (Belsky and Nerworski, 1988). Insecure children, on the other hand, tend to be anxious about their parents' availability and show little confidence in their reaction to the world. Because human infants are so totally dependent for so long they need to know that they can depend on the outside world. If their basic needs are met, they are thought to develop basic trust in parents, and thus to evolve a nucleus of self-trust, which is indispensable for later development.

When children's needs are not met, their physical, cognitive, intellectual, and emotional development is quite likely to be arrested. In infancy curtailed development will tend to show itself in insecure attachment and delayed psychosocial development; in pre-school children it will be manifested in disturbance of social and emotional behaviour, and in school-age children it will show itself in serious learning deficits and behavioural problems.

Dimensions of child's developmental needs and failure-to-thrive

Health

Failure-to-thrive can be caused by physical illness. For example, illnesses such as central nervous system malformations can interfere with the complex regulations of appetite, sucking, swallowing, and digestion. Infection may make the infant too lethargic or weak to eat. On the other hand, disorders such as cleft lip may have little impact on the primary aspects of feeding, but may interfere with the parent-infant feeding interaction style and this may secondarily disturb the feeding process. As Woolston (1984) observes, some physical illnesses as diarrhoea may primarily be a result of the malnutrition. However, the diarrhoea may also exacerbate the feeding disorder by making the infant less efficient at calorie and fluid absorption. Some children would require medical examination and testing to exclude possible organic reasons for their FTT.

Measuring weight, height and head circumference

The primary feature of children with failure-to-thrive is a disturbance or poor physical growth. But how do we know that a child's growth is cause for concern? During the first two years after birth an infant's weight, height, head circumference and general psychosocial development are routinely recorded either by a health visitor or at a baby clinic. We know that not all children grow and develop at the same speed and that there is some variation. In order to see how well a child is developing its measurements are normally compared to growth charts which show the expected range of measurements from that particular population of children at a particular age. If a child is showing a growth rate lower than most of the population then this is taken to be cause for concern and the child is diagnosed as failing-to-thrive. Investigations are then made to discover the cause of the growth problems in order to identify the best treatment or intervention. Assessments are sometimes carried out by the medical profession, e.g. paediatrician, if it is thought that there might be an organic reason for failure-to-thrive, and health visitors or social workers doing psychosocial assessment. Occasionally child psychiatrists or psychologists are involved when cases are more complex. However, it is important to mention that practitioners and researchers have disagreed when exactly a child's growth failure is serious enough to give cause for concern. Maggiori and Lifshitz (1995) concluded that the central issue in defining failure-to-thrive is not the terminology by which it is described, but the choice of growth indices by which it is identified.

With regard to physical measurements, weight-for-age, height-for-age, and weight-for-height, have all been used alone or in combination. Growth charts applicable to each sex are used which give the range of expected growth at various ages, although there is no general agreement as to which charts are most appropriate. Stuart and National Centre on Health Statistics (NCHS) charts are most often employed.

Regardless of what chart is used, these measures are commonly divided into centiles (percentiles). The simplest common definition of growth failure appears to be a drop below the 3rd centile for weight for children of that age (Batchelor, 1996; Boddy and Skuse, 1994). Only 3 per cent of children in the population will fit into this category. Furthermore, to state that a child is failing-to-thrive, a child's weight needs to remain for a period of time, e.g. one month below either the 3rd or 5th centile (Wilensky et al., 1996).

Apart from being below the 3rd or 5th centile the child can fall down across centiles, e.g. from 50th to the 25th or 10th centile. This might simply indicate natural slimming, but it can also indicate some traumatic events, e.g. abuse, abandonment, separation, anxiety, or development of some serious diseases. In such cases special attention needs to be paid in order to identify the reason for the loss of weight.

Feeding/eating

The most common factor in failure-to-thrive is the feeding/eating behaviour of those children. Most studies identified feeding difficulties over a prolonged period of time (Ayoub and Milner, 1985; Iwaniec et al., 1985a; Pollitt, 1975). Hampton (1996) suggested that the only common factor in children with non-organic failure-to-thrive was the presence of feeding difficulties. The evidence arising from different studies has shown badly organised and anxious meal-times and more difficulties in feeding among families with children who are failing-to-thrive than is the case with controls (Dawson, 1992; Iwaniec, 1991; Skuse et al., 1994). Mothers are reported to be less sensitive, infants more negative while being fed, and vocal interaction infrequent in comparison with control groups. Drotar et al. (1981); Drotar et al. (1990); Hanks and Hobbs (1993); and Iwaniec (1983) found that the majority of children in their samples had experienced significant feeding problems such as spitting up, storing food in their mouths, poor sucking and appetite refusal to take solids, rumination, and long-time feeding. Feeding difficulties tended to emerge soon after birth. For example Raynor and Rudolf (1996) reported that a concerning number of mothers described difficulties in feeding their infants starting in the first three months of life.

Skuse et al. (1994) found that a substantial number of their non-organic FTT infants were reported as having slept through feeds during the first year of life, and their parents were less likely to wake them for feeds. The authors pointed out that some mothers woke their babies for the feed but many did not and found that the children who slept through the feeds had lower weights for their age. Iwaniec (1995) reported maternal lack of awareness that a child was extremely thin and was offered an inadequate amount of food for its age. Additionally, a child's slow feeding was often interpreted as not being hungry and consequently was not given enough food. Tables 1 and 2 provide a sample daily eating record and details of interactional styles.

Malnutrition

Research and practice evidence indicates that FTT children are severely under-nourished. Hanks and Hobbs (1993) concluded from their research that the issue with children who fail-to-thrive was caloric rather than protein or any other specific dietary deficiency. This suggests an inadequate quantity of food, rather than a problem with the quality.

There may be several reasons why a child may ingest an inadequate amount of food. The child may simply eat less than other children. These children also do not show an interest in food. It has been known for the parents to over-dilute expensive formula feeds in order to save money, whilst not realising that the child's dietary requirements will not be met

Table 1: Daily eating record (a sample).

Date	Time	Food amount	Method of feeding	Time taken	Mother's feelings
Wednesday 20 October	8.30 a.m.	½ Weetabix, a little milk	Being fed	45 minutes	exhausted, depressed, bad start to the day
	10.00 a.m.	100 mls milk		10 minutes	
	11.45 a.m.	½ potato, 2 pieces of carrots, few pieces of lamb, gravy	Began herself, but then refused to swallow meat. Mother ended up liquidising the child's lunch and feeding it to her, almost by force	1 hour 20 minutes	Angry and depressed
	3.00 p.m.	3 spoons of yoghurt, 1 biscuit	Fed herself	20 minutes	Very tired
	5.30 p.m.	1 chip, 2 spoons of baked beans	Being fed, refused to eat fish		Gave up, asked her father to feed her
	7.00 p.m.	Cup of drinking chocolate		10 minutes	

Table 2: Interactional styles and characteristic behaviour: description of interaction behaviour.

Carer's feeding style	Behaviour of carers	Reaction of children
Forceful, impatient, and angry	Rushing child to eat, getting easily frustrated and angry, screaming, shaking, smacking, frequent force-feeding, anxious.	Refusal to eat, crying, choking, vomiting, stretching out, fearful and apprehensive, uneasy when in the carer's company. Little intake of food.
Unconcerned and neglectful	Failure to respond to child's signal of hunger and distress. Fed irregularly and in a haphazard way. Not appropriate food given. Seldom picked up when fed.	Lethargic, withdrawn, sleep a lot. Little movement, seldom heard. Looking detached and sad. Little intake of food.
Not persistent and passive	React to stress with high anxiety. Tend to get depressed and helpless. Low self-esteem. Give up easily, unable to cope and to exert authority.	Strong willed, persistent, irritable, getting their own way, manipulating, miserable. Persistent refusal to eat, to swallow and chew. Little intake of food.
Determined and coaxing	Preoccupied with feeding. Generally resourceful, patient, try different ways to manage, try different food. Anxious about child's poor growth.	Long feeding periods, faddiness, spitting, storing food in mouth, heaving, refusal to chew. Stubborn and difficult to distract. Little intake of food.

Hathaway, 1989). Another possibility is that the child ingests the same caloric intake as other children but, for some reason, is not able to make the best use of it.

Infants and young children who fail-to-thrive may also have some organic features that contribute to, but do not explain, their growth failure. For example, it has been shown that in otherwise healthy FTT infants, significant degrees of oral motor dysfunction are common, such as problems with sucking, chewing, and swallowing (Iwaniec, 1995; Lewis, 1982; Skuse, 1993). Consequently, parents may be faced with a significant yet subtle and often unappreciated obstacle to ensuring the child ingests adequate nutrition for growth.

Contextual features, such as inappropriate positioning during feeding may also compound these problems, or a distracting place where the child is being fed like the main living room, and it was found that twice as many infants who were failing-to-thrive had habitually been fed with a bottle propped in their mouth. Direct observation of feeding style would be beneficial for assessment purposes and then for devising treatment and intervention.

Education

Developmental Delays

It is widely recognised that a child's early experiences can have long lasting effects on their later development (Rutter, 1995). Cases of non-organic failure-to-thrive are particularly worrying since these children show poor developmental outcomes, particularly for mental abilities (Dowdney et al., 1987; Illingworth, 1983; Reif et al., 1995; Skuse et al., 1994) and effects can be long lasting (Iwaniec, 1995, 2000; Iwaniec and Sneddon, 2001). The detrimental effects of early malnutrition may be extensive given the rapid period of growth, particularly brain growth. Nearly all of a child's brain growth and synaptic connections occur by age two, but if the protein and calories are not present to support that growth, it cannot occur. Grantham-McGregor et al. (2000) concluded that children younger than two years of age are particularly vulnerable to the effects of malnutrition, since head circumference and height in the first 24 months are more significant predictors of IQ at 11 years of age than more recent or concurrent measure. A further concern is that once stunting of growth is established in the first three years these children may be reluctant to increase their intake, even if offered more food at a later stage. Woolston (1984) defines developmental delay as either a deceleration of the acquisition of new developmental milestones or actual regression in certain areas. The measurement of these developmental delays may be particularly useful for prognosis. For example, Corbett et al. (1996) found that even in relatively mild FTT there are long-term adverse cognitive deficits and that a velocity-based measure could be a useful predictor of cognitive outcome. It was found that IQ can be reduced by 10-20 points which are potentially reversible if positive changes occur in a child's life or if appropriate intervention and treatment take place (Hutcheson et al., 1997; Iwaniec, 1995; Kristiansson and Fällström, 1987). Reif et al. (1995) found that, compared to a group matched for age, sex, social class and ethnic affiliation, five years after assessment, children with FTT had more learning difficulties and evidenced developmental delays also in language, social and emotional areas.

Developmental delays here are also associated with poor stimulation and a low level of interaction at home. Some of these children are neglected both physically and emotionally, so there is limited verbal, social, and emotional contact between care-givers and the child, which in turn leads to poor developmental attainments.

Emotional and behavioural development

It has been found that many children who fail-to-thrive present themselves as temperamentally difficult or slow-to-warm up. These temperamental attributes, it is claimed, may diminish the mother's ability to nurture (Pollitt and Eichler, 1976). Infants and young children with growth failure have been described as both fussy, demanding, and unsociable, or lethargic, slow-moving, and undemanding (Gagan et al., 1984; Iwaniec, 1985a; Skuse, 1985). They vocalise less and tend to use low-level undifferentiated communication signals such as fussing and whining. They frequently avoid social contact with their mothers and spend less time initiating social interactions with a stranger (Wolke et al. 1990). Many research findings demonstrate that children, by the nature of their physical or psychological make-up, can exert an influence on their parents' interactions and feelings (Herbert, 1988). Certain inborn attributes can seriously worsen relations between parents and children: congenital characteristics like irregularity in biological functions, unadaptability, hypersensitivity, withdrawal responses to new stimuli, and high intensity and frequent bad moods, can make them particularly difficult to care for and to enjoy. The child's characteristics and its responses can arouse pride, or, alternatively, resentment, guilt or helplessness in parents, and can lead to poor attachment and bonding (Iwaniec, 1995).

Self-care skills

Socialisation is the major developmental task of all children, teaching them step-by-step to become more independent and able to do things for themselves. Different developmental stages expect mastering of self-care skills. These skills will be learned if a child is given the opportunity to try and experiment to do things alone or with a little help from carers. Neglected children and children who fail-to-thrive tend to be delayed in self-social care areas, partly because of low mother-child interaction, indifferent relationship and poor stimulation (Hanks and Hobbs, 1993). The level of attention iven to the child needs to be taken into onsideration as well as parental awareness as o when and how they should encourage elf-skills learning. When assessing the family areful attention should be paid to identifying ealistic and unrealistic expectations of the arents, as to what a child can or cannot do at a ertain age. There are simple milestone neasurements available, or any health visitor an assist in developmental assessment. Child bservation is a good way to put knowledge of evelopmental theory into practice.

Dimensions of parenting capacity

General overview

am always amazed how well the majority of eople, especially young ones, adapt to their arenting role and become wholly successful nd caring parents. They do this job effectively nd willingly in spite of many other demands n their time and energy. Let us look at what ood parenting requires, and what stands in the vay of good parenting.

Adequate parenting requires a number of kills that are far from being simple – part ommon sense, part intuition, part empathy, nd part of what we have learned from being arented as children. Most parents successfully arry out the complex tasks involved in hild-rearing, using a variety of methods in very liverse family, cultural, and social ircumstances. Some, however, find bringing up hildren difficult, frustrating, and unrewarding. 'here are many reasons why some parents are nadequate in their parenting role. Contemporary parents are often inexperienced n the care of children. They may be naccustomed to babies because they were brought up in small families and were not given esponsibilities for caring for their younger iblings, as was the case in past years. They may ave been brought up themselves in neglectful nd uncaring homes, or have been abused or ll-treated and have had no opportunities to cquire a better parenting style and understanding of children's developmental needs. They might be living in adverse social nd economic circumstances that may affect the quality of everyday child-care. Some might be ll, have learning disabilities, or suffer from lepression, so they cannot tune into the child's motional needs. Additionally, lack of support nd guidance, as well as social isolation brought bout by diminished extended family and community resources (from where traditionally help was provided) contribute to poor and often ill-informed parenting. Growing numbers of single, young, and immature mothers, often living in poverty (who are socially isolated and unsupported) are unprepared for the demands of child-rearing and therefore unable to provide basic physical and emotional nurturance for their offspring.

Dimension of parenting capacity in failure-to-thrive

Basic care

Failure-to-thrive children, like all children, require basic provision of physical care, such as food, shelter, clothing, appropriate hygiene, and adequate medical care. Failure-to-thrive children's physical care is reported to be inadequate, such as provision of the appropriate quantity of food for the child's age, regularity of feeding/eating, and the manner in which the child is handled during eating/feeding time (Iwaniec, 1991; Skuse et al., 1994). The following questions need to be asked when assessing physical care of the child:

- is the child regularly fed?
- is the child given enough and the right food for the child's age?
- are the signals of hunger or satiation properly interpreted?
- is the manner of feeding comfortable and anxiety free?
- is there availability of food?
- is there awareness of child being too thin, small, or unwell?
- is the child's medical-care being seen to, such as: medical examinations, vaccination, eye and hearing tests, etc?
- is medical advice being sought when the child is unwell?
- are medical or other welfare agency appointments being kept?
- do the parents administer required medication for the child?
- is there recognition and concern about the child's well-being?
- is the child appropriately dressed for the weather?
- is the child changed and clean?
- are the sleeping arrangements adequate?
- is the safety for the child observed?
- is the child supervised when playing outside?
- is the child provided with fresh air and outdoor activities?

- is the child protected from the use of alcohol, a smoking environment, and other unhealthy and damaging substances?

Parental characteristics

Adequate parenting may depend on many factors. Cognitive and socio-economic characteristics of the care-givers are important to examine in relation to FTT children. Low maternal education is considered to be a risk factor (Drotar and Sturm, 1988). Skuse et al. (1994) found that mothers of children who began growth faltering before six months of age were found to have significantly higher IQs than mothers whose children began growth faltering after six months of age. Sometimes non-organic failure-to-thrive can result from lack of knowledge about parenting and children's developmental needs. Some of the parenting deficits are easy to correct, requiring simple instructions (e.g. what to feed, how to dress, how to bath); others might require developmental counselling and more intensive parent-training. For example, a care-giver may not understand the importance of feeding formula preparation and, trying to save money, may over-dilute the more expensive formula so that it lasts longer, while not realising that this means the child will be inadequately nourished. The following parental characteristics and functioning have been identified:

- frequent depressive moods;
- low self-esteem;
- feeling helpless and inadequate;
- distorted perceptions and attitudes towards the target child;
- anxious and apprehensive to ask for help;
- little affection and positive interest shown to the child;
- limited interaction with the child;
- finding the child difficult to manage and to enjoy;
- physical and emotional distancing from the child;
- either rigid or chaotic in their parenting;
- socially isolated; and
- limited support.

Ensuring safety (Ensuring the child is adequately protected from harm or danger)

Failure-to-thrive children are associated with physical abuse and neglect and more often than not with emotional maltreatment (Blizzard and Bulatovic, 1993; Iwaniec et al., 1985a). Older toddlers are often deprived of food, locked in the bedroom for a long time, and punished physically by being smacked and at times quite hard. Skuse et al. (1996) reported that a number of children in their sample were sexually abused as well. Practitioners need to be alert to possible physical and occasionally sexual abuse when assessing failure-to-thrive children. Additionally, due to emotional rejection, some of these children are exposed to cruel punishment, e.g. like putting a child into a bath of cold water in the middle of winter for soiling, or locking a child in a dark cupboard or shed. In severe cases of long-term duration children harm themselves, e.g. cutting themselves with a knife or sharp object, setting fire, or head-banging. Children who display this behaviour require urgent conferencing and immediate action. Most FTT children can be helped in the community.

Emotional warmth (Ensuring the child's emotional needs are met)

It is now widely accepted that a child needs a close, confident, and caring physical and emotional contact with the caregiver in order to grow well, be healthy, and develop vigorously. The absence of such continuing nurturance and physical intimacy can bring about anxiety in the child, fretting, and disruption of biological functions. It has been recognised that infants and small children deprived of warmth, parental care, and lack of responsiveness to their emotional needs, may develop profound depression or acute withdrawal with consequent lack of appetite, loss of weight, and serious developmental delays (Bowlby, 1988). One of the indices of basic trust and security in an infant is stable feeding behaviour. In order for eating to be nutritionally beneficial and enjoyable it requires conditions that denote a relatively benign and calm state of psychosomatic harmony.

Researchers, such as Drotar (1991), Iwaniec (1995), and Raynor and Rudolf (1996), have argued that failure-to-thrive is a result of emotional neglect demonstrated by lack of interest in the child, absence of physical contact (such as holding, cuddling, smiling at, playing, initiating communication, responding to the child's signals of distress), and being insensitive to the child's nurturing needs. Additionally,

arental attitudes towards these children are
eported to be indifferent or negative. The
motional bond between the child and parent
ends to be weak, as demonstrated by low
requency of mutual interaction and reported
ick of pleasure at being together and enjoying
ie child's company. Consequently, such
arental behaviour does not facilitate
evelopment of secure attachment as a source of
afety and reassurance when in distress.

Parent–child interaction

'arent–child interaction is a two-way process,
vhich powerfully affects the way parents and
hildren relate to each other, perceive each
ther, and influence each other's behaviour. The
uality and quantity of mutual interaction is not
nly determined by the parental behaviour
owards the child, but also by the child's input
whether positive or negative) that affects this
wo-way process. If parents receive positive
eed-back from the child, like smiling, taking
ood, responding to attention, then parents will
ry to engage with the child more often. On the
ther hand if a child gives back little in terms of
howing pleasure in seeing the parent, then the
are-giver will interact less. There are many
easons why FTT children are passive and their
esponsiveness is more flat. Being
inder-nourished brings about lethargy and
vithdrawal which, in turn, creates an
mpression that the child prefers to be left alone.
Consequently, parent–child interaction is poor
in quality, infrequent and of short duration.
Children who fail-to-thrive tend to be nervous
and apprehensive when in the parent's company,
which indicates a painful and anxiety-provoking
interaction and relationship with the care-giver
(Iwaniec, 1999). When observing parent–child
interaction and exploring the quality of the
emotional bond during the early stages of a child's
life, it is often apparent that disappointment, or
unfulfilled dreams of a perfect child, are turned
against the offspring. A downwards spiral of
destructive interactions rolls on, preventing
development of secure bonding of parent to child.

Parent–child interaction is at the core of
indicating the quality of relationship and
general well-being of failure-to-thrive children.
The following checklists provide useful
information about the frequency and quality of
interaction between the FTT child and parents;
between the FTT child and siblings; and the
child's responsiveness and reaction when in the
parents' company.

Tables 3 and 4 provide an assessment
measure of parent–child interaction, and the
quality of emotional relationship between
parents and child.

Often	Indicates good quality of parenting and positive relationship with the child.
Seldom	Indicates emotional neglect and necessity to provide family support to stop escalation of negative feelings and poor provision of nurturing.

Table 3: Observation checklist: child.

Visit No. _____ Assessor _____ Name of Client _____

Child's reactive and proactive behaviour	Often	Seldom	Almost never
1. Playing freely			
2. Laughing/smiling			
3. Running			
4. Talking freely			
5. Comes for help			
6. Comes for comfort			
7. Cuddles up to mother/father			
8. Responds to affection			
9. Responds to attention			
0. At ease when they are near the child			
1. Joins in activities with other children			
2. Is not frightened when approached by mother/father, or corrected			
3. Eats/feeds satisfactorily			
4. Asks for food – indicates hunger			
5. Seems to be at ease during feeding/eating time			

Table 4: Observation checklist: parents.

Father's/mother's reactive and proactive behaviour	Often	Seldom	Almost never
1. Talking to the child			
2. Looking at the child			
3. Smiling at the child			
4. Making eye contact (loving)			
5. Touching (gently)			
6. Holding (closely, lovingly)			
7. Playing			
8. Cuddling			
9. Kissing			
10. Sitting the child on the lap			
11. Handling the child in a gentle way			
12. Giving requests (as opposed to commands)			
13. Helping the child if it is in difficulties			
14. Encouraging the child to participate in play and other activities			
15. Being concerned about the child			
16. Picking the child up when it cries or when it is hurt			
17. Answering the child's questions			
18. Not ignoring the child's presence			
19. Emotionally treating the child the same as other children			
20. Handling children consistently			

Almost never   Indicates severe risk of emotional abuse and prevention of developing secure attachment to parents.

Stimulation

Stimulation means promotion of the child's learning and intellectual development through encouragement of cognitive stimulation.

In order to help children to understand the world around them and help them to make sense of things they observe and hear, a great amount of parental attention is required to inform the child's learning on a daily basis. Most parents do that automatically. They point out different things to the child, saying what it is, they attract the child's attention to a new object or experience, show them pictures, or demonstrate how the toy works. Parents also do things deliberately with children to stimulate their learning and to enhance the child's curiosity about things around them. Parents will read or play with them, using age-appropriate material to get them involved. They will take a child, for example, to a farm to show them animals, so the child can link real things with pictures in the book. Later on, they will guide their social learning, instruct them in what is right or wrong, and reason with them to promote better understanding and problem-solving through play.

Infants need attention and stimulation to help them develop basic skills like sitting, crawling, walking, talking, and the social behaviour of participation and sharing. Parents of children who fail-to-thrive spend little time with them and do not involve them in family activities. Their interaction with the child tends to take place when it is absolutely necessary, such as feeding, bathing, changing, and even then it tends to be salient with little communication and stimulation taking place. Many failure-to-thrive children are being reared in social isolation, spending a lot of time in the cot in the bedroom or in the pram in the garden or a different room. It is not surprising that these children suffer from developmental delays because of severe lack of stimulation and social isolation.

When assessing these children the level of parental involvement, both physical and verbal must be taken into consideration. It is necessary to establish how much time is spent with the child on an average day and what is the content of mutual involvement. Direct observation is a good method to assess parental involvement and availability.

Guidance and boundaries

This comprises enabling the child to regulate their own emotional state and develop an internal model of conscience and appropriate behaviour, while also promoting pro-social inter-personal behaviour and social relationships.

In order for children to be well prepared for life and to become well-adjusted, they must acquire a vast amount of information about the environment in which they live, the culture to which they belong, and the prevailing moral code that guides their behaviour. Thus, a child's socialisation process will depend upon parental ability, awareness, willingness, and motivation to give the necessary information, to provide an appropriate model of behaviour, to supervise, and to guide social-learning in order to lay the foundation for future life and well-being. By observing appropriate parental behaviour and being provided with discrimination learning as to why certain things are painful to others and should not be done, and what is pleasurable and appropriate and should be done, would help the child to develop a good sense of empathy and fairness. Teaching socially appropriate behaviours in relation to self and others needs to start in infancy and expand during the toddler stage. Assessment needs to cover: existence of fair rules and routines; boundaries of what can and cannot be done; understanding of the rules; provision of sensitive instructions; and guidance and supervision. Additionally, children have to learn to consider the needs of others, learn to share and wait, and to control frustration and anger.

The above parenting requirements are seldom evident in families who neglect their children and whose emotional commitment, for whatever reason, is inadequate. Failure-to-thrive children suffer from that omission of child-rearing.

Stability

Stability involves provision of a stable and nurturing family environment, which is considered to be persistent and predictable for all family members. Many children who require social-work assessment are exposed to extremely unstable family life and functioning. Frequent changes of homes, partners, and daily life create a sense of confusion and helplessness on the one hand, and emotional disturbance on the other. Sensitive and vulnerable children are at particular risk of developing behavioural and emotional problems if they are responded to in an unpredictable way. They tend to become nervous, anxious, or apprehensive when in the

caregiver's company, or when they are approached by them to do something. Some, however, become aggressive or defiant as a result (Herbert, 1988; Iwaniec, 1994). Many children who fail-to-thrive tend to live in the families who lack social structure and cohesion and there is often lack of unity, social roles, and mutual support (Iwaniec, 1997).

Table 5 sets out the questions that need to be asked when assessing parenting.

Family and environmental factors
General overview

Parents have responsibility to provide the quality of care which will promote the child's healthy, happy, and vigorous development, but in order to fulfil these obligations their needs as parents and family have to be met too. Parents, as people, have certain genetic requirements, such as basic material needs for shelter and subsistence, and psychosocial requirements for support, security, recognition, approval, guidance, advice, assistance, education, and resources. The essential needs of reasonable shelter and financial provision are seen as foundation elements of life and, if unattended to, can create such an overpowering set of needs themselves, as to make it pointless to consider others.

Over and above these, more specific parents' needs arise at different times in the family cycle and with change of situation or life style. It is not enough to assume that intellectual understanding and competence at skills of parentcraft are sufficient to make for a satisfactory family environment. Emotional responses also require understanding, their proper interpretation, sensitivity, and willingness to accommodate other people's feelings within the family.

Nevertheless, parents are adults and are quite rightly expected to take the child through its early life journey in a responsible manner. There is no doubt that parenting entails sacrifices of time, money, interest, and energy, and that parenting creates, as well as interferes with, life opportunities.

Family history and functioning

Family stress has been observed as more common in families with children who are failing-to-thrive (Iwaniec et al., 1985a). These include chronic illnesses in the parents, siblings, or extended family; prior divorce, current

Table 5: Assessment of parenting.

The following questions need to be asked when assessing parenting.

Is there evidence which would indicate:
- acceptable/unacceptable physical care, e.g. feeding, dressing, changing nappies, bathing, keeping clean and warm, acceptable sleeping arrangements, safety
  As evidenced by

- positive/negative attitudes towards parental duties and responsibilities
  As evidenced by

- positive/negative attitudes towards the child
  As evidenced by

- parental life-style which might be contributing to the child's neglect and abuse
  As evidenced by

- harmful habits (alcohol, drug-abuse, criminal behaviour, prostitution)
  As evidenced by

- personal circumstances affecting positive parenting (single parents, poor housing, poverty, social isolation, poor health, unemployment, mental illness, immature personality)
  As evidenced by

- parents intellectual capabilities – level of education
  As evidenced by

- passivity, withdrawal, inertia – learned helplessness
  As evidenced by

- parental childhood experiences of parenting
  As evidenced by

- are parents aware of their children's developmental needs?
  As evidenced by

- are they concerned about the child's physical and psycho-social well-being?
  As evidenced by

- do they show affection and demonstrate a positive bond with the child?
  As evidenced by

- what is the level and quality of parent-child interaction?
  As evidenced by

- what help and assistance were provided for parents to overcome parenting difficulties?
  As evidenced by

- what use did they make of the help available to them?
  (a) level of co-operation with workers
  (b) working constructively towards set goals
  As evidenced by

- are they able to understand what is going wrong in their parenting and are they able and willing to work at it?
  As evidenced by

---

separation, emotional tension between parents, single mothers with young children, depression, social isolation, and lack of available support (Drotar et al., 1981). In addition to the above-mentioned factors, family life is often seen to be filled with conflict and tension, rather than being a source of emotional support (Hathaway, 1989). It is of enormous advantage to have a good network of social support to help cope with these demands. However, several studies have found that the mothers of non-organic failure-to-thrive children are socially isolated, depressed, lacking energy and initiative to organise their lives in a more enjoyable way (Bithoney and Newberger, 1987). Mothers are thought to be less available to bond with a baby when their emotional resources are depleted (Drotar and Malone, 1982). Good assessment o

amily functioning may help in devising
ppropriate intervention such as couple
herapy. In order to understand the current
ituation a good family history should be taken,
vhich might shed light on our understanding of
resenting problems and to address these when
lanning intervention.

ncome

TT is also associated with poverty. Children
om low-income families are lighter and shorter
han those living in better homes and having
etter incomes (Dawson, 1992). As almost all
tudies of FTT have been done in low-income
opulations little is known about FTT in affluent
nes. However, classifying into social class can
ometimes be misleading. For example, Skuse et
l. (1994) examined two groups of children who
rere FTT; one with early onset (within six
nonths of birth), and one with later onset (after
ix months of birth). Although both groups had
imilar amounts of money coming into the
ouse, there were different patterns of
nanaging money. Iwaniec's (1983) sample
onsisted of 40 per cent of middle-class families,
vhere there was no financial hardship but a
igh level of emotional indifference and marital
nstability.

Housing

ssessment of accommodation is considered to
e fundamental when looking at children's and
arents' needs. Failure-to-thrive children are
ften brought up in impoverished housing,
adly heated, in poor state of repair, and damp.
: has been found (Iwaniec, 1983) that some of
ne children have frequent colds and infections,
ften due to poor heating and inadequate
lothing. Additionally, frequent changes of
ousing because of rent arrears or conflict with
eighbours prevent establishing meaningful
ontact and mutual support with neighbours
nd a wider community. It has been reported
Hanks and Hobbs, 1993) that basic living
menities which are poor have a negative
npact on a child's health and safety.

Employment

'ailure-to-thrive is associated with low-income
amilies and general economic hardship. Many
arents tend to be unemployed and live on
arious benefits. Poor growth is often
mbedded in a context of family economic
disadvantage (Drotar et al., 1990). Children
living in families who have been unemployed
for a considerable time or have never been at
work are lighter and shorter than children who
live in better-off homes (Dawson, 1992).
However, those parents who are employed tend
to be happier, better organised, more mature
and, as a rule, engage in providing family
support to resolve the child's poor growth.

Family's social integration

Families of FTT children tend to be socially
isolated. They have little contact with
neighbours and are inclined to avoid people in
order to escape criticism and open disapproval
of their parenting style. As their self-esteem is
low, they anticipate rejection from people living
in the same community. Many such families'
life-style, such as alcohol abuse, children's
unkempt appearance, and often poor social
behaviour, denies those children the
opportunity to make friends and establish social
contacts outside the family. Parents too seldom
interact and get support from people living near
them. As a result they become isolated,
unsupported and consequently depressed.
These, in turn, have serious effects on children,
especially infants and toddlers, as their mothers
become physically and emotionally unavailable
and unable to meet their basic needs.

Community resources

It is now widely recognised that availability of
necessary facilities and suitable services in the
community, where the service-user resides,
serves as a buffer to prevent abuse and neglect
and better developmental outcomes for
children. An easy access to health services,
schools, and day services (such as family
centres, nurseries and playgroups) enables
clients to use these services more independently
when they are needed. This is particularly
important for parents whose children require
frequent medical and social-care attention.
Failure-to-thrive children need to be seen by the
GP and health visitor quite frequently to start
with to monitor their weight, height, and head
circumference . Parents also need advice and
help with prevailing feeding/eating problems.
As some FTT children are developmentally
delayed they might need day-care services to
help them make good the developmental deficit.
Iwaniec (1983) found that families living near, or
having easy access to the Health Centres

frequently took their FTT children there and received the necessary advice and reassurance which, in turn, benefited the children. More importantly, however, it was the manner in which those parents were dealt with which counted. Sadly some were treated as time-wasters, neurotic, and irrational, as there was nothing physically wrong with the child. Those who were given a sympathetic ear and opportunity to discuss worries regarding a child's poor growth and development also managed to resolve some of the eating problems much quicker. Good awareness of what and who is available in the neighbourhood may help social workers facilitate child and family needs.

Concluding comments on the Assessment Framework

The Assessment Framework is a good guide for practitioners to do their work. There is, however, nothing new or revolutionary about it, apart from avoiding words such as risk, abuse, and dangerous parenting. The philosophy underpinning the Framework of Assessment means to be universal, applicable to all children in need, and based on the child's developmental requirements. If those developmental needs are to be met, at appropriate stages, then the 'wait and see' approach has to be avoided, in order to eliminate escalation of problems leading to significant harm. There is no doubt that there needs to be better assessment of children and of parenting capacity done on a multidisciplinary basis, followed by appropriate and targeted intervention, to resolve presenting problems. Failure-to-thrive children have to be assessed and helped on a multi-disciplinary basis, as are other children at risk or in need of services. Table 6 sets out the process and stages of involvement in FTT cases.

It is well known that intervention is likely to be most effective in providing better results for children when it is done early in a child's life or the problem development. Stepping in early, as a preventative measure, will secure better outcomes for the child, will be cheaper in the long run, and less hurtful for everybody. However, there need to be time limits within which improvement has to take place. Children cannot wait indefinitely as they grow fast and problems grow with them at a remarkable speed. If parental capacity cannot accommodate the child's needs, and services provided are not used or refused, then alternative arrangements need to be made promptly and decisively. It is suggested (Adcock, 2001) that adoption or placement with a suitable relative should be

Table 6: Process and stages of involvement in failure-to-thrive cases.

Stage 1:	Identifying that child's weight is below expected norms and its general well-being is questionable.
Stage 2:	Advice and help provided by the health visitor re. feeding, caring and management or GP.
Stage 3:	If there is not improvement, and parents are doing their best, referral to the paediatrician to investigate any possible organic reason for the child's poor growth and development.
Stage 4:	Medical investigation if felt to be necessary.
Stage 5:	If there is non-organic reason for failure-to-thrive, and child welfare continues to cause concern, referral to the Social Services for psychosocial assessment and care plan in the community.
Stage 6:	More serious cases (if there is evidence of rejection, emotional indifference or more serious neglect) to be conferenced.
Stage 7:	Treatment/intervention programme to be worked out and negotiated with the care-givers.
Stage 8:	Monitoring child's growth and development – either in outpatients clinic, by GP, or health visit, until child's growth is appropriate for the chronological age.
Stage 9:	Monitoring child/care-givers interaction and relationship and general well-being of the child by the social worker and/or health visitor.
Stage 10:	Case closed when there is evidence of systematic improvement in child's growth and development and care-givers/child relationship for at least three months.
NOTE:	Failure-to-thrive children should be dealt with on a multi-disciplinary basis. Good communication and co-ordination between social workers, doctors and health visitors, schools, nurseries etc. is essential.

considered without delay if there is no change. This new thinking as to how to deal with children with poor parenting prognosis for change, and whose needs are unlikely to be met while living with parents, is based on numerous findings from committees of enquiry and research commissioned by the Department of Health. However, one questions the availability of family-support services, which, if provided promptly and for long enough, might do the job effectively under Section 17 of the Children Act without reverting to more drastic measures. Most parents care about their children and, providing that help is given at the right time and in the right amounts, then change may occur.

Nevertheless, there are parents who cannot provide good enough parenting for various reasons and whose children are permanently neglected, and therefore deprived of opportunities to meet their potentials. Prompt decision, following comprehensive assessment, is essential to avoid negative snowball effects and to facilitate meeting developmental needs.

Widom (1996), cited in Adcock, 2001, described the compounding effects of a negative process in failure-to-thrive in the following way:

Deficits or dysfunctional behaviours at one developmental period will lay the groundwork for subsequent dysfunctional behaviours. Deficits, manifest at one stage, continue to exert an influence at the next stage unless an intervention occurs. For example, malnutrition in infancy may lead to impaired intellectual or cognitive functioning in toddlers which, in turn, lead to impaired performance as an adult.

Iwaniec's (2000) 20-year follow-up study of children who failed-to-thrive confirmed Widom's above statement.

References

Adcock, M. (2001) Significant Harm: Outcomes and Management. Paper presented at Guardian Ad Litem conference on Significant Harm, Belfast.

Ayoub, C.C. and Milner, J.S. (1985) Failure-to-thrive: Parental Indicators, Types and Outcomes. *Child Abuse and Neglect.* 9: 491–9.

Batchelor, J.A. (1996) Has Recognition of Failure-to-thrive Changed? *Child: Care, Health and Development.* 22: 4, 235–40.

Belsky, J. and Nezworski, T. (1988) Clinical Implication of Attachment. In Belsky, J. and Nezworski, T. (Eds.) *Clinical Implications of Attachment.* Hillsdale: Lawrence Erlbaum.

Bithoney, W.G. and Newberger, E.H. (1987) Child and Family Attributed of Failure-to-thrive. *Journal of Developmental and Behavioural Pediatrics.* 8: 32–6.

Blizzard, R.M. and Bulatovic, A. (1993) Psychological Short Stature: A Syndrome With Many Variables. *Baillière's Clinical Endocrinology and Metabolism.* 6: 3, 637–712.

Boddy, J.M. and Skuse, D.H. (1994) Annotation: The Process of Parenting in Failure-to-thrive. *Journal of Child Psychology and Psychiatry.* 35: 3, 401–22.

Bowlby, J. (1988) Developmental Psychiatry Comes of Age. *The American Journal of Psychiatry.* 145: 1–10.

Corbett, S.S., Drewett, R.F. and Wright, C.M. (1996) Does a Fall Down a Centile Chart Matter? The Growth and Developmental Sequelae of Mild Failure-to-thrive. *Acta Paediatricia.* 85: 1278–83.

Dawson, P. (1992) Should the Field of Early Child and Family Intervention Address Failure-to-thrive? *Zero to Three.* 20–4.

Dowdney, L., Skuse, D., Heptinstall, E., Puckering, C. and Zur-Szpiro, S. (1987) Growth Retardation and Developmental Delay Amongst Inner City Children. *Journal of Child Psychology and Psychiatry and Allied Disciplines.* 28: 529–41.

Drotar, D. and Malone, C. (1982) Family Oriented Intervention with the Failure-to-thrive Infant. In Klaus, M.H. and Robertson, M.O. (Eds.) *Birth, Interaction and Attachment, Exploring the Foundations for Modern Perinatal Care.* USA: Johnson and Johnson Baby Products Pediatric Round Table Series, 104–11.

Drotar, D. and Sturm, L. (1988) Prediction of Intellectual Development in Young Children With Early Histories of Non-organic Failure-to-thrive. *Journal of Pediatric Psychology.* 13: 281–96.

Drotar, D. (1991) The Family Context of Non-organic Failure-to-thrive. *American Journal of Orthopsychiatry.* 61: 23–34.

Drotar, D., Eckerle, D., Satola, J., Pallotta, J. and Wyatt, B. (1990) Maternal Interactional Behaviour With Non-organic Failure-to-thrive Infants: A Case Comparison Study. *Child Abuse and Neglect.* 14: 41–51.

Drotar, D., Malone, C., Negray, J. and Dennstedt, M. (1981) Psychosocial Assessment and Care for Infants Hospitalized for Non-organic Failure-to-thrive. *Journal of Clinical Child Psychology*. 63–6.

Frank, D. and Zeisel, S. (1988) Failure-to-thrive. *Paediatric Clinics of North America*. 35: 6, 1187–206.

Gagan, R.J., Cupoli, J.M. and Watkins, A.H. (1984) The Families of Children Who Fail-to-thrive: Preliminary Investigations of Parental Deprivation Among Organic and Non-organic Cases. *Child Abuse and Neglect*. 8: 93–103.

Grantham-McGregor, S.M., Walker, S.P. and Chang, S. (2000) Nutritional Deficiencies and Later Behavioural Development. *Proceedings of the Nutrition Society*. 59: 47–54.

Hampton, D. (1996) Resolving the Feeding Difficulties Associated With Non-organic Failure-to-thrive. *Child: Care, Health and Development*. 22: 4, 273–84.

Hanks, H. and Hobbs, C. (1993) Failure-to-thrive: A Model for Treatment. *Baillière's Clinical Paediatrics*. 1: 1, 101–19.

Hathaway, P. (1989) Failure-to-thrive: Knowledge for Social Workers. *Health and Social Work*. 14: 2, 122–6.

Herbert, M. (1988) *Working with Children and Their Families*. Leicester: British Psychological Society, Routledge.

Hutcheson, J.J., Black, M.M., Talley, M., Dubowitz, H., Berenson Howard, J., Starr, R.H. and Thompson, B.S. (1997) Risk Status and Home Intervention Among Children With Failure-to-thrive: Follow-up at Age 4. *Journal of Pediatric Psychology*. 22: 5, 651–68.

Illingworth, R.S. (1983) *The Development of the Infant and Young Child*. (8th edn.) Edinburgh: Churchill Livingstone.

Iwaniec, D. and Sneddon, H. (2001) Attachment Style in Adults Who Showed Failure-to-thrive as Children: Outcomes of a 20-Year Follow-up Study of Factors Influencing Maintenance or Change in Attachment Style. *British Journal of Social Work*. 31: 179–95.

Iwaniec, D. (1983) *Social and Psychological Factors in the Aetiology and Management of Children Who Fail-to-thrive*. Unpublished PhD thesis: University of Leicester.

Iwaniec, D. (1991) Treatment of Children Who Fail to Grow in the Light of the New Children Act. *Newsletter of the Association for Child Psychology and Psychiatry*. 13: 3, 21–7.

Iwaniec, D. (1994) Neglect and Emotional Abuse in Children Who Fail-to-thrive. *Northern Ireland Journal of Multi-disciplinary Child Care in Practice*. 1: 2, 15–27.

Iwaniec, D. (1995) *The Emotionally Abused and Neglected Child: Identification, Assessment and Intervention*. Chichester: John Wiley and Sons.

Iwaniec, D. (1997) An Overview of Emotional Maltreatment and Failure-to-thrive. *Child Abuse Review*. 6: 370–88.

Iwaniec, D. (1999) Lessons From 20-Year Follow-up Study on Children Who Failed-to-thrive. *Child Care in Practice*. 5: 2, 128–39.

Iwaniec, D. (2000) From Childhood to Adulthood: A 20-Year Follow-up Study of Children Who Failed-to-thrive. In Iwaniec, D. and Hill, M. (Eds.) *Child Welfare Policy and Practice: Current Issues Emerging from Child Care Research*. London: Jessica Kingsley.

Iwaniec, D., Herbert, M. and McNeish, A.S. (1985a) Social Work With Failure-to-thrive Children and Their Families. Part 1: Psychosocial Factors. *British Journal of Social Work*. 15: 243–59.

Kristiansson, B. and Fällström, S.P. (1987) Growth at the Age of 4 Years Subsequent to Early Failure-to-thrive. *Child Abuse and Neglect*. 11: 35–40.

Lewis, J.A. (1982) Oral Motor Assessment and Treatment of Feeding Difficulties. In Accardo, P.J. (Ed.) *Failure-to-thrive in Infancy and Early Childhood, a Multidisciplinary Approach*. Baltimore: University Park Press, 265–98.

Maggioni, A. and Lifshitz, F. (1995) Nutritional Management of Failure-to-thrive. *Pediatric Clinics of North America*. 42: 4, 791–810.

McMillen, P. (1988) Infants Thrive with Failure-to-thrive Program. *Health Progress*. 70–1.

Pollitt, E. and Eichler, A. (1976) Behavioural Disturbances Among Failure-to-thrive Children. *American Journal of Diseases of Children*. 130: 24–9.

Pollitt, E. (1975) Failure-to-thrive: Socioeconomic Dietary Intake and Mother Child Interaction Data. *Federation Proceedings*. 34: 7, 1593–9.

Powell, G.F., Brasel, J.A. and Blizzard, R.M. (1967) Emotional Deprivation and Growth Retardation Stimulating Idiopathic Hypopituitarism: Clinical Evaluation of the Syndrome. *The New England Journal of Medicine*. 276: 23, 1271–8.

Raynor, P. and Rudolf, M.C.J. (1996) What do we Know About Children Who Fail-to-thrive. *Child Care, Health and Development*. 22: 4, 241–50.

Reif, S., Beler, B., Villa, Y. and Spirer, Z. (1995) Long Term Follow-up and Outcome of Infant

With Non-organic Failure-to-thrive. *Israel Journal of Medical Science*. 31: 8, 483–9.

Rutter, M. (1995) Clinical Implications of Attachment Concepts: Retrospect and Prospect. *Journal of Child Psychology Psychiatry*. 36: 4, 549–71.

Skuse, D. (1985) Non-organic Failure-to-thrive: A Reappraisal. *Archives of Disease in Childhood*. 60: 173–8.

Skuse, D. (1993). Identification and Management of Problem Eaters. *Archives of Disease in Childhood*. 69: 604–8.

Skuse, D., Albanese, A., Stanhope, R., Gilmore, J. and Voss, L. (1996) A New Stress-related Syndrome of Growth Failure and Hyperphagea in Children Associated With Reversibility of Growth Hormone Insufficiency. *Lancet*. 348: 9024, 353–8.

Skuse, D., Gilmour, J., Tian, C.A. and Hindmarsh, P. (1994) Psychosocial Assessment of Children With Short Stature: A Preliminary Report. *Acta Paediatricia Supplement*. 406: 11–6.

Skuse, D., Reilly, S. and Wolke, D. (1994) Psychosocial Adversity and Growth During Infancy. *European Journal of Clinical Nutrition*. 48: 113–30.

Skuse, D.H. (1989) Emotional Abuse and Neglect. *British Medical Journal*. 298: 1692–4.

Wilensky, D.S., Ginsberg, G., Altman, M, Tulchinsky, T.H., Ben Yishhay, F. and Auerbach, J. (1996) A Community Based Study of Failure-to-thrive in Israel. *Archives of Disease in Childhood*. 75: 145–8.

Wolke, D., Skuse, D. and Mathisen, B. (1990) Behavioural Style in Failure-to-thrive Infants: A preliminary Communication. *Journal of Pediatric Psychology*. 15: 2, 237–54.

Woolston, J. (1984) *Failure-to-thrive Syndrome: The Current Challenge of Diagnostic Classification*. Paper presented at the Failure-to-thrive Symposium, Ontario Centre for the Prevention of Child Abuse, 70–85.

Wright, C.M. and Talbot, E. (1996) Screening for Failure-to-thrive: What are we Looking For? *Child: Care, Health and Development*. 22: 4, 223–34.

Wynne, J. (1996) Failure-to-thrive: An Introduction. *Child: Care, Health and Development*. 22: 4, 219–221.

Chapter Sixteen

Domestic Violence and Children: Making a Difference in a Meaningful Way for Women and Children

Caroline Rowsell

Introduction

Children have often been called 'forgotten victims' or 'hidden victims' of domestic violence and historically statutory agencies have viewed separately the abuse of women to the abuse of their children. However, research has consistently suggested that the most likely context to find child abuse is where domestic violence is present, and vice versa (Stark and Flitcraft, 1988). However, refuge organisations have been noticing the connections for over 30 years, and have campaigned tirelessly throughout this time for other professionals to sit up and take notice. In making these connections publicly women's organisations have had to take some considerable risks, particularly as knowledge and awareness of domestic violence is still minimal, and abused women are very often still misunderstood and held to blame for the abuse that they suffer at the hands of known men. There is little doubt that in making the connections in this climate has led to some women experiencing inappropriate and heavy-handed interventions from child protection agencies.

The *Framework for the Assessment of Children in Need and their Families* (DoH, 2000) clearly outlines how to assess children's needs in relation to their developmental needs, the context of their family and the environment in which they live, and the ability of their parents to parent effectively. However, I have concerns that despite a great deal of research evidence now existing that demonstrates the impact of domestic violence upon women and their children, the Framework appears to be very limited, and fails to address fully the dynamics and complexities of domestic violence. This in itself is not surprising, as despite greater public awareness and political commitment at national and local levels to tackling the problem of domestic violence, meaningful change has been slow to occur.

This chapter seeks to: define domestic violence; explode some of the common myths; identify the impact upon women and their children; to identify some of the limitations of the framework; and encourages practitioners to broaden their knowledge and awareness of domestic violence in order to achieve positive outcomes for abused women and their children. In it I argue that given the difficulties that all child protection agencies face in trying to protect children from abuse, in the context of domestic violence the most cost effective form of child protection is to protect, support and empower their abused mothers. It is not intended that this chapter should be a definitive guide to undertaking a child protection assessment, and the author advises that all practitioners should refer to local child protection procedures, and to Calder (forthcoming) and Hester et al. (1998).

Prevalence of domestic violence

In the main domestic violence is perpetrated by men against women with whom they have, or have had, intimate relationships. This is not to suggest that domestic violence does not occur between other family members, or in same sex relationships, but overwhelmingly research suggests that domestic violence is a gendered issue, with over 90 per cent of its victims being women. It is now widely accepted that all women are vulnerable to violence and abuse regardless of their age, race, class, sexuality or ability, and that the violence and abuse they experience is often hidden, condoned, or colluded with by members of the communities including agency professionals, in which they live. Contrary to popular myth there is little evidence that women who have abused mothers, or have themselves experienced abuse as children, are any more likely than other women to experience domestic violence as adults. Whilst it is extremely difficult to give accurate incidence and prevalence figures,[1] of violence against women due to under-reporting and under-recording, research studies consistently suggest that domestic violence is likely to be experienced, at some time in their lives, by between 20–50 per cent of all adult women in heterosexual relationships.

The importance of shared language and definitions of domestic violence

Very often the public, including professionals, find it very difficult to accept these prevalence levels, and I believe this is because we are still unclear as to just what the definition of domestic violence is. The fact that domestic violence is an umbrella term used to describe a wide range of behaviours is often misunderstood, leading to an over-emphasis by practitioners upon physical violence,[2] and the presence, and impact, of sexual violence, emotional, psychological and financial abuses often being ignored or minimised (Hester et al., 1998). The fact that there is no one common definition of the term 'domestic violence' is problematic for all of us, particularly practitioners (Kelly, 1988; Maynard, 1993; Lloyd, 1997). We need to work to a shared definition of exactly what we mean by the term 'domestic violence' if we are to be explicit not only about what constitutes domestic violence, but also; the circumstances in which it occurs; whether women define themselves as victims; whether men are named and held to account as the main perpetrators; and who is responsible for deciding what change needs to take place, and in what context that change will occur.

The violence and abuse women experience can be actual, attempted or threatened and includes (but is not exclusive to) being: slapped; pushed; hit; bitten; knifed; thrown; burnt; strangled; suffocated; kicked; scalded; punched; abused by his use of a weapon; ignored; belittled; isolated from family and friends; raped (vaginally, anally or orally); sexually assaulted by the use of implements; forced or coerced into engaging in a range of unwanted sexual acts; forced to get pregnant; forced to have an abortion or sterilisation; prevented from having an abortion or sterilisation; prostituted; made to engage with, or in, pornography; kept in financial deprivation (kept short of money; taking her money; kept constantly in debt); psychologically tortured; denied sleep; starved; having to dress as the man determines; urinated on; threatened with deportation; actually sent back to her country of origin; sworn at; mutilated and tortured; constantly criticised; subjected to extreme jealousy and

possessiveness; having her property and personal possessions destroyed; and forced to accept the abuse of family pets. In addition the woman may also find that the man may threaten or carry out threats to abuse, harm or remove her children.

The importance of deconstructing myths and stereotypes

Contrary to popular myth the men who perpetrate this violence are not sick, mad, poor communicators, under stress, alcoholics or drug addicts (although sometimes these issues may co-exist), but are ordinary men who choose to use this behaviour to control and dominate women. Traditionally practitioners have bought into these myths, and have rarely held men accountable, which as a result has led to women and children experiencing higher levels of danger and damage. Buying into the myths has also allowed us to blame women for the abuse they experience, and our strategies, policies and practices have been sadly lacking and ineffective as a result. Deconstructing these myths starts to help us to think about how we view women who are victims, how we view men who perpetrate, and informs how we should consider working with this issue.

The impact of domestic violence on women

Living with a violent partner can have far reaching short and long term impacts upon women physically, socially, emotionally and psychologically (Cambell et al., 1994; Hoff, 1990), although it will vary greatly for each individual woman and the circumstances that she finds herself in. Apart from the obvious physical harm that women may suffer, domestic violence can include women experiencing: sleep deprivation, isolation, depression, loss of confidence, self-harm, and an increased tendency to commit suicide; miscarriage, stillbirth and foetal abnormalities; difficulties in mothering and caring for their children; in homelessness and in some instances being deported; being prevented from gaining employment and/or training opportunities; increased sick leave from employment or being forced to give up employment; the development of coping strategies such as alcohol or drug abuse; forced or unwanted sex can result in pelvic problems; and can also result in a woman experiencing severe menstrual problems, sexually transmitted diseases or any kind of urine infection, vaginal or anal tearing, and of course unintended pregnancy; in some instances women may commit minor criminal offences to survive on a day-to-day practical basis, or serious criminal offences (such as killing a partner) as a strategy of self-preservation. There is little doubt that living with domestic violence has a hugely negative impact on the lives of women.

Pregnancy and children as a risk factor

Whilst many women are vulnerable to domestic violence, being pregnant or having small children has been acknowledged as a particular risk factor (Amaro et al., 1990; Helton et al., 1987; Gazmararian, 1996; McFarlane et al., 1992; McFarlane et al., 1998; Noel and Yam, 1992; Parker et al., 1993; Peterson, 1997). Many women report that the onset of physical violence occurs during pregnancy, or where it is already a feature that it increases in frequency and severity during this time. Some men use repeated pregnancy, as a tactic to maintain power and control, after all it is very difficult to leave your abuser if you have a number of small children. Very often the abdomen becomes the focus of physical assaults during pregnancy, and some babies are miscarried, stillborn or born disabled as a result.

Many women are repeatedly raped by partners, and a significant number of women will become pregnant as a consequence of sexual violence. Without any doubt women will then have to engage with a whole range of difficult issues in relation to their pregnancy, and the child that they have conceived and given birth to, will be a constant reminder of their abuse. Professionals will need to find a way of creating time, and space, for women to talk about their experiences of rape, and feelings towards their child, without making the assumption that she will not be able to effectively mother, or pose any greater risk.

Abusive men will often prevent women from seeking medical attention and it is important that health professionals are alive to this possibility. Where a woman does not attend ante-natal/post natal checks it is all too easy to view her as a difficult, or a non-compliant patient, rather than a woman who is being prevented from attending by her abuser. Some men will accompany women, and whilst this may be a man just wanting to be fully involved

in the pregnancy and birth process, it can also be a sign that a man is controlling his partner, and reducing her opportunities to disclose her abuse.

Pregnancy is also a time where we stop thinking of a woman as an individual, and see her as part of a couple, the next step being the creation of the family. Whilst I am not suggesting that this is necessarily a bad thing, it is important to remember that to view her as part of a family unit rather than an individual woman significantly reduces the professional's opportunity to ask questions, and her ability to disclose her experiences of violence and abuse. Therefore, all professionals need to take the lead in creating time and space at every visit to talk to women on their own. However, it is important that professionals engaged in this work are assisted to develop high level skills to enable them to carry out this intervention in a meaningful and sensitive way.

The impact of domestic violence on mothering

Society still has, despite years of campaigning by women, expectations of mothers that are very different from those of men who are fathers. Women are expected to be the homemakers, carers, nurturers, and protectors, whilst men are expected to be the head of the family, the disciplinarians, the main breadwinners and in control. Mothering is a tiring and exhausting business at the best of times, and most women will have the ideal text book definition of motherhood as their primary aim. An abused woman may have chosen to have her children to compensate for the abuse she has experienced, and she may well throw herself 100 per cent into being the best mother possible. However, her ability to mother and care for her children may well be significantly affected by her physical, mental and emotional state and at times achieving effective mothering will be almost impossible, which may well increase her feelings of failure as a mother.

A woman's mothering style may change significantly when the man is at home, and this can create a great deal of confusion for her children. She may well use abuse herself to pre-empt even worse abuse that could be perpetrated by her partner if she fails to keep the children in check or under his rules of control. Some abused women believe that they can protect their children from being directly abused by the man by keeping them quiet, out of his way, by using violence against the children themselves to pre-empt worse abuse by the man, or by not challenging his behaviour in front of them. For the vast majority of abused women, caring for, and protection of, their children are their primary concern. However, many women underestimate both the impacts of witnessing or overhearing violence upon their children, and the man's opportunities to directly abuse children without their knowledge. Women will sometimes believe that they have genuinely protected their children from the abuse, and may well be shocked later on to find out from professionals (or indeed their children) that their children were aware of the abuse, the extent of their knowledge, and that fact that they may have been directly abused themselves.

Professionals need to be alive to the fact that some men will deliberately set out to prevent women from parenting effectively, and women will often be forced to choose between their partner and caring for their children. Life becomes a series of unwanted compromises, and abusive men will use her ineffective parenting against her, by threatening to expose her to child protection intervention agencies, or by threatening to remove her children from her care.

Clearly, living with a violent man has considerable impacts on a woman's whole life and, for some women, the physical and psychological effects of living with a violent and abusive partner may make mothering very difficult to achieve in a way which would hold up to the scrutiny of child protection professionals. Given this it is important that professionals, when assessing the woman's parenting capacity, include all of the following inter-related factors: the type of violence and abuse the woman is experiencing; how long she has been in a violent relationship and whether she has experienced violence and abuse at any other time in her life; the severity and frequency of the violence and abuse that is perpetrated against her by the man and how she makes sense of this; the level of control that the man imposes upon her relationship with her children; how she perceives herself as a mother; the extent to which her physical, emotional and mental health are affected by the violence and how this subsequently impacts upon her ability to mother; and how the children individually and collectively make sense of and respond to the abuse.

Seeking help and resisting abuse

Failure to understand the dynamics between abused women and violent men can lead to professionals ignoring the power and control that men have over women in our society, and concentrating on individual factors which relate directly to the woman they are working with, rather than the behaviour of abusive men (Hanmer, 1996). This often leads them to believe that women are passive in their responses, and do not seek help or resist their abuse as a result (Mullender, 1996). Very often women are blamed for the violence and abuse they experience, by their abusers and agencies alike (Hanmer, 1996; Mullender, 1996), and women are often criticised for not seeking help or resisting the violence in some way that is logical and visible to those around them (Hoff, 1990; Barnett and LaViolette, 1993; Deltufo, 1995). In fact research suggests that many women do actively try to resist violence and abuse, and make all sorts of attempts to get help and support (Dobash et al., 1985; Hoff 1990; Kelly, 1988).

Why don't women just leave?

Without any doubt the question I am most asked in the work that I do, (especially as professionals become more aware of the impact of domestic violence upon children) by professionals at all levels of agencies, is why doesn't a woman just leave? The simplicity of this as a response is understandable, but one of the key problems that we must overcome if we are to improve strategic thinking, policy development, and practice in a way which truly makes a difference for women and children. Just as we have the myth of the perfect mother, we also have the myth of the perfect family, and thinking our way out of these myths is vital if we are to create appropriate support and resources, and assist women to access them.

The socialisation of women has taught us that we exist in the main to be nurturers, protectors and to keep our family together. Whilst this socialisation may be very useful to society in order that we can bring up children within a stable environment, it poses a major problem for women who want to leave a violent relationship. We have socialised women to be primary caregivers and to forgive the wrongs done to them in order to maintain their family. Leaving a violent relationship means withholding forgiveness and making the decision to 'break up' your family, both of which place women outside of society's expectations of them.

On average a woman will be physically assaulted 35 times, and will contact between 5 and 12 different agencies before they receive an appropriate response. Therefore, women are faced, often alone, with complex issues when they are considering their future in a violent relationship. These complexities will be further compounded by the responses of those around them, and this is particularly problematic where responses are negative or inconsistent from agencies. Negativity and inconsistency lead to confusion, fear and inactivity, and professionals need to bear in mind that a woman bases her responses to them not only on the here and now, but past agency responses to either herself and/or other women that she knows. If she, or others, have been let down in the past then professionals have to overcome her fears, regain her trust, and deliver services effectively on each and every occasion.

For some women their partners will have spelt out in no uncertain terms what they will do to her (and/or her children) if they are found, and this will be further compounded where she feels agencies have previously failed her, or her perception is that they will be unable to protect her if she leaves. However irrational it sounds, staying may be preferable because there is a degree of safety in knowing where he is, and what he is likely to do. Leaving may take away her ability to predict his next move, or to gauge his mood or reaction, and expose her to the unknown at a time where she feels most vulnerable and isolated. In effect, far from giving her back some control over her life, leaving may eradicate, or reduce, what little degree of control she feels she has over his behaviour.

A woman may well believe (quite rationally in a number of instances) that others will hold her to blame for the man's behaviour, and be deeply ashamed and scared of not only him, but also the consequences for her and her children if she attempts to disclose her abuse. This is particularly problematic for women who may have developed risky coping strategies (e.g. prescribed and non-prescribed drug use, alcohol misuse) or have mental health problems as a result of the abuse they are experiencing, as this will have significant effects not just on the outcome of child protection interventions, but also on those in civil family court cases. Indeed the irony is that women who have struggled to

survive against all odds will be the most likely to be dealt with more punitively by child protection agencies, and are far more likely to lose custody of their children even where there is no direct abuse of them.

In addition, some women will experience problems linked to the fact that they may already be experiencing additional oppressions,[3] or are frightened that they will be discriminated against by agencies when seeking help. It is vital that practitioners understand that these oppressions will present very real dilemmas for women when they make decisions about disclosure, seeking help and leaving.

Despite all of this some women will try to escape from the situation they are in by removing themselves and their children from the home. When fleeing women report that they seek support from a range of sources, some will go to family and friends, others will go into refuges, or seek help from other agencies. However, the vast majority of abused women are critical of the agencies that they approach, and report that they often receive negative or inconsistent responses to their requests for help, and that this in itself often affects any future decisions that they make. Given that society's responses to abused women are still not always positive, and verge from passivity, to blame, through to open hostility, woman have a lot to overcome before they can even contemplate leaving at a macro, never mind a micro level.

The process that women have to go through when deciding whether or not to leave is therefore complex, and fraught with dangers and difficulties. Whilst for child protection practitioners leaving may be seen as a logical goal to be achieved to ensure that safety is achieved for children (and in some cases this may well be true) for many women it exposes them to additional risks both from their ex-partners, and in some cases adverse agency agendas. It also may well fail to protect children in the longer term as mothers find themselves having to comply with family court judgements around issues of contact and residency. Telling a woman all her problems will be solved if she leaves is at best naïve, at worst evidence of incompetent practitioners failing to see the situation in its entirety.

Use of coping strategies

To live with a violent man takes courage, strength and resolve, especially where agencies have failed to respond appropriately. It will deplete a woman's energy levels greatly, as her whole life is controlled by the need to ensure that both she and her children can survive. To think herself out of this situation may take additional energy that she cannot summon up without consistent, co-ordinated and unconditional support over a period of time that may not fit in with child protection time-scales. However, many abused women will try to minimise their pain and suffering by developing coping strategies. It is important to note that where women have themselves also been abused as children, the range of coping strategies used are generally greater, and self-destructive strategies are more than twice as likely to be used.

The most common strategy used by women is to withdraw or switch off from the world around them. Given that many abusive men use isolating tactics to control women, and keep them away from their family and friends, and that some women report that the violence they experience leads to depression, this seems a logical response to the situation that they are in. For child protection practitioners this withdrawal may be viewed at best as unhelpful, at worst as non-compliance with the system, and she may experience more punitive responses than other women may. In these instances women find themselves drifting through the child protection system seemingly cut off from the process, and practitioners need to find a way of breaking through the woman's isolation that has become her survival jacket.

Some women may use alcohol, prescribed or non-prescribed drugs to block out or cope with the abuse that they suffer. Where this usage becomes visible and problematic, or women develop profound mental health problems that mean they are struggling (or failing) to care for their children effectively, at this point women may come to the attention of child protection agencies. Intervention at this stage will often focus on the symptoms (with little or no attempt to make the connections to abuse) and fail to have the desired effect.

Whilst women will need help with their health problems, these interventions will fail to deliver unless the woman has opportunities to disclose her abuse and be appropriately supported through the resulting issues. It is not surprising that abused women are far more likely to attempt or commit suicide than those who are not abused, and often these women are already in contact with health services.

Given this point, it is important to note that appropriate support services available to women with the most complex of needs are still sadly lacking, and there is an urgent need for the development of women centred services and practice.

The potential impact of ignorance, inertia and inadequate agency/community responses

The aggregate effect of women and children not receiving appropriate responses to help seeking behaviour, or appropriate and consistent support to end the abuse, is that they may be left with little or no option than to choose progressively more negative, or risky, coping strategies in order to escape the violence and survive. Use of these often may lead to women being in contact with (and often at odds with) child protection agencies, mental health services, or the criminal justice system, and mean that they are not only coping with the reality and effects of violence and abuse, but are also dealing with the repercussions of the very actions that were designed to get them through the violence and abuse in the first place.

There is little doubt that where a woman's or child's family, friends, agencies and community all respond with sensitivity, speed and consistency to domestic violence and deliver seamless services, the potential for a positive outcome is increased dramatically. Given the complex needs of women and children no one agency alone can meet their needs, and this means more than ever that agencies must work together in partnership, sharing understanding, definitions, and information. Practitioners have a responsibility to check out a woman's history with other agencies, although no information collected will not mean abuse hasn't happened, but just hasn't been adequately recorded.

Children's experiences of domestic violence

The fact that children are impacted by living within a home where domestic violence is perpetrated against their mother is actually now well researched and documented (Bowker, Arbitell, McFerron 1988; Carter and Schechter, 1997; Dobash, 1977; Edleson, 1997; Hendessi, 1997; Hester and Pearson, 1998; Hughes, Parkinson, Vargo, 1989; Humphreys, 1997; Maxwell, 1994; McGee, 1996; McGee, 2000;

Morley and Mullender, 1994; Mullender et al., 2000; Mullins, 1997; NCH, 1994; Saunders et al. 1995; Stark and Flitcraft, 1988;) and the Government paper *Working Together to Safeguard Children* (DoH, 1999) highlights that child protection agencies must make the connections between the abuse of children and their mothers, and include it in all levels of their policies, strategies and practice.

Witnessing or overhearing abuse

We know that in 90 per cent of instances of physical violence children are in the same or the next room, and that a third of children present during an incident of violence will try to intervene and protect their mother from the man's abuse.[4] Given these facts children of abused women are not only damaged by witnessing and over-hearing violence, but are also exposed to violence as a consequence of getting caught in the 'cross fire', or as a result of their attempts to protect their mother.

Children will also witness the aftermath of episodes of violence, including their mother being distressed or depressed, or suffering from physical injuries, which may significantly impact upon their mother's ability to care for them physically and emotionally. Children will be aware on a daily basis of the unpredictability of the situation in which they live, the atmosphere that exists, and the fear and intimidation, which means that the man is able to rule and terrorise everyone in their home. Many children will be shocked, embarrassed, and blame themselves for the violence (as their mothers do also) and will look desperately for solutions within themselves to end the violence. Many children (especially older children) will fantasise about hurting, or killing the man, as a way of stopping the violence.

Witnessing, overhearing or living with the aftermath of violence leaves children frightened, distressed, and anxious about their own, their sibling's and their mother's safety. Witnessing or overhearing violence means that the consequences of being threatened by the man, or hearing him make threats against their mother, are all the more real to children. They have real (rather than imaginary) pictures in their heads, and do not have to imagine the consequences of these threats, they know them, can feel them, can smell them, can predict them, and in this context the direct abuse of children is easy, and quick to achieve.

Direct physical/psychological abuse of children

We now know that somewhere between 50 and 70 per cent of children living with an abused mother will be directly abused by the man also. Children may be used by the man as part of the violence perpetrated against women, with children used as physical or psychological weapons, and being forced, coerced or encouraged to side with the man and encouraged to participate with him in the abuse of their mother. Many children who are killed at the hands of fathers/father figures are killed as a direct result of the man wanting to punish their mothers, and the significance of the presence of domestic violence has often been ignored and minimised by professionals, often despite previous pleas and protestations by the woman (O'Hara, 1994). This is particularly the case where children are killed after separation during contact visits with fathers.

Links to sexual abuse

The links between domestic violence and child sexual abuse are still being made (and we urgently need more research to be conducted into this area) but research conducted by Farmer and Owen (1995) found that 40 per cent of children living with an abused mother had been sexually abused by the man. Foreman's (1995) research into the backgrounds of mothers of sexually abused children found that 100 per cent had histories of domestic violence. Clearly practitioners need to be alive to these possibilities.

Differences for children in families

Not all children are treated the same within families, and this leads to confusion for children who experience violence and abuse where siblings do not. The man may single out children, in positive or negative ways and this may lead to feelings of confusion, anger, guilt and sadness by themselves, their siblings, and their mother. It is important to acknowledge that some children will display (on the surface) little or no evidence of abuse, and these are the children in families that lead to confusion for professionals. Their own needs are ignored, whilst the behaviour of their outwardly more disruptive siblings can be written off as related to themselves, rather than the abuse they and their mothers are experiencing.

Furthermore, how children have made sense of the violence, and whom they hold responsible, will have a profound impact on how they feel about their father and their mother. Women will often have to face the fact that their children will choose their father over them, despite their own abuse (and in some cases the direct abuse of their children), and may lose them to him in the short or longer term. These experiences often have hugely negative, far-reaching impacts on relationships between mothers, children, and their siblings.

Additional issues that may affect the impact of domestic violence upon children

Whilst professionals are now beginning to consider how age, gender, and the factors above will impact individual children, often little, or no attention, is paid to issues of race, class or disability. Just as their mothers will find it more difficult to leave violent relationships where these and other oppressive factors are present, children will find that additional obstacles (both internal and external) will need to be confronted and overcome if they are to resist, cope and disclose their experiences. Whilst there is little research evidence to assist us here (and again these are areas that all must be further investigated) professionals must consider these issues when working with children.

Child contact

Courts often still make the assumption that contact with fathers is always in the best interests of the child, despite a great deal of anecdotal and research evidence to the contrary (Hester and Radford, 1994). This issue of Contact is a contentious one,[5] and whilst failed or broken attachments undoubtedly carry the risk of significant emotional harm happening to children (Bowlby, 1980; Fahlberg, 1994; Howe et al., 1999; Rutter, 1981) for children involved in domestic violence continued contact with a father who is also violent may have a range of profound consequences for the children themselves, and their mothers.

Disclosure

Many children will disclose their experiences of domestic violence and abuse, although this may not always be by openly talking of the abuse, but in a range of ways that those around them

do not always pick up upon. Not being believed previously, or the fear of not being believed, seemed to be the primary reason why children may choose not to tell. This seems to be completely rational given that research suggests that when children decide to tell it is not uncommon for their disclosure, particularly where sexual abuse is a feature, to be met by anger, denial and rejection (Eastel, 1994; Macleod and Saraga, 1987).[6] Research has demonstrated that where children are not believed, and receive poor or inadequate support, the effects of domestic violence and abuse are more extreme and longer lasting (Wyatt and Mickey, 1988).

Whether children receive positive or negative responses to disclosure has profound consequences in relation to: how they themselves make sense of the abuse that is perpetrated against both themselves and their mothers; who they hold responsible; their hopes for the future and the options available to them for survival; and in some cases the future relationships with those that they had chosen to disclose to.

Children's resistance to and ways of coping with domestic violence

Given that domestic violence is such an isolating experience for children, resisting and seeking help is often a lonely thought to contemplate and carry through. Experiencing any kind of abuse involves a misuse of power and an abuse of trust between the abusive adult and the child (Working Party on Violence Against Women and Children, 1993). In addition, children may also blame the non-abusive mother in that they often struggle to understand their mother's apparent refusal to stand up to the man, or leave him, which ultimately may lead to feelings of anxiety, distress and them feeling unprotected and at risk of further abuse. Given the power differential that exists between children and the adults who abuse them, any action children take to resist abuse are likely to be problematic, and expose them to further risk and danger.

Children experiencing domestic violence still need to get through their daily lives and just like their mothers they are likely to develop coping strategies to help them deal with their own and their mother's abuse. Age is a significant factor in that whilst younger children are likely to be restricted to the displaying of physical symptoms and distress, as children get older they are more likely to display behavioural and emotional problems, and to run away or look for other forms of escape. The most common coping strategies reported by older children are: to play truant from school; to be badly behaved or really naughty; to run away; to become withdrawn and depressed; to use alcohol or drugs; or to use cutting or other self-destructive behaviours.

All of these coping strategies can have negative consequences both in the short and the long term. Not going to school has obvious outcomes in relation to a child's educational attainment, but also means that they are having to take themselves somewhere else during the day other than home or school, and this can mean that the child may put themselves at further risk of abuse and danger. In addition, poor or erratic behaviour may lead to negative labelling, resulting in this becoming the focus of any intervention rather than the abuse and violence that is happening at home.

Conducting a child protection assessment where domestic violence is a feature

When considering how women and children may have been impacted by violence and abuse, and how they have managed to cope, it is important that a balanced picture is presented. Representing women and children as merely victims suggests that they have no agency (Baskin and Sommers, 1993) and are not able to make decisions and choices that are about resisting and surviving violence and abuse. Although anyone who experiences violence or abuse is undoubtedly victimised by their experience Kelly et al. (1996) contest that viewing women and children as survivors, instead of merely victims, reflects the sheer fact that many do physically survive,[7] often against tremendous odds. However, this survival can often only be achieved by the use of resistance tactics, and the development of resistance and coping strategies, that may not automatically be viewed as rational and logical by society in general, or those around them.

In order to conduct a thorough assessment we need to think about the Assessment Framework in some detail. The investigation and assessment of the three inter-related systems (development needs of children, family and environmental factors, and parenting capacity) is without doubt an obviously extremely useful tool for practitioners. However, there are some areas that warrant further clarity and thought

before conducting an assessment where domestic violence is a feature.

In some senses the triangle is flawed in that whilst it makes some reference to the different role played by mothers and fathers (father figures), it actually lumps them both together when looking at parental capacity, and we may find ourselves talking about 'family violence' rather than 'domestic violence'. The problem with this is that we start from the premise that there is a dual level of responsibility, that each parent is able to contribute equally to the child protection process, and in many cases the judgement concentrates on the capacity of the women to parent and protect rather than on the effect of the man's violence on the woman and her children. All too often the focus of child protection assessments are on women, and this means that we are asking women to sort out the problem and operate as our agent, rather than including men and assisting them to take responsibility for the violence. It may well be worth child protection agencies assigning different practitioners to each parent (and then co-working) in order to ensure that the needs of women and children are more accurately identified, and to ensure that men are given an opportunity to talk about the violence. In this way the professional can achieve a far more accurate child protection assessment. There are obvious issues of safety here, particularly for female workers, and issues of men working with men where collusion may be sought and entered into. Both of these issues need careful thought and planning by child protection managers and practitioners.

Direct work with women

In order to conduct a thorough and useful risk assessment for children, we must enable and empower women to disclose their experiences, and consider its impact upon their own and their children's lives. It is important to recognise that naming violence is often very hard for women to do for a number of complex reasons, including: not wanting to accept that the situation she find herself in is serious; being scared of what the man will do if she tells someone else about his behaviour; the fear that she will not be believed, or that if she is she will be pushed into making decisions that she is not yet able or ready to contemplate; and being scared that agencies may have their own agendas including removing her children.

There are significant benefits for child protection agencies in the blanket screening of all women in contact with their services, and monitoring and recording the abuse that they and their children experience. There is evidence to suggest that when agencies introduce blanket screening conducted in a sensitive and meaningful way that the disclosure rate of domestic violence will increase from about one third to two thirds of women. Screening should occur at the initial visit and on every subsequent occasion, to maximise women's opportunities to tell us about their abuse.

Being asked the questions does not necessarily lead to disclosure by women. Research (Rowsell, 2000) suggests that women, even when blanket screening is in place, will fail to disclose for a range of reasons including: the fear of not being believed; the gender of worker; a perceived lack of follow up support; previously poor experiences when disclosing, or being placed on a referral circuit that means women feel out of control and over-loaded by agency roles and responsibilities; some women are simply not ready (hence the importance of keeping asking the questions); the blocking of the abuse out of their minds as a way of coping; issues of mistrust and the poor quality of relationship between women and workers; and being worried about confidentiality and partners being informed about the disclosure.

Given that contact with the child protection agencies is stressful for women, and they may be asked for a great deal of information in a short period of time by practitioners, whether these questions are heard when asked, and subsequently responded to, may be dependent on a number of factors, including how the question is asked, in what context, and by whom. Abused women are skilled at assessing body language, dissecting oral messages, and making predictions on what another person will do next – after all they have had to become skilled at these to survive. Research with women consistently suggests that being honest, and open, and asking questions in a direct work is more likely to result in her being enabled to disclose. Therefore, it is important that the right practitioners are chosen to undertake this work, and are equipped with the awareness, knowledge and tools in order to do this sensitively, consistently and in a way that will empower and enable women to disclose.

Importance of confidentiality

It is also important that practitioners understand that a differential approach must be taken to confidentiality in relation to women and their partners, from a sheer safety point of view there cannot be the same rule applied to abused women and the men who perpetrate violence against them.

Essential components for conducting an initial assessment with a woman

A useful checklist for conducting an assessment with women is outlined in Table 1 overleaf.

Questions to ask women

The following screening questions are merely for guidance (and others may be more appropriate to use in specific situations with women):

1. Do you get support at home, who from and how often?
2. How does your partner help you?
3. Is everything all right at home between you and your partner?
4. We all have rows occasionally, tell me do you ever argue or row with your partner?
5. What happens when you argue or row?
6. Does your partner get jealous, and if so how does he behave when he is jealous?
7. Have you ever been in a relationship with anyone who ever hurt you?
8. Has anyone ever hit, punched, kicked, or done anything that has hurt you physically?
9. Does your partner ever make you feel frightened or scared by his behaviour?
10. Does he call you names, or shout, or threaten you in any way?
11. Where are your children when your partner behaves like this?
12. Does his behaviour frighten them?
13. Have they ever got hurt when he has been hurting you?
14. Many women tell me that their partners are not always nice to them, and can be cruel either physically or emotionally – does this ever happen to you? (Use Duluth Power and Control Wheel – and ask the woman if her partner ever behaves in any of the ways identified. Explain that the wheel was put together by women who were experiencing or had experienced domestic violence).
15. You have a nasty looking bruise/cut/scratch/burn, can you tell me how they happened and when?

Table 1: Assessment considerations with women.

Element of assessment	Considerations, benefits, potential outcomes
All women should be routinely asked questions about domestic violence, and told that this is routine. This should be done calmly as practitioner anxiety or being in an emotional state can put the woman off disclosing.	Need to create a safe place that can meet her needs,* with a high degree of privacy, and away from the man. Will reduce tension felt by woman who may well suspect that the practitioner knows something. Will give positive messages to woman that DV is common and on the agenda for all. Will not only create space for every woman to disclose, but will increase practitioner's skills in asking the questions and responding to disclosure effectively.
It should be made clear that the purpose of asking these questions is to ensure that she and her children are safe.	Will reduce resistance and encourage disclosure as the woman believes that the practitioner will not just hear the disclosure but will be able to support her to be safe. It also will raise the issue of the potential impact upon her children, and means that she has to consider her own safety alongside her own.
Explain agency confidentiality issues, that any information she shares with you will not be disclosed to the man unless she agrees with this and has a safety plan to accommodate it, the boundaries and exceptions to confidentiality.	Will ensure that women know that information they share with workers is confidential, and will not be told to the man. Ensures that women know that some information cannot be kept confidential and must be shared within and across agencies.
Workers should ask questions gently, and in a non-blaming way.	A range of questions needs to be asked, and there is some issue about who asks the questions, how and when. Whilst some woman may feel comfortable in disclosing to a male others won't, and this should be openly discussed between professionals and strategies be in place to accommodate this.
It should be made clear that if women choose to disclose that this will not result on her children being removed from her care unless the risk to the children is serious.	Telling women the truth, will allay their fears and will counter-act any threats the man may have made to her previously in relation to her children. Ensures she understands agency agendas.
Where women do not disclose at this stage, it should be made clear that they can come back to the worker at any time in the future should this become an issue.	It is important to leave the door wide open, to send signals that tell women whilst they are not yet ready to disclose, that they may, and can do so, in the future.
If disclosure occurs it is important to remember that she may only tell the bare minimum. One way of finding out more is to ask about the first incident, the last incident and the worst incident of violence.	Gives the practitioner an opportunity to explore the spectrum of abuse, the severity and the time span. Gives the woman an opportunity to snapshot without having to think about the whole at the first disclosure – this may be too much for her to bear. Prevents probing for too much detail, in the first instance.
Use the Duluth Power and Control wheel (see 'Making an Impact') to explore with women the type and range of abuses they may have experienced.	This will mean that women have an opportunity to engage with the range of abuses they may have experienced, will help them share practitioner's definition of abuse, and will tell them that abuse is common and they are not alone.
Document what the woman tells you, in her words, ensuring that you have her explicit consent to do so. Make sure that she knows that some things are not negotiable.	Will provide evidence for assessment, and evidence for future criminal/civil action if required.

Table 1: Continued.

With her permission photograph and/or use a body chart, date, sign (both you and the woman) any visible injuries, or arrange for this to be done by health/police. Ensure that she is able to access medical attention, and is encouraged to report her injuries to the police.	Will provide evidence for future criminal/civil action if required. Will ensure that health risks are minimised.
Document fully all disclosures, and add any concerns that you may have to her notes factually and accurately. This is very important if the woman's explanation of the situation/injuries is not consistent with worker findings.	Will ensure that all information is recorded, and that workers and subsequent workers can track the case appropriately.
Discuss options available to her. Women should be given a package with information about all these services, and engaged in a discussion about where they can keep this information so that the man cannot find it.	Practitioners need to be fully aware of all available services, systems of referral and access points and thresholds (if any).
If she isn't ready to leave/doesn't want to leave conduct an assessment of safety, and agree a safety plan with her if appropriate.	Some women will have a safety plan but formalising it with her will check that it is in place, is viable, that she knows she has options, gives her a degree of control, and demonstrates that she is thinking about her safety and forward planning. In some circumstances the level of risk may be so great that practitioners are left with no option but to remove children if the women refuses to engage with the reality of the situation.

16. Your partner seems very concerned about you and your injuries, sometimes men behave like that when they have hurt a woman and she has injuries, did he do anything to you?
17. Has your partner ever destroyed your possessions, or things that he knows are important to you?
18. Has your partner ever followed you, checked up on you, does he ring you constantly?
19. Does your partner withhold sex or reject you sexually in a way which makes you feel punished, or rejected?
20. Does your partner ever persuade or coerce you to have sex when you really don't want to?
21. Does your partner make you do things sexually that you really don't like, don't enjoy or hurt you?
22. Does your partner threaten to, or abuse your children?
23. Does your partner ever drink, or take drugs? What happens when he takes them, how does he behave around you, your children?
24. Tell me about the first time your partner abused you, the last time, the worst time?

Safety planning with women

Where women indicate that they are not yet ready to leave then the practitioner has to decide whether trying to coerce or force a woman, by threatening to remove her children will be counterproductive in the longer term. Without a doubt this means that the practitioner will have to make an assessment of risk. It is important that in order to make a thorough assessment of risk to children, the practitioner asks themselves the following:

1. Is the woman accepting that she is abused or disclosing the abuse?
2. Does the woman recognise the scale and impact of the abuse that is being perpetrated against her?
3. Is the abuse getting worse, increasing in frequency and severity?
4. How does she cope on a daily basis – what coping strategies does she use, and how risky or successful are these to her and her children?
5. Does she have any mental health problems, if so is she in contact with appropriate support agencies?

6. Has she made previous attempts to leave, how successful have these been and what have been the problems, have there been barriers to leaving?
7. What involvement has there been from other agencies and how does she feel this has impacted upon her life (positive or negative)?
8. Which agencies does she trust and could these agencies be brought in to increase her safety?
9. What does she believe has been the impact upon her children, is the likely future impact upon her children, and how can she take action that will minimise risk of harm to her children?
10. Has she previously raised concerns about her children, and have these been met with useful interventions?
11. To what degree does the woman seem to be compliant with the child protection process (the practitioner needs to be able to work out whether disinterest, anger or non-compliance is as a result of her abuse and previous experiences or a genuine refusal to take seriously the concerns that may be held)?

Safety planning

Where the practitioner decides with the woman that risk is acceptable, then s/he will often need to assist a woman to formulate safety plans. These should include as a bare minimum:

1. Identifying with her what she will do if an incident of violence occurs, how will she ensure her own safety.
2. Identifying ways of trying to minimise the risk to her children, getting them out of the room, sending them to get help etc.
3. Her being able to identify somewhere safe that she and her children can go to in an emergency.
4. Always carrying a list of important/emergency numbers.
5. Packing a bag which contains a spare set of clothes for herself and the children, important documents, important photographs, a spare set of keys for the house/car, a bit of money if possible, and if possible get the bag out and store it with a trusted friend.
6. Ensuring that she is in touch with key support agencies i.e. Women's Aid, Rape Crisis, Police Domestic Violence Unit etc.,

and calls them when needed, particularly if a crisis occurs.

7. Being able to access a good solicitor who will be able to explain legal options, panic will be reduced if she knows her rights.

8. Getting a trusted friend to ring or check on her at least once a day-using key words that will identify to her friend whether she is safe or needs help is very important.

It is often helpful to agree the safety plan with the woman, and formally record it. This should then become an integral part of the work that the practitioner undertakes to evaluate whether the woman's situation improves or deteriorates over an agreed time period. In this way the practitioner can assist the woman to review her situation on an on-going basis, and ensure that their own assessment is updated and appropriate decisions made as necessary. Where the level of risk assessed relates to parenting issues, then it is of vital importance that the practitioner is realistic in what a woman can achieve if she is living with violence and abuse, or the threat of it from a previous partner. However, the attempts a woman may make to comply with, and achieve child protection goals may be deliberately undermined or thwarted by the perpetrator, and practitioners need to find a way of establishing whether the woman won't or can't co-operate.

Abused women deserve honesty and openness, and the system needs to become transparent so that women understand their own role and responsibility within the child protection process, and are clear about the consequences of non-compliance. It is the practitioner's responsibility to ensure that this happens.

Direct work with men who perpetrate domestic violence

It is now widely accepted that in order to effect meaningful change that all stakeholders need to be actively involved in the process. Change necessary for child protection reasons is no different. Whilst I accept that there are often a minimal number of appropriate resources available to assist men to take responsibility for violent behaviour, the best outcome can only be achieved when practitioners work directly with men to do just that. However, men have become good at avoiding intervention, and we have become good at allowing this to happen. However, the process of engaging with men is complex and needs to be thought through by

child protection agencies. Social workers are not taught how to engage with men, and often lack the skills needed to do so, and therefore often consciously or unconsciously exclude them from the process. Any intervention needs to be undertaken by a skilled practitioner who has an excellent understanding of domestic violence and the men who perpetrate it. Men need to be working on not only understanding how and why their behaviour occurs, but also how they can develop their own plan of safety that will keep their partners and children safe. Practitioners need then to actively include men as a matter of urgency, because unless they do so how can they truly assess the level of risk posed, or work out a long term effective intervention strategy. But this should never be done in a way which compromises the safety of women and children.

Just as with other agencies, the best tactics men can employ when working with child protection practitioners are to: absent themselves from the child protection process in a practical sense by being unavailable; to minimise, deny and blame the woman thereby convincing the practitioner that there is no problem, or that the problem is the woman; and/or to intimidate practitioners and use the process as a way of silencing women and children. However, there is some evidence that when practitioners refuse to allow men off the hook, and actively seek to engage them in the process, that they will and do talk about violence and abuse, even if this is only in a very piecemeal way to begin with.

Practitioners working with men on men's re-education programmes report that the most effective way to engage with men is to ask them general questions to begin with, followed by very specific questions that demonstrate that the practitioner knows that violence and abuse is present, and is presuming that the man should and will take responsibility for its perpetration. It is vital that the language used by practitioners is not that of the counselling or therapeutic, as research suggests that men have learnt how to avoid these kinds of techniques, or use them to their own advantage e.g. to assume victim status. Therefore practitioners need to ask questions of men directly, that tell them quite clearly that we know abuse is present, and allow them to assess against the following:

1. How willing is the man to co-operate and comply with the child protection process?

2. How does the man's version of events/his relationship compare with the woman's?
3. Does he have a history of violent behaviour, particularly against other women/children?
4. If so, what has been the outcome of this behaviour?
5. To what degree does he minimise his abuse, deny the abuse, or blame the woman?
6. How aware is he of the impact of his behaviour on the women and the children?
7. To what degree does he accept responsibility for his behaviour?
8. To what degree does he seem likely to respond to intervention?
9. How willing is he to leave the relationship if this is necessary for child protection reasons?
10. Are there currently any charges being laid against him, and what are his bail conditions?
11. Does he have any alcohol or drug misuse?
12. Does he have any mental health issues?
13. To what degree does the practitioner feel confident that they can work with the man, and how far will his/her own safety be compromised?

Impact of domestic violence on children and the safety of the women and children

How can we measure the impact of domestic violence on children? Just as women are unique, so are their children. The way children respond to, make sense of, and assign responsibility for domestic violence is dependent upon a range of factors including:

1. Whether the child themselves has overheard, witnessed or been directly abused by the man.
2. Whether the man is encouraging the child to take his side or take part in the abuse of their mother or siblings.
3. The type of abuse experienced by themselves, their siblings and their mothers.
4. Its severity, frequency, and duration.
5. The quality of the child's relationship with its mother, and its siblings. (This is even more significant where the child is being singled out, encouraged to participate in the abuse of their mother or siblings, or being overtly or covertly abused by the man directly).
6. The child's own use of positive or negative resources and coping strategies and the implications of these (e.g. some children will

throw themselves into school, others will truant).

7. Whether the child is given opportunities to disclose, and is subsequently believed by those important to them.
8. How family members and significant others respond to the violence and abuse.
9. The quality of the child's support networks and those available to their mother.
10. The quality, speed and sensitivity of agency interventions (if any have occurred).
11. The level of tolerance within the child's community to domestic violence and child abuse in general.

Essential components to include when working with children

There is no blanket approach that we can take to assess how each child will be affected, and this often leads to a great deal of confusion for professionals, particularly where children in the same family are affected in different ways, and to different degrees. However, just as with their mothers children will often respond best to direct questions asked in a way that is most appropriate to each child's age and stage of development. In planning the assessment process with each child practitioners will need to assess and collect information in order to assess the impact of domestic violence and the level of risked posed to the child (see Table 2 overleaf).

Conclusion

There is little doubt that child protection agencies need to take greater account of how domestic violence impacts upon children when undertaking child protection assessments. Whilst it is important that we ensure that children's needs are identified, considered and met, it is vital that we do not do so at the expense of women who are themselves victimised. Given the difficulties that all child protection agencies face in trying to protect children from abuse, in the context of domestic violence the most cost effective form of child protection is to protect, support and empower their abused mothers and hold men who perpetrate it accountable.

However, meeting children's needs once identified remains a huge issue for practitioners given that the vast majority of local authorities still fail to fund specific services for children experiencing domestic violence. This leaves

Table 2: Assessing children: some considerations.

Element of assessment	Considerations, benefits and potential outcomes
Assess child's level of awareness, and feelings about, violence and abuse being perpetrated upon its mother.	Will enable practitioner to identify how much the child is aware of the abuse, the level of risk that is being experienced by the child, and begin to raise issues of responsibility. Will enable practitioner to share this with mother (and perpetrator if appropriate).
What is the quality of the child's relationship with its mother?	Will enable the practitioner to gain greater insight into the impact of abuse on each child, and how this is impacting the child's relationship with its mother. Will identify key areas of concern, and present practitioner with a clear pathway in any therapeutic work to be undertaken.
What is the quality of the child's relationship with the perpetrator?	Will help the practitioner identify whether the child holds the perpetrator responsible for the abuse, whether the child is being manipulated by the perpetrator, and whether on-going contact with the child is likely to be safe or not.
What is the quality of the child's relationship with each of its siblings?	Will identify strengths and weaknesses in sibling dynamics, and identify clear areas of therapeutic work that will need to be undertaken with each child.
What role does the child play within its family, and has it been given or assumed responsibilities that are beyond its years or capabilities?	Will identify where the child is being asked to assume too much responsibility, and will assist practitioner to make judgements on how this is impacting upon the child's health and developmental needs. Will again identify how therapeutic work may be used to deconstruct unhealthy family dynamics.
Assessment of child's general health and all areas of development, including assessment of: physical health and growth and development; social skills and ability to function in different social situations; intellectual and educational development, including understanding, school attendance, performance and the way the child presents; emotional development including child's moods, confidence levels, self-esteem etc. This will need to be done by liasing with health, education and other relevant agencies.	Will enable practitioner to consider total impact, identify problem areas, and identify differences between siblings. Will also ensure that other professionals are alive to the issues and the risks, and direct resources appropriately.
What strategies does the child have in place to cope/use to cope?	Will assist to identify impact of abuse on child, and identify level of risks being taken by the child in order to cope or to cope with violence and abuse.
What support networks are in place for the child, what other significant adults are involved in the child's life?	Will identify to what degree each child has support networks, whether these are appropriate or not, whether these can be extended or tapped into by the practitioner. Will also provide practitioner with a greater picture as others may be approached and asked to assist with the assessment process.

practitioners with huge dilemmas and this is an issue that Directors of Social Services Departments and their senior officers responsible for the provision of services to children really need to address as a matter of urgency. In most instances the only services available to children are those provided by refuges, and children have to therefore physically be resident in a refuge before these can be accessed.

Unlike the statutory sector, many refuges employ specific children's workers whose role is to work directly with mothers, and their children, to help them understand and come to terms with their experiences of violence and abuse. The work they do reflects the philosophy that children deserve services in their own right, and the interventions provided are often of an extremely high standard and are of vital importance to the achievement of a positive outcome for children. However, these services very rarely attract long term local authority funding, instead they are funded in the main by short-term grants (Lottery, Children in Need and Comic Relief), and resources very rarely extend to meeting the needs of children in the community, who have not been in refuge accommodation.

Whilst I firmly believe that if child protection practitioners use the Assessment Framework, together with an increased knowledge and awareness of domestic violence, then it is possible to make a positive difference for women and children experiencing domestic violence. However, to identify children's needs and then not be able to meet them post-assessment cannot continue. Child protection agencies therefore have a responsibility to define all children living with, or surviving domestic violence, as children in need and commission and provide appropriate services. Not to do so is evidence that we continue to fail mothers and their children.

Notes

1. In relation to domestic violence Jalna Hamner (cited in Ball, 1995, page 2–6) argues that incidence will always be higher than prevalence, given that half of women who report domestic violence experience more than one assault, and that men who abuse one woman are likely to be serial abusers.
2. This said, it is important to recognise that women experiencing physical violence are more likely to be physically injured than

other victims of violence (Home Office, 1996), and physical assaults undoubtedly can lead to a range of injuries, hospital treatment, disability, disfigurement, and death with almost half of all women murdered in England and Wales being killed by a partner or former partner (Home Office, 1995; Mirrlees-Black, 1995).
3. Black women, women with disabilities (physical, sensory impairment, learning), women with mental health problems, women with substance misuse problems, older or very young women, women who are travellers, lesbians, women working in the sex industry etc.
4. Abrahams (NCH, 1994) found that three-quarters of children had directly witnessed the physical abuse of their mothers, and that 10 per cent had witnessed sexual violence and assaults.
5. Practitioners will find reports and guidance notes published by WAFE particularly useful to view in relation to child contact issues.
6. Macleod and Saraga (1987) assert that this is not surprising given that abusers create a web of secrecy, fear and often implicate the child, causing the child to believe that they are somehow to blame for the abuse. Therefore, disclosure and being believed become difficult for a child to visualise.
7. It is also important to acknowledge that not all girls or women survive violence and abuse and may actually die as a direct or indirect consequence.
8. Needs may include: a venue where she feels comfortable and safe, disability access and facilities, an appropriate interpreter if English is not her first language, sign language interpreter if she has a sensory impairment, female worker if she prefers (should always be considered as a first option), a support worker if she already has a good, existing relationship with someone else, the opportunity to be accompanied (although important to ensure that this is willingly).

References and bibliography

Abrahams, C. (1994) *The Hidden Victims: Children and Domestic Violence.* London: NCH Action for Children.

Amaro, H., Fried, L, Cabral, H, and Zukerman, B. (1990) Violence During Pregnancy and Substance Use. *American Journal of Public Health.* May 80: 575–9.

Ball, M. (1994) *Funding Refuge Services: A Study of Support Services for Women and Children Experiencing Domestic Violence.* Bristol: Women's Aid Federation.

Ball, M. (1995) *Domestic Violence and Social Care: A Report of Two Conferences Held by the Social Services Inspectorate.* London: Department of Health.

Barnett, O.W. and La Violette, A.D. (1993) *It Could Happen to Anyone: Why Battered Women Stay.* London: Sage Publications.

Baskin, D. and Sommers, I. (1993) *Females Initiation into Violent Street Crime. Justice Quarterly,* 10: 4, 559–81.

Bowker, L.H., Arbitell, M. and McFerron, J.R. (1988) On the Relationship between Wife Beating and Child Abuse. In Yllo, K. and Bogard, M. (Eds.) *Feminist Perspectives on Wife Abuse.* Newbury Park: Sage Publications.

Bowlby, J. (1980) *Attachment and Loss, Volume III: Loss, Sadness and Depression.* New York: Basic Books.

Calder, M.C. (forthcoming) *Children Living With Domestic Violence: Empirically Grounded Frameworks for Intervention.* Dorset: Russell House Publishing.

Campbell, J.C., Miller, P., Cardwell, M.M. and Belknap, R.A. (1994) Relationship Status of Battered Women Over Time. *Journal of Family Violence.* 9: 99–111.

Carter, J. and Schechter, S. (1997) *Child Abuse and Domestic Violence: Creating Community Partnerships for Safe Families, Suggested Components of an Effective Child Welfare Response to Domestic Violence,* Family Violence Prevention Fund, http://www.fvpf.org/fund/materials/speakup/child . . . abuse.html

Deltufo, A. (1995) *Domestic Violence for Beginners.* New York: Writers and Readers.

Dobash, R.E. (1977) *The Relationship Between Violence Directed at Women and Violence Directed at Children Within the Family Setting.* Appendix 38, Parliamentary Select Committee on Violence in the Family, London: HMSO.

Dobash, R.E., Dobash, R.P., and Cavanagh, K. (1985) The Contact between Battered Women and Social and Medical Agencies. In Pahl, J. (Ed.) *Private Violence and Public Policy: The Needs of Battered Women and the Response of the Public Services.* London: Routledge and Kegan Paul.

DoH (1999) *Safeguarding Children.* London: TSO.

DoH (2000) *Framework for Assessing Children in Need and Their Families.* London: TSO.

Easteal, P. (1994) *Voices of Survivors.* North Melbourne, Australia: Spinifex Press.

Edleson, J.L. (1997) *The Overlap Between Child Maltreatment and Woman Battering.* University of Minnesota, http://www.mincava.umn.edu/papers/overlap.htm

Epstein C. and Keep, J. (1995) What Children Tell Childline about Domestic Violence. In Saunders, A., Epstein, C., Keep, J. and Debbonaire, T. (Eds.) *It Hurts Me Too: Children's Experiences of Domestic Violence and Refuge Life.* Bristol: WAFE.

Fahlberg, V. (1994) *A Child's Journey Through Placement.* London: BAAF.

Farmer, E. and Owen, M. (1995) *Child Protection Practice: Private Risks and Public Remedies – Decision Making, Intervention and Outcome in Child Protection Work.* London: HMSO.

Foreman, J. (1995) *Is there a Correlation Between Child Sexual Abuse and Domestic Violence? An Exploratory Study of the Links Between Child Sexual Abuse and Domestic Violence in a Sample of Interfamilial Child Sexual Abuse Cases.* Glasgow: Women's Support Project.

Gazmarian, J.A., Lazorick, S., Spitz, A.M., Ballard, T.J., Saltzman, L.E. and Marks, J. (1996) *Prevalence of Violence Against Pregnant Women. Journal of the American Medical Association.* 275: 1915–20.

Hanmer, J. (1996) Women and Violence: Commonalties and Diversities. In Fawcett, B., Featherstone, B., Hearn, J. and Toft, C. (1996) *Violence and Gender Relations: Theories and Interventions.* London: Sage Publications.

Helton, A., McFarlane, J. and Anderson, E. (1987) Battered and Pregnant: A Prevalence Study. *American Journal of Public Health.* 77: 1337–9.

Hendessi, M. (1997) *Voice of Children Witnessing Domestic Violence: A Form of Child Abuse.* Coventry: Coventry Domestic Violence Focus Group.

Hester, M. and Pearson, C. (1998) *From Periphery to Centre: Domestic Violence in Work with Abused Children.* Bristol: Policy Press.

Hester, M., Pearson, C. and Harwin, N. (1998) *Making an Impact: Children and Domestic Violence, a Reader.* Illford: Barnardos, NSPCC, University of Bristol and DoH.

Hester, M. and Radford, J. (1996) *Domestic Violence and Child Contact: Arrangements in England and Denmark.* Bristol: Policy Press.

Hoff, L.A. (1990) *Battered Women as Survivors.* London: Routledge.

Home Office (1996) *British Crime Survey*. London: Home Office.

Howe, D., Brandon, M., Hinings, D. and Schofield, G. (1999) *Attachment Theory, Child Maltreatment and Family Support*. Basingstoke: MacMillan Press.

Hughes, H.M., Parkinson, D. and Vargo, M. (1989) Witnessing Spouse Abuse and Experiencing Physical Abuse: A Double Whammy? *Journal of Family Violence*. 4: 197–209.

Humphreys, C. (1997) *Case Planning Issues Where Domestic Violence Occurs in the Context of Child Protection*. Coventry: Coventry Social Services Child Protection Unit.

Kelly, L. (1988) *Surviving Sexual Violence*. Cambridge: Policy Press.

Kelly, L., Burton, S., and Regan, L. (1996) Beyond Victim or Survivor: Sexual Violence, Identity, and Feminist Theory and Practice. In Adkins, L. and Merchant, V. (Eds.) *Sexualising the Social Power and the Organisation of Sexuality*. London: Macmillan.

Lloyd, M. (1997) Defining Violence Against Women. In Bewley, S., Friend, J. and Mezey, G. (Eds.) *Violence Against Women*. London: RCOG Press.

Macleod, M. and Saraga, E. (1987) Abuse of Trust. *Journal of Social Work Practice*. Nov. 71–9.

Maynard, M (1993) Violence Towards Women. In Richardson, D. and Robinson, V. (Eds.) *Introducing Women's Studies*. Hampshire; Macmillan Press.

Maxwell, G. (1994) *Children and Family Violence: The Unnoticed Victims*. New Zealand: Office of the Commissioner for Children. http://www.mincava.umn.edu/papers/nzreport.htm

McFarlane, J., Parker, B., Soeken, K. and Bullock, L. (1992) Assessing for Abuse During Pregnancy: Severity and Frequency of Injuries and Associated Entry into Pre-Natal Care. *Journal of the American Medical Association*. 267: 3176–8.

McFarlane, J., Parker, B., Soeken, K., Silva, C. and Reel, S. (1998) Safety Behaviours of Abused Women after an Intervention During Pregnancy. *JOGNN*. 27: 1. 64–9.

McGee, (1996) *Children's and Mother's Experiences of Child Protection Following Domestic Violence*. London: NSPCC.

McGee, C. (2000) *Childhood Experiences of Domestic Violence*. London: Jessica Kingsley.

Mirrlees-Black, C. (1995) *Estimating the Extent of Domestic Violence: Findings from the 1992 British Crime Survey*. London: Home Office Research and Planning Unit.

Morley, R. and Mullender, A. (1994) Domestic Violence and Children? What do we know from research? In Mullender, A. and Morley, R. (Eds.) *Children Living With Domestic Violence: Putting Men's Abuse of Women on the Child Care Agenda*. London: Whiting and Birch Ltd.

Mullender, A. (1996) *Rethinking Domestic Violence: The Social Work and Probation Response*. London: Routledge.

Mullender, A., Kelly, L., Hague, G., Malos, E. and Imam, U. (2000) *Children's Needs, Coping Strategies and Understanding of Woman Abuse*. Economic and Social Research Council.

Mullins, A. (1997) *Making a Difference: Working with Women and Children Experiencing Domestic Violence*. London: NCH.

NCH Action for Children (1994) *The Hidden Victims: Children and Domestic Violence*. London: NCH.

Noel, N.L. and Yam, M. (1992) Domestic Violence: The Pregnant Battered Woman. *Women's Health*. 27: 871–84.

O'Hara, M. (1994) Child Deaths in the Context of Domestic Violence: Implications for Professional Practice. In Mullender, A. and Morley, R. (Eds.) *Children Living With Domestic Violence: Putting Men's Abuse of Women on the Child Care Agenda*. London: Whiting and Birch.

Parker, B., McFarlane, J., Soeken, K., Torres, S. and Campbell, D. (1993) Physical and Emotional Abuse during Pregnancy: A Comparison of Adult and Teenage Women. *Nursing Research*. May/Jun. 24: 173–8.

Peterson, R., Gazmarian, J.A., Spitz, A.M., Rowley, D.L., Goodwin, M.M., Saltzman, L.E and Marks, J.S. (1997) *Violence and Adverse Pregnancy Outcomes: A Review of the Literature and Directions for Future Research*. American Journal of Preventative Medicine. 13: 5, 366–73.

Rowsell, C. (2000) *Closed Eyes, Covered Ears, Silenced Women, Inevitable Consequences? Women on Probation and their Experiences of Violence and Abuse*. Unpublished Masters research thesis. Leeds Metropolitan University.

Rutter, M. (1981) *Maternal Deprivation Reassessed*. London: Penguin Books.

Saunders, A., Epstein, C., Keep, G. and Debbonaire, T. (1995) *It Hurts Me Too: Children's Experiences of Domestic Violence and Refuge Life*. London; Childline.

Stark, E. and Flitcraft, A. (1988) Women and Children at Risk: a Feminist Perspective on Child Abuse. *International Journal of Health Services*. 18: 1, 97–118.

Working Party on Violence Against Women and Children (1993) *When Children Tell*. Glasgow: Women's Support Project.

Wyatt, G. E. and Mickey, M.R. (1988) Mediating Factors to Outcomes for Children. In Wyatt, G.E. and Powell, G.J. (Eds.) *Lasting Effects of Child Sexual Abuse*. London: Sage Publications.

Chapter Seventeen

Children at Risk of Illness Induction or Fabrication (Fabricated or Induced Illness): How Helpful is the Assessment Framework?

Gretchen Precey

Introduction

One of the most complex forms of abuse encountered by child protection practitioners involves the deliberate induction of illness or fabrication of symptoms or interference with treatment programmes of a child by their carer causing them to suffer significant harm. This pattern of behaviour was originally described by Professor Sir Roy Meadow in 1977 (Meadow, 1977) and given the name Munchausen Syndrome by Proxy (FII).

Both the Department of Health (2002) and the Royal College of Paediatrics and Child Health (2001) have recommended that the name to describe this form of child abuse now be referred to as Fabricated or Induced Illness (FII) rather than Munchausen Syndrome by Proxy. The reason for the change of name is to ensure that the focus of concern is on the child by describing the nature of the risk to which they are exposed rather than the behaviour of the person who is perpetrating the abuse. For this reason I shall use the term Fabricated or Induced Illness (FII) rather than Munchausen Syndrome by Proxy (MSBP) throughout this chapter.

The challenges to those professionals undertaking assessments where FII is suspected are immense. These are often children who have long medical histories encompassing a plethora of health problems and social care workers and carers who may present as committed to their child, faultless in their dedication to seeking help and extremely knowledgeable in the details of their child's symptoms and condition.

This chapter will examine the role of the *Framework for the Assessment of Children in Need and their Families* (DoH, 2000) in assisting child welfare professionals in untangling and making sense of the often confusing and sometimes fatal processes associated with FII. I shall begin by describing some of the characteristic features of FII and offer several general thoughts on approaches to assessment in these cases. I do not propose to give a very detailed account of the Assessment Framework itself as that is thoroughly discussed elsewhere in this volume (Calder, Chapter 2) but will focus instead on the specific benefits and limitations that I believe the Framework entails in its application to concern about FII. Finally I shall comment on recently released guidance by the Department of Health that has the effect of compensating for what the Framework lacks in providing information for practitioners undertaking assessments involving induced/fabricated illness.

Features of Fabricated or Induced Illness

Fabricated or Induced Illness is a condition whereby the child, usually under the age of five, suffers harm through the deliberate action of the main carer, in most cases the mother, but which is duplicitously attributed by her to another cause. For example actual suffocation of the child may be reported as cot death or intentional poisoning as caused by an accidental overdose. The child may also be harmed by unnecessary or invasive medical treatment based on symptoms that are falsely described or consciously manufactured by the carer (Brighton and Hove Child Protection Procedures, 2000).

There are a number of presentations which, under certain circumstances, may lead the practitioner to be concerned that FII might be a possibility. A list of some of those circumstances includes:

- Failure to thrive (sometimes through deliberate withholding of food).
- Fabrication of a number of medical symptoms, especially where there are no independent witnesses to the event itself. Among these symptoms are:
  - convulsions
  - pyrexia (high temperature)
  - cyanotic episodes (reported blue tinge to the skin due to lack of oxygen)

– apnoea (stops breathing)
– allergic reactions
– asthmatic attacks
– unexplained bleeding (especially anal or genital or bleeding from the ears)

Frequent unsubstantiated allegations of sexual abuse, especially when accompanied by demands for medical examinations.

Frequent accidental overdoses (especially in very young children).

Failure of a child to respond to treatment which should assist their recovery (carer may be obstructing drips or tampering with medication).

Non-attendance at school, in excess of what a medical explanation would warrant.

Applications for financial help e.g. Disability Living Allowance or other services e.g. residential special school that depend on proof of severity of child's medical condition as threshold criteria.

These victims of FII are often pre-verbal, therefore the paediatrician or GP, who in many cases are the first to suspect illness induction/fabrication, are dependent on the carer for a history of the child's symptoms. It frequently takes time for a pattern to begin to emerge whereby the child is not responding to a course of treatment as expected or there are unusual features in the child's presentation or the sheer weight of the number of visits to medical professionals will cause the doctor to become suspicious about the veracity of the mother's reporting. Schreier and Libow (1993) found that this increased the average length of time from onset of symptoms to identification of abuse in FII cases compared to other forms of maltreatment. Of the 362 cases they looked at the average length of time to identification of abuse was greater than six months in a third of the cases and over a year in a fifth of the cases. Because they are 'thinking the unthinkable' in the context of ill children and mothers who are often very plausible and caring, doctors want to be as certain as they can be that what they are dealing with is actually child abuse before reporting it to social services. One study (McClure, 1996) found that 85% of notifying paediatricians considered the probability of their diagnosis of FII as 'virtually certain' before a case conference was convened. This means that in cases of suspected FII the abuse often goes on longer before it is recognised and professionals who have contact with the family

are sometimes divided as to their respective definitions of the true nature of the problem.

Although Fabricated or Induced Illness is a very dangerous form of child abuse, and Schreier and Libow (1993) estimate that 10% of mothers who deliberately induce or fabricate illness in their children ultimately kill them, it is also very rare. The aforementioned epidemiological study carried out by McClure et al. (1996) found an annual incidence of FII of 0.5 per 100,000 in children under 16 years of age and at least 2.8 per 100,000 for children aged one and under. Extrapolating those figures to the general population the authors estimate that the incidence of FII in a hypothetical district of 1 million would be expected to show just one child per year harmed in this way. (p58).

Although the condition is rare my clinical experience of working with such cases is that they are extremely time consuming in the amount of material to be gathered and analysed and the number of people in the professional system who are involved. One particularly complex case I worked with involving the 'accidental' poisoning of two young boys took over a year to unravel and understand and progress (Precey, 1995). It is not just the information gathering and assessment that is difficult but also the emotional impact on the professionals involved because of the very skewed reality one enters when beginning to work with this condition. I have found dealing with FII among the most perplexing and pre-occupying forms of child protection work I have ever undertaken.

Those children who survive the experience of having suffered illness fabrication or induction sometimes suffer significant long-term consequences related to the nature of the abuse. Bools and Jones (1999) give some examples of what some of these consequences can be:

• Delay in speech and language or motor development as a result of distress.
• Development of feeding disorders as a result of unpleasant feeding interactions.
• Dislike of close physical contact and contact because it recalls episodes of smothering.
• Development of attachment disorders as a result of the mother–child relationship being over-controlled.
• Low self-esteem as a result of not being able to understand why they have been abused in this way.

- Having no or poor quality of relationships with peers because their opportunities for social interactions are restricted.
- Under-achievement at school because of frequent interruptions in their attendance.
- Development of abnormal attitudes to their own health.

Children who are abused in this way for long periods of time can become victims of distorted reality such that they find themselves so enmeshed with the perpetrator in the fabrication of their symptoms that they come to adopt a similar belief system for themselves (Precey, 1998). Little research has been done retrospectively on the impact on adults who are victims of FII as children. A small scale study undertaken by Libow (1998) found that 70 per cent of adults victimised in childhood sought psychological help with problems such as suicidal thoughts, anxiety, depression, low self-esteem, intense generalised rage and symptoms of post-traumatic stress disorder. Most of these adults made direct connections between their childhood experiences and their current difficulties.

Children with an existing impairment which requires ongoing medical treatment can also be subject to illness induction and fabrication (Schrier and Libow, 1993). This is an even more complex set of circumstances to assess especially as the scope for interfering with treatment and medication and manipulation of symptoms is so much greater for already disabled children (Precey and Smith, forthcoming).

Siblings of the affected child are also at risk although research findings vary as to the rate of morbidity. McClure's study, cited above, found that in 42 per cent of families with more than one child a sibling had previously suffered some form of abuse. Meadow (1990) reported that in a group of 27 children who were found to have been suffocated by their mother there were a total of 33 older siblings of that cohort. Within that group of siblings 15 were still alive and 18 had died.

Although men are sometimes perpetrators in the induction or fabrication of illness in children or are knowingly complicit in the process, it is women who are by far more likely to injure children in their care in this way. McClure et al. (1996) put the figure at 85 per cent of abusers in FII cases being women, usually mothers. Schreier and Libow (1993) estimate that number

to be as high as 95 per cent. For this reason mothers are usually the focus of assessment with fathers often being either absent or marginalised in the family dynamics. It has also been recognised by Adshead (2000) and Polledri (1996) that the mother's own family of origin is frequently an influential feature in her behaviour towards her child. In a previous paper (Precey, 1998) I examined some of the issues for assessment in working with mothers who induce illness in their children including examples of inter-generational transmission of pathology between mother and daughter. The need for detailed exploration of family functioning, sometimes over a number of generations, has obvious implications for the depth and length of the assessment process.

Children who are the victims of FII are clearly children in need and especially in need of protection from this often virulent form of significant harm. But how well served are practitioners by the *Framework for the Assessment of Children in Need and their Families* in attempting to gather and analyse information and formulate care plans when there are concerns about Fabricated or Induced Illness?

Applying the Assessment Framework to FII concerns

Positive aspects of the framework in FII assessments

Multi-agency working

This multi-agency approach is clearly an advantage when working with Fabricated or Induced Illness. Horwath and Lawson (1995) demonstrated the necessity of all agencies being included in a co-ordinated assessment where concerns about induced or fabricated illness are manifest. Police officers, health visitors, social workers, paediatricians, nurses, teachers, GP's, playgroup and nursery staff and psychiatrists all may have a part to play in the detection, assessment, monitoring and safeguarding of children subjected to this form of abuse. There frequently is a deliberate campaign by the perpetrator to mis-inform the people working with her. This can have the effect of splitting the professional system in FII cases. Or the mother herself is so plausible that the professionals involved sometimes take sides according to those who believe and don't believe in her culpability without the perpetrator having to do anything herself to bring that about. An ssessment that sets out to involve all rofessionals from the beginning and o-ordinate their views and roles in an rganised way will result in a piece of work that eeps its focus on the needs of the child rather han the wranglings of a fragmented rofessional system.

Once FII has been identified the treatment spect of the work will also require a well o-ordinated care plan that recognises the role hat each agency has to play in service provision o meet the needs of both the parents and hildren in the family. The multi-agency rientation of the Framework is potentially of reat assistance in this aspect of working with amilies in the aftermath of the identification of lness induction and fabrication.

ocus on the child

Another principle underpinning the Assessment ramework (DoH, 2000, p10) is the expectation hat the assessment will centre on the needs of he child and not allow him or her to become ost in other issues the family may be facing. his is especially important in FII where the ehaviour of the parent concerned may be very izarre. One of the pitfalls of work in this area as been an over emphasis on 'proving' athology in the perpetrator and paying nsufficient attention to the impact of her ehaviour on the developmental needs of the hild. With the clear expectation that ssessments are now to be child-centred it is to e hoped that there is less likelihood of that appening.

In a case I was involved in recently the nother claimed to have a PhD in child sychology, even producing a certificate (which ppeared to have been manufactured on her omputer) to prove it. The fact that her qualifications' were not commensurate with the ob she held as a shop assistant and that she was ompletely unable to understand or follow hrough on any of the professional advice she vas given on managing the behaviour of her hildren was the focus of considerable attention y the assessment team. A child centred pproach to this situation would concentrate on he importance of understanding what impact er belief in her qualifications had on the needs f the children rather than focusing too much on vhy she had to perpetuate this fantasy. In this ase the meaning of her belief system did have n impact on the children. It caused her to view erself as more highly qualified than the child

psychologist whom she was seeing for help with the children's behaviour. The mother said that, because she had a doctorate and the CAMHS staff member did not, she had no faith in what the psychologist said, and saw no need to follow any of her advice on behaviour management.

As Reder and Duncan (1999) remind us, it is essential to take a systemic view of the child's situation rather than focus on any one piece of information in isolation. They place great emphasis on the fact that 'it is context that gives meaning to behaviour' (p6). In requiring that we undertake assessments within the context of the child and their world as the focus of the proceedings, the Assessment Framework helps us not to be too distracted by the often bizarre behaviour of the parents in cases of FII.

Assessment of all children in the family who are in need

Another key concept associated with the Assessment Framework is the expectation that all the children of the family who are deemed to be in need should be assessed and not just the child about whom there are immediate concerns. As mentioned above, in cases of induced and fabricated illness it often happens that a number of children in the family are victimised, usually surreptitiously. Practitioners must be aware of the needs of those children as well if they are to be safeguarded.

Negative aspects of Assessment Framework in FII assessment

Whilst some of the concepts underpinning the Framework in assessments where FII is at issue are helpful there are a number of ways in which it is inadequate and, in some respects, potentially dangerous when applied to work with induced/fabricated illness.

Analysis of risk

One of the main flaws of the Assessment Framework is that it fails to assist practitioners with the analysis of risk. Whilst there is no question that it is in the best interests of children and families for statutory services to intervene in a less heavy handed way and at an earlier stage, the Assessment Framework is wrong to demote the centrality of the importance of risk assessment work to just one among many needs that vulnerable children and families may experience. Risk assessment requires a particular set of skills and attitudes as demonstrated by Dalgleish (2000 and Chapter 5). He discusses some of the tensions between approaches to assessing children in need and for risk assessment and warns that both the information gathering process and thresholds used for taking action are not identical in these two forms of assessment. In comparing systems used for assessing risk in a variety of countries Dalgleish comments that:

> The UK Assessment Framework doesn't ask the user to summarise their overall assessment (of risk) and just provides a way of organising the case information needed for an assessment ... very little guidance is given on how information collected during an assessment is integrated to provide such a risk assessment.
> (p2–3)

This is also the view of social workers I interviewed recently for a research project I undertook on the role of assessment in social work (Precey, 2001). The view of one of the social workers I spoke to was that, whilst she found the guidance helpful in showing up neglect and emotional abuse issues, she had doubts about the place of risk assessment within the Framework:

> I don't see at all where we could fit in immediate risk assessment. There should be something like a 5 point risk assessment checklist included to be carried out prior to the 35 day assessment ... it's all too 'wishy washy' on risk.
> (p64).

There is no scope for being 'wishy-washy' on risk when it comes to undertaking assessments of children in danger of suffering induced or fabricated illness. Careful planning, tight co-ordination of the professional system, a knowledge of the main features of behaviour often associated with FII and an informed analysis of the information gathered are all essential in this very high risk, complex form of child abuse.

Partnership with parents

The Assessment Framework puts great emphasis on working in partnership with parents and seeks to include their views and those of their children throughout the assessment process. The objective of working in an open and inclusive way with families who are being assessed is a cornerstone of good professional practice and should be encouraged wherever possible. However this must be tempered with realism about the fact that it is not always safe or desirable to be involving and

sharing information with parents at every step of the assessment process. This is particularly true in dealing with concerns about FII.

Many of the parents I have worked with deliberately promote themselves as caring, committed to getting the best treatment for their children and knowledgeable about the details of their illness. On many levels they are meeting their child's needs whilst at the same time perpetrating covert acts of abuse that put their children at risk. One mother I worked with referred herself for parenting classes so she could have better insight into her children's behaviour, bought her 6-year-old son a pager so they both could be in touch with each other if he needed her for any reason and was a stalwart of the school PTA. Simultaneously she was factitiously describing her son's increasingly frequent and severe convulsions to the many medical professionals she consulted. This culminated in him being on excessively high doses of carbamazapine, which in itself was damaging to him.

The assessment of this mother according to the parameters offered by the Assessment Framework would have indicated that she was doing an admirable job of meeting her child's needs especially in the difficult context of her son's acute 'epileptic' condition. The reality behind that picture is that she nearly killed him. The Framework in its current form has little to offer practitioners dealing with these circumstances of overt compliance and care and covert deceit and harm.

The dimension of 'ensuring safety' in the domain of Parenting Capacity is probably the closest the Framework comes to really acknowledging that all children may not be safe in the care of their parents but its terms seem very anodyne compared with what experienced child protection practitioners often encounter. The dimension of ensuring safety is described in the Framework as follows:

> Ensuring the child is adequately protected from harm or danger. Includes protection from significant harm or danger, and from contact with unsafe adults/other children and from self-harm. Recognition of hazards and dangers both in the home and elsewhere.
> (p21)

This is clearly not the blueprint for a comprehensive risk assessment. In the case of FII it is ironic that the 'unsafe adults' in the child's world may well be doctors who, acting on the mother's information about the child's symptoms, are harming the child through invasive medical procedures or unnecessary medication.

The Assessment Framework appears to be predicated on the assumption that parents will have a mainly benign influence on the lives of their children. Unfortunately, those of us who have had experience in dealing with parents who maltreat their children, including those who induce or fabricate illness, know that this is not always the case. Dale (2001) also make this point. In a recent report on a continuing NSPCC study of 2-year-olds who were at risk of serious physical abuse (2001) he makes a strong case for more rigorous assessment procedures in the 'ensuring safety' dimension. Dale considers what the Assessment Framework has to offer and find it wanting:

> *Our view is that the framework will do little to assist with the systematic assessment of cases of serious injuries to babies and infants where there are discrepant or disputed explanations . . . the framework inclines toward a view of abusing parents as helpless and poor – doing their best in difficult circumstances*

Sharing information

In keeping with the Data Protection Act 1998 and the Human Rights Act 1998, especially article 8 which guarantees right to privacy in family life, the Assessment Framework places great emphasis on the need to seek parental consent before information is shared between agencies. It does acknowledge that 'in any potential conflict between the responsibilities of the professionals towards children and towards other family members, the needs of the child must come first' and that safeguarding the child must be the first priority (3.56).

My experience of consulting to local authorities on FII cases since the implementation of both the Framework and the Human Rights Act is a growing anxiety about withholding information from parents. It is unfortunate that the Assessment Framework does not expand more specifically on the real dangers that can obtain to a premature disclosure of information to parents in a number of child abuse arenas including FII. Schreier and Libow (1993) reported that one of the most dangerous times in an investigation where factitious illness is suspected is immediately following the sharing of information with the mother of what the concerns are. They recommend that arrangements be in place to safeguard children before such an interchange takes place.

Although the Framework makes no mention of the potential risk involved in working in partnership with parents where FII is an issue the DoH itself tackled this matter in guidance issued in 1995:

> *Such is their (the parents) deviousness that it is dangerous for professionals to make their concerns explicit before they have sufficient evidence to ensure the adequate protection of the child. It is important for the agencies with statutory responsibilities to seek expert advice before they invite such family members to engage in decision-making or any level of partnership.*
> (DoH, 1995).

Would that the current Assessment Framework contained guidance that was as accurate in reflecting some of the hard realities and dilemmas on involving parents in the assessment process.

Timescales

Calder has dealt with the issues raised by timescales in Chapter 2, but I would like to examine the timescales from the point of view of their impact on the quality of assessment where there are concerns about the induction and fabrication of illness in children.

I have already discussed the notion that, because of the complexity of this form of child abuse, it is common to have a longer period of time elapse between the first indication of suspicion and the decision to undertake a full-blown assessment. Furthermore, these are almost always situations where there are extensive medical records on children and a large and complex professional network involved. Careful planning and co-ordination are of the essence and are unlikely to be accomplished in such a rigid time scale. To adhere to the necessity of an assessment concerned with fabricated/induced illness being finished in 42 working days for the sake of complying with Department of Health guidelines sacrifices good practice on the altar of bureaucratic procedure. This may result in the assessment being completed within the timescales but at the potential cost of less than thorough information gathering and analysis, and at worst increased risk to the children.

In a case I was recently involved with one of the variables in the mother's care of the children was the toxic influence of her own mother with whom she lived and was emotionally enmeshed. During the course of the assessment she finally succeeded in obtaining her own property and began to live apart from her mother for the first time. A crucial piece of information for the assessment is the potential for the mother to establish herself as a separate household and resist the proclivity of her mother to interfere. But that will take some time to be known, almost surely more than the time remaining since the core assessment 'clock' started ticking.

The Assessment Framework also allows for specialist assessments, which are permitted to exceed the time limits but whose contribution and status are not well defined by the guidance. In cases where induced or fabricated illness is suspected it is very likely that specialist assessments in the form of psychiatric/psychological input will be commissioned. The Framework says that the core assessment should carry on and be completed within the 35-day time scale and 'appropriate services should be provided whilst awaiting the completion of the specialist assessment' (p3.11). In cases of FII this provision of service may be very dependent upon the outcome of the specialist assessment and shouldn't proceed until all the information is known. In one family I worked with the mother was seeking a diagnosis of autism for both her children and assistance in claiming the higher rate Disability Living Allowance on that basis. The diagnosis of autism previously made on her children was now being reconsidered in the context of new information that had come to light regarding the possibility that the mother manipulated the information she supplied to paediatricians in order to achieve the diagnosis. Most of the services she was requesting were connected with the autism being confirmed. In this example it would have been quite wrong for the services she was requesting to have been provided until the specialist assessment was complete.

Another impact of the pressure exerted by timescales is the implications for engagement with both the children and the carers concerned. Engagement with families where illness induction or fabrication is suspected is a particularly skilled and delicate process (Precey, 1998). Often the children are committed to their belief in the reality of their own illness, such as the 12-year-old girl I once saw who used a wheelchair in the presence of her mother because of the severity of her 'rheumatoid arthritis', yet the school have photos of her taking part in a sponsored walk without her

wheelchair. There is clearly a discrepancy in reality here for both the mother and daughter and finding an approach to begin to untangle that is very challenging and takes time. This may not be achievable in the timescales allowed by the Framework.

Genograms

A surprising omission from the Framework is any mention of the importance of the construction and use of genograms in assessment work. This has been an essential component of my practice in child protection work and particularly in working with families where there are concerns about FII (Precey, 1998). It is one thing to know from a chronology that a mother has had 6 pregnancies in 8 years and only 2 surviving children, but to see that represented in a genogram has much more of an impact. Also the construction of a genogram itself may be the only point of agreement between a worker and a client where their respective realities are so different. But even then genograms can be useful in showing up discrepancies. One family genogram I did showed the mother having had twins that died as a result of cot death, but there was no mention of this in her medical records. Unravelling with her the story of why that might be, proved a useful component of the assessment.

The omission of the use of genograms in the Assessment Framework also runs counter to the findings of Reder and Duncan who recommend their effectiveness in child protection work (1999). 'The value of a genogram is that it also highlights important information about the family's history that is missing and needs to be sought'(p12).

Supports to evidence-based practice

The Assessment Framework requires that assessments be evidence based and make use of theoretical frameworks. To this end the Department of Health has commissioned a wealth of supporting information to assist practitioners in ensuring that they understand some of the key theories and concepts that inform assessment practice, such as Bentovim and Bingley-Miller (2001); Cleaver et al. (1999); Cox (2001); Horwath (1999); Jones and Ramchandani (1999); Ryan (2000). It is surprising then that given the ever-increasing knowledge base and body of literature, Schreier nd Libow (1993), Eminson and Postlethwaite 2000), Horwath and Lawson (1995), concerned vith FII abuse it receives no mention in any of hose documents.

Recording forms

To accompany the Assessment Framework the Department of Health has devised lengthy recording forms, some in excess of 40 pages ong, that are banded by age group so as to nsure that the child's developmental level is aken into account by the assessor.

These are the forms that social workers are sked to complete when undertaking core ssessments, albeit with input from other professionals who have knowledge of the amily. Well over half of each form is dedicated o information gathering, much of it in the ormat of binary tick boxes. The analysis section onsists of one blank page. The prescriptive ature of the forms is not conducive to relaying nformation gathered or analysis undertaken in ituations as unique and complex as those ssociated with cases of induced or fabricated lness. Another social worker I interviewed for ny research told me about his concerns that the ssessment records were so confining that they prevented me being able to use them to tell the amily's story' (Precey, 2001).

Applying concerns about nduced/fabricated illness to the Framework for the Assessment of Children in Need and their Families

t may be helpful to bear in mind the following practice points when using the Recording Forms hat accompany the Assessment Framework to onsider the needs of children about whom here are concerns regarding risk of harm due to deliberate induction or fabrication of illness by heir carers.

As mentioned above, a detailed chronology of vents in the life of each child is often an ndispensable assessment technique for unscrambling the complex histories that usually ccompany cases of induced or fabricated lness. This chronology should include a horough examination of the child's medical notes which will probably require close ollaboration with the child's Health Visitor, GP nd other medical specialists. It is also helpful to note absences from school in the case of older hildren. Working with the Headteacher, EWO nd school nurse is usually essential in

obtaining this information and understanding its meaning. If using the DoH Recording Forms for the Framework, sections B/K2 and B/K3 may be the most appropriate place for this information to be located.

Although the Framework requires a separate assessment for each child it is important not to consider children's histories in isolation from each other. Often patterns emerge regarding similarities in onset of symptoms or variations in focus of attention e.g. as one child's health improves that may be accompanied by a deterioration in the health of a sibling (see section B/K4 in the DoH recording forms).

The medical history of the main carer, usually the mother, is often significant, as well as other details of her background. Details of her medical history should be included if possible, although consent and disclosure of information will be an issue in all matters to do with obtaining health records. Because the circumstances of the mother's own family of origin are often significant where illness induction/fabrication is suspected (Polledri, 1996; Precey, 1998; Schreier and Libow,1993) information on her background is important, sometimes including interviews with members of her own family, especially the child's maternal grandmother. For this reason the section in the Recording Forms that covers 'Issues affecting parents'/carers' capacity to respond appropriately to the young person's needs' should be completed in detail.

Although the Assessment Framework Recording Form does not specify the inclusion of a genogram, in cases where illness induction is suspected this can be a very valuable tool both for information gathering and analysis (Precey, 1998; Reder and Duncan, 1999). It may be helpful to append a detailed, multi-generational genogram to the Framework Recording Forms and refer to it when considering the analysis of the information that has been collected.

Although the Recording Forms are set out with a number of tick boxes in the headings under each of the dimensions, my view is that, whilst they may give pointers towards issues to consider in each of the dimensions, they may not always assist in analysing the key considerations when FII is suspected. It may be less confusing for the social worker to concentrate on the dimensions alone and not try to transfer information into the tick boxes. The following Practice Pointers are offered to assist social workers in applying the dimensions of the Framework when assessing children at risk of induced or fabricated illness.

Dimensions of child's developmental needs

Health

As stated above a detailed medical history is essential in tracking concerns about FII. Additionally information relevant to the child's health could be contained in this dimension heading:

- Numbers of presentations to the GP, A&E and other hospital admissions should be logged to build up a picture of the history of her use of medical services on the child's behalf.

It is also significant to note how the parent may be using medical services. When attending with her child at the surgery does she tend to see the same GP or deliberately see other doctors in the practice or locums or make exceptional use of out of hours service? The tendency to 'doctor shop' and sometimes deliberately falsely report the advice or diagnosis made by one medical practitioner to another can be a feature of induced illness (Meadow, 1977).

- To what extent does she seek second opinions either by other GPs or among the specialists to whom the child has been referred?
- How informed is she about the details and latest research concerning her child's condition? Many mothers who seek to induce or fabricate illness in their children go out of their way to become 'experts' in the field, sometimes in an attempt to elevate their status in the eyes of the medical profession or to be more accurate in the creation of the symptoms she is trying either to induce or fabricate in her child.
- How does the child's condition impact on the mother's prestige and self image? It is not unknown for mothers who induce illness to have children who become 'poster children' for particular conditions or who themselves receive considerable vicarious satisfaction for the attention the child is receiving.(Artingstall, 1999).
- Certain medical conditions may be more common than others in their likelihood of being exacerbated, induced or fabricated. Among these are epilepsy, bowel disorders,

autism, food allergies, skin complaints and Chronic Fatigue Syndrome (M.E.). This is especially true in very young children where the medical practitioner is almost entirely dependent on the mother's report of the child's symptoms and response to treatment.

- Does the child have an existing, bone fide impairment? Manipulation of therapeutic interventions and symptoms may be even more difficult to disentangle from the effect of the impairment in these situations (Schreier and Libow, 1993; Precey and Smith, forthcoming).

Education

- Very often children's education is disrupted by erratic attendance due to their 'illness'. It can be helpful to track the child's illness presentation and school attendance to determine if any significant patterns emerge.
- There are sometimes also discrepancies in how the child actually performs in school and the description of their ability provided by the parent (Precey, 1998). Is there a difference in how the school and the parent view the child's limitations?
- It may also be the case that the objective for the mother in inducing or fabricating illness in her child is to achieve a placement for the child in a particular school for children with special needs.

Emotional and behavioural development

Because of the underlying hatred that the mother sometimes feels for the child or what the child may represent to her (Polledri, 1995) some children in whom illness is induced or fabricated may show signs of insecure attachment. Observation of the relationship between mother and child could be recorded in this dimension. The child may come to realise that they are most acceptable to the parent when they are ill and seek to maximise this behaviour in the mother's presence.

Identity

How possible is it for the child to distinguish for themselves when they are ill or well? How much does this definition rely on reference to the abusing parent?

Initial research with 'survivors' of FII has shown that many report problems with recognising illness and health in themselves (Libow, 1995).

Family and social relationships

To what extent is the child able or allowed to develop relationships outside of the family? Children in whom illness is induced or fabricated are sometimes quite isolated by the perceived restrictions of their 'condition'. Or it may make the parent anxious to allow the child too many experiences outside the family that could call into question the child's existing reality as 'ill'.

Social presentation

What impact does the child's illness have on how they are perceived by others?

How much significance does the child come to attach to being ill, being in hospital, undergoing treatment regimes?

To what extent is the child aware of a particular mode of their social presentation making them more or less acceptable to their parent, with the effect that the child seeks to promote that impression in order to gain parental approval?

Self care skills

How much has the child become involved in their own treatment, what significance is placed on this by the parent?

Is the child deliberately discouraged from becoming more independent in order to maintain the mother's need to be indispensable to the child perhaps thereby continuing to attract the attention that accrues to her from that? There may also be financial gain to be achieved in terms of enhanced rate of benefit if the child remains dependent.

Dimensions of parenting capacity

Basic care

The ability of the parent to provide appropriately for the child's medical needs is usually one of the main themes in the assessment of induced/fabricated illness. Brief reference to that may be included in this section if it has been covered in depth elsewhere e.g. the dimension of 'health'.

It is also the case that mothers who otherwise show impeccable overt basic care of their children can display extreme, unexpected lapses which is in fact a feature of their abusing behaviour. I have come across several cases of mothers whose overall basic care is faultless but inexplicably neglect specific aspects of their child's basic care, for example allowing their child to become cold to the point of near hypothermia.

Ensuring safety

Again the duplicity of parental behaviour can be a feature here. This can take the form of care that seems exceptionally safe but with extreme, unexpected lapses, for example the mother of a young baby who worries excessively about her child and appears to cosset the baby whilst at the same time indiscriminately leaving the infant with people she hardly knows.

Emotional warmth

Is the meeting of the child's emotional needs, being valued etc. contingent on the child being ill? Is the mother able to imagine what life would be like if the child were well, and how does she think of the child in those circumstances?

Older children may be drawn into a 'folie a deux' with the mother by which they come to believe in their own fabricated symptoms and behave accordingly in order to secure the mother's attention and emotional support (Precey, 1998).

Stimulation

Stimulation required to help a child achieve their social and intellectual potential may be manipulated by the parent in order to achieve the image of the child she is trying to create. Mothers seeking to have their child diagnosed as having learning disabilities or autism may attempt to understimulate them or create a bizarre environment for them that may elicit the type of behaviour they are attempting to reinforce.

Guidance and boundaries

To what extent are the guidance and boundaries provided by the parent contingent on a particular definition of the child's condition that the parent themselves has been instrumental in achieving? The child's ability to regulate their own emotions and behaviour may be very bound up with the illness that the parent has sought to induce or create. Thus the child's capacity for genuine autonomy becomes compromised.

Stability

How much and for what reason has the family moved house, especially to different parts of the country where they can access a new network of medical services? The propensity for carers to re-locate to a new area, especially if they think that professionals may be becoming suspicious about the symptoms they are describing in their children or that the treatment they have been given is unnecessary, has been well documented (Schreier and Libow, 1993).

Dimensions of family and environmental factors

Family history and functioning

The importance of a thorough family history in assessing concerns about induced or fabricated illness has been mentioned above. Brief reference could be made to it in this section if it is dealt with more extensively elsewhere in the Recording Form.

Wider family

Again it is important to have background information on other members of the family, especially the maternal side if the mother appears to be the abuser.

In decisions about alternative placement of children where FII is suspected it is usually inadvisable to place them with close family members, especially if they do not share the concerns of professionals about the safety of the main caregiver (Precey, 1995). Placement completely outside of the wider family network can sometimes be the most effective way of ascertaining the influence of the parent on the maintenance of the child's symptoms.

Housing

The fact that housing is often more than adequate for the family's needs and material conditions are good can distract practitioners from looking more closely into what may be going on within the family where concerns about induced/fabricated illness are present.

It may also be the case that carers are unexpectedly negligent in seeking re-housing or adaptations to their existing premises that would in fact enhance the quality of life for the child concerned.

Employment

In some familys where FII is suspected fathers may be absent due to the demands of their employment, such as being stationed away with the armed forces. In my own clinical experience induction of illness in children, sometimes to the point of death, may be a deliberate strategy on the part of the mother to keep her partner closer to home.

It is also my experience that very few of the mothers I have worked with, although often well qualified (or at least claiming to have qualifications) are employed outside the home or in jobs that are commensurate with the educational status they claim for themselves. The demands on them of their child's 'condition' becomes a full time job in itself.

Income

The high standard of living enjoyed by some families who induce or fabricate illness in their children may mislead practitioners who are investigating abuse, and make them less likely to suspect the parent's behaviour.

It may also be the case that where the benefit attracted by the child's illness or disability is an important component of the family's income, there could be more incentive to infantalise the child or exaggerate their symptoms so that the higher level of benefit can be maintained.

Family's social integration

In the range of possible levels of social integration, families where there are concerns about induced/fabricated illness are often located on the extreme ends of the spectrum. Sometimes they are very isolated and interact with few people in the community or they can be excessively involved in many activities often with a focus on issues involved with their child's 'condition'.

Community resources

As with the above dimension, my own experience would suggest that families where illness induction/fabrication is an issue tend to be at one extreme or the other. Some families seem deliberately not to want to know about or to use resources that could assist themselves or their child cope with their illness. The effect of this can be to reduce the chances of recovery for the child. Other parents present as vociferous campaigners on behalf of their child. This is sometimes to the point of the campaign, rather than the child themselves, becoming the main focus of their activity.

New developments in DoH guidance

In August of 2002 the Department of Health went some way towards redressing the lack of information for child welfare professionals dealing with concerns about child abuse involving induced or fabricated illness by publishing guidance entitled *Safeguarding Children in Whom Illness is Fabricated or Induced* Issued under Section 7 of the Local Authority Social Services Act 1970 the Guidance supplements *Working Together to Safeguard Children* (1999) and should be used in accordance with *The Framework for the Assessment of Children in Need and their Families* (2000).

This document contains information about procedures to be followed in safeguarding children who are at risk of harm through illness induction or fabrication, the roles of the various agencies involved, factors to consider in the decision making process at case conference and guidelines for undertaking Covert Video Surveillance. It also assists practitioners with helpful clinical and contextual information on FII by including a section on 'Lessons from Research and Experience'. Whilst still requiring that the Assessment Framework timescales are adhered to when assessing cases of Fabricated or Induced Illness, the Guidance does accept that some of the procedures in safeguarding children need to be modified to allow for the very complex nature of this type of enquiry. For example it is recognised that, in cases of FII, it may be necessary to hold a series of multi-agency strategy meetings before embarking on the fifteen-day investigation period that leads to a decision about the convening of a Child Protection Case Conference (para 3.28).

The Guidance also includes more specific advice about how to apply the dimensions of the Framework in assessing families where there are concerns that illness has been fabricated or induced in the child (para 3.48). It makes reference, for instance, to the necessity of obtaining thorough information on the child's health status and differentiating where possible between presenting symptoms which may be organic in cause and those which may be related to abuse. The importance of obtaining histories of both parents and attending to the circumstances of the child's siblings is also acknowledged in the Guidance.

One of the greatest strengths of the Guidance is the clear recognition that, because of the dangerousness of this form of abuse and the often duplicitous nature of the parent's behaviour, protecting the child must take priority over sharing information with parents at an early stage.

> While professionals should .seek, in general, to discuss any concerns with the family, and, where possible, seek their agreement to making referrals to Social Service, **this should only be done where such discussion and agreement-seeking will not place the child at increased risk of significant harm**.
>
> (para 3.12)

Even after completion of the initial assessment the Guidance recommends that professionals should continue to be guarded in sharing information with parents.

> Upon completion of the initial assessment, Social Services together with the medical consultant responsible for the child's health care . . . should decide on the next course of action. At this stage careful consideration should be given to what parents should be told, when, and by whom, taking account of the child's welfare . . . Concerns should not be raised with a parent if it is judged that this action will jeopardise the child's safety.
>
> (para 3.18)

Clearly the issuing of *Safeguarding Children in Whom Illness is Fabricated or Induced* is to be welcomed as a way of bridging the gaps in the Framework concerning the assessment of Ell. The fact that the Guidance has been issued separately to both Working Together and the Assessment Framework and, at sixty-nine pages, is in itself nearly half as long as each of those two documents is problematic. Although it is meant to be 'incorporated' into local ACPC child protection procedures and into the Assessment Framework process, the fact that it exists in a 'stand alone' format is likely to reduce the probability of it being used for the purposes for which it was intended. It would have been preferable to have the key points included in the body of Working Together and the Assessment Framework with perhaps a chapter in *The Child's World Reader*, which summarises some of the main theoretical and research information on FII that is relevant to assessment work. This may have rendered the many useful points made in this document more accessible to busy practitioners and therefore more likely to be used.

References

Adshead, G. (2000) The Hand that Rocks the Cradle: Morbid Care Giving and Sudden Death in Infants. Lecture given on 2 March Munchausen Syndrome by Proxy and Sudden Infant Death: Thinking the Unthinkable. London: Pavilion Publishing.

Artingstall, K. (1999) *Practical Aspects of Munchausen by Proxy and Munchausen Syndrome Investigation*. London: CRC Press.

Bools, C.N. and Jones P.D.H. Factitious Illness by Proxy. In David T.J. (Ed.) *Recent Advances in Paediatrics*. London: Churchill Livingston.

Brighton and Hove Area Child Protection Committee (2000) *Child Protection Procedures*. Brighton and Hove Area Child Protection Committee.

Cleaver, H. Unell, I. and Aldgate, J. (1999) *Children's Needs, Parenting Capacity: The Impact of Parental Mental Illness, Problem Alcohol and Drug Use, and Domestic Violence on Children's Development*. London: The Stationery Office.

Dale, P. (2001) Risk Radar. *Community Care*. 21 Jun.

Dalgleish, L. (2000) *Assessing the Situation and Deciding to do Something*. paper presented at the 13th International Conference on Child Abuse and Neglect, Durban South Africa September.

Department of Health (1988) *Protecting Children: A Guide for Social Workers Undertaking Comprehensive Assessments*. London: HMSO.

Department of Health (1995) *Child Protection: Messages from Research*. London: HMSO.

Department of Health (1995) *The Challenge of Partnership in Child Protection: Practice Guide*. London: The Stationery Office.

Department of Health (1999) *Working Together to Safeguard Children*. London: The Stationery Office.

Department of Health (2000) *Framework for the Assessment of Children in Need and their Families*. London: The Stationery Office.

Department of Health (2000a) *Assessing Children in Need and their Families: Practice Guidance*. London: The Stationery Office.

Department of Health (2002) *Safeguarding Children in Whom Illness is Fabricated or Induced*. London: The Stationery Office.

Department of Health and Bentovim, A. and Bingley Miller, L. (2001) *The Family Assessment*. London: The Stationery Office.

Department of Health and Cleaver, H. (2000) *Assessment Recording Forms*. London: The Stationery Office.

Department of Health and Cox, A. (2001) *The Home Inventory* London: The Stationery Office.

Department of Health, Cox, A. and Bentovim, A. (2000) *The Family Assessment Pack of Questionnaires and Scales*. London: The Stationery Office.

Eminson, M. and Postlethwaite, R.J. (2000) *Munchausen Syndrome by Proxy Abuse: A Practical Approach*. Oxford: Butterworth Heinemann.

Horwath, J. (Ed.) (1999) *The Child's World: Assessing Children in Need*. (Reader). Leicester: NSPCC.

Horwath, J., and Lawson, B. (Eds.) (1995) *Trust Betrayed?: Munchausen Syndrome by Proxy – Interagency Child Protection and Partnership With Families*. London: National Childrens Bureau.

Jones, D. and Ramchandari, P. (1999) *Child Sexual Abuse: Improving Practice from Research*. Oxford: Radcliffe.

Libow, J. (1998) Munchausen by Proxy Victims in Adulthood: A First Look. *Child Abuse and Neglect*. 19: 1131–42.

McClure, R.J., Davis, P.M., Meadow, S.R., and Silbert, J.R. (1996) Epidemiology of Munchausen Syndrome by Proxy, Non-accidental Poisoning, and Non-accidental Suffocation. *Archives of Diseases in Childhood*. 75: 57–61.

Meadow, R. (1977) The Hinterland of Child Abuse. *The Lancet*. ii: 343–5.

Meadow, R., (1990) Suffocation, Recurrent Apnoea and Sudden Death. *Journal of Paediatrics*. 117: 351.

Parton, N. (Ed.) (1997) *Child Protection and Family Support: Tensions, Contradictions and Possibilities*. London: Routledge.

Polledri, P. (1996) Munchausen by Proxy and the Perversion of the Maternal Instinct. *Journal of Forensic Psychiatry*. 7: 371–85.

Precey, G. (1995) On First Encountering Munchausen Syndrome by Proxy, a Guide for Beginners. in *Trust Betrayed?: Munchausen Syndrome by Proxy, Inter-agency Child Protection and Partnership with Families*. London: National Children's Bureau.

Precey, G. (1998) Assessment Issues in Working With Mothers Who Induce Illness in Their Children. *Child and Family Social Work*. 1993: 3.

Precey, G. (2001) *The Role of the Social Work Assessment in Child Care Proceedings*. unpublished dissertation for Masters Degree in Child Studies, London: Kings College.

Precey, G. and Smith, K. (forthcoming) *The Fabrication or Induction of Illness in Children with Complex Needs: Thinking the Truly Unthinkable*.

Royal College of Paediatrics and Child Health (2001) *Fabricated or Induced Illness by Carers*. London: RCPCH.

Reder, P. and Duncan, S. (1999) *Lost Innocents: A Follow-up Study of Fatal Child Abuse*. London: Routledge.

Ryan, M. (2000) *Working with Fathers*. London: The Stationery Office.

Schreier, H. and Libow, J. (1993) *Hurting for Love: Munchausen by Proxy Syndrome*. NY: Guilford Press.

Chapter Eighteen

A Framework for Assessing Parents with Mental Health Problems

Amy Weir

Purpose and content

The purpose of this chapter is to consider the particular circumstances which need to be considered when assessments are made of children whose parents are affected by mental illness. It considers and recommends:

- How the Assessment Framework needs specifically to be applied in this area of practice and makes particular reference to the need for joint working between mental health services and children's social work.
- What areas and additional factors need to be covered in the assessment.
- Which frameworks can be used to help workers know how to make sense of the information collected and to determine levels of risk and levels of support required.

There is a growing number of books about this area of work. A list of references for further reading about the issues is also provided.

Introduction

There has been an increasing awareness during the last few years of the need to ensure that the needs of children whose parents have mental health problems are identified and fully considered. There has also been more acknowledgement that their parents also need to be supported effectively to care for their children. Of course, that does not mean that all children whose parents are affected by mental illness will be in need. Many parents affected by mental health problems care well and safely for their children without additional extra-familial support. Being a parent with a mental health problem does not of itself mean your children will be more vulnerable or even in danger. As Channi Kumar put it:

Most mentally ill mothers don't abuse children and most abusive mothers are not considered mentally ill.
(Kumar, 1997).

However, there are many children, who are affected by their parent's mental health

problems, who do not receive any particular attention. Their needs are often ignored or neglected whilst the services involved concentrate on addressing the needs of the mentally ill parent. Despite national guidance to the contrary, the needs of many children will not be considered even when their parents' needs are being assessed and met through mental health services.

How much of an issue is this?

It is very unclear how many dependent children are living with, and cared for, by parents or carers who have mental health problems. However, there is some indication from national surveys, such as OPCS 1996, about how many children may be affected by parental mental ill health. From the evidence available, it is likely that a significant proportion (at least 20%, probably 30%, and perhaps more) of adults known to mental health services have children (Falkov, 1998).

Children whose parents have mental health problems are generally at greater risk of experiencing a range of problems when compared with the general population. Emotional difficulties, cognitive delays, psychiatric disorders, academic underachievement and poor peer and family relationships are some of the problems which have been identified in surveys of these children. There is also significant representation of these children on child protection registers and in fatal abuse. Some of the children – depending on the nature of their parent's mental illness, may have an increased likelihood of genetic transmission of the same condition.

There is, therefore, a significant number of children who are likely to be affected by parental mental illness. Below is a list of some key facts and figures which put in context the incidence and significance of this area of work.

Mental illness and parents

- All adults in the UK have a 1 in 4 chance of experiencing a period of mental illness (covering the wide range of severity) during their lifetime.

- 5.7 million (12.6 per cent) of the adult population are suffering from a mental illness at any one time.
- 30 per cent of mentally ill adults have dependent children under 18 years.
- 3.8 per cent of all parents with dependent children have a mental illness – something like 1.7 million adults and something like 2.5 million children.
- Care in the community and the availability of community given drug therapies means that mentally ill parents and their dependent children spend more time together.
- 33 per cent to 75 per cent of parents whose children are known to children's services experience mental health problems; more than 33 per cent of mothers of children on social work caseloads were found to be moderately to severely depressed (Shepherd, 1997). At least 25 per cent of children who are the subject of child protection conferences have a parent with mental health problems; Parental mental illness is an important factor in children entering the care system (Weir and Douglas, 1999).

Children of parents with mental health problems

- Approximately 10,000 children and young people are caring for a mentally ill parent.
- 33 per cent to 66 per cent of children who have a mentally ill parent will be adversely affected; i.e. 33 per cent of the children will themselves develop significant psychological problems or disorders and a further 33 per cent will have less severe emotional and behavioural difficulties.
- 1.4 million children (12 per cent of the total child population of 11.6 million) will experience an emotional and behavioural disorder during their childhood.
- 33 per cent of children with emotional and behavioural disorders have a parent with a mental health problem (Weir and Douglas, 1999).

Whatever the precise incidence of these families is in the population, there is likely to be an increased vulnerability for many children in families affected by mental illness. As a result, assessment processes need to ensure that their needs are identified and that the additional support, services and sometimes protection required is provided. Whatever the particular circumstance, there is a need always to consider the protective and resilience factors which exist for the child as well as the vulnerability and risk factors in the situation.

Key service issues

Several organisational factors influence how effectively the needs of children affected by parental mental health can be met. The service delivery contexts to children and families who are affected by mental illness are quite separate. This separation is becoming even more marked as unified mental health service trusts outside local authority structures are developed in line with the National Service Framework for Mental Health. This increasing service specialisation and structural separation means it is not possible to provide a single, coherent or integrated service response to meeting their needs without considerable effort and explicit requirements that this must be provided.

The legislative framework for children and adults is also quite different. Mental health services and children and family services each have their own separate legislative frameworks with associated Guidance and Regulations on policy and practice. There has been some attempt to bring these together and to ensure a consistency and coherence in practice; however, there are still gaps and issues about ensuring that practice and policy between, and even within, agencies are coherently managed.

There has been a lack of a holistic, co-ordinated approach to the development and maintenance of values, knowledge and skills across the needs of parents and their children – particularly within mental health services. Other difficulties follow from this. There are different priorities for adult and children's services. Information exchange and issues of confidentiality are an additional concern since there is no unified approach to this across health and social service agencies. Staff in the separate services therefore, are likely to lack knowledge of each other's systems, priorities and skills to assess the other family members unless these shortfalls are specifically tackled locally.

What are the implications for Assessment?

Currently, two separate assessment systems operate for families affected by mental illness, – the mental health Care Programme Approach for the parent affected by mental illness and the children's Assessment Framework for the child.

The problem is that a single referral may contain child care needs, mental health needs, a carer's needs, possibly substance misuse, and more, but the needs may not be approached from all the required angles and, if they are, several different agencies may be involved.

There is, therefore, a significant requirement for practitioners to work across professional and agency boundaries. Unless this happens, the quality of assessment and intervention which is needed for children affected by mental illness will not be achievable. Working in this way is very demanding. Hallett (1995) in her study of inter-agency co-ordination in child protection concluded that good inter-agency working is difficult to achieve. The study identified a number of potential problem areas relating to different domains and perspectives, which include:

- Different professional perspectives and frames of reference about the nature of child abuse and of intervention.
- Different agency mandates and operational priorities.
- Organisational tendencies towards autonomy.
- The time and other resource costs of collaborative work; and interpersonal difficulties of trust and openness, gender and status differentials.

However, the study showed some optimistic pointers to what can be achieved through sustained attention to the process of inter-agency work:

> . . . the study revealed a high degree of co-ordination, a relatively clear division of labour, a dependable set of assumptions about role performance, and some degree of convergence (or at least tolerance of difference) of professional values and paradigms among core workers.
> (Hallett, 1995).

The key issue is, that to work successfully in this way, does require considerable commitment and perseverance at practitioner level. The professional differences in background, culture and understanding will all affect our practice and ability to co-operate with other professionals unless they are explicitly acknowledged and addressed.

It also requires top down support at the most senior levels in agencies to endorse and encourage exchange and joint working. If communication between staff and agencies is poor, risks to both children and their parents inevitably increase. There is substantial evidence that structures and organisational systems make a significant difference to the quality of service delivery. Adrian Falkov's study of Part 8 reviews relating to child deaths suggested that the core conclusions about each of the thirty-two deaths were strikingly similar:

> Service provision is fragmented and there is poor inter-agency communication. In general, professionals working with children lack expertise in adult mental health and there is insufficient emphasis on child welfare and child protection amongst adult psychiatric services.
> (Falkov 1996).

There is no doubt that the capacity for both individuals and agencies to work across a range of professional and agency boundaries is particularly important for families affected by mental illness.

There is a further potential area of difficulty in this area of practice. The differences in professional remits between mental health and child care social workers can result in conflictual outcomes. These potentially conflictual circumstances are very much a mirroring of the possible conflict which may exist between the needs of the children and of the affected parent.

Ensuring that high quality assessments of children of parents with mental health problems are carried out is a challenge. They require effective cross-agency collaboration and, if this is not achieved, the consequences may be serious. Poor collaboration and a lack of joint working may result in unco-ordinated, duplicated assessments, planning and intervention. The benefit of sharing and contrasting the information available will be lost and the separate assessments will not inform each other. Information is not likely to be shared appropriately and the separate, narrow perspectives adopted may be rigidly maintained. Above all, the opportunity to share information, skills and expertise across professional disciplines, in the best interest of both child and parent, is likely to be frustrated. At the same time, intervention may be delayed or avoided because it is seen as the responsibility of the other specialism.

Ensuring that the needs of children of parents with mental health problems are appropriately addressed and that all the information and factors are fully considered is a challenging area of practice. It requires considerable commitment but also additional expertise and the capacity to work effectively across agency and professional boundaries.

The key ingredients

There are some key ingredients of good assessments for children affected by parental mental health which need to be put in place as well if the best outcomes for children and their families are to be achieved.

The Assessment Framework and associated practice Guidance from the Department of Health provide much useful information about what should be considered and covered in carrying out an assessment of need of a child. The intention here is not to repeat the basics of the approach which is covered in that Guidance and elsewhere in this book. However, there are some particular aspects and issues for assessing the needs of children affected by parental mental health which need considering.

The four statements below signpost an approach to assessment which will ensure that the complexity and multi-factorial nature of making assessments of children affected by parental mental illness is successfully captured.

Complex systems approach

In understanding how to apply the Assessment Framework to best effect for children affected by their parent's mental illness, it is necessary to appreciate the dynamic and complex nature of the parenting circumstances for these families:

- Parental mental illness affects children, not necessarily adversely.
- Mental illness can affect the capacity of parents to parent and the resulting parent-child relationship. Parents may not be able to address the needs of their child safely or adequately as a result of their illness. Children and young people may have to assume some inappropriate and additional responsibility of caring for their parent.
- Caring for children affects the mental health of the parent. The challenges of parenting can precipitate and influence the parent's mental illness.
- Children's mental health and development needs have an impact on parental mental health.

The assessment and care planning processes have to take account of all these angles. The assessment itself has to consider comprehensively and inclusively not only the needs of the child, the parent's capacity to parent but also the parent's overall general level of functioning. This needs to be a comprehensive and inclusive process to achieve a rounded assessment which covers all the angles. The main focus for the child care practitioner must be to concentrate on ensuring that the child's needs are being met. However, there must also be an awareness and assessment by the child care practitioner of the parent's needs and level of functioning generally as well as the specific issue of addressing and considering their capacity to parent.

The interdependence of the circumstances of the vulnerable adult and their child means that the assessment process needs to go beyond only considering the narrower purview of parenting capacity. This does not mean that any additional needs identified in the adult should be met by the child care practitioner worker but they need to be identified and not just ignored. If additional needs in the parent related to their mental health are identified, then contact with mental health colleagues should be made. The importance of working closely with mental health colleagues and sharing information is crucial in ensuring that good assessments are made and that effective responses are made. Child care practitioners need to be able to assess the parent's needs at least to some degree as well as the child's. Child care practitioners should have some training – both in qualifying and post qualifying training, and preferably experience in understanding and identifying mental health needs. This enables them to identify when a child's needs are not being fully met by the parent. By the same token, there is a reciprocal need for adult services practitioners to have knowledge and understanding of children's needs through training and practice experience. For all practitioners, the professional supervision provided must be competent to embrace this agenda too and make explicit the needs to consider all the issues in the family.

Comprehensive and inclusive approach

Specialisation of services has produced some positive results for specialist area of activity and client groups. However, as far as the children of parent's affected by mental health problems are concerned, it results in some intrinsic obstacles to successful assessment and intervention for both child and parent. Many practitioners can feel de-skilled and disempowered to enter each other's specialist territory; staff believe they do not have the skills to assess the adult and to assess the child. As a result, they may avoid such assessments and decisions because of their apparent or perceived de-skilling. Mental health practitioners, for example, may see the responsibilities too narrowly in the following way – it is your job to make decisions about risks to children not mine and, it is my job to make decisions about risks to adults, not to children. In this way, practitioners and the separate services in which they are operating may work in a blinkered fashion focusing only on their own clients, their particular part of the family system. Child care and mental health practitioners need to work together. They need to be seen to be working together to gain the confidence and trust of the parent that the purpose is to work together in the interest of their child, which must be the paramount consideration.

Differential and dynamic approach

The child may be affected in several different ways by their parent's mental health problems and the assessment process needs specifically to look out for and to take account of these different possibilities:

- The symptoms and nature of the mental illness itself will have a differential impact depending on the kind of symptoms – how severe they are and how long they have been in place.
- The degree and nature of the child's experience or involvement of the parent's symptoms and behaviour also needs to be considered. If the child is incorporated into the parent's delusional thoughts or considerations of self-harm, this is likely to pose a significant risk to the child's safety. If the mental illness of the parent makes their behaviour more aggressive and prone to violence, this may pose a risk to the child physically and emotionally. Alternatively if the symptoms disconnect the parent from reality and makes them over-passive, then the child may be neglected or may become inappropriately responsible for the parent.
- The treatments, particularly medication, given to the parent may affect their capacity to parent. Some medication can slow down responses and cause loss of motivation and lethargy which would clearly impact on how well a parent could meet the child's needs. If the parent is not taking the required medication to control their mental health condition and capacity to function, this too may affect their parenting capacity.

- There is evidence that if the parent has additional difficulties – so called, dual diagnosis – such as substance abuse, learning disability – as well as mental health difficulties, the implications for the child will be more serious (Reder and Duncan, 1999).
- If the parent's social and psychological functioning are affected by the mental illness – however slightly this appears to be the case – this may affect the parent's capacity to relate consistently and coherently to their child. This will have a variable impact on the child depending on his/her developmental and emotional stage of development. A study by Falkov in the mid-1990s showed that – even when the parent appeared to be well – there were significant levels of measurable stress in the child.
- Separations and discontinuities in parenting may impact on the child's development and well-being. This may result from the parent's illness because of time in hospital or substitute parenting having to be provided even at home. The significance of this needs to be factored into the assessment process and in care planning. It is important to listen to children and to provide them with opportunities to talk through their experience and understanding of what is happening.
- Additional socio-economic disadvantage, social isolation and poverty as well as the parent's mental illness may provide a multiplier effect and are likely to add to the degree of impact on the child. The assessment and intervention provided needs to ensure that this is fully factored in and support provided to manage these issues.
- The impacts on children of mentally ill parents from groups who are marginalised and discriminated against, such as ethnic minorities are also likely to be more significant as there is a potential for the mental health issues and issues of discrimination to compound each other.

Protective and vulnerability factors

The impact of parental mental illness on children is affected by a range of different factors. The outcome for the child will be affected by a range of such other issues:

- The child's access to significant others – particularly the other parent and the mental well-being of the other parent.
- The child's age and stage of development when mental illness is first evident in a parent

– the older the child, the less vulnerable to severe impact and the younger the more vulnerable in every dimension.

- The child's individual resilience and coping capacity.
- The 'style' of parenting historically in the family and prior to mental health difficulties in the parent – indifferent or neglectful parenting can render a child particularly vulnerable.
- The wider social support available to the child from extended family, friends, teachers or other adults.

Assessment of risk of neglect or abuse

All mental illness can affect the capacity to parent and sometimes the impairment may be so serious that the behaviour of the parent may pose significant risks to the child. An element of the assessment process needs to evaluate the risks to the child resulting from the parent's symptoms and behaviour. Any observed or possible risk to the child resulting from their parent's capacity to care will need to be weighed against what preventive and protective circumstances exist to deal with that risk.

Some factors to consider about the parent's mental illness were discussed earlier. More specifically, there are some mental health conditions which most certainly are likely to pose considerable risk to the child:

- Severe post-natal depression and puerperal psychosis carry particular risks for babies and young children and several child fatalities have occurred in these cases.
- Continuous or frequent substance misuse – drugs and/or alcohol – may lead to dangerously low levels of parental care and supervision and neglect. Several children have died as a result of their parent's unavailability or pre-occupation.
- Psychopathic disorder, where the parent is impulsive, needy and committed to instant gratification, can lead to direct physical or emotional abuse, or the needs of the parents being given priority over those of the children. As mentioned above, the child may have been attributed a role in the parent's delusional behaviour.
- Chronic psychosis can result in physical or emotional neglect of children. The condition itself and the medication required for treatment may both impact on the capacity of the parent to care safely.

When a mentally ill parent is the sole carer for a child, this is also likely to increase the level of risk because of the level of protection available on a day-to-day basis.

The framework and the hierarchy of issues

The Assessment Framework spells out the seven dimensions to consider when assessing a child's needs. These all need to be considered in assessing children of parents with mental health problems but the factors outlined above need to be overlaid within these areas. The three sides of the Assessment Framework triangle – the child's developmental needs, parenting capacity and family and environmental factors – bring together the three domains which should be considered. However, concentrating particularly on assessing the needs of children with mentally ill parents, considerable detail should be paid to the full circumstances of the parent. Any aspect of a child's development and well-being can be affected by a parent's mental health. The degree of affect, if there is any, will depend very much on the nature and severity of the problems of the parent, the developmental stage and resilience of the child and the absence or existence of additional protective factors within the child's environment.

Considerable skill and expertise are required to bring together and understand all the possible protective and stressor factors for the child. There is no simple direct equation between the effect of the parent's mental health state and the outcome for the child's development, safety and well-being. The assessing practitioner needs to gather as much information as possible, to engage as actively as possible with the child and the parent, to seek additional expertise, as required, about the mental health needs and to use all this to consider what intervention will promote the child's welfare most effectively. This will include actively working to support the parent, whenever possible, to parent effectively as well as promoting the child's welfare and safety. The child care practitioner needs to assess the parent's general level of functioning as well as how competently they seem to be meeting the child's needs. A systems approach to child, parent and family is needed in assessing, analysing and planning for each of the components of the child's circumstance. Only in this way can the interactions and influences between the child, the parent and the mental health issues be fully identified, understood and managed.

For the child care practitioner, there will be a hierarchy of issues to consider both in carrying out the assessment of the child's needs, the parent's capacity to parent and the parent's needs in relation to the mental heath problems:

- Are the child's needs, referring to the seven dimensions, being met and is the child safe?
- What intervention might be needed to meet the child's needs?
- How can the parent's parenting be supported and promoted – through casework and practically? How can other supportive relationships for the child – in and outside the family – be encouraged? How can other vulnerabilities and sources of stress for the child (and the parent) be reduced?
- How can any specific issues for the child arising from the parent's mental illness – including any possibilities of discontinuity in the care of the child – be best managed to promote the child's welfare?

Considering the child's needs and the parent's issues and weighing up how best to assess and then intervene for the child's benefit requires the complex systems approach suggested above. The overall context in which children are being reared and how well parents are able to manage themselves and their children's needs has to be considered. This also provides information about what additional resources parents may need to care for their children. There also needs to be adequate consideration of the environment – the cultural and ethnic background of families to ensure that this is considered and understood.

Various attempts have been made to develop frameworks for assessing the quality and level of family functioning. For families affected by mental illness, a level of family functioning framework is also useful. It enables all the domains mentioned above to be considered together. Patricia Crittenden tried to review the research evidence for predicting the likelihood of future child abuse in families in relation to the severity of the first abuse. However, when she found that it was not clear that such a relationship could be demonstrated she reconsidered what alternative schema might work to promote children's safety and welfare. Crittenden has advocated a 'family competence' approach to understanding and assessing the

overall context of family life – what the child experiences; families are seen as managing along a continuum of competence. This continuum of competence could also reflect dynamically the degree to which mental illness may be affecting the parents' capacity to cope at any point or over a period of time. This is a conceptual framework which can be particularly beneficial in making the complex assessments which may be necessary when considering how to intervene for children affected by parental mental health.

Crittenden suggested five different levels of family functioning.

- *Independent and adequate*. These families are able to assess and manage their needs through their own resources combined with professional support which family members actively seek and use when needed.

  For instance, the parents make use of universal family support services such as attending child health clinics and consult the health visitors and GP about care of the children. A mother may experience a minor degree of post-natal depression for which she draws on the support of her health visitor, GP and her partner.
- *Vulnerable to crisis*. The family needs short term i.e. less than a year, information, advice and support.

  For instance, mother has had a schizophrenic episode following the birth of her second child but has responded well to treatment and is recovering well and coping with caring for the children with day care support.
- *Restorable*. The family needs so much external support that intervention on many levels, over a long period of time (e.g. 2-5 years) with extensive casework and a substantial commitment of resources will be needed to preserve the family and to restore it to independence.

  For instance, father is suffering from schizophrenia and his behaviour can be violent with likelihood of associated risk to the children who are presenting behavioural problems at school.
- *Supportable*. Family needs are so great relative to family competencies and available intervention that long term continuous case management and intervention are necessary to enable the parents to rear their children successfully. For instance, the children have

suffered physical abuse from their mother who suffers from a manic-depressive disorder but she is currently responding to and co-operating with treatment.

- *Inadequate.* Essential family needs cannot be met by current services and intervention; children must be placed in more supportive environments.

For instance, mother suffered psychotic breakdown two years ago and has since been diagnosed as having schizophrenia and is in hospital with no likelihood of discharge in the foreseeable future.

This approach of considering the competence of families to parent and the level of support needed to maintain or improve their level of competence is a useful means of considering the needs of children and families affected by mental illness. It can complement approaches which focus on assessing the needs of children and on assessing how 'well' mentally ill parents are. It is crucial therefore, that where there are serious concerns about a parent's capacity to parent, that not only the mental state of the parent but also their parenting capacity – level of family functioning achievable – are both assessed together.

The resolution of a parent's mental illness – whether this is a short term or longer term improvement – cannot automatically be assumed to indicate that the parent can adequately parent their child. As discussed earlier, several levels of assessment need to be considered: the context of the parent-child relationship, the developmental needs/attainment of the child, and the availability of family and social support for mentally ill parents. This model is one means of doing just that and it is incorporated into a suggested operational framework further on in this chapter.

Collaboration and openness of practice

As discussed earlier, essential ingredients for good practice in this area for child care social workers must include collaboration with other professionals and agencies – particularly adult mental health services but also child and adolescent mental health services. It must be a given in this area that information and expertise is shared and exchanged. Networking locally and knowing who your counterparts in mental health are necessary if full and competent assessments are to be produced.

Confidentiality and information exchange is an issue which can seriously muddy the waters as far as joint working is concerned. This is particularly so now that mental health and children's services are structurally so separate. An effective service for children and families affected by mental illness cannot be provided without clear lines of communication between agencies and the exchange of information. Considerable progress has been made recently in developing a shared understanding between health and social services agencies about the need to share information when there are concerns about the safety and welfare of children. However, concerns about the responsibilities of Caldicott Guardians, data protection requirements and, more recently, the possibility of Human Right Act challenges has made this potentially an even more confused and confusing territory.

All recent guidance has made it clear that, although patients and clients should normally expect any information about them to be confidential, this expectation may be varied when the safety or health of children is of concern. When any information could be beneficially exchanged in the interests of a child between professionals or agencies, then it would be appropriate, whenever possible, to inform the parent, and sometimes child or young person that this is the case and to gain their confidence, engagement in the process and consent. An openness and directness about discussing the parent's mental illness and its impact on their parenting and the impact on the child would also assist in clearing the lines on the issue of confidentiality. Such a transparent approach is also much more likely to produce a better outcome for the child. If an understanding is also developed with the parent about what s/he wants the child to know about the mental illness and the parent can be assisted to be as open about it as possible, this will also be beneficial to the child. The child will be enabled to understand the illness and not speculate about whether, for example, they have caused it or are ill too.

A comprehensive framework for assessment and intervention

An example is described here of how local interagency protocols and other arrangements can be used to improve practice for children of mentally ill parents across and within the different agencies involved. We need to ensure that the needs of children and their mentally ill parents are addressed together and that appropriate plans are made to meet the needs of each. This requires some bridge building and crossing.

One means of bridging the structural and practice gap, which we have to bridge, is to ensure that all professionals in contact with families affected by mental illness have clear guidance about what factors to consider in their own assessment and when they should exchange information with their colleague professionals in the other speciality.

In 1999, a common framework was developed for the joint operation of children and mental health services for families affected by mental illness in the London Borough of Camden. Crittenden's framework for describing levels of family functioning was used to develop the protocol. It included all arrangements for referral, assessment and care planning. It also covered training needs, confidentiality and the roles of mental health and child care practitioners.

The protocol was developed from a clear starting point that, whatever the framework used, when working with families affected by mental illness, professionals need to consider whether the needs of children are being met and whether the capacity of parents to meet those needs is sufficient. The protocol was written on the basis that existing assessment processes – the Assessment Framework and the Care Programme Approach – would continue. The Assessment Framework's seven dimensions, mentioned previously, gave the template for considering children's needs. The context of the parent's capacity to parent and the family and environmental circumstances provided the broader canvas within which and through which these needs are met. However, the protocol allowed practitioners to bring together all the information to form a shared assessment of the full circumstances of the child and the parent.

The basis for adopting this approach was the view that professional activity needs to be directed, whenever possible, to supporting children and their families rather than to undermining the capacity which they have. In order to do this coherently for the parent and safely for the child, it was essential to have an agreed understanding between mental health and child care practitioners and awareness of all the issues and needs.

Fundamental to the approach was the principle that we all – mental health and children's services – would be operating and trained together to meet the needs of children affected by parental mental illness. The success of shared practice development depends on achieving a shared vision and understanding of the service to be developed. As discussed above, there also needed to be consideration of the requirements for information exchange and for confidentiality and how this could be managed. The particular circumstances of each family – including ethnicity, culture and gender and the views of service users need to be considered in building up the local protocol.

The model of assessment and service delivery presented here considers and spells out how and when children and families and mental health services can and should work closely together in assessment and intervention.

Referral and initial response

The process for possible initial routes which a referral may take were drawn up (Figure 1). It was predicated on the policy that firstly, when there are concerns about the mental health of a parent or about their parenting and safety or welfare of their child, referral about these issues should be approached from a joint perspective between children and families and mental health services. There should be *a shared, planned response* with prompt exchange of information and consultation, leading to an initial response depending on the urgency or severity of the concerns.

Specifically, referral and assessment of needs should be managed along continuum of need. There should be an exchange of information between specialist teams initially about risk and safety either for the parent or the child. If there are urgent needs and issues, then an urgent response will be made to the needs. Two other levels of joint response are suggested depending on the degree of need and it is also acknowledged that some families will require no external support outside the family. Four levels of need and response are defined in Figure 2 and, as follows:

Urgent: Acute Concerns: explicit child protection concerns and/or mental health emergency
Significant: Parenting or Mental health Concerns: care of children causes concern but does not require urgent child protection response and/or parental mental health is cause for concern but does not require urgent assessment.

Figure 1: A model of referral/initial response for children and families afffected by mental illness.

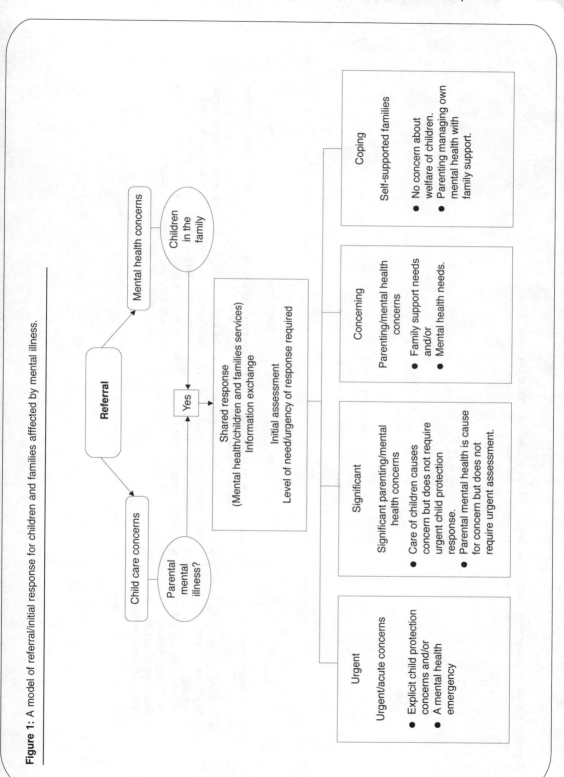

Figure 2: A model of assessment and care planning for children and families affected by mental illness.

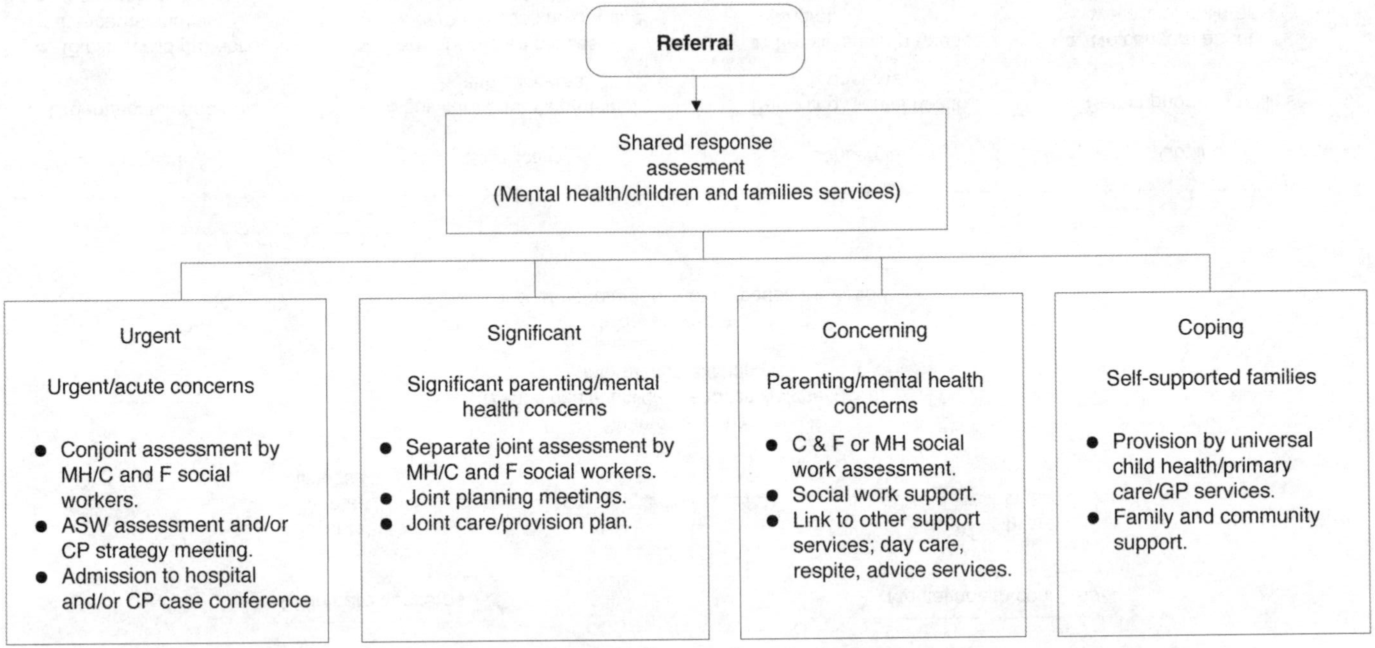

Referral

↓

Shared response
assesment
(Mental health/children and families services)

Urgent

Urgent/acute concerns

- Conjoint assessment by MH/C and F social workers.
- ASW assessment and/or CP strategy meeting.
- Admission to hospital and/or CP case conference

Significant

Significant parenting/mental health concerns

- Separate joint assessment by MH/C and F social workers.
- Joint planning meetings.
- Joint care/provision plan.

Concerning

Parenting/mental health concerns

- C & F or MH social work assessment.
- Social work support.
- Link to other support services; day care, respite, advice services.

Coping

Self-supported families

- Provision by universal child health/primary care/GP services.
- Family and community support.

Figure 3: Assessment and care planning: levels of intervention.

Referral/assessment along continuum of need	Response/assessment and care planning
Urgent: Acute Concerns: explicit child protection concerns and/or mental health emergency.	**Urgent needs:** At the most urgent or severe level of need, there should be a conjoint assessment by both children and families and mental health workers working together closely. Plans should be developed together and reviewed jointly.
Significant: Parenting or Mental health Concerns: care of children causes concern but does not require urgent child protection response and/or parental mental health is cause for concern but does not require urgent assessment.	**Significant Needs:** Children and families and mental health workers should make separate assessments of need but work together to formulate care plans with the family.
Concerning: Issues about Parenting/Mental health: there is a need for support to the family and/or for mental health service support for the parent.	**Concerning:** Either children and families or mental health services could assess needs and provide support either family support services (such as day care) and/or supportive mental health services (such as counselling).
Coping: Self-Supported Families. There is no concern about the welfare of children and parent is managing own mental health with family and primary care support.	**Coping:** These are parents with mental health problems who are able to function adequately and to care appropriately supported by universal and primary care services as well as family.

Concerning: issues about Parenting/Mental health: there is a need for support to the family and/or for mental health service support for the parent.

Coping: Self-Supported Families. There is no concern about the welfare of children and parent is managing own mental health with family and primary care support.

Assessment and care planning

Following the first referral information and immediate assessment of needs, it may be necessary to make further enquiries depending on the level of concern or need. The levels of assessment and intervention which may be required by children and families affected by mental illness are summarised in Figure 3.

This model aims to address the problems of bridging the cross sector boundaries of client-based specialisms. The complimentary perspectives of both children and families and mental health workers are essential in order to provide a holistic and comprehensive service to children and families affected by mental illness. Ultimately, interpreting and managing the different levels of concern will depend on the quality of professional judgement and decision-making available. Arrangements need to be in place locally to ensure that information

and concerns can be exchanged and discussed. Staff will need the experience and training required to make the model operate effectively.

Service and practice development

The assessment and intervention framework described above needs to be supported and underpinned with service and practice developments. These ensure that it is embedded in local practice and that a consistent and coherent approach locally is maintained and monitored.

- **Training Together**
  In practice terms, practitioners from each speciality require training together and opportunities thereafter to exchange views. Training programmes enable this to happen. There are training needs for a wide variety of professional staff across pre and post-qualifying courses. There are considerable advantages to joint, inter-agency and inter-professional training.
- **Joint Practice Models**
  Professionals within mental health and children and families services also need to develop combined practice models. Senior managers within each agency need to consider what organisational and structural frameworks will facilitate the exchange of

information and good practice in working together.

A model local protocol is included in Appendix 1. and this could be used to develop an appropriate response to assessing and meeting the needs of children affected by parental mental illness.

Conclusion

There is a need to ensure that services fit the needs of child and parent. The assessment and intervention provided needs to strike the balance between support of the parent and monitoring and ensuring the safety of the child. Above all we need to avoid having an unco-ordinated, haphazard service in this area of need with either mental health services or children's services vying for control or neglecting the needs of either the child or the parent. Adults with mental health problems need an effective service to enable them to parent as well as they can. However, having the capacity and motivation to be an effective parent is that adult's responsibility which if that condition cannot be met, then children's services with other family members must work to ensure that the child is safe and secure. The concept of the parenting role and the necessity of maintaining it as a part of the treatment / therapeutic plan for the adult is unsupportable if it endangers the child's safety and welfare. Seeking to maintain a child with a parent who is too ill to care supposedly for the child's sake is equally dangerous.

This whole area of practice is about the potential conflict of interest between child and parent. There are rights and responsibilities on both sides which need to be weighed in the balance. But it is the child's interest which must be paramount because of his/her vulnerability.

Summary of key points

- The need for a holistic, family systems approach to assessing the needs of children affected by parental mental illness.
- The assessment must include:
  - The child's health, development, well-being and safety on all the child needs dimensions the Assessment Framework.
  - The level of parenting and the quality of the parent-child relationship.
  - The general functioning of the parent, the current mental state of the parent and the history of illness and own parenting.

  - The family and environmental context, protective and stress factors for the child and parent.
  - An overall evaluation of family competence and of the degree to which the child's needs can and are being met, using the Crittenden framework.
- Important to listen to and explain to children what is happening.
- Need to ensure that the long view is taken of children's needs, taking account of the child's developmental needs and timescales.
- Assessments need to take account of the unpredictability and variability of some mental illnesses and the fact that the parent's mental state may be more or less stable over time; there may be a need for regular review and re-assessment in some cases.
- Collaboration and joint working with mental health practitioners is essential both to complete accurate assessments but also in subsequent work with the family since treatment and care for the mentally ill parent in both acute episodes and continuing care may be required
- Local joint protocols – between mental health and children's services – and senior endorsement are good practice to ensure good quality assessments and service delivery.
- Child care practitioners should have access training about adult mental health, preferably as a part of joint training with mental health colleagues about how to assess needs most effectively.

References

Australian Infant, Child, Adolescent and Family Health Association (2001) *Children of Parents Affected by a Mental Illness*. Scoping Project.

Becker,S., Aldridge,J. and Dearden,C. (1998) *Young Carers and Their Families*. Oxford: Blackwell Science.

Cleaver, H. Unell, I. and Aldgate, J. (1999) *Children's Needs: Parenting Capacity*. London: The Stationery Office.

Cowling, V. (1999) *Children of Parents with Mental Illness*. ACER Press.

Crittenden P. (1993) Severity of Maltreatment. In Hobbs, C. J. and Wynne, J. M. (Eds.) *Clinical Paediatrics; Child Abuse*. London: Balliere Tindall.

DoH (1996) Building Bridges: A Guide to Inter-agency Working for the Care and Protection of Severely Mentally Ill People. Brighton: Pavilion Publishing.

Falkov, A. (1996) *Study of Working Together Part 8 Reports: Fatal Child Abuse and Parental Psychiatric Disorder*. London: Department of Health.

Falkov, A. et al. (1998) *Crossing Bridges: Training Manual and Reader for Working With Mentally Ill Parents and Their Children*. Brighton: Pavilion Publishing.

Gopfert, M., Webster, J., and Seeman, M.V. (Eds.) (1996) *Parental Psychiatric Disorder*. Cambridge: Cambridge University Press.

Hallett, C. (1995) Inter-agency Co-ordination in Child Protection. *Studies in Child Protection*. London: HMSO.

Howarth, J. (2001) *The Child's World: Assessing Children in Need*. London: Jessica Kingsley.

Hugman, R. and Phillips, N. (1993) Like Bees Round the Honeypot. *Practice*. 6: 3, 193–205.

Kumar, R. (1997) Personal communication.

NISW (2000) *Working at the Interfaces Within and Between Services: Appropriate Care for the Children of Mentally Ill and Substance Abusing Parents*. London: NISW.

Reder, P. and Lucey, C. (Eds.) (1996) *Assessment of Parenting: Psychiatric and Psychological Contributions*. London: Routledge.

Reder, P. and Duncan, S. (1999) *Lost Innocents*. London: Routledge.

Sheppard, M. (1997) Double Jeopardy: The Link Between Child Abuse and Maternal Depression in Child and Family Social Work. *Child and Family Social Work*. 2: 91–108.

Sieff Foundation (1997) *Keeping Children in Mind: Balancing Children's Needs with Parents' Mental Health*. London: Sieff Foundation.

University of Manchester (1996) *Learning Materials on Mental Health: An Introduction Vol. 1 and Risk Assessment Vol. 2*. DoH.

Weir, A. (1994) Split Decisions: Issues in Child Protection and Mental Health. *Community Care*. Dec.

Weir, A., Douglas, A (Eds.) (1999) *Child Protection and Adult Mental Health: Conflict of Interest?* London: Butterworth-Heinemann.

Appendix 1: Services for Children and Families Affected by Mental Illness

A Joint Service Protocol for the Assessment and Care Management of Parental Mental Health Problems

1. Purpose

- To provide a clear framework for service provision to families affected by mental illness.

- To ensure that integrated, well co-ordinated services are provided to children and families affected by mental illness.

- To provide an agreed framework for planning and undertaking the joint assessment of risk for Assessments (including ASW Assessment) under the Mental Health Act 1983, the NHS and Community Care Act 1990 and Assessments (including Child Protection Assessment) under the Children Act 1989.

- To develop and improve communication and overall service co-ordination between the children in need and the community mental health teams to enhance the quality of services provided.

2. Service Principles

- Paramountcy of child's welfare and safety.
- Needs-led approach to engagement with and management of needs and risks posed by vulnerable adults.
- Children are usually best brought up within their own families and support should be provided to enable this whenever possible.
- Inter-professional and inter-agency working together across boundaries.
- Appropriate professional confidentiality and respect for service users.
- Valuing and appreciation of diversity.

3. Background

With increasing separation between service areas and growing specialism within service areas, there is a need to ensure that a strategic approach is adopted to joint working and to the exchange of information between service for adults and children. For parents affected by mental illness, there is a clear need to ensure that the style of working in services matches the needs of those clients.

- There is a need for integrated and co-ordinated services to parents with mental health problems to support their parenting.
- Many parents with mental health problems successfully care for their children with the support of family and friends.
- However, the children of parents with mental health difficulties are more likely to require additional services and support as children in need; they are more likely to experience health or developmental delay and may require alternative care at times.

- Some children and young people whose parents have mental health problems may be required to assume additional responsibilities for their parent, themselves and other children in the family.
- Some mentally ill parents will not be able to care safely for their children and the children may be exposed to abuse, including fatal abuse, in a few exceptional cases without appropriate protection. Falkov's 1996 study of 100 child deaths identified parental psychiatric disorder as a factor in one third of the cases.

4. A Joint Approach to Assessment and Care Management

Strategic inter-agency frameworks are in place for both mental health services – within the community care plan and the local care programme approach and care management policy – and for children's services within the children's service plan. This protocol sets out to establish a clear framework at operational level for the sharing of information about the needs of children and parents affected by mental illness. It also proposes a framework for joint and conjoint assessment between children in need social workers and community mental health workers.

At all times, the paramount consideration for all professionals must be the welfare and best interests of the child.

The provision of appropriate mental health services for parents will reduce the likelihood of difficulties for the children of the family. Family support will play an important role in reducing stress on parents and in enhancing their capacity to parent effectively. There is a growing awareness of the need to ensure that the needs of children and their mentally ill parents are addressed together and that appropriate plans are made to meet the needs of each.

One means of bridging the practice gap is to ensure that all professionals in contact with families affected by mental illness have clear guidance about what factors to consider in their own assessment and when they should exchange information with their colleague professionals in the other specialty.

When working with families affected by mental illness professionals need to consider whether the needs of children are being met and whether the capacity of parents to meet those needs is sufficient.

Professional activity needs to be directed, whenever possible, to supporting children and their families rather than to undermining the capacity which they have.

Local arrangements for jointly addressing these needs need to be developed and implemented. A model for local policy and procedure to achieve this is described here.

The success of shared practice development depends on achieving a shared vision and understanding of the service to be developed. There needs to be consideration of the requirements for information exchange and for confidentiality and how this could be managed. The particular circumstances of each family, including ethnicity, culture and gender and the views of service users need to be considered in building up the local protocol.

The model presented here attempts to consider how and when children and families and mental health services can and should work closely together. Figure 1 outlines the possible initial routes which a referral may take.

4.1 Referral and initial response

Staff in the community mental health and children in need services should identify on referral all cases where an adult with mental illness has parental responsibilities. Such families will require support and assistance, particularly if the children are less than five years old. There is enormous benefit to be gained from sharing concerns and skills about particular families. On referral there should be contact between the two services to consider whether the family are known to the other service and to discuss whether any information needs to be shared.

When there are concerns about the mental health of a parent or about their parenting and the safety or welfare of their child, referral about these issues should be approached from a joint perspective between children and families and mental health services.

There should be a shared response with prompt exchange of information and consultation, leading to an initial response depending on the urgency or severity of the concerns. **Referral and assessment should be regarded as being along a continuum of need**

There should be an exchange of information between specialist teams initially about risk and safety either for the parent or the child. Different levels of response are required depending on the urgency or significance of the needs or concerns. If there are urgent needs and issues then, an urgent response must be made to the needs. Two other levels of response are suggested depending on the degree of need and it is also acknowledged that some families will require no external support outside the family. Four levels of need or urgency for response are described in Figure 1as follows:

4.1.1. **Urgent or acute concerns** about child protection or urgent mental health problems.

4.1.2 **Significant parenting or mental health concerns** where the care of children causes concern but does not require an urgent child protection response or parental mental health is cause for concern but does not require urgent assessment.

4.1.3 **Concerning parenting or mental health issues** where there is a need for support to the family or for mental health service support for the parent.

4.1.4 **Coping self-supported families** where there is no concern about the welfare of children and the parent is managing their own mental health with family and primary care support.

4.2 Assessment: 'joint' and 'conjoint' according to level of concerns or needs. Response assessment and care planning

Following initial enquiries and assessment, it may be necessary to make further assessment depending on the level of concern or need and staff in each service should work together in the interests of the family. The needs identified again need to be regarded along a continuum with the variable response required. Four levels of intervention are suggested again (Figure 2).

4.2.1 **Urgent needs:** At the most urgent or severe level of need, there should be a **conjoint assessment** by both children and families and mental health workers working together closely. If possible staff should visit the family together and plans should be developed together and reviewed jointly. A joint planning meeting or case conference will be required.

4.2.2 **Significant needs:** Children and families and mental health workers should make **separate assessments of need but work together** to formulate care plans with the family. Each specialist professional should form a separate assessment of the issues but they would co-operate subsequently to produce a joint or shared view of the

situation and what support is required. The need for a joint planning meeting should be considered and how the needs will be assessed should be agreed at the point of referral.

4.2.3 **Concerning:** Either children and families or mental health services could assess needs and provide support, either family support services (such as day care) or supportive mental health services (such as counselling).

4.2.4 **Coping:** These are parents with mental health problems who are able to function adequately and to care appropriately supported by universal and primary care services as well as family.

The aim of working together is to address the problems of bridging the cross sector boundaries of client based specialisms. The complimentary perspectives of both children and families and mental health workers are essential in order to provide a holistic and comprehensive service to children and families affected by mental illness. Ultimately, interpreting and managing the different levels of concern will depend on the quality of professional judgement and decision-making available. Arrangements need to be in place locally to ensure that information and concerns can be exchanged and discussed. Staff will need the experience and training required to make the model operate effectively.

5. Case Management/Allocated Cases

5.1 Packages of care and support
Families affected by mental illness need:

• Treatment and care for the mentally ill parent in both acute episodes and continuing care.
• Support for the family as a whole on a holistic basis – to give them the knowledge and skills to be able to cope as a family; for children, this means they have to be able to make sense of what is happening and to be able to complete developmental milestones through to adulthood; it may also mean protection when parenting is inadequate or abusive.

The level of provision will varying according to the needs identified. (Figure 3). In cases where there is continuing work involving both the children in need and community mental health team, it is essential that there is effective communication, joint planning and an integrated programme of care. For instance, the attendance of a parent at a mental health day centre might be complimented by day care provision for the children.

In some families, children and young people may have to assume additional responsibilities because of their parent's mental health difficulties. These 'young carers' will need particular support and will be eligible for a carer's assessment of need as well as for assessment as a possible child in need.

5.2 Management of child protection concerns
When there are concerns about the safety or welfare of children and that they may be at risk of harm from neglect or abuse, these must be discussed with the line manager, referred to the duty social worker in the children in need centre. A strategy for dealing with the concerns must be agreed. The details of the referral concerns should be confirmed in writing.

All staff working with families need to be aware of the child protection procedures and to have received training in child protection. Attendance at strategy meetings, case conferences and core group meetings is expected of staff from both services.

6. Interagency Collaboration

In formulating joint assessment and care planning for families affected by mental illness, there needs to be an acknowledgement of the significant role which primary care services such as GPs and health visitors play in supporting parents in the community. Wherever possible, they should be included in any joint planning meetings. As wide a range of other relevant agencies and professionals as possible should be included in any plans to support parents.

7. Strategy for Training Together

In practice terms, practitioners from each speciality require training together and opportunities thereafter to exchange views. Training programmes will enable this to happen.

There are considerable advantages in joint, interagency and inter-professional training and this will be commissioned for staff working in. This will add to the existing ACPC workshop training about parental mental health which has been provided over the last few years.

7.1 Training will be established to provide an understanding of the applicable legislation and guidance, to examine practice issues and to develop good working relationships between the two services.

7.2 The protocol will be introduced to staff – particularly as part of their induction – and there will be a rolling programme of training for mental health and children in need staff.

7.3 Community mental health team staff should receive regular updates on child care issues and about family support services in the Borough as part of their ongoing training. Similarly, children in need staff will receive regular information about developments in mental health services.

8. Confidentiality and the Exchange of Information

An effective service for children and families affected by mental illness cannot be provided without clear lines of communication between agencies and the exchange of information. Considerable progress has been made recently in developing a shared understanding between health and social services agencies about the need to share information when there are concerns about the safety and welfare of children.

All recent guidance has made it clear that, although patients and clients should normally expect any information about them to be confidential, this expectation will be varied when the safety or welfare of children is of concern.

Mental health and children in need assessments should be exchanged so that there is a clearly agreed view of the circumstances of the child and the family.

9. Service Evaluation and Quality Review

9.1 The protocol and any arising service issues will be reviewed annually by the senior manager officer responsible for mental health and children in need services.

9.2 Performance indicators will need to be developed to ensure that joint assessment and collaboration is taking place.

Chapter Nineteen

Parental Alcohol Misuse and Compromised Child Care: A Framework for Assessment and Intervention

Martin C. Calder and Anne Peake

Introduction

In our society, alcoholic drinks are widely consumed, socially acceptable and indeed thought desirable in many contexts. Alcohol is often associated with status, power, conviviality, attractiveness, and achievement (Collins, 1990, p1). It is thus very difficult to determine what problems are and are not alcohol-related. In 1987, the population of England and Wales spent £17 billion on alcohol, equivalent to £370 for every adult in Britain (Faculty of Public Health Medicine, 1991). In 1996, £189.5 million was spent on promoting alcohol (Alcohol Concern, 1997). Yet taken in excess, it may also lead to damage and even death to the drinker and others. Many definitions of alcohol misuse have been proposed, and the common criteria appear to be:

- Interference with life functioning, including personal, work or family.
- Continued use despite adverse consequences.
- Psychological or physical dependence.
- Loss of control over drinking.
- Withdrawal symptoms upon discontinuation of drinking.

(Nastasi and DeZolt, 1994).

When a person with an alcohol problem is in a family where there are children, there are often concerns about the welfare or safety of the children. This chapter endeavours to provide a framework for examining the presenting problems of a family/professional network where an adult has an alcohol dependency problem. The framework conceptualises the problems in terms of elevated/lowered risks to children in the same household and offers a framework to guide professional intervention.

The size of the problem

It is impossible to give precise figures for the number of children and young people who are living in families where alcohol is misused because so much alcohol misuse is hidden and because many studies examine adult rather than parental drinking. HMSO (1996) provided figures suggesting that in England and Wales 8.5 million people (6 million men and 2.5 million women) drink above the medically recommended levels of 21 units per week for men and 14 units per week for women and nearly 3 million people are alcohol dependent.

Alcohol Concern postulates that up to 800,000 children may be involved in the UK (Brisby et al., 1997) reflecting that up to seven per cent of parents are problem drinkers. Alcohol Concern (1997) also identified that:

- One person in 25 in Britain is dependent on alcohol causing severe problems for their families as well as themselves. Heavy drinking is a common factor in family break-up – marriages where one or both partners have a drink problem are twice as likely to end in divorce as marriages where alcohol problems are absent.
- There were over 28,000 hospital admissions in one year due to alcohol dependence or the toxic effects of alcohol.
- Problem drinkers are 40-50 times more likely to commit suicide, while 66 per cent of parasuicides are likely to have alcohol problems (Saunders, 1984).
- Alcohol is a factor in 40 per cent of domestic violence incidents.
- Alcohol is a factor in a third of child abuse cases.

Houston et al. (1997) reported that they heard about problem drinking from twice as many children in lone-parent families as one would expect from the child population as a whole, and that drunken parenting is more common in lone-parent families headed by a father than a mother.

Evidence-based material and parents who misuse alcohol

There is clearly a substantial proportion of social work clients who are experiencing alcohol-related problems. Yet at the same time a number of studies also indicate that social workers lack knowledge and confidence in this area, often resorting to stereotyping, wonder if intervention is justified or may be a waste of time and tend to be excessively reliant upon general practitioners or psychiatrists (Collins, 1990, p4). Fanti (1987) also found that between 3 per cent and 6 per cent of all social workers employed in Britain have serious alcohol problems.

Workers need to be aware that whilst we will utilise the research that is available, we do so with caution as children of all ages tend to be grouped together; few studies have comparison groups; there is a lack of longitudinal studies; and there is an over-emphasis on drinkers in treatment rather than being drawn from the general population. On a more positive note, the available studies do portray a high level of consistency in the findings. We should consider the research as a compass to give us some direction but recognising that we need to select the right map. For a detailed analysis of the research in the area of alcohol and family processes, the reader is referred to Jung (2001, p365–95).

Determining whether to respond

In many situations of parental alcohol misuse, professionals wait until the family hits a crisis, partly created by parental resistance to acknowledge they have a problem and to access specialist service provision. Workers have a responsibility to protect children through supporting the parents to function better and to remove the stigma, privacy and fear of the consequences from the children. The evidence demonstrates that these children are children in need. The adverse effects of parental alcohol abuse on children can be significant without the provision of a service.

In looking at whether the threshold for accessing a social work service is met locally, workers need to consider whether the parental alcohol misuse is affecting their parenting, impacting directly or indirectly on the children, and requires further assessment and/or a detailed package of support.

Impact factors for children

Most people who consume alcohol do not have a drink problem and there is no evidence that the responsible use of alcohol by parents has bad effects on children. However, there is a growing body of material surrounding the

experiences of children who live with parental alcohol misuse (Houston et al., 1997; Laybourn et al., 1996) that identifies some important messages for workers.

The way that parental drinking affects children is highly complex. Various aspects of the child's situation interact with each other to produce different levels and time-scales of impact. Laybourn et al. (1996) developed a useful model for explaining the impact of parental drinking on children (see Figure 1) that we will use in an adapted format as our map and compass for the chapter.

Parental drinking and its side effects have an impact on children at two levels.

- The immediate emotional impact – how the situation makes them feel, which is in turn affected by their understanding of the alcohol consumption and its effects.
- The long-term impact on personality, emotional well-being and social functioning.

These are both mediated by the child's coping mechanisms and by the actions of significant others which may offset or exacerbate the effects of drinking. This area is explored later in this chapter and in Calder et al. (2001).

Morehouse (1979) identified the principal concerns for children when living in problem-drinking families:

- They worry about the health of the drinking family member, particularly a parent.
- The general unpredictability and inconsistent behaviour of family members may lead to the children developing feelings of anger, insecurity, fear and distress.
- The lack of support from the non-drinking family members, particularly from parents, can lead to a child feeling isolated.
- Violence and arguments at home may involve children. They may see them taking place or they may be the recipients, resulting in severe short-and long-term upset.
- The lack of positive attention to the children can lead to feelings of being unloved and unwanted.
- Sometimes the children may feel they are in some way responsible for the problem drinking at home.
- Inappropriate behaviour by family members towards the children can cause confusion and fear. This includes sexual abuse.
- The loss of friends due to the embarrassing family life.

Figure 1: Adapted from 'The impact of parental drinking on children'.

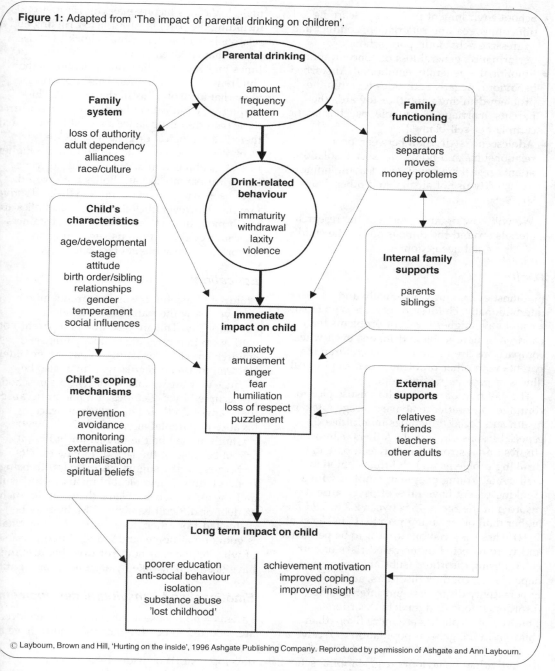

The communication and expression of these concerns can be difficult for children to achieve. The provision of alcohol information may be effective in allowing the child to understand that the situation is not of their own making and this could be accompanied by concrete coping suggestions (Fanti, 1990, p145).

Velleman (2001) identified four areas where parental alcohol problems lead to a high risk for children:

- Anti-social behaviour and conduct disorder – delinquency, truancy, aggressive behaviour, hyperactivity, temper tantrums.

- School environment problems – learning difficulties, reading retardation, conduct and aggressive behaviour, poor school performance, general loss of concentration.
- Emotional – generally emotionally disturbed behaviour, negative attitudes towards the problem-drinking parent, or towards the parents' marriage as a whole, psychosomatic complaints, self-blame.
- Adolescence – division between peer relationships and home life; social isolation, attention-seeking behaviour, leaving home early, early use of alcohol and other drugs (p179–80).

We will now organise some of the research materials around the dimensions of the child's developmental needs domain.

Health

In almost every study, nationally and internationally, children of parents who misuse alcohol have higher levels of problems than the children of non-problem drinkers, even when comparisons are made with the children of parents with other problems, such as physical illness or psychiatric difficulties.

The children of people who misuse alcohol continue to experience above average rates of health and social difficulties in adulthood, especially sons of alcoholic fathers. Almost all studies find a strong link between parental drinking problems and children's emotional well-being. Young people in families with a drinking parent have rates of psychiatric disorder at the age of 15 between 2.2 to 3.9 times higher than other young people (Lynskey et al., 1994). These associations appear to be pervasive and were reflected in increased risks of both externalising disorders (substance misuse and dependence, conduct disorders, attention deficit hyperactivity disorders) and internalising disorders (mood and anxiety disorders). Children of alcoholics are more likely than children in the general population to receive a diagnosis of conduct disorder and often show the individual behaviours (e.g. skipping school, stealing, poor impulse control) associated with this disorder.

Velleman and Orford (1993) found that young people with problem drinking parents were more likely than a control group to start using alcohol and other drugs at a younger age, and use alcohol in a 'risky' fashion, or have problems with their alcohol use (particularly

males). Various factors may contribute to this, including the parents' attitude to drinking and a relative lack of supervision. Schuckit (1991) found that children of alcoholics have a four times higher-risk of becoming alcoholics than children of non-alcoholics. This supports the view that alcohol 'runs in the family'. This finding may indicate either that children learn these patterns of substance abuse at home or that there is a biological or genetic basis for alcoholism. Cadoret et al. (1980) found a higher rate of alcoholism in adopted children whose biological parents are alcoholics than would have been expected on the rates in their adoptive families. However, the offspring of alcoholics are much more likely than others to be abstainers (Harburg et al., 1990), thus suggesting an important environmental factor in play.

Education

Children of alcohol misusing parents might achieve below their attainment level educationally. This may be due to a parent not getting up in a morning to take younger children to school or failing to encourage older children to attend regularly. It may also be because they are unable to concentrate in school preoccupied by difficulties at home or because they cannot do their homework in peace because of parental arguments (Cork, 1969).

Children may be the targets for bullies at school because of the lack of money for clothes or because of the stigma associated with being from a family where alcohol misuse is an issue and the associated problems there can be such as debt or difficult behaviour. Many may be distracted from their schoolwork, fearing what is going on at home, and may be tired because of what happens at home or tired because they have been kept awake by arguments at night.

Emotional and behavioural development

Parents who misuse alcohol and their children are reported to be at higher risk and to have a variety of subsequent problems in emotional development (Woodside, 1986), such as depression and low self-esteem. However, these are not specific to children of alcoholics, but to people reared in dysfunctional families. Streissguth (1986) identified emotional and behavioural difficulties in alcohol-exposed children including hyperactivity, distractibility restlessness, lack of persistence, and impulsivity. Other studies have identified oppositionality, aggression, poor peer relationships, emotional reactivity, irritability, reactivity, over-dependence and rigidity (Harden, 1998).

Identity

Children of alcoholics are more likely than their peers in families where alcohol misuse is not an issue to experience negative life events and less likely to experience positive events. High levels of negative events in turn are correlated with symptoms of depression and anxiety (Nastasi and DeZolt, 1994). Research with the general population provides additional support for the association of family disharmony (e.g. marital conflict, parent-child relationship difficulties) and adjustment difficulties that persist into adulthood (Velleman, 1992). This research suggests that marital conflict is the most powerful predictor among family environment variables (e.g. divorce, poverty, mental health problems of parents) of child and adolescent anti-social and delinquent behaviour. All these factors and the others described in this chapter contribute to a child's sense of identity.

Family and social relationships

The children of problem drinkers may assume a considerable weight of responsibility for tasks within the family. They may assume tasks directly from the drinker, or they may take on some of the non-drinker's roles when the non-drinker assumes more of the drinker's former responsibilities. This means that not only will they miss out on the care, attention and responsiveness normally given by parents, but they may have to assume a parenting role (physical chores such as cooking, cleaning or taking the younger children to school and emotional responsibility towards a parent who turns to them for company, advice and emotional support) especially if they are the eldest child and this often means that their own childhood is lost. They may also be called on to undertake potentially embarrassing tasks associated with personal care, such as cleaning up after sickness or incontinence. Such demands that children take on responsibility, which is too heavy or inappropriate for their age or stage of development, may have negative consequences for the child's development. One such inappropriate role is caring for younger siblings it often involves emotional demands or

stressful experiences that are inappropriate for the child's stage of emotional maturity (Cork, 1969) and unhelpful for the younger siblings.

Many children describe being left with a drinking parent as one of isolation, fear, low standards of care, and their emotional needs being ignored (Houston et al., 1997). They experience neglect, as money for food and clothes is spent on drink, or the parent is too incapable too often and so children, clothes, kitchens, bathrooms are left dirty. Constant and binge drinking can take no account of children's routines (Laybourn et al., 1996)

Both parents may try to hide excessive drinking from the children. The drinker's unusual behaviour is often explained as 'illness' to conceal its real nature. However, even very young children are aware that what is happening in the family is quite different from their normal experience of illness and may be worried and confused about it. When they discover the real explanation, children may be sworn to secrecy. This injunction is usually observed and often unnecessary: most children are acutely aware of the mystery and anxiety surrounding the alcohol-related behaviour and are very reluctant to risk exposing the dark family secret, even if they are not fully aware of the social stigma and associated attitudes of ostracism and rejection. Children may thus feel unable to share their experience with peers or with adults and are left to deal with their feelings such as anxiety, fear, hostility, anger, with no avenue of expression or possible relief. Problems of social isolation, feelings of shame about the family, fear of rejection by friends, and other outsiders, and difficulties in making and keeping friendships are problems.

Fanti (1990) found that children often take psychological responsibility for their parents, form alliances against the drinker and the family closes itself off from outsiders to preserve the drinking as a secret. Where professionals intervene, this does not necessarily resolve the problems. On the contrary, this often fuelled the pressure to deny the problem and keep the whole business secret. Reticence and secrecy often characterise their lives. This can mean that their misery and their difficulties are invisible. They lack trust and are thus difficult to help. Clearly there is a professional obligation to make their assistance accessible to such families to overcome such an obstacle.

Children may be let down repeatedly, either on special occasions such as birthdays or school events, as well as promises to cease drinking which are constantly broken. Broken promises can lead to strained family relationships and a lack of trust. The child may develop anxiety, phobic and depressive states and may also attempt self-harm (Seixas, 1979).

Children often describe being ground down to an appalling sense of worthlessness by constant criticism, moaning and yelling. When they do receive any love or warmth it is when the drinking parent has been drinking and this is often inconsistent and unreliable. Many talk of feeling unloved and unwanted, and sometimes being told as much; of fear that the parent will injure themselves, set the house on fire, or that they will die. Jones and Houts (1992) have suggested that negative consequences are more likely when drinking is combined with verbal criticism and inhibited communication about feelings. Laybourn et al. (1996) uncovered children experiencing denigration, name-calling and threats, which all found very distressing.

Laybourn et al. (1996) found that one side effect of heavy drinking which had an unexpected impact on children was cessation of the drinking. For some children, non-drinking periods could be just as traumatic as drunken episodes. The withdrawal symptoms which drinkers experienced made them morose, bad-tempered or sensitive to disturbance. People experiencing alcohol withdrawal may complain of insomnia, agitation and hallucinatory states, depression, suicidal intent, sexual problems and self-neglect (Faculty of Public Health Medicine, 1991). Recovery can also pose new problems for the child: lax parents tighten up discipline and demands; drinkers expend a lot of emotional energy on their efforts to stay off alcohol permanently, reducing what they could give to their children; individual and group counselling takes up a lot of time, so lessening the time with the children; other psychological and emotional problems, masked by alcohol previously, emerge and have to be addressed; and reconciliation between previously warring partners could mean the child felt excluded (p59-60).

Further relevant issues are explored in the family domain later in this chapter.

Social presentation and selfcare skills

Virtually all children whose parents have an alcohol problem feel lonely and 'switched off', both from relationships within their family and

with other people (Brisby et al., 1997). Children may resist bringing friends home because they are too ashamed or embarrassed and they can't be sure what state their parent will be in when they get home. 'To be tormented with embarrassment and shame at their parents' behaviour, fearful of their friends or others finding out, or to have to hide the truth and take the full emotional impact of a problem drinker takes an immense toll of their self-esteem, and of their respect for their parents and themselves (Houston et al., 1997). Their confidence is also eroded.

Positive impact factors

Laybourn et al. (1996) have noted that we cannot assume that all the effects on children will be negative or that children will have difficulty coping. Many children do not realise the extent or seriousness of their parents' drinking, viewing it with amusement or indifference. Most children of alcoholic parents do reasonably well and some even shine. It is thus important to identify protective and supportive factors, which enable some children to cope well despite a parent's heavy drinking.

Some children describe positive effects of drink on their parents, for example depressed people cheered up, others become genial and generous, less 'narky' and more loving (Laybourn et al., 1996). Some describe the drinking as enjoyable, seeing the drunken behaviour funny. Whilst some children enjoyed the relaxed freedom from adult control, this had immediate potential safety issues and in the longer-term might shift to becoming indifference in schoolwork, and even contribute to poor school performance and attendance. Some children felt they achieved greater insight into other people's problems. Others identified beneficial side effects, such as enhanced academic motivation, improved coping skills, concern for others in difficulty and greater family closeness (Laybourn et al., 1996). In some families, alcohol may assist family functioning and play a part in maintaining family stability.

Resilience and protective mechanisms

Protective factors that ameliorate negative outcomes for these children are important. The results of studies have shown that children who have better outcomes have had more peer support, are more likely to have had a supportive and nurturing relationship with the non-addicted parent and to have lived in a family with structure and routines. Negative outcomes were related to having fewer financial resources, greater disorganisation, and to earlier parental loss as a result of divorce, death, or other factors (Emshoff and Anyan, 1991).

Some children are remarkably stress-resistant to trauma and a number of factors may contribute to such resilience. Some are external, such as educational opportunities and supportive adults, but others are internal such as abilities, talents, temperament and self-esteem (Werner, 1986).

Laybourn et al. (1996) found that whilst the impact on children varied with age, most children started to see their parent's drinking behaviour as abnormal when they were between eight and ten. Many of these children made proactive efforts to deal with parental drinking, either by trying to tackle the drinking problem itself or handling the emotions aroused by it. They did so in a variety of ways. Some retreated to their rooms to keep away from the sight of the drinking and resultant behaviour (although they could still hear the arguments); some kept a careful eye on the drinker for warning signs, motivated by a need to know what was going on; some focused their energies on other activities, which could include the expression of their anger and frustration through anti-social behaviour (male) or pro-social behaviour (female); or they internalised their feelings of anger and frustration through self-blame, resulting in isolation from peers. Where children had close relationships with the non-drinking parent, they had a positive role model of living with an alcoholic, and they received support and advice on how to cope with the drinker, emotional support, and this gave a sense of responsibility shared. Where children shared their experiences with siblings, this facilitated the sharing of problems and often led to relief and a reduced risk of self-blame. Grandparents were also a significant source of support.

Children seem to survive quite well as long as the level of family conflict is low, parents enforce family rules in a reasonably consistent way and there is some sort of regular pattern to life. They also benefit if the drinker acknowledges that it is his or her problem and not the children who are to blame (Brisby et al., 1997). For a more detailed review of the literature on risk, resilience, vulnerability and protective mechanisms, the reader is referred to Calder et al. (2001).

Parenting Capacity

A parent with a drinking problem causes all sorts of havoc within a family: the problem disrupts the cohesion of the parental and family relationships, or one or both parents may emotionally withdraw from the child. The child may respond in a variety of ways, probably leading to lowered self-esteem, anxiety, emotional detachment, perceived isolation, and so on. They may also develop ambivalent and conflicting attitudes to alcohol – negative because it causes so many problems, yet positive because parents have modelled the use of alcohol as a way of coping with problems, albeit a not very effective one.

(Velleman, 2001, p180).

The impact of heavy drinking on children acts through its effects on parental behaviour and competence, affecting parenting skills, contributing to inconsistency, poorer monitoring and supervision. There are several reasons for this. A drinking parent may swing between loving, entertaining, withdrawn, depressed, violent and argumentative, all within a very short space of time.

When parents become aggressive when drunk, this is frightening to most children. They will experience emotional ups and downs with them witnessing arguments and separations, not always being clear about how serious a situation will become. Many children described further uncertainty and insecurity of living in families where domestic violence is a regular occurrence (Houston et al., 1997). Close to half of the wives of men at an alcoholism clinic reported violence and physical harm from their husbands (Orford et al., 1975). O'Farrell and Murphy (1995) found that married men undergoing alcoholism treatment were four times more likely to have physically abused their wives than demographically matched non-alcoholic males.

When children witness domestic violence against the other parent or the home, this represents a frightening threat to the person and place, which normally provide a strong sense of security for children. Some children may become involved in protecting one parent from the other, often by physically intervening in domestic violence incidents; whilst others may be mediators between them. Many may have seen their parents' unconscious, injured and bleeding, vomiting or incontinent and have had to deal with these situations (Brisby et al., 1997). Some children may stay away from school or not go out to visit friends in order to try and prevent a parental argument or to protect a parent (Wilson and Orford, 1978). It is likely that children brought up by violent parents model their behaviour on this example and learn that violence may be an effective means to control others or to express feelings of frustration or hostility. For more detailed discussions of the impact of domestic violence on children the reader is referred to Rowsell (Chapter 16) and Calder (forthcoming).

Some children can be violent towards one of their parents, usually the drinker. Some attack the drinking parent in order to protect the non-drinker whilst others use violence as a way of releasing pent-up emotions (Wilson, 1980). Younger children sometimes report feelings of frustration and helplessness because they are not strong enough to stand up to an aggressive parent or to protect one parent from the violence of another.

In some circumstances, the children and their non-abusive parent will leave the home (for a Women's Refuge) which can be more distressing and compound the damage done by the actual behaviour they either witnessed or were caught up in. This may be because they often have to change schools, leave close friends and family behind. In some cases, the children witness the non-drinking parent turn to drink due to the pressures of their new situation. For mothers who had insufficient money to leave, then the children are subjected to an ongoing, often escalating, pattern of abuse (see Calder, forthcoming, for a review). Marital conflict is frequently cited by women as a reason for starting to drink heavily or for seeking help (Wilson, 1980).

The drinker's preoccupation with alcohol-focused activities can lead to the partner taking on full organisational responsibilities for the family. In effect, the partner begins to function as a one-parent family, with an additional dependant – their problem-drinking partner. The responsibility entailed in not only dealing single-handedly with everyday family affairs, but also coping with alcohol problems, can lead to considerable emotional strains for the partner. There becomes less time to relax and take care of their needs. As daily life deteriorates and become crises, the partner may blame him/herself for not coping, experiencing anxiety and depressive states, instead of looking to the drinking partner to help the family (Fanti, 1990, p130). They may experience sexual difficulties in the relationship (Wilson, 1984), suffer increasing social isolation as old friends are lost and new friends may be focused

exclusively on the drinking lifestyle. The drinker thus controls their partner's life and the more control they have, the less opportunity the spouse has to leave. In many cases, the woman will assume the role of breadwinner and be working full-time outside the home as well as taking full responsibility for the domestic management and the care of the children. Not surprisingly, women in this position are frequently exhausted, physically and emotionally, and may show a number of symptoms of physical or psychological disturbance (Wilson, 1980, p112). In some circumstances it is the non-drinking parent who abuses the children as a response to the stress they feel trying to keep the family together.

There are other possible outcomes from the impact on the spouse. Firstly, they may need to escape themselves and leave the children with the drinker, probably as they feel they have nowhere to go and no means of supporting the children. Secondly, they may turn to drink themselves as a coping mechanism, particularly where domestic violence is heavily featured or they may be responding to their own history, which may be why they were sought as a partner by their spouse. Kent (1990) identified that women's self-worth can be undermined by such heavy drinking, inducing a downward spiral of self blame, guilt, helplessness, and increased drinking develops as alcohol problems become more severe.

Whilst some alcoholic parents are able to sustain basic responsibilities (such as physical care) and are proud of this achievement, we always need to explore whether they have provided the children with the necessary attention, affection and emotional security.

Heavy drinking increases the likelihood of absenteeism from work or job loss, which has knock-on effects for family income. In adults, alcohol is associated with depression, anxiety and other psychiatric problems, including suicide. Physical health may also be affected, as alcohol is associated with disorders of the stomach, liver and brain.

Alcohol use has an increased prevalence in persons with psychiatric disorders (Mueser and Kavanagh, 2001) and this presents multi-faceted challenges for workers. These include accurate diagnosis, consideration as to whether they are treated separately or in an integrated way, and whether there is any real potential for sustained or significant change. For a detailed discussion of change, see Chapter 2.

Family and environmental factors

Children do not respond to parental drinking in isolation. Both the drinking and children's reactions are part of a complex set of inter-relationships and activities within the household. Parental alcohol misuse clearly affects all aspects of family functioning. The ordinary routines of family life are fraught with difficulties because drinkers tend to behave in unpredictable ways, swinging between aggressive and violent, silently withdrawn, or talkative and emotional (Brisby et al., 1997). Indirect consequences of drunken behaviour include separations, multiple changes of address and financial problems. Some changes associated with periods of abstaining also created difficulties (Laybourn et al., 1996).

Alcohol misuse is thus usually a problem for the whole family. It affects not only the person who is dependent but all those who come into regular contact with them, especially family members. It is also believed that families with alcohol problems are dysfunctional and, for this reason, do not provide the optimal environment for rearing children. The extent of the effects depends on the extent to which the child's environment is affected. This depends on how 'dysfunctional' the family is or becomes, how much other pathology is present, the extent to which addiction affects the family's financial status, and how the relationship between parent and child is maintained or impaired.

Two patterns of dysfunctional families have been described as associated with addiction: these are the 'enmeshed' family and the 'unorganised' family (Coles, 1995b).

Enmeshed families

Families of middle-class alcoholics are often described as enmeshed because they limit contact with others outside the family who might provide social support or stimulation for the children. This pattern is believed to be due to unspoken rules that operate in such families: don't talk and don't trust. These rules have been developed to protect the current organisation of the family and support the denial of the alcohol misuse within such families. Children's needs may be ignored because the family's attention is focused on the parent who is drinking. The parent's behaviour often has to be carefully monitored to avoid negative consequences. The family lives are often characterised by inconsistency and uncertainty. Discipline may be dependent on whether or not the parent is drinking. Family rules may apply in one situation and forgotten in others. A parent who is affectionate and considerate when sober may be violent and inconsiderate when intoxicated. Promises made in one state may not be remembered in another. Parents who misuse alcohol may not have the time, energy or judgement that are required for competent parenting. In addition, alcohol is a disinhibitor: that is, it may either impair judgement or provide the excuse for behaving impulsively so that the individual who would not usually react violently may do so when drinking. Similarly, sexual abuse of children often occurs in families where substance abuse is common, and the alcohol may be disinhibiting or may be used as an excuse for conduct the abuser wishes to indulge in anyway (see Calder, 1999; 2000; 2001 for detailed discussions on this point).

Unorganised families

This pattern is often seen among underprivileged individuals but can be observed in middle- and upper-class families as well. In the unorganised family, the family structure may be more open because of a lack of consistent rules about behaviour, lack of supervision of children, single-parent status, financial problems, and similar factors. Children in such situations are often neglected because there may be no adult available to care for them when their parent is using alcohol, and they may be abused sexually because of a lack of supervision. Children's basic needs may be overlooked because no one may be taking responsibility for providing for them. Children in such families can have many different responses, although a frequently identified pattern is the 'parentified' child ('young carer') who takes on the care of younger siblings as well as of the incompetent parent. The family environment may not support or facilitate the child's learning, and academic goals for the child may be subservient to more immediate needs for drink seeking and other activities. Children are often described as lacking in self-esteem and as having more psychopathology than other children (Emshell and Anyan, 1991). When children have learned that their alcohol-misusing parent is not trustworthy, they may fail to trust other people they encounter, which will limit their ability to interact in the world. Some children may fail to establish an appropriate attachment to a caregiver during their first few years and this can create a range of future problems, including a lack of empathy for others.

Alcoholism is thus characterised as a family disease in that family members participate in the dysfunctional behaviour of the alcoholic by assuming individual and complementary dysfunctional behaviours. The family's attempts to cope with the alcoholic follow a progressive course, paralleling the progression of alcoholism. Thus, as the alcoholism worsens the family takes more extreme measures in order to adjust. The initial coping mechanism is denial, with family members denying that a problem exists by simply not talking about it or by adjusting family responsibilities so that the alcoholic's neglect of routine tasks is not apparent. The next stage involves attempts to eliminate the problem (discarding the alcohol or encouraging the alcoholic to get help). When such efforts fail, the family system may become more disorganised. Family members are then more likely to initiate efforts to reorganise in order to create a sense of normality. When these fail, one or more family members may try to escape (e.g. through divorce, running away). Finally part of the family may try to reorganise itself in order to meet the needs of some of the members. This may involve one or more of the members seeking professional help (Nastasi and DeZolt, 1994).

Communication in families with alcohol problems is often circular and non-productive, consisting of a large proportion of nagging, bickering, sarcastic comments, and sharp rebukes (Paolino and McCrady, 1977). It is not uncommon to find that the whole family rarely talks together and that family members find difficulty in giving direct expression of needs, dissatisfactions or appreciation (Wilson, 1980). Communication within the family may become disrupted (content and emotional quality). Drinking parents may be silent, incoherent, sentimental or garrulous (Brisby et al., 1997).

Fanti (1990) argued that the problems for the family can be broken down into three main areas: physical, psychological and social:

1. Physical: The family may experience alcohol-related poverty leading to nutritional neglect, insufficient fuel, clothing and poor housing conditions. Holidays may be rare and other family treats, such as eating out together and day trips may be similarly infrequent or absent.

2. Psychological: Wegscheider (1981) suggests that each family member takes on a specific family role in an attempt to counterbalance the difficulties brought on by problem drinking. These roles enable the family to function despite its alcohol focus, keeping together a system that would otherwise fall apart. The roles are set out in Figure 2.
3. Social: The family as a whole may experience gradual social isolation from relatives and friends. Any new family friends are more likely to have a similar alcohol-focused life themselves. In families with serious hardship, statutory agencies may become involved in helping the family to resolve short-term crises and to place boundaries on family behaviour where these have not been internally set.

When one family member ceases to play his/her allocated roles within the family, other members must take over the vacant role positions if the family unit is to continue to function. Taking an additional role responsibility may place a strain on the individual concerned, which can lead to symptoms of physical and psychological disorder. Thus role changes, increased role responsibility and the failure to take on vacant role positions are important factors mediating the impact of a crisis such as alcoholism on family members (Wilson, 1980, p111).

Drinking patterns are relevant to any discussion on family roles. Women often drink at home, alone, often drinking steadily throughout the day, only rarely becoming intoxicated to the point of losing control or being unable to do their housework (Dahlgren 1978). In contrast, men more typically drink in company, out of the home and may be more likely to become very drunk on each drinking occasion. The ability of the drinker to perform family roles, and thus the extent of role change within the family, will depend greatly on the frequency of intoxication, the time of day when drinking occurs, and the extent to which drunkenness is incapacitating.

The timing and frequency of drinking is likely to have important consequences. Seilhamer et al (1993) indicated that children are more adversely affected by their father's drinking when this occurs in the early evening – the usual 'prime time' for father-child interaction. The pattern of drinking by the parent will affect the degree of exposure the child has to the

Figure 2: Family roles (Wegscheider, 1981).

Roles	Description
The enabler	The family member who is emotionally closest to the problem drinker usually takes on the role of 'the enabler'. Their role is to support the alcohol misuser, allowing them to function as freely as possible whilst avoiding their drinking consequences. The enabler delays the crises that may threaten the problem drinker, which in turn threaten the family stability. They regularly cover for the drinker's behaviour and take over the responsibility for maintaining the family. Where the problem drinker is a parent, the enabler is usually the spouse. The enabler is most likely to be the eldest child where the problem drinker is a single parent.
The hero	Their role is to be the figurehead of the family in terms of achievement and they become the symbol on to which the family pins its fantasy that everything is OK. As such, they are denied demonstrating how they feel and this reinforces the need to do better each time to gain praise. They tend to have low self-esteem, feeling guilty and inadequate as they may be unable to reach the distant targets they constantly set for themselves. Typically, the hero is the eldest child in the family with one or more parents with drinking problems.
The scapegoat	They attract attention through troublesome behaviour. Always defiant and anti-social, they become the hook on which to hang the family's troubles. At times of impending family crisis, the scapegoat acts to distract the family from the possible problem, rescuing the family by attracting attention to their own behaviour. They are openly blamed for all the family's troubles – the 'black sheep' of the family.
The lost child	Like the scapegoat, 'the lost child' fails to secure regular family attention and through unassertive behaviour, unlike the scapegoat, causes no difficulties. Almost invisible to other family members, the lost child is isolated, unadventurous, and has poor self-worth.
The mascot	The 'mascot' has much in common with the scapegoat and the lost child. They are the family joker, providing the light relief in a stressful environment. Often inappropriate in action, they compulsively fight for attention through humour, which disguises their own real sense of fear.

consequences. Where the parent returns home in an incapable, aggressive or depressed state, the children may be fearful and apprehensive as a result. Where the parent does not get very drunk, the children may be less afraid or upset by the drinking, although they may be confused about inconsistent behaviour and even disapprove of it quite strongly. The amount of marital conflict or violence may similarly depend upon the frequency of drinking episodes, the presence or absence of aggressive moods accompanying drinking or drunkenness, or the ability of the drinker to perform tasks within the family (Wilson, 1980).

There is a potential for families to split into opposing camps with children allied to one or other of the parents. The parents may compete for the children's loyalty. Whilst this is often the non-drinking parent as they are more likely to offer the child protection, offering support and advice about coping with the drinker, there are costs if they have to act as informers, monitoring the drinking consumption of the drinker (Laybourn et al., 1996). Many children lacked respect for the drinking parent either because they were allowed to run riot or because they viewed their behaviour with embarrassment and contempt.

From an ecological perspective, the experiences a child has within their family context provide them with a frame of reference for interpreting other social environments and for guiding social interactions in other contexts. As the individual seeks or elicits similar experiences across contexts, the cognitions and behaviours initially learned within the alcoholic family are reinforced and become characteristic patterns for interpreting and interacting with other social contexts. Unless other frames of reference and interpersonal experiences are provided for the developing child, the experiences within the alcoholic family are expected to have long-term influence on the individual's adjustment both within and outside the family system (Nastasi and DeZolt, 1994).

Laybourn et al. (1996) identified that alcohol is part of our culture and problem drinking has to be seen in the context of what is considered 'normal' and socially acceptable. They found that in certain areas of poor housing and high unemployment, some parents clearly regarded heavy drinking as a way of life rather than a shameful secret. It also appears that in certain areas a degree of heavy drinking is considered acceptable for men, particularly if it takes place in the evenings. Again, this creates little embarrassment or need for secrecy. They found a different kind of heavy drinking norm in middle class families, associated with party going and entertaining among friends who all drank in similar fashion. In some rural areas, the pub is the focus of community life, and thus considered an essential venue for social and practical networking.

A framework for intervention

Alcohol-related problems involve health problems, psychological problems and social problems. In this respect, people who drink too much are no different to other social services' clients, and consequently the services they require are no different (Collins and Keene, 2000). Social workers are most likely to intervene in circumstances which may be causes and/or consequences of excessive drinking, bereavement, domestic violence, relationship difficulties, problems in parenting, sexual abuse, and mental and physical ill-health (Kent, 1990, p101). In the child protection arena, many parents dispute their problems are attributable to alcohol. There are various reasons why this may be so: a level of denial which means the drinker doesn't admit it is a problem; uncertainty about who might help; guilt or shame which might prevent an open discussion of all the facts surrounding a problem (Leckie, 1990, p45).

Assessment of the adults drinking is a key skill for workers and should preferably be undertaken jointly with a specialist alcohol service provider. Workers do need to obtain information about the amounts of alcohol consumed, types of alcohol consumed, length of time that alcohol has been consumed, frequency of alcohol consumption, setting/location for drinking, companions' for drinking, physical effects, psychological effects, social/relationship effects and legal/financial issues. It is by exploring such areas and broader aspects such as family history and relationships, education background, and present or past contact with other agencies that social workers and the adult

would be jointly in a better-informed position to assess strengths, weaknesses, stage of change, possible tasks for intervention, and targets for change (Collins and Keene, 2000).

It is not always easy to put together the interrelationships between individual personalities, their use of drink, its history, and their family and social functioning. Collins and Keene (2000) provided us with a useful framework to consider the above (see Figure 3 overleaf).

The more the extreme the drink problem, the more the user's psychological state will be influenced. Pre-existing levels of anxiety and depression will be exacerbated by drinking and provide additional impetus for it. What matters are that the two interact and can accelerate drinking. Poor relationships and difficult family life will be made worse by problem drinking and problem drinking can escalate. Equally, positive interactions can be established so that reduced drinking can lead to improved self-esteem, lower levels of anxiety and depression and better relationships with family and friends. The key point is that various aspects of a problem drinker's life may need to be worked on and just reducing or stopping drinking may not be sufficient in itself (Saunders, 1994). The interface or interaction between drinking behaviour, the individual's psychological state and social functioning, all offer possibilities for effective intervention. Billings and Moos (1983) found those who had overcome drink problems had significantly higher levels of family support, job satisfaction (where possible) and fewer negative life events and better coping skills. Havassy et al. (1991) found that close friends, sound partner relationships and strong group affiliations were significantly associated with moving away from, and successfully avoiding, drink problems. Thus there is an obvious need to focus on social as well as psychological functioning and social workers are ideally placed to help in such matters.

In order to deal with alcohol misuse it is necessary to provide support to prevent the kind of problems that cause it (such as stress and depression), help with the kind of problems that arise from it, and to deal with physical and psychological dependency. Collins and Keene (2000) developed an assessment grid (see Figure 4 overleaf) to provide a structure for understanding, identifying and assessing different types of alcohol problems. This can and should be used at the outset and then

Figure 3: Adapted from Saunders (1994).

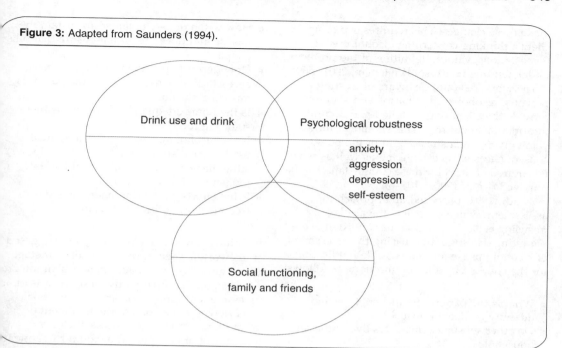

Figure 4: Assessment grid (adapted from Collins and Keene, 2000).

Problems	Intoxication	Heavy use	Dependency
Social	Relationships	Financial problems Unemployment Criminal offences	Isolation Sexual problems Self-neglect Lack of social and life skills Homelessness
Psychological	Mood swings	Depression Anxiety	Depression Anxiety Poor self-esteem Disinhibition and aggression Suicide attempts Hallucinations Paranoia
Physical	Accidents/assaults Lack of motor coordination Hangovers	Ill health Blackouts	Tolerance of large quantities of alcohol Withdrawal symptoms Craving for alcohol Delirium tremens Epileptic fits

eriodically repeated as the process of tervention unfolds and the client's problems nd needs change.

Workers need to understand the drinker's ehaviour in the context of their life as a whole mily, employment, social) and in working ith the client to identify the pros and cons of their drinking pattern. The social worker also needs to make a careful assessment of the client's alcohol use, their drinking behaviour, severity of drinking, the severity of harm and the effects of use, and the degree of difficulty the client might experience in changing the pattern, and how ready they are (if at all) to try and make these changes. This requires exploring the client's thinking concerning alcohol use (expectations, values, definition of the problem, understanding its cause) (Velleman, 2001, p69).

The worker should be aware of existing or potential alcohol-related harms and should provide the client with detailed and accurate information about this. This should include being given a realistic account of the possible consequences of their drinking as well as what is required of them for these circumstances to be removed (Kent, 1990, p105–6).

Swadi (1994) proposed an approach to assessment, which considers the alcohol misusing behaviour within the context of overall parenting. He suggested basing the assessment of alcohol misuse and its possible implications for the child on a series of questions as follows:

- What is the pattern, frequency, type and quantity of alcohol misuse?
- Do other substance mis-users live in the same household?
- How dependent is the parent on other alcohol users for their social interaction?
- Are the children involved in the alcohol misuse?
- What is the pattern of childcare when the parent is under the influence of alcohol?
- Are the children protected from exposure to the alcohol and its effects?
- What is the effect on child care of any criminal activity or imprisonment, or of absences when drinking?

- How is the money obtained to sustain the misuse and does the parent ensure that bills are paid?
- How dependent is the provision of basic necessities on whether or not the parent is misusing alcohol?
- Is the home adequately clean and is there sufficient food?
- Is the alcohol misuse accompanied by a psychiatric disorder and what effect does either have on the parent's cognitive state and judgements?
- What efforts have been made towards treatment and with what results?

Collins and Keene (2000) go on to suggest a framework for action consisting of four stages (see Figure 5 below). Each stage has an integral assessment. The first, motivation, consists of an assessment of motivation and motivational interviewing. The second, the treatment or counselling for change process, includes assessment of change and action for treatment or counselling for change. The third stage is maintenance, which includes assessment for maintenance of change and the actual maintenance of change. Finally, relapse prevention consists of assessment for intervention at relapse and return to change, and maintenance of it.

Collins and Keene (2000) go on to provide us with a framework to match individuals with appropriate interventions commensurate with their stage in the change process, and this is

Figure 5: Framework for action.

Intervention	Assessment grid
a. Motivational interviewing	Assess for motivation
b. The treatment/counselling for change process	Assess for treatment/counselling for change
c. Maintenance of change	Assess for maintenance of change
d. Relapse intervention	Assess for reintervention and return to change

Figure 6: Issues for the children.

Stage	Features	Focus of intervention
Pre-contemplation	Lack of concern about drinking. Benefits of drinking outweigh costs.	Harm reduction. Increase commitment to change. Inform and educate about healthy, and consequences of unhealthy drinking. Encourage making links between drinking and impact factors for the children and the family.
Contemplation	Considering stopping or reducing drinking. Wanting information. Some awareness of drinking linked with concerns for children.	Increase consciousness of problem and commitment to change behaviour by information giving, motivational interviewing, assessment and self-monitoring of drinking.
Action	Making active, committed efforts to stop or cut down drinking. Wanting to use help. Seeing costs of drinking.	Behavioural self-control, monitoring of drinking, setting goals, modifying lifestyles, social skills training, using problem solving methods, changing behaviour.
Maintenance	Maintain behaviour change, reduced drinking, or no drinking.	Continue commitment to new behaviours, new lifestyle. Vigilance to risky situations. Relapse prevention and management.

Figure 7: Indicators for and against controlled drinking (Velleman, 2001- from Heather and Robertson, 1983 and Ward, 1988).

Those more likely to succeed with controlled drinking	Those more likely to succeed with total abstinence
• Those choosing controlled drinking • Those who are younger • Those in employment • Those with a family around them • Those with a shorter history of misuse • Those with less physical, mental, or social harm caused by their drinking • Those with lower consumption before coming for help • Those showing no signs of physical dependence	• Those choosing abstinence • Those who are older • Those who have no social stability in terms of stable relationships, employment and accommodation • Those with less support from family or friends • Those with a longer history of heavy drinking • Those suffering from physical damage such as liver disease, or mental damage such as memory loss • Those who have tried and failed to control their drinking • Those who are more severely dependent in terms of having more physiological indices, such as more severe withdrawal, high (or reversed) tolerance, etc.

more likely to lead to a successful outcome which we have adapted to focus on issues for the children (see Figure 6 above).

Velleman (2001) provided some useful indicators for and against controlled drinking (see Figure 7 above), which is useful when setting realistic targets for the drinking parent.

In most relationships when a partner's drinking is causing overt physical, practical or emotional problems, the other partner will experience conflict and distress. The woman needs to be given 'permission' to talk about the

role alcohol plays in her personal and family relationships. She needs to be given clear and honest information about whether what she talks about will be passed on to anyone else. She needs to be shown that the worker is 'on her side' and will work with her at her own pace. She will need to unload her fears, anger, and feelings of loyalty, confusion and self-blame. Confrontation between the woman and her partner often follows such an unloading (Kent, 1990, p119).

There will likely be multiple relationship problems that need exploring. The worker needs to understand the drinking behaviour and needs of the adult, but to be always very clear about the point at which it infringes the rights of the child. Velleman (2001) suggested that we assess the following:

- Family structure: the way a family is structured often provides a useful insight into both how problems may have evolved and how they might be tackled. Family structure can include such issues as who has the power; who does what; what are the age and sex boundaries.
- Family processes: how does the family conduct itself? Where are the alliances? Where is the hostility – at which individual or set of individuals, or at which alliance is it directed? Families usually have a state to which they return if events knock them off balance.

- Family history: is crucial if we are to uncover signposts to the origins of the problems. For example, is there a history of problem drinking, or other excessive behaviour, in either side of the family?
- Family patterns of communication: Who talks to whom, about what, and when? Who keeps secrets from whom? Who has alliances with whom and about what?
- Family functioning: what does the family do easily/with difficulty? What are these things and how can they be used to develop an intervention strategy to help the family?
- Family life cycle: where are they (such as the recent birth of a baby, death of a family member, someone leaving home)? How has this affected the problem and why has this problem presented now?
- Family crisis: what is the crisis and how has it affected the family? (p176-7).

A framework for assessing the risks to children

1. Factors related to the alcohol/drug dependency

Elevated Risk
- Total denial
- Lack of information about the cycle of addiction
- The person with the alcohol/drug dependency has no insight into factors underpinning his/her dependency
- Behaviour under the influence of alcohol/drug which poses a risk to children
- Extreme loss of personal control when using or as a result of using alcohol or drugs
- Drink/drugs/equipment are left around the house
- The person with an alcohol/drug dependency problem has a social network of others who are dependant or dealers, who come into contact with the children
- Distance/or lack of availability of assessment/treatment resources
- Unwilling to join and regularly attend a treatment programme
- Refusal to co-operate with Child Protection worker
- Unemployment

Lowered Risk
- Admission of the problem or partial admission of problem
- Knowledge of the cycle of addiction
- Awareness of the context/trigger factors in the dependency problem
- The person who has the dependency problem and/or the partner priorities the needs and safety of the children
- Clear evidence of very controlled alcohol/drug use
- An adult in the household ensuring the drink/drugs/equipment used by the person with the dependency problem is out of reach of children
- The social network around the family is one where the misuse of alcohol/drugs is recognised as harmful
- Local resources for the assessment/treatment of people with alcohol/drug dependency problems
- Willing to attend treatment programme
- Co-operation with Child Protection investigation workers and system
- The demand of regular employment which acts as external inhibitors

2. Factors relating to the partner

Elevated Risk
- Partner who also has alcohol/drug dependency problems
- Partner refusing to talk about the alcohol or drug dependency partner's problems and behaviour
- Socially isolated partner of the person who has the dependency problems
- Alcohol/drug dependency which is hidden from family
- Partner who is victim of violence or aggression from the person with a dependency problem
- Absence of a personal supportive relationship

Lowered Risk
- Partner who does not have an alcohol/drug dependency problem
- Partner who is aware of the alcohol/drug dependency and is able to talk about it
- Network of practical social and emotional support for the partner of the person with dependency problems
- One or more adults in the family network aware of the alcohol/drug dependency problem
- Partner who is able to act independently and has positive self regard
- A supportive partner

3. Concerns about the children

Elevated Risk
- Parents with personal problems past or present which mean the needs and care of the children are not a priority
- House which is in disarray, dirty, with demonstrated lack of attention to safety for children
- Babies/small children who are physically dependent on care
- Alcohol/drug dependency problem of the parent leaves children emotionally isolated
- Children unaware of the causes of the behaviour of the alcohol/drug dependent person
- Children missing school
- Children not coping with work in school
- Children have relationship problems with peers/adults
- Children isolated from extended family/local community

Lowered Risk
- Parents prioritise the needs and care of the children
- House is clean and safe, children are physically cared for
- Age/developmental stage of the child which means child is able to manage some self-help successfully
- Children have regular access to emotional support from a supportive adult.
- When children can name the problem of alcohol/drug dependency problem to concerned others
- Children attend school regularly
- Children cope with school work at a level commensurate with age and ability
- Children making socially appropriate relationships with peers/adults
- Adult in family/community network available to offer care and support to children

4. The professional system

Elevated Risk
- Absence of timely professional intervention
- Lack of co-operation between the professional network
- Conflict within the professional network
- Only short-term work and support is available

Lowered Risk
- Possibility of prompt supportive professional intervention over time
- Information sharing and co-operation between agencies in the professional network
- Shared professional understanding of the problem and the ways to intervene
- Planned intervention consistently available over time

Conclusions

The severity of the effect of drinking on children varies from family to family. Children, like adults, have differing needs, which will change as they grow older and their situations change. It is for these reasons that any assessment should consider the broad range of potential impacts of parental alcohol misuse. In considering outcomes from the core assessment, workers need to consider the ability of the parent to control their alcohol misuse, the quality of the parent-child relationships, the child's overall presentation, behaviour, self-esteem, and levels of attainment. This information will inform the decision as to whether the child can remain living at home safely. Improving family functioning is likely to reduce the long-term harm caused to children in such situations.

References

Alcohol Concern (1997) *Measures for Measures: A Framework for Alcohol Policy.* London: Alcohol Concern.

American Psychological Association (1993) *Violence and Youth: Psychology's Response.* Summary report on violence and youth. Washington, DC: APA.

Bays, J. (1990) Substance Abuse and Child Abuse: The Impact of Addiction on the Child. *Pediatric Clinics of North America.* 37: 881–904.

Billings, A. and Moos, R. (1983) Psychosocial Processes of Recovery Among Alcoholics and Their Families. *Addictive Behaviour.* 8: 205–18.

Brisby, T., Baker, S. and Hedderwick, T. (1997) *Under the Influence: A Report on the Needs of Children of Problem Drinking Parents.* London: Alcohol Concern.

Cadoret, R.J., Cain, C.A, and Grove, W.M. (1980) Development of Alcoholism in Adoptees Raised Apart From Biologic Relatives. *Archives of General Psychiatry.* 37: 561–3.

Calder, M.C. (2000) *The Complete Guide to Sexual Abuse Assessments.* Dorset: Russell House Publishing.

Calder, M.C. (2001) *Juveniles and Children Who Sexually Abuse: Frameworks for Assessment.* (2nd edn.) Dorset: Russell House Publishing.

Calder, M.C. (forthcoming) *Children Living With Domestic Violence: Empirically-grounded Frameworks for Assessment and Intervention.* Dorset: Russell House Publishing.

Calder, M.C. with Skinner, J. and Hampson, A. (1999) *Assessing Risk in Adult Males Who Sexually Abuse Children: A Practitioner's Guide.* Dorset: Russell House Publishing.

Calder, M.C. with Peake, A. and Rose, K. (2001) *Mothers of Sexually Abused Children: A Framework for Assessment, Understanding and Support.* Dorset: Russell House Publishing.

Coles C.D. (1993) Impact of prenatal alcohol exposure on the newborn and the child. Clinical Obstetrics and Gynaecology 36(2): 255–66.

Coles, C.D. (1995) Children of Parents Who Abuse Drugs and Alcohol. In Smith, G.H., Coles, C.D., Poulsen, M.K. and Cole, C.K. (Eds.) *Children, Families and Substance Abuse: Challenges for Changing Educational and Social Outcomes.* Baltimore: Paul H Brookes Publishing Company, 3–23.

Coles, C.D. (1995b) Addiction and Recovery: Impact of Substance Abuse on Families. In Smith, G.H., Coles, C.D., Poulsen, M.K. and Cole, C.K. (Eds.) *Children, Families and Substance Abuse: Challenges for Changing Educational and Social Outcomes.* Baltimore: Paul H Brookes Publishing Company, 25–56.

Collins, S. (Ed.) (1990) *Alcohol, Social Work, and Helping.* London: Tavistock/Routledge.

Collins, S. and Keene, J. (2000) *Alcohol, Social Work and Community Care.* Birmingham: Venture Press.

Cork, R.M. (1969) *The Forgotten Children: A Study of Children With Alcoholic Parents.* Toronto: Alcoholism and Drug Research Foundation of Ontario.

Dahlgren, L. (1978) Female Alcoholics: III Development and Maintenance of Problem Drinking. *Acta Psychiatrica Scandanavia.* 57: 325–55.

Edelstein, S.B. (1995) *Children With Prenatal Alcohol and Other Drug Exposure: Weighing the Risks of Adoption.* Washington DC: CWLA Press.

Emshoff, J.G. and Anyan, I.L. (1991) From Prevention to Treatment: Issues for School-Aged Children of Alcoholics. In Galanter, M. (Ed.) *Recent Developments in Alcoholism. Volume 9: Children of Alcoholics.* NY: Plenum Press, 327–46.

Faculty of Public Health Medicine (1991) *Alcohol and the Public Health.* London: Macmillan.

Fanti, G. (1987) Clients Aren't the Only Ones With Alcohol Problems. *Community Care.* 16th Apr. vi–viii.

Fanti, G. (1990) Helping the Family. In Collins, S. (Ed.) *Alcohol, Social Work and Helping.* London: Tavistock/Routledge, 125–52.

Goddard, E. and Ikin, C. (1988) *Drinking in England and Wales in 1987, OPCS Social Surveys Division, SS1283*. London: HMSO.

Hamilton, C.J. and Collins, J.J. (1981) The Role of Alcohol in Wife Beating and Child Abuse: A Review of the Literature. In Wolfgang, M.E. (Ed.) *Drinking and Crime: Perspectives on the Relationships Between Alcohol Consumption and Criminal Behaviour*. NY: The Guilford Press, 253–87.

Harburg, E., DiFranceisco, W., Webster, D.W., Gleiberman, L. and Schork, A. (1990) Family Transmission of Alcohol Use. *Journal of Studies on Alcohol*. 51: 245–56.

Harden, B.J. (1998) Building Bridges for Children: Addressing the Consequences of Exposure to Drugs and the Child Welfare System. In Hampton, R.L., Senatore, V. and Gullotta, T.P. (Eds.) *Substance Abuse, Family Violence, and Child Welfare: Bridging Perspectives*. Thousand Oaks, Ca: Sage Publications, Inc, 18–61.

Havassy, B,, Hall, S. and Wassermam, D. (1991) Social Support and Relapse: Commonalities Among Alcoholics, Opiate Users and Cigarette Smokers. *Addictive Behaviour*. 16: 235–46.

Heather, N. and Robertson, I. (1983) *Controlled Drinking*. (2nd edn.) London: Methuen.

HMSO (1996) *Living in Britain: Results from the 1994 General Household Survey*. London: HMSO.

Houston, A., Kork, S. and MacLeod, M. (1997) *Beyond the Limit: Children Who Live With Parental Alcohol Misuse*. London: ChildLine.

Jenson, J.M. (1997) Risk and Protective Factors for Alcohol and Other Drug Use in Childhood and Adolescence. In Fraser, M.W. (Ed.) *Risk and Resilience in Childhood: an Ecological Perspective*. Washington, DC: NASW Press.

Johnson, J.L. and Rolf, J.E. (1990) When Children Change: Research Perspectives on Children of Alcoholics. In Collins, R.L., Leonard, K.E. and Searles, J.S. (Eds.) *Alcohol and the Family: Research and Clinical Perspectives*. NY: The Guilford Press, 162–93.

Jung, J. (2001) *Psychology of Alcohol and Other Drugs: A Research Perspective*. Thousand Oaks, Ca: Sage Publications, Inc.

Kent, R. (1990) Focusing on Women. In Collins, S. (Ed.) *Alcohol, Social Work and Helping*. London: Tavistock/Routledge, 96–124.

Laybourn, A., Brown, J. and Hill, M. (1996) *Hurting on the Inside: Children's Experiences of Parental Alcohol Misuse*. Aldershot: Avebury.

Leckie, T. (1990) Social Work and Alcohol. In Collins, S. (Ed.) *Alcohol, Social Work and Helping*. London: Tavistock/Routledge, 43–66.

Lynskey, M.T., Fergusson, D.M, and Horwood, J.L. (1994) The Effect of Parental Alcohol Problems on Rates of Adolescent Psychiatric Disorders. *Addiction*. 89.

Mueser, K.T. and Kavanagh, D. (2001) Treating Comorbidity of Alcohol Problems and Psychiatric Disorder. In Heather, N., Peters, T.J. and Stockwell, T. (Eds.) *International Handbook of Alcohol Dependence and Problems*. Chichester: John Wiley and Sons, Ltd, 627–47.

Morehouse, E.R. (1979) Working in the Schools of Children of Alcoholic Parents. *Health and Social Work*. 4: 4, 144–62.

Nastasi, B.K. and DeZolt, D.M. (1994) *School Interventions for Children of Alcoholics*. NY: The Guilford Press.

O'Farrell, T.J. (1990) Sexual Functioning of Male Alcoholics. In Collins, R.L., Leonard, K.E. and Searles, J.S. (Eds.) *Alcohol and the Family: Research and Clinical Perspectives*. NY: The Guilford Press, 244–71.

Orford, J. (1985) Alcohol Problems and the Family. In Lishman, J. and Horobin, G. (Eds.) *Approaches to Addiction*. London: Kogan Page.

Paolino, T.J. and McCrady, B.S. (1977) *The Alcoholic Marriage: Alternative Perspectives*. NY: Grune and Stratton.

Rosett, H. and Weiner, L. (1984) *Alcohol and the Foetus: a Clinical Perspective*. NY: Oxford University Press.

Saunders, B. (1994) The Cognitive Behavioural Approach to the Management of Addictive Behaviours. In Chick, J. and Cantwell, R. (Eds.) *Seminars in Alcohol and Drug Misuse*. London: Gaskell.

Schukit, M.A. (1991) A Longitudinal Study of Children of Alcoholics. In Galanter, M. (Ed.) *Recent Developments in Alcoholism. Volume 9: Children of Alcoholics*. NY: Plenum Press, 5–19.

Seilhamer, R.A., Jacob, T. and Dunn, N.J. (1993) The Impact of Alcohol Consumption on Parent-Child Relationships in Families of Alcoholics. *Journal of Studies on Alcohol*. 54: 89–98.

Seixas, J. (1979) *How to Cope With an Alcoholic Parent*. Edinburgh: Canongate.

Stafford, D. (1992) *Children of Alcoholics*. London: Piatkus.

Streissguth, A.P. (1986) The Behavioural Teratology of Alcohol: Performance, Behavioural and Intellectual Deficits in Prenatally Exposed Children. In West, J. (Ed.)

Alcohol and Brain Development. NY: Oxford University Press.

Swadi, H. (1994) Parenting Capacity and Substance Misuse: An Assessment Scheme. *ACPP Review and Newsletter*. 16: 237–44.

Velleman, R. (1992) *Counselling for Alcohol Problems*. London: Sage.

Velleman, R. (1993) *Alcohol and the Family*. London: Institute of Alcohol Studies.

Velleman, R. (2001) *Counselling for Alcohol Problems*. (2nd edn.) Thousand Oaks, Ca.: Sage Publications.

Velleman, R. and Orford, J. (1993) The Importance of Family Discord in Explaining Childhood Problems in the Children of Problem Drinkers. *Addiction Research*. 1: 39–57.

Ward, M. (1988) *Helping Problem Drinkers: A Practical Guide for the Caring Professions*. Canterbury: Kent Council on Addictions.

Wegscheider, S. (1981) *Another Chance: Hope and Health for the Alcoholic Family*. Palo Alto: Science and Behaviour Books.

Weiner, L. and Morse, B. (1988) FAS: Clinical Perspectives and Prevention. In Chasnoff, I.J (Ed.) *Drugs, Alcohol, Pregnancy and Parenting*. Boston: Kluwer.

Wilson, C. (1980) The Family. In Camberwell Council on Alcoholism (Eds.) *Women and Alcohol*. London: Tavistock Publications, 101–32.

Wilson, G.T. (1984) Alcohol and Sexual Function. *British Journal of Sexual Medicine*. Feb/March, 56–8.

Wilson, C. and Orford, J. (1978) Children of Alcoholics: Report of a Preliminary Study and Comments on the Literature. *Journal of Studies on Alcohol*. 39: 1, 121–42.

Wilson, G.S., McReary, R., Kean, J. and Baxter, C. (1979) The Development of Preschool Children of Heroin Addicted Mothers. *Pediatrics*. 63: 135–41.

Woodside, M. (1986) Children of Alcoholics: Breaking the Cycle. *Journal of School Health*. 56 448–9.

Chapter Twenty

The Assessment of Parental Substance Misuse and its Impact on Childcare

Michael Murphy and Fiona Harbin

Introduction

This chapter is not just about the assessment of childcare; it is about the difficult situation where family life, parenting and childcare are affected by significant parental substance misuse. The chapter begins by examining the crossover between substance misuse and parenting and subsequently the crossover between the childcare and substance misuse systems. It continues by exploring the usefulness, in this area of work, of the Assessment Framework (DoH, 2000), suggesting ways that the new framework can be developed and augmented to prove more effective in this assessment area. It ends with a discussion on the inclusion of the child's perspective and begins to explore what follows our assessment.

In a society in which substance use is the norm for many young people and parents, it is important to distinguish between *use* and *misuse* of substances. For the sake of this chapter we will use substance dependence as the key indicator of substance misuse. SCODA's definition of dependence is as follows:

> *'a compulsion or desire to continue taking a drug, or drugs in order to feel good or avoid feeling bad. The compulsion or desire is usually initiated following previous repeated use of the drug and is difficult to control'*

> (SCODA, 1997).

Our definition of a parent will be a wide one, including all those who take on a parenting role with regard to a given child. This includes parents, other involved family members, foster carers and any other adult carers.

This chapter does not concern itself with the misuse of alcohol, (as this is more fully detailed with by Calder and Peake in the previous chapter), but the majority of assessment issues we address will also be relevant to alcohol misuse. Many parents use a number of substances (poly-use) often including alcohol. It is also relatively common for some people who change their drug use, to begin to misuse alcohol as a substitute for the original drug.

The crossover

Much has been written about the increasing use of illegal drugs in Britain in the 1980s and 1990s (Harbin and Murphy, 2000; SCODA, 1997). One of the most disturbing aspects of this increase has been the significant increase in the misuse of drugs by women of childbearing age (Macrory and Harbin, 2000). More concerning is the fact that many of these women will not be receiving appropriate services (Kearney, 2001). Women and men often do not stop using substances when they have children, and the arrival of children does not seem to make substance misuse less likely (even though becoming pregnant and having a child are often significant motivators to change). Most parents do not 'choose' to become dependant on substances, it just happens as a sequel to use and other problems in their lives. Thus family life and substance misuse become significantly wrapped up in one another. This wrapping up or crossover is not a simple process. One of the jobs of a good assessment is to try to unravel the reality behind the intertwining of family life and substance misuse.

Furthermore, research from the USA has indicated (Murphy et al., 1991) that the closer one approaches the stage of legal intervention in child protection, the more substance misuse is likely to be significantly represented in your sample. When a family does come before the court, the problems that they bring may be more exaggerated than those families who do not misuse substance: 'Parents with documented substance abuse were significantly more likely to have had previous charges of child mistreatment, more likely to be rated as presenting high risk to their children, more likely to reject court-ordered services, and more likely to have their children permanently removed' (Murphy et al., 1991, p208). This research from the USA certainly seems to be confirmed by our experience in Bolton, the area in which we work (Harbin and Murphy, 2000). Forrester (2000) also notes the close connection between the use of heroin and alcohol with registration for neglect in Bermondsey.

Changing patterns of substance misuse can also have a serious impact on child protection systems as a whole. Dore et al. (1995) document the significant increase in child protection caseloads that accompanied the rise in crack cocaine use in the USA in the 1980s.

Inter-system and inter-agency working

All children and families have contact with a number of different agencies in the course of their daily lives. So, good childcare assessments should include a significant input from all these agencies that have contact with the child: 'An important underlying principle of the approach to assessment in this guidance, therefore, is that it is based on an inter-agency model in which it is not just social services departments which are the assessors and providers of services' (DoH, 2000, p14). One weakness of the early drafts of the framework was that it relied too heavily on social services' exclusive involvement in assessments.

However, because of the substantial crossover between the clients of substance and childcare systems, it is also essential that, where substance misuse is an issue, the staff from the substance system should also be included in the assessment process. As well as interagency, these assessments also need to be *inter-system* in nature.

One important factor in this crossover is that these two major systems have become used to separate ways of working: 'The two modern systems (substance misuse and childcare) have developed independently of each other, following their own paths without much regard for the direction or purpose of the other' (Murphy and Oulds, 2000, p113). This separate development continues to the present day, but in most areas, both systems acknowledge the crossover between their clients and their domains: 'it has become clear that the two systems have much in common, not least that they share individual clients, families and mutually impacting concerns' (Murphy and Oulds, 2000, p121). Unfortunately, the level of collaboration between substance and childcare systems varies considerably from locality to locality (Murphy and Oulds, 2000).

McKellar and Coggans (1997) report that substance workers in Glasgow recognise problems within users' families but are not necessarily sure about what to do with them: 'Some 80 per cent of respondents reported that they would feel it was part of their remit to take some form of action about such cases, *though less than half said that they ever refer them to another agency and only about a third suggested that they themselves intervene*' (p57). Forrester (2000) comments on the low involvement of specialist substance practitioners in child protection conferences in Bermondsey:

> In the 34 most recent case conferences involving substance-using parents, only four specialist substance use workers were invited. It is not clear whether this reflects a lack of involvement of specialist workers with these families or those specialist workers were not invited to conferences. It is certainly of concern that only two of these workers attended.
>
> (p242).

Kearney et al. (2000) comment on the gap of information around this crossover: 'the work generated by mental health and substance misuse, especially in the case of alcohol, is under-recognised and under-estimated. Existing information and recording systems do not capture the size of the problem across the various teams in SSDs. Interviews with practitioners in children's services suggest that 50 per cent to 90 per cent of families on child care caseloads have parental mental health, drug or alcohol problems'(p48).

So although the significant crossover between substance misuse and childcare is well established, the crossover between childcare and substance systems and procedures seems quite variable. This variability will have considerable impact on the type and quality of assessments that take place within families where substance misuse is an issue.

Assessment

It is important, right at the start of our deliberations, to examine and question our assumptions about this area of assessment. Macdonald (2001) reminds us that bias, error and assumptions can all negatively impact on our assessment work. In the area of substance misuse, many societal assumptions, biases and prejudices can affect our judgement: 'To suggest that all parents who suffer from problem drug use present a danger to their children is misleading. Indeed, much research indicates that in isolation, problem drug use of a parent presents little risk of significant harm to children' (Cleaver et al., 1999, p23). The

Figure 1: The potential impact of substance abuse.

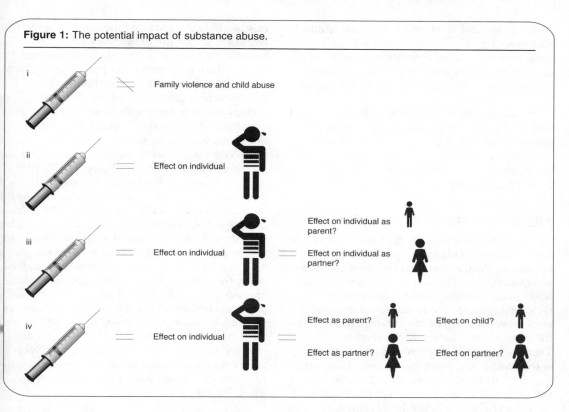

Government agrees with Cleaver's conclusion and insist on the importance of good family assessments to measure the impact of substance misuse on individual children and their families: 'it is important not to generalise, or make assumptions about the impact on a child of parental drug and alcohol misuse. It is, however, important that the implications for the child are properly assessed' (DoH, 1999, p9). This chapter is all about that proper, holistic assessment of the interaction between children, parents and their substance misuse.

In summary, substance misuse in families is *not* tantamount to child abuse. Substance misuse *will* have an impact on the individual adult, which *may* have an impact on their parenting capacity, which in its turn *might* effect the development of the individual child (Figure 1).

The job of the assessment is to discover the impact of the particular style and type of substance use on the parenting capacity of adults in that particular family, and then to gauge that combined impact on the development and safety of individual children within that family (see Figure 1 above). The process then should indicate the appropriate threshold or level of response to the child and

its family (e.g. that the family use drugs recreationally with little or no impact on childcare, or perhaps that this child is a child in need, or that this child is in need of protection).

It is worth noting here that some child care systems operate in a way that either offers a child protection investigation or, if the family does not reach the child protection 'threshold', offer no service at all (Calder, Chapter 2; DoH, 1995). In this area of work, with many different types of substance use and many different types of family lifestyles and problems, a system which allows for other preventative interventions (as well as the powerful child protection intervention) may be extremely useful. Jones and O'Loughlin (see Chapter 8) explore Bolton's graded process of intervention, which can hold families outside the protection system and yet still promotes inter-agency collaboration at an early stage.

The extra complication of having to measure across system boundaries (see below) reflects the extra importance of doing good assessments in this area. In order to be able to predict or measure the child's experience of being parented, we don't just have to measure their development, their parents' parenting and their wider family and community. We need to attach all this to a good assessment of parental substance use and an accurate measurement of how much and in what ways this impacts on parenting and childcare (see Hackett, Chapter 9).

It is also worth remembering that assessments will not just be concerned with the impact of substance misuse. Many families will have substance use as one problem among many, and those other issues also need to be included within our assessment process.

Engagement, denial, taboo and secrecy

The proper assessment of all types of substance misuse can be made much more difficult because of the taboo and secrecy that surrounds problematic use. This taboo and secrecy often leads to an unwillingness to engage with childcare agencies and is often mirrored and felt even more strongly by the children involved in the assessment (Harbin, 2001; Kearney, 2001). The key to proper engagement and partnership is the style of the workers concerned (Bates et al., 1999) and the most important component of that style is the reassurance that the client (both parent and child) will not be devalued, patronised or stigmatised in the assessment encounter (see Calder, Chapter 2; Kearney, 2001).

The contribution of the Assessment Framework

In the early 1990s, within Bolton ACPC area, we developed some assessment tools to assess the crossover between substance misuse and childcare. In 1997 these were altered to accommodate the new SCODA guidelines (SCODA, 1997). However, in 1999 we welcomed the draft of the Assessment Framework because of its common framework and language that we hoped would help practitioners work more easily across agency and system boundaries. We still see the Framework's ability to include many practitioners, in a single assessment process, as its most positive aspect.

However there are some weaknesses or disadvantages inherent in the Framework (see Chapter 2). In this area of assessment work three weaknesses stand out clearly. The first is that because of the insistence on measuring strengths and capacity, rather than weakness, gaps or risk, (DoH, 2000, p13–14) some impact of substance

misuse 'lifestyle' may be ignored. The second weakness is that the Framework offers no specific mechanism to include adult oriented issues which may impact on parenting capacity and child development (even though the government is intent on making childcare systems more in tune with adult problems and systems). Although the Working Together document advises us to: 'recognise the complementary roles of adult and children's services in health and social care' (DoH, 1999, p11) the Framework offers us no obvious mechanism to do so. In a similar way the pack of questionnaires and scales (DoH, 2000) gives us little to help assess alcohol use and nothing to help us with the assessment of drugs. Therefore we need to develop the Framework in such a way that helps us look at weaknesses as well as strengths and assists us in the measuring and analysing of adult-oriented issues, (in this case parental substance misuse). The third weakness that has been much discussed in previous chapters is that of timescales. To do a good interagency and intersystem assessment, with a family with significant substance problems, will probably take much longer than the allotted 'core' 35 days.

Developing the Assessment Framework

There are two complementary models that we have developed in Bolton ACPC to help make the Assessment Framework 'fit' our needs in this area of work. The first model is a simple add-on section to the Assessment Framework triangle. The crucial difference between it and the Framework is an assessment of substance use and all its constituent parts (What used? how much? when? where? who with? lifestyle implications? etc.), which may be done by childcare or substance workers. This 'use' is then tracked across the model to establish what impact this use has on parenting capacity. This then carries on by examining the impact on the child's developmental needs. This model offers a simple means of integrating parental substance misuse into the Assessment Framework (see Figure 2).

The second model offers a more tailor made response to the specific issue of parental substance misuse within families. Section One of the model closely resembles the first section in the previous model offering a way of assessing parental use of substances. This is then tracked into Section Two, which again offers a way

Figure 2: Adapting the framework to address substance misuse.

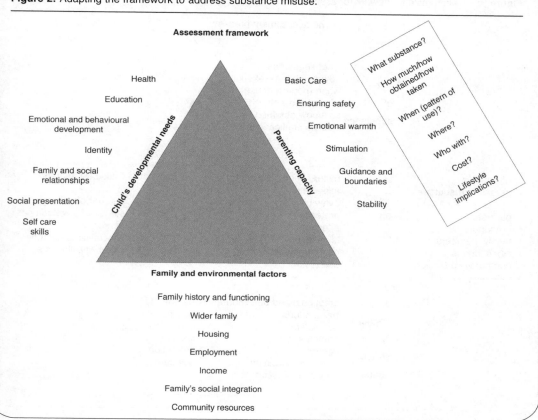

Assessment framework

Health

Education

Emotional and behavioural
development

Identity

Family and social
relationships

Social presentation

Self care
skills

Child's developmental needs

Parenting capacity

Basic Care

Ensuring safety

Emotional warmth

Stimulation

Guidance and
boundaries

Stability

What substance?

How much/how
obtained/how
taken

When (pattern of
use)?

Where?

Who with?

Cost?

Lifestyle
implications?

Family and environmental factors

Family history and functioning

Wider family

Housing

Employment

Income

Family's social integration

Community resources

based largely on the Assessment Framework) of measuring the impact on parenting. Section three examines the impact on the needs of the child. The crucial difference, within this model, is that it offers two sections that moderate the ability to parent within families, or parenting capacity (see Figure 3).

The first, *Alternative Parenting Resources* is a way of measuring those factors that may assist in delivering a parenting service within the family. These include the availability of other partners, grandparents and extended family and community parenting support. (It is worth noting here that there is something within substance misuse that seems to promote the involvement of grandparents and other family members with substance misusing families).

The second *Childcare Demand* is a way of attempting to measure the changing levels of childcare demand within the family that *parenting capacity* has to deal with. So instead of assuming that the level of childcare demand will remain the same, we need to assess those factors that will increase or lower that demand – number, age, personality, illness/disability of children and so on. A crucial irony, where a baby is born to a substance-using mother, is that the childcare demand from that baby may be significantly exaggerated by withdrawal, irritability and so on (Macrory and Harbin, 2000) whilst the parent's ability to respond may also be impeded by their substance use.

In spite of the criticism of the 'Orange Book' (DoH, 1988) that 'set' questions within were believed to be too prescriptive (explored by Calder in Chapter 2), we have found that practitioners really value some guidance about what questions should accompany the model. What follows are a number of 'prompts' that we have developed to help make the models work. Once again, let us remind ourselves that it is really important to measure strengths as well as weaknesses in families, as strengths can assist and predict change.

Figure 3: An alternative framework for assessment.

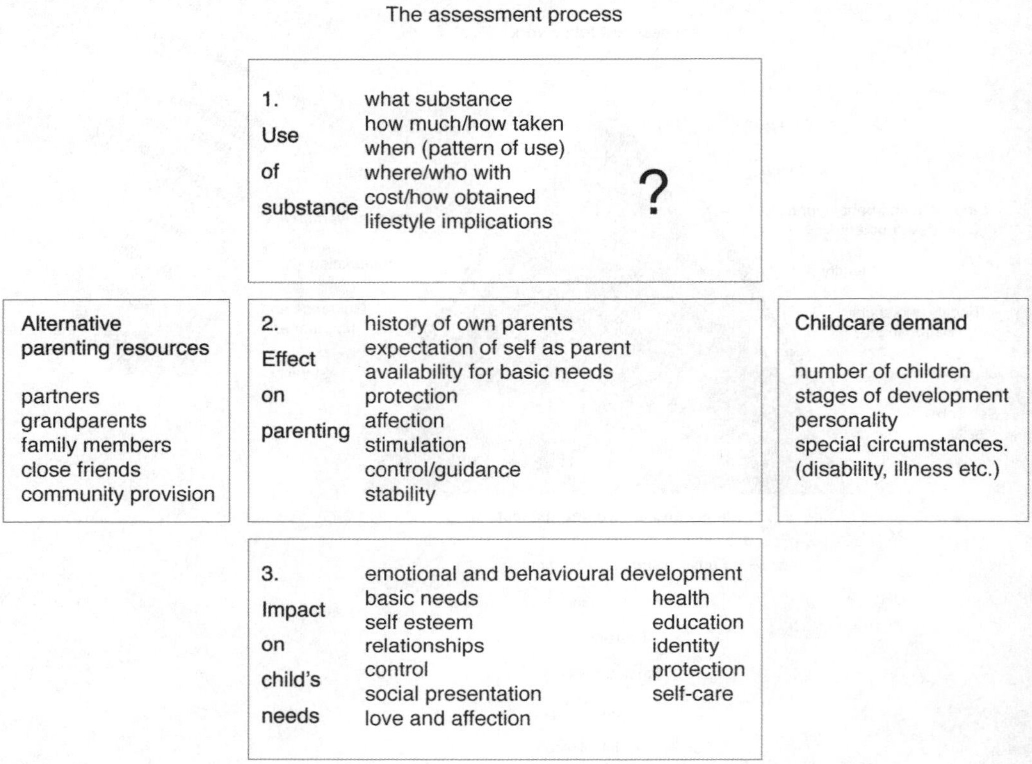

The assessment process

1. **Use** **of** **substance**	what substance how much/how taken when (pattern of use) where/who with cost/how obtained lifestyle implications

?

Alternative parenting resources partners grandparents family members close friends community provision	**2.** **Effect** **on** **parenting**	history of own parents expectation of self as parent availability for basic needs protection affection stimulation control/guidance stability	Childcare demand number of children stages of development personality special circumstances. (disability, illness etc.)

3. **Impact** **on** **child's** **needs**	emotional and behavioural development basic needs health self esteem education relationships identity control protection social presentation self-care love and affection	

Section 1 (in both models) seeks to assess the relationship of the adult with the substance that they are using.
Useful Questions may include:

1. What substances are being used?
   Are more than one substance being used together?
2. What is the pattern of use?
   – When?
   – Where?
   – How much?
   – How taken?
   – Who with?
   – How has this pattern changed in the last few years
3. How funded?
   – How much is the weekly cost of the substance?
   – How is the substance obtained?
4. What are the lifestyle implications of this use?
5. Is the substance use experimental, recreational, binge using, chaotic or

dependent? Has the individual made attempts to alter their pattern of substance use? Were they successful? If not why not?
6. Is there any evidence of mental health problems alongside the substance use?
7. Do the parents see their substance use as harmful to themselves or to the children?
8. Will parents accept help from relatives, voluntary or statutory agencies?
9. Do they see change as desirable or possible?

Section 2 concerns the impact on parents and parenting capacity in the assessed family.

1. What is the adult's experience or history of being parented?
2. Is there a history of substance misuse in their family?
3. What are their expectations of themselves as parents?
4. How well do they, as parents, meet their children's basic needs (food, clothing and warmth)?
5. How well do they ensure safety/protection

6. Do they offer emotional warmth (love and affection)?
7. Do they offer stimulation?
8. Do they offer control, guidance and boundaries?
9. Do they offer stability?
10. Are levels of childcare different when a parent is using, than when not using?
11. How are the children cared for while substances are being procured?
12. To what extent is the child exposed to the substance using lifestyle?
13. How safely are substances and paraphernalia stored and disposed of within the family home?

Section 3 concerns the child's development needs.

How is the child's health, are they attending health groups, are there any ongoing illnesses/appointments?
Are the children attending school regularly? How well are they doing academically? How well are they doing socially (have they got any friends)?
Are the children reaching their developmental milestones? Are the children engaging in age appropriate activities?
How is the children's emotional and behavioural development?
What is the childs identity? Do they have low or high self-esteem?
How are the child's relationships with their family and peers?
Are any of the children taking on a parenting role with the family?
How do the children present themselves socially? Do they have good self-care skills?
Are the children aware of the substance use? Can they talk to anyone about this? What is their subjective experience? How do they deal with their anxiety about substance use (if they have any)?

Section 4 seeks to assess alternative parenting support and family and environmental factors.

Is there a drug free partner, grandparent, other relative, or close family friend? Are they aware of the substance use?
How much are they involved with the care of the child?
Are there any community resources that would help with parenting?
Do parents and children associate primarily with other substance users/non-users/both?

5. Is housing adequate and does the family move frequently?

Section 5 seeks to measure the changing childcare demands within the family.

1. How many children are there in the family?
2. What are their ages?
3. What are their responsibilities?
4. Do the parents see any of the children as being particularly demanding?
5. Are there any other special circumstances (illness, disability, and use of substances)?
6. In case of pregnancy what has been the early history/health of previous children? What are the predicted early health issues for this child?

Analysis

This is the most important part of the assessment, where we should take all the information that has been gathered and make sense of it in terms of the following questions:

- Is the substance use significantly affecting parenting capacity? If so how?
- Is the substance use and associated behaviour significantly impacting on the child's health and safety, education, emotional and social development? If so how?
- What are the resources and strengths in this family? How might they impact on the care of the child?
- What is the parents understanding of and attitude to the need for change? What change might be acceptable and attainable?

Thresholds

The two main outcomes of the assessment should be to establish what services or therapeutic response are required by the child and family (see below), but also where on the child concern 'thresholds' does this particular family sit. To be successful in dealing with childcare concerns a system needs to employ a number of different thresholds (not just the child protection one) in order that the needs of the child and family can be appropriately dealt with. If all we possess in our threshold 'toolkit' is the 'hammer' of child protection, then we tend to respond to every demand as though it is a nail, when often it may be a screw, a tack or even a drawing pin!

Assessment and treatment/being creative

What follows this assessment process? Is it acceptable (or ethical) to measure or assess without then using that assessment to help to create some positive change? Isn't the point of the assessment to measure and discover where services, support, therapeutic work, challenge and change are required?

If parents or children are being significantly affected by substance misuse, even though that effect does not reach the 'threshold' of inclusion in the child protection system, how do we offer them appropriate help?

Change around both substance misuse and parenting capacity are difficult to achieve and yet, paradoxically, parents achieve both types of change all the time. Murphy (1991) reminds us that where there is significant parental substance misuse, change in the substance arena must occur before parenting change becomes possible.

Creative/inter-agency responses

But change and the delivery of appropriate services are not easy in the childcare or substance misuse fields. Sometimes families and their children will find it difficult to access even the services that are most readily available (Elliott and Watson, 1998). Sometimes the services that are provided take no account of the separate needs of substance users who are also parents (Kearney, 2001).

One key factor that seems to be emerging from feedback from children and parents (Harbin, 2001; Kearney, 2001) is that creative, inter-agency provision, particularly that which offers a one-stop place of help to parents and children, offering assistance with both substance and childcare issues, may prove beneficial. In our area a resource that combined substance and childcare help, centre-based and home-based assistance has proved valuable to all members of the family (Harbin, 2001).

Use of the voluntary sector

It is essential to properly include not just the statutory sector but the voluntary sector from both the substance and the childcare fields. It is often the voluntary sector, which holds the energy and the permission to be bold and creative around change and treatment. This boldness and creativity (although often creating anxiety in the statutory sector) is often the key t change in families and in systems.

Including the Child

It is tempting when completing assessments to talk only to the adults involved and not includ children and their subjective experience. It is particularly important in this area of work to include how the child feels about their family experience (Laybourn et al., 1996). If we are to put the child at the centre of our assessment, w need to understand their assessment of their situation. There is a substantial body of literature about the child's experience (Brisby e al., 1997, Houston et al., 1997, Kearney, 2001, Laybourn et al., 1996, Mahoney and MacKechnie, 2001) that seems to show a wide variation in that subjective experience. We may use this literature to both understand the diversity of the child's experience but also to begin to discover how to uncover that subjectiv experience and use it in our assessments. Although children will normally show some reluctance to talk about substance issues (usually because of stigma, shame and the fea of negative consequences) once this initial reluctance is overcome children often have strong opinions that they will want to share (Harbin, 2000; and Kearney, 2001). The positive that children will report in this area can be ver similar to those of other children in non-using families, but we have discovered that some children's negative experiences may follow a pattern of anxiety, isolation, inappropriate responsibility, separation and exposure to offending and exploitation.

Conclusion

This chapter has been concerned with a particularly difficult yet crucial aspect of assessment: how to make an assessment of the impact of significant parental substance misuse on the care, wellbeing and development of children. The chapter has looked at the crossover between substance misuse and childcare systems, and discovered that there ar significant indicators from research of the crossover and inter-relationship between substance and childcare problems. The chapter goes on to emphasise the importance of working in an inter-agency and inter-system way that involves substance and childcare agencies working and assessing in a collaborative fashion. The evidence from different systems u

nd down the country indicates a great
ariability in the level and sustainability of this
nter-agency collaboration.

The chapter then continues to examine the
eneral issues concerned with assessment in this
rea. The importance of not letting our judgement
e affected by societal prejudices, or by the false
ssumption that substance misuse automatically
eads to child harm. We have looked at the
ontribution of the Assessment Framework and
xamined some of the weaknesses of the
ramework. The chapter then outlines some
evelopments of the Assessment Framework that
elp bridge the gap between the Framework's
hildcare assessments and the need to include
dult oriented substance assessments. The chapter
nds with a discussion of the need to include
hildren's own subjective experience within our
ssessments and the further need to develop
reative, inter-agency services and treatment
ptions, to usefully follow our assessments by best
neeting children's and families' needs.

References

ates, T., Buchanan, J., Corby, B., Young, L.
(1999) *Drug Use, Parenting and Child
Protection:Towards an Interagency Response.*

risby,T., Baker, S. and Hedderwick, T. (1997)
*Under the Influence: Coping With Parents Who
Drink Too Much.* London: Alcohol Concern.

leaver, H., Unell, I. and Aldgate, J. (1999)
Children's Needs: Parenting Capacity. London:
HMSO.

)oH (1988) *Protecting Children: A Guide for Social
Workers Undertaking a Comprehensive
Assessment.* London: HMSO.

)oH (1995) *Child Protection: Messages from
Research.* London: HMSO.

)oH (1999) *Working Together to Safeguard
Children.* London: HMSO.

)oH (2000) *Framework for the Assessment of
Children in Need and their Families.* London:
HMSO.

)oH (2000) *Framework for the Assessment of
Children in Need and their Families:
Questionnaires and Scales.* London: HMSO.

)ore, M., Doris, J. and Wright, P. (1995)
Identifying Substance Abuse in Maltreating
Families: A Child Welfare Challenge. *Child
Abuse and Neglect.* 19: 5, 531–44.

:lliott, E. and Watson, A (1998) *Fit to be a Parent.*
Salford: PHRRC.

'amularo, R., Kinscherff, R. and Fenton, T.
(1992) Parental Substance Abuse and the
Nature of Child Maltreatment. *Child Abuse and
Neglect.* 16: 475–83.

Forrester, D. (2000) Parental Substance Misuse
and Child Protection in a British Sample. *Child
Abuse Review.* 19: 235–46.

Harbin, F and Murphy, M. (Eds.) (2000)
Substance Misuse and Childcare. Lyme Regis,
Dorset: Russell House Publishing.

Harbin, F. (2000) *Therapeutic Work With Children
of Substance Misusing Parents.* In Harbin, F and
Murphy, M. (Eds.) *Substance Misuse and
Childcare.* Lyme Regis, Dorset: Russell House
Publishing.

Harbin, F (2001) *The Connaught Square/Safer
Families Project.* Conference Paper 7/12/2001.

Houston, A., Kork, S. with MacLeod, M. (1997)
*Beyond the Limit: Children Who Live With
Parental Alcohol Misuse.* London: Childline.

Kearney, J., and Taylor, N. (2001) *The Highs and
Lows of Family Life* Research Report 7/12/2001

Kearney, P., Levin, E., and Rosen, G. (2000)
*Alcohol, Drug and Mental Health Problems:
Working With Families.* London: NISW.

Laybourn, A., Brown, J. and Hill, M. (1996)
*Hurting on the Inside: Children's Experiences of
Parental Alcohol Misuse.* Aldershot: Avebury.

Levin, E., Kearney, P. and Rosen, G. (2000)
Fitting it Together. *Community Care.* 3/8/2000.

Macdonald, G. (2001) *Effective Interventions for
Child Abuse and Neglect.* Chichester: John
Wiley and Sons.

Macrory, F and Harbin, F. (2000) Substance
Misuse and Pregnancy. In Harbin, F and
Murphy, M (Eds.) *Substance Misuse and
Childcare.* Lyme Regis, Dorset: Russell House
Publishing.

Mahoney, C. and MacKechnie, S. (2001) *In a
Different World.* Liverpool: DAAT.

McKellar, S. and Coggans, N. (1997) Responding
to Family Problems: Alcohol and Substance
Misuse. *Children and Society.* 11: 53–9.

Murphy, J., Jellinek, M., Quinn, D., Smith, G.,
Poitrast, F. and Goshko, M (1991) Substance
Abuse and Serious Child Mistreatment:
Prevalence, Risk and Outcome in a Court
Sample. *Child Abuse and Neglect.* 15: 197–211.

Murphy, M and Oulds, G. (2000) Establishing
and Developing Cooperative Links Between
Substance Misuse and Child Protection
Systems. In Harbin, F. and Murphy, M. (Eds.)
Substance Misuse and Childcare. Lyme Regis,
Dorset: Russell House Publishing.

SCODA (Standing Conference on Drug Abuse)
(1997) *Drug Using Parents: Policy Guidelines for
Inter-agency Working.* London: LGA Publications.

Chapter Twenty-One

Unborn Children: A Framework for Assessment and Intervention

Martin C. Calder

Neither the Assessment Framework or its predecessor provide an adequate framework for conducting pre-birth risk assessments. This chapter will describe a holistic framework which was devised by an inter-agency working group in Salford: which explores the process for the assessment, the multiple possible components which may be appropriate to a wide range of presenting circumstances, and a matrix to determine the level of projected risk once the baby has been born.

Introduction

A core assessment should always be commissioned when there appears to be a risk of significant harm to an unborn baby. The question regarding at what point in the pregnancy child protection procedures should be invoked to consider the foetus is a complex one. There is an argument for suggesting that the earlier in the pregnancy the better, to enable appropriate preventative action. This might be in relation to the foetus itself, if the lifestyle of the mother is placing the integrity of the foetus at risk – e.g. through some form of substance abuse – as early intervention provides much opportunity of reducing such harm. Alternatively, the action might be in relation to planning protection for after the birth – if it is assessed that there is a need to provide particular support services or a change of living accommodation when the child is born. In most circumstances, the earlier the plans can be made to do this the better. Other action might be in relation to assessing the parent's ability to care for the future child appropriately – and the longer the time available for such a period of assessment the more thorough and comprehensive such an assessment can be. However, there do remain powerful ethical arguments against early intervention, not least of which centres on the possible impact of such intervention on considerations by the mother about seeking a termination of the pregnancy (within 24 weeks in the UK at the present time, under the Abortion Act (1967), (Barker, 1997).

Given that most pregnancies are identified within the first three months, there is some flexibility about the point, and in which forum the pre-birth risk assessment is formally commissioned. I would advocate that a multi-disciplinary planning meeting take place at around 20 weeks gestation (with the exception of concealed pregnancies, and where it is imperative to elicit the police information i detail through an early child protection conference). This should be attended by the identified midwife, the local family centre, the likely health visitor, the parents and the social worker. Ideally, the family GP should attend, but it may be more realistic for the health visito to collate any relevant health information (psychiatric, medical, and relevant social history, including a review of the GP records) and bring it to the meeting. Given the expectation that a core assessment is completed within 35 working days of being commissioned local practice and procedure should ensure tha this particular process is exempt and that ther is power to suspend as long as it is clearly identified when it will start, what form it will take, and when the outcome will be considered It may be appropriate to do an assessment quickly if (a) a pre-conception assessment is requested or (b) parents want the choice of termination if removal is the outcome.

The task of the initial planning meeting would be to collate all the relevant family history and determine whether a formal pre-birth risk assessment should be commissioned, and what form it should take. There are a number of different circumstances ir which a planning meeting will need to be convened to consider the need for a comprehensive pre-birth risk assessment:

- Where previous children in the family have been removed because they have suffered harm.
- Where a schedule one offender (or someone found by an initial child protection conferenc to have abused) has joined a family. For

detailed frameworks for the assessment of risk in sexual abuse, see Calder (2000).

- Where concerns exist regarding the mother's ability to protect.
- Where there are acute professional concerns regarding parenting capacity, particularly where the parents have either severe mental health problems or learning disabilities.
- Where alcohol or substance abuse is thought to be affecting the health of the expected baby, and is one concern amongst others.
- Where the expected parent is very young and a dual assessment of their own needs as well as their ability to meet the baby's needs is required.

In most cases, either the same parents/adult carers or one parent with a new partner are expecting (or sometimes only planning) to have another child. The risks can be either single e.g. risk of sexual abuse, or multiple, e.g. inadequate parenting coupled with emotional, physical or sexual abuse. Many years have often elapsed since the previous intervention, so there is a need to tread carefully as the parents often come to the work with a pre-determined view about professionals and invariably fear a negative outcome.

There are several professional issues that need acknowledging and addressing with the professionals at the outset of any pre-birth risk assessment. They include:

- The perceived and actual consequences of making a wrong decision in high-profile, high concern cases.
- The consequences for professionals of deciding for removal at birth – possibly lengthy and demanding legal proceedings.
- Feeling bound by the conclusions or views of previous professionals and any variation now may be perceived as disloyal.
- The number of factors for consideration in the assessment that are rarely part of the professionals direct experience.
- The emotive nature of such work, particularly when coupled with a strong view about removing children at birth.

The following components should be considered for each commissioned assessment, and they could usefully be used as an agenda for the planning meeting to ensure that all the relevant areas for the presenting case are considered:

- Definition of the problem. What is the purpose and scope of the assessment?
- Ante-natal, medical and obstetric history.
- Full social history.
- Current family structure, extended family and potential support.
- The parental relationship and family support.
- Family functioning and strengths.
- Previous abuse or convictions, including any previous assessments, with any increased acceptance of responsibility or major changes.
- Family attitudes towards previous action or professional involvement, and ability to engage them in the current intervention process. (Note. It is important to engage *both* parents in the assessment process).
- Assessment of non-abusing parent's ability to protect.
- Understanding of expected baby's needs and ability to meet them.
- Future plans.
- Alcohol using parents and anticipated health problems.
- Drug using parents and anticipated health problems.
- Measuring the family's potential for, and motivation to, change.
- Determining the way forward: the risk factors.

The professionals and the family should then construct a written agreement which sets out clearly the agreed tasks, roles, responsibilities and time-scales. It should also identify the need for any specific assessment, e.g. psychiatric or psychological (processing it if resources permit) and appoint a co-ordinating professional (usually the social worker). For further details on these issues, the reader is referred to Calder and Horwath (1999). Once the work has been completed, a planning meeting should be arranged to consider what further action, if any, is needed, and whether an initial child protection conference should be convened to consider whether registration and any legal action is necessary.

Exploring the identified components

Definition of the problem

It is essential that professionals and the family address the concerns at an early stage to ensure there is no confusion about why a particular assessment package has been constructed. Workers have a duty to set out clearly for the parents a statement of their concerns, the process and content of the assessment and what the expected child needs to be protected from. They also need to be advised about the potential consequences of non co-operation. This allows the parents to clarify the outcome needed and decide whether they can make the necessary changes in a time-scale commensurate with the expected child's needs. In some cases, this will only become clear as the assessment itself unfolds, but workers should punctuate the work with feedback to accommodate this. It is sometimes useful to assess a parent's motivation to address the concerns at the outset of the assessment and re-gauge these at the end of the formal assessment to see if any change has been noticed.

Ante-natal care: medical and obstetric history
Pregnancy itself creates special circumstances/ influences on both parents, which need to be accommodated by the workers. For example, pregnancy has a major impact upon their present lives, affecting both their behaviours as well as their relationships. Pregnant women's health and responses to external factors change during pregnancy. The physiological, emotional and social influences effecting and affected by this change will determine, to some extent, how representative their behaviours are, their state of health and the functioning of key relationships.

Ante-natal care is usually provided on a shared care basis by Midwives, General Practitioners and Hospital Consultants. Care begins as soon as pregnancy is confirmed and continues until a minimum of 10 days post-partum up to a maximum of 28 days post-partum. The named midwife (geographically attached to a GP) will provide women with choices about the place of birth and the type of care they would like to receive. A booking interview is carried out at around 8-12 weeks of pregnancy, either in the woman's home or in the GP's surgery according to the woman's wishes.

During the booking interview the midwife is collecting information, which will build into a full medical and social history (now held on computer). When all the data is assimilated, the midwife is then able to assist the woman in making informed choices about the care she receives and advises on the suitability of her choices. The midwife will discuss with the woman the pattern of care, which is thought to

most suit her needs. A holistic approach, taking into account the woman's social history will be provided. The information collected usually includes:

* name
* age/DOB
* address
* next of kin
* marital status
* partner support
* family support family structure
* occupation
* ethnic origin
* planned/unplanned pregnancy
* feeling about being pregnant
* dietary intake
* medicines or drugs taken before and during pregnancy
* alcohol/cigarette consumption
* previous obstetric history including:
* number of children, dob of children, names, current health status.
* miscarriages and termination's of pregnancy
* information regarding chronic and acute medical conditions, surgical history and psychiatric history i.e. previous depression, suicide attempts.

Post-natal care will be provided either completely in the home in the case of home births or where the birth occurs in hospital or the GP unit the initial post-natal care will be on the post-natal ward. Hospital stays are getting shorter with many women going home 6 hours after the birth but, 12–48 hours are the routine lengths of stay. Post-natal care is then transferred to the named community midwife who will then visit regularly according to need. The Health Visitor attached to the women's GP will have been notified during the pregnancy, some do an ante-natal visit, others write to mothers in the first week of life and arrange a primary visit at around the tenth day of life. Midwives will often transfer the care of mother and baby over to the Health Visitor following the tenth day visit. Midwives can however continue to provide care up to 28 days post delivery.

Full social history

Anyone wanting to promote changes in clients must first obtain a comprehensive understanding of the total context in which the behaviours occur.

(Lazarus, 1976, p25)

A detailed social history is essential and should not differ from a social history taken in any other situation. The social history is designed to collect information which will help understand the parents developmental experiences which may be contributing to the identified concerns; whether any contemporary factors might have increased the concerns or risks; as well as being an excellent mechanism for engaging the parents via a routine, non-threatening process (see Calder et al., 2001 for a review). Workers can use this component to evaluate their ability and willingness to recount events.

There are no boundaries to a social history, although most embrace their family of origin; the quality of their parenting; their early life experiences; social, educational, medical, marital, occupational, criminal (and sexual) history. For detailed guidance on this, the reader is referred to Calder (1999; 2001). We should consider complications during the pregnancy and birth; developmental issues, including their milestones; peer and sibling relationships; school performance; family relationships; drug and alcohol abuse; general impulsivity; anger levels; self-esteem; social skills and competence; and past psychiatric history.

Current family structure, extended family and potential support

It is essential that we establish full details of the immediate and extended family, including dates of birth, full names and addresses, so that full checks can be done on relevant criminal and child protection history. There are very real advantages to using eco-maps and genograms for this purpose, and further guidance on adapting them to different cultures can be found in Congress (1994) and Hardy and Laszloffy (1995).

The parental relationship

The parental relationship is crucial and needs to include information on how they met, why they stay together, how their relationship has developed and changed, what the good and bad parts of their relationship are, the number of children each has had previously, domestic violence, etc. The workers need to focus on the parental relationship and their individual physical, intellectual and emotional abilities/control; as well as the effect of a baby on the parental relationship. Workers need to establish which parent is likely to provide the main care for the expected baby. Changes in the parental relationship in the context of previous abuse, family violence, drug or alcohol use, and environmental factors such as housing and unemployment need to be understood as either superficial or fundamental. Workers need to consider the relevance of problems in any previous relationships and the impact this may have on their current relationships. Workers need to explore the previous family unit within which any previous abuse occurred and consider the positives and the negatives about the new relationship and any changes that remain outstanding. Workers should explore who they are now, their current lifestyle and what has happened since the removal of their previous children.

Family functioning and strengths

It is important to look at the current family functioning, particularly lifestyle, roles and responsibilities, and how they envisage adapting to the arrival of a newborn baby. This should include the stability and quality of family life, the extent of agreement on raising children, family rules, the identification, management and resolution of conflict, whether they support or undermine each other, particularly around colluding with each other to deny the problems, and their strengths and capabilities.

Working with family strengths is proving to be an excellent mechanism to foster working relationships without excluding the need to focus on risk. It is a more acceptable way of looking at how to manage risks. It recommends that we focus on individuals by focusing on their capacity, talents, competencies, possibilities, visions, values and hopes. It is not enough to assume that strengths exist in the absence of any identified weaknesses. The most heavily weighted factors when judging a family's strengths are their level of co-operation, aspects of their parenting, and aspects of their social system. A major consideration as part of strengthening families is promoting their abilities to use their existing strengths in a way that produces positive changes in family functioning. For a detailed discussion of the strengths perspective, the reader is referred to Calder (1999b) and Saleebey (1992, 1996).

Previous abuse and convictions

It is imperative that workers research written and verbal accounts of past events: gain descriptions from those involved, and collect and codify reports/statements. They need to allow for the probability that previous records will be extensive as well as held in numerous places (e.g. court section; police; archives; family centres, etc), as well as the reality that many are incomplete or disorganised. If possible, workers should try and speak to the workers at the time of the previous abuse to assist them in their preparation.

In assessing the previous abuse, workers should consider the following factors:

- The category and level of abuse. Workers also need to consider the ages and the gender of children previously removed, and whether there is a predicted pattern of continuing abuse against either a particular sex or age band.
- What happened? Why did it happen? What else was happening? Workers need to acknowledge the 'filter' that time places on past events, and this requires that they consider carefully the context and significance. Even where the factual information uncovered is thorough, they need to contextualise the decision-making to allow them to accurately translate the significance of past events for the purposes of predicting future risk.
- The parents' explanation for, and view of, the abuse (then and now), testing the congruence of individual accounts and that of professionals. Incongruity should be fed back to parents to enable them to move on and provide alternative explanations/change their story. It may be that we do not know who perpetrated the previous abuse, so we need to explore who might have done it.
- The ages of the parents at the time may be relevant now. For example, they may have been very immature as 15-year-old parents when the last abuse occurred and they are now wanting to be assessed as more mature and responsible 25 or 30-year-old adults.
- The acceptance of responsibility for the abuse (has there been a criminal or civil court finding of responsibility?). Where do the parents **now** place responsibility for what happened in the past? Workers are often left with the task of finding explanations and establish responsibility for the abuse years on from the events themselves. If no-one admits or accepts responsibility for past abuse, then our conclusion is that future children are not safe. If there is no believable acceptance of responsibility for or explanation of the abuse

forthcoming, it is essential that a way forward be identified. For example, workers should actively facilitate parents to again address responsibility for the abuse; find realistic, congruent and 'felt' explanations; and address the need for change from their current position. See Calder (1999) and Calder (forthcoming) for a review of denial and engagement strategies. Some families may never accept any responsibility for the previous abuse, but they may have changed their attitudes towards working with professionals to look at the future risks and safety of the expected child. Workers may often have to consider whether the plans for the future, regardless of the past, can adequately protect the expected child.

- The parents' concern/understanding for the abused child. What understanding do they have of the impact of their past abuse on the children – then, now and possibly in the future? If workers can elicit this information from the child themselves, then it can be a powerful tool to use to get them to look at issues around victim empathy.
- Any previous assessments, with outcome and recommendations. If the couple accept some responsibility for the abuse; offer a believable explanation; recognise the impact of the abuse on past children; work can concentrate on why children were abused in the past; what has changed since, that would indicate future children would be safe; what needs to change for future children to be safe; and to evaluate likelihood of this change-within what time-scale for the children. Workers need to be aware that it is unrealistic to predict future risk with the mathematical accuracy applied to the solution of a mathematical problem. This is particularly true when looking at the chances of a particular risk materialising. In many cases it is usually difficult to do more than place these chances within a fairly broad band, such as 'negligible', 'very high', or 'about 50:50' – and even then it may be hard to avoid an appreciable amount of speculation. However, it is usually easier to predict the likelihood of a risk materialising in the future if that risk has actually materialised in the past, than if it is, as yet, a purely hypothetical risk. However, the seriousness of the harm already done is not a predictor that future harm will be more or less serious, only that the likelihood of it is increased, unless relevant interventions can be made that will

lessen that risk (Calder, 2002).Workers do need to be cautious about making decisions for children if they hold either incomplete or biased information.

In this section, it is important to consider the seriousness of the previous abuse, and how the parents' either individually or together have cared for previous children. This may be their own birth children or children they have been responsible for. The abuse of previous children is not a bar to caring for future children, although the parents attitude towards that abuse and their attitude towards the child is a factor where there would need to be significant and fundamental change.

Family attitudes towards previous action/professional involvement, and ability to engage them in the current intervention process. (Note. It is important to engage both parents in the assessment process)

Much of the success of the assessment depends on the relationship between the workers and the family, and what their understanding is of the assessment task. However, in many of the cases where a pre-birth risk assessment is commissioned, individual professionals and their agencies will have taken decisions/actions that have affected families fundamentally, i.e. the removal of their children. This can lead to acute difficulties for the current workers, particularly if both sides have become entrenched in their positions. Workers can sometimes feel bound by the assessments and decisions they have inherited – as any change may be construed as disloyal.

It is important that professionals remain loyal to one another (co-working is essential) if families are hostile or resistant. It is always worth pointing out to the parents that there will be a need for a similar assessment to be undertaken whenever they present with a pregnancy or join with a new partner with children.

Professionals should try to avoid expressions of over-concern, avoid moralistic judgements, avoid criticising the client, avoid making false promises, avoid displays of impatience, avoid ridiculing the client, avoid blaming the client for their failures, avoid dogmatic utterances, and respect their right to express different values and preferences from your own (Ivanoff et al., 1994) – if they want to engage the parent.

Working in partnership is not about sharing power, but about working together towards a common goal. Parents should be allowed to have a reasonable level of understanding about the assessment process; give their views as well as receiving and debating the views of the professionals; and having a time limit to ensure they are clear where the goalposts are – as any failure to do so will lead to them opting-out of the process (plus distancing them from the experience/decision) – until the next pregnancy (Calder, 1995).

There is a need to engage partners (usually men) in the assessment to maximise the accuracy when predicting future risk (see Calder, forthcoming b). It is useless to have undertaken a parenting assessment of the mother in isolation when the principal risk is believed to be the (male) partner. Workers may sometimes struggle to engage men in assessments (see O'Hagan, 1997 for a review) where they do not hold any parental responsibility for the foetus and are not able to have any say in decisions affecting them pre-birth.

Assessment of non-abusing parent's ability to protect

We need to establish whether they are new partners (in which case we need to examine who they are-their own personal history; how they view what has happened in the past-how critical/uncritical; realistic/unrealistic are they?), or long-standing partners, party to the old abuse (in which case we need to explore what has changed regarding their understanding /view of past abuse; their acceptance of responsibility for a failure to protect or collusion with the abuse; their view of past children and the effects the abuse has had on them; what has changed, and for whom, particularly when changes may have occurred only because there were no children living within the family; what sort of change it is – temporary or permanent/fundamental or superficial ; and what the potential for change is in the light of previously expressed concerns?).

Smith (1994) has provided us with a useful preliminary framework for assessing non-abusing parents' capacity to protect, strengths, weaknesses and areas for change, which includes:

- Position regarding the abuse or conviction – immediate and now? What information do they have, and who was this provided by? Can other information (police, medical, judicial) be provided to assist the mother move from her disbelieving position?

- Feelings towards the child – anger, sympathy? Who do they blame, and why?
- Did they have a role in the investigation of the previous abuse? Was it helpful or a hindrance? To whom, and in what way?
- Position regarding responsibility for the abuse – is easier if the perpetrator has taken full responsibility, but the message has to be that this is where the full responsibility rests in all circumstances.
- Perceived options – do they have sufficient resources to provide their own solutions? Can they co-operate with the statutory agencies? A task centred approach with a clearly defined outcome is important.
- Relationship history – do they have to choose their child or their partner? Are they highly dependent on male partners? Do they have a history of violent and abusive relationships?
- Other vulnerabilities – physical disabilities, including hearing and visual impairments, chronic physical illness, psychiatric illness, or any condition which isolates them from independent help.
- Recognition of future risk situations and their ability to manage them safely for the child.

Calder et al. (2001) have significantly extended the assessment components to include: position regarding the child's disclosure; feelings towards the child post-disclosure; their role in the disclosing process; their role in the sexual abuse; their knowledge of the abuse taking place; their position regarding responsibility for the abuse (what are they responsible for?); the mother's distress to the disclosure/consequences; their definition of the risks compared to the professionals, the abuser and their extended family/community; their perceived options; the relationship and co-operation with the agency (throughout the process); their expression of feelings; openness regarding the sexual abuse; knowledge of sexual offending behaviour generally and specific to their partner; knowledge of effects of child sexual abuse on the victims – generally and specifically to their children (empathy); position regarding self-protection work: what do their children know now? Their ability to identify indicators in both the offender and the children; the mother's relationship with her children; her present attitude and relationship with the abuser;

general parenting; social history: including their family background, health and medical history, including lifestyle stress (alcohol and drug use); interpersonal relationships (positive and negative, e.g. domestic violence); anger, aggression and assertiveness; self-esteem and self-concept; social skills and competence; and social support networks. Sexual history, including any history of sexual abuse, and denial around the current issues. Outcomes will look at safe care: strategies for managing risk (short- and long-term); contact; desire for reunification, with reasons; their understanding about treatment programmes; and any agreed priorities for change. Extra-familial sexual abuse will be covered separately.

Workers need to bear in mind that the uncertain nature of the assessment, particularly around the mother's ability both to protect as well as respond to her expected child, needs to be explored and understood. Despite this, they do need to determine at the end of the assessment whether the non-abusing parent is capable of making the transition to becoming a protective parent. If not, then the baby should not remain in the care of the parents.

Understanding of expected baby's needs and ability to meet them

It is probable that this section will always be completed by a family centre and further detailed guidance can be found in the City of Salford Community and Social Services Directorate (2000).

It is important to consider how the parents, individually and together, feel and respond towards their expected baby. The parents' developing sense of attachment to their expected baby is a useful measure of the quality of the likely attachment between the parents and the child at birth.

It is important to look at how individuals build relationships and whose responsibility they feel it is. It is worth noting that many parents may be unable to articulate a response to such questions, but this does not always mean that they are unable to form strong bonds with their children.

There is a need to look at their understanding of the child's anticipated basic needs and whether they will be able to meet them in a time-scale commensurate with their developmental level. The baseline is establishing whether the parenting will be 'good-enough' to meet the baby's needs.

Future plans

Workers have to consider the future family and should include answering questions about:

- How realistic are the parents' plans for the future?
- Have they considered the impact of a future child on their relationship/lifestyle?
- Do they consider that such an impact might be 'negative'?
- Is it safe for the child to be placed with these parents?

Workers do have to allow for the fact that many pregnant women have a restricted or unrealistic view of their relationship with their unborn child during pregnancy and of their anticipated relationship with the child once born.

If no one admits or accepts responsibility for past abuse, then the conclusion should be that future children are not safe, whatever other strengths have been identified.

Alcohol or drug using parents and anticipated health problems

Drug issues

The parents should be advised either to attend the local community drugs team or get their GP to review their drug regime, taking into account the past history of the user, their motivation and their current situation as well as the demands of the pregnancy. Treatment options can then be discussed with them and include maintenance, partial reduction or complete withdrawal during pregnancy. It may not be desirable for the woman to withdraw completely from drugs before the birth because the additional stress that she may experience during pregnancy may precipitate a crisis in an already chaotic lifestyle, which may result in harm to the baby. In addition, a parent in a withdrawal crisis may be unable to look after a child adequately, as it can impair people's capacity to tolerate stress and anxiety.

The woman needs to be encouraged to book at the ante-natal clinic as early as possible in the pregnancy to ensure they receive advice on general health issues and counselling (SCODA, 1989). However, pregnant drug users are often reluctant to come forward to ante-natal care or to admit to their drug use, because of the fear that the expected child may be taken away at birth. As a result, many do not access ante-natal care until late in pregnancy or when they are in labour. However, it is worth noting that pregnancy can act as an incentive to cease or stabilise drug use, e.g. by prescribing methadone.

Professionals need to assess carefully the mother's and/or partners understanding of the potential effects of their substance abuse on the expected child. This always has to include factors such as social supports, parenting skills, the parent-child relationship and family resources (Azzi-Lessing and Olsen, 1996). The parents need to have some idea about the criteria by which professionals will begin to be concerned about the foetus, e.g. failed ante-natal appointments, continued use of street drugs (Kearney and Aldridge, 1989). Given the potential vulnerability of children pre-natally exposed to alcohol or drugs, and/or the challenging behaviours exhibited by children born to substance abusing mothers, the parenting skills of the primary caregiver (usually the mother) become more important.

Further explanatory information on the issues of drug use in pregnancy, also embracing how to assess risk can be found in Bays (1993) who explores the impact of addiction on the child and Coleman and Cassell (1995) who explore the direct and indirect effects of drugs and alcohol, both on the individual as well as family life. (Coleman and Cassell, 1995). The reader is referred to the Local Government drug forum/SCODA policy guidelines (1997) for detailed information on the issues relating to drug-using parents and Murphy and Harbin (Chapter 20).

Alcohol use

The first twelve weeks of pregnancy is when the embryo is developing and the potential teratogenic effects are likeliest. The teratogenic model explains negative consequences of prenatal exposure in terms of direct damage to the foetus caused by exposure in gestation. This model assumes that both physical defects and behaviour problems observed neonatally and during later childhood are the direct result of exposure to a teratogen, which leads to observable deficits in cognitive, emotional and behavioural outcomes (Wilson, 1977). It is popularly assumed that prenatal exposure to alcohol is always associated with negative outcomes. This assumption rests on the idea that these psychoactive substances are teratogens (that is they are chemicals that cause damage to the developing foetus leading to physical birth effects).

Table 1: Factors affecting outcome in children pre-natally exposed to alcohol (Coles, 1995, p10).

1. Genetic and/or physical vulnerability: suggesting that some individuals may have more tendency to be affected by exposure than others.
2. Drug type and drug action (see Table 2 below).
3. Type of exposure: dose, duration during gestation and timing (daily or binge use).
4. Maternal health, access to heath services and prenatal care.
5. Pregnancy complications (e.g. Prematurity).
6. Status variables: (such as postnatal caregiving factors, the immediate family environment, and the general social environment i.e. Socio-economic status), as well as the developmental process itself and the many factors that are known to affect it, e.g. particular behaviours of family members, the caregiver's style, and specific and significant events, such as the loss of a parent, which affect the developing child.
7. Availability of services: prevention, education and treatment.

When a pregnant woman drinks alcohol it crosses the placental barrier, into the baby's blood stream and then to the developing brain. Ideally pre-conceptual care and advice should be sought when attempting to conceive. The advice is to follow the guidelines for safe drinking in pregnancy. The risk to the foetus increases as the mother's alcohol consumption increases but it is not clear whether there is a safe limit for alcohol intake in pregnancy below which there is no risk. It is likely that there may be critical stages in the development of the embryo when it is especially vulnerable to alcohol. The latest guidelines from the Royal College of Obstetricians and Gynaecologists is:

1. No adverse effects on pregnancy outcome have been proven with a consumption of less than 120 grams of alcohol (around 15 units) per week.
2. Consumption of 120 grams (15 units) or more per week has been associated with a reduction in birth weight.
3. Consumption of more than 160 grams (20 units) per week is associated with intellectual impairment in children.

Based on our current knowledge, it is difficult to identify accurately the risk of exposure in any given individual (Coles, 1995). Most women spontaneously reduce alcohol during pregnancy and since the problems exposed with alcohol exposure have become better known, many women have avoided drinking all together. However, Rosett and Weiner (1984) estimated that 5–10 per cent of pregnant women drank at levels high enough to place their foetuses at risk. Fortunately, foetal alcohol syndrome (FAS) does not occur that frequently. However, it is estimated that FAS has an incidence of 0.3–1 per 1000 live births (Abel and Sokol, 1991). There is

Table 2: Problems noted through alcohol use in pregnancy (Coles, 1995, p11).

- foetal wastage
- facial dysmorphia
- persistent growth retardation
- central nervous system damage/intellectual deficits
- cardiac abnormalities
- neonatal withdrawal
- failure to thrive
- vision and hearing problems
- long-term effects

a wide range of possible outcomes of alcohol use in pregnancy and Table 1 lists some of the factors that are believed to contribute to the impact of alcohol on the foetus and the child. It is important to remember that alcohol may have different effects on both mother and child because of their biochemical actions.

The impact of alcohol consumption during pregnancy on the physical development of children is well established. Intrauterine growth retardation has been found in alcohol exposed infants, due to poor maternal nutrition, the direct effects of alcohol on the foetus, and alcohol's interference with foetal nutritional intake. Alcohol exposed children are often exposed with failure to thrive and growth retardation is often sustained throughout childhood. Neuro-behavioural outcomes include irritability, poorer habituation and orientation, increased tremors, poorer arousal, disturbances of sleep, poorer motor tone and development, and diminished spontaneous movement (Harden, 1998).

A spectrum of specific patterns of physical sequelae exists in children chronically exposed to alcohol in utero, ranging from foetal alcohol effects (FAE) to the more severe foetal alcohol syndrome (FAS). The three primary features of FAS are pre- and post-natal growth retardation, central nervous syndrome dysfunction and facial dysmorphology (Coles, 1993). Other features of FAS include intra-oral deformities, vision and hearing deficits, cardiac problems, hypotonia, poor co-ordination and skeletal malformations. Neuro-behavioural outcomes have been documented such as feeding difficulties, sleep irregularities and hyperactivity Weiner and Morse, 1988). In contrast, children with FAE usually do not have all three types of physical health impairment and often do not display these difficulties throughout childhood.

Children with FAS display severe cognitive impairments, such as mild to moderate mental retardation, with accompanying language and perceptual difficulties (Rosett and Weiner, 1984). Children without the full-blown syndrome also have lower intelligence, language and academic achievement scores. Factors that impede academic functioning have also been noted with these children, including difficulties in reasoning, problem solving, memory, and auditory and visual-motor processing (Coles, 1993).

In the neonatal period, sudden infant death syndrome (SIDS) is approximately five times higher than average among all groups of substance abusers (Regan et al., 1987).

Measuring the family's potential for, and motivation to, change

Workers need to estimate the prospects of change: such as a lessening of acute risk factors, or issues such as compliance, the likely response to intervention, and the means through which change might be achieved. The process of expected change always has to be placed in a short time-scale, because of the expected baby's pressing needs for parenting.

There are a number of useful tools for looking at the prognosis for change and the parent's motivation for achieving change. Tony Morrison 1991) produced an excellent continuum of motivation (see Figure 1), which shows clearly whether the parents motivation for change is only because of external pressures (e.g. threatened or actual legal intervention, known as external forces) or because they themselves recognise the need for change to ensure the expected child is safe (known as internal forces). The greater the internal force, the better the future prognosis, and vice-versa.

Figure 1: A continuum of motivation (adapted from Morrison, 1991, p34).

___

Internal motivators

___

- I want to change.
- I don't like things as they are.
- I am asking for your help.
- I have resources to help solve this.
- I think you can help me.
- I think things can get better.
- I have other support, which I will use to encourage me.
- I accept that I am doing something wrong.
- I accept what you say needs to change.
- I accept that others are right (family, friends, community, agencies).
- You defining the problem clearly helps.
- I understand what change will involve.
- I accept that if I do not change, you will take my children away.
- I can change if you do this for me.
- I'll do whatever you say.
- I agree to do this so the family can be reconstituted.
- It's your job to solve my problem.
- You are my problem.
- I am right and you are wrong.
- I don't have any problems.

___

External motivator

It is important to assess their motivation to sustain any work that has been identified. Questions such as the following may help workers:

- Why is it important that I change?
- Do I have the ability to change?
- What does change really mean?
- What will I have to do that I can't do now?
- What will I not have to do that I do now?
- Who can help me change and in what way?
- What (if anything) have I tried to change in the past, and was it successful? (Calder, 1997).

Determining the way forward

When the assessment identifies a risk of significant harm to a child then an initial child protection conference should be convened. It needs to consider the nature of the risk by collating and weighting various factors, identifying any inter-relationship between factors, and any information which has remained unknown.

The following framework (see Figure 2) allows workers to analyse the future risks and

Figure 2: Risk estimation: a framework for practice (adapted from Corner, n.d.).

Factor	Elevated risk	Lowered isk (Inc. protective factors)
The abusing parent.	• Negative childhood experiences, inc. abuse in childhood; denial of past abuse. • Violence/abuse of others. • Abuse and/or neglect of previous child. • Parental separation from previous children. • No clear explanation. • No full understanding of abuse situation. • No acceptance of responsibility for the abuse. • Antenatal/post-natal neglect. • Age: very young/immature. • Mental disorders or illness. • Learning difficulties. • Non-compliance. • Lack of interest or concern for the child.	• Positive childhood. • Recognition and change in previous violent pattern. • Acknowledges seriousness and responsibility without deflection of blame onto others. • Full understanding and clear explanation of the circumstances in which the abuse occurred. • Maturity. • Willingness and demonstrated capacity and ability for change. • Presence of another safe non-abusing parent. • Compliance with professionals. • Abuse of previous child accepted and addressed in treatment (past/present). • Expresses concern and interest about the effects of the abuse on the child.
Non-abusing parent.	• No acceptance of responsibility for the abuse by their partner. • Blaming others or the child.	• Accepts the risk posed by their partner and expresses a willingness to protect. • Accepts the seriousness of the risk and the consequences of failing to protect. • Willingness to resolve problems and concerns.
Family issues (marital partnership and the wider family).	• Relationship disharmony/instability. • Poor impulse control. • Mental health problems. • Violent or deviant network, involving kin, friends and associates (include drugs, paedophile or criminal networks). • Lack of support for primary carer/unsupportive of each other. • Not working together. • No commitment to equality in parenting. • Isolated environment. • Ostracised by the community. • No relative or friends available. • Family violence (e.g. Spouse). • Frequent relationship breakdown/multiple relationships. • Drug or alcohol abuse.	• Supportive spouse/partner. • Supportive of each other. • Stable, non-violent. • Protective and supportive extended family. • Optimistic outlook. • Previous efforts to address the problem, e.g. Attendance at relate, have secured positive and significant changes (e.g. No violence, drugs, etc). • Supportive community. • Optimistic outlook by family and friends. • Equality in relationship. • Commitment to equality in parenting.
Expected child.	• Special or expected needs. • Perceived as different. • Stressful gender issues.	• Easy baby. • Acceptance of difference.
Parent-baby relationships.	• Unrealistic expectations. • Concerning perception of baby's needs. • Inability to prioritise baby's needs above own. • Foetal abuse or neglect, including alcohol or drug abuse.	• Realistic expectations. • Perception of unborn child normal. • Appropriate preparation. • Understanding or awareness of baby's needs. • Unborn baby's needs prioritised.

Figure 2: Continued.

Factor	Elevated risk	Lowered isk (Inc. protective factors)
Parent-baby relationships. (contd)	• No ante-natal care. • Concealed pregnancy. • Unwanted pregnancy/identified disability (non-acceptance).. • Unattached to foetus. • Gender issues which cause stress. • Differences between parents towards unborn child. • Rigid views of parenting.	• Co-operation with antenatal care. • Sought early medical care. • Appropriate and regular ante-natal care. • Accepted/planned pregnancy. • Attachment to unborn foetus. • Treatment of addiction. • Acceptance of difference-gender /disability. • Parents agree about parenting.
Social.	• Poverty. • Inadequate housing. • No support network. • Delinquent area.	
Future plans.	• Unrealistic plans. • No plans. • Exhibit inappropriate parenting plans. • Uncertainty or resistance to change. • No recognition of changes needed in lifestyle. • No recognition of a problem or a need to change. • Refuse to co-operate. • Disinterested and resistant. • Only one parent co-operating.	• Realistic plans. • Exhibit appropriate parenting expectations and plans. • Appropriate expectation of change. • Willingness to consider changes in lifestyle. • Clear about changes and affect on relationship. • Willingness and ability to work in partnership. • Willingness to resolve problems and concerns. • Parents co-operating equally.

possible protective factors when reaching some decisions on the way forward with the case.

Concluding remarks

The use of this framework should help us move from a reactive, crisis-led response to a more considered, proactive, and needs led response. The aim of the assessment is to accurately identify the level of anticipated risk and look at whether this risk is manageable or not. Our goal is to try and enhance the prospect of maintaining the baby with their parents, either through an inter-agency child protection plan or a detailed package of support. A good plan should ensure that everyone is clear about what will happen when the baby is born and for the pre-birth risk assessment conclusions to be reviewed once the baby has been born and the actual observation of parenting can be started.

References

Abel, E.L. and Sokol, R.J. (1991) A Revised Conservative Estimate of the Incidence of FAS and its Economic Impact. *Alcoholism: Clinical and Experimental Research*. 15: 514–24.

Azzi-Lessing, L. and Olsen, L.J. (1996) Substance Abuse-Affected Families in the Child Welfare System: New Challenges, New Alliances. *Social Work*. 41: 1, 15–23.

Barker, R.W. (1997) Unborn Children and Child Protection; Legal, Policy and Practice Issues. *The Liverpool Law Review*. XIX: 2 219–29.

Bays, J. (1993) Substance Abuse and Child Abuse: The Impact of Addiction on the Child. In Hobbs, C.J. and Wynne, J.M. (Eds.) *Child Abuse*. London: Bailliere Tindall, 121–47.

Calder, M.C. (1995) Child Protection: Balancing Paternalism and Partnership. *British Journal of Social Work*. 25: 6, 749–66.

Calder, M.C., Hampson, A. and Skinner, J. (1999) *Working With Adult Males Who Sexually Abuse Children: A Practitioners Guide*. Dorset: Russell House Publishing.

Calder, M.C. (1999b) Towards Anti-oppressive Practice With Ethnic Minority Groups. In Calder, M.C. and Horwath, J. (Eds.) *Working for Children on the Child Protection Register: An*

Inter-agency Practice Guide. Aldershot: Arena, 177–209.

Calder, M.C. (2000) *The Complete Guide to Sexual Abuse Assessments.* Dorset: Russell House Publishing.

Calder, M.C. (2001) *Juveniles and Children Who Sexually Abuse: Frameworks for Assessment.* (2nd edn) Dorset: Russell House Publishing.

Calder, M.C. (2002) A Framework for Conducting Risk Assessments. *Child Care in Practice.* 8(1): 7–18.

Calder, M.C. (forthcoming) *Children Living With Domestic Violence: Empirically Grounded Frameworks for Assessment and Intervention.* Dorset: Russell House Publishing.

Calder, M.C. (forthcoming b) *Towards effective practice with involuntary clients.* Dorset: Russell House Publishing.

Calder, M.C., Peake, A. and Rose, K. (2001) *Mothers of Sexually Abused Children: A Framework for Assessment, Understanding and Support.* Dorset: Russell House Publishing.

City of Salford Community and Social Services Department (2000) *Family Assessments.* Dorset: Russell House Publishing.

Coleman, R. and Cassell, D. (1995) Parents Who Misuse Drugs and Alcohol. In Reder, P. and Lucey, C. (Eds.) *Assessment of Parenting.* London: Routledge, 182–93.

Coles, C.D. (1995) Children of Parents' Who Abuse Drugs and Alcohol. In Smith, G.H., Coles, C.D., Poulsen, M.K. and Cole, C.K. (Eds.) *Children, Families and Substance Abuse: Challenges for Changing Educational and Social Outcomes.* Baltimore: Paul H Brookes Publishing Company, 3–23.

Congress, E.P. (1994) The use of Culturagrams to Assess and Empower Culturally Diverse Families. *Families in Society.* Nov. 531–40.

Corner, R. (nd) *Pre-birth Risk Assessment: Developing a Model of Practice.* Carmarthen: NSPCC.

DoH (1988) *Protecting Children: A Guide for Social Workers Undertaking a Comprehensive Assessment.* London: HMSO.

Hardy, K.V. and Laszloffy, T.A. (1995) The Cultural Genogram. *Journal of Marital and Family Therapy.* 21: 3, 227–37.

Ivanoff, A., Blythe, B.J, and Tripodi, T. (1994) *Involuntary Clients in Social Work Practice: A Research-based Approach.* NY: Aldine de Gruyter.

Kearney ,P. and Aldridge, T. (1989) Drug Abuse and Child Care. In Sills, P. (Ed.) *Child Abuse: Challenges for Policy and Practice.* Wallington, Surrey: Reed Business Publishing.

Lazarus, A.A. (1976) *Multi-modal Behaviour Therapy.* NY: Springer Publishing Company.

Local Government Drug Forum/SCODA (1997) *Drug Using Parents : Policy Guidelines for Inter-agency Working.* London: Local Government Management Board.

Morrison, T. (1991) Change, Control, and the Legal Framework. In Adcock, M., White, R. and Hollows, A. (Eds.) *Significant Harm: Its Management and Outcome.* Croydon: Significant Publications, 85–100.

Regan, D.O., Ehrlich, S.M. and Finnegan, L.P. (1987) Infants of Drug Addicts: At Risk for Child Abuse, Neglect, and Placement in Foster Care. *Neurotoxicology and Teratology.* 9: 315–9.

Rosett, H.L. and Weiner, L. (1984) *Alcohol and the Foetus: A Clinical Perspective.* NY: Open University Press.

Saleebey, D. (1996) The Strengths Perspective in Social Work Practice: Extensions and Cautions. *Social Work.* 41: 3 296–305.

Saleebey, D. (Ed.) (1992) *The Strengths Perspective in Social Work Practice.* NY: Longman.

SCODA (1989) *Drug Using Parents and Their Children: Issues for Policy Makers.* The second report of the National Local Authority Forum on Drugs Misuse, in conjunction with SCODA. London: Standing Conference on Drug Abuse.

Smith, G. (1994) Parent, Partner, Protector. In Morrison, T. et al. (Ed.) *Sexual Offending Against Children.* London: Routledge, 178–202

Chapter Twenty-Two

Assessments Using an Attachment Perspective

David Howe

Introduction

Most children, even those in situations of abuse and neglect, develop a selective attachment relationship with their main carer. What is of particular interest to child care practitioners and attachment researchers is the quality and character of the attachment. Very different developmental prospects are associated with each pattern of attachment. Moreover, particular attachment patterns form within particular caregiving environments. Therefore key to understanding children's behaviour, mental states, and developmental prospects is the ability to fathom how parent-child relationships shape young, growing minds.

In this sense, attachment is more than just another perspective. It offers a theoretical framework within which to make sense of the complex relationship between the quality of parenting, children's development and the character of the environment. An assessment framework, such as that offered by the Department of Health (2000), that encourages practitioners to gather more and better information is to be welcomed. But the key question remains: What is to be done with all the information once it has been collected? Although there are a variety of suggestions in the new assessment framework about how the facts and figures might be categorised and ordered, what is still largely missing is a theoretical driver, something that *explains* what is going on and how all the disparate bits of information might be linked, including the carer's parenting capacity, the child's developmental needs, and family and environmental factors. It is theories that help *make sense* of facts.

For example, a geologist might make a large number of observations and collect a myriad of facts about a volcano including the viscosity of the magma, how much gas is dissolved in the molten rock, the chemical composition of the liquid melt, and land movements. But none of these in themselves will help the geologist predict whether this particular volcano will erupt violently and catastrophically or smoulder

and extrude quietly and benignly. The earth scientist needs to know how volcanoes work as complex, dynamic, physico-chemical systems if they are to predict future courses of event. Theories of mantle flows, plate tectonics and the formation of volcanoes help the geologist interpret the particular facts about this specific volcano. For example, if the magma is acidic, viscous, and rich in dissolved gases and the volcano is located in a continental mountain chain bordering an oceanic plate, they might expect the eruption to be violent and dangerous. All the measurements and observations gathered about a particular volcano have to be interpreted with reference to the theory before an explanation, prediction and recommendation can take place.

In similar fashion, no amount of information about a particular child and their family tells the practitioner what is actually going on psychologically, developmentally and interpersonally. Explanations and understandings depend on empirical facts being seen as surface manifestations of a deeper psychosocial order in which complex cause and effect relationships occur. In this way, behaviours can make conceptual sense. Theoretical connections can be seen between say, a carer's mental state and a child's behaviour. If the practitioner can begin to appreciate how minds work, including his or her own as it is affected by emotionally challenging work, what previously might have been puzzling and frustrating can become understandable and interesting, thus freeing the worker to become more emotionally available, confident and compassionate.

Developmental attachment theory not only provides the conceptual tools to make sense of parents and children in need, it also directs the practitioner what to look for and how to look for it. In short, an attachment perspective sees a much more dynamic relationship between carers, their parenting capacity, and children's development.

Key to this approach is a time dimension. It is impossible to make sense of current behaviours and states of mind, whether of the parent or the child, without understanding people's relationship history. Assessments therefore need to gather information not only about children and their relationship history but also gain as full a picture as possible of the parent's own socio-emotional experiences as a child, adolescent, and adult. As we shall see, an attachment-based assessment can happily use the information generated by the Department of Health's *Framework for the Assessment of Children in Need and their Families*, but it thinks about it in a way that links the carer's relationship history to his or her current emotional, cognitive and behavioural capacities which in turn create the psychosocial environment in which the child's biopsychosocial development takes place.

Practitioners using developmental attachment theory have to acquire knowledge of and expertise in the extensive research base and thinking that now informs modern attachment theory. There are no short cuts to this knowledge, but conscientious study rewards the practitioner with many dividends including the ability to understand how parents and their behaviour affect children and their behaviour, how families emotionally impact on practitioners, and which interventions are likely to be most appropriate in particular cases.

A brief review of the main theoretical features of modern attachment now follows (for a fuller treatment of the subject the interested reader is referred to one or more of a number of good introductory texts that are now available e.g. Cassidy and Shaver, 1999; Goldberg, 1999; Heard and Lake, 1997; Howe et al., 1999).

The attachment system

The human infant is vulnerable and dependent. To enhance survival, the baby arrives with a number of pre-programmed, automatic behavioural systems already in place. These systems are triggered by environmental stimuli. The attachment system is activated when the young child feels anxious, distressed, frightened or confused. It triggers attachment behaviour which is designed to get the vulnerable infant into close proximity with an adult who provides protection, comfort and care. Attachment behaviour includes the emission of distress and engagement signals including crying, clinging, fretfulness, smiling, following, and displays of vulnerability. The normal effect of attachment behaviour is either to bring the attachment figure to the child or to propel the child to the attachment figure. A child who feels unprotected or without care is likely to experience strong feelings of fear and distress. These are basic emotions, the experience of which is highly likely to lead to attachment behaviour. The two essential components of competent care giving are therefore the provision of protection and care.

Children are also born prosocial. Attachment theory recognises a universal human need to form close affectional bonds. In fact, attachment is a special type of social relationship between infants and their carers involving an affective bond in which children learn to regulate their emotions (Bowlby, 1979). Infants find social stimuli particularly engaging, and they appear eager to experience and make sense of themselves and other people, psychologically and socially. The combination of attachment behaviour, which for most children involves regular interaction with parents, particularly mothers, and prosocial behaviour, results in infants forming a clear-cut attachment to a primary selective attachment figure and possibly a small number of secondary attachment figures by around seven months of age. And with the attachment bond come not only care and protection, but also an affectional relationship which leads to psychological and social understanding.

Young brains are also programmed to make sense of experience. If the infant is to maximise care and protection, and hence survival, a key experience of which to make sense is the mind and behaviour of the attachment figure. Psychologically speaking, how does she work? How can I make sense of her? How can I elicit care and protection and have my needs met?

The other basic requirement if the infant is to increase their chances of survival, is to make sense of not just the other, but also the self. Indeed, the very sense of self only becomes possible as the young mind interacts with others. This being the case, the quality of the interaction with the attachment figure will affect the sense of self that emerges out of the child's relationship with their carers. This is why attachment theorists take such an interest in the quality and character of the parent-child relationship. Indeed, the work of neuroscientists, such as Schore (1994), remind us that young brains enter the world programmed to organise themselves in the light of their experience – the brain is a self-organising developmental structure. If children are to function as competent social beings, then not only must the young brain learn to make sense of physical experience, but it also has to make sense of psychological experience, including the mental make-up of the self, the other, and the cultural context in which parents and their children find themselves. If a child fails to understand the way thoughts, feelings and behaviour interact and affect each other, both within minds and between minds, social life in that cultural context is destined to become very difficult. Indeed, it is this very difficulty that brings so many children to the attention of child welfare agencies.

Secure attachments

Children who find themselves in relationship with parents whose care giving is broadly sensitive, loving, responsive, attuned, consistent, available and accepting develop *secure attachments*. Parents are interested in and alert to their infant's physical needs and states of mind. They are anxious to understand their child and to be understood by their child. The more each party in the relationship understands the mind of the other, the more co-ordinated, co-operative, effective and satisfying is their relationship likely to be. If the child feels loved and understood, the child will develop a cognitive representation (an internal working model) of the self as lovable and psychologically intelligible. If attachment figures show interest and concern, and respond sympathetically to needs, the child will mentally represent others are potentially interested, available and responsive at times of need. In the face of stress and challenge, secure children have a positive view of others as available as a resource.

The richer, more textured, consistent and open are the communications between parent and child, the more psychological information the child has of which to make good sense of both the self and the other. This is particularly true in the case of emotions and states of arousal. Children need to recognise, understand and regulate their emotions if they are to become competent social players. In relationship with carers who are consistent and open, accurate and reciprocal, not only do children have the maximum amount of psychological and behavioural information on which to draw, but they also have information which is relatively accurate and undistorted. With the help of their carers and an increasingly

sophisticated understanding of their own mental states, secure children remain relatively organised under stress. Negative feelings do not easily overwhelm or psychologically threaten them.

In rich, two-way relationships, children quickly recognise that other people have minds and what goes on in those minds in terms of thoughts and feelings, beliefs and intentions, hopes and desires helps *explain* their behaviour and helps *predict* their actions and responses. Children learn quickly that other people are also dealing with them as intentional beings; that they are trying to understand the mental state of the child's self to work out their feelings and thoughts, needs and behaviour in order to respond most appropriately. Out of such relationships, securely attached children develop a positive view of self, good self-esteem and self-efficacy, and a recognition that both one's own and other people's behaviour can be explained psychologically (the ability to 'mentalise') and that the psychosocial world can make sense. People who are able to look at themselves objectively, and evaluate openly and without distortion their own and other people's mental states (what Fonagy and Target (1997) call reflective-function) generally show the highest levels of social competence, including satisfactory relationships with peers, partners and their own children. Children who fail to develop good reflective function or 'metacognition' (thinking about thinking) find it difficult to contain thoughts and the strong feelings they engender.

Insecure attachments

Some children find themselves in attachment relationships in which there are distortions, errors and omissions in the psychological communications that take place between them and their carers (Crittenden, 1997). As the quality of shared information affects the quality of mind achieved by the child, deficits in communication increase the risk of children forming an insecure attachment. Insecure attachments are also associated with reduced reflective-function, and more negative representations of self and others. In general, the different patterns of attachment related behaviour are underpinned by different strategies adopted by children to regulate their emotional reactions. As affect regulation is acquired with the help of the child's primary caregiver, the child's strategy will be inevitably a reflection of the caregiver's behaviour towards them (Fonagy, undated, p3). Three basic patterns of insecure attachment are recognised: avoidant/defended, ambivalent (resistant), and disorganised/controlling.

Avoidant attachments

Carers who feel anxious and irritated when their own children make emotional demands on them tend to distance themselves as infants signal their distress. Furthermore, rather than attempt to understand the child and his or her state of mind, carers prefer to impose on the child their own views of how 'good' children should behave and see themselves. These imposed definitions typically see 'good' children as those who do not make emotional demands on parents. Parents who reject attachment behaviour and intrude into the mind of the child their own ideas of how children should behave and see themselves, generate a distinctive type of care giving known as 'rejecting' or 'dismissing'. The infant has to try and understand this caregiving environment in order to adapt and maximise the care and protection available under the psychological conditions generated by the parent.

Children who develop *avoidant* attachments adapt to 'rejecting' caregiving by downplaying and inhibiting their emotions and feelings of need. They *over-regulate* their emotions. In effect, they deactivate their attachment behaviour as a way of increasing parental acceptance, responsivity and availability. They earn most parental attention when they behave as they believe the parent would prefer them to behave. Characteristic of avoidant children is therefore a tendency to be emotionally independent, self-sufficient, self-contained, and compliant, at least in the presence of the carer. Thus, the parent-child relationship, which is *predictably* and *consistently* unresponsive to displays of negative affect, deprives the child of exposure to the full range of the emotions. The child therefore learns what is required to stay on the right side of her carer, but does not learn how to elicit care and protection. Indeed, intimacy and emotional closeness, which in the past increased the child's fear of rejection and hurt, tend to be avoided. These mechanisms mean that for the avoidant personality, being in a state of need and emotional arousal increases feelings of anxiety.

Ambivalent attachments

In contrast, carers who remain underinvolved with their children are experienced as *inconsistent*. In the child's mind, there is no relationship between their behaviour, whether or not the carer responds, and if they do respond, what type of response might follow. The carer is more sensitive to whether or not she believes her child loves and accepts her than she is of the child's needs. The parent is relatively insensitive to the child's internal states. She is slow to respond to signals of distress, including the child's attachment behaviour.

In attempts to increase parental responsivity, children increase their displays of distress, including crying, fretting, whining, attention-seeking behaviour, fussing, fractiousness and being very demanding. In effect, they hyperactivate their attachment behaviour in an attempt to overcome the caregiver's insensitivity. This hyperactivated attachment strategy seeks to increase the parent's predictability. The pattern associated with this attachment strategy is known as *ambivalent* because the child desires an increase in parental responsivity but also feels angry that parental care and protection cannot be taken-for-granted. When attention is won, the child does not trust the parent to remain involved and so resists being soothed and comforted so that the pattern is also referred to as a *resistant* attachment. In this adaptation, the child's emotions remain under-regulated. There is a preoccupation with and hypersensitivity to other people's emotional availability and interest. One of the consequences of this preoccupation is that the child plays poorly, becoming easily distressed at the prospect of being left alone either psychologically or physically. If the child, or indeed adult, feels that the other's interest is being lost or withheld, attention-seeking behaviour increases even further. Anxiety and anger remain heightened, and caregivers find it difficult to provide reassurance. In turn, carers begin to feel increasingly anxious, uncertain and angry.

If the 'hyperactivated' attachment strategy fails, the individual experiences despair and depression, although it is usually not too long before they precipitate some drama or crisis as they provoke other people into some kind of reaction. Children show poor concentration, are easily distracted, and frequently display moodiness and feelings of helplessness. By

nder-regulating emotional arousal, the
dividual feels that they can increase other
eople's predictability and consistency. They
egin to control other people's previous
npredictability through coercive behaviour
sing, in particular, strong displays of emotions,
cluding threat, anger, need, desire and
eduction. However, those on the receiving end
f this unregulated, demanding and needy
motional style can soon feel drained, angry and
chausted with the result they attempt to
ithdraw and even give-up on the relationship,
ereby confirming the ambivalent person's fear
at other people can't be trusted and will
ventually let you down.

isorganised/controlling attachments

lthough feeling insecure, both the avoidant
nd ambivalent patterns witness an attempt by
e child to organise their attachment
ehaviour, either by its deactivation or
yperactivation, in order to maximise the
tachment figure's availability. However, some
ildren find themselves in more complex
lationship environments. Carers who frighten
eir children, intentionally or otherwise,
resent their infants with a psychological
ilemma. Fear normally activates attachment
ehaviour, which as we have seen, is designed
 propel the infant into close proximity with
e attachment figure where he or she might
xpect to experience feelings of safety,
motional containment, comfort and care. But if
e attachment figure is the source of the fear,
e child experiences simultaneous feelings of
scape and approach which cannot be resolved.
[aving experienced the caregiver as a source of
oth danger and reassurance, fear and
ttachment are out of balance. The child cannot
rganise an attachment strategy to increase
elings of care and protection – hence the
ehaviour is described as *disorganised* or
isoriented*. For example, in the presence of their
aregiver, distressed infants might freeze,
isplay head banging, or show confused
voidance/approach behaviours.

Disorganised attachments are commonly
ound in children whose carers are physically
nd/or sexually abusive, severely neglectful,
eavy abusers of alcohol and/or drugs,
ronically depressed, disturbed by unresolved
elings of loss and/trauma, the victims of
omestic violence, or any combination of these.
 short, disorganised attachments are most

likely to be observed in children who have
experienced abuse and neglect, which is to say
caregiving which is both dangerous *and*
unpredictable, frightening *and* inconsistent. In
these environments, children can find no
strategy that enables them to regulate their
emotions. Children whose attachment behaviour
is classified as disorganised in infancy are at the
greatest risk of developing maladaptive
behaviours and mental health problems.

However, with maturation, disorganised
children develop overlays of organisation based
on one or more *controlling* strategies (for a more
detailed treatment of this subject, see Cassidy
and Shaver, 1999; Howe et al., 1999; Solomon
and George, 1999). For example, children whose
parents are rejecting and physically abusive
often develop *compulsively compliant* behaviours
in relationship with their caregivers. In an
extreme form of avoidance, these children
suppress displays of need, attachment
behaviour and emotion. They quickly become
independent, self-contained and self-sufficient.

Other children might experience their carers
as needy, and unable to care or protect
themselves never mind the child. For young
children, this is frightening. Carers whose own
needs drown those of their children include
those who are regularly beaten up by their
partners, addicted to alcohol or drugs, suffer
major depression, or feel helpless under stress
and states of unresolved trauma. One way for
children to establish a relationship with such
carers is to worry about and care for them in
acts of *compulsive caregiving*, also known as
'parentified behaviour' or role reversal. These
are anxious, stressed children who try to
maintain a false, brittle cheerfulness, fearing the
loss of their parent, if not physically, then
emotionally and psychologically.

Children whose parents are both abusive and
neglectful have particularly difficult caregiving
environments in which to survive. Their world
is one of unpredictable violence and random
neglect. They experience parents as either out-
of-control and aggressive, or helpless and
needy. Such parents appear to have abdicated
their role as carer and protector (George and
Solomon, 1996). In these conditions, children
avoid being cared for – for them, care implies
danger and hurt. They seek to be in control
rather than be controlled. These children have
survived by trusting only themselves. The result
is that children, often from a very young age
become bossy, aggressive, violent, self-abusive,

self-endangering, fearful, helpless, sad, and extremely difficult to look after whether by their biological parents or new, substitute carers. These *aggressively-controlling* children are often diagnosed as suffering a disorder of attachment and present child care agencies with some of their most taxing cases.

There are also compound versions of these controlling strategies in which children can switch between compliance, parentification, and fearful-aggressive controlling behaviours. These children can be perplexing unless the practitioner understands the origins of these disturbed behaviours and dissociated states of mind.

Conducting an assessment

The first task in carrying out an assessment is to collect as much observational and descriptive information about the child and his or her family as possible. The Assessment Framework certainly helps but it tends to lack an historical dimension, vital if the quality of care provided by the parents and the child's behaviour are to make sense. A number of research procedures and instruments now exist that help increase our understanding of adults' and children's attachment behaviours and states of mind. These include the strange situation procedure, projective storytelling, drawing tasks, and the Adult Attachment Interview. However, interpretation of this material generally requires specialist training which can be long and expensive. In spite of this limitation, child care practitioners generally score over researchers in the sense that the knowledge they acquire about parents and their children is often extremely detailed and informed. Such knowledge can be found in files, gained on visits to see how people interact in their home setting, acquired in conversation with teachers and health workers, and gathered at case conferences.

As an attachment-oriented assessment seeks to understand children's states of mind, mental representations and behaviours in terms of their attempts to adapt to, make sense of and survive in a particular caregiving environment, information is first organised and ordered into three dynamically connected domains:

1. The carer's own behavioural and relationship history as a child, adolescent and adult.
2. The quality and character of the caregiving environment, both in the past and the present.

3. The child's behaviour and relationship style both in the past and present, and in different social contexts (for example, home, family, nursery, school, peer group). The child's behaviour and relationship style provides clues about his or her attempts to adapt to, make sense of, cope with, function and survive in his or her caregiving environment.

In practice, the information gathered in each of these domains will, at best, be partial and incomplete. Nevertheless, there is usually enough for the practitioner to hypothesise the state of mind and mental representations (internal working model) of the caregiver or the child. Equally important, it is also possible to hypothesise from the characteristics of one domain the likely characteristics of the other two. For example, if a child shows a particular range of needs and behaviours, the research evidence available would suggest that these needs and behaviours are typically associated with particular parenting and caregiving styles. The practitioner can then check out what is known about the caregiving style of the parent to see how well it matches the hypothesis based on the child's observed needs and behaviours. If there is a reasonable match, the practitioner can have increased confidence in the hypothesis and the psychological dynamics that link particular caregiving environments with certain development needs and behaviours in children. This allows the assessment to go beyond mere description to more sophisticated levels of explanation and diagnosis, which in turn inform decision making, treatment plans, support strategies, and case management. The following example illustrates the process.

A case of parental rejection and abuse, and an aggressive child

Josh

Josh is seven years of age. When he was three, he was asked to leave his play group where he had been persistently aggressive towards other children, pushing and prodding them, and hitting them with toys. At home, his mother, Joanna, said that he 'got under' her feet. Although occasionally Josh shouted back at and became angry with his mother, he tended to be watchful. A health visitor observed that he seemed anxious to please his mother, although she also mentioned that he looked a rather sullen little boy. Josh's step-father worked as a long-distance lorry driver and tended to be at ome only at weekends. His mother said he ever misbehaved when his (step) Dad was round: 'He wouldn't dare.'

When Josh started school, he was soon in rouble for 'disruptive behaviour' which, according to his teacher, meant he was forever ghting with other children, not just at laytimes but also during class. He said that ther children started it by 'winding' him up. Ie always appeared to have a 'stern' look. This nade him unpopular with other children. An ttack by a group of older boys left him bruised nd hurt, but he didn't cry, simply saying 'I on't care; they're all pricks.' However, his eacher said she had a touch of sympathy for osh. On one occasion after she had complained o his mother about his behaviour, he came into chool the next day with the faded marks of a allpoint pen on his forehead where his mother ad written in capitals ARSEHOLE. Around the ame time, a neighbour reported that she had een Josh standing in the garden late one ebruary night without a coat. When she asked im why he was out so late, he replied that he vasn't allowed back in the house until he had :ooled down' and was shivering with cold. She aid he looked 'perished' but wasn't crying or isibly upset. When the neighbour knocked on he door to tell Josh's mother that she thought it vas time for him to be let indoors, she was told o 'Mind her own sodding business' and that if vou had to live with Josh, you'd bury him in ne garden never mind just make him stand nere. No little brat is going to tell me what to o, the bossy little bugger.'

nterim hypothesis

Although the description of Josh and his ehaviour is sketchy, a number of themes begin o emerge. Josh is aggressive, particularly with is peers. Although there are hints that he has een 'bossy' with his mother, his general emeanour with his parents tends to be :ompliant'. His mother punishes him in ways nat are 'power assertive' – verbal abuse, umiliation, physical harshness. Josh rarely hows his emotions. These descriptions are onsistent with young minds that feel ncomfortable displaying need and strong eelings. The child's internal working model epresents the self as self-contained and other eople as emotionally unavailable, rejecting nd, if strong, dominating. If other people are erceived as weak, in turn the child believes

they should expect to be dominated, often in an aggressive manner. Children who suppress their own needs and affect and show mixtures of compliance, bossiness and aggression suggest an adaptive strategy based on a deactivation of their attachment system (avoidance) and an increasing tendency to develop controlling behaviours, often aggressive in nature, designed to keep the frightened self as safe as possible.

Research findings suggest that the parenting style of children with these needs and behaviours are typically disengaged and rejecting. The carer's own relationship history, including childhood, is likely to have been emotionally harsh and depriving. Research also predicts that such parents tend to keep practitioners at a distance, and although they might treat the authorities 'correctly', they rarely encourage anything other than the most formal relationship. It is not unusual for practitioners to find parents with these characteristics intimidating, legalistic and liable to make regular and frequent formal complaints to higher authorities.

The next step in the assessment is to see whether the facts support the interim hypothesis. If there is only scanty information available, the hypothesis might indicate that the practitioner needs to collect more information or make further observations, either to support, modify or disconfirm the hypothesis.

The character and quality of the caregiving environment generated by Joanna, Josh's mother.

Joanna describes her upbringing as 'strict'. Her mother emigrated to Canada with her boyfriend when Joanna was three, leaving her and her younger brother in the care of their father. Not long after the separation, he remarried. Joanna says her step-mother was 'horrible'. She favoured her own son, Joanna's half brother, who was five years her junior. As the only girl, Joanna was made to do all the chores. Her step-mother was rarely satisfied with Joanna's standards or achievements. If her step-mother felt the dishes that Joanna had just washed were not sufficiently clean, she was made to do them all again. When Joanna was late returning home from school, she was either made to beg for her dinner by sitting like a dog with its paws in the air (which seemed to amuse her step-mother) or sent to bed early without anything to eat. Joanna said she was often beaten with a leather belt for misdemeanours. Joanna entered residential care when she was fifteen as a result of increasing levels of violence between her step-mother and herself. Little is known of her experiences in late adolescence and early adulthood.

Joanna had a violent relationship with Josh's father. As a little boy, Josh witnessed many rows, most of them ending up as physical fights. His parents eventually separated. Joanna met Mal, her current partner, three years ago. She has said that Josh and his difficult behaviour isn't going to spoil the relationship she has with Mal. She believes that Josh misbehaves deliberately: 'He only does it to wind me and Mal up. He's a little bastard and I've just about had enough of him. I've tried but he goes too far. I'm not sure I like him anymore. He's very hard work and I'm just really fed up with him and I just couldn't be bothered and I'm sick of going down to that school of his and seeing those teachers. I wish I'd never met his Dad and then I wouldn't be having all this shit now.'

Joanna did not ask for social work involvement. The original referral came as an anonymous phone call accusing Joanna of being unfit to care for her son. The caller had seen Josh walking to school on his own, a journey that involved crossing a busy road. From the outset, Joanna made it clear that social workers would have no automatic right to visit and 'snoop into her business.' She insisted that they telephone in advance to make an appointment at hours that were convenient to her. These times included weekends as well as late evenings. However, more recently Joanna has said that Josh has behaviour problems that 'he's probably got from his Dad who was a head-case.' The choices she gives social workers are either to stop interfering or to remove Josh. She never initiates contact. Her manner with professionals is frosty and impatient with barely concealed irritation. The social worker, on the few times that she has been let into the house, failed to see any evidence of the presence of a young boy – there were no toys visible, no photographs of Josh on display, no drawings or paintings on show either in the kitchen or living room.

Analysis and explanation

In broad terms, the hypothesis about the likely character of Josh's caregiving environment is supported by the evidence. Josh's behaviour can therefore be seen as adaptive in that it has helped him to make sense of himself and others, at least in the context of the relationship he ha had with his mother. However, what might be functional in one environment might be dysfunctional in another. His understanding o his own mind and the minds of others is the product of his interaction with those with whom he has had a close relationship, including thei states of mind and mental representations of se and others, including him.

In terms of developmental attachment theory if Josh and his needs and behaviours are to be understood, sense has to be made of the way Joanna's relationship with her son has affected his ability to understand and regulate his emotions. Difficulty in dealing competently wit others has resulted in Josh getting into trouble more and more often both at home and at schoo An assessment which offers an explanation of the psychological dynamics of the situation allows decisions about Josh to be made with greater confidence. It also suggests the best courses of practical action. In Josh's case, the practitioner needs to decide whether Josh has any future with his mother, and if he does, wha work and with whom (Joanna, Josh, Joanna an Josh, the whole family?) would be necessary an the most effective. If the decision was made to place Josh in substitute care, an attachment-oriented assessment would also highlight the likely impact that his internal working model would have on both his behaviour and on his new carers. The assessmer would therefore indicate the kind of guidance and support the new carers would require to help them meet Josh's developmental needs.

In the case of Josh, the assessment seeks to link the characteristics of the caregiving environment, his behaviour and its strategic purpose, and his internal working model (mental representation of self, others and relationships):

1. *Caregiving environment, including caregiver's own relationship history.* Joanna's own childhood was strict and emotionally harsh She lost her own mother as a toddler. She suffered humiliation and rejection. These experiences are likely to adversely impact o her parenting capacities. Not having experienced much love as a child, she is uncomfortable with both her own states of need and those of others. She anticipates rejection and defends against it by either being disengaged, aggressive, or self-contained.

The research evidence indicates that carers who feel anxious when their own children make demands on them typically react by 'rejecting' displays of need and attachment behaviour. They show little interest in wanting to understand the mind of their child and what might be causing them distress, preferring to impose their own semantic definitions on what is and is not appropriate: 'Little boys who get hurt don't cry' or 'Worthy children don't make demands on their parents; therefore if you make demands on me, this means you are not a worthy child and unworthy children deserve to be punished.' Joanna believes that the harsh parenting which she received in her own childhood is the best way to handle Josh. Like other 'rejecting' and abusive carers, Joanna's cognitive schemata of other people, including her own child, is that unless checked or avoided, other people will attempt to dominate and subjugate you, and the self will be rejected if one seeks to have one's own needs fulfilled. Typically, Josh's emotional needs and attachment behaviours trigger caregiving that is controlling, hostile, critical, anxious and punitive. Joanna attributes motives to Josh that are either irrational or distorted – for example, that even as 3-year-old, she believed he was winding her up 'deliberately.' These inappropriate beliefs would often lead to harsh punishments. Joanna expresses little pleasure or satisfaction in her role as a mother. She expects Josh to be independent and non-needy. Whenever he fails to meet her age-inappropriate expectations – which given the unreasonableness of her expectations he is bound to do – she either belittles him, dismisses him as 'a waste of space', or punishes him.

Behavioural and developmental sequelae of rejected (and abused) children: Josh is beginning to show a number of behaviours common in children who have suffered emotional rejection and abuse. He is aggressive with his peers which makes him unpopular. In a manner not unlike his mother's relationship with him, he quickly attributes hostile intent to others, even when the stimulus is objectively neutral. For example, eye contact made casually by another child might be interpreted as a hostile act by Josh, who then aggressively demands to know what the other child is 'staring at'. He sees acquiescence, being apologetic, showing his feelings and being needy as weakness. He values only strength and power. Only if he perceives the other as more powerful and potentially dangerous than himself does he show compliance. He still shows wariness with his step-father, but increasingly his behaviour with his mother is shifting from watchful containment to bossy aggression and dismissal. Under stress, which he experiences frequently, he shows anger. His facial expression is sullen.

3. *Internal working model, mental representations and adaptive strategies*: Josh's behaviours and relationship style can be understood as examples of an avoidant/ controlling attachment. Although his mother's behaviour is hostile, it is consistent and predictable. Josh knows that his mother is likely to be emotionally most rejecting when he makes the greatest demands on her caregiving – in other words when he displays careseeking behaviour. It is hurtful and frightening to feel rejected by your caregiver at those very times when you most need her care and protection. Perversely, the strategy that appears to maximise her availability and responsiveness is to inhibit attachment behaviour, downplay negative emotional states, and develop self-sufficiency and self-containment. However, in Josh's case, even this strategy appears to have received only partial success. Often at times of fear (for example, witnessing violence between his mother and biological father, being rejected by his mother when in a state of distress), his attempts to organise his attachment behaviour have failed to increase his feelings of security. In infancy this leaves the child's attachment system in a state of disorganisation.

But with maturation, children in frightening environments develop various controlling strategies in which they attempt to provide themselves with their own care and protection. This can take a wide variety of forms. In the case of Josh, his psychological survival strategy appears to have been one of aggressive control. His experience has been that when others are allowed to be in control, he feels either in danger or in a state of psychological hurt. Thus, Josh has survived and adapted by inhibiting displays of negative affect and neediness, being in control rather than being controlled by others, and reacting aggressively whenever he perceives danger or being at the mercy of more powerful and dangerous forces.

All of this comes at a considerable developmental cost. By suppressing and denying his feelings, Josh will fail to understand emotions in both himself and other people. The world of relationships and social intercourse requires emotional literacy and psychological competence. A lack of empathy makes social relationships confusing and difficult, which is stressful. And under stress, we know that Josh reacts with anger and aggression. These are not attractive characteristics. They will make it more likely that Josh will be rejected by his peers, perpetuating the vicious circle. So, although Josh has learned how to minimise being rejected and frightened by his carers, he has not learned how to elicit care and protection, warmth and unconditional love.

The state of mind and internal working model that Josh develops within this caregiving environment is also characteristic of an avoidant/controlling attachment. He will mentally represent his self as one unworthy of love, care and protection. His self-esteem will therefore be low. In the past his experience of being close and dependent is one of rejection, even danger. Therefore, he will feel anxious and frightened whenever others move into his psychological and physical space. This insight has important implications for new carers. He will feel least anxious when he is in control which will include being independent and emotionally without need. Other people cannot be trusted or expected to meet one's needs for care and protection, love and intimacy. Children who have developed avoidant strategies have learned not to ask for their caregiver's help in times of need and distress. They act as if nothing is wrong when in a distressed state. If these behaviours are imported into new relationships, foster carers or adoptive parents can easily feel that they are not needed or wanted by the child, which is disappointing and even hurtful. New carers can find themselves beginning either to back off, deactivate their caregiving or ignore the child (Stovall and Dozier 1998).

It appears to Josh that love, attention and relationships are in short supply and allocated on the basis of power. Only the strong get what they want out of relationships. Therefore power and aggression appear to be the basis on which relationships work.

Although insecure attachment patterns represent an attempt by children to cope with their caregiving environment, each comes at a particular developmental price. In Josh's case, he has learned to adapt by over-regulating his emotions and not trusting adults to be psychologically available or responsive at times of need. His mother's rejection and frightening behaviour mean that in his mind the relationship between attachment and fear has become disturbed. As a consequence, all close relationships will be experienced by Josh as a confused mix of desire, anger and fear which will lead increasingly to his behaviour becoming unpredictable and socially incompetent. An avoidant/controlling attachment strategy, though designed to try and protect him from mental hurt and pain, nevertheless cuts him off from key bits of psychological information about himself and other people. In particular, failure to recognise the part that emotions play in interpersonal life will mean that Josh will not fully understand the complex relationship between thoughts, feelings and behaviour both in himself and others. Confusion will increase the likelihood of Josh becoming socially withdrawn or aggressive.

The above assessment not only helps to make sense of Josh and his mother, it also suggests the most appropriate interventions and best form of case management. In this particular case, initial work might usefully concentrate on working psychotherapeutically with Josh's mother, Joanna to help her improve her 'mentalising' capacities and sensitivity which in turn would increase her interest in and ability to understand her own as well as Josh's mind. The caregiving environment is always the most powerful influence on children's behaviour and state of mind. If it is possible to work with willing parents, this is generally the preferred focus of intervention with young children. This developmental work might also be strengthened by setting up specific 'play' and interactive sessions between Josh and his mother. Joanna would be encouraged to analyse and reflect on her behaviour with Josh (for example, by video-recording a planned interaction). Joanna might be asked to think about how her behaviour might be affecting Josh and vice versa. She might be encouraged to think about what he might be feeling. These, and similar chniques, have been shown to increase arents' 'reflective function', which is to say eir ability to recognise and understand the elationship between thoughts, feelings and ehaviour and how these affect mental states oth in the self and their child. Parents who are and explore mental states with their hildren have been shown to promote secure tachments and improve their children's notional intelligence and social skill.

However, the assessment might predict that anna would be unwilling to explore and eflect on her own mentalising processes, in hich case direct work with Josh would become e prime focus of intervention. In extreme cases f rejection, this might lead to Josh being emoved from the care of his mother. But hether he is removed or not, Josh will need elp in recognising the part that his own inner ental experiences play in the way he nderstands and conducts his social life. hildren can be helped to develop netacognitive control' and understand that the ehaviour of the self and others is organised by ental states composed of thoughts, feelings, eliefs and desires. Such help might be rovided by a play therapist, a teacher who romotes peer support and interest, substitute rers, or indeed anyone in a position to provide secure and understanding relationship in hich the child develops his or her nentalising' and reflective capacities. All close d important relationships are capable of elping children feel more positive about emselves. Responsive, interested and vailable relationships help children disconfirm eir insecure working models of self, others d relationships. More positive models of self n improve self-esteem, one of the most potent silience factors in any child's psychological ake-up. Positive, affirming relationships might cur between a child and their teacher, new rer, peer group or therapist.

The case of Josh and his mother is a relatively mple one of emotional rejection. The same pproach can be used in more complex cases in hich we meet compounds of two or more risk ctors including passive neglect, disorganised eglect, physical abuse, sexual abuse, epression, alcohol and drug problems, ultiple placements, periods of institutionalised re, domestic violence, and unresolved loss d trauma in the mind of the parent. In tachment terms, it is not sufficient merely to cognise or describe problematic parenting or disturbed caregiving. The fundamental purpose of an attachment-based assessment is to see how children's minds and mental states form in these difficult environments where care and protection cannot be taken-for-granted. Understanding this helps practitioners decide what specific things must be done, with this particular parent or child, to help children feel safe, protected and cared-for.

Conclusion

In child care and family work, classifying attachment styles, whether in children or adults, in itself has only limited value. It has to be remembered that in any normal population of either children or adults, around 40 to 50 per cent of individuals will be classified as insecurely attached. Clearly, in most cases there is nothing pathological or clinically significant about being assessed as insecurely attached. In this restricted sense, not a great deal can be made of the suggestion that this child or that parent has an insecure attachment. The vast majority of children brought to the attention of child care agencies show insecure attachments. It is the nature, type and degree of insecurity that is more important in the clinical arena. In particular, the complex category of disorganised and controlling attachments is likely to be the most frequently met in child welfare agencies in which children suffer major disturbances in the balance between fear and attachment.

The key task in assessing children's and parents' attachments is to understand their adaptive value in the context of the caregiving/careseeking relationship, including what happens when these adaptive strategies generalise to other relationships. This understanding then provides the practitioner with a powerful picture of how the child (and parent) perceive the world of relationships, process thoughts and feelings, mentally represent themselves and others, and handle close and important relationships. All of these characteristic ways of thinking, feeling and behaving become particularly pronounced under conditions of stress. Stress, whether interpersonal or environmental, not only increases insecure people's attachment styles, insecurely attached people perceive and experience more situations as stressful than secure individuals.

In this sense, an attachment-oriented assessment requires a detailed knowledge and understanding of the social and environmental context in which the child is attempting to develop, function, cope and survive. Much of the attachment-based research relevant to child care and family work looks at how different caregiving environments put children's socio-emotional development at risk, and how these risks affect children needs, behaviour, relationship and educational capacities. There is now a growing body of research on children's attachment strategies in environments where there is parental violence, drug and alcohol misuse, emotional rejection, physical abuse, sexual abuse, neglect, depression, and learning difficulties.

Attachment-sensitive assessments are therefore not seen as additional to or separate from frameworks for assessing physical abuse or failure to thrive or parents with mental health problems. Attachment-sensitive assessments begin with attempts to describe and understand the characteristics of the caregiving environment, both at a point in time and over time, in which a particular child happens to have fetched. In their attempts to cope with, adapt to and make sense of themselves and others in this particular caregiving environment, young minds and the brain structures that underpin them develop and form. At heart, attachment-based assessments are designed to understand children's and parents' states of mind, including the way they perceive and represent themselves and others in interaction, and how these mental states affect behaviour, relationships, parenting, and approaches to learning and work. No simple check-list, schedule or accumulation of facts will help practitioners achieve this level of understanding and professional authority. An attachment-based approach requires practitioners to become highly knowledgeable about children's psychological development, particularly their social and emotional development. Pre-programmed to interact and make sense of the world about them, the particular caregiving environment in which a child happens to find herself will have a profound effect on her mental development.

Good assessments aid sharper, more focused interventions. Attachment-oriented assessments remind us of the healing power of good quality relationships at any stage in the lifespan, for parents as much as children. However, an attachment perspective also recognises that many treatment methods and supportive techniques might be brought into play if they help carers improve their availablity, sensitivit and 'mentalising' capacities, or allow children t experience themselves as competent and worth of love and protection, and able to understand their own and other people's minds. Cognitive therapies, long-term support, material help, family therapy as well as more specific attachment interventions can all be considered The key skill is in recognising which technique lend themselves best to parents' and children' states of mind. For example, carers with a preoccupied and ambivalent state of mind ma well be very enthusiastic about brief solution-focussed therapy, but an attachment theorist would not expect a successful outcom Long term, low-tech supportive approaches often work better with carers with ambivalent/preoccupied attachments. However, a carer with a dismissing, avoidant state of mind would be much more likely to b interested in and engaged by the more cognitively based techniques, including brief and systemic therapies. Differential diagnoses and treatments are therefore necessary if effective work and decision-making is to be achieved when working with children.

References

Bowlby, J. (1979) *The Making and Breaking of Affectional Bonds*. London: Tavistock.

Cassidy, J. and Shaver, P. (1999) *Handbook of Attachment*. New York: Guilford Press.

Crittenden, P. M. (1997) Truth, Error, Omissio Distortion, and Deception: The Application Attachment Theory to the Assessment and Treatment of Psychological Disorder. In Dollinger, S.M.C. and DiLalla, L.F. (Eds.) *Assessment and Intervention Issues Across the Life Span*. Mahweh, NJ: Lawrence Erlbaum Associates. 35–76.

DoH (2000) *Framework for the Assessment of Children in Need and their Families*. London: TSO.

Fonagy, P. (undated) *Attachment, the Development of the Self, and its Pathology in Personality Disorders*. http:// www.psychomedia.it/pm/modther/ probsiter/fonagy-2.htm

Fonagy, P. and Target, M. (1997) Attachment and Reflective Function: Their Role in Self-organization. *Development and Psychopathology*. 9: 679–700.

George, C. and Solomon, J. (1996) Representational Models of Relationships:

Links Between Caregiving and Attachment. *Infant Mental Health Journal.* 17: 198–216.

Goldberg, S. (1999) *Attachment and Development.* London: Arnold.

Heard, D. and Lake, B. (1997) *The Challenge of Attachment for Care giving.* London: Routledge.

Howe, D., Brandon, M., Hinings, D. and Schofield, G. (1999) *Attachment Theory, Child Maltreatment and Family Support: A Practice and Assessment Guide.* Basingstoke: Palgrave/Macmillan.

Schore, A. (1994) *Affect Regulation and the Origin of the Self: The Neurobiology of Emotional Development.* Hillsdale, NJ: Erlbaum.

Solomon, J. and George, C. (Eds.) (1999) *Attachment Disorganisation.* NY: Guilford Press.

Stovall, K. C. and Dozier, M. (1998). Infants in Foster Care: An Attachment Theory Perspective. *Adoption Quarterly.* 2: 55–88.

Further reading

Cassidy, J. and Shaver, P. (1999) *Handbook of Attachment.* New York: Guilford Press.

Goldberg, S. (1999) *Attachment and Development.* London: Arnold.

Howe, D., Brandon, M., Hinings, D. and Schofield, G. (1999) *Attachment Theory, Child Maltreatment and Family Support: A Practice and Assessment Guide.* Basingstoke: Palgrave/Macmillan.